Organized Crime:
Uncertainties and Dilemmas

Edited by

Stanley Einstein
The Middle Eastern Summer Institute on Drug Use

and

Menachem Amir
The Hebrew University, Jerusalem, Israel

D1713214

Production Manager: Cindy Moors
Cover designed by Ronit Berson

Contents

Prologue to the Series

UNCERTAINTY is an international, interdisciplinary monograph series of topic-focused issues publishing invited state-of-the-art analyses one or more times a year. Each issue will contain a minimum of 6-8 review articles. They will focus on an issue, problem or process, which remains unresolved. The topics will be ones that significantly affect the quality of life of the individual and the nature and effective functioning of our institutions, communities and of society-at-large. Authors will help you, the reader, to move from concepts, definitions, theories, paradigms and their "demands," to the implications of current generalizable empirical data, to the future of the issue's topic, noting remaining unresolved issues, the barriers to their understanding, planning and implementation and suggesting future research.

Each issue will include:
- *ABSTRACTS*
- *REFERENCES*
- *GLOSSARIES*
- *RESOURCES*: Lists of selected printed, auditory and visual materials from governmental and private organizations which the interested reader can write to for further information.
- *GRAPHICS:* Graphic materials, designed to help you, the reader, "see" the issues, their parameters, "demands" and (inter) relationships, directions, potency, stability and valences.

UNCERTAINTY, the monograph series, is designed as a forum for minimizing individual and systemic uncertainties, to promote exploration of selected vital human concerns and to maximize the needed openness for preventing premature closure as we examine, think about and create new paradigms of change. In our increasingly complex world in which solutions all too often raise or themselves become problems the paradox of the lawfulness of unpredictability is our reality; notions of *control, predictability* and "*cause and effect*" are mythical messages. In our complex world the concept of predictability changes. The answer to the question: "Tell me what will happen?" *always* has some degree of uncertainty. "Tell me what is plausible, likely, to anticipate" is reasonable. The answers could be the same, scientifically speaking, but the meanings will be different. In our complex world, the dynamics of reality do not play dice, even though to all appearances, and to "common sense," life and reality is experienced as a dice game.

UNCERTAINTY is and can be a stimulus and tool for you.

Both the authors in each volume and the editors welcome queries and feedback.

The Editors

'It is not a fact it's a real story'
  - Yiddish folk saying

Acknowledgments

Many people have made it possible for this volume to move from an 'interesting idea' to an actual publication. The willingness of professionals and students, friends, colleagues and strangers to take the necessary time from their busy personal and professional responsibilities for this project continues to serve as an ongoing source of joy to both of us.

Phil Williams' suggestion for involving graduate students with known and experienced professionals in this transnational, globalizing volume has resulted in a most satisfying meld for the editors...and hopefully for you, the reader. We have learned a great deal.

Without David Nelken there would have been no connection. The technical help and support given so freely by Pamela Trbovich and Randy Pearson (Ridgeway Center for International Security Studies, University of Pittsburgh), by Eyal Ben-Levi (Jerusalem M-M Treatment Center), Yossi Gadot (Department of Psychology Lab., Bar Ilan University), Gil Shimon (American Cultural Center – Jerusalem), Navah Jacob-Fanani, (Faculty of Law, Hebrew University, Jerusalem), the Abstract translators – Lina Nazzal Abu Dayyeh, B.S.Pharm., Palestine National Authority (Spanish), Marina Barham, MA, Palestine National Authority (Arabic), Professor Lidya Belostky, Faculty of Law, University of Tel Aviv, Israel (Russian), Dr. Fu Hua Ling, The University of Hong Kong (Chinese), Dr. Gert-Jan Meerkerk, IVO, Rotterdam, The Netherlands (Dutch), Professor Mauricio Lima, Universidade Federal de Pelotas, Brazil (Portuguese), Dr. Fransceso Scandale, Israel (Italian), Dr. Urban Weber, Frankfurt, Germany (German), Dr. Molly Milesi-Wilson, Israel (French), Professor Minoru Yokoyama (Japanese), and the graphic designer of this volume and of the *Uncertainties* series, Ronit Berson, was and remains beyond what the editors expected. We are most grateful to each of them.

Our families and friends were most patient as we attempted to meet the demands of this volume. Their support made it possible for us to continue.

And of course this volume, as the series, would not be possible without John Irwin, who demonstrated his belief in two strangers and their dream.

Lastly, my our grandchildren, Shira, Jamie, Nimrod, Adi, Hilla and Matan inherit a world of less violence, corruption and crime, with the necessary caring, sensitivity, empathy and concern for others.

Perhaps all of this can best be summed up by the above quoted folk saying.

List of Figures

List of Tables

List of Contributors

Howard Abadinsky, Ph.D., is Professor of Criminal Justice and Sociology at Saint Xavier University in Chicago, Illinois.

Joseph Albini, Ph.D., is Professor Emeritus of Criminology, Department of Sociology, Wayne State University, Detroit, Michigan.

Menachem Amir received his Ph.D. at the University of Pennsylvania. He is a member of the permanent faculty and a Professor of Criminology at The Institute of Criminology, Hebrew University, Jerusalem, Israel.

Margaret E. Beare, Ph.D., is Director of the Nathanson Centre for the Study of Organized Crime and Corruption, York University, North York, Toronto, Canada.

Lauren L. Bernick, MPIA, University of Pittsburgh, Ridgway Center for International Security Studies.

Sung-Kwon Cho was a Ph.D. student of Professor Lupsha. He is currently a university professor of Latin American Studies in Seoul, South Korea.

John Daly, MPIA, University of Pittsburgh, Ridgway Center for International Security Studies.

Mag. Maximilian Edelbacher, Chief of Viennese Major Crime Bureau (burglary, fraud, forgery and prostitution) is a lecturer for the Middle European Police Academy and at the Vienna University of Economics and Business Administration.

Prof. Stanley (Shlomo) Einstein, Ph.D., clinical and social psychologist, researcher, academician, lecturer, journalist, radio interviewer, author, editor, consultant and conference organizer.

Dr. Hualing Fu is a research fellow in the Faculty of Law, the University of Hong Kong.

Dr. Mark Gaylord is an Associate Professor of Sociology at the City University of Hong Kong.

Michele Gideon, MPIA, University of Pittsburgh, Ridgway Center for International Security Studies.

Sal E. Gomez, MPIA, University of Pittsburgh, Ridgway Center for International Security Studies.

David Hess, MPIA, University of Pittsburgh, Ridgway Center for International Security Studies.

Prof. Brunon Holyst is the head of the Department of Criminology and Criminalistics, University of Lodz, Lodz, Poland.

Robert J. Kelly, Ph.D., is Broeklundian Professor of Social Science at Brooklyn College and The Graduate School and University Center of the City University of New York.

Peter A. Lupsha, Ph.D., is Senior Research Scholar at the Latin American Institute, University of New Mexico and Professor Emeritus of Political Science.

Frederick T. Martens is the Executive Director (Ret.) of the Pennsylvania Crime Commission.

Kenneth Myers, MPIA, University of Pittsburgh, Ridgway Center for International Security Studies.

Letizia Paoli, Ph.D., is a researcher in the Department of Criminology of the Max-Planck-Institut für auslandisches und inter-nationales Strafrecht.

Gary W. Potter is Professor of Police Studies, Eastern Kentucky University.

Jeffrey Ian Ross, Ph.D, is an Assistant Visiting Professor at Baltimore University.

Sarah L. Shannon, University of Pittsburgh, Ridgway Center for International Security Studies.

Mark Shaw, Ph. D., is head of Crime and Policing Policy at the Institute for Security Studies, a non-profit think-tank based in Johannesburg, South Africa.

Dr. Phil Williams is Director of the University of Pittsburgh's Ridgway Center for International Security Studies and Professor of the Graduate School of Public and International Affairs at the University.

Prof. Minoru Yokoyama completed his B.A in Law and an M.A. in both Criminal Law and Sociology at Chuo University, Tokyo. He is a professor and the former Dean of the Faculty of Law at Kokugakuin University, Tokyo, Japan.

You take
a bit of fire, a bit of water,
a bit of rabbit or tree,
or any little piece of man,
you mix it, shake well, cork it up,
put it in a warm place, in darkness, in light, in frost,
leave it alone for a while -
though things don't leave you alone- and that's the whole point.
And then
you have a look - and it grows,
a little sea, a little volcano,
a little tree, a little heart, a little brain,
so small you don't hear it pleads
to be let out
and that's the whole point, not to hear.
Then you go and record it all, all the minuses or
all the pluses, some with an exclamation-mark,
all the zeros, or all the numbers, some with an
exclamation -mark,
and the point is that the test tube
is an instrument for changing question -
into exclamation - marks.
And the point is
that for the moment you forget
you yourself are
In the test tube.

Miroslav Holub
On the Test Tube
in *Brief Reflections*

Introduction

In spite of the developments in criminological theory and research, the accumulation of data on frequencies, regularities and patterns of crimes, including the characteristics of offenders, victims, the crime organizations and the reactions to crime and to criminals, a great deal of uncertainty continues to exist regarding these aspects of the criminal phenomenon.

The same uncertainties exist with regard to *organized criminality,* and *organized crime* -local, national or international.

Each contributor, in this growing field, gives their own definition of organized crime (OC), but it is not always clearly stated nor does a general agreement exist about *the definition.* So too, in this volume, it seems that the analytic differentiation between *organized criminality* and *professional criminality* and *organized crime* is often blurred. The former is a phase in the development of organized crime and does not necessarily become organized crime. While organized crime contains the elements of organized criminality, and uses organized criminality, (see Shaw in this volume) organized crime has its own special elements. These include:

- greater continuity of structure and activities
- greater *rationality in structure and activities* (in the licit an illicit economic arenas) and
- their attempts to gain *control over the licit and illicit markets* and/or *geographical areas.*

It should be remembered that whereas we make a distinction between economic, social and political organized crime, the focus and discussions in this volume are mainly about economic organized crime.

Another common thread, which emerges from the studies, is the *globalization of organized crime*, with the explanations given for the processes of OC's internationalization (Williams). There are differences among the "branching out" of national organized crime groups towards *cross-border*, regional or *transnational* activities. Analyses are presented of these differences in terms of the group's strengths, expertise and wealth, which are needed to be able to enter the international arena.

Controversies continue to exist about the necessary conditions, which give rise to, and precipitate, the emergence of local, state, and international organized crime.

It would appear, from the studies in this volume, that organized crime emerges as a *functional necessity* when the State or its policies fail to deliver goods and service (including justice, peace, security or employment) to sectors of society which demand these goods and services. The "price" which organized crime imposes on society to deliver these goods and services include violence, corruption and the violation of civil, human rights and democratic values (Lupsha). Whereas "failures" in democracies can explain the observed emergence of organized crimes in stable democratic societies, contributors to this volume document another important consideration. Organized Crime can emerge when societies and States undergo sharp and extensive social, economic and political changes, which weaken the State's legal and regulatory agencies. The examples given are the transition from non-democratic regimes to more democratic and free market societies (Holyst, Shaw). Under such conditions organized crime further weakens the State and its economics; although some view this as being a temporary or transitional phase. Some work, however, suggests the consideration of a condition of symbiotic *institutionalization* of organized crime in which OC may, and indeed has, become a "partner" via intimidation and corruption of the State's political and economic systems (i.e. Holyst, Lupsha, Shaw, Williams).

In deciding to create this volume we did not approach this project with any prior or preferred theory or position to describe and to explain the phenomenon of organized crime. What emerges from these studies is what is already known regarding the theories about organized crime, about its structure and activities in both illicit and legitimate markets. Organized crime is shaped by local, regional and global conditions and *changes* in the economic, social and political legal systems. We have, however, included studies on the developments in existing organized crime groups, a number of them documenting a decline in their power (Italian groups in the United States), others noting the emergence of new groups in the local scene (African-American entering the international arena) (Kelly, Abadinsky); with the examples of other powerful groups, on the local level, being able to enter the international arena (Paoli).

We have decided to arrange the studies in this volume in the following way:

1. *Theory and Meta-theory*: First the international, legal and regulatory framework (Mueller). Second, international, social, economic, political and other conditions and developments which (can) explain the globalization of organized crime (Lupsha, Williams).

2. *National and regional levels of description and analysis of organized groups*: The emphasis is once again on social and political developments, including historical descriptions of the emergence of organized crime groups with their special characteristics. Thus there are studies on social change and OC in former East European communist block countries (Holyst), in changing mainland China (Fu and Gaylord), and in South Africa (Shaw), which, like Russia, moves toward democracy and a free market economy.

   The history of organized crime and its current structure and activities is documented in the studies on Austria (Edlelbacher) and Israel (Amir). Both stress the role of immigration in the development of organized crime in their countries. The studies analyzing Japan's *Yakuza* (Yokayama) and OC groups in Italy (Paoli) document for us yet another change which led to the emergence of organized crime. This was the movement from feudalism to that of a modern state and in Japan, after the processes involved in the democratization of the Japanese political and social system.

3. Topics of special *activities or enterprises* of organized crime or facets of OC which aside from "money laundering" are relatively rarely published about: These include the art - OC nexus (Bernick), the global sex trade (Shannon), a comprehensive overview about money laundering (Hess, et al) and State-organized crime (Ross).

4. The last topic deals with the *reaction of the State*, namely the criminal justice system: Each contribution to this volume discusses in some manner the legal and criminal justice measures taken against organized crime. Whereas Mueller's article, which opens this volume charts the attempts of the UN and other international bodies to combat organized crime, Lupsha documents, as a caveat, what we are likely to be faced with when the State and its legal systems become corrupted; Nelken's analysis pinpoints the problems which can confront the criminal justice system in dealing with the globalization developments of organized crime.

We are aware that this is not a comprehensive overview of this complex, dynamic and confusing field. We are aware that numerous important topics have not been included (foreign laborers and OC, illegal immigration and OC, child adoption and OC, human organs for transplants and OC, the Internet and OC, unions and OC, etc.) and that additional relevant areas of the world are missing. We made efforts to involve authors who are experts in these areas but their schedules and previous commitments did not allow them to participate.

Part I
Theory and Meta-
theory

1 Transnational Crime: An Experience in Uncertainties

Gerhard O.W. Mueller

Abstract

The paper describes the developments in the definition of transnational and international crime in the deliberations of the UN agencies. Once a basic agreed definition was reached, member states of the UN and NGO organizations were asked to describe 18 categories of crimes that have international characterizations and impact, although some may seem local in their nature.

The eighteen categories are reviewed, emphasizing their scope and patterns, existing resources and needed measures to combat these crimes. Dealt with are such crimes, with transnational characteristics, as: money laundering, terrorism, art and intellectual theft, piracy, computer crimes, environmental crimes, etc.

These crimes "suffer" from uncertainties as to the very definition of the concept of transnational crime, needed research, and needed viable measures or criteria.

The very definition of the concepts of **transnational** *and* **international crimes** *need research and measures called for in order to effectively combat them.*

Key Words: Transnational crimes, types of transnational crimes, United Nations definitions

Introduction

The concept *transnational crime* is in itself wrapped in uncertainty. The media and, indeed, many criminologists, think of any form of criminality, which transcends even a single international frontier as "international" crime. That is far from accurate. The concept of transnational crime was first placed before the profession at the Fifth United Nations Congress on the Prevention of Crime and the Treatment of Offenders (Geneva, 1975). Agenda item 5 of that Congress was concerned with "Changes in Forms and Dimensions of Criminality Transnational and National."[1] Similarly, that Congress dealt with the topic "Violence of Transnational and Comparative International Significance."[2]

In the intervening decades *"transnational crime"* has assumed the meaning of "criminal activities extending into, and violating the laws of, several countries."[3] Thus, *"transnational crime"* is distinguishable, at one pole, from *"international crimes."* These are crimes which are recognized by international law (whether customary or by convention) in which the entire world is victimized and which are recognized by both international criminal courts (such as the current international war crimes tribunals for the former Yugoslavia and

Rwanda, or the projected permanent international criminal court) or by national criminal courts of jurisdictions adhering to international conventions.

At the other pole we find local crimes whose commission and prevalence are influenced by factors beyond the boundaries of the affected jurisdiction. In a totally globalized world economy, there are very few local crimes that are not somehow impacted by foreign factors.[4]

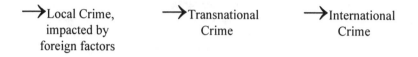

The borders of the three types of crime noted above are fluid, and the concepts are somewhat overlapping. Many transnational crimes have evolved into international crimes, namely as soon as a convention defines them as such. By the same token, "local crime impacted by foreign factors" fluidly moves into the category of transnational crime, namely when the country of origin, by legislation, turns the impacting activity into a crime by change of legislation, e.g., the banking laws.

Nevertheless, using the concept of transnational crime as a starting point, the United Nations Crime Prevention and Criminal Justice Division has succeeded in identifying eighteen transnational crime categories. Neither individually, nor by type, nor collectively by category, do transnational crimes conform to the definitions and categorizations found in penal codes, although they approximate groupings of penal code offenses or, indeed, some international crimes.

The United Nations Secretariat distributed, for the first time, as part of its Fourth United Nations Survey of Crime Trends and Operations of Criminal Justice Systems, an additional questionnaire to governments. It hoped to gain a first impression on the prevalence and impact of transnational crime, descriptively and statistically through responses to it.[5] Following is a listing of the derived eighteen categories of transnational crime.

- Money-laundering
- Terrorist activities
- Theft of art and cultural objects
- Theft of intellectual property
- Illicit traffic in arms
- Aircraft hijacking
- Sea piracy
- Land hijacking
- Insurance fraud
- Computer crime
- Environmental crime
- Trafficking in persons
- Trade in human body parts

- Illicit drug trafficking
- Fraudulent bankruptcy
- Infiltration of legal business
- Corruption and bribery of public officials as defined in national legislation and of party officials and elected representatives as defined in national legislation
- Other offenses committed by organized criminal groups

Interestingly enough, most criminal activities falling into these categories, are in the nature of organized crime.[6] Most of the crime categories are the product of the relatively recent globalization of the economy, of communications and of transportation.[7]

The governments that received the United Nation's added questionnaire had considerable difficulties responding to it. Having been sent to 193 States, fifty states responded; and of 88 international and non-governmental organizations who received the questionnaire, 10 replied. Nearly all States had definitional problems; few had statistical information (noting that statistical categorizations could not be applied); and some merely sent in copies of relevant legislation. Nevertheless, a good start was made, and with time and patience future such questionnaires may transform this area of uncertainty into one of certainty. In the ensuing, I shall comment on the eighteen transnational crime categories.

1. Money Laundering

This category of transnational crime ranks number 1 on the list, because of it massive impact on the economy of the entire world. Money laundering is an activity aimed at making illegally attained funds seem legitimate. Consider that, in a little village, a poor householder has been struggling for years to patch his roof and feed his cow. All of a sudden, he orders the roofer to put a new roof on his cottage. He also buys a car and sends his kids to summer camp. The villagers will ask questions: Where does the sudden wealth come from? And so it is nationally and internationally, but the villagers' curiosity is augmented by laws requiring the divulgence of bank deposits of $10,000.00 or more, and by many other legislative devices. Consider now that a considerable part of he financial gain of the world's citizens is ill-gotten, for example by bribery, corruption, black market activities and transactions outside the tax laws, and especially by dealing in contraband -- weapons, stolen goods, art and cultural heritage, and particularly drugs. It has been estimated that annual sales of the illegitimate international drug market run between $300 and $500 billion, with the American drug economy alone generating up to $50 billion in sales annually. What can the drug barons do with this enormous wealth? In America, nothing, because the money is "dirty." But if the money were to be "laundered," somehow, overseas, it could return to the U.S. to buy anything, entire industries, commercial enterprises, real estate, and a voice in politics.

The drug barons, and other owners of ill-gotten gains, have devised many schemes to launder dirty money, including bogus real estate transactions, purchases of gold (many times consisting of lead bars with a coat of gold), sales (real or fictitious) of art and antiques. However, the standard method remains the physical transfer of cash out of the country (e.g., by plane or ship or by trucks and trailers with false bottoms); deposit of such cash abroad, followed by a series of international (electronic) transfers, at the end of which the source is untraceable. The money seems "clean" and finds itself being legitimately invested in the economy -- albeit controlled by organized crime.

The true dimensions of money laundering are largely unknown. Criminologists have just begun to assess this phenomenon adequately.[8] Nevertheless, policy research (especially by the Financial Transaction Task Force of the Group of Seven (highly industrialized countries) has resulted in remedies. Some of these center on countries with secretive banking laws, aimed at making information available to investigators. Yet only five of the responding States could provide any data on the prevalence of the problems.

2. Terrorist Activities

Americans were largely unaware of the international scope of terrorist activities, primarily because their homeland had remained unaffected. This naivete changed with the growing awareness that Americans and American interests and installations abroad had become targets of international terrorists. But only the bombing of the World Trade Center (NYC) in February of 1993, by an organized group of Mid-Eastern terrorists, alerted Americans to the vulnerability of their own country as simply being a part of the global village in which terrorists seek to accomplish their purposes. The destruction of PAN AM Flight 103 in 1988, and the bombing on opening day of the Centennial Olympiad (July 27, 1996), will not be the last reminder of American vulnerability.

The governments of the world -- excepting a few who derived national benefits from international terrorism -- have long hoped that, as grievances could be solved by negotiation and settlement, terrorism would decline. This has happened to some extent, but every settlement of a grievance leaves some hard-liners dissatisfied. Consequently, some terrorism continues, aided by the contemporary easing in international transportation and communications.

Much scholarly inquiry has been directed at understanding and explaining international terrorism.[9] There have been some legislative responses. As a matter of fact, a network of international conventions is in place to deal with international terrorism. International judicial and police cooperation has been vastly improved. Yet, there is no international machinery in operation to assure the arrest or adjudication of international terrorists, and criminologists have yet to arrive at theoretically sound explanations which would help deal with a problem which knows no international boundaries and which, most often, is directed at the transportation industry.

Sixteen States provided data on terrorism in their jurisdictions.

3. Theft of Art and Cultural Objects

This category obtained a high number three ranking because of its potential for denuding entire cultures and nations of their cultural heritage. Tombs and monuments have been plundered since the times of the Pharaohs. But with the development of modern tools, and the high demand for cultural objects, as well as the ease of transport, international plunderers and thieves have developed a system, which can strip an entire region or country of its valuable cultural heritage.

There is no country that has not been victimized. We must add to the historical heritage of each country its more contemporary contributions, the arts that have been produced over the last few centuries. An estimated $4.5 billion of fine art is stolen every year -- for sale on the international market. A database lists 45,000 stolen art objects, with an increase of 2,000 items a month. It appears that the world's cultural heritage, and its art, are the object of a vast international enterprise aimed at redistributing, and thereby totally disorienting the world's cultural heritage for the profit, of an as yet ill defined international criminal organization -- or organizations.[10]

With one exception,[11] criminologists have paid scant attention to this phenomenon, though the industry has endeavored to come up with some practical solutions.[12]

Eleven States were able to provide statistical information.

4. Theft of Intellectual Property

The "theft of intellectual property" includes the unauthorized use of the rights of authors, performers, and of copyright and trademarks. There is obviously a high temptation to reproduce works of protected originators at a fraction of franchise (or similar) costs, especially in countries with relatively unregulated economies. Yet the destructive impact on the economy of producing or originating countries is immediately apparent -- though hard to assess in monetary terms. One type of theft of "intellectual property," namely the illegal copying of software, has been quantified by the U.S. Software Publishers Association; it mounts to an astounding loss of $7.5 billion annually.[13] The counterfeiting of protected values, such as copyrights, is not something to be accomplished by minor, individual entrepreneurs. It requires coordination, management, and a system of distribution. That, frequently, requires governmental collusion.

Despite extant international agreements, and in the absence of criminological underpinnings, this transnational crime category is a problem without a certain solution. Statistical information is largely unavailable.

5. Illicit Traffic in Arms

Local, regional or national armed conflicts, which plague today's world on every part of the globe, would not be imaginable without an international network of weapons producers and suppliers. This is a shadowy world beyond the reach of statistical assessment. Yet if episodic evidence were to be trusted, it is a world with relatively few actors. These actors, likely, form a network of uneasy alliance, often in congruity with governmental agencies.

National legislation to deal with illegal arm trades appears to be of only theoretical significance. Accurate information is lacking -- despite the fact that weapons and munitions are traceable. Criminological information on the illegal arms trade is also lacking. Yet, the largest portion of the world's homicides is potentially traceable to the illegal international trade in arms.

The most lethal part of the world's illegal arms trade centers on the illegal transfer of nuclear materials. It is clear now that since 1992, on at least five occasions, several relatively small quantities of nuclear material, including pure plutonium, have been diverted from nuclear facilities in former Soviet republics and offered for sale in Germany and other countries west of Russia. This is an indication that controls at the source are inadequate.

First indications are that the diversions of nuclear material which have occurred so far were carried out by small groups of individuals, rather than by organized crime, for motives of individual gain (or possibly to assist in financing totally underfunded former Soviet laboratories and scientists?). Most of the efforts were amateurish, and none of the material apparently reached a viable buyer. Indeed, most were the result of "sting operations." In several cases the thieves, transporters, and the public have been exposed to radiation hazards -- in itself a not insubstantial danger.[14] Criminologists have been caught by surprise. There have been few criminological responses up until the present.[15]   At this point, government have cooperated to control nuclear materials at the source. Controls beyond the sources do not appear to be cost-beneficial, yet the potential harm is vast.

Eighteen States were able to provide some statistical information on the illegal arms trade.

6. Aircraft Hijacking

The system for curbing and responding to the illegal interception or destruction of aircraft is in place. Yet at the moment I am writing this, an Algerian domestic airliner, a well as a Spanish airliner en route to Cuba, have been hijacked. Both episodes ended with all passengers safe.

The airlines industry had been plagued by aircraft hijackings in the 1970s and into the 1980s. While a few such incidents were attributable to individuals who demanded ransom, most were political with typical terrorist characteristics, seeking to demonstrate the ability of the terrorist organization to strike at vulnerable targets almost anywhere in the world and propagating their cause or ideology.

Since the entire world community was affected, especially diplomats and politicians, whose mobility depends on air travel, the reaction to the flood of aircraft hijackings was swift and effective. The industry itself reacted effectively by increasing security measures. Most importantly: the early pronouncements by UN organs, that the causes of such terrorism must be removed by ameliorating or removing the underlying reasons for terrorist resort to violence, now appear to have been prophetic. Many grievances have been resolved, yet some remain, and every resolution by compromise leaves some parties dissatisfied. Hence we must accept the possibility that airplane hijackings will be with us for some time, though on a significantly decreased scale.

The criminological literature on this phenomenon is considerable, centering on the profiles of hijackers, causes, regions, carriers involved, etc., all of which has led to the improvement of controls. Moreover, airplane hijacking/destruction has been moved into the category of international crimes.

7. Sea Piracy

Virtually forgotten until the mid-1970s, sea piracy resurfaced on three fronts since then:

- The illegal narcotics drug smuggling from South and Central America into the United States initially relied heavily on yacht and fishing vessels captured at sea or ports, after owners and crew were killed. Several thousand vessels were victimized. As the drug trade became prosperous, it could rely on purchased or (illegally) chartered vessels.
- At the roadstead of Lagos, Nigeria and the narrow shipping channel of the Malacca Straits -- as well as in several other comparable sea lanes -- the opportunity of deriving some benefit by attacking commercial vessels at anchor or moving at slow speed attracted thousands of marginalized young men in Africa, Southeast Asia, and Latin America, to attack ships and to steal valuables (including cargo), sometimes with the loss of crew lives. Such piracies (often not piracies in the international law sense, since they occurred in the territorial waters of States) reached a high level of frequency (one-a-day), but are on the decline now, thanks largely to the research and policy activities of the International Maritime Bureau (IMB, London) of the International Chamber of Commerce (Paris), the International Maritime Organization (UN), and the research of a number of criminologists.[16]

While the problem has been ameliorated, it has by no means ended. Prudent shipping lines order "piracy watches" on their vessels in affected waters. National and regional maritime law enforcement agencies maintain closer watch, and the IMB maintains a special branch office in Kuala Lumpur to monitor developments.

There have been allegations, though never concrete proof that the piracies in South East Asia were controlled by one (or a few) organized crime groups (including one linked to armed forces). While this may seem likely, the simultaneous appearance of piracy in so many parts of the world cannot be attributed to a single organization; it remains a criminological challenge.

Obviously, the pirates of the various affected maritime sites do operate as criminal gangs.

Data was obtained from five States.

8. Land Hijacking

The inclusion of land hijacking in the UN's listing of transnational crimes was a surprise.   At the national level, hijackings of trucks had been well documented as a form of robbery or theft. But the world economy has changed. Long distance trucking from Eastern to Western Europe or from the Central Asian republics to the Baltic States, is now a reality, involving a high percentage of goods transported transnationally. Unhappily, the opportunity to divert such cargoes has increased proportionately.

It is telling that only four States responded to this item on the UN questionnaire. At this point the evidence is entirely episodic but seems to point to the involvement of organized groups. Predictably, the problem will increase due to the porosity of borders, the growth of organized crime (especially in Eastern Europe), and the paucity of data and criminological analysis.

9. Insurance Fraud

The insurance industry is internationally linked, especially through reinsurance and other methods of spreading risks and benefits. Thus, local insurance fraud ultimately affects all insurers, and all insured, worldwide.

The global dimension of the problem has not been calculated. Australia reported an annual loss through fraudulent claims of $1.7 billion (Australian) annually and for the United States the loss likely amounts to $100 billion annually.[17]

Unknown is the extent to which organized crime is involved in insurance fraud. But whether it is, or is not, should not affect the determination of the industry to protect itself and its clients. My prediction is that organized crime will see the opportunity of organizing the fraudulent claims business, either by consolidating little entrepreneurs in individual spheres (e.g., maritime insurance fraud) or by infiltrating the industry itself, possibly to the point of controlling companies.

10. Computer Crime

Just as computers serve legitimate commerce (and government), the Internet is equally accessible to organized crime. While there is no indication that the Internet has been taken over, or is even marginally influenced by, organized crime, criminal organizations are relying on the communication opportunities which the Internet affords and must be planning to control as much of the electronic superhighway as they can.

Extant criminological research on computer criminality deals with individual perpetrators, some of whom amassed fortunes by abusing the Internet. Current estimates of losses through computer crime range up to $8 billion annually.[18] Australian estimates are at the level of $700 million (Australian) annually, within the nation.

We unfortunately lack necessary criminological information, although criminologists take an increasing interest in the development of legal and other protections.[19]

11. Environmental Crime

Well into the mid 20th century, degradation of the environment was regarded as a matter to be controlled by local authorities. Indeed, it was not until the first United Nations Congress on the Environment (Stockholm, 1972) that the global dimensions of environmental degradation, and thus the need for its control were recognized. In the quarter century since Stockholm much has been achieved in recognizing environmental danger, quantifying them, and devising control mechanisms (treaties, legislation and ultimately technology) in order to divert these dangers. Criminological research has contributed a great deal in this regard.[20]

The victims of environmental crime are the population of the entire world. Yet any of these victims are also perpetrators. More particularly, manufacturers may be viewed as the possible inner circle of perpetrators when they avoid or circumvent controls, including avoidance by collusion in the process of creating control schemes. This has become particularly apparent when industries relocate into developing countries where control schemes are non-existent or have been tailored for the convenience of foreign industries, often through bribery, corruption and other forms of collusion. Disclosures and condemnations may have had a wholesome effect in some industries (e.g., the petroleum industry), but have had little impact overall.

Poor nations prefer industrialization, including employment and gross national product increases, over a clean environment. Organized crime has found its own not inconsiderable niche in the environmental industry, especially in improperly transporting and disposing of waste, especially hazardous waste. Yet, legitimate industries are virtually forced to deal with organized crime.[21]

Powerful international organizations, including the UN, the European Union (EU) and professional non-governmental groups, e.g., the International Association of Penal Law, exert relentless pressure for the creation and enforcement of standards.

Eleven States provided information on environmental criminality.

12. Trafficking in Persons

Original forms of trafficking in persons included the slave trade and the white slave trade (traffic in women). Although the slave trade may be a matter of the past, the traffic in persons is on the increase, including:

- the transport of illegal immigrants, often resulting in involuntary servitude
- the transport of women for purposes of prostitution

- the transport of migratory laborers to work under slave-like conditions
- the transport of household workers from developing countries
- the transfer of children for adoptions not sanctioned by law

For the most part, laws are in place to prevent the illegal trafficking in persons. Their enforcement is another matter in a world with increasingly porous borders. The problem is bound to increase as the populations of a stagnant Third World press for settlement in the relatively prosperous countries of northern climates.

Much of the illegal population flow is controlled by organized crime.[22] The newcomers in the industrialized countries, being largely unemployable, are forming a new marginalized class, likely to be exploited, but also contributing to crime and unrest. Yet, as the papers presented at the conference of the International Scientific and Advisory Council of the United Nations Programmes in Crime Prevention and Criminal Justice (ISPAC) have demonstrated, a number of States have dealt unsuccessfully with the influx of illegal immigrants, turning them from an economic liability into an asset, with little if any impact on the crime rate.

13. Trade in Human Body Parts

The first kidney transplant was performed in 1954, the first lung transplant in 1963, and the first heart transplant in 1967. By now close to half a million kidneys have been transplanted. Transplant surgery has become a highly specialized branch of medicine, and the supply of transplantable organs has spawned a very large industry. In the United States of America, sixty-nine transplant agencies have been established and federal and state laws seek to control their activities.

Yet at any given moment, 35,000 people are waiting for a transplant (and the number increases by fourteen percent annually), thus, the demand far outstrips the supply (The number of potential donors in the U.S. is estimated to about 12,000). Consequently, an illegitimate industry has sprung up which provides a service by which recipients are flown to a usually developing) country where organs can be procured virtually on demand. "Donors" may in fact have been murdered for their organs, or they are children of poor parents sold for their organs, at extremely low prices.

The professional journal *Magazin fur die Polizei* published the first exposure on the illegal trade in body parts in 1993.[23] As a result, commissions of inquiry have been created in a number of countries, some of which passed regulatory legislation -- of doubtful enforce ability.[24] There is a shadowy border between the legal referral to donors, and the illegitimate market which accesses donors in Third World countries. The latter is reported to be controlled by organized crime operating out of Western Europe.

Only one state provided data on this problem range.

14. Illicit drug trafficking

The illicit traffic in narcotic drugs is entirely controlled by organized crime networks, loosely related with each other geographically, as well as at the various levels of production and marketing, and by type of narcotic drugs. The criminological literature exploring this phenomenon from every angle is vast but by no means clear in terms of policy implications.[25] With the Single Convention on Narcotic Drugs (1961), the Convention on Psychotropic Substances (1971) and the United Nations Convention against Illicit Traffic in Narcotic Drugs and Psychotropic Substances (1988), a theoretically perfect international legal structure to control this traffic is in place. Yet its application and enforcement suffers from the following shortcomings:

- The UN structure to oversee this treaty scheme is inadequate, being woefully underfunded (The United Nations International Drug Programme, Vienna, Austria).
- Similarly underfunded are comparable national and regional programs.
- Nations differ vastly on their emphasis (e.g., interdiction vs. repression and control vs. tolerance vs. treatment approaches).
- Some of the most important countries of origin suffer from corruption at all levels -- due to the vast income base of the trade -- thus affecting enforcement.
- Corruption similarly affects law enforcement in many countries.
- Most developing and newly democratic countries lack the legal and technical infrastructure necessary to implement the treaties, though a new UN program to assist these countries by providing technical and legal assistance is now in place to remedy this shortcoming.

No other form of transnational and organized crime is as costly in terms of human and national financial suffering as the illicit trade in narcotic drugs (See money laundering above).

Thirty-eight States were able to provide data on transnational narcotic criminality.

15. Fraudulent Bankruptcy

The internationalization of commerce has turned fraudulent bankruptcy from a local into a transnational crime. The dimensions of the phenomenon are largely unknown. Evidence is anecdotal but includes information that organized crime, after acquiring an enterprise, may subject it to bankruptcy when the gains thereof exceed the expectations of profit. There is need to strengthen national enforcement efforts and for these to cooperate internationally.

Twelve States provided data on fraudulent bankruptcy.

16. Infiltration of Legal Business

This topic arises out of topic one, above, as it is the logical and temporal sequence of money laundering, the principal objective of which is seemingly legitimate investment. At this point the existing information permits no quantitative or qualitative assessment of the phenomenon, but it must be considered that the drug trade alone has between $200 and $500 billion to invest in the market. At this rate one could theoretically predict the time at which the world's economy is controlled by organized crime.

No State would provide data on this phenomenon.

17. Corruption and Bribery of Public Officials as Defined in National Legislation and of Party Officials and Elected Representatives as Defined in National Legislation

Notwithstanding that bribery of party officials is not punishable in several countries, all other forms of bribery encompassed by this title are prohibited by penal codes. The problem lies with the enforceability of such laws, in both developed and developing countries, particularly with respect to international investments and trade. Disguised as "commissions," "consultancies," "agency or attorneys' fees," bribes have become necessary cost of doing business worldwide. Nor is the practice universally condemned. Traders and investors have often proclaimed that it cannot be their business to improve the business/political ethics in countries with which they have commercial relations.[26]

A recently established international non-governmental organization, *Transparency International* (Berlin), has undertaken the formidable task of investigating international business ethics. Among its accomplishments are:

- The publication of a country-by-country bribery index, rating political/business corruption, as assessed by international traders.
- Pressing for national legislation abolishing the tax-deductibility of bribes.
- Seeking international governmental cooperation in criminalizing the bribing of officials, by the law of the bribe-giver's country.
- Strengthening international cooperation among non-governmental organizations, such as the International Chamber of Commerce.
- Creating independent watchdog mechanisms, such as industry self-control, ombudsmen, independent private sector inspector generals (IPSIG).

International political/business corruption is rapidly gaining worldwide attention. The 13th International Congress of the International Society for Social Defense (Lecce, Italy, November 1996) was entirely devoted to this topic, which affects all international business, yet only eighteen States could provide data.

This new emphasis on business bribes has already yielded some concrete results. Thus, the OECD meeting of April, 1996 resulted in the agreement of twenty-six nations to end the tax-deductibility of business bribery.[27]

18. Other Offenses Committed by Organized Criminal Groups

This catchall category permitted governments to report on problems encountered that could not be easily included in the seventeen definite categories. The catchall category may include a number of criminal activities more in the nature of local (domestic) crime impacted by forces beyond the borders. For example, both North America and Western Europe are experiencing large-scale automobile theft with the transport of stolen vehicles abroad. Organized criminal groups control these criminal activities. They impact adversely not just individual owners, but the insurance industry. Undoubtedly, effective international law enforcement cooperation must be maintained to deal with this and similar problems.

Summary and Conclusion

A review of the eighteen categories of transnational criminality recently identified by the United Nations demonstrates the vast impact which these criminal activities have on individuals, various branches of the economy and the world economy itself, resulting in a tax on every citizen of the world which may become unbearable and which is totally unnecessary. Individuals and individual commercial enterprises can do relatively little to protect themselves from these dangers. Thus, increased international cooperation among nations has been recognized as the *sine qua* for dealing with transnational criminality. The United Nations Commission on Crime Prevention and Criminal Justice, a 40-nation body, at its Fifth Session (Vienna, 21-23 May 1996) has unanimously adopted an omnibus resolution to deal with transnational crime. This resolution calls for measures to:

- Provide international law enforcement cooperation and assistance
- Prevent the operations of criminal organizations in national territories.
- Provide for effective extradition or prosecution of offenders.
- Share information and provide international technical assistance.
- Strengthen action against international terrorism.
- Fight against illicit drug trafficking.
- Strengthen the ability to detect and interdict the movement across borders of offenders, smuggled persons, firearms, explosives, as well as materials and components designed for use in the manufacture of nuclear, biological or chemical weapons.
- Strengthen the system designed for the prevention of money laundering.

- Strengthen professionalism but also the involvement of all sectors of society in combating and preventing transnational crime.
- Design new measures for the prevention of bribery and corruption.

Additional draft resolutions are dealing with transnational organized crime, ecological criminality, the illicit trafficking in children, firearms, and international crime prevention and criminal justice cooperation.[28] These draft resolutions were subsequently approved by the Economic and Social Council and largely endorsed by the General Assembly, with requests for action by the Secretary General.[29]

In matters of crime prevention and criminal justice, the record of the United Nations has been exemplary. But ultimately, success will depend on the political will, and the governmental capacity of governments to work toward the achievement of common goals.[30]

Independent thereof, all affected industries and entities, e.g., the insurance industry, ecology-sensitive manufacturing, the computer hardware and software industry, the transportation industry, would be well advised to protect themselves by industry-wide self-control. Nevertheless, as yet, the problem of transnational crime is marked by uncertainty in every respect, including its definition, quantification and control. There is, however, a developing body of scholarly inquiry.[31]

*Gerhard O.W. Mueller, J.D., LL.M., Dr.jur. (h.c.) Distinguished Professor, Rutgers University, School of Criminal Justice. Chief (Ret.), United Nations Crime Prevention and Criminal Justice Branch. He has published numerous articles and books focusing on American as well as international comparative criminal law and criminology and has made many presentations at professional conferences.*

Notes and References

1 United Nations, Department of Economic and Social Affairs, Fifth United Nations Congress on the Prevention of Crime and the Treatment of Offenders -- Report Prepared by the Secretariat, A/CONF.56/l0 (1976), p. 9.

2 Ibid., para. 84, p.15

3 F. Adler, G.O.W. Mueller, and W.S. Laufer, (1994) *Criminal Justice*, New York: McGraw-Hill, p. 567.

4 G.O.W. Mueller, "International Criminal Justice: Harnessing the Information Explosion--Coasting Down the Electronic Superhighway," *Journal of Criminal. Justice Education* (in press)

5 A/CONF.169/15/Add.1, of 4 April 1995

6 Several recent symposia have concentrated on a variety of transnational, especially economic, crimes. See G. Arzt et al., (1992), *Effective and Innovative Countermeasures Against Economic Crime* (Takashi Watanabe, ed.), Resource Material Series No. 41, Tokyo United Nations Asia and Far East Institute for the Prevention of Crime and the Treatment of Offenders; J. Reuvid (ed.), (1995), *The Regulation and Prevention of Economic Crime Internationally*, London: Kogan Page.

7 e.g., global imports rose from $330 billion in 1960 to $3,500 billion in 1990. Air traffic volume increased from 26 billion passenger miles in 1960 to 600 billion in 1992 -- and that was only the start of true globalization which occurred with the collapse of the Soviet Union.

8 C. A. Intriago, (1991), *International Money Laundering*, London: Eurostudy; W.C. Gilmore, (1992), *International Efforts to Combat Money Laundering*, Cambridge, England: Grotius; P. Bernasconi (ed.), (1995), *Money Laundering and Bank Secrecy*, The Hague: Kluwer Law International.

9 Several journals are devoted entirely to terrorism. See *Terrorism* (New York); *Studies in Conflict and Terrorism*, (London); *Violence, Aggression, Terrorism*, Danbury, CT. For research on the drug-terrorism connection, see R. Clutterbuck (1990), *Terrorism, Drugs and Crime in Europe after 1992, London: Routledge;* R. Ehrenfeld, (1990) *Narco Terrorism*, New York: Basic Books.

10 P. Reuters, (1993), "High-Tech Art Sleuths Snare Thieves," *C.J. International*, 9(4): 6

11 Truc-Nhu Ho, (1992), *Art Theft in New York City: An Explanatory Study in Crime Specificity* Ph.D. Dissertation, Rutgers University.

12 R. Blumenthal, "Museums Getting Together to Track Stolen Art," *New York Times*, July, 16, 1996, pp. C13, C15.

13 N. D. Voss, (1996), "Crime on the Internet," *Jones Telecommunications and Multimedia Encyclopedia*, Drive D:\Studio, Jones Digital Century.

14 "For Sale -- Nukes: Deadly plutonium from Russia's vast nuclear network is turning up on the European market. Who is buying-- and can they be stopped?" *Newsweek*, August 29, 1994, pp. 30-31; B. W. Nolan, 'Formula for Terror,' *Time*, August 29, 1994.

15 L. Johnston (1994), "Policing Plutonium: Issues in the Provision of Policing Services at Nuclear Facilities and for Related Materials in Transit," *Policing and Society*, 4(l): 53-71; Williams and P. H. Woessnar, (1995), *Nuclear Material Trafficking: An Interim Assessment*, Pittsburgh, PA: Ridgway Center for International Security Studies.

16 E. Ellen, (1995), "The Dimensions of International Maritime Crime," in M. Gill (ed.), *Issues in Maritime Crime: Mayhem Sea*, Leicester, UK: Perpetuity Press, 1 95, pp. 4-11; E. Ellen (1990), "Contemporary Piracy," *California Western International Law Journal*,

21:123-128; M. Gill, (1995), *"Crime at Sea: A Forgotten Issue in Police Co-operation,"* Leicester, UK: Centre for the Study of Public Order; G.O.W. Mueller and Freda Adler, (1985), *Outlaws of the Ocean,* New York: Hearst Marine Books; G.O.W. Mueller and F. Adler, (1992), "Piraterie: le 'Jolly Roger' flotte a nouveau les Corsaires des Caribes," *Revue Internationale de Criminologie et de Police Technique,* 4:408-424.

17 National Insurance Crime Bureau, Fax of July 29, 1996.

18 British Banking Association estimate. See L. E. Coutoria, (1995), "The Future of High-technology Crime: A Parallel Delphi Study," *Journal of Criminal Justice,* 23(1): 13-27.

19 See U. Siber (1992), *The International Emergence of Criminal Information Law,* Koln: Carl Heymanns Verlag.

20 S. M. Edwards, T. D. Edwards and C. B. Field (eds.), (1996) *Environmental Crime and Criminality,* New York: Garland Publishing, with 11 individual essays.

21 W.D.Hyatt and T.L.Trexler, "Environmental Crime and Organized Crime: What will the Future Hold?" in S.M. Edwards et al., op. cit., supra pp. 245-262.

22 Ko-lin Chin (1990), *Chinese Subculture and Criminality: Non-traditional Crime Groups in America,* Westport, CT: Greenwood.

23 B. Buse and N. Donges, (1993), "Illegaler Organhandel," *Magazin fur die Polizei,* 203: 4-7. See also Dae H. Chong, (1995), "A New Form of International Crime: The Human Organ Trade." *International Journal of Comparative and Applied Criminal Justice,* 19(1): 1-18.

24 P. S. Young, "Moving to Compensate Families in Human Organ Market'', *New York Times,* July 8, 1994, p. B7

25 P. Williams and C. Flores, (1994), "Transnational Criminal Organizations and Drug Trafficking," *Bulletin on Narcotics,* 46(2): 9-24; M. Woodiwiss (1993), "Crime's Global Reach," in *Global Crime Connections,* (eds) F. Pearce and M. Woodiwiss, Houndmills and London: Macmillan, pp. 1-31; B. Bullington, "All about Eve: The Many Faces of United States Drug Policy," in Pearce and Woodiwiss, (eds.) *Global Crime Connections,* pp. 32-71; Nicholas Dorn and Nigel South, "After Mr. Bennett and Mr. Bush--U. S. Foreign Policy and the Prospects for Drug Control." in Pearce and Woodiwiss, *Global Crime Connections,* pp. 72-90; G. Alexander, (ed.) (1991), *Western State Terrorism,* New York: Routledge.

26 See, in general, 'Crime Prevention and Criminal Justice in the Context of Development: Realities and Perspectives of International Cooperation,' in *International Review of Criminal Policy,* 41/42:1-19 (1993). See also M. Clarke et al., Selected Papers Presented at the Second Liverpool Conference on Fraud, Corruption and Business Crime, *Corruption and Reform,* 6 (1991): 207-303; F. Pearce and M. Woodiwiss, (eds.) (1993), *Global Crime Connections: Dynamics and Control,* Toronto: University of Toronto Press.

27 M. Simons, 'U.S. Enlists Rich Nations in Move to End Business Bribes' *New York Times,* April 1, 1996, p. 10.

28 ISPAC Newsletter, vol. 4, No. 15, July 1996.

29 United Nations, General Assembly, Crime Prevention and Criminal Justice, Progress Made in the Implementation of General Assembly Resolutions 50/145 and 50/146, Report of the Secretary General, A/51/327, of 1 October, 1996.

30 For an assessment of Japan's responses to transnational crime, see Toyoji Saito, (1994), "Japanese Response to the New Norms of Crime: Crime and Justice in the Era of Globalization," *Konan Law Review* (Japan), 35 210-232.

31 For a starter, see R. D. Atkins (ed.), (1995) *The Alleged Transnational Criminal,* The Hague: Kluver Law International.

Mere anarchy is loosed upon the world,
The blood-dimmed tide is loosed, and everywhere
The ceremony of innocence is drowned;
The best lack all conviction, while the worst
Are full of passionate intensity
-- Yeats, The Second Coming

2 Getting Rich and Getting Even: Transnational Threats in the Twenty-First Century

Phil Williams

Abstract

This paper examines the threats to national and international security posed by transnational criminal organizations and transnational terrorist groups. It contends that the emergence of these threats can be understood as a result of two processes -- globalization and the crisis of state authority -- both of which contribute to a contraction of the domain of state authority. The impact of various aspects of globalization-diasporas and ethnic networks, the growth of trade, the development of a global financial system, and the development of global information communication systems, ·and the emergence of global cities -- are examined. Future trends in organized crime and terrorism are also explored.

Key Words: Organized crime, transnational, globalization, terrorism

Introduction

Microbes are often more dangerous to one's health and well being than more visible threats. They are also more pervasive, more difficult to detect, more difficult to avoid and more difficult to counter. Security threats in the post-Cold War world have many of the same qualities. While there are still potential dangers from states that deploy large-scale military power, threats to national and international security are no longer restricted to such states. Security threats now come in many different guises, extend well beyond military power, emanate from a growing variety of actors, are no longer linked inexorably to territory and, paradoxically, stem in part from developments that traditionally have been regarded as positive and benign in their effects.

Globalization, in particular, a development that has long been hailed by liberal institutionalists as holding out the promise to transcend the parochial power struggles of a Hobbesian world, has provided new opportunities for the emergence of transnational threats. Such threats are the theme of this article, with particular attention given to the activities of transnational criminal organizations (TCOs), drug trafficking organizations and transnational terrorist groups.

The major paradox of the Cold War world was that security rested upon threats that would have been disastrous to implement. The major paradox of the post-Cold War world is that, in some respects, power and wealth can be a source of weakness rather than strength. Similarly sophistication, particularly in technology, is becoming a source of vulnerability rather than protection. The new world has seen not so much a multiplication of potential targets -- these have always been there -- but an increase in both the attractiveness of many targets and in the capacity of "sovereign free actors" to exploit or destroy them.[1] The structured chess and poker analogies of nuclear deterrence have given way to a world in which there are fewer rules, and in which norms of behavior and conventions of restraint are no longer compelling. If the dominant theme of Cold War competition was the game of "chicken," the dominant theme of the post-Cold War era is cacophony.

There are many games being played simultaneously, overlapping with and impinging on one another. The playing field has become more fluid and less definable, the areas for offensive and defensive operations more problematic and the players more varied and less predictable. Moreover, it is not always clear whether particular actions are intended to exploit or to destroy. Counterfeiting of the U.S. dollar, for example, can be either a deliberate effort to undermine the stability and integrity of the United States currency or simply an illicit way of obtaining greater wealth.

In considering the threats posed by TCOs and by transnational terrorist organizations, it is tempting to conclude that there is a blurring of the two kinds of groups. After all, transnational criminal organizations, such as the Italian Mafia and the Colombian cartels, have used terrorist attacks against their home states in an attempt to deter or disrupt vigorous law enforcement campaigns and ensure an environment conducive to a continuation of their criminal activities. Moreover, with the end of the Cold War, proxy factions in civil wars can no longer count on support from superpower patrons, while there has also been a marked decline in state sponsorship for terrorism.

In these circumstances, terrorist organizations, insurgency groups and participants in ethnic conflicts have turned to criminal activities in order to obtain the resources to continue their political and military struggles. This is evident, for example, in the relatively large number of Tamils who have been arrested in Western Europe and the United States for drug trafficking. While some were engaged in the drug business for personal gain, others were "clearly linked to fund-raising for the Tamil Tiger separatists" looking to use the profits to prosecute their political and military struggle in Sri Lanka.[2] Similarly, during the war in Bosnia there were frequent reports regarding the exchange of drugs for arms.

Not surprisingly, there are also growing links between criminal and terrorist organizations. Both operate in the same murky world, and on occasion, see mutual benefit in deals involving weapons for illicit products or services. At times, there are natural synergies; in other cases the alliances or cooperative ventures are somewhat unexpected with both criminal and terrorist organizations displaying a remarkable capacity to transcend ideological antipathies for the sake of mutual gain. Peruvian drug traffickers and Shining Path guerrillas, for example, have worked together, while in Colombia the drug trafficking cartels have had an ambivalent but nevertheless continuing relationship with groups such as the FARC and M-19. Whether forged out of convenience or necessity, however, such links enhance the capacity of both criminal and terrorist organizations and make the threats they pose even more formidable.

Important as these tendencies are, they point to an overlapping of activities and a mixture of cooperative and conflicting relationships between the two kinds of organizations rather than towards convergence. In the final analysis, terrorist and criminal organizations have very different objectives that set them apart from one another. Terrorist organizations generally seek radical political change in support of a religious, political or ideological cause and try to bring this about directly or indirectly through violence. Their political goals range from global revolution to rectifying specific grievances against particular governments. Whatever the particular goals in specific cases, however, the driving impulses are invariably political in nature.

For criminal organizations, in contrast, the dominant leitmotif is the accumulation of wealth. Insofar as criminal organizations try to influence the political situation, whether at the local or the national level, such efforts are usually designed to protect and promote their illicit enterprises and to ensure that the risks they face from law enforcement remain low. For terrorist groups, in contrast, criminal activities such as drug trafficking and arms trafficking are simply a means to an end.

These differences in objectives are accompanied by equally profound, although not immediately obvious, differences in means. For terrorist groups, violence is not incidental to their activities or simply the key factor differentiating them from other political activists; rather it is their raison d'être and their defining characteristic. For transnational criminal organizations, the use of violence is something which -- as many observers have noted -- sets them apart from licit corporations, but is certainly not as central to their functioning as it is to the terrorist group.[3] Violence is an instrument that transnational criminal organizations often employ selectively and rarely use indiscriminately. Moreover, it is used to enforce internal discipline, to eliminate or weaken rivals and to coerce victims more often than it is used directly against governments.

Violence against state authorities is generally eschewed in favor of the other major instrument of transnational organized crime -- corruption. Transnational criminal organizations prefer to work within the existing system as long as this is malleable. In so far as they have political objectives, these are aimed against specific law enforcement policies rather than designed to overthrow the existing power structure. Cooperation is generally the preferable alternative and it is only where this has not worked -- or where the state authorities are deemed to have reneged on their side of the bargain, as in Italy in the 1980s -- that criminal organizations resort to terror tactics.

If one kind of organization wants money to facilitate its terror activities while the other occasionally uses terror to protect its business activities, they both use the same infrastructure of globalization and both are able to exploit the crisis of authority and legitimacy that has taken place in many states. Nevertheless, divergent aims and priorities represent a potential source of tension between the two kinds of groups. Transnational criminal organizations want profit and the continued ability to exploit the financial and other systems that could increasingly become the target for destruction or disruption by terrorist organizations. Acknowledging the differences between terrorist and criminal organizations, therefore, is crucial. In both cases, though, it is essential to understand the reasons for their emergence, their future directions and what can be done about them. Accordingly, this paper sets out to answer several broad questions:

- Why have transnational threats emerged?
- What forces, trends and developments are likely to shape their future direction?
- What are the major trends in transnational threats?
- What, if anything, can be done about these threats?

The Emergence of Transnational Threats

Explaining the emergence of transnational threats is relatively easy. In large part, transnational crime has grown out of the economic interdependence and globalization processes that have for so long been regarded by liberal commentators as a stabilizing and pacifying influence in international relations, the same developments (discussed more fully below) that have encouraged the growth of licit economic activity have also helped to promote illicit activity. In effect, transnational organized crime represents the dark side of interdependence. As such, it poses major challenges to national and international security, both feeding off and exacerbating insecurity, instability and economic and political dislocation. Transnational organized crime, like transnational terrorist activity, is fed by war, ethnic strife, political upheaval and the crisis of state authority that exists in large parts of the world. It has also become an unwelcome concomitant of the transition from centralized, authoritarian political systems and command economies towards liberal democracies and market economies. In short, the post-Cold War world is one in which there are new opportunities for transnational crime and terrorism, new markets for illicit products and continued incentives to exploit these markets.

In addition, "sovereign-free" actors are developing an increased capacity both for exploitation and disruption. Although there is not a complete absence of countervailing pressures, there is only a very patchy implementation of policies designed to prevent and control criminal and terrorist activities and mitigate the consequences of their actions. In effect, the emergence of the global village has been accompanied by a loss of authority by the traditional guardians. The elders of the village (governments) no longer have the power to determine and enforce the rules of village life or the capacity to control the activities that take place.

As a result of the globalization of trade, finance, investment, technology, communications and information systems, the domain of state authority has contracted significantly. States no longer have the same degree of control over the information, people, money or commodities that, in one way or another, flow across their borders. To some this has been welcome. The process of globalization has led many corporate executives in particular to embrace the idea of a borderless world and the twilight of national sovereignty.[4]

Operating transnationally in the new global market has become a central characteristic of the modern corporation. But the very things that have made it possible to move goods, people and money through the global economy have also facilitated the movement of "dirty money" and contract killers as well as the transportation of drugs, arms and illegal aliens. Just as borders no longer provide an impediment to licit business activity, they are no longer a barrier to illicit activities. In short, globalization has provided new opportunities and capabilities for TCOs and transnational terrorist organizations. There is a double irony here. Although globalization has reduced the importance of borders and undermined traditional conceptions of national sovereignty as impediments to criminal and terrorist activities, borders and the formalities of sovereignty continue to impede efforts by governments to respond to such activities. While transnational criminals and terrorist groups operate in what is, in effect, a borderless world, law enforcement still operates in a bordered world -- even if the borders themselves are often contested - that seriously reduces its effectiveness.

The developments involved in globalization are the result of long term secular trends that are impossible to reverse. Simultaneously -- and connected in part, but only in part, to this -- in many states there has been a loss of legitimization and authority. This does not mean that the state system has completely lost its hold; in some cases of civil strife -- such as Yugoslavia -- even where there has been an almost complete failure of the state and a reversal to tribalism and ethnicity as the basis for political action, the conflict still centers around the form the state should take, in terms of either its territorial or ethnic composition. Even where the particular form of the state is contested, in most cases the state as such remains the primary source of both identity and allegiance for the majority of the population.

Yet, in some instances there is also a growing sense of alienation towards the state and government authority per se. This is evident even in the United States where distrust of the government has been a major factor in the rise of the militia movements. In states in transition, there is the added problem that the citizenry has lost not only authoritarian rule, but also the economic and social safeguards that often accompanied it. Hyperinflation and unemployment throughout a large part of the former Soviet Union have created conditions of economic hardship.   At the same time, the opportunities in the legitimate economy have -- for most people - been very circumscribed.   Such a situation provides both pressures and incentives for involvement in criminal activity as one of the few available routes to economic betterment.

The twin processes of globalization and the crisis of state authority have produced a fundamental challenge to global governance -- and will continue to do so.[5] If globalization has become a dominant theme during the last quarter of the twentieth century, there is no evidence that the processes involved have run their course. Indeed, globalization is more likely to intensify rather than abate in the early decades of the next millennium.   Moreover, since globalization involves highly profitable economic and social interdependencies, efforts at reversal would have such debilitating consequences for legitimate trade and financial flows that they have become virtually impossible.   Beneficial as it might be for criminal and terrorist organizations, globalization is here to stay -- and governments and law enforcement agencies need to adapt accordingly.

Similarly, the crisis of state authority and the inability of many states to meet the needs and demands of their citizens will continue to have profound implications for the future development of both domestic and transnational threats. These highly diverse developments have not only made it impossible to eliminate conditions that facilitate the activities of transnational terrorist and criminal organizations, but have also resulted in what can best be described as a new form of geopolitics. While traditional geopolitical competition based on power and territory is unlikely to disappear, it is accompanied by a new form of geopolitics based on very different considerations and centering around new actors. The geopolitics of transnational threats differs in many respects from traditional geopolitics in which control of natural resources and critical geographical areas was central. Yet, like its predecessor, the new geopolitics rests on a series of interlocking and complementary features of global politics and economics that helps to explain not only the growth of transnational threats but also why they are likely to intensify rather than abate.

TRANSNATIONAL THREATS AND THE NEW GEOPOLITICS
Developments at the Global Level
Although the term "globalization" has long been used, it was only with the end of the Cold War in 1989, the subsequent demise of the Soviet Union in 1991 and the breakdown of barriers between East and West that the process became truly global.   The following analysis identifies several crucial components of this process and considers their implications for both the present and the future of transnational threats.

Mobility of People
To a greater extent than ever before the free movement of people, information, and ideas has become truly global -- and this trend is likely to intensify. At one level it is very simple. Air traffic in particular has provided the easy mobility that facilitates international business meetings, international

vacations and travels on a scale that is unprecedented. Among the countries that account for particularly large numbers of passengers arriving in the United States by air are France, Germany, Britain, Mexico and Canada.[6] Also significant, however, are the Bahamas, the Dominican Republic and Jamaica -- all countries that have increasing links to the drug trafficking industry.[7] There is nothing to indicate that the upward trend in mobility is likely to be reversed over the next ten to fifteen years. On the contrary, one of the most significant results of the collapse of the Soviet Union has been the emergence of new air routes to and from regions such as Central Asia that were previously inaccessible. Direct connections, for example, now exist between Tashkent and London, and Tashkent and New York with a brief stop in Amsterdam. This allows new business linkages but also facilitates the movement of drug traffickers from areas of production to the large consumer markets in Western Europe and the United States.

The other and more complex aspect of mobility of people is migration. Migration is far from a new phenomenon, and has long been propelled by the desire to escape poverty and carve out a better life. The extent of migration has never been as great as it is today, however, with some estimates claiming that there are now well over 100 million migrants worldwide.[8] Sarah Spencer has distinguished among factors which facilitate migration, factors which encourage it and factors which necessitate it.[9] One of the most important facilitating and encouraging factors has been transnational social networks that "tie potential immigrants to actual residents in the receiving countries, whether through families, information dispersion or labor recruitment."[10] The necessitating factors include famine, conflict and repression.

There has been a vast explosion in the number of refugees in the world from 4.6 million in 1978 to over 18 million (with 6 million in Africa and 5 million in the Middle East) by 1993.[11] Unless the political and economic upheavals of the post-Cold War world abate significantly, the refugee problem is likely to increase. So too is migration. The difficulty, however, is that developed countries such as Germany that are the targets for migrants, have unemployment problems that have reduced the demand for outside labor, creating a disconnection between supply and demand. Another problem is that in countries such as the United States there is growing political opposition to continued migration flows and demands for greater restriction on entry. One result of this is that those who are unable to acquire legal access to a target state often try to enter the country illegally. When the pressures that generate legal migration encounter obstacles, they simply create illegal migration patterns that can all too easily be exploited by organized crime.

Immigration into the United States during the 1980s reached its highest level since the 1900s with over seven million people entering the country. Another 4.5 million immigrants arrived between 1991 and 1994.[12] Western European countries such as France, Italy and Germany have also had a major inflow both from the South and from the East -- although the massive exodus from Eastern Europe predicted by many observers has not taken place. In addition to the legal migrants, of course, there are also the illegal immigrants. Over a million illegal immigrants were apprehended by the United States border patrol in 1994. Yet it is estimated by the United States Department of State that between 100,000 and 120,000 Chinese illegally enter the United States every year. In the case of Western Europe, there are about two million immigrants annually and at least 300,000 illegal immigrants.[13]

Many demographic analyses suggest that migration, driven in large part by economic necessity, will continue. Between 1991 and 2025 the global workforce will increase by around 1.48 billion people of whom 1.4 billion will be in the developing world.[14] With over 40 million would-be workers entering the job market every year in the developing world and finding that jobs are simply not available, the potential for increased migration and diasporas is enormous. And if developed states fail to open up to increased immigration then illegal immigration will increase enormously. All of this has important implications for transnational criminal and terrorist organizations and activities:

- Most migrants, of course, are law-abiding citizens. Yet among those who emigrate, there are inevitably members of criminal organizations who bring with them their criminal skills and knowledge and their criminal affiliations and contacts. Chinese, Nigerian, Italian and Russian diasporas have all contained significant criminal elements. This should not be surprising; when criminal organizations come under pressure in their home state, either from law enforcement or as a result of internecine warfare, one response of some of the members is to migrate to areas and states where the risks are lower and conditions are generally more congenial. The Sicilian diaspora of the 1960s and 1970s to places as diverse as Australia, Venezuela and Germany is a good example. Eventually this became a major asset as La Cosa Nostra increasingly became involved in transnational activities.[15] The Cuntrera family in Venezuela became a key factor linking Italian organized crime and cocaine supplies from Latin America. Similarly, during the 1970s and 1980s, some of those allowed to emigrate from the Soviet Union were criminals, and provided a foundation for criminal activities in the United States and Israel that subsequent Russian émigré groups were able to consolidate and extend.
- Greater mobility has increased the capacity of criminal organizations and their individual members to elude national criminal jurisdictions where they are high priority targets. It has been claimed that Cambodia, for example, has become a haven for fugitive crime, largely because of its lack of extradition treaties. Reportedly, in 1995 between 150 and 300 of Interpol's most wanted fugitives were using Cambodia as a safe haven.[16]

- The increase in business, personal and leisure travel as well as the increase in migration exacerbates the difficulties confronting governments in their efforts to monitor and control access to and exit from their national territory. The need to expedite passport checks sets limits to what can be achieved at entry and exit points.
- There is likely to be a marked intensification of alien smuggling. The trends described above suggest that there will be growing diversification in the nationality of illegal immigrants as well as continued increases in their number. The corollary of course is the consolidation and extension of what can best be described as human commodity trafficking and increased profits to those who organize and facilitate illegal entry into the United States, Western Europe and other developed countries.[17]
- Air transport has provided unprecedented opportunity for individuals or groups to enter a country, commit a crime or series of crimes or engage in terrorist activity, and then depart before they are caught. Contract killers can be brought in to Brighton Beach from Yekaterinburg, fulfill their contract, and depart again before the crime has even been discovered.
- The ethnic networks resulting from diasporas provide links with the home bases of criminal and terrorist organizations. These networks are an important resource for many transnational criminal organizations; they provide cover, recruits and transnational linkages that facilitate illicit activity. And because immigrant communities are difficult for law enforcement to penetrate, they provide a built-in security mechanism. Tactics such as wiretapping that the FBI used effectively against the Mafia are far less effective when targeted against criminal networks, such as the Nigerians or Chinese, able to use a variety of different dialects to confound efforts at electronic eavesdropping. Nor is it easy to find informers in immigrant communities, which are notoriously reluctant to contact let alone cooperate with law enforcement.
- Ethnic networks make it difficult for governments to distinguish between external and internal threats posed by transnational criminal and terrorist organizations. Because of the tendency of governments to compartmentalize problems, this can all to easily result in either interagency competition over roles and missions or the problem falling through the cracks.

Increased Trade Flows

One of the major components and underpinnings of globalization has been the vast growth of international trade, a process greatly facilitated by the free trade system set up after the Second World War. Lowering of tariffs, the creation of free trade arrangements and the gradual integration of the former Soviet bloc into the global trading system have all encouraged steep increases in global trade during the 1990s. One indicator of this growth is the increase in the number of dry cargo containers in use worldwide. Between 1990 and 1994 the availability of cargo containers jumped from under six million to over eight million. There has also been an increase in the amount of world seaborne trade. Apart from a temporary downturn in the mid-1980s resulting from lower demand for crude oil, the increase in the amount of sea-borne trade has been fairly constant and forecasts through to 2005 suggest that this upward trend will continue.[18] Once again this provides an environment that is highly conducive to the activities of transnational criminal organizations and, to a lesser extent, terrorist organizations. There are several ways in which criminals and terrorists benefit from continued increases in global trade:

- The opportunities to embed illicit goods in licit are multiplying and the risk of detection is likely to fall from what is already a low figure. The list of illicit products has also expanded and includes not only arms and drugs, but also fauna and flora, art and antiquities, CFCs, hazardous waste and nuclear materials. Problems of inspection and monitoring will become even more formidable than they are at present. The United States typically inspects about four percent of the containers coming into the country, while in many other countries the capacity for inspections is even lower. As container trade continues to grow, inspections will pose even less of a barrier to smuggling.
- The number of targets for terrorist activity is increasing with ports and container ships providing targets that can be hit fairly easily and with relatively low risk. Similarly, the number of opportunities for piracy is also increasing. Indeed, during the last several years there has been a serious increase in the incidence of piracy, especially in the seas around Indonesia, off the coast of Somalia and near Brazil. The International Maritime Bureau's Regional Piracy center in Kuala Lumpur reported ninety-two cases of piracy in 1994, 170 in 1995 and 175 in 1996.
- The opportunities for smuggling weapons of mass destruction into the United States and other potential target countries are increasing significantly. During the 21st century the container bomb is likely to become a more serious threat than the ballistic missile -- and may be even harder to stop.
- The number of opportunities for financial maritime fraud is increasing along with the number of ship-borne containers. Cargoes and in some cases the ships are declared lost when in

fact the cargoes have been illegally sold. This problem of "phantom ships" has been around for some years, but is likely to become an even more frequent occurrence.

- The number of opportunities to use false invoicing for imports to the United States and Western Europe, and other major importers is increasing, thereby providing greater opportunities for money laundering and the repatriation of profits from illicit activities.

In short, the expansion of licit trade has been accompanied by an expansion of illicit trade and an increase in the availability of opportunities to divert or disrupt the flow of licit commodities. The global trading system has become a smuggler's paradise and is likely to remain so as the opportunities continue to expand faster than the constraints or obstacles to criminal activities. The global trading system, of course, was the initial manifestation of globalization. Gradually, its importance has been overtaken by the development of the global financial system. And if anything criminal enterprises find this even more congenial than the vast increase in world trade.

The Global Financial System

A major component of the new geopolitics is the financial infrastructure -- a system that links countries, banks and other financial institutions such as brokerage houses and stock markets, currencies and investment portfolios in a global exchange mechanism that operates twenty-four hours a day. Reflecting the revolutions in communications and information technologies this system is reliant on what Joel Kurtzman has termed *"megabyte money."*[19] As he notes most money now appears as symbols on computer screens and is best understood as a network which includes all the world's markets -- stocks, bonds, futures, currency, interest rate, options, derivatives and so on.[20] If money has in some respects been transformed, it nevertheless retains its flexibility and can be moved from continent to continent and owner to owner, through a global system of electronic transfers that incorporates clearing mechanisms such as Chips, Swift and Fedwire. In effect, money can disappear, and even though anti-money laundering agencies such as Financial Crimes Enforcement Network in the United States and Austrac in Australia can often trace "dirty money," catching up with it and confiscating it is another matter altogether.

One of the major characteristics of the global financial system is that it is not under state or government control. As Kurtzman has noted, the financial economy is akin to an electronic commons that is owned by the people using it. Money is transmitted rapidly and easily from one node on the network to another with very limited oversight or regulation.[21] To some extent governments and Central Banks have themselves to blame for this situation. As Helmut Schmidt once observed, during the 1980s central banks:

> did not see that they were losing their grip over the over markets when they allowed commercial banks to establish offshore affiliates...they are not really cooperating closely

> *enough to prevent the internationalization of financial flows*
> *without an international controlling agency. Nowadays you*
> *have one worldwide stock exchange. Nobody is controlling it.*
> *You have one worldwide money market.   Nobody is*
> *controlling it.*[22]

If this situation arose in part through a lack of both foresight and oversight, once the process of deregulation had started, governments tended to embrace it, engaging in what was effectively a *"competition in laxity."*[23] Yet even without government participation and encouragement, major change was inevitable, facilitated by technology and driven in part by the massive increase in the number of transactions and the move from an investment economy to a transaction economy or what Susan Strange termed *"casino capitalism."*[24] The implication of government involvement in this process of competitive deregulation, however, was that the increased volume of financial business was not matched by the development of regulatory measures.

This situation may be getting even worse. The increase in the number of monetary instruments, the increased number of financial transactions -- such as futures and derivatives -- that are not necessarily linked directly to real products, the growing use of cyber-money and smart cards, new banking methods such as correspondent banking and the use of representative offices and foreign branches, all make monitoring and control of the global financial system extremely difficult if not impossible.

Some governments, of course, have attempted to provide safeguards against money laundering in their jurisdictions, seeking to regulate both banks and non-bank financial institutions. The OECD's Financial Action Task Force, under the impetus provided by the United States, has been at the forefront of efforts to ensure anti-money laundering regulations are in place among the member states and to extend the nascent regime to other countries. While the FATF has had some successes, however, these have been modest. The global banking system can be divided into three main sectors -- a relatively well-regulated zone in which there is strict regulation against money laundering, the offshore banking havens that place a premium on secrecy and the unregulated zone in countries of the Former Soviet Union and parts of the developing world where appropriate norms, procedures and conventions have not yet been established.

One astute observer has argued that "the combination of the internationalization and deregulation of banking in the 1980s effectively furnished both legitimate corporations and criminals with a protective shield of secrecy that undermines control efforts."[25] While this is correct so far as it goes, it does not convey the whole picture. The privatization of former communist economies and the introduction of a commercial banking sector have added another massive obstacle to efforts to establish a global anti-money laundering regime. As banks in Russia are integrated into the global financial system they bring with them those elements of organized crime that exert direct control or indirect influence over their activities.

Another problem is that divergent levels of regulation ensure that efforts to prevent the global financial system from being used for money laundering and other illicit transactions have little impact and simply push money laundering activities from areas where they are illegal to countries where the origin or source of money is irrelevant. Even in well-regulated systems where efforts have been made to impose safeguards through "due diligence" requirements and know your customer rules, and the will to prevent money laundering is clearly present, it is still virtually impossible to distinguish "dirty money" (i.e. money earned through illicit activities such as drug trafficking) from clean money. In most of the world, however, not only are there few efforts to prevent money laundering but also no distinction is made between clean and dirty money. In effect, money is money and its source is irrelevant. This is not surprising. For both developing economies and economies in transition, capital flight tends to be more of a problem than laundering the proceeds of illicit activity. In Belarus and other countries in the former Soviet Union, incoming money tends to be welcomed as foreign investment whatever its source.[26] Even if legislation against money laundering is enacted, therefore, it will not necessarily be implemented vigorously. In sum, unless there is universal adherence to norms of financial transparency, and general adoption and implementation of laws and regulations directed against money laundering, laundering activities simply relocate from one venue to another.

In one sense, the problems that come from possible criminal exploitation of the global financial system are simply a subset of the much larger problem of state control and regulation of a vast array of transnational financial activities. Even so, it is possible to identify several ways in which the global financial system can be exploited by transnational criminal organizations, drug trafficking and terrorist organizations.

The system has many points of access and makes it possible to trade anonymously, to move money rapidly and easily and to obscure the origin and ownership of money making thereby obscuring the distinction between dirty and clean money. Indeed, the mobility of capital parallels that of the transnational criminals themselves and could not be better suited to the activities of transnational organized crime. "Megabyte money" is enormously difficult to track and to control, while the creation of new stock exchanges combined with the growing popularity of future options and derivatives makes effective policing impossible. "Hot money" has simply become too hot to catch and seize.

The offshore banking sector provides attractive opportunities for the transfer and secretion of funds in places where they are relatively safe from identification and seizure by law enforcement. Although some efforts are being made to "clean up" and regulate this sector, this is likely to be a long struggle -- not least because offshore banks are also havens for tax avoidance and tax evasion schemes.

As "cyber-money" and "smart cards" become increasingly popular they are likely to be fully exploited by criminal organizations for money laundering and other activities including the circumvention of exchange controls. The U.S. State Department's International Narcotics Control Strategy Report in March 1997 paid considerable attention to this issue, noting that:

> *high speed, worldwide transfers that are a part of the cyberpayment technology add complexity to law enforcement's ability to trace criminal activity and recover illicit proceeds. And there are important international jurisdictional issues. Some cyberpayment systems are being designed to operate internationally and use multiple currencies. Thus one of the challenges facing law enforcement and the international community will be determining jurisdictional authority in a global economy.*[27]

This does not augur well for efforts to combat money laundering.

Some of the new trading schemes encourage a risk taking mentality that often goes hand win hand with disregard for regulation. Indeed, as Jessica Mathews has noted, the global financial system is a "space without rules" that is "made to order for those who operate without them."[28] A system in which a Nicolas Leeson can operate without supervision -- thereby leading to the collapse of Barings Bank -- is a system that is easily exploited by the successors of Meyer Lansky, the accountant for the mob who is generally acknowledged as the inventor of modern money laundering.

The integration of Russian banks into the global system carries with it very considerable dangers since, according to many reports, between forty and eighty percent of these banks are either under the direct control of organized crime or heavily influenced by criminal groups.

There are increased opportunities for repatriation of profits from illicit activities. Much of what is popularly termed money laundering is not so much about disguising or cleaning money as it is about repatriating it from the host state to the home state of the criminal organization where it can be used with impunity. In many cases -- Nigeria is an obvious example -- the home state does not inquire very closely about the source of the money.

The global nature of the system and the anonymity it affords makes it easier to provide financing for criminals or terrorist groups active in host states. The global financial system with its major nodes in "global cities" provides an attractive set of targets for terrorist activity. Because the system is global and highly reliant on electronic networks it probably has some redundancies built in. Nevertheless, terrorists, by coordinating strikes in several different locations, might be able to do serious damage to the functioning of the system and create a financial crisis of unprecedented gravity.

The global financial system provides a myriad of new opportunities for the mixing of crime and terrorism in ways that manage to send a political message while also being very lucrative. Purchases of future options for foreign countries' wheat crops prior to biological attacks on the United States' wheat crop could allow those involved to get rich and get even. Such initiatives are essentially hybrid activities that do not fall neatly into traditional categories of crime or terrorism, but they are feasible contingencies and should be treated very seriously.

The global financial system offers opportunities to transfer money simply, quickly and clandestinely, thereby facilitating the corruption of government officials. This helps to ensure the maintenance of safe home bases for transnational criminal organizations as well as to facilitate the flow of illicit commodities.

The Rise of Global Cities and Mega-Cities

A fourth dimension of the new geopolitics is the emergence of global cities, a category that encompasses not only the obvious candidates such as New York, Los Angeles, Miami, London, Paris, Frankfurt, Tokyo, Hong Kong and Moscow, but that also extends to Rio de Janeiro, Johannesburg, Bangkok, Lagos and the like. Such cities have large cosmopolitan populations connected to one another by advanced telecommunications that form the major and minor nodes of the global financial and trading systems and provide transportation links both to one another and to the national hinterlands they serve. Some of these cities are national capitals, while a small number have also become mega-cities (i.e. cities with over eight million inhabitants).

The number of mega-cities increased from ten in 1970 to twenty in 1990; by 2000 there are expected to be twenty-eight such cities.[29] Most of these cities are hosts to an influx of people coming from rural areas in search of economic opportunity. In practice, aspirations are rarely fulfilled and most of new urban dwellers find that they have merely traded a life of rural destitution for one of urban destitution. As Wally N'Dow, head of the Habitat II Conference has noted, there are now more than 600 million people officially homeless or living in life-threatening urban conditions. More than one billion lack sanitation. "A low-grade civil war is fought every day in the world's urban centers. Many cities are collapsing. We risk a complete breakdown in cities. People feel alienated."[30] Nor are conditions likely to improve in the near future as the number of mega-cities continues to increase and governments find it increasingly difficult to provide not only an appropriate level of services but also effective governance. Perhaps nowhere else is Robert Kaplan's somewhat apocalyptic vision of the coming anarchy likely to be as prescient as in mega-cities.[31]

Such cities provide an urban environment in which survival takes precedence over the rule of law, in which alienation and anger are rife, and in which localized street gangs become the dominant form of social organization. The most ruthless and efficient of these gangs are likely to develop into more significant and powerful criminal organizations. In this sense, mega-cities and global cities are likely to act as incubators for modern organized crime groups superseding port cities such as Marseilles, which traditionally had this role.[32]

For some individuals, of course, solace and bonding will be found not in crime but in forms of political, social and economic activism that could all too easily become transformed into new forms of economic-based terrorism. In other words, the rise of global cities and the spread of mega-cities have several consequences for transnational threats:

- Such cities are excellent incubators for criminal and terrorist groups. They provide anonymity and encourage the kinds of survival skills and bonding mechanisms that underpin all successful criminal enterprises.
- Urban youth provides an excellent recruitment pool for existing transnational criminal organizations and is also likely to play a large part in the formation of new groups. The kind of gang activity that has developed in Los Angeles, the drug trafficking groups that dominate the *favelas* in Rio de Janeiro, and the organized crime groups that have become so prevalent in Moscow all provide variations on the same theme.
- Mega-cities are likely to be a breeding ground for a new radicalism rooted either in the desire for revenge against individuals, corporations and states which exploit the poor or in a fervent wish to destroy what one cannot hope to have.
- Global cities and mega-cities provide excellent opportunities for the establishment of links among criminal organizations and between criminal and terrorist organizations. Cities like Rio de Janeiro have already witnessed the development of a kind of criminal cosmopolitanism in which criminals of various nationalities work side by side, a form of cooperation that often endures and extends beyond the city and ultimately beyond national borders. In one instance a group of Nigerians and Ghanaians led by a Russian was trafficking in drugs to the United States and Western Europe.

The Growth of Global Information Systems

Another component of the new geopolitics is the development of global information and communication systems that are linked to -- and complement -- the global financial and transportation systems. Although it is possible to talk about the emergence of a global information system, however, it is a system in which some countries are much more advanced than others are. In developing countries and countries in transition the level of computerization are still relatively low. In post-modern states such as Japan, Western Europe and the United States, however, sophisticated computer and information systems have become key components of the economy. Moreover, as corporations and governments have downsized they have turned to technology for greater efficiencies at lower costs. The result has been considerable increases in both sophistication and dependence.

Technology has been embraced enthusiastically and with little attention to inadvertent vulnerabilities that might result. As David Gompert has noted: reliance on information technology has grown much faster than our grasp of the vulnerabilities inherent in the networks, systems and core technologies that knit the nation together.[33] Moreover, if anything the trends are accelerating rather than slowing down. An important RAND report highlighted several dimensions of this continuing technological momentum: the cellular revolution, the expansion of the Internet and the World Wide Web, increased connectivity among computers, the growth of electronic commerce, the growth in activist use of the National Information Infrastructure (NII) and the Global Information Infrastructure (GII), and the increased reliance of the Department of Defense on the commercial switched telephone and public data systems.

At the national level in the United States, the information infrastructure is used to control oil and gas pipelines, electric power grids, transportation systems, banking transactions and the health care system as well as many commercial enterprises.[34] Consequently, this infrastructure is a very tempting target.

This is particularly true of the Department of Defense. According to a GAO report in Spring 1996, the Department of Defense uses over 2.1 million computers, 10,000 local networks, 100 long-distance networks, 200 command centers, and 16 central computer processing facilities or Mega-Centers. There are over two million Defense computer users and an additional two million non-Defense users that do business with the Department. Not surprisingly, this system has certain vulnerabilities. Preventing and sometimes even detecting intrusions has proved highly problematic. Only about 1 in 500 attacks is detected and reported even though there are around 250,000 attempted intrusions per year. Those attacks that have been detected have involved the theft, alteration, or destruction of data and software systems.[35] Commercial systems almost certainly have similar problems, although assessing the extent of these is difficult as corporations seek to avoid publicity that might encourage copycat attacks.

In short, the new global and national information infrastructures represent a new set of vulnerabilities that can be exploited by transnational criminal organizations and by terrorists as well as by disgruntled individuals. Indeed, it is in the area of information technology that there is perhaps the greatest diffusion and democratization of threats to security as well as a decoupleing of the traditional linkages between territorial integrity and security. In the past, threats to national security have generally been associated with large accumulations of power and resources, and efforts at territorial aggrandizement. National security has required a capacity -- either through one's own efforts or through a shrewd policy of coalition building -- to defend against such aggrandizement by other states. Physical invasion of territory or physical destruction of resources and wealth along with the coercive power that came from the capacity for such actions were the major threats. They have not disappeared and it would be foolish to suggest that they are a thing of the past. But there now exists a new set of vulnerabilities that are wholly independent of territory or physical resources.

Ironically, these vulnerabilities are also asymmetrical: the greater the level of sophistication, the greater the vulnerability. As societies become more dependent upon linked communication and information systems the possibility that these systems will be compromised or disrupted becomes more salient, and the resulting consequences more catastrophic. The disruption of the systems that facilitate national and global financial transactions, stock markets, air traffic control, the collection of taxes, the operation of social security, let alone key components of the military, intelligence, and law enforcement infrastructures, could have far-reaching effects on the ability of society and government to function effectively.

Moreover, the capacity to engage in actions that produce catastrophic disruptions in the national and global information infrastructures is also becoming more widespread. What one journalist has termed the "democratization of high technology" has been accompanied by a new form of individual empowerment, the positive side of which is the growth of computer literacy and the negative the emergence of the hacker/cracker sub-culture.[36] Several RAND Corporation analysts made the same point in a different way when emphasizing the low entry costs to engage in offensive strategies in cyber-space, the price to develop a high-performance Information Warfare capability is low and is available to a wide range of participants. Unlike previous high-performance weapons technologies, new potential information warfare weapons can be developed by skilled individuals or groups residing anywhere within the GII.[37]

One person with a computer, a modem and the requisite knowledge and skills has the capacity to wreak considerable havoc on national and global information systems, even those that have security mechanisms and fire walls. Moreover, there are multiple opportunities for the hacker to protect his own anonymity through a process that is the "cyberspace" equivalent of the establishment of front companies. Most hacking, of course, has simply involved efforts by the hackers to display their skills. Yet as this form of individual empowerment becomes more closely linked to transnational criminal organizations or terrorists the potential vulnerabilities loom very large.

We should expect a growing convergence between organized crime and white-collar crime, as criminal organizations use the information infrastructure as the mechanism for both old and new forms of financial fraud. This is particularly likely in Russia and other states of the former Soviet Union where businessmen have frequently been coerced by criminal organizations into committing fraudulent acts.

Threats of violence and kidnappings of family members have forced law-abiding businessmen to commit fraud. If transnational criminal organizations will look to use the global information system primarily for new avenues for financial gain, they will also have the capability to inflict major damage on the system. National and global information systems open up not only new opportunities for fraud and embezzlement but also for disruption and extortion. To the extent transnational criminal organizations feel threatened by law enforcement efforts then they might engage in disruptive activities of this kind. Alternatively, exhibiting a capacity to damage crucial nodes in the information and communications infrastructure could itself enhance the coercive power of these groups. Vulnerabilities in national and global information infrastructures provide transnational criminals with at least the potential for developing and exploiting new forms of bargaining power.

The growth of information technology and the speed and ease with which information can be transmitted provides greater opportunities for theft of data and intellectual property -- and make such activities almost impossible to prevent or control. There are increased nodes of vulnerability especially at the points where the virtual and the real meet.[38] Tampering with data and software in the virtual system could have major repercussions in the physical world, involving such things as disruption of air traffic control systems, tempering with automated computer controlled pharmaceutical or food production, and interfering with financial transactions. Although such activities are often described as cyber-terrorism, this is a misnomer in that the consequences are not limited to the world of cyber-space but are felt in very telling ways in the physical world. It is simply that there are new instruments through which terrorists can attack society.

The dependence on information systems also provides some opportunities for terrorist activities that can damage a target government but that do not necessarily kill innocent civilians. As Arquilla and Ronfeldt note the advantage of this is that it avoids the opprobrium that otherwise can seriously damage the cause of the terrorist and therefore, could provide the best of all worlds.[39] At the same time, the extent to which such actions become a source of publicity is uncertain.

There are novel opportunities for extortion. Criminal organizations can use threats to computer and information systems in order to extort large payments from companies that find it preferable to pay up rather than lose their capacity to operate effectively in a very competitive business environment. In Britain, it was reported in June 1996 that a number of companies, banks and trading house had paid over 600 million dollars to avoid having their computer systems shut down or disrupted.[40] Although the accuracy of these reports was challenged, this is almost certainly a trend for the future. And unless potential targets of "cyber-extortion" manage to reduce their vulnerability they are likely to continue at the mercy of those groups that have developed a capacity to inflict serious damage on what has, in effect, become the central nervous system of corporations and financial institutions. Three characteristics of these threats stand out: they are anonymous; the perpetrator would prefer acquiescence of the target to implementation of the threat; and the objective is financial gain.

Another consequence of the growth of information systems and their vulnerability is that it will become even more difficult to differentiate between an accident and an act of terror. A shutdown in the system and the loss of data may result from an internal problem or an external attack -- and in some cases it may be impossible to determine the cause. Closely related to this is the possibility that there will be a significant time lag between the attack itself and the manifestations of the attack in the physical world. In effect, this is equivalent to the incubation period of a virus, when the victim is not aware of what could prove to be a life threatening condition.

As the RAND "day after" exercises have demonstrated, the growing reliance on computerized and linked information systems has rendered the United States homeland vulnerable to what is, in effect, a new strategic threat. "Given the increased reliance of the U.S. economy and society on high-performance computer networks, U.S. infrastructures represent a new set of 'strategic' targets. Threats against key NII targets may have an extremely coercive value, while outright attacks may have a powerful disruptive effect on the national decision making authority. U.S. borders will not provide sanctuary from this kind of conflict."[41] This could act as a great leveler or equalizer -- something that could prove particularly important not only in regional conflicts but also when the United States attempts to take offensive actions against transnational criminal and terrorist organizations. The United States may be the only remaining superpower but it is also becoming Goliath in a world of many Davids.

The global information revolution is something that, as yet, has not been fully exploited by either transnational criminal organizations or transnational (or even national) terrorist groups. The development of national and global information systems that have out paced appropriate safeguards and security measures, however, provides new targets and new opportunities for such groups. To expect that they will fail to exploit these opportunities would be a mistake. Indeed, information networks are a natural for exploitation by groups that are themselves heavily reliant on network structures.

The Growth of Transnational Networks

Unfortunately for the analysis of organized crime, the dominant paradigm has been that of the Mafia family with a hierarchical structure and specialized roles and responsibilities. Although this model has been challenged on a variety of grounds it has retained its pre-eminence in law U.S. enforcement, partly because it provides an attractive and relatively straightforward target. The reality is much messier and generally involves a looser and more fluid structure of groups and individuals that coalesce and break up according to both need and opportunities. One report on organized crime in the Netherlands concluded that while there are between thirty and forty well-organized gangs, "thousands of criminals operate on their own initiative, sometimes with one another and sometimes against one another." Consequently, organized crime in the country is best understood as "a diffuse and constantly changing network of individuals and groups."[42] This is almost certainly a more appropriate description of contemporary organized crime than the more familiar family hierarchy.

This does not mean that family is insignificant. Family and kinship ties are often an important component of what Peter Lupsha has termed "networks of affiliation."[43] The ties that bind criminal organizations are also based on more extensive social mechanisms such as common ethnicity or shared experience (e.g. in prison, or in street gangs) or even in the Chinese case the notion of *guanxi* or reciprocal obligation that can span generations and continents. These binding mechanisms create a basis for trust and make it difficult for law enforcement to penetrate or infiltrate the organizations.

Network organizations also have the advantage that they are fluid, highly adaptable, and resistant to disruption. They have a degree of resilience that other forms of organization lack. The network is an ideal form for maintaining organizational integrity; because networks are characterized by considerable redundancy, linkages can be maintained through a variety of different connections. If some of the connections are broken they can be replaced, enabling the organization to reconstitute itself without great difficulty. Furthermore, even if the periphery of a network is infiltrated, the core can still be insulated through the imposition of safeguards and careful restriction in the number of connections to the leadership. In large part such advantages are obtained through what is termed loose coupling, an arrangement which provides protection through insulation. In organizations or systems where the components are tightly coupled, disturbance or dislocation in one component can create a damaging chain reaction. In contrast, "loose coupling gives time, resources, and alternative paths to cope with the disturbance and limits its impact."[44]

The value of network structures is increasingly being recognized in the commercial and industrial world where some businesses are finding that alternatives to traditional hierarchy are both more efficient and more effective in terms of innovation and the achievement of goals. Transnational criminal organizations, however, have been in this position for some time, and have instinctively developed a form of organization that offers distinct advantages over any other -- advantages that are increasing as a result of the information and communications revolutions. Indeed, there are several implications of the growing importance of transnational network structures that need to be identified:

- What are commonly referred to as cellular structures adopted by many terrorist organizations are, in effect, loosely coupled networks in which there is sufficient duplication and redundancy that the elimination of particular cells can have only a modest impact. Indeed, "many revolutionary and terrorist organizations are adopting networked command structures that are segmented and polycephalous (i.e. having a number of commanders who are positioned at various nodes but who are able to exert strategic control over the whole network."[45] This makes them even more difficult to destroy or even neutralize the network.

- The possibility of new forms of cooperation among criminal organizations is enhanced by reliance on networks. As Arquilla and Ronfeldt have noted in a brilliant study entitled *The Advent of Netwar*, the network form of organization is becoming a new source of power especially "for actors who have previously had to operate in isolation from each other and who could or would not coalesce into a hierarchical design."[46] Criminal organizations that jealously guard their own prerogatives and independence and that would find merger unacceptable are both able and willing to engage in extensive cooperation through networks.

- Criminal organizations tend to extend their influence into the licit sectors of the economy, society and government by extending their network using coercion, co-option, or corruption as necessary. This serves to prevent or undermine law enforcement activities. The difficulty for those trying to attack networks is that it is often unclear how extensive the network is, let alone where the crucial and linkages located.

The Growth of Global Communication Systems

The growth of global information systems has gone hand in hand with the development of global communications. At its most obvious, the spread of telecommunications, fax machines, electronic mailboxes and the like, has opened up many more opportunities for cross border contacts and the development of more extensive networks. In some ways this has served to establish and entrench the dominance of Western popular culture in many parts of the world; but it has also helped to create global markets for licit and illicit products alike. If global communications have created more homogenous markets, however, they have not dispelled inequalities among potential consumers. In fact the globalization of communications has served to highlight and accentuate social and economic inequalities.

As the Commission on Global Governance has noted, the number of absolute poor, the truly destitute, was estimated by the World Bank at 1.3 billion in 1993, and is probably still growing. One fifth of the world lives in countries, mainly in Africa and Latin America, where living standards actually fell in the 1980s. Several indicators of aggregate poverty -- 1.5 billion lack access to safe water and 2 billion lack safe sanitation; more than 1 billion are illiterate, including half of all rural women - are no less chilling than a quarter-century ago.[47]

The difference in the era of global communications is that those who live in abject poverty are becoming increasingly aware that everyone does not share their predicament. One result of this is that the poor segments of the population are less likely passively to accept their fate. There are several implications of all this:

- The imperative to design global marketing strategies is as relevant to those who trade in illicit products as for those who provide licit goods and services. Illicit drugs, for example, have become a truly global product. In the last few years new forms of drug use have spread to areas such as South Africa and the former Soviet Union where substance use was traditionally a much more restricted activity.

- There is a market for drugs even in the poorest segments of the population where narcotics provide an escape from the harsh realities of day to day existence.

- The other result of the growing awareness of inequalities is likely to be the desire either to become wealthy - by whatever means necessary -- or to strike out in retaliation at those who possess the wealth and are seen as exploitative. In short, the global communications revolution is also likely to enhance the recruitment process for both criminal and terrorist organizations.

- There are massive target audiences for acts of violence -- something recognized as long ago as the Palestinian attack at the Munich Olympics, but that is no longer dependent on the global spotlight being in one place. In light of the global communications revolution terrorism is no longer merely theater -- it is now global theater. And terrorists themselves can create the stage rather than relying on a pre-existing stage.

It is clear from all this that globalization represents an implicit attack on state authority and sovereignty from above. This assault, however, is all the more serious because it is accompanied by an attack on state legitimacy from below.

DEVELOPMENTS AT THE STATE LEVEL
The Crisis of Authority and Legitimacy

The demise of the nation state has been long predicted, but states retain their position as the dominant organizing device for political life. As discussed above, control of the state remains the major prize in civil wars and ethnic conflicts. At the same time in many states there has been a reduction in both internal cohesion and the capacity to govern. The dominant theme of the 1990s is the collapse of totalitarian forms of government in the former Soviet Union and their tacit abandonment elsewhere. While this was initially hailed as a victory for both democracy and market economies, it has also brought with it a collapse of social controls that have had all sorts of unforeseen consequences central to the new geopolitics. Part of the problem is that the change has come in most cases from the top and has not been based on a well-developed civil society in which there is respect for the law, a sense of obligation to the community, and a recognition of the importance of norms of behavior, of self-restraint and of the boundaries of permissible action.

In some developing states too, the combination of weak government and weak civil society has also provided a basis for organized crime. Colombia became the corporate headquarters of the global cocaine trade both because of the weakness of the state and because of what might be termed an "uncivil society" dominated by a history of violence.[48] This facilitated the development of large criminal organizations that, in effect became a "state within a state" and that developed sufficient power to confront if not defeat the government. State weakness of course is far from new. The weakness of the Italian State in the nineteenth century is generally accepted as one of the major causes of the rise of La Cosa Nostra in Sicily. Indeed, some observers argue that one reason the Mafia became so deeply entrenched in Sicily is that it provided the protection and contract enforcement that is normally the preserve of the state, but that the Italian government was incapable of offering.[49]   What is novel, therefore, is not so much the weakness of particular states, but the prevalence of such cases.

Indeed, in the new geopolitics, the crucial variable is not power so much as it is authority -- or rather, the lack of it. Criminal organizations flourish in those countries where authority has been eroded (or never properly established) and the state is weak. Such organizations not only thrive on political instability but also exacerbate the consequences of the breakdown of authority structures that occurred in an increasing number of states during the 1980s and the first half of the 1990s. The era of the failed nation-state is also the era in which organized crime has become a major problem both domestically and across national borders. One of the crucial factors in the emergence of organized crime and drug trafficking in many of the countries of Eastern Europe and the Former Soviet Union is the weakness of the new states. Few states in transition have effective criminal justice systems to assist in the struggle against organized crime: they have no legislation that allows them to target criminal organizations as such, or that facilitates witness protection schemes, asset forfeiture, and electronic surveillance, all of which are essential in efforts to combat organized crime. Furthermore, in many of these states, banking regulations are notably lax, thereby providing an attractive environment for money laundering both by indigenous criminal organizations and by groups from elsewhere. Weak state capacity, however, goes beyond the absence of appropriate legislation. Massive social and economic dislocation, hyperinflation and unemployment, a limited tax base, and a multiplicity of demands on the state have contributed to the under funding of law enforcement, which typically has poor transportation, limited communications systems and relatively unsophisticated computer equipment. These trends have also removed the social safety nets that existed before the collapse of communism -- thereby placing enormous pressure on the citizenry.

In addition, the lack of avenues for advancement in the licit economy has provided enormous incentives for those with entrepreneurial skills and ambitions to migrate to the illicit economy. In short, the pressures and incentives for the development of criminal organizations have greatly outweighed the constraints. In effect, the erosion of social controls occurred at the very time they were most needed.[50]

Perhaps nowhere have such developments been more obvious and more alarming than in Russia's diminution of control over its inventory of nuclear materials. At the same time, poor economic conditions and the lack a regulatory framework for the transition to capitalism has encouraged the development of a culture in which everything is for sale. The result has been a process of nuclear material leakage from Russia that is likely to continue for some time and that could all too easily be exploited by both criminal and terrorist organizations.[51]

Even where the state has the capacity to take effective action against organized crime, a government may acquiesce in criminal activities either because there is a recognition that these activities provide certain benefits to the state (through export earnings for example) or because portions of the population benefit from them (because of localized multiplier effects in the economy). Transnational criminal organizations often portray themselves as positive forces in society and the economy, providing jobs that would otherwise be unavailable and offering services that the government has failed to provide. Some groups are highly paternalistic.

The Japanese Yakuza's provision of food parcels and other assistance during the Kobe earthquake was not really out of the norm. Pablo Escobar had a housing program called "Medellin without slums," while the drug lords of Rio de Janeiro occasionally provide food and hospital transportation for the inhabitants of the *favelas*. Such actions are part of what might be called the Robin Hood syndrome in organized crime, but are calculated rather than altruistic. A supportive population makes it easier to obtain counter-intelligence that is useful when governments and law enforcement agencies go on the offensive, while paternalism also tend to create a degree of public sympathy for criminal organization that makes such offensives less popular and, therefore, less likely. This is not to ignore the alienation of the population that occurs when transnational criminal organizations embark on offensives of violence against the state authorities. Short of this, however, the degree of tolerance for organized crime -- and the fact that many of its activities are consensual -- compounds the difficulties faced by many governments.

Corruption offers another way in which transnational criminal organizations can nullify or disarm the home state. When individuals or groups within government benefit directly as a result of the continuation of the criminal activities, then their desire to prevent those activities and destroy the organizations that engage in them is likely to be minimal. Indeed, "the extensive penetration of such groups into the state sector has immunized most transnational groups from the law enforcement controls of their home countries."[52] Such corruption can reach a level where there is a virtual partnership between the criminal organization and the government that embrace one another in a symbiotic relationship.[53]

In other words, criminal organizations prosper in a safe home base that may be based on the weakness of government (lack of capacity to do anything about the criminal organizations), the acquiescence of government (lack of will to do anything about it) on corruption or collusion. In the last two of these the distinguishing feature is simply the extent of the corruption. In the corrupt state, key figures in government provide protection to the criminal organizations -- as Andreotti allegedly did in Italy and as state officials seem to be doing in Russia. In the collusive relationship, the government has gone beyond the recipient of benefits provided by the criminal organization to become a partner in criminal enterprise -- as Noriega did in Panama. Collusion of this kind is based on mutual convenience and shared greed. Another form of collusion is that between government and terrorist organization. In these cases, however, collusion is usually based less on greed or expediency and more on common values and a shared antipathy to the major target of terrorist action. Terrorist groups, of course, have long operated from sanctuaries provided by states that have sponsored and supported their activities. If much terrorist activity has traditionally been an extension of state policy, however, we are also likely to see the emergence of terrorist groups based in states that are not necessarily sympathetic to their activities but that are unable to do anything about them.

Acting from a "sanctuary" or safe haven criminal and terrorist organizations are able to extend their criminal activities into other countries, often developing important regional networks and sometimes extending their operations globally. The irony is that whatever the internal condition of the home state, so long as it retains nominal control over its territorial base, it is recognized as a sovereign entity by others.

Weakness, acquiescence, and corruption are not in themselves a justification for external intervention in a state system in which respect for sovereignty remains one of the most important norms (although one that was frequently violated on grounds of national security during the Cold War). National sovereignty is almost invariably exploited by criminal organizations in an effort to ensure that the home base remains safe from foreign law enforcement activities. At the same time as they try prevent the emergence of a strong home state and to protect themselves from domestic law enforcement, criminal organizations (and we may see this pattern emulated by terrorist organizations) use national sovereignty as a barrier to the law enforcement agencies of other states -- even while they themselves are routinely violating the sovereignty of these other states in pursuit of profit and access to markets. Perhaps the most striking example of this was the way in which the Colombian drug organizations campaigned against Colombia's extradition treaty with the United States. Contending that the treaty was a challenge to Colombian national sovereignty, the drug trafficking organizations initiated a campaign of violence and propaganda that led ultimately to a rescinding of the agreement. Such opportunism notwithstanding it is clear that borders are important for criminal organizations only because they represent different levels of risk and demarcate different markets; in almost every other way they are irrelevant. The implications of all this is:

- Transnational criminal organizations operate from home bases where the risks they face are low and which act as sanctuaries or safe havens. From these home bases they can engage in criminal activities with impunity. Even if host states take action against the local or national subsidiaries of the major organizations, they are unlikely to have a decisive impact so long as the center of gravity or corporate headquarters of the criminal organization remains out of reach. Russia and other states of the former Soviet Union, Nigeria, and Mexico are simply some of the more obvious of the safe havens for TCOs. Colombia was also a safe haven for the Cali Cartel until the United States succeeded in pressuring the Samper government into decisive action against the leadership. Such successes, however, are more than outweighed by the reverses: the number of sanctuaries has increased significantly through the 1980s and 1990s because of the weakness, acquiescence or corruption of states.

- Terrorist organizations have a slightly less congenial environment in that they lack the capability to buy government support. Nevertheless, there are still some states such as Libya that work closely with political terrorists and regard their activities as a natural extension of state policy. Increasingly, terrorist organizations are also likely to take advantage of the weakness of specific states in establishing the home base for their activities. As such groups become more diverse it will be more difficult for governments to identify them let alone counter their activities.

- The use of corruption and the development of collusive relationships exemplify the growing sophistication of criminal organizations that are concerned not only with increasing their profits but also with preventing and controlling the risks they face from law enforcement. Crime organizations develop comprehensive practices and procedures to protect themselves from law enforcement infiltration and to mitigate the consequences of law enforcement successes against them.

The collapse of the Soviet Union brought a new set of opportunities for criminal organizations to acquire and sell not only state property, strategic metals and minerals, icons, art and antiquities, but also armaments and even, on occasion, nuclear materials. It will be some time before the new opportunities are blocked by the re-establishment of effective control mechanisms.

The Prevalence of Ethnic Conflicts

The other major development at the national level has been not simply the loss of state authority but the disintegration of some states into warring factions. Even during the Cold War the majority of wars took place within national boundaries; since its end, this tendency has become more pronounced. Between 1989 and 1992 there were 82 armed conflicts in which more than 1,000 people were killed. Of these conflicts, 79 were internal.[54] The tendencies towards fragmentation are in many ways the complete antithesis of those towards globalization. Yet they pose an equally profound challenge to nation-states -- albeit from within rather than without. The "retribalization of large swaths of humankind by war and bloodshed" offer good business opportunities for criminal organizations while also providing the kind of environment in which the losers resort to terrorist activity as a way of continuing their struggle.[55]

Ethnic conflicts, for example, offer numerous opportunities for trafficking in arms. Indeed, they are sometimes characterized by arms-for-drug-deals as ethnic groups seek ways of acquiring the means to continue the armed struggle. This has been an important feature of the war in Yugoslavia and has been replicated elsewhere. Linkages between the warring parties and criminal organizations willing to take the risks of dealing with them tend to be mutually beneficial. In some cases, however, the criminal organizations are cut out as the participants in conflict engage in criminal activities of their own, a phenomenon one journalist has described as "fighters-turned-felons."[56] The IRA provides an excellent example of this. This phenomenon seems likely to grow as ethnic factions, insurgency movements, and terrorist groups all find it more difficult to obtain state sponsorship for their activities. Criminal endeavors provide a substitute that enables them to finance and sustain their political struggles. Close relationships have also been forged between criminal organizations and revolutionary or guerrilla movements. Ideological antipathies have been no barrier to alliances of convenience. When in Peru a few years ago, El Vaticano, one of the country's most prominent drug traffickers was sentenced to imprisonment, it was not for his drug trafficking but for his cooperation with the Shining Path guerrillas.

This is not to deny that, on occasion, political instability and military conflict pose problems for criminal organizations -- traffickers bringing heroin to Western Europe from Southwest Asia, for example, had to find alternatives to the Balkan route as a result of the conflict in Yugoslavia. For the most part, however, criminal organizations flourish amidst such conditions -- as is evident in the two states that are the largest producers of opium, Burma and Afghanistan, both of which are torn by ethnic and tribal conflict and are home to major drug trafficking organizations. It is difficult, therefore, to avoid the conclusion that "whatever form they take - guerrillas going criminal or finding mafia allies, mafias profiting from war - the links between war and crime are growing stronger in the 1990's."[57] In the short term, not only do these links add to the profits that accrue to transnational organized crime, but they also tend to perpetuate conflicts, encourage terrorism and make enduring peace more elusive. They may also encourage the emergence of new forms of hybrid organizations that are part criminal organization, part terrorist, and part mercenaries, who provide specialized forms of violence against either competitors or government forces. In short, ethnic conflicts have significant implications for transnational criminal and terrorist activities:

- They provide incentives to engage in criminal activity in order to fund political struggles.
- They create and perpetuate hatreds that transcend national boundaries and the immediate locale of the conflict and that can lead to an extension of terrorist activities.
- They provide a large cadre of well-trained specialists in

violence with the knowledge and expertise that can be directed against governments or used by criminal organizations as they engage in struggles for dominance with each other. The growing professionalization of violence makes these groups even more formidable adversaries for governments. It is not coincidental that some of the factions involved in the war in Bosnia have provided "hit-men" for organized crime activities in Austria and elsewhere in Europe.

Indeed, the implication of this analysis is that governments will find themselves facing criminal organizations that are not only sophisticated in the use of corruption and techniques of co-option but that also have the capacity to initiate a level of violence going well beyond that perpetrated by traditional organized crime groups. Indeed, the next section attempts to draw out more fully the implications of the developments discussed above for the way in which criminal and terrorist organizations are likely to evolve in the next ten to twenty years.

TRENDS IN TRANSNATIONAL THREATS
Trends in Transnational Terrorism

One of the implications of the preceding analysis is that there is enormous scope for a much more diversified terrorist threat -- in terms of the groups themselves, the instruments they use and the target sets available. Furthermore, as terrorist groups become more varied, they are also likely to be less predictable. Terrorist groups that are the product of some kind of national independence movement (e.g. the Basque, ETA, and the Irish Republican Army) are likely to continue their struggle in the future. So too are Middle Eastern terrorist groups whose activity is directed against the state of Israel and its supporters. While these latter groups are not synonymous with radical Islamic organizations they do overlap with them. The groups themselves are highly fluid subject to both fractionalization and factionalization. Increasingly they are being joined by groups whose allegiance to a political cause is less clear, targets are less obvious and are far less predictable. There are two kinds of groups in particular that seem likely to become an increasingly important part of the terrorist scene:

- The first groups are those likely to arise from continued poverty and despair in the developing world. With their predicament accentuated by a global media that can hardly avoid highlighting the gap between the "haves" and the "have-nots," the increased radicalization of the poor, especially in Africa, may well be unavoidable. Ironically without the Marxist alternative that promised a form of economic redemption, the main motive could simply be the desire to highlight their plight and to ensure that greater efforts are made to alleviate it. At the same time, the desire for revenge on those who are seen as the exploiters could also become a

powerful impulse. In turn this could lead to the emergence of
terrorist groups whose targets are the symbols of wealth and
power, such as the key institutions of the global financial
system or transnational corporations whose offices and
personnel display the kind of wealth that members of the
indigenous population can hardly imagine let alone attain.
Kidnappings of personnel, bombings of banks and attacks on
corporate offices are likely to become even more common
occurrences than they are at present as the politically
disaffected are joined in the terrorist ranks by the
economically deprived.

- A second kind of terror group that could become much more
common is the transnational cult group -- particularly in the
remainder of the 1990s and the early years of the next
millennium. The difficulty with these groups is that they are
unpredictable, the targets of their activity are not always
obvious, and their rationale is difficult for outsiders including
intelligence agencies to understand. The capacity to predict
and forestall their activities, therefore, will be problematic at
best. Such groups will often have low visibility, only being
recognized as a problem after they have initiated a terrorist
campaign. They will also tend to have radicalized, nihilist,
and somewhat bizarre philosophies that are closer to the
ramblings of Charles Manson than to the more familiar tenets
of radical Marxism or radical Islam. Aum Shinrikyo had
some of these characteristics and, in some respects, could be
the prototype for the transnational terrorist threat of the twenty
first century.[58] There are several characteristics of the Aum
that may be difficult for other groups to emulate -- its
membership (40 to 60,000 worldwide with 3 times as many in
Russia as Japan); its assets of over 1.3 billion dollars; the
extent to which it infiltrated key sections of government,
industry, law enforcement and the military; and its
transnational reach, which included extensive activities in
Russia, the United States and Australia. Nevertheless, Aum
Shinrikyo's efforts to recruit scientists to develop weapons of
mass destruction, the production of chemical weapons -- sarin,
phosgene and sodium cyanide -- as well as its efforts to
develop biological weapons (anthrax and botulism) and to
acquire exotic but deadly viruses such as Ebola - provide what
could unfortunately be a foretaste of things to come.
Moreover, as Bruce Hoffman has noted, Aum Shinrikyo's
willingness to inflict large-scale civilian casualties crossed a
threshold that can never be reinstated.[59] Even though Aum
Shinrikyo was unsuccessful in its efforts to create a catalytic

conflict between the United States and Japan, it has certainly been a pioneer -- and where Aum Shinrikyo has led, others may be only too willing to follow. The real danger will arise if these groups are like Aum Shinrikyo in their ability to operate effectively beyond the radar screens of most intelligence services and thereby obtain strategic surprise.

Matching the diversification of terrorist groups is an increase in terrorist targets. One of the consequences of the triumph of democracy is that there are more and more states which are reluctant to impinge upon fundamental freedoms of their citizens in the name of protecting national security. The result is the predominance of soft targets that continue to be readily accessible. Moreover, as suggested above, the information infrastructure provides both a set of targets and a set of channels for striking at these targets. One of the intriguing results of this is the increased opportunity for separation between a terrorist action and its consequences. Tampering with air traffic control systems could cause as much destruction as several bombs placed aboard airliners, but could be achieved at a distance and with a very low risk that the perpetrators will be captured. By threatening airline safety and disrupting schedules such actions could also create havoc with the conduct of business. It is not inconceivable that these measures could be part of a carefully orchestrated assault on the national and global information infrastructures including the global financial system.

Equally important could be the shift in terrorist methods. The loss of life to terrorism has thus far been relatively small. This could change in the future as terrorist groups exploit not only the vulnerability of information systems but also the availability of the components and materials for weapons of mass destruction. The ease with which weapons of mass destruction can be manufactured should not be exaggerated. In spite of its wealth and all its efforts Aum Shinrikyo failed to develop biological weapons or to deploy a chemical weapon system with high lethality. Nevertheless, too much comfort should not be taken from this. Radioactive material smuggling from Russia is extensive. That there have been very few cases involving weapons grade material is some comfort to those who are concerned only about proliferation, but does not mean that even some of the lower grade materials could not create widespread death and destruction if used in conjunction with conventional explosives. The availability of radioactive materials provides opportunities for the creation of crude but effective radiological weapons.

It is also worth emphasizing that Aum Shinrikyo's failure was in the delivery not in the chemical weapon itself. Nor is it wholly inconceivable that transnational terrorist groups from the developing world will be able to use rare but highly virulent diseases such as the Ebola virus as crude biological weapons. Biological toxins are also widely used in research and are not as stringently controlled as might be expected even in the United States. The degree of control in developing nations may be even lower.

Trends in Transnational Criminal Organizations

One of the most telling developments of the 1990s for transnational criminal organizations has been the emergence of a variety of countries as safe havens. Unless present trends are reversed the number of sanctuaries for criminal organizations is likely to increase. Acquiescence could be transformed into active support and collusion, especially in poorer countries. Such countries are likely at best to tolerate and at worst to welcome criminal organizations so long as these organizations provide benefits to the economy, whether in terms of providing criminal capital as a substitute for foreign direct investment or as an economic multiplier. In the mid-1990s, the Seychelles offered citizenship and immunity from extradition to several Mafia leaders in return for the payments of substantial sums of money. In the event, pressure from the United States forestalled the implementation of this scheme. Nevertheless, it highlighted some of the problems encountered by those states that adopt a hard line towards TCOs. They have to contend not only with the criminal organizations themselves, but also with states offering -- through necessity or choice -- support and sanctuary to such organizations. In this connection, it is worth emphasizing that one of the problems with efforts to deal with transnational criminal organizations is that these organizations are not an unmitigated evil. In some states they are regarded with tolerance and occasionally even affection.

Hand in hand with the spread of safe havens there is likely to be a growing diversity of criminal organizations. There are several dimensions to this. One is that successful criminal enterprises encourage emulation. This helps to explain, for example, why many Ghanaians have followed Nigerians into drug trafficking, so much so that in Britain the problem is referred to not as Nigerian but as West African. Another is that as one kind of ethnic group become more entrenched, secure and successful in its activities, it will look for mules, couriers or other rank and file members who do not fit law enforcement profiles. The growing diversity of groups will pose considerable problems, as such groups are likely to be not only outside the experience of domestic law enforcement but also outside that of much of the national security and intelligence community. Dealing with unknown quantities adds enormously to the fragility and frustrations of predictive assessments.

The growing diversity of groups is likely to be matched by a growing diversity of the products traded by transnational criminal organizations. These products will include any licit goods where tax differentials across borders make smuggling very attractive (cigarettes); goods that are prohibited but for which there is demand (drugs and CFCs); goods for which demand greatly exceeds supply (organs for transplant surgery); and goods which promise high levels of profits (materials and components for weapons of mass destruction).

There is also likely to be a consolidation and a gradual blurring of different kinds of crime and of the organizations perpetrating them. Organized crime and white-collar crime are becoming increasingly difficult to distinguish as Russian criminal organizations, in particular, engage in elaborate schemes for financial fraud. Indeed, in the United States Russian criminal organizations have been very successful in Medicare fraud in California, in running a gasoline tax evasion scheme in New Jersey and New York and in car insurance fraud nationally. Although they have also engaged in extortion and vice, fraud has been their most lucrative activity.

Similarly, actions that have traditionally been associated with terrorism could also become the hallmark of certain organized crime groups. Conversely, terrorists could use extortion as a means of obtaining funding. All this suggests another closely related trend: that towards an increase in the level of violence threatened or implemented by TCOs. Large-scale violence, for example, has been predominantly the province of terrorist organizations. Yet, in the future, the threat of large-scale violence as an instrument of extortion could become much more frequent. The availability of the capabilities to engage in such threats is already apparent. The implication of all this is that criminal organizations could increasingly obtain access to destructive capabilities that could be used for extortion against states, cities or corporations. Proving credibility will simply require that those being extorted find evidence that the organization really does have the material to inflict considerable harm. Similarly, criminal organizations, by acquiring the expertise of skilled hackers, could threaten to disrupt or corrupt major communications and information systems, as well as to obtain access to bank and corporate funds. There have been enough examples of this already to raise alarm bells. And although the widespread availability of powerful encryption tools will enhance computer security, it will also make it much more difficult for law enforcement to track electronic communications by criminal organizations.

Another trend that could prove even more disturbing, if rather less dramatic, is that criminal organizations might well move from corruption and co-option of political elites to more direct control of political power. Bolivia in the early 1980s provides an example of a state being governed for a short time by what was, in effect, a *narcocracy*. The pattern for the future is likely to involve not only more cases of this but also more enduring rule by criminal organizations, albeit with a veneer of respectability and legitimacy. The rise of the "outlaw state" will pose considerable difficulties for efforts by the international community to create regulatory regimes or norms of behavior to deal with transnational organized crime. Efforts to achieve a global money laundering regime currently encounter major difficulties but will be even more problematic where criminals control governments and prevent them from joining such efforts. An even more disturbing scenario is one in which several powerful states fall under criminal domination and take concerted action to obstruct efforts by the international community to initiate more vigorous measures against transnational organized crime. Should this occur, it is not inconceivable that one of the main fissures in international politics would be that between "outlaw states" and law-abiding states. The clash would be not one of civilizations, but between criminal cultures and those upholding the rule of law.

As well as moving to more direct control of political power transnational organized crime could move from infiltration to control of licit businesses. This has certainly happened already in certain economic sectors (the construction industry and waste disposal are very obvious examples) and in certain cities and regions, but could become much more widespread. There are signs of this in Russia where organized crime has taken control of large sectors of the economy, including a significant portion of the banking industry. This endows criminal organizations with advantages that go beyond those they currently enjoy: when one controls or owns the bank, for example, it is not necessary to worry about suspicious transactions reports, even if there is legislation mandating such reports. Moreover, developments of this kind can all too easily take on their own momentum. Control of some businesses might be extended into other areas through the use of coercion for competitive advantage. The implication of all this is that BCCI could be not a footnote to the 1980s so much as a model for the twenty first century -- albeit one in which the barriers to external investigation and control are more difficult for law enforcement to overcome.

It is also likely that there will be a consolidation of strategic alliances among criminal organizations. The late 1980s and early 1990s witnessed several meetings between various bosses of the criminal worlds. Characterizations of these meetings as "criminal summits," leading to the emergence of global criminal syndicates, tended to inflate the threat posed by these meetings. Nevertheless, it is clear that criminal groups are engaging in cooperation at both strategic and tactical levels. Many of their alliances are one-off, but others tend to be more sustained and to involve an expectation of future cooperation. Moreover, the real cooperation comes not at so-called summit meetings but at the level of practical criminal operations. It has recently been reported, for example, that both Colombian drug traffickers and Russian criminal organizations are increasingly prevalent in Aruba. As one official noted:

> the drug barons flourish thanks to corrupt public servants and politicians...on Aruba and the Netherlands Antilles. Each time you see the same pattern; Everywhere...the Colombians appear with their cocaine, they bribe government functionaries and politicians at every level. And the latest development is that the Russian mafia has also established itself in the Caribbean area in order to do business directly with the Colombians.[60]

This is to be expected. The efforts of law enforcement provide a continued incentive for criminal organizations to cooperate. Just as strategic alliances have become more pervasive and entrenched in the licit business world so they are likely to become an even more central feature of the operations of transnational criminal organizations.

Another trend is towards greater sophistication. This is reflected in the growing use of specialists by TCOs, particularly the use of financial specialists for money laundering and the employment of mercenaries or military veterans for security. In the future criminal organizations are likely to recruit information technology specialists. Indeed, such people are likely to become as important for criminal enterprises as they have become for licit businesses and will provide new offensive options. Equal attention is likely to be given to defense against law enforcement and hostile governments. Some criminal organizations have already developed sophisticated three-pronged strategies that allow them to prevent, control, and absorb the risks they confront from law enforcement. Maintaining a congenial environment through corruption is obviously the best ways of preventing risk. Yet attention is also given to defensive measures that rely on good counter-intelligence obtained through infiltration of government and law enforcement agencies. Criminal organizations have also developed ways of protecting their assets and minimizing the penalties that the members incur when they are brought to justice. This multi-tiered approach may not always be sufficient to prevent inroads against particular organizations but it certainly complicates the task of law enforcement.

The Worst Case Scenario

On the basis of all this it is possible to devise a worst case scenario for the years 2005 to 2010, the main features of which are:

- Growth in number of safe havens for transnational criminal groups and terrorist organizations that, in more and more cases are based not on weakness or acquiescence but on corruption and collusion.
- An increased number of money laundering centers that are resistant to efforts to impose control and regulation and see this as an effort by the "haves" to ensure that the proceeds of crime do not come to the "have-nots."
- Increased linkages among criminal organizations themselves and between them and terrorist organizations which serve to make criminal organizations more violent and terrorist organizations more criminal.
- Increased capacity of both criminal and terrorist organizations to exploit technological vulnerabilities, especially in information infrastructures for both violence and extortion.
- A further breakdown of the inhibitions against the use of weapons of mass destruction by terrorist organizations.
- A further erosion of the capacity of intelligence organizations to penetrate or monitor criminal and terrorist organizations and their activities thereby resulting in more strategic surprises.
- The consolidation of symbiotic relations that are virtually impossible to unpackage and that sabotage efforts to provide global regimes against terrorist and criminal organizations and their activities.
- More and more licit businesses driven out by "unfair" competition from the illicit and more and more industries that

are dominated by criminal organizations.

- A Russia in which the dictatorship of the communist party has been replaced by a democratic front government that has minimal impact on a state apparatus in which symbiotic linkages with criminal organizations are pervasive.
- A growing supply of synthetic drugs that are more powerful than heroin and opium and that make use of the surplus technological expertise available throughout the former Soviet Union.

There are other dimensions that could easily be added -- but this gives a flavor of the kind of situation that could very easily develop if present trends go unchecked. While some components of this worst case situation could prove unavoidable, others could be prevented by effective counter-actions. The worst case is not inevitable.

Policy Responses

It is impossible in a paper of this kind to enunciate a comprehensive policy response to transnational threats. Nevertheless, it is possible to highlight several key principles that should inform and provide a basis for the formulation of specific strategies.

In efforts to level the playing field against transnational organized crime and transnational terrorist groups it is essential to adopt a holistic approach. Organized crime and terrorist are not merely law and order problems and cannot be dealt with simply by increasing the amount of resources devoted to law enforcement. A holistic approach must incorporate efforts to modify the environment in which criminal and terrorist organizations emerge and flourish, attacks on the integrity and viability of the organizations themselves, efforts to inhibit their activities by removing or reducing the markets for illicit products whether drugs or protection services, and the confiscation of their assets.

The environmental modification has several pillars: re-establishing strong and legitimate government where it is weak or acquiescent, transparency where there is corruption and collusion, and effective criminal justice systems where they do not yet exist. This requires that criminal justice assistance have a much higher priority and become the post Cold War equivalent of military assistance during the Cold War years. Such actions would increase the level of risk faced by TCOs, making it harder for them to protect their assets, organizational integrity and the leadership. It would also go some way towards the elimination of safe havens from which they can conduct their criminal enterprises. Only when the level of risk faced by criminal organizations from state policies is both considerably higher than it is at present and more evenly distributed among states will it be possible to go beyond forcing their relocation and to make real inroads. At the same time, it is necessary to identify and remove perverse incentives for criminal activities.

In Russia, for example, prohibitive taxation rates encourage widespread tax evasion by businesses. Information about these businesses is often obtained by criminal organizations through their direct control over banks or their capacity to coerce or bribe bank officials. And when the businesses are approached, they are both vulnerable to extortion and willing to pay criminal taxes that are less than government taxation. Creating an environment that is less conducive to the growth of criminal and terrorist organizations also requires that sustainable development become more than a catch-phrase and that efforts are made to mitigate some of the worst consequences of urban poverty. Without systematic efforts in this direction, getting rich through crime and getting even through terrorism are likely to become dominant aims of more and more people in developing countries.

Another -- and much more controversial -- approach is to encourage the legitimization of both criminal and terrorist groups. This is an approach that is not always palatable, but one that could have some payoffs. It requires not only recognizing that at least some political terrorist groups might have legitimate grievances, but also a willingness to take measure to remove these grievances, while simultaneously encouraging the participation and legitimization of the group in some kind of peace process. As for criminal organizations, amnesties for members who are willing to leave the illicit business could encourage the process of legitimization that has helped to weaken the Mafia in the United States. When Lee Iacocca replaced Lucky Luciano as the role model for Italians in the United States, the Mafia lost the basis for continued dominance of the criminal world.[61] This process was accelerated, of course, by the successes of the FBI and by the growing challenge from other ethnic criminal organizations.[62] Nevertheless, it provides a model that might be worth considering, especially in relation to Russia where criminal groups often display real entrepreneurship.

Both this alternative and those policies designed to create an environment less conducive to the growth of criminal and terrorist organizations are not measures that will have immediate or short-term impact. In the meantime, therefore, it is necessary to pay attention both to defensive or control measures and to steps that can be taken to mitigate the consequences of criminal or terrorist actions. Priority should be given to protecting the national and global information infrastructure. Steps to minimize the vulnerabilities of those systems that are particularly attractive as terrorist targets or as targets for criminal extortion should be taken as a matter of urgency. It is also necessary to develop a much greater rapid response capability to contain incursions that occur in spite of efforts at prevention, and to establish enough redundancy to mitigate the consequences of system disruption when defensive measures fail. A similar mix of prevention, control and mitigation should be devised to ensure the integrity of financial institutions and other businesses that are likely to be prime targets for organized crime. In some cases this requires more and better regulation; in other cases a process of deregulation and greater competition might oe more effective.

In terms of efforts to control terrorist and criminal organizations, it is essential to go beyond strict hierarchical or bureaucratic solutions and develop new networks that are as flexible as the organizations they are trying to counter and that combine various forms of expertise. The Center for Disease Control, for example, could become as important as the Pentagon in responding to certain kinds of threats to United States security. Exploiting synergies and developing capacities for rapid response are critical to effectiveness terrorist and criminal organ. Networks should be both multi-jurisdictional and transnational in scope.

In terms of intelligence, the need is partly to cast the net wider and try to avoid situations where new groups like Aum Shinrikyo can achieve a form of strategic surprise. Less obvious groups need to be monitored and particular attention given to the destitute areas of mega-cities that are likely to generate the terrorists of the future. As far as TCOs are concerned attention needs to be given to devising models that build on the current level of understanding of these groups. Research on their origin, development, and maturation is crucial to providing preventive measures and devising reversal strategies to rollback their evolution. It is also necessary to identify the major triggers that enable criminal groups to advance from predatory to parasitic organizations and ultimately to develop symbiotic relationships with government officials.[63] As well as looking at the context within which the groups operate, their network structures need to be examined in an attempt to identify key nodes of communication and vulnerability that, if destroyed, would have a major impact on the capacity of the network to function. Another fruitful area is the decision processes of these groups, in particular the information on which they base their profit-making and risk management strategies. Obtaining this would offer new opportunities to provide misinformation that could lull criminal organizations into a false sense of security or encourage them to take actions that would prove damaging.

More consideration also needs to be given to patterns of activity especially the ways in which criminal organizations circumvent law enforcement efforts. What tends to happen in many cases is that law enforcement creates a form of displacement in which criminal activities simply relocate to areas of lower risk. During the first half of the 1990s, for example, Uzbekistan introduced tough measures against the cultivation and trafficking of drugs. The result was simply to drive these activities across the border into Tajikistan where government and law enforcement agencies were much weaker. Similarly, an inadvertent and undesirable consequence of law enforcement successes against the Cali cartel in Colombia has been the growing importance of Mexico in the drug trafficking industry. In other words, combating organized crime and drug trafficking is a policy arena in which it is important to think through the possible consequences of "success." In some cases, success against one criminal organization can simply open the way for its replacement by others who prove even more ruthless or efficient. By predicting displacement and replacement consequences of this kind, however, it might be possible to forestall them and use a more effective "squeeze strategy" against TCOs or drug trafficking organizations.

Even with such initiatives the obstacles to effective national and international responses to transnational organized crime and terrorism are formidable. A more favorable future requires a coordinated international approach incorporating agreement on goals, agreement on means or instruments, and effective implementation involving extensive and dense cooperation among states and law enforcement agencies. It requires far greater inter-operability if not complete harmonization among legal systems (especially in relation to extradition and mutual legal assistance), the creation of public private partnerships that create more serious barriers to the infiltration of organized crime into licit business and industry, and the elimination of safe havens or sanctuaries for transnational organized crime. It also requires education campaigns to reduce demand for illicit products, thereby removing the markets that much organized crime requires. Greater use could also be made of technology to combat organized crime, terrorism, and drug trafficking. The difficulty is that such initiatives require first of all a recognition of the scale of the problem and the challenges it presents to security on the part of a generation of decision-makers in the United States and other leading countries which grew up with the Cold War paradigm and an exclusively military conception of security. Unless decision-makers recognize that there is a new form of geopolitics which differs in critical respects from traditional geopolitics, their capacity to devise effective strategies against organized crime and terrorism is certain to be limited. Even if there is such recognition, however, and governments do develop innovative and imaginative strategies, there are still limits to what can be achieved. Transnational organized crime, terrorism, and drug trafficking cannot be eliminated. Reducing them to "acceptable levels" where they no longer pose a threat to security and can be treated as law and order problems is perhaps the most that can be achieved. And even this is a daunting task.

Dr. Phil Williams is Director of the University of Pittsburgh's Ridgway Center for International Security Studies and Prof. of the Graduate School of Public and International Affairs at the University. Phil Williams has a BA (with First Class Honors) from the University of Wales, Swansea, a M. Sc. (Econ) from the University College, Aberystwyth and a Ph.D., in Political Science from the University of Southampton, England. He has taught at the universities of Aberdeen, and Southampton and during the 1980s directed several projects on international security at the Royal Institute for International Affairs. He joined the University of Pittsburgh in January 1990.

Dr. Williams has published extensively in the field of international security including Crisis Management (1976), The Senate and U.S. Troops in Europe (1986), and (with Mike Bowker) Superpower Detente: A Reappraisal (1987) and has co-edited books on Superpower Competition and Crisis Prevention in the Third World (1990), Security in Korea: War Stalemate and Negotiation (1994), as well as volumes dealing with the Carter, Reagan and Bush Presidencies. During the last three years his research has focused on transnational organized crime and drug trafficking and he has written articles on these subjects in Survival, Washington Quarterly and the Bulletin on Narcotics, Temps strategique, and Criminal Organizations as well as the 1994 Strategic Survey published by the International Institute for strategic Studies. In addition, Dr. Williams is editor of the journal Transnational Organized Crime and member of the editorial board of Substance Use and Misuse. He is also co-author (with Ernesto Savona) of the background papers prepared for the World Ministerial Conference on Transnational Organized Crime, held in Naples, November 1994, and is a consultant for both the United Nations Crime Prevention Branch and the United Nations Drug Control Program (UNDCP). During 1995 he spent several months in Belarus preparing a paper for UNDCP on organized crime and drug trafficking in the country. During February, March, and April 1996, he visited Vienna and Tashkent completing a similar study dealing with organized crime and drug trafficking in Central Asia. In 1996 he and Pail Woessner published an article on nuclear smuggling in Scientific American. He has testified on transnational organized crime to the House Committee on International Relations and was part of a small group of specialists invited to meet the US National Security Council staff to discuss international organized crime. Dr. Williams has also been a consultant to Orion Scientific, for whom he worked on the risk management strategies adopted by drug trafficking organizations. He is currently preparing a major book on transnational organized crime. He recently prepared a Special Double Issue of the journal Transnational Organized Crime focusing on Russian organized crime.

Notes and References

[1] 'Sovereign-free' is the term coined by James Rosenau (1989), *Turbulence in World Politics*, Princeton NJ: Princeton University Press.

[2] Charles Hanley, "Increasingly, guerrillas financed by drugs," *Toronto Star*, December 29, 1994 p. A19.

[3] For a fuller analysis of definitions of organized crime see Michael D. Maltz, "Defining Organized Crime," in Robert K. Kelly, Ko-Lin Chin, and Rufus Schatzberg, (eds.) (1994), *Handbook of Organized Crime in the United States*, London: Greenwood Press, pp. 21-37.

[4] See Kenichi Ohmae (1990), *The Borderless World*, New York: Harper; and Walter B. Wriston (1992), *The Twilight of Sovereignty*, New York: Scribners.

[5] Roy Godson and William J Olson have written very perceptively about the governance problem. See, for example, their (August 1993) *International Organized Crime: Emerging Threat to U.S. Security*, Washington: National Strategy Information Center.

[6] See *National Transportation Statistics 1996*, Washington: Department of Transportation. Fuller details can be found in Table 17 on p. 85.

[7] Ibid.

[8] James Purcell, Director General of the International Organization for Migration claimed that in 1994 including refugees, asylum seekers and clandestine immigrants there were over 120 million migrants in the world. See his Preface to Nino Falchi (March 1995), *International Migration Pressures*, Geneva: International Organization for Migration, p. 18.

[9] Sarah Spencer (2-3 November 1995), "Security Implications of Global Migration" Paper presented at the Seminar on Global Security beyond 2000, University of Pittsburgh.

[10] Kevin Olson and Hanne Fugl (Dec. 1995-Jan 1996), "Why They Keep Coming: Immigration and Transnational Social Networks," *Center for West European Studies Newsletter*, University of Pittsburgh.

[11] Sarah Spencer, op cit. p. 3.

[12] *1994 Statistical Yearbook of the Immigration and Naturalization Service* (February 1996), Washington: Department of Justice, p. 25.

[13] "The New Trade in Humans, " (5 August 1995), *The Economist*, p. 45.

[14] These figures are drawn from Nino Falchi, op. cit. p. 18.

[15] Alison Jamieson (Summer 1995), "The Transnational Dimension of Italian Organized Crime," *Transnational Organized Crime* Vol. 1. No.2, pp.151-172.

[16] See *International Herald Tribune*, 17 Aug, 1995.

[17] The term human commodity trafficking is developed in Capstone Report on Transnational Organized Crime completed at the University of Pittsburgh in 1994.

[18] UNCTAD (1995), *Review of Maritime Transport 1994*, Geneva: United Nations, p. 11.

[19] Joel Kurtzman (1993), *The Death of Money*, New York: Simon and Schuster, p. 15.

[20] Ibid, pp.15-17.

[21] Ibid, p.92.

[22] Helmut Schmidt, quoted in Ibid, p.92.

[23] Philip Cerny (ed.)(1993), *Finance and World Politics*, Aldershot: Elgar, p. 15.

[24] Susan Strange, "From Bretton Woods to the Casino Economy," in S. Corbridge, N. Thrift and R. Martin (1994), *Money, Power and Space*, Oxford: Blackwell, pp.49-62 at

p.59.

25 Nikos Passas (1993), "Structural sources of international crime: Policy lessons from the BCCI Affair," *Crime, Law and Social Change,* volume 20, pp.293-309 at p.293.

26 This was made very clear to the author in interviews with bank officials in Belarus in the summer of 1995.

27 *International Narcotics Control Strategy Report 1996* (March 1997), Washington: Department of State.

28 Jessica Mathews (April 24, 1995), "We Live in a Dangerous Neighborhood," *Washington Post,* p. 19.

29 David Clark (August 1996), *Urban World/Global City,* London: Routledge, pp. 46-47.

30 Wally N'Dow, quoted in "The Urbanizing World: Megacities; Bane or Boon," *World Press Review,* p.8.

31 See Robert D. Kaplan (February 1994), "The Coming Anarchy," *The Atlantic Monthly.*

32 The point about port cities is made in Peter Lupsha (Winter 1986), "Organized Crime: Rational Choice not Ethnic Group Behavior: A Macro Perspective," in *The Law Enforcement Intelligence Analysis Digest,* pp. 1-7

33 See David C.Gompert, "Keeping Information Warfare in Perspective," RAND Review.

34 Roger C. Molander, Andrew Riddile, and Peter Wilson (1996), *Strategic Information Warfare: A New Face of War,* Santa Monica: RAND.

35 *Information Security: Computer Attacks at Department of Defense Pose Increasing Risks Report* (May 1996), General Accounting Office, GAO AIMD-96-84.

36 Nicholas Wade (September 1994), "Method and Madness; Little Brother," *New York Times,* Volume 4 security 6, p.23.

37 Molander op. cit. p. 15.

38 This point was made by Barry Collin at a conference on "Terrorism and the New World Disorder" organized by the Office of International Criminal Justice, University of Illinois at Chicago on 9 August 1996.

39 John Arquilla and David Ronfeldt (1996), *The Advent of Netwar,* Santa Monica: RAND.

40 "City Surrenders to 400 Million Pound Gangs," (2 June 1996), *The Sunday Times,* London.

41 Molander op.cit. p. 16.

42 See "Netherlands: International Connections of Organized Crime," (28 February 1996), *Amsterdam De Volkskrant.*

43 I am grateful to Peter Lupsha for this term.

44 Charles Perrow (1984), *Normal Accidents,* New York: Basic Books, for a fuller analysis of tight and loose coupling. The quote is from p. 332.

45 Arquilla and Ronfeldt, op. cit

46 Arquilla and Ronfeldt, op. cit

47 Commission on Global Governance, *Challenges to Global Economic Governance.*

48 This is argued very persuasively by Francisco Thoumi, the foremost specialist on the Colombian drug economy

49 Diego Gambetta (1993), *The Sicilian Mafia: The Business of Private Protection,* Cambridge: Harvard University Press.

50 For a fuller analysis of Russian organized crime see Phil Williams (ed.) (1997), *Russian Organized Crime: The New Threat?* London: Cass.

51 See Phil Williams and Paul Woessner (January 1996), "The Real Threat of Nuclear

Smuggling," *Scientific American.*

52 Louise Shelley (Winter 1995), "Transnational organized crime: an imminent threat to the nation-state?" *Journal of International Affairs*, Vol. 48, No.2, pp. 463-489.

53 This concept has been most fully developed in the writings of Peter Lupsha.

54 Figures quoted in Spencer, op. cit. p. 3.

55 Benjamin R. Barber (1995), *Jihad versus McWorld*, New York: Times Books, p. 4.

56 Hanley, op cit.

57 Hanley, op cit.

58 Staff Statement, A Global Proliferation of Weapons of Mass Destruction: A Case Study on the Aum Shinrikyo, Global Proliferation of Weapons of Mass Destruction, Hearings before the Permanent Subcommittee on Investigations of the Committee on Governmental Affairs United States Senate, 104th Congress, First Session, Part I, October 31 and November 1, 1995.

59 Quoted in Ibid.

60 Quoted in Pieter den Hollander and Willem Vergeer (25 May 1996), "Crocodiles in the Swamp," *Rotterdam Algemeen Dagblad,* p. 49.

61 Peter Reuter (Summer 1995), "The Decline of the American Mafia' Public Interest," No.120.

62 See William Kleinknecht (1996), *The New Ethnic Mobs*, New York: Free Press.

63 This three stage model is most fully developed in the writings of Peter Lupsha. See his "Organized Crime" in the third edition of William Geller (ed.) *Local Government Police Management*, ICMA.

Glossary

Global cities - cities with large cosmopolitan populations (New York, Los Angeles, Miami, London, Paris, Frankfurt, Tokyo, Hong Kong and Moscow, but also extends to Rio De Janeiro, Johannesburg, Bangkok, Lagos, and the like) which are connected to one another by advanced telecommunications, that form the major and minor nodes of the global financial and trading systems, and provide transportation links both to one another and to the national hinterlands they serve. Such cities have national capitals, while a small number have also become mega-cities, i.e. cities with over 8 million inhabitants.

Globalization - the emergence of a variety of systems or activities that are global rather than national or regional in scope and that are generally not controlled by states.

Guanxi - binding mechanisms of reciprocal obligations that can span generations and continents which create a basis for trust, making it difficult for law enforcement to penetrate or infiltrate the criminal organizations.

Megabyte money - A term created by Joel Kurtzman to denote the transformation of most money into symbols on computer screens and which is best understood as a network which includes all the world's markets -- stocks, bonds, futures, currency, interest rate, options, derivatives and so on. This transformed money nevertheless retains its flexibility and can be moved from continent to continent and owner to owner, through a global system of electronic transfers that incorporate clearing mechanisms such as Chips, Swift, and Fedwire.

Mega-city - a form of global city with populations of over 8 million inhabitants. The number of mega-cities increased from 10 in 1970 to 20 in 1990; by 2000 there are expected to be 28 such cities. Most of these cities are hosts to an influx of people coming from rural areas in search of economic opportunity. In practice, aspirations are rarely fulfilled and most of new urban dwellers find that they have merely traded a life of rural destitution for one of urban destitution. Such cities provide an urban environment in which survival takes precedence over the rule of law, in which alienation and anger are rife, and in which localized street gangs become the dominant form of social organization. The most ruthless and efficient of these gangs are likely to develop into more significant and powerful criminal organizations. In this sense, mega-cities and global cities are likely to act as incubators for modern organized crime groups superseding port cities such as Marseilles which traditionally had this role.

Narcocracy - Bolivia, in the early 1980s, provides an example of a state being governed for a short time by criminal organizations which moved from corruption and co-option of political elites to more direct control of political power. The pattern for the future is likely to involve not only more cases of this but also more enduring rule by criminal organizations, albeit with a veneer of respectability and legitimacy.

Networks of affiliation - contemporary organized crime can be best understood as a *'diffuse and constantly changing network of individuals and groups'* with binding ties based upon family hierarchy, social mechanisms such as common ethnicity or shared experience (e.g. in prison, or in street gangs).

Transnational organized crime - organized crime that typically crosses national boundaries and operates in more than one country.

Terrorism - use of violence by non-state actors, often directed against civilian populations, for political objectives.

Part II
Selected Regions of Organized Crime

3 Organized Crime in Eastern Europe and Its Implications for the Security of the Western World

Brunon Holyst

Abstract

This article reviews the organized crime situation in Eastern European states and notes the threats that this presents to the Western world. Political and economic transformations in former socialist bloc states exerted an impact upon shaping the dynamics and structure of crime. Changes taking place in all domains of life are exploited by criminals who are increasingly connected internationally. Weakness in state apparatus and the subsequent loss in its monopoly for the administration of justice, gaps in the law, social unrest, a considerable lowering in the standard of living, in conjunction with systemic corruption in public, economic and political life creates a particular web of 'pathological' institutional ties.

International currency connections, world financial transactions, commodity exchange as well as the opening of frontiers will lead to an even greater internationalization and professionalism in OC activities.

The chief threat posed by organized crime is due to its flexibility; (it takes on many forms) which permits it to profit from the same freedom and social opportunities as those, which are enjoyed by the conventional, legitimate, legal, social and economic society. The situation in East Europe is likely to facilitate political criminalization.

Key Words: Political criminalization, OC flexibility, Social unrest, Systemic corruption

Introduction

The fall of the totalitarian system in all states of the former Eastern bloc had an indubitable impact upon the dynamics and structure of crime. Following are but a few of the associated issues which merit mention. They include examples of the impact exerted by the fall of totalitarian systems in Central and Eastern European states upon the dynamics and structure of crime:

- the weakening of police structures;
- the loosening of the degree of administrative-police control;
- the facilitation of possibilities of traveling abroad;
- the facilitation of possibilities for undertaking economic activity;

- liberal tendencies in the penitentiary system.

Criminals make increasingly frequent use of political and economic changes. A weak state apparatus, gaps in the law, and social unrest contribute to a rising crime rate. We are dealing with an increase in:

- crimes against life and health;
- crimes against property (both groups are connected with aggression, violence and ruthlessness towards victims);
- the use of firearms against both victims and intervening police officers;
- crimes involving the settling of accounts, including commissioned murders;
- the professionalization of crime groups;
- the growing number of crime groups;
- the "internationalization" of crime;
- the growing number of juvenile felons;
- the growth of crime connected with the drug traffic.

Many countries witness growing social protest due to a considerable reduction of the living standard of the majority of society, as well as ever more profound and unjustified differences in the material standing of various social groups. This phenomenon affects, for all practical purposes, all countries of the region in different degrees and forms. The strongest unrest has been observed, or still is ongoing, in Bulgaria, Romania and in Albania.

The transition from a state-planned economy to its private-market counterpart is accompanied by a certain objective contradiction. This is the contradiction between the necessity of applying a monetary and fiscal policy, which introduces so-called "hard budget" restrictions into the economy, on the one hand, and the retention of economic properties -- both state enterprises and farms -- on the other hand. This type of maintenance expresses habits that originated under the conditions of mild budget restrictions and the so-called "seller-market" which consisted of a permanent supremacy of "demand" over "supply."

In almost all of the countries in question, the police experience serious financial and staff crisis as well as lack necessary technical equipment. The police forces believe that the greatest problem faced by them, and society, is the increasing brutality of the perpetrators. Time, training and the police officers' necessary adaptation are required in order to effectively counteract the violent, ruthless and organized world of criminals.

Crime in socialist Poland remained a subject surrounded by an air of mystery. This situation was created by two factors. First, the exaggerated optimism which is characteristic of Marxist doctrine about the penal law -- that professional and organized crime had no raison d'être under socialist system conditions. The phenomenon of professional crime was not emphasized in the work involved in penal legislation, passed in 1969, in prison rules or principles of law enforcement tactics and techniques. The overwhelming majority of forces and measures at the disposal of law enforcement investigation agencies were designed to combat so-called political crime.

Secondly, numerous, extensive areas of the "black-market" and the accompanying procedures of smuggling remained directly connected with a multitude of state agencies. Individuals occupying key positions in the state bureaucracy simultaneously engaged in criminal activity. They made use of their official roles and were capable of concealing their criminal activities. The greatest scandals involved officials connected with state administration organizations; in particular with the Ministry of the Interior.

It should be emphasized that the legal system dating from the communist period no longer corresponds to the new political and economic conditions. The law simply must be adapted to the standards of the European Union.

Obtaining information about organized crime in Eastern Europe is associated with a number of difficulties. For almost fifty years, crime was taboo subject. Certain old habits concerning the disclosure of the causes of organized crime have been retained. The organizational structure of this form of crime (e.g. hierarchy, specialization, degree of secrecy) do not facilitate investigation.

This chapter is based on information about organized crime which was provided by various sources (scientific studies, conference and symposia material, published statistics, assessments made by police and prosecutors, interviews with police officers, judges, prosecutors and undercover sources, e.g. information received from criminals). Much of the data comes from international and national conferences. Not all sources of information can be revealed.

We can anticipate that a widening range of information will accompany the development of organized crime. Scientific research will become more comprehensive. Up until now studies have generally been fragmentary, focusing only on selected topics or areas, e.g. economic (the "gray zone") or on types of crime, e.g. the illegal production and sale of narcotics, or the white slave trade.

Finally, we need to consider that the situation in many countries of East Europe is defined by international events, and in particular by the disintegration of the Soviet Union. Relations with these new states have not created, up until now, a necessary perspective for the full development of political and economic relations in this part of the Continent.[1]

Russia and Belarus regard the access of Poland, Hungary and the Czech Republic to NATO as highly controversial, while Ukraine looks rather favorably upon these Polish efforts.

The liberalization of international tourism has changed the structure of crime, and organized crime is assuming all of the features of an international phenomenon. Examples of the impact of such liberalization upon crime include car thefts in Western Europe and the sale of stolen goods in countries of the former Soviet Union and wide-scale drug smuggling.

The new political and social reality has not developed an equally novel system of values. Hence the significance of accenting axiology (the science about values or a certain theory of values) in an analysis of contemporary trends in crime.

The conception of being rich remains extremely attractive. The accumulation of wealth becomes a direct value, a value in itself. Obsessive greed is accompanied by pathological envy caused by the awareness that others are better off or are living differently. Greed and envy are strong emotions. They debilitate human intelligence, give rise to stress and to frustration, and provoke pathological forms of behavior. People driven by these emotions lose their ability to perceive things as they are in reality, commit errors, and change illusory successes into ultimate failures. The irrational nature of human deeds appears at ever level of the social hierarchy.

These circumstances are the reason for the appearance of phenomena, which can be recognized as new to their dimension, character and international connections. They include murders committed against the background of settling criminal accounts, terrorist acts, the white slave trade, economic crimes, the arms trade, smuggling of radioactive material, car thefts, duty and across-the-border crimes, thefts of artworks, armed band robberies and assaults against convoys carrying money and valuable objects.

A Review and Assessment of Organized Crime in East Europe
Belarus

It remains extremely difficult to estimate the dimension of organized crime in Belarus due to scarce information and the level of work performed by the local organs of prosecution. Information provided by the Ministry of the Interior documents that the recent period -- and in particular the year's 1992--1996 - has witnessed the emergence of organized groups, which predominantly commit thefts, extortion, robbery and crimes against property. For example, the Polshkov group in Minsk was composed of experienced lawyers and was involved in audacious crimes. During the arrest of Polshkov -- charged with organizing the assassination of his partner -- and other group members, the police requisitioned 30 guns and 27kgs of narcotics.

Another criminal group uncovered in Minsk, and led by Mitranovich, Steshits and Filipovich, dealt in assault, extortion, and car thefts. Its liquidation revealed a machine gun, four grenades, four gas pistols, a "sawed off" gun, a large cache of ammunition and three telephone listening devices. Observers note the rapid growth of organized crime connected with nightlife and drugs.

The rising intensity of the white slave trade is particularly vivid. An excellent example is the activity pursued by Israeli citizens in Minsk, who under the pretext of guaranteeing employment in Israel, force Belorussian women to work as prostitutes. At the time of arrest, the perpetrators possessed numerous blank passport documents, as well as seals and stamps used by official passport departments.[2] A similarly organized group discovered in the Homel region included members of the police force. Over forty organized criminal groups had been uncovered, and more than 1,000 persons detained from January 1993 to June 1994. Over two hundred firearms were requisitioned (machine and submachine guns, howitzers and ammunition), together with more than 1,200kgs of narcotics, money and currency, worth over a million dollars, and 2,100kgs of precious metals. Recent estimates put the number of organized crime groups in Belarus at about seventy, with a total of 3,000 members. Approximately 150 leaders head the groups.

Bulgaria

Bulgaria has become the scene of a veritable explosion of crime, and in 1993, the number of felonies exceeded 240,000. At the same time, the detection of the perpetrators is declining, and averages thirty-four percent. During the 1980s the average annual number of crimes committed in Bulgaria totaled 50,000. In 1994, over 220,000 crimes were registered and the crime coefficient per 100,000 persons was 2,779. A particularly dangerous phenomenon is the rising number of murders committed and attempted (900), and rape (744). Serious bodily injuries grew by 26 percent, robberies by 7.7 percent (6,640 cases).   Approximately four percent of robberies were committed using firearms. The number of car thefts grew by over eight percent (17,593 cases).

There is a tendency towards an increase on organized crime. This is particularly so for narcotics trade (791kgs of narcotics were discovered along the countries frontiers in 1994). Bomb attacks are also spreading (200 in 1994).

Both the police and the courts are unprepared for this crime growth. During this period, due to changes in the political and economic systems, more than 1,000 judges and prosecutors were dismissed. Currently, seventy percent of the judges have only three years of experience. The police force has many vacancies (3,000 to 4,000). Bulgarian law and the penal code more specifically, call for changes. Penal procedures have been in force since 1968, and no longer correspond to democratic changes.[3]

Bulgaria is considered to be an East European supporter of international terrorism. The country is used as a base for terrorism due to its central location; a crossroads between the East and the West. A growing number of gangs deal with the drug traffic since Bulgaria offers the cheapest narcotics. Illegal trade in artworks, especially, icons, is on the rise, and annual profits are put at $6 billion dollars.[4]

The Czech Republic

Recent crime statistics confirm a great rise in crime and an unfavorable development of its structure throughout former Czechoslovakia. The Federal Ministry of the Interior has noted that in 1990, in comparison with 1989, the number of murders increased by two-thirds, armed robbery by 400 percent, and burglaries by 300 percent. The number of rape cases has grown by one-third and the number of intentional bodily injuries by 30 percent. Equally significant is the appearance of heretofore-unknown types of robberies, murders and brutal crimes using violence, whose perpetrators use firearms and modern technology for overcoming obstacles. An accompanying phenomenon is the emergence of organized criminal groups. This development of crime has a highly unfavorable impact on young people, and increases civic fear.

During the 1990-1993 period, The Czech Republic witnesses a threefold rise in crime; during some years the increase was 12 percent. The greatest increase in crime was registered in 1993; in 1994 there was a slight decline by 6.5 percent and it remained the same in 1995. Table 3.1 documents the Czech crime development tendencies.

Studies document that 49 percent of all citizens consider the level of security in the Czech Republic to be "bad" or "very bad" while 45 percent regard the level of security in their places of residence as "good" or "very good."[5]

The Czech Republic is the scene of a growing activity pursued by about thirty large criminal groups which specialize in the theft and smuggling of artworks, illegal drug traffic, and prostitution. Czech authors indicate that the increase of crime in the previous political formation makes it necessary to take into consideration also the political factor.

Its citizens treated the undemocratic state with indifference, and, as a result, many of them did not observe the norms established by the state. So far, the new, present-day form of the state has not won civic trust and the overcoming of crime in a free and democratic society proves to be a difficult task. Institutions occupying crucial positions in the professional combating of crime have not gained their identity. This is predominantly so for the police. The implementation of the legal norms of the new democracy, passed by the parliament, still encounters assorted obstacles.

Phenomena contradictory to law and social welfare win more space thanks too increasingly extensive areas of social relations. An atmosphere of universal dissatisfaction and social tension expands this space also. The number of crimes is on the rise. Foreign criminal groups are making their appearance on the domestic crime scene. In this situation, a further development of an unfavorable crime structure in the Czech Republic and Slovakia can be anticipated.[6]

Hungary

The crime rate in Hungary started to grow in 1977, and its upward progress became distinctly rapid in 1987. The structure of crime was subject to considerable changes, and new forms of crime made their appearance. The emergence of the category of so-called "international crime" in the mid-1970s meant that:

- the number of crimes committed by foreigners grew;
- an ever larger number of Hungarians committed crimes abroad;
- the activity of organized international criminal groups intensified.

Table   3.1: Czech crime rate trends, 1989-1994

Year	1989	1990	1991	1992	1993	1994
Economy	13,463	7,145	8,249	11,850	18,431	18,440
(a) %	90.51	73.71	82.91	83	77.09	85.46
General	85,552	192,492	258,020	314,256	357,978	332,123
(b) %	70.37	32.33	28.11	26.26	25.97	2.49
Crimes against property	59,681	166,638	231,372	287,059	327,183	300,352
(c) %	59.51	25.05	22.61	21.5	21.02	22.87
Violent crimes	11,958	17,812	18,715	18,571	19,820	20,177
(d) %	92.54	70.67	70.12	69.76	72.61	76.32
Crimes against morality	7,004	2,521	1,924	1,843	2,048	2,240
(e) %	97.84	85.84	83.84	81.23	82.67	86.12
Total no. Crimes	120,788	216,852	282,998	345,205	398,451	372,427
%	77.48	38.38	33.28	31.4	31.73	34.77

a. Illegal production of spirits, corruption, etc.
b. Crimes against property, morality and others.
c. Thefts, burglaries, fraud.
d. Murder, bodily injury, robbery, extortion.
e. Rape, white slave trade, sexual abuse of minors, etc.

These groups basically committed duty and customs crimes (smuggling), currency crimes and assorted burglaries, thefts of artworks, etc. Hungary is currently the main transit country for drug smuggling in Central and Eastern Europe, and frequently plays the role of the destination in the drug trade.[7]

During the 1980s, Hungary witnessed the emergence of so-called organized crime, i.e., group crime, well concealed, and with a division of tasks among group members. One of the symptoms of this form of crime is "laundering dirty money." Hungary is free of mafia-type crime, which is closely associated with the political elites of a given state.

Local criminal groups prefer three types of felonies:
- crimes against property i.e. burglary and organized extortion (payment in return for protection);
- the management of luxury prostitution and the emerging industry;
- customs and currency crimes (specialists estimate that the perpetrators of this category of crime number several thousand).

What sort of social dependencies and phenomena can explain this state or condition? Apparently, due to the fact that Hungarian society was completely disillusioned with the socialist system, and that its members still feel uncertain in the new reality, many of them harbor the conviction that in an unstable situation a person can act as he wishes. Such an approach constitutes a socio-psychological rule. A total economic, social and political crisis has produced a situation which is best characterized by the Durkheim model: society as a whole has succumbed to *anomie*, creating a crisis which has affected the system of values, norms and morality of that society. The characteristic features of a total social crisis are deviations from behavioral norms, occurring on a great scale.

New development in the wake of the pacific revolution of 1989 is difficult and exhausting. The market economy is being introduced at great costs, and entails unemployment, impoverishment of the population, uncertainty of existence, and an enormous rise in crime.[8]

Organized crime in Hungary has involved various nationalities since 1980, most specifically Turks and Albanians who dealt with drug trafficking. Democratic transformations in Romania meant that in Hungary Romanians turned to the white slave trade. Newly created Romanian-Hungarian-Gypsy criminal organizations initiated co-operation with criminals from Moldavia and the Ukraine.

Criminals from the former Soviet Union -- predominantly from Russia, Ukraine and Chechnya -- pose a serious threat to the domestic security of Hungary.

A characteristic group is the Chinese, whose organized crime develops on the basis of various enterprises. Although approximately 2,500 Chinese have official residence permits the police estimate that their actual number totals 15,000.   Identification difficulties and their organization structure are not conducive for effectively combating them.[9]

The crime rate in Hungary during the years 1984-1994 manifested a tendency to increase as is documented in Table 3.2. The crime co-efficient in Hungary, whose population is 10.5 million, is 1,470.5 per 100,000 inhabitants in 1984, and 3,789.2 in 1994.[10]

Table   3.2: Crime rates in Hungary, 1984-1994

Year	Crimes	Year	Crimes
1984	157,036	1990	341,061
1985	165,816	1991	440,370
1986	182,867	1992	447,215
1987	188,397	1993	400,935
1988	185,344	1994	389,451
1989	225,393		

The position of the police in this situation is extremely difficult. Faced by a threefold growth of crime, the police must be reorganized in order to fulfill its new tasks. The police in Hungary, similar to other states of the former socialist bloc, served the interests of their ruling party. The new democratic system is restoring to the police their original functions. The police are mandated to serve the *whole of society* and to be concerned with the *security of the citizens.*

Estonia

Table 3.3 documents the number of crimes registered by the police during the 1990-1993. The number of murders has grown extremely rapidly. In 1990, there were 137 such cases, and three years later, 328. Crimes against the person: robbery, assault, and rape are on the rise. Thefts of firearms are becoming increasingly frequent (33 in 1992, and 48 in 1993); the same holds true for the use of such arms during criminal activity. Organized crime groups have divided the terrain of Northeastern Estonia into spheres of influence, and demand payments in return for the "protection" of persons and property.

Table 3.3: Registered crimes and crime rates in Estonia, 1990-1993

Year	1990	1991	1992	1993
Registered Crimes	23,207	31,748	41,254	37,136
Crime Rates/ 100,000	1,504	2,029	2,641	2,468

The highest crime level is observed in Tallinn, and the Ida-Virsuk and Narva regions, and the lowest on the islands of Western Estonia.

Organized crime, which encompasses the uppermost ranks of state authorities, constitutes another extremely important problem. It is estimated that criminal groups have perpetrated twenty to twenty-five percent of the total number of committed felonies. The dominating forms of crime include illegal export of metals, "laundering dirty money," corruption, and frauds in the food industry. The crime rate among "white collar" workers is rising.

Lithuania

During the transition from a planned to a market economy, Lithuania neglected to take sufficient early notice of the new threats, and did not create suitable protection against the "gray zone," a situation also known in Poland. Capital was obtained by resorting to corruption and violence, and conditions conducive for the legitimization of criminal incomes were created. Negative aspects of legal nihilism came to the fore. In the opinion of V. Rachkauskas, the popularization of criminal motivation for amassing wealth, already present in social consciousness, gained strong impact among young people and minors. It strengthened criminal organizations, and influenced gang competition as well as the hierarchy of the criminal world. At present, Lithuanian organized crime groups maintain close contacts with gangs and their bosses in Western Europe, as well as on other continents.

The criminal police of the Lithuanian Republic are predominantly engaged in combating such forms of organized crime as: smuggling non-ferrous metals, missile materials, alcohol, cigarettes, controlling trafficking in drugs and arms, car thefts, production of counterfeit money, counteracting illegal immigration, preventing international prostitution and procurement, as well as, financial activities and other frauds committed under the cover of non-existent firms.

A form of crime which is accompanied by enormous sums of money, unregistered and untaxed, is associated with the increase in murders "by order," both within as well as the Republic's borders. These crimes involve bomb assaults, street warfare, kidnapping, "rackets," and all forms of "settling" gang accounts. More often than not the victims are innocent passers-by. The first cases of "commissioned murders" are being noted.

In its struggle against crime, the Lithuanian police stress the introduction of order into legal regulations. The law on "preventive detention," devised and passed through the initiative of the police in December 1993, permits the detention of a person who is suspected of preparing crimes -- defined in the penal code as banditry or membership in a criminal group. Detention, with the prosecutor's approval, lasts for sixty days.

This law was followed by legal acts concerning the protection of witnesses (their concealment) and the legal responsibility for crimes committed by members of organized groups, a law raising penal liability for the illegal storage and trade in fire arms, ammunition, explosives, and many others.

In 1993-1994, members of approximately eighty criminal groups, the majority of who also act outside of Lithuania, were brought to justice as a result of legislative, organizational and detection-reconnaissance campaigns as well as joint efforts conducted together with Latvia, Belarus, the Kaliningrad region of Russia and Poland. The overall crime rate was stabilized (in 1994, an average of 144 crimes was registered in the course of twenty-four hours, thirty-six less than the previous year). General crime detection improved by over 8 percent for a total of 42.4 percent.

Despite these positive aspects, it merits stressing that Lithuania is witnessing an increase in serious crimes, committed with particular cruelty and with the use of firearms and explosives. Attacks against property (arson and explosions) are becoming more frequent and the number of car thefts as well as commissioned crimes, also committed abroad, have not declined.[11]

In Lithuania, the data from an eight-year period (1988 to 1995) documents that quantitative (statistical) indications of crime have increased greatly. The number of reported crimes has almost tripled, from 21,337 to 60,818; the level of crime (coefficient/10,000 inhabitants), from 58.2 to 163.6; while the number of perpetrators has doubled, from 12,746 to 22,069, and the number of convicted persons has increased more than twice per annum, 8,002 in

1988 and 18,344 in 1995. The number of imprisoned persons has increased continuously, from 29 percent to 40 percent.

Although the rate of the growth of reported crimes has slowed down, the problem itself has reached a rather high level (in 1994 - 157.4; in 1995 -163.6), particularly as regards latent, i.e. concealed cries, the rate and scale of which are insufficiently analyzed and controlled (especially in the economic arena). We are dealing, by contrast, with a low degree of registered crime detection (less than half of the crimes are detected: in 1994 - 40.8 percent).

Qualitative (structural) changes with crime remain unfavorable. This holds true for the growing number of serious violent felonies; premeditated homicide rose from 143 cases in 1988 to 502 in 1995 (attempted crimes are not included); premeditated bodily injuries and violent crimes which are committed with mercenary motives and against property, with the use of weapons, explosives, etc. 177 to 299.

Crimes against property prevail in the crime structure (about 75 to 80 percent) and increased the general crime rate in 1988-1995.

Alongside "traditional" crime (thefts, etc.), new "non-traditional" forms and types of crimes have developed. These include economic, organized and professional crimes (against property, extortion, contraband/smuggling, tax avoidance, forgery, crimes connected with corruption, drug trafficking, prostitution, etc.).

Unfavorable territorial redistribution of crime is being noted and this is increasing throughout the country. It is accompanied by the phenomenon of "crime-import-export" (to and from the East and West: *transnational crime*).

Basic changes in the criminal's characteristics are still taking place and new strata of criminals are emerging: professional, organized criminals, socially maladjusted individuals (e.g. alcoholics, drug user, unemployed, those fired from their jobs, homeless, etc.). Relapse to crime is increasing and young people and minors are increasingly becoming involved in criminal activities. For example, the rate of juvenile delinquency was 1.5 times higher during 1990-1995 than the rate of the population increase within that age group and exceeded the general crime rate (especially in 1994-1995 and up until the present time). This is a dangerous trend, because currently approximately half of all individuals with criminal records, and approximately three-quarters of felons, who have been convicted on charges of violent crimes, are aged 14 to 29. Such a trend, if not stopped, can induce the rise of a new criminal "wave" in the near future.[12]

Moldova

As in many other countries, organized crime in Moldova has permeated those branches of business which facilitate the "laundering" of "dirty money," i.e. banks, saving banks, private joint stock companies, etc.

The local police uncovered fifty-seven organized criminal groups and the prosecutor's office arrested two hundred and five of their members by June 1994.

Criminal control over legal business consists of investments in the private or state sector of the economy and obtaining illegally gained capital. Another documented phenomenon involves taking over an entire enterprise, or part of it, in return for the debts of businessmen who have been involved in illegal activities or in gambling. The third method is blackmail. One of its forms is known in Russia as "rackets;" the extortion of payments in return for actual or supposed protection of a firm's interests.

The mafia structure which is emerging as organized crime in Moldova, corrupts state officials, including police officers, and the justice administration. As a result, for example, OC obtains information about the privatization of the state sector and economic contracts, and insures itself needed protection against legal liability.

Car thefts, smuggling and trade in stolen cars are a particularly serious facet of Moldova's OC activities. Moldova has also become a supply source for the white slave trade, providing women for brothels in the West, Turkey, Egypt and Syria. Criminal groups are continuously engaged in battles for leadership and spheres of influence and frequent use is made of local or hired criminals for this.

A characteristic feature of Moldavian OC is the reinforcement of the economic base of criminal environments. Criminal "authorities" (in Russian such bosses are known as super-thieves -*vor v zakone*) organize a joint fund from illegally obtained means, as well as from dues paid by the rank-and-file "soldiers" of the criminal underworld.

Mafia crime in the Republic of Moldova is a recent phenomenon and for the time being it remains restricted to several small OC groups. Nevertheless, it constitutes an urgent warning for the local police.[13]

Poland

Poland's period of transformations, within the political and economic system, inaugurated in 1989, coincided with a rapid growth in crime, as documented by the following data:

Table 3.4: Registered crimes in Poland, 1989-1996

Year	1989	1990	1991	1992
Registered Crimes	547,589	883,346	866,095	881,076

Year	1993	1994	1995	1996
Registered Crimes	852,507	906,157	974,941	897,751

Source: Chief Police Headquarters, Warsaw 1996

Although the crime rate dropped slightly in 1996 (approximately six percent), the number of particularly brutal felonies remains at a very high level, and the use of fire arms and explosives while committing them has increased.

Last year, 1,134 people were killed this way in Poland. The perpetrators were minors in 36 cases - 26 in 1995. Further data documents 628 armed thefts, 1,519 armed robberies and 5,885 cases of armed extortion.

Data provided by the main Police Headquarters, during the first two months of 1997, document that operational control involved over 340 crime groups and 4,424 individuals, including 453 foreigners.

In 1996, the Polish police "neutralized" 143 OC groups; prosecutors and the courts arrested 182 suspects -- chiefs of gangs. Sixteen channels for narcotics trafficking were destroyed 49 groups that committed robbery, assault and extortion were eliminated. Members of 17 groups that specialize in theft, modification and legalization of stolen cars were detained. Eighteen cases of corruption involving official labor exchanges, departments of communication, passport departments, municipal guards, border guards, customs offices and the police were uncovered. There were eight cases of "money laundering."

Table 3.5: Crimes certified according to select legal classifications, 1989-1995

Legal Class	1989	1990	1991	1992	1993	1994	1995
Murder	556	730	971	989	1,106	1,160	11,341
Rape	1,160	1,840	1,921	1,919	1,976	2,039	2,267
Bodily injury	8,588	10,415	12,956	13,795	16,646	18,454	18,901
Participation in fight or assault	2,988	3,935	5,553	6,060	7,285	9,223	10,600
Theft of property	105,129	158,785	139,507	125,074	134,089	180,514	211,602
Robbery extorting	90,067	16,217	17,094	17,715	21,034	23,574	26,868
Burglary	218,581	431,056	355,896	330,741	314338	304,293	304,899
Traffic offenses	21,075	29,141	35,568	30,753	29,578	32,030	35,005

Source: Chief Police Headquarters, Warsaw 1996.

Public security and public order are particularly threatened, since the serious offenses reveal a distinctly growing trend. A total of 1,298 suspects were detained; 680 of them were arrested.

For several years now, certain unfavorable phenomena in the structure of crime have become more marked, in particular:
- the threat of crimes against life, health and property, combined with aggression, violence and ruthlessness towards the victim;
- the use of firearms against victims and intervening police officers;
- the number of account-settling crimes, murder, manslaughter, robbery and criminal terrorism;

- the number of criminal groups and their growing professionalism: many crimes are committed in a well-planned and organized way;
- the demoralization of juveniles, whose symptoms include a greater number of crimes;
- the participation of citizens of foreign states in criminal groups active in Poland.

Police findings document that Poland has become the center of activity pursued by several score of professional criminal groups, specializing in the following categories of crime:

- the illegal production and distribution of narcotics and psychiatric drugs (16 groups);
- international trade in stolen cars (13 groups);
- smuggling of highly taxed commodities (11 groups);
- circulation of counterfeit money (7 groups);
- illegal trade in radioactive material and rare metals (4 groups);
- illegal arms trade (2 groups).

This list does not include criminal groups associated with the white slave trade.

Poland has been divided between criminal groups. The most dangerous group, composed of organizers, heads and members, includes about four hundred persons. There are an additional sixty criminal groups, originating in Russia, Ukraine and Lithuania, as well as several international groups, predominantly from former Yugoslavia, are present in Poland.

The internationalization of OC in Poland remains on the rise. Cocaine sales are the domain of branches of world Mafiosi, including the South American drug cartel, with Poles acting as couriers. Ukrainians and Russians often commit murder by order. Thirty-one foreigners were suspected of this crime in 1996.

The main Police Headquarters claims that at present the number of the most dangerous Polish gangs totals eleven. Some groups range between a few members up to twenty members others, such as the Pruszkow gang, include several hundred "soldiers."

Although Polish gangs began appearing during the 1970s, Poland manifested criminal activities during its previous economic period. For example, Polish criminal groups stole national property of considerable value.

The opening of Poland's frontiers in 1989 offered new opportunities for the development of organized crime. Its Polish variant has taken on the features of an international phenomenon.[14]

The dynamic growth of contacts between Polish criminal groups and their counterparts in other countries gives rise to extreme anxiety. Studies have indicated the international composition of certain criminal groups active in Poland. Member include in Polish citizens, Western European criminals as well as criminals from the former Soviet Union; with a distinct predominance of the latter. Organized crime groups consisting of Vietnamese citizens has been noted in Poland recently. These particular groups maintain close ties with Vietnamese criminal organizations that have been active in Western Europe for quite some time.[15]

The Public Studies Department polled a representative Polish sample of 1,010 adults, January 18 and 19, 1997. Over three-quarters of respondents believed that Poland was the scene of mafia activity. The existence of a mafia organization was confirmed by almost eight out of every ten adults, based upon their own experience, the opinion of the milieu, media information or statements made by politicians. Residents of towns usually declare the presence of the mafia in Poland; fear of the mafia is expressed by over 61 percent of all respondents. This attitude is "caused" by the fact that mafia activity is perceived as a threat facing all citizens (34 percent of responses).

Criminal activities in Poland which are regarded as being new due to their dimensions and international links, include: car thefts, crimes connected with drugs, and the illegal gold trade.

Interpol estimates that Poland has become an international sales center of cars stolen in the West, which subsequently find their way to Moscow, St. Petersburg, Kaliningrad, Lviv, Ivanofrankivsk (Ukraine), Brest and Vitebsk (Belarus). A Polish-Russian-German car theft mafia is responsible for their theft, "import" into Poland, across the border transit and sale. Co-operation between the Kaliningrad militia and the Gdansk police has made it possible to detain one of the Polish-Russian criminal gangs specializing in stolen cars.

Many regional well-organized criminal groups deal in car theft in Poland. For example, criminal groups in Szczecin, Slupsk, Gdansk, Suwatki, Bialystok, Warsaw, Wroctaw, Poznan, Kalisz, Katowice and Lublin are involved. The most powerful criminal groups are found in Gdansk, Warsaw, Szczecin and Poznan. The prices of stolen cars are 20 to 30 percent percent lower than official used car prices. Car thieves fill "special orders," particularly for types of cars (particularly Mercedes, VW and Audi), their color and outfitting.

Criminals in Poland maintain contacts with gangs operating in Stockholm, Munich, Hamburg, Vienna, Paris, Brussels and The Hague.

A specialized stolen car smuggling gang consists of local as well as overseas members, number of:

- the organizer;
- perpetrators of car thefts;
- carriers/deliverers;
- receivers;
- others (e.g., producers of necessary counterfeit documents, state, customs, financial administration officials, etc.).

Drug addiction in Poland has achieved the dimensions of a serious social problem.[16] Poland is increasingly viewed as being a country involved in the transit and smuggling of narcotics.

The general situation concerning the "abuse" of and the illegal trafficking in narcotics in Central and Eastern Europe has deteriorated as a consequence of political changes, the opening of frontiers, and the geographic location of the region. Circumstances accompanying economic and social changes increase the demand for narcotics, and produce a marked escalation of drug connected crime.

The central location of Poland in Europe, the rapid development of international contacts, as well as liberal laws pertaining to drug-related crimes facilitate co-operation between criminals from various countries.

The opinions presented by Interpol and United Nations experts as well as police information document that Poland has found herself to be in the very center of international criminal groups' interests and search for new routes for smuggling cocaine, heroin, hashish and marijuana. Polish legislation concerning drug addiction has chosen a prevention-medial treatment model rather than its repressive counterpart.[17]

Narcotics illegally produced in the former Soviet Union are increasingly available in Western Europe, and the shortest route of delivering them to the Western markets leads across Poland. The routes in question are:

- from the Far East, functioning for the past twenty years;
- the Balkan route, beginning Turkey -- heroin is smuggled across Poland to Western Europe in trucks; this is the route used for heroin produced in the "Golden Crescent": Afghanistan, Pakistan and Iran;
- cocaine from South America -- in the course of the last two years, Polish law enforcement uncovered 800kgs of cocaine from Colombia, Ecuador, Peru and Bolivia;
- West African, used for supplying Europe with marijuana and hashish; a recently intercepted transport of 6.5 tons of marijuana, discovered in Hamburg, was addressed to Poland, and ultimately was to reach the Netherlands;
- the former Soviet Union -- all narcotics, with the exception of cocaine, are sent to Poland where they are distributed or smuggled further on.

Poland is the largest producer of amphetamine, second only to the Netherlands, which it supplies to Scandinavia and Germany.

The drug "abuse" and narcotics illegal trafficking situation in Poland is systematically deteriorating. The number of addicts is growing, and amphetamine, smuggled into Germany and Sweden, is becoming a universally "abused" substance, next to "Polish heroin."

High quality amphetamine is the newest product of underground Polish laboratories. The dimensions of this production, smuggling and trade, as well as the ensuing profits, still remain undefined. Estimates made by Western drug addiction specialists provide much food for thought. Their findings claim that Poland has over 200 laboratories of this type; 15 of them being situated in the environs of Warsaw, Lodz and Szczecin. Recent trials of amphetamine smugglers and traffickers disclosed only the "small fish;" the producers continue to earn great sums of "dirty money."

From what has been noted, Poland could be described as a "bridge" between the East and the West, serving the smuggling and transit not only of narcotics and psychiatric drugs but also radioactive material, non-ferrous metals and arms.[18]

Effectively combating international OC exceeds the capabilities of any single state. Narcotics, produced in the poor regions of the world are predominantly "sold" to prosperous states. The profits obtained from the illegal sales of drugs surpass sums spent on armament and constitute an uncontrolled instrument of power.

The illegal export of gold from Poland totals one ton in a given year. In 1993, the Polish police received numerous signals that there was a large demand for gold and other precious metals in the market. OC groups "cornered" gold next to currency exchanges and pawnshops as well as at auctions of old coins. Gold was also purchased from Russians, Belorussians and Ukrainians, to be melted down and sold in Germany, Austria and France. These reactions are highly profitable, reaching profits of 10 to 20 percent.

Poland's Main Police Headquarters predicts that a growth in smuggling of precious metals should be anticipated in the near future given that the price of these commodities is lower in Poland than in Western Europe. It is known that groups preparing themselves for smuggling the gold, which has been collected, are working in several larger Polish towns. Gold is being purchased from Bulgarians, Czechs, Rumanians and Russians. The Poles are also selling their gold jewelry, amassed over the years, since it is loosing value and its owners simply lack money for everyday expenses.

A new Polish OC activity is the expansion of "protection" by Polish gangs. Yet another example are "social agencies" which play the role of brothels. Paradoxically, they are regarded as a source of income by the mafia, the state treasury and the police. The mafia demands protection money, the state treasury collects taxes paid by the officially acting agencies, and the police treat them as an excellent source of information and, at times, free-of-charge sexual services. The money obtained in this way is much safer than gains from drug trafficking.[19]

"Money laundering" is a new offense in Poland. Controlled economy conditions, prevalent up to the 1990s, did not permit private persons take part in such operations. The establishment of currency exchange centers in 1998 made it possible to "launder" money. The progress of privatization also permits the investment of illegal capital in the assets of private enterprises.

Changes in Poland's political and social system in recent years have far-reaching effects on crime transformations, including economic offenses. We must also take note of the transformations of the perpetrators themselves. A category of criminals who hold a high position in the social and political hierarchy, and who treat their economic activity, conducted by dishonest means, as normal business ventures has come into being in Poland. Furthermore, they often involve workers of enterprises as well as high ranking state officials, parliamentarians, and celebrities into this illegal activity, by offering them profitable posts in business or by sponsoring political parties. Economic scandals disclosed by the mass media and information about the participation of individuals from high levels of state authority have become the object of lively social interest and shocked public opinion.

Data and information obtained from both domestic and international sources document that the greatest threat is posed by the following forms of economic crimes:

- the activity of organized criminal groups;
- crimes concerning capital and bank turnover;
- customs and across-the-border crimes;
- tax crimes;
- abuses accompanying ownership transformations;
- the corruption of economic and local administration officials;
- crimes against creditors in the economic turnover and the seizure of property.

Previous bank regulations and the absence of an efficient information dissemination system, on the one hand, as well as the prohibition of surveying suspect operations and examining documents by specialized services, on the other hand, contribute to the presence of large-scale frauds committed to the bank's detriment. Simultaneously there have been new criminal activities associated with securities (checks, bonds and stocks) turnover and insurance.

The liberalization of economic activity and border traffic regulations has resulted in an uncontrolled flow of both people commodities. An increasing amount of crime is linked with an international turnover achieved by companies and individuals as well as foreigners and firms from abroad.

Poland is confronted with the functioning of organized crime groups specialized in smuggling alcohol, cigarettes, electronic equipment and other goods. An equally considerable threat is posed by fictitious "export," re-export and transit of commodities whose actual destination is the domestic market. Frequently foreign firms and individuals are contracted to counterfeit documents. Export in return for bribes continues to be a confirmed fact.

Groups and firms specializing in organizing smuggling to Poland are being established abroad. Poland is used as an open market, and the organizers are frequently former or current Polish citizens, residents of Germany and Austria, two countries that act as sources for the largest transports of alcohol, cigarettes, electronic equipment, etc. Criminal contacts across Poland's eastern border are gaining impetus; the smuggled articles include cars, non-ferrous metals, mercury, and works of art. Poland also comprises a territory for the transit of commodities intended the extremely absorbent market of the former Soviet republics.

Russia

The earliest information concerning crime in the Soviet Union was presented to journalists as late as 1989. Prior to then data about "social pathology" was kept secret.[20]

Crime in Russia has been growing rapidly since 1990 in the aftermath of the collapse of the economy, political instability, and violence.[21] This fact is confirmed by data from the 1990 to 1994 period. Data in Table 3.6 documents facets of this process. The number of registered murders (Table 3.7) also documents a progressing trend.

Table 3.6: Dynamics of crime in Russia, 1983-1994

Year	Number of registered crimes	Crime coefficient per 100,000 inhabitants
1983	1,402,694	992.4
1984	1,398,239	987.0
1985	1,416,935	989.8
1986	1,338,424	929.9
1987	1,185,914	816.9
1988	1,220,361	833.9
1989	1,619,181	1098.5
1990	1,839,451	1242.5
1991	2,167,964	1463.2
1992	2,760,652	1856.5
1993	2,799,614	1887.8
1994	2,632,708	1770.5

Table 3.7: Dynamics of violent crime in Russia,* 1985-1994

Year	Registered murders and attempted murders	Co-efficient	Registered severe bodily injury
1985	12,160	8.5	28,381
1986	9,434	6.6	21,185
1987	9,199	3.3	21,100
1988	10,572	7.2	26,639
1989	13,543	9.2	36,872
1990	15,566	10.5	40,962
1991	16,122	10.9	41,195
1992	23,006	15.5	53,873
1993	29,213	19.6	66,902
1994	32,286	21.7	67,706

*These cited figures do not convey the dimension of crime in Russia.

Victor Iliukhin, Chairman of the Security Committee, declared in an interview published in "Rossiyskaya Gazieta," March 22, 1995, that 10 to 12 million crimes are committed annually in Russia. The same source maintains that Russian crime groups have an army of 100,000 men at their disposal and that the heads of mafia organizations are members of state authorities, e.g. the Parliament.

Crime has also become a political topic,[22] with "law and order" politicians such as Vladimir Zhirinovsky calling for harsher treatment of offenders.

According to Iliukhin, 118 to 120 billion dollars leave Russia each year by illegal channels. Similarly, 20 percent of Russia's crude oil "leaks out" of the country. The mafia controls 55 to 60 percent of capital and 81 to 85 percent of the shares of all privatized enterprises. In 1995, an organized criminal band in Yakutsk threatened to blow up the main heat-generating plant, while another mafia, this time in Vladivostok, blackmailed local authorities that it would poison the water mains. The gangsters demanded ransom in both cases.

Russian OC, described by the local population as the "mafia," shows little resemblance to the structure of contemporary international criminal cartels. It rather brings to mind a large number of criminal networks focused on bribery, trade in commodities, and facilitating other assorted illegal activities. There is no control center at the top. There are various arrangements between the criminals and those who pay "dues" in order to retain their business position.

The police had identified over 1,000 criminal gangs by 1990. The Russian reality is that various members of political and police agencies are either involved in criminal activity or ignore it. Almost every citizen has contact with the "shadow economy" by purchasing articles on the black market and commodities produced by state enterprises, or by taking part in illegal currency transactions.[23]

Starting from the government chauffeur, who has access to "free-of-charge" gasoline, sold on the black market, and then resold in the streets from, euphemistically called "mobile gas stations," to cleaning women in hotels, who steal every possible article for their own use or to exchange for another commodity. This range of illegal activity has become an accepted part of life.

One needs to consider that the ruble, which has no value on the international market, continues to lose domestic value as a result of growing inflation and a flourishing currency trade market. The population was permitted to change rubles for dollars in November 1990 in order to weaken the currency black market. The dollar is employed in international "money laundering." It is also used for purchasing foreign commodities, which are subsequently sold at excessive prices on the black market.

Numerous government and police functionaries, even if they are not engaged in the "shadow economy," do not feel any need to combat it in a situation in which goods are scarce on the domestic market, especially in large towns. Corruption has become endemic; in the majority of cases inconsistency is one of its characteristic features. In order to survive and help their families, police officers often accept food free of charge or become involved in various illegal campaigns.

The Russian Minister of the Interior declared, in a meeting with President Yeltsin, that the Russian economy was steadily succumbing to criminalization. The Interfax Press Agency noted that during 1996 economic crimes grew by 2.5

times compared to 1995. An estimated $300 billion was taken out of the country illegally.[24]

During an international conference held in Prague, dealing with "money laundering" in Eastern and Central Europe, Sergei Shibayev, an expert in the accounting firm of Coopers & Lybrand, claimed that the Russian economy has lost about $60 million due to the exit of capital caused by political and economic instability, as well as, Russia's high taxes. Some sources estimate that the total sum of Russian capital leaving the country reaches $100 million. Russia's central bank issued permission to transfer $800 million abroad; exports of any other sums are illegal. "If you were to have high taxes and an unstable economic situation, and those are the prime reasons for the exit of capital from Russia, then you would face the same problem," declared Shibayev.

The Russian economy is experiencing a profound payment crisis. Enterprises do not have sufficient funds for paying for deliveries or they themselves do not receive payments for supplied goods and services. Many do not pay taxes or delay paying workers' wages. Additionally, in many branches of the economy, groups appeared which were connected with organized crime. Shibayev maintains that the mafia controls about 41,000 enterprises as well as many banks. "We shall not achieve a stable situation in Russia by combating the effects; it is the causes of the problem that have to be liquidated," he adds.

It follows from his studies that a universal form of transferring money abroad are prepayments by foreign firms for the delivery of commodities or services which are never realized. The capital is located mainly in Switzerland, Germany, Cyprus or Great Britain as well as closer to Russia -- in Hungary or the Baltic States.

Sergei Shibayev did not mention the size of the capital located in other countries of Eastern Europe, stressing that it is extremely difficult to determine the sums involved. John Taylor, chief advisor of the European Reconstruction and Development Bank, claims that the breakdown of the "pyramid" system in Albania is connected with "money laundering," which hinders healthy business and building free market economies.

David Bickford, senior consultant in the London firm of Inter Access Risk Management, said that the global criminal product is estimated at about one billion U.S. dollars, of which 70 percent is connected with drug trafficking. All of this "dirty money" is "laundered" somewhere with the assistance of intermediaries from the West.[25]

Police authorities are most disturbed by people who actively engage in, and support, organized crime. It is estimated that the number of people holding official posts and involved in this sort of activity is very high.[26]

The level of the penetration of crime in Russia is unprecedented. An article on the front page of *Izvestia* on January 26, 1994 reported that the Russian mafia now controls 70 to 80 percent of all private business and banking. The Russian mafia seems to be even more pervasive than its Sicilian counterpart. Most important, the Russian mafia possesses major impediment for healthy economic recovery. That does not mean that with a strong mafia that there can be no growth. Indeed, there is. But it tends to be a distorted kind.[27]

In order to understand the structure of Russian organized crime it is necessary to become acquainted with its system, which is basically unknown in the West. An additional complication stems from the variety of racial and ethnic groups, representing a wide array of cultures and languages. For all practical purposes, each ethnic group (Tartar, Azerbaijani, Ukrainian, etc.) creates its own criminal syndicate which deals with financial manipulations, illegal trade in alcohol and cigarettes, prostitution, etc. In many instances, criminal groups influence political decisions.

Consider that in Russia itself, there are approximately 3,500 to 4,000 criminal groups. Members of these mafia are usually well educated (31 percent are university graduates), and well armed. The assorted mafias have at their disposal modern communication equipment, often produced in the United States and Canada.

Another dangerous phenomenon is the spreading of corruption within penal prosecution agencies. This is particularly so for the traffic and industrial police in Moscow, St. Petersburg and Voronezh.[28] Mafia members are beginning to cooperate with criminal organizations; i.e. Poland, Germany, Austria, Sweden and even China.

In Moscow, gangs are more inclined to resort to violence, are well armed and do whatever they want to do in many areas of the town. Various ethnic groups openly conduct gang warfare in the streets and attempts are made to divide the town into spheres of influence, as was the case in the United States during the 1920s and 1930s.

The Russian mafia has become specialized in the illegal export of strategic materials (oil, copper, nickel, zinc, and timber), in the production of counterfeit money, and money laundering for their criminal gains, primarily by drug traffic.[29] Europol and Interpol assume that Russian private banks had "bleached" approximately $80 billion for Italian mafia bosses in 1995.

One of the purposes of opening the National Interpol Bureau in Moscow in October 1990 was to combat OC. The bureau employs 21 police officers (compared to 124 in the U.S. and 17 in Poland). It received 10,000 inquires during its first year of work (40 percent came from Germany). Ninety percent of all independent states, which emerged after the collapse of the Soviet Union, are transit countries for the illegal drug trade. Special campaigns have secured thousands of tons of narcotics.

The Russian Ministry of the Interior has at its disposal 12 million criminal files. This is one of the largest criminal registers in the world. The database contains information pertaining to offenders who had been sentenced to at least three years imprisonment. Annually, this information center receives five million inquiries, forwarded by Russian law enforcement agencies and Interpol.

The penal responsibility of mafia members is illusory[30] and a new social group is emerging with the assistance of the KGB.[31]

Ukraine

The Ukrainian economic crisis, resulting from conditions created by modest attempts at the introduction of a market economy, is conducive for the growth of crime, including its organized variant. The latter is connected predominantly with the private economic sector, banking, the financial-credit system and foreign trade.

The rapid development of organized crime in the Ukraine constitutes an enormous hazard for the functioning of state structures. Criminals aim at subjugating the economic sphere of life, controlling privatization, dominating the labor market, and exerting an impact on state policy.[32] There is a criminal division of national property and revenues by means of the "racket", blackmail, theft, and control over the functioning of the economy. This situation leads to the obliteration of the boundary between organized criminal and economic activity.[33]

Robbery and robbery with extortion are committed increasingly frequently against businessmen, petty entrepreneurs, and traders in market places. Extortion also affects foreign firms in Ukraine. Five such cases of attempted extortion were frustrated at the end of 1993. Extortion is usually committed under the pretext of collecting financial "dues" owed by a given firm. The Georgian-Ukrainian firm "Dzhordzhiya," for example, forced the Bulgarian firm "Bilet-CD-Ltd" to pay $37,000 in return for undelivered products.

Organized criminal groups are particularly interested in the banking and credit-financial system, which makes it possible to legalize "dirty money-profits." The most frequent crimes associated with financial turnover include the fraudulent confirmation of credits, as well as forged checks, foreign banks obligations and mortgage securities required to obtain high credits.[34]

The introduction of an electronic bank clearing network, in January 1994, made it possible for an organized crime group to appropriate millions of dollars from one of the commercial banks in the Crimea. The firm in question transferred the money to its account and then changed it to dollars.

Another recent phenomenon is the rise of organized crime in Ukrainian foreign trade. From 1993 to the middle of 1994, prosecution agencies uncovered over 300 crimes committed by organized crime groups; 60 offenses were associated with foreign investments. A case in point is the activity pursued by the management of the "Ukraina" enterprise and the "Kolo" agricultural firm (in the Lviv region). Together with representatives of a certain Czech firm, they illegally exported at least 450 tons of coal, about 700 tons of assorted metals, 37 tons of synthetic rubber, and 567 tons of pharmaceutical acid. Profits from these transactions made their way to foreign banks.

A serious threat is posed by crime connected with smuggling radioactive material, toxic waste and firearms. In 1993, for example, eleven crimes involving the theft and smuggling of radioactive material were discovered. An organized crime group established after a merge of the Odessa-based

"Tezaurus" enterprise and the "Lider" firm, tried to smuggle sixty phials containing uranium 235 and 239 into Lebanon.

An equally serious problem is the smuggling of cars stolen in Germany, Poland, Hungary and other parts of Europe, which are intended for the Ukrainian market.

There has been a rapid rise in illegal immigration in recent years. More than 4,000 people, illegally crossing the frontier, were detained during the first four months of 1994. The majority of them came from Southeast Asia, Africa, and the near and Middle East. This crime usually involves organized groups employing Ukrainian citizens and foreigners.

The anxiety of the Ukrainian prosecution agencies is reinforced by being confronted by the internationalization of Ukrainian OC.[35]

East European Organized Crime --A Threat to Other States

Nuclear offenses are a new OC phenomenon. There is a real danger that terrorist groups or individual perpetrators will use nuclear material to commit serious crimes, or will threaten to do so.[36]

Discussions were held, predominantly in the United States, at the beginning of the 1970s, on the hazards of atomic energy being used by criminals, particularly by terrorists.[37] The German literature neglected this potential crime up until the 1990s. Only spectacular cases of illegal importing of atomic waste and the smuggling of nuclear material (plutonium used for the production of nuclear arms was requisitioned in Germany for the first time in 1994) stimulated discussions. The mass media and professional public opinion began to discuss the forms and range of nuclear crime in Germany during the 1990s, and the possibilities for combating it. These discussions were basically caused by two factors.

Firstly, the disintegration of the Soviet Union has created an unstable Central and Eastern Europe. This holds true for the economic, social and military situation in states which emerged after the collapse of the Soviet Union and for other Central and Eastern European countries. Nuclear crime did not begin to play a specific role in Germany until 1991-1992, when notice was taken of the first cases and their subsequent growth (1990, 4 cases; 1991, 41 cases; 1992, 158 cases; 1993, 214 cases; 1994, 267 cases). An increasing, regional intensification of this type of crime was noted around Frankfurt am Main, Bavaria and Baden-Wurttemberg.

It is impossible to comprehensively review Central and Eastern European nuclear crime with the information which is available. Several cases, however, are capable of shedding additional light on the problem. For example, in December 1994, 2.7 grams of uranium dioxide was uncovered in Prague. In this particular case, uranium 235 was enriched by 86.7 percent. This was the discovery of the largest amount of nuclear material for the production of nuclear arms. The offenders came from the Czech Republic, Belarus and Tadzhikistan. The overwhelming majority of cases uncovered in Germany also points to Central and Eastern European countries being the sources of nuclear material.

The proof necessary to enable German prosecution agencies to locate a specific institution as being the actual source will remain unobtainable until the establishment of the necessary cooperation with the authorities of the relevant countries of origin. Experts maintain that there are still some 120 to 150 tons of plutonium in the Russian Federation itself. This amount could be increased annually by a ton taking into account the local production potential.

There is, to date, no official data concerning the dimension of the illegal trade in nuclear material within the European Union. In the middle of 1994, the government of the German Federal Republic knew of only five such cases among the member states of the Union during the 1990 to 1994 period. Several instances of trade in nuclear material have been uncovered in Austria since 1991. These involved, as a rule, apparent possessions of nuclear material, and the sellers proved to be frauds. Information provided by state security organs, documents that Austria usually acts as a transit country, and does not have a suitable market. Thus, for reasons of "criminal geography," Germany is that member of the European Union which is most affected by nuclear crime. In addition to Austria, the roles of transit states are played by Scandinavia and the Baltic countries, as well as, Poland, the Czech Republic, Romania, Bulgaria, Hungary and Switzerland.

The Future of Organized Crime in East Europe

Organized crime can also lead to political implications. At present, mention is made of the growing political nature of this form of crime and the criminalization of politics. Political conflicts at the uppermost pinnacles of power are not conducive for combating organized crime.

Organized crime will continue becoming more important in terms of both its quality and quantity. International currency connections, world financial transactions, the exchange of goods and commodities, as well as freedom of movement, lead to an even greater internationalization and professionalization of activities carried out by crime groups. Following the opening up of Eastern European states, the already existing differences between Western European legal, social and economic structures will be accompanied by new elements whose impact upon the development of organized crime cannot be assessed fully. The prime threat posed by organized crime arises from their being flexible (assuming numerous forms), and that it enjoys the same freedoms and social opportunities as conventional society and legal economies do.

The path from criminal to political terrorism is not a lengthy one. Self-jurisdiction expands in those situations when the state, which has a monopoly for the administration of justice, is weak. As a result of this one should consider the possibility that terrorism, and terror as a technique, could also encompass the world of politicians. The previously noted conference that was held in Washington in 1994 established that organized crime poses a greater hazard for Western democracy than the "cold war."[38]

FBI director Louis Freeh, speaking before the U.S. Senate Foreign Relations subcommittee, warned that Russian organized crime groups had made strong gains in a broad range of criminal activities, such as tax fraud, drug trafficking and insurance scams. Freeh said that the activity of these groups is "a mounting threat to the safety and well-being of Americans." Former CIA director James Woolsey echoed Freeh's concerns, adding that Russian criminal groups are linking up with the mafia, Chinese Triads and Latin American drug cartels in such a way that their being an economic and security threat has become a global concern. Freeh further noted that organized crime groups have stolen an estimated $500 million, from the Russian economy. The overall profits of OC groups were estimated to range between $200 and $300 billion annually. Many officials are particularly concerned about the capability of Russian criminals to secure and to traffic in nuclear warheads.[39]

Former President of the Bundeskriminalamt, Hans Ludwig Zachert, drew attention to the ongoing brutalization by criminals under the impact of mafia organizations from the East. OC groups from the Far East, Eastern Europe, South American drug cartels, and La Cosa Nostra have "invaded" Germany because of her central location in Europe.[40]

Beginning efforts are being made by various countries to protect themselves against the East European mafia. For example, a police unit in Toronto was mandated, in 1994, to combat crime groups from Russia and other parts of East Europe. This is most relevant given that numerous Russians emigrate to the United States and Canada in order to develop criminal networks.[41]

The threat of East European OC is an ongoing one. Heads of the Italian mafia meet with Russian OC gang bosses in Vienna on a regular basis. Various estimates maintain that Russian funds, frequently "dirty," are invested in 1,500 Austrian firms and that Austria is being used by the Russian mafia to "launder" its money. Other criminal activities include the white slave trade, drug trafficking, and control over prostitution.[42]

This review of East European organized crime and criminality can be read as a caveat for the need for ongoing, effective international cooperation in order to achieve and maintain the necessary guarantees, and state, of security in the face of a growing threat by increasingly growing, better organized and cooperating criminal groups.

*Professor **Brunon Holyst** is the head of the Department of Criminology and Criminalistics, University of Lodz, head of European Post-Graduate Studies of Crime Problems, former director of the Institute of Crime Problems in Warsaw,*

former President of the Polish Society for Mental Health. He has taken an active and senior role in international and national organizations (International Society for Criminology, Polish Society of Forensic Medicine and Criminology, Polish Criminalistics Society, member of the scientific board of several Polish institutes) and has made numerous presentations at international congresses, conferences and symposia. Author of 45 books, approximately 300 papers, editor-in-chief of 29 books, the journals Eurocriminology and Mental Health and various series: Criminological, Criminalistic and Penitentiary Studies (22 vols.), *Social Pathology-Prevention (10 vols.) and Criminality in the World (18 vols.). His research interests covered the broad fields of criminology, forensic psychology and criminalistics. He has created numerous scientific concepts (i.e. penal victimology).*

Notes and References

1 B. Holyst, *Kryminologia* (Criminology) 5th edition (1994), Panstowowe Wydawnicto Naukowe, Waszawa,, pp. 175-208.

2 Paper read by the delegation of the Ministry of the Interior of Belarus given at the III International Conference of the Criminal Police/Militia in Poland 'Legionowo 94.

3 S. Stalev (1996), "Lagebild und Politik der inneren Sicherheit in Bulgaren," (The domestic security situation and policy in Bulgaria), in R. Pitschas, *Politik und Recht der inneren Sicherheit in Mittel-und Osteuropa,* Jehle Rehm, Munchen, Berlin, pp. 233-234.

4 "Bulgarian: Mehr Verbrechen," (Bulgaria: More crimes) (1994), *Die Polizei,* 9, p. 23.

5 S.Kosik, *Sicherheitsrisiken in der Tscechischen Republik und Gegenmassnahmen* (The security risk in the Czech Republic and methods of opposing it) in, R. Pitschas, (ed.), op. cit., pp. 143-145. See also: J. Musil, *Grenzuberschhreitende polizeiliche Kooperation als kulturelle Herausforderung an die Tscechische Republik* (Trans-border police co-operation).

6 B. Holyst (1995), "Die neuen Richtungen in der Entwicklung de organisierten Kriminalitat in Osteuropa," (New trends in the growth of organized crime) in: *Mittelleuropaische Polizeikademie,* Lehrbrief, 2, p. 46.

7 Ungarten: Drogenumschalagplatz (Hungary: New localization of the turnover) (1994), *Die* Polizei, 12, p.337.

8 I.Tauber (1992), "Die Revolution und Kriminalitat" (Revolution and crime), *Die Polizei,* no.5.

9 L. Korinek, "Grenzuberschreitende polizeiliche Kooperation als kulturelle Herausforderung an die Republik Ungarn" (Transborder police cooperation as a cultural challenge for the Republic of Hungary), in R. Pitschas, ed., op. cit. pp.188-189.

10 I. Schikinger, "Lagebild und Kriminlitatsentwicklung und Bekampfungsstrattegien in Ungaren unter besonderer Berucksichtigung transnationaler Aspeket und der /aufgaben und Funktionen der Hochschule fur Polizeioffiziere" (The situational and developmental tendencies in crime as well as strategies for combating crime in Hungary, with particular attention paid to the transnational aspects, tasks and functions of the Higher Police Academy), in, R. Pitschas, (ed.) op. cit., p.208-209.

12 E. Kurapka (1996), "Problems and perspectives of complex crime investigation in Lithuania," in M. Pagon (ed.), *Policing in Central and Eastern Europe,* Ljubljana : College of Police and Security Studies, p. 369.

13 B. Holyst, "Die neuen Richtungen in der Entwicklung der organisierten Kriminalitat in Osteurope," op. cit., p.47.

14 B. Holyst (1993), "Organized crime in Poland," *EuroCriminology,* (5-6):145-177.

15 W. Plywaczewski, J. Swierczewski (eds.) (1996), *Policja polska wobec przestcepczosci zorganizowanej* (Polish Police and Organized Crime), Szczytno: Police Academy.

16 Estimated data from: B. Holyst (1996), *Narkomania: Problemy prawa i Kryminologii* (Drug Addiction: Legal and Criminological Probems), Warszawa, pp. 28-30 (police and health service data).

17 See B. Holyst, *Narkomania,* op. cit., chapter VI, p. 118.

18 J. Serdakowski, "Zorganizowana przestepczosc narkotykowa w Polsce" (Organized drug crime in Poland), in *Policja polska wobec przestepczosci zorganizowanej,* op. cit. pp.197-202.

19 W. Stykowska, "Przestepczosc zorganizowana zwiazana z zyciem nocnym" (Organized crime connected with night life), chapter on the dimensions of prostitution, in *Policja Polska wobec Przestepczosci Zoeganizowanej*, op. cit., pp.210-212.

20 See: J. Swierczewski, M. Merta and W. Mocarski, "Przestepczosc zorganizowana w wybranych panstwach bylego ZSRR," (Organized crime in select states of the former Soviet Union), *Policyjny Biuletyn Szkoleniowy*, p. 30.

21 J. Gilinskij, "Umbruch und kriminalitat in Russland" (The breakthrough and crime in Russia), in *Mitteleuropaische Polizeiakamie*, op.cit., pp. 17-23; The real threat from Russia: crime is exploding, *Los Angeles Times*, May 30,1994, Metro, part B, p.6, col. 3.

22 J. Steele (1994), *Eternal Russia: Yeltsin, Gorbachev and the Mirage of Democracy*, Cambridge, Mass: Harvard University Press.

23 D. Cheisev (August 13, 1994), "Mafia cashing in on Moscow's economic chaos," *Inter Press Service*.

24 "Kriminalitat verhindert Gesundung der Russischen Wirtschaft" (Crime as an obstacle for curing the Russian economy) (1997), *Der Kriminalist*,2, p.69.

25 Quoted according to the Polish daily *Rzeczpospolita* no. 40, February 17, 1997.

26 D. Ward (1991), "Organized crime, corruption add to law enforcement problems," *Crime and Justice International*, 1 (7); W. Milutenko (1992), "Wie bedrohlich ist die russische Mafia?," *Magazin fur die Polizei*, 3; USSR Ministry of Interior (1992), "Organized crime: survey response," *International Criminal Police Review*, 434, p. 29-35.

27 M. I. Goldman (January-February 1996), "Why is the mafia so dominant in Russia?" *Challenge*, p. 39.

28 A. Waksberg (1991), *The Soviet Mafia*, New York: St. Martin's Press; see also Y. Solomenko (December 18, 1993), "St. Petersburg gangsters push for economic power," *Izvestia*, p. 10; A. Higgins (May 3, 1994), "Gangster activity in St. Petersburg is spectacular, bloody and on the increase," *The Independent*.

29 E. Weisskopf, "Russia in Transition: Perils of the Fast Track to Capitalism," in J. A. Frieden, D. A. Lake (eds.), *International Political Economy* , New York, p.475-489.

30 "Russia's Mafia: More crime than punishment," *The Economist* July 9, 1994, p.13.

31 M. Waller (1994), *Secret Empire: The KGB in Russia Today*, New York: Westview Press.

32 Paper read by the delegation of the Ukrainian Ministry of the Interior at the III International Conference of the Criminal Police/Militia, op. cit.

33 J. Swierczewski, op. cit., p. 31.

34 Ibid, p. 32.

35 Ibid, p. 32.

36 A. Kohl and P. Krrvert (1996), "Przest Lepczo~c nuklearna i nuklearny terroryzm w Niemczech" (Nuclear crime and nuclear terrorism in Germany), in B. Holyst, E. Kube, R. Schulte (eds.), *Przest~epczosc zorganizowana w Niemczech i w Polsce* (Organized Crime in Germany and Poland), Warszawa, p.189.

37 M. Willrich and T. Taylor (1974), *Nuclear Theft: Risks and Safeguards*, Cambridge, MA.

38 R. Godson and J. Olson (1995), *International Organized Crime: Emerging Threat to U.S. Security*, Washington D.C.

39 D. Ward and J. Serio (July-August 1994), "Violent crime increases amid growing criticism of police," op. cit., p.4; see also J.E. Jennings, "Controlling political violence: Russia and South Africa," *Crime and Justice International*, p.5, 6; J. Serio (1993), "Organized crime in the former Soviet Union: New directions, new locations," *Crime and Justice International*, 9, pp.15-20.

40 H. L.Zachert (1994), "Kriminalitatsgefarhrdung der Wirtschaft" (The criminal threat to the economy), *Kriminalistik*, 8, p. 361.

41 "Kanada: Sondereinheit gegen Ost-Mafia" (Canada: the police versus the Eastern Mafia) (1994), *Die Polizei*, 9, p. 264.

42 V. Pankov (October 2, 1995), "Ost mafia sucht num im Westen Operationbasis," *Die Presse*, p.4.

4   The Development and Control of Organized Crime in Post-Apartheid South Africa

Mark Shaw

Abstract

Organized crime has grown dramatically in South Africa's new democratic order. While some forms of organized crime - notably gang activity in the Western Cape- did exist under apartheid rule, this did not constitute a threat, and indeed, street level gangs were often used by state agents to disrupt anti-apartheid activists. While public and political pressure is mounting on the issue, South African law enforcement agencies are ill-prepared for the task of countering large scale organized criminal activity. Yet, it is critical that interventions occur now: South African criminal organizations, while numerous, are still relatively fragmented and vulnerable to focused police action. One major current weakness, however, is the lack of understanding and analysis of the size, shape, structure and potential growth paths of South African organized crime.

Key Words: South Africa, Organized crime, Policing, Transitions

Introduction

Organized crime is a little-understood phenomenon in newly democratic South Africa. Public attention has been focused on other, more visible areas of criminality, and the South African Police Service (SAPS) has only recently begun to counter the problem. Yet, organized crime has grown dramatically since the transition to democracy began in the country in 1990.

The growth in organized crime has caught South African law enforcement agencies unprepared. The policing agencies of the South African State are struggling to make the conversion from authoritarian control to democratic forms of policing. The SAPS and other state law enforcement institutions do not yet have the resources or technical expertise to cope adequately with organized crime. Given that organized crime was never a priority under apartheid rule – indeed, there is evidence that local criminal gangs were used to disrupt the activities of pro-democracy activists – it is now difficult to measure the extent of its growth since 1990.

Current (although tentative) intelligence estimates indicate that organized crime has doubled under the new government. SAPS strategic intelligence estimates suggest that there are currently about 700 *"extremely well financed and superbly armed"* crime syndicates operating in and from South Africa.[1]

According to SAPS organized crime officers, almost half of these operations are based in and around Johannesburg.

These estimates of organized criminal activity are based on the collation of information from police and other intelligence sources according to police definitions (although these are still contested) of "syndicated crime." In South African police parlance a crime syndicate is defined broadly as a well organised and structured group with a clear leadership corps, which is involved in different criminal activities such as drug trafficking, vehicle theft or money laundering. Such syndicates have well-established contacts with national and international criminal organisations, cartels or mafia groupings.[2]

While varying in form and structure, South Africa organized crime syndicates share a number of common characteristics: a hierarchy of control, with clearly designated systems of promotion and payment; sophisticated procedures, often via legitimate business interests, to launder money obtained by means of illegal activities; and the use of weapons to ensure that "business" routes are protected and potential competitors eliminated. However, senior police officers concede that there is still much to learn about the development of organized crime in South Africa.

The lack of understanding of the growth of organized crime in South Africa has been the result of a general failure to properly analyse the phenomenon. There is little if any substantial work on the development of organized crime in the country and the growth, size and shape of criminal groups is poorly understood. Organized criminal operations have benefited: lack of analysis has meant that attempts to police the problem have often been poorly co-ordinated and the attention of policy makers has, until recently, been diverted to other seemingly more urgent police transformation issues. This article constitutes the first comprehensive attempt to record the growth of organized crime in the country and assess the capacity of the state to counter it.

Organized Crime in Transition

Comparative evidence suggests that organized crime grows most rapidly in periods of political transition and violence, when state resources are concentrated in certain areas only and gaps emerge in which organized criminal groups may operate. The most notable example is the former Soviet Union: the collapse of communist rule allowed the emergence of literally thousands of criminal organisations involving current and former members of the establishment.[3]

The formation of new states, the breakdown of old ones and the establishment of competing centres of power is hardly a new phenomenon. The growth of the earliest recorded forms of organized crime in Sicily more than a century ago was the result of weak government, and strong ethnic and family linkages. Even when stronger forms of governance were exerted from the Italian mainland in the 19th century, and again in the 1980s, organized crime proved to be remarkably adaptive, altering its operations and forging new linkages to ensure continued profits.[4]

In South Africa, these and other forces have been at play. Before the collapse of apartheid, South Africa was considered not to have had an organized crime problem. This was only partly true: in the Western Cape increasingly organized gangs had forged links with foreign criminal organisations in East Asia in order to obtain narcotics, particularly Quaaludes or (in South African terminology) Mandrax. Local gangs were often used to target anti-apartheid activists in exchange for police turning a blind eye to their activities.[5] Towards the late 1980s tightly organized and ethnically based organized crime emerged in the form of the "Boere Mafia" (literally farmers mafia). Involved in a range of criminal activities, these groups were soon infiltrated and broken by the police. Significantly, however, the Boere Mafia appeared to recruit former members of the security forces and had right wing political connections.[6]

Generally however organized criminal activity (notwithstanding the criminal activities of the state itself) were poorly developed given that the country was largely cut-off from the rest of the world and engaged in a near civil war. While criminal organisations were used by both sides to smuggle weapons and disrupt opponents, political considerations were always predominant. Although there is little available evidence to substantiate it, there must have been a significant growth in local organized crime syndicates in the final days of apartheid rule and the first year of the new democracy. The security forces at the time were largely occupied with political issues and despite the conversion of the (political) Security Branch into the Criminal Intelligence Service, the shift in emphasis was slow.[7]

The advent of democracy in the country heralded an increase in organized criminal activity. Senior SAPS officers point out that when apartheid ended, border controls were weakened, thus creating new potential areas of operation for organized crime. This also occurred at a time when transnational criminal operations were expanding; just like "legitimate" multinational businesses East Asian, Nigerian and Eastern European groups bought into local South African criminal operations and expanded them, or contracted subsidiary organisations to conduct their work for them. Stricter controls at points of entry into North America and most European states, southern Africa's favourable position on the drug trafficking routes between the Far and Middle East, the Americas and Europe, and its accessibility via land, sea and air made it a lucrative area for illegal business.

Given these factors, a recent report by the World Economic Forum cited South Africa as having an organized crime problem second only to Colombia and Russia.[8] In truth, the report provides an inaccurate reflection of the actual extent of the problem in the country. Primarily the growth of organized crime has been much more fragmented and (although there are notable exceptions) does not involve former members of the security establishment to the same degree as in the former Soviet Union.[9] Like Russia however the growth of organized crime has been a feature of the political transition to a democratic order. The opening up borders, the weakening (or inappropriateness) of the policing institutions of the state and the volatile regional context have all contributed to the growth of organized crime.

In sum, four factors should be taken into account when measuring the extent to which organized crime has developed in South Africa since the transition to democracy:

- The degree to which various organized crime groups have consolidated either through merger or structured co-operation;
- The role that ex-members of the apartheid security forces play in relation to organized crime;
- The degree to which organized criminal groups have been successful in penetrating the state and corrupting officials;
- The degree to which foreign organized crime groups operate within the country and have forged links with local crime syndicates.

South African organized crime remains relatively fragmented and on current evidence, the extent of organized crime in South Africa remains difficult to gauge accurately. According to SAPS intelligence reports, 192 organized crime syndicates with a combined figure of 1,903 primary suspects are currently known to be operating in South Africa and are under police surveillance. The majority of these syndicates specialise either in drug trafficking (96 syndicates), vehicles related crimes (83 syndicates), and commercial crime (60 syndicates) or in any combination of these crimes. At least 32 of the 192 known organized crime syndicates in South Africa operate internationally, while the criminal activities of 150 of these syndicates are at present restricted to countries in sub-Saharan Africa.[10] (See Table 4.1)

The estimated number of crime syndicates is not in itself important. The development of organized crime, for example, could be much more advanced if there were only two but extremely well developed criminal operations. Thus, the relative fragmentation of organized crime in South Africa suggests that there is a "window period" in which appropriate policing interventions can make a substantial difference. Organized crime, despite (or perhaps because of) its rapid growth, remains comparatively "disorganised" and is vulnerable to well targeted policing interventions. Given the connections between criminal syndicates and street level gangs, law enforcement interventions need to concentrate equally on both.

According to SAPS definitions syndicates are seen as more sophisticated organisations operating on a wider level than gangs, which are considered to be criminal organisations of a lower order of influence and sophistication. Gangs may often be employed by syndicates to do the dirty work at street level, with the latter often acting to co-ordinate the activities of different gangs. The Western Cape in particular has had a problem with gang related activities. While anti-crime vigilante action has now become a feature of the politics of the Western Cape, this has served largely to consolidate local gangs[11] (who just

Table 4.1 National and provincial perspectives on the focus of activities of organized crime syndicates

Criminal Activity / Province	National	Eastern Cape	Northern Cape	Mpuma-langa	Gauteng	KwaZulu-Nat	Northwest	Northern Provence	Western Cape	Free State
Number of OC Crime Syndicates	192	27	16	12	45	45	12	8	19	8
Drug Trafficking	96	17	3	5	29	16	7	3	10	6
Counterfeit Money and Laundering	9	1	1	0	2	3	0	1	0	1
Communications Crime/Fraud	46	2	12	2	13	9	0	2	2	4
Falsification/ Forgery	5	1	0	0	1	0	1	0	1	1
Corruption	8	1	0	1	2	2	0	1	1	0
Bribery	7	1	6	0	0	0	0	0	0	0
Soliciting	6	0	6	0	0	0	0	0	0	0
Diamond and Gold Related	38	3	15	3	2	8	5	1	0	1
Aluminum, Copper, Chrome, etc.	6	0	1	1	1	0	2	1	0	0
Stolen Goods Related	8	2	3	0	1	0	0	2	0	0
Theft	7	2	2	0	3	0	0	0	0	0
Housebreaking	3	0	1	0	1	0	0	0	1	0
Murder & Robbery	25	2	7	0	5	2	0	2	1	6
Firearms Related	26	7	2	0	1	6	2	3	3	2
Highjacking	10	1	0	0	5	2	0	0	0	2
Truck & Freight Related	6	0	1	0	1	2	0	0	2	0
Vehicle Related	69	8	2	3	21	20	2	5	3	5
Taxi Violence	3	1	0	0	0	0	0	1	1	0
Gang Related Crime	4	4	0	0	0	0	0	0	0	0
Intimidation & Other Violence	1	0	0	0	0	0	0	0	1	0
Chinese Triad Related	1	0	0	0	0	0	0	0	1	0
Prostitution	3	0	0	0	1	0	1	0	1	0
Endangered Species Trade	5	1	0	0	0	1	1	2	0	0
Stocktheft & Theft of Game/Poaching	6	5	0	0	0	0	0	0	0	1
Total	398	59	62	15	89	71	21	24	28	29

Note that a single syndicate may be involved in more than one category of crime. More than one syndicate may also be involved in a specific category of criminal activity.

months ago were engaged in vicious turf battles) into a larger umbrella structure, known as "The Firm," in an attempt to ensure a unified front against vigilante activity.[12]

Two factors make the policing of the gangs in the Western Cape potentially problematic. Firstly, the fact that before 1990 the then South African Police actively used criminal gangs to disrupt activities aimed at undermining the Apartheid State. The police (much of the new organized crime units are formally members of the Security Branch) have displayed some reluctance in arresting and bringing to trail former allies in the political struggle.[13] While these connections have been undercut over time, there is some potential for these old linkages to be re-established should organized crime continue to gain in power, resources and influence.

Second, gangs operate in many of the most destitute areas of the Western Cape and often provide the only means of livelihood for whole communities. Policing organized crime in the South African context cannot be separated from high levels of poverty in certain areas and the ease at which "foot soldiers" can be recruited for comparatively high levels of reward.[14]

Apart from the 194 syndicates identified above the SAP have targeted a range of criminal organisations for observation and information. Such "target groups" are potential criminal organisations, to be classified as such once information on their structure and activities is complete. Approximately 500 target groups with a combined figure of 1,184 primary suspects have been identified for attention in this way.

Most of these organized crime operations concentrate on southern Africa, dealing in a wide variety of commodities and engaging in a number of illegal activities. These include a lucrative trade in drugs, gold and diamond smuggling, vehicle theft, commercial crime, and arms smuggling. Significantly, the activities of organized crime syndicates are often inter-linked. For example, in Southern Africa, vehicle theft and robbery are linked to the illegal arms trade in Mozambique, while drug trafficking is connected with motor vehicle theft and money laundering in Zambia.

At least 16 of these 500 organized crime groups operate internationally, with the criminal activities of 403 of these target organisations at present restricted to countries in sub-Saharan Africa. As in the case of the known syndicates, the Tactical Research Unit of the SAPS's Crime Information Management Centre has determined that the majority of the target groups specialise in drug trafficking (194 target groups), vehicle related crimes (106 target groups), commercial crime (97 target groups) or any combination of these crimes.[15] (See Table 4.2)

South Africa has emerged as a major transhipment point for narcotics trafficking after the transition to democracy ended the country's international isolation. Contributing factors include the its geographic position on major trafficking routes between the Far and the Middle East, the Americas and Europe, the rapid expansion of international air links, a well developed transportation infrastructure, and modern international telecommunication and

Table 4.2 National and provincial perspectives on the focus of activities of organized crime target groups

Criminal Activity	National	Eastern Cape	Northern Cape	Mpuma-langa	Gauteng	KwaZulu-Nat	Northwest	Northern Provence	Western Cape	Free State
Number of OC Crime Syndicates	500	107	84	80	85	43	53	22	19	7
Drug Trafficking	194	62	48	33	17	13	13	3	5	0
Counterfeit Money and Laundering	8	3	0	2	1	0	2	0	0	0
Communications Crime/Fraud	86	9	16	1	40	8	1	0	7	4
Falsification/ Forgery	3	0	0	0	0	2	1	0	0	0
Corruption	1	0	0	1	0	0	0	0	0	0
Bribery	6	0	6	0	0	0	0	0	0	0
Soliciting	9	0	9	0	0	0	0	0	0	0
Diamond and Gold Related	46	4	26	2	9	3	2	0	0	0
Aluminum, Copper, Chrome, etc.	5	0	0	0	3	1	1	0	0	0
Stolen Goods Related	3	1	2	0	0	0	0	0	0	0
Theft	8	4	0	0	0	4	0	0	0	0
Housebreaking	3	3	0	0	0	0	0	0	0	0
Murder & Robbery	14	3	6	3	0	2	0	0	0	0
Firearms Related	20	15	1	1	0	3	0	0	0	0
Highjacking	11	4	0	4	0	1	1	0	0	1
Vehicle Related		24	3	18	1	25	15	2	5	2
Taxi Violence	2	0	0	0	0	0	0	2	0	0
Gang Related Crime	2	2	0	0	0	0	0	0	0	0
Intimidation & Other Violence	1	1	0	0	0	0	0	0	0	0
Endangered Species Trade	4	0	0	0	0	0	0	3	0	1
Stocktheft & Theft of Game/Poaching	78	23	6	24	0	0	12	13	0	0
Total	599	158	123	89	71	62	48	23	17	8

Note that a single target group may be involved in more than one category of crime. More than one target group may also be involved in a specific category of criminal activity. It is furthermore possible that the criminal activities that some target groups are involved in, have not yet been fully identified.

banking systems. Long, porous borders and weak border control, including undermanned ports and numerous secondary airports, give traffickers nearly unlimited access to South Africa.

Drug trafficking in particular provides the resources on which other forms of illegal activity can be built. Mozambique has emerged as a major transit point for heroin, hashish and Mandrax being smuggled into the Southern African region, as well as for drugs destined for the Northern Hemisphere. Given the end of the civil war there – and South African supply of weapons to one of the protagonists – Mozambique has become the region's main source of illegal firearms.16[3] There is a ready market for these weapons among other crime syndicates and criminal gangs operating in South Africa and elsewhere in Southern Africa.

The need to move illicit goods has meant that the largely unregulated transport sector in the country has served as the breeding ground for organized crime. A dramatic expansion in the number of mini-bus taxis plying their trade within the larger cities and on long distance routes have not surprisingly given rise to turf wars for profitable routes, as well as the growth of tightly organised taxi organisations who employ "hit squads" to eliminate potential competitors and actively engage in the corruption of state officials.[17]

The growth and consolidation of a few powerful figures in the taxi industry constitutes a classic case of the overlap between legitimate and illegitimate business and development of organized crime. Given their capacity for mobility, taxi operators are useful partners (or in some cases initiators of) smuggling networks across the sub-continent. State attempts at regulating the industry are proceeding slowly and while there have been some successes these have been undercut by high levels of corruption and weak law enforcement.

The growth of crime (and in particular organized crime) has led many at the highest echelons of the new government to argue that organized crime is a project of many of those opposed to democracy – a conspiracy to undermine the new state. The reality is more complex.

Former members of the apartheid security forces are indeed heavily involved in crime; ex-members of the security forces have been active in drug trafficking, weapon smuggling and prostitution rings. In these cases there are some parallels between the cases of the former Soviet Union and South Africa: most particularly was the increased power and access to resources of particular military and policing units during the closing days of communist and apartheid rule. In the main these are former operatives from the murky world of special forces whose transition to the world of crime was an easy step from covert operations which often co-operated with criminals.[18] For example, South African military intelligence networks were involved in the late 1980s with smuggling of contraband ivory and rhino horns both in an attempt to gather intelligence in neighbouring states and to raise money for additional military projects.[19]

In turn, government now fears that the rapidly developing private security industry, which employs many who received their training in the apartheid security state, constitutes a safe haven for organized criminals. Again, blanket distinctions are dangerous. The industry, which outnumbers the public police by three to one, is fragmented and internally competitive and does not in itself constitute a threat to the state.[20] What is clear however is that some security "companies" are involved in the training of paramilitary forces, the smuggling of arms and organized criminal activity. Ironically, the private security industry does serve a useful function in the post-transition environment: without the employment opportunities it provides for former combatants, criminal activity might be a much more appealing alternative for disgruntled former soldiers, police and intelligence officials.

Also of concern to the new government is growing levels of corruption (some of which can be linked to organized crime) across state institutions. Organized criminal operations in Colombia and Russia however have penetrated the state to a much greater extent than is the case in South Africa. While current estimates suggest that there is fairly wide-scale (and increasing) levels of corruption in the lower echelons of the criminal justice system (that is, among the police, Department of Justice officials and among prison staff) this has not yet permeated to higher levels.

While the exact number of corruption charges laid against the police is difficult to determine given that they do not result in automatic suspensions, internal police figures show that about 2,834 police officers were investigated for criminal offences during 1996. While many are still ongoing, these investigations have however led to few prosecutions often due to the fact that evidence is difficult to obtain and police officials are unwilling to give evidence against each other. SAPS anti-corruption unit estimates however suggested that the problem of corruption is fairly widespread in particular in vehicle theft units and the South African Narcotics Bureau (SANAB). In the Johannesburg area one in four police officers were being investigated for a criminal offence in 1996.

Public perceptions that the SAPS is increasingly corrupt, undermine attempts at transformation of policing in South Africa and uncut confidence in the ability of the police to undercut growing levels of criminality. While the causes of corruption are complex they relate in most cases to the weak implementation of controls and poor management practices. Anti-corruption unit members also make it clear (although this is the case for all units in the SAPS) that they were significantly under resourced and understaffed. If not countered quickly and innovatively, it is possible that the SAPS will be affected by institutionalised forms of corruption.

There is an unfortunate paradox for South Africa here. Organized crime operates best in the context of a corrupted state and organised business sector – not one that has completely broken down. The existence of a relatively strong but penetrated state (as in the case of South Africa) allows organized crime the luxury of using state institutions for profit, remaining relatively free from prosecution while continuing to operate in a comparatively stable environment. Failed states mean higher costs for organized crime: without state "assistance" and infrastructure, there may be greater costs involved in securing crime fiefdoms, which come closer to "warlordism" than organized crime operations.

Apart from the growth of localised variants of organized crime outlined above, international organized crime groups have increasingly become active in South Africa. The operations of the following groups constitute the greatest threat:

- *Russian Mafia*: Available information indicates that Russian citizens are involved in the activities of a number of criminal groups in several southern African states particularly, Angola, Botswana, Mozambique, Namibia, Swaziland and South Africa. The Russian Mafia groups concentrate mainly on diamond and weapon smuggling, corruption, fraud and money laundering schemes, as well as investment in legitimate business. For example, police intelligence reports show how Russian citizens residing in South Africa simultaneously have contacts in Mozambique to facilitate weapons smuggling to South Africa, while a private Russian business group is currently attempting to sell stockpiles of Russian armaments and ammunition to countries on the African continent. An agency will, according to current information, be set up to facilitate the marketing and distribution of the weaponry. Officials in the Mozambican planning agency are reported to have close contacts with the Russian Mafia in South Africa.[21]

- *Chinese Triads*: SAPS intelligence assessments argue that the growth of Chinese Triad activity in the country is closely related to the growing number of Chinese illegal immigrants entering the country. Triads in particular have been involved in the smuggling of endangered species or products derived from such species. Recent police operations in the Western Cape have reaped some benefit. Various Chinese criminal syndicates have been uncovered and some leaders and members apprehended in connection with a variety of crimes ranging from abalone smuggling, prostitution, murder, blackmail and the possession of unlicensed firearms. An almost unprecedented array of state policing agencies were involved in the investigations. Among others these included: the Western Cape Organized Crime Investigation Unit, SANAB, SAPS Internal Security, the Illegal Immigration Investigation Unit, the Endangered Species Protection Unit and the Department of Sea Fisheries. (The diversity of agencies engaged in the investigation of organized crime and the problems associated with this will be discussed below).[22]

- *Nigerian Organized Crime groups*: The growth of Nigerian organized crime groups in South Africa over the last five years has been phenomenal. Organized crime assessments completed by the South African government indicate substantial activity by Nigerian organized crime groups in South Africa. Despite this there have been comparatively few arrests and fewer successful prosecutions. Street level drug officers in Johannesburg admit that they are largely unsuccessful in countering Nigerian and central African criminal organisations and parts of inner city Johannesburg are increasingly dominated by the activities of Nigerian and central African "drug lords."[23]

The response of the South African public to rising levels of crime is increasingly a vocal one. Political leaders, who originally regarded issues of state transformation as more important, have taken note and the police are under increased pressure to investigate and prosecute those involved in organized crime. The media have given extensive coverage to the issue of crime and there is a growing interest in reporting on organized criminal activities. However, to date, most press coverage remains event specific with little in-depth press investigation or coherent analysis of organized crime.

Given levels of poverty in the country and the culture of lawlessness bred during apartheid (and the fight against it) some communities do indeed tacitly support the operation of organized crime. This is changing rapidly however and community responses to crime are increasingly to take action themselves when the police appear to be ineffective. Thankfully, organized criminal activity – with some minor exceptions – has largely lacked ethnic or tribal parameters. There is also little evidence that politicians at the level of national or provincial government have connections with organized crime. Indeed, it is positive to note that given the public outcry on the issue, should a clear link be made between senior politicians and organized crime, their political careers would be in ruins. Church and business leaders have been particularly outspoken in condemning criminal activities.

These factors have resulted in intense (and growing) public pressure for action against crime in general and organized crime in particular. State law enforcement institutions are currently ill prepared to actively counter the problem. At the outset, the diversity of foreign and local organized crime operations in South Africa may contain both advantages and drawbacks for policing. Monitoring two or three large organisations in any areas may be easier than watching hundreds. At the same time, though, a diversity of competing organisations provides some opportunities for more sophisticated forms of control, exploiting divisions and fostering competition between syndicates.

Central to any policing strategy should be an attempt to prevent the consolidation of organized crime operations.

Once firmly established, organized crime operations are immensely difficult to eradicate. Indeed, South Africa may have already entered a stage where this is no longer possible. While still fragmented, organized crime in South Africa is increasingly sophisticated and is rapidly countering attempts by the state to clamp down on its activities. Also, state law enforcement institutions will remain weak and dominated by questions of internal transformation for the foreseeable future.

Thus, much research work still needs to be done on organized crime in South Africa. While detailed work is available on the operations of organized crime in Europe and North America, there is little literature either on South African syndicates or on organized crime in South Africa as a whole. To begin to police the problem innovatively it will be essential to better understand the growth of organized crime networks. Four guidelines are appropriate in this regard:

- A focus must be given to the changing commodities that organized crime networks trade in and potential new commodities they seek to obtain. The introduction of drugs such as "crack" into the South African market suggests that drug syndicate operations may change over time to accommodate changing market conditions.
- The dynamic connections between various syndicates and street-level organisations, and their linkages to the state and external criminal organisations in turn, is an important measure of the maturation of organized crime in the country. A solidifying of operations, the targeted penetration of the state apparatus and the emergence of a number of prominent figures will all signal growth stages in the development of organized crime operations in the country.
- The reaction of organized crime syndicates in response to policing interventions should be a key area of concern. Criminal operations may change their shape and structure in reaction to some forms of policing, or may specifically target police agencies either for corruption or violent retribution.
- Violence, which can be linked to organized crime operations, should be carefully monitored to assess the stages of development exhibited by crime syndicates. Ironically, periods of comparative peace may signal the growth and consolidation of organized crime rather than its demise.

The growth of organized crime in South Africa from 1990 however has not been accompanied by a criminal justice system or specialised police agencies, which are well placed to analyse and counter the problem. Responses to organized crime have generally been fragmented and there is a general lack of co-ordination both between the various policing agencies but also across the departments of the criminal justice system.

The National Crime Prevention Strategy (NCPS), a cross-departmental plan aimed at achieving greater co-ordination serves as the cornerstone of state strategy against criminality.[24]   The NCPS outlines a comprehensive set of programmes to deal with organized crime.   These range the improvement of information technology resources to infrastructure upgrading.   One year after its launch however it is generally conceded by its drafters that little concrete has been achieved.   NCPS implementation has been characterised by a complex set of committees and has been plagued by the failure to set clear objective s for delivery.

A key weakness of the NCPS was a neglect to confront the country's growing illegal drug trade.   A draft strategy for the control of illegal drugs has now been formulated.   However, the strategy is regarded as too ambitious (it is based on the British drug prevention plan), ignoring the weakness of provincial and local government structures.   The strategy has been some time in the making and it is not clear when it will be released under which department it should fall.

One area where some progress has been made however is the drafting of legislation, which aims to tighten the legal framework in which organized criminals operate.   These include the drafting of legislation aimed at, among others, allowing the confiscation of the profits of crime and the prevention of money laundering.[25]   These initiatives were taken largely as a result of foreign pressure particularly from the United States and Great Britain.[26]   Most of the battery of legislation is regarded by international experts as being comprehensive, although law enforcement officers and prosecutors concede that it is one thing to have a comprehensive set of laws, and quite another to enforce them.

Indeed, the effective prosecution of organized crime assumes a degree of efficiency in the state's criminal justice system.   This is still some way off and the criminal justice system is characterised by multiple blockages, which are not easily fixed in the short term.   Any attempt at improving the policing of organized crime will be hampered without an effective institution to process offenders once a crime has been committed.   Currently, all departments in the criminal justice system are characterised by poor moral and weak middle management.   Some old order civil servants are disillusioned and new or recently promoted officials have little experience and (often deliberately) receive no support.

Within the criminal justice system the investigation and gathering of information in relation to organized criminal groups is spread across a number of SAPS units and intelligence agencies.   These include, among others, the organized crime units of the SAPS, SANAB, the Commercial Branch, vehicle theft units, the Endangered Species Unit, the Diamond and Gold Branch, various SAPS anti-corruption units, SAPS Internal Security (formerly Security

Branch), the National Intelligence Agency (NIA), Military Intelligence (MI) and the South African Secret Service (SASS).

Thus, one of the key challenges in the policing of organized crime operations is increasingly the co-ordination between the various units involved. While there appears to be growing support for the establishment of a single national investigative agency similar to the United States Federal Bureau of Investigation (which Deputy-President Thabo Mbeki is said to be in favor of), no concrete plans have been formulated in that regard.

Given the current fragmentation however the exact budgetary amount, which is allocated for the policing of organized crime, is difficult to determine. The difficulty of determining exact expenditure on any function is not confined to organized crime: the SAPS budget is notoriously difficult to interpret with it being impossible, for example, to determine the exact expenditure at individual police stations. The lack of clarity with which money is allocated to various functions makes it difficult to measure performance in relation to resources.

Currently expenditure is probably around 10 percent of the total budget of R11.9 billion a 15 percent increase on the previous years expenditure of R9.8 billion. The NCPS has been allocated R406 million for the financial year 1997/98 for a range of cross-departmental programmes, some of which relate to organized crime. A significant component of the police budget is spent on paying informers: reward money in 1996 for informants amounted to R45.4 million, exceeding the budgeted amount. While a "substantial portion" of this is said to relate to organized crime it is unclear the degree to which the reward money resulted in convictions.

The lead agencies mandated with the investigation of organized crime are the various provincial and national organized crime units of the SAPS. These are relatively new with coordinated investigations only beginning some time after 1990. These units are supplemented by the resources of the Crime Intelligence Service (formally the Security Branch, responsible for "political crimes" under apartheid) as well as those of the NIA. Both of the latter agencies generally collect intelligence around the operation of organized crime groups either through a request by organized crime investigators or on their own initiatives. Insiders admit that there is some degree of infighting between the agencies involved with particular animosity (although this is not something new) between the NIA and the various units of the SAPS.

SANAB, the SAPS agency responsible for drug related law enforcement, is regarded by foreign governments as the most effective drug policing institution in the region. SANAB officers themselves informally admit however that they are losing the struggle against the illegal trade in narcotics given a lack of resources. The Johannesburg branch of SANAB for example has only twelve drug enforcement officers.

In particular, much more attention needs to be given to border control initiatives. The South African National Defence Force (SANDF) is currently tasked with border control although constitutionally it is the responsibility of the SAPS. Police officers however continue to staff border control points. A key weakness remains a poorly organised customs and revenue service responsible for the control of imports and exports through ports of entry. Foreign customs and excise experts concede that while some success is being achieved, falling morale and lack of skills and resources are serious obstacles.

Despite the weaknesses outlined above, it is clear that many of the resources of the apartheid security state have been refocused on the issue of organized crime. South Africa has a degree of comparative advantage here given a history of authoritarian policing which among other things included advanced systems of electronic surveillance and eavesdropping. It is clear from the figures quoted earlier, for example, that between the various state agencies involved that a large number of criminal organisations are monitored.

Apart from the impressive number of criminal organisations being monitored, however, comprehensive surveillance and targeted investigation appears to be restricted to comparatively few organisations. Table 4.3 illustrates the number of dedicated organized crime projects run by the SAPS organized crime units as well as the number of projects being conducted by specialised units in relation to a number of priority crimes as at March 1997.[27]

Table 4.3: SAPS organized crime projects

Category of organized crime	No. of projects
Drugs	37
Vehicles	18
Endangered species	3
Diamond and gold	15
Commercial crime	6
Firearms	9
Taxi violence	5
Corruption	8
Hijackings of freight	3
Armed robbery	2
Gang related violence	1
Housebreaking	1
TOTAL	**108**

While, given the number of syndicates identified, the total number of organized crime and related projects is relatively small some success has been achieved through this focused method of investigation. The first three months of 1997, for example, saw the arrest of twenty-three suspects for drug related organized crime offences and a further nine in relation to motor vehicle theft and firearm smuggling syndicates. However, if the policing of organized crime is to prove successful in the longer term there is an urgent need to expand the ability of the state to investigate a wider diversity of criminal groups.

In any event, police measures of their success – such as numbers of arrests or amount of contraband seized – provides a poor reflection of progress against organized crime. Little or no attention is paid to monitoring whether or not criminal groups have been eliminated and there is an urgent need to develop a more sophisticated mechanism to assess the total threat of organized crime in the country.

While recording numbers arrested, police figures seldom illustrate what success is obtained in relation to prosecutions. This is largely the result of the fact that detectives have been poorly equipped for policing the new democracy. The conversion from a confession based system of criminal justice (with many "confessions" extracted under torture) to one which relies on the collection of evidence has been slow. New order policy makers have also little expertise in the area (the division is head by an ex-ANC military officer) and improving the SAPS's investigative capacity is only receiving attention now, some three years into the new democracy.

Indeed, one of the key weaknesses identified in a NCPS report on *Re-engineering the Criminal Justice System* is the lack of skills of police investigators.[28] That often results in poorly completed case dockets and unsuccessful prosecutions. While these problems are more likely to occur at the level of the ordinary station detective, it does suggest that there is not a pool of talent among detectives to continue to staff specialised units. The problem of lack of skills in the area of detection is a deep-seated one. South Africa's detectives have always been a threatened breed; under apartheid the quick road to promotion for bright and ambitious officers was through the security branch; in the new order the fast track is uniform or visible policing.

This has been exacerbated in the past year by the large numbers of experienced detectives leaving the services for the more handsome pickings of the private sector and by the difficult of replacing these skills (One important loss has been Niels Venter, the Commissioner in charge of policing organized crime.). As it is detectives are underrepresented in the structure of the SAPS: the total number of detectives is 18,000 in a service of 138,000. Of the 18,000 about 6,000 detectives work within specialised units at either national or provincial level concentrating on organized crime and related issues.

Currently there are few incentives for detective work: uniformed officers work four days on and four days off, good detectives (many in specialised units) often work seven days a week with no overtime, under poor and dangerous conditions with little support. Most detectives, often with no training (only about 26 percent have been on a detective course), carry upwards of 50 case docket. There is no mentoring or assistance programme to speak of (although there are some exceptions in specialised units) and the vast majority of new detectives have to find their own way. There is also a high degree of inexperience: only 13 percent of all detectives have over six years experience.

Prosecutors in the Department of Justice are generally inexperienced and a poorly managed programme of affirmative action has weakened the Department's capacity. Some pockets of excellence however do remain particularly in the various offices of attorneys-general. Specialised units of prosecutors who deal specifically with complex organized crime cases have been established in most provinces. The key to their success is a close working relationship with specialised police units and the appointment of senior advocates and not police officers to direct investigators.

The Office for Serious Economic Offences (OSEO) also plays some part in organized crime prosecutions. Staffed by about 20 skilled prosecutors and accountants OSEO is well placed to investigate complex fraud cases. The unit however has been plagued by an inability to compete with private sector pay scales and some important posts remain unfilled.

The National Intelligence Agency (NIA) is also increasingly involved in the monitoring of criminal organisations. With an estimated 3,000 analysts and operatives and a proven technical ability the Agency is well placed to support the police. However, effectiveness has been blunted by the loss of skilled personnel either disillusioned with the new order or able to find better paying jobs in the private security sector. Effectiveness has also been blunted to some extent by ongoing efforts at rapid organisational transformation. It is currently unclear to what degree NIA monitoring has been of great support to the police. Agency insider's claim that evidence passed to the police is not always well handled and many in the intelligence community believe that NIA officials should be given policing powers. The budget of the NIA has increased dramatically since 1994; much of this money appeared to be used on paying off intelligence officers from the old order and recruiting new ones. However, insiders suggest that the substantial resources focused on political violence in KwaZulu-Natal (which has tailed off) can be redeployed on organized crime and related issues.

SASS, the foreign intelligence agency, is tasked with the collection of information on organized crime in foreign countries. Most resources in this regard are concentrated in Southern Africa although SASS staffers concede that organized crime is only one of a range of foreign intelligence priorities. Military intelligence concentrates largely on weapon smuggling and the monitoring of movement across the country's borders.

The extent to which organized criminal groups operate not just in South but Southern Africa emphasises the importance of regional attempts to control the problem. Unless the region can be made more secure from the threat of organized crime policing efforts in South Africa will be undermined. Regional efforts at policing organized crime have developed to some degree since 1994. The Southern African Regional Police Commissioners' Cooperation Organisation (SARPCO) and the Inter-State Defence and Security Committee are not yet being optimally utilised to combat organized crime in the region. Apart from the setting up of an electronic link between policing agencies in the various countries and the initiation of meetings between the various heads of police much of the co-operation remains largely at the level of rhetoric although a number of successful operations have recently been completed.

Part of the problem of regional policing, however, is the differing capacities of the various agencies involved. South African law enforcement institutions, despite their problems, are far better resourced and skilled than their regional counterparts. Recent operations in Zambia and Mozambique have thus had to be carried almost entirely by the SAPS. Despite this, co-operation among regional intelligence structures has improved dramatically although it is still too early to determine whether this will have an impact on the growth of organized crime. The Regional Information Liaison Office (RILO) has been established to co-ordinate intelligence collection efforts in relation to organized crime. However, these efforts will remain constrained by the weakness of such state agencies in countries like Mozambique and Angola emerging from protracted civil wars. This is a key point: better policing at home will only have a limited effect without a strong regional effort to counter organized crime.

Conclusion

The issue of organized crime is becoming of increasing significance in South Africa. However, the level to which organized crime has developed in the country has not reached the same point as in other societies such as Russia and Columbia. Current evidence suggests that organized crime remains comparatively fragmented and high-level state structures relatively unpenetrated. There are some positive features in the current scenario: South African organized crime groups do not have large numbers of émigrés in other countries (unlike, for example, Nigerians) to constitute an immediate threat to Western democracies or (although to a lesser extent) other African countries. There are however real dangers: weak institutions in the criminal justice system are increasingly open to corruption, more active policing could bring a greater consolidation of criminal groups and the growth in linkages between internal and local groups could strengthen over time. These factors suggest that the time for critical intervention be within the window period of the next three years.

State responses to date have been inadequate. Most clear is the lack of co-ordination and information sharing between the various agencies involved. Over time there is a real need to begin to investigate the possibility of establishing a single national specialised investigative agency to pool resources and skills. While this may be some way off key decision-makers have mooted the idea. Current evidence suggests that while state agencies have been fairly successful in monitoring the activities of a wide-ranging number of criminal groups they have been less successful in bring perpetrators to trail. Part of the problem relates to limited resources that are concentrated on a relatively small number of high focus investigative projects.

While it is difficult to determine the exact amount of resources which are focused on policing organized crime there is some agreement (at least among police officers) that a lack of skills and resources constrains specialised units from taking on more cases. A key problem is the failure of the SAPS to produce a strong core of experienced and skilled detectives who could be recruited into more complex and specialised investigations. This will result in a key long-term weakness which will be difficult to resolve. While the role of outside agencies (particularly NIA) is useful, the SAPS will always remain the lead department and its detectives will be central to the fight against organized crime.

Apart from the weakness among the investigative arms of the police it is clear that some of the largest obstacles are to be found in the institutional weaknesses of the criminal justice system itself. Unless the reactive components of the system can be reformed any attempt to control crime generally, and organized crime specifically, will be hamstrung from the beginning. In the short term one immediate result of weak institutional controls is the growth in corruption in lower levels of the system. This may have potentially serious consequences if it becomes institutionalised.

Falling morale in the police service and the lack of political direction accentuates many of the problems outlined above. While legislation has been drafted and policy formulated political leadership has shown little ability to drive the process of implementation. This may be particularly serious in the longer term in relation to establishment of a single national investigation unit. A poorly designed and implemented national agency may have more serious implications for policing than the current (all be they fragmented) institutional arrangements.

Aside from institutional reform, it is clear that the problem of organized crime in South Africa cannot be isolated from the problems of organized crime in the Southern African region more generally. Any counter strategy needs to give a heavy focus to regional initiatives. Unfortunately, compared to South Africa, many countries in the region lack the most basic skills and equipment for dealing with the issue. This may have long term consequences for attempts to adequately confront the problem at home when at least some of the problem lies on the country's borders. Current arrangements suggest a realisation of the problem although regional structures established so far have operated for too short a period to determine their effectiveness.

Central to any policing strategy – whether regionally or nationally focused – should be an attempt to prevent the consolidation of organized crime operations. Once firmly established, organized crime groups are immensely difficult to eradicate. In the final analysis, however, the development of organized crime is related as much to the effectiveness of policing as to the institutional strength of the state. Assessing the growth of organized crime cannot then be divorced from broader issue of governance and economic development. The weaker the state becomes over time the more likely that criminal organisations will form parallel and competing points of power which will be difficult to displace.

Mark Shaw, *Ph.D., is head of Crime and Policing Policy at the Institute for Security Studies, a non-profit think-tank based in Johannesburg. He has published widely on South African defence, intelligence, policing, crime and conflict resolution issues. He works closely with the ministry of safety and Security in Pretoria and is currently part of a ministerial team tasked with writing the White Paper on Safety and Security which aims to map key policing challenges for the country from 1998 to 2003. Dr. Shaw is a consultant to a number of South Africa's companies. During South Africa's transit ion to democracy, and while on secondment from a post as !\senior researcher at the Centre for Policy Studies in Johannesburg, he worked as a violence monitor and analyst.*

Notes and References

[1] W. Grove (22-24 May 1995), "A perspective on organized crime in South Africa," SAPS, Organized Crime Conference, Bramshill, United Kingdom.

[2] SAPS Organized Crime Unit, Anti Organized Crime Measures, August 1997.

[3] Among a burgeoning literature on the growth of organized crime in Russia, see James Sherr (February 1995), *Russia, Geopolitics and Crime, Conflict Research Centre*, 49.

[4] See Diego Gambetta (1996), *The Sicilian Mafia*, Cambridge, MA: Harvard University Press.

[5] There is very little literature on organized crime under apartheid. For an excellent study of the gangs in the Western Cape, see Don Pinnock (1984), *The Brotherhoods: Street Gangs and State Control in Cape Town*, Cape Town: David Phillip.

[6] There is no comprehensive analysis of the Boere Mafia. Perhaps most interesting however was the degree to which the Boere Mafia suggested that a democratic state would herald greater involvement of ex-security force members in crime.

[7] Mark Shaw, "Point of Order: Policing the Compromise," in Steven Friedman and Doreen Atkinson (eds.) (1994), *South African Review* 7: The Small Miracle, Johannesburg, Ravan.

[8] *Business Day* (14/04/97), Johannesburg.

[9] See for example, Graham Turbiville (Winter 1995), "Organized Crime and the Russian Armed Forces," *Transnational Organized Crime*, Vol. 1, No 4.

[10] SAPS, Crime Information Management Centre, The Incidence of Serious Crime: January to March 1997, Quarterly Report 2/97, 13 June 1997, pp. 23-46.

[11] See Mark Shaw (Spring 1996), "Buying Time? Vigilante action, crime control and state responses," *Indicator SA: Crime and Conflict*, No 7.

[12] Wilfried Scharf and Clare Vale (1997), "The Firm: Organized Crime comes of age during the transition to democracy," unpublished paper, Institute of Criminology, University of Cape Town.

[13] See Gavin Cawthra (1993), *Policing South Africa: The SAP and the Transition from Apartheid*, London: Zed.

[14] Antoinette Louw and Mark Shaw (1997), *Stolen Opportunities: The Impact of Crime on the Poor in South Africa*, Institute for Security Studies, Monograph 14.

[15] SAPS, *Quarterly Report 2/97*, pp. 23-44.

[16] Glenn Oosthuysen (1996), *Small Arms Proliferation and Control in Southern Africa*, Johannesburg: The South African Institute of International Affairs, pp. 39-53.

[17] Anthony Minnaar and Sam Pretorius (1996), *A Year of Living Dangerously: Hitmen, Corruption, Competition, Conflict and Violence in the Taxi Industry, 1994-1995*, Pretoria: Human Sciences Research Council.

[18] "The role of the former CCB and Associated Organisations in organized crime in South Africa," unpublished paper, Institute for Security Studies, August 1997.

[19] See D. W. Potgieter (1995), *Contraband: South Africa and the International Trade in Ivory and Rhino Horn*, Cape Town, Queillerie.

[20] For a more detailed overview of the industry, see Mark Shaw (1995), "Privatising Crime Control? South Africa's private security industry," in Shaw, *Partners in Crime Political Transition and Changing Forms of Policing Control*, Johannesburg: Centre for Policy Studies.

[21] Institute for Security Studies, Organized Crime in South Africa, unpublished briefing paper, July 1997.

[22] Ibid.

[23] See Mark Shaw (November 1996), "The growing threat of Nigerian organized crime in South Africa," *SA Exclusive.*

[24] National Crime Prevention Strategy, Departments of Correctional Services, Defense, Intelligence, Justice, Safety and Security and Welfare, Pretoria, May 1996.

[25] Four key pieces of legislation have been drafted and three have been enacted. These are as follows: International Co-operation in Criminal Matters Act, 1996; The Proceeds of Crime Act, 1996; The Extradition Amendment Act, 1996; and, the Money Laundering Control Bill, 1997.

[26] There have for example been a number of high level delegations on the issue and both the U.S. and British governments have stationed law enforcement officers, including FBI, DEA and custom officials, in South Africa.

[27] SAPS Quarterly Report, 2/97, pp. 23-44.

[28] Re-engineering the Criminal Justice System, A joint project of the Ministries of Safety and Security, Justice, Welfare and Correctional Services and Business against Crime, June 1996.

5 Economic Reform and "Black Society": The Re-Emergence of Organized Crime in Post-Mao China

Mark S. Gaylord and Hualing Fu

Abstract

China's cultural heritage includes an organized crime tradition, which dates back hundreds of years. Throughout the first half of the 20th century, China's "secret societies" enjoyed an intimate relationship with Chiang Kai-shek's Nationalist government. After the communists came to power in 1949, however, Mao Zedong moved quickly to crush what he correctly saw as a potential source of opposition to his new government. For nearly 30 years, organized crime in China disappeared, submerged along with other institutions of the earlier era. In the post-Mao China, however, organized crime (called hei shehui, *or "black society") has not only reappeared but is now widespread. "Black society" is an all-encompassing term from small bands of highwaymen to organized crime groups with thousands of members. By design, it is hidden from view, obscured by secrecy, corrupt officials and the hopelessly blurred distinction between private and public sectors.*

Key Words: Black society, Chinese Communist Party, Corruption, Economic reform, Triads.

Introduction

Organized crime is arguably the least understood, and most controversial, of all types of crime today. Nevertheless, criminologists and law enforcement officials generally agree on three points. First, that the term refers to the illegal activities connected with the management and coordination of racketeering (organized extortion) and the vices (Block and Chambliss, 1981). Second, that it exists because some members of society display a strong and persistent demand for illegal drugs, gambling, prostitution, loan-sharking, and increasingly, arts, arms, body parts, babies, etc. Third, organized crime has developed a structure that makes it possible to provide such illegal goods and services on a regular basis (Beirne and Messerschmidt, 1991).

What they do not agree on, however, is the nature of that structure. One school of thought believes organized crime comprises modern, bureaucratic, corporate-like groups that are governed at the national level (Cressey, 1969). Akin to their "upperworld" counterparts, these groups seek to monopolize their industries by expanding in size and forming large cartels of national and even international scope. According to this school, the structure of so-called "crime families" resembles that of formal organizations; there is a clear division of labor and chain of command; tasks and responsibilities are assigned according to members' skills and abilities; rules and regulations govern members; activities; promotion is based on merit and membership is restricted. Thus, it is claimed, crime families operate as their legitimate counterparts in terms of leadership, management and professionalism (Pace and Styles, 1975).

The other school of thought argues that organized crime is made up of small, fragmented and ephemeral enterprises. This definition suggests flexible and adoptive networks that can readily expand and contract to deal with the vagaries of an uncertain environment (Potter, 1994). A number of similarly minded researchers have focused on the entrepreneurial nature of organized crime. Their studies describe transitory alliances of risk takers who seize opportunities to earn large profits on their investments (Block 1983; Reuter, 1983). Apart from a relatively small core group, most associates are brought in as needed to provide special services. These groups vary in their level of organization but most are best understood as task forces, or small groups of people assembled to perform a particular piece of work. Their members are united by a shared interest in making money rather than by common heritage, kinship or desire to form and maintain corporate-like business enterprises.

Thus it is clear that the two major schools of thought on the nature of organized crime describe realities that stand virtually at opposite ends of a continuum.

Traditionally, Chinese organized crime has been described as historically rooted, embedded within a tightly knit ethnic group, international in scope, highly organized and willing to use violence to solve conflicts. A number of recent studies have focused on the Triads in Hong Kong and the Tongs in North American Chinatowns (McKenna, 1996; Chin, 1990). These studies claim Chinese crime groups such as the *14K, Sun Yee On, United Bamboo, Flying Dragons* and *Fuk Ching* have formed a highly organized criminal underworld that preys on the silent and frightened masses (Posner, 1988). Other criminologists and law enforcement officials, however, question this description, particularly in relation to international drug trafficking. Instead, they claim that most Chinese drug traffickers are entrepreneurs who operate within flexible, adaptive networks that expand and contract in response to changing levels of opportunity and risk (Dobinson, 1993).

In our view, however, neither the traditional model nor its alternative provides a viable framework for analyzing Chinese organized crime, particularly within China itself. Field research suggests these groups cannot be so easily classified. In our experience, Chinese crime groups range along a "*continuum of organization*." As Barlow (1994) has noted, there are *degrees* of organization. The concept of a continuum of organization allows us to examine and interpret Chinese organized crime from a broad perspective that encompasses a range of organization. We suggest that there is considerable variation among Chinese crime groups: some are highly organized with extensive national and international connections, while others are loosely structured open systems. Still other groups exhibit mixed characteristics (Zhang and Gaylord, 1996).

Organized Crime in Pre-Communist China

China's cultural heritage includes an organized crime tradition that dates back hundreds of years. It is widely believed the first Triad "secret society" was founded in the late Ming or early Qing period by monks of the Shaolin Temple, and formed part of a patriotic resistance movement in protest against the Manchu rulers who had overthrown the Ming dynasty in 1644 and formed the Qing dynasty (Morgan, 1960).

This view has been refuted in recent years by Chinese and Western historians using archival evidence discovered on Taiwan and the Chinese mainland since the mid-1960's (Cai, 1964; Zhuang, 1980). It is now believed that the first such society, the *Tiandihui* (Heaven and Earth Society), was founded at the Goddess of Mercy Temple in Fujian province in 1761. One of the major purposes of the *Tiandihui* was to create, through the rituals of sworn brotherhood, a mutual aid society for China's lowliest migrants. An underlying cause of the *Tiandihui's* formation was the rapid population growth and resultant severe economic dislocation during the early Qing period. Those who lost their means of livelihood or who did not have access to land were forced to migrate from their indigenous communities in order to earn a living. In southeast China, one of the strategies for those displaced from their villages was to create organizations of their own for self-protection. The subsequent expansion of the *Tiandihui* was linked to the migration patterns of China's lower classes. As new arrivals came into contact with the most marginalized residents of their host communities, the *Tiandihui* gradually became part of the social fabric of more settled communities and became a vehicle for such activities as robbery, feuding and rebellion (Murray, 1993).

A century later, before Sun Yat-sen established the Chinese Republic, he appealed to secret societies to come forth and help him. He traveled the world, visiting Chinese communities and asking for their help in toppling the Manchu regime and establishing a modern republic (Ma, 1990). To encourage their financial and organizational aid, Sun praised the putative "nationalistic, anti-Manchu origins" of secret societies, hoping to rally the latent patriotism of North American and Southeast Asian societies, which historically had been rather more like mutual aid societies than "cabals of rebels-in-waiting" (Ownby, 1993:6).

Later, in his bid to control China, Sun's successor, Chiang Kai-shek, repeatedly turned to secret societies, which by then had become deeply involved in prostitution, gambling and the opium trade. In fact, Chiang, as Sun before him, was a Triad member, and relied so heavily on his Triad allies that they served as generals, soldiers, spies, businessmen and hired thugs in his Kuomintang, the Chinese Nationalist Army (Dubro and Kaplan, 1986).

By the beginning of the 20th century, the opium trade, which had been inflicted on China by the British, had fallen into the hands of the Chinese underworld following what Seagrave (1985:331) calls Britain's "moralistic turnabout." After the Shanghai Opium Commission of 1909 and the International Opium Conference at the Hague in 1911-1912, China's suppression of domestic opium cultivation led gradually to a shift in consumption to imported morphine and heroin from Europe and to the centralization of Shanghai's Triads, notably the Green Gang, over China's now illicit opiate trade (McCoy, 1992).

By 1923, Shanghai drug syndicates were annually importing over 10 tons of heroin from Japan and Europe to meet the growing consumer demand. In the early 1930s, with Japanese laboratories in north China producing large quantities of narcotics and a network of Russian and Greek smugglers living in Shanghai, China began supplying America's illicit market, by then the world's second largest market. Simultaneously, Shanghai's Green Gang leader, Tu Yueh-sheng, emerged as the city's leading drug dealer and a key intelligence operative for Chiang's Nationalist Government, an alliance that protected Tu's narcotics network from the regime's highly publicized (but largely symbolic) anti-opium campaign of the 1930s. The ultimate basis of Tu's remarkable power lay with his political patrons. Indicative of his control, the head of the government's Opium Suppression Bureau, created by Chiang in 1933, was an active member of the Green Gang (McCoy, 1992).

Although Mao Zedong praised and wooed the secret societies before 1949, intending to incorporate them into his revolutionary course (Brady, 1982), after the communists came to power Mao moved quickly to crush what he correctly saw as a potential source of opposition to his new government. Hundreds of leaders from the *Yi Guan Dao* (Way of Basic Unity) and the *Ge Lao Hui* (Society of Brothers and Elders), in particular, were imprisoned (Hood, 1992). Many others were summarily executed by the simple expedient of a bullet to the back of the head.

Tens of thousands of their followers fled before and after the Communist take-over in 1949. Many made their way to Hong Kong where the Green Gang opened heroin refineries in the early 1950s. But after suffering reverses in a struggle with local Triads for control of the colony's heroin trade, the Green Gang faded by the mid-1950s and was replaced by local syndicated who traced their origins to nearby Swatow (Shantou) on China's south coast (Dubro and Kaplan, 1986; McCoy, 1992).

Today it is generally agreed that the Communist Revolution ended China's long nightmare with narcotics addiction. It did not, however, put an end to the Triads. Wherever Chiang's army fled, Triads went along: less successfully to Hong Kong, but also to Taiwan and, from the south of China, into the Golden Triangle and other parts of Southeast Asia where they have since flourished (Kaplan, Goldberg and Jue, 1986).

Economic Reform and Black Society

For 30 years, organized crime in China disappeared, submerged along with other institutions of the earlier era. But appearances can be deceptive. Following the historic Third Plenum of the Eleventh Central Committee of the Chinese Communist Party (CCP), in December 1978, China moved to modernize its economy, including the key decisions to "open up to the outside world" (*kaifang*) and to create a "socialist market economy." For nearly two decades now, China has been engaged in a pell-mell transition marked by sharp social and ideological conflicts. While the transformation has awakened long-dormant energy and initiative, it has come at a price. Most notably, economic development has widened the income gap between city and countryside, spawned official corruption on a massive scale, and witnessed the emergence of thousands of "economic gangs" (*jingji banghui*), secret societies and other criminal organizations.

One new structural source of corruption has been the creation of a hybrid, dual-track economy (planned and market) in which there are two forms of prices: state price and market price. In theory, these prices are restricted to their respective spheres: state prices for materials and products distributed or produced according to central planning, and market prices for materials and products not subject to state control (Gong, 1993). In practice, however, the result has been a significant increase in so-called "back-door" transactions, as insider's profit from price differentials in the public and private sectors. Cadres or *gaogan zidi* (children and other blood relatives of high-level cadres) have used their privileged access to scarce goods and materials only to resell them in China's burgeoning free market. In the rush to earn quick profits, cadres in effect have appropriated state organizations, thus gaining for themselves and their offspring financially advantageous position. This situation has led to artificial scarcities and contributed to soaring urban inflation as raw materials and finished products have been diverted from state to the market sector. In short, the reforms have created opportunities for those with the right sort of connections to benefit from access to scarce goods, inside information and disparate pricing systems. In China, this and other forms of "red-collar crime" (Los, 1988) are rampant and have been on the rise ever since Deng returned to power in the mid-1970s (Gaylord and Levine, 1997).

As with Leninist systems elsewhere, corruption has been a perennial problem in the People's Republic of China (PRC). The Chinese government has experimented, since the early 1950s, with numerous systems of control: internal administrative audits, separate control commissions, discipline inspection bureaus and mass campaigns, all to no avail (Findlay and Chiu, 1989). The problem is that Leninist systems structurally generate clienteles and networks of personal ties, while at the same time making them politically illegitimate. Control over appointments and promotions within the bloated administrative bureaucracies of these systems make the party an efficient vehicle for distributing patronage and exchanging favors. Patronage allows such officials as party secretaries and cadres to form power bases and networks of personal ties. In China these reciprocal exchange relationships are denoted by the term *quanxi* (Meaney, 1991).

Although corruption is not a new phenomenon in the PRC, its current vast scale represents a major change from the past. Until recently, Baum (1994) argues, the extent of corruption in China was limited by the relatively small financial rewards and relatively high social and political costs involved. Under Mao, the party's egalitarian, anti-bourgeois ethos made it extremely risky for anyone to engage in the conspicuous pursuit or consumption of wealth. Where corruption did exist, it tended to be rather localized and limited in scale; much of it involved cadres extorting "donations" of various kinds, including money, consumer goods and sexual favors from members of their work units. In the more permissive "to get rich is glorious" environment of post-reform China, however, the cost/benefit calculus has changed dramatically. There now is a manifold increase in both the incentive to engage in corruption (in the form of substantially greater economic payoffs and diminished ideological restraints) and the opportunity to do so (presented by the gap between a newly decentralized, weakened state economic apparatus and a newly strengthened, semi-autonomous local cadre corps). With stakes thus raised and transaction costs lowered, corruption and economic crime have flourished.

Throughout the nearly 20 years of China's "reform and opening" policy, social change has been a mixed blessing. Crime has more than doubled and unemployment, divorce and suicide rates all point to a dramatic deterioration in the quality of life. Previously, average citizens had not been allowed a private life exempt from the scrutiny of officialdom. Even officials who had sought to link power to privilege had faced "struggle meetings," rectification movements and, in some instances, People's Tribunals (Brady, 1982). In the towns, the party had controlled all jobs. In the countryside, it had bought all produce and owned all land. Individuals had been bound to their work-units (*danwei*), which had allocated housing, education and health care. By these means, and by the often-savage punishment of resisters, the party elite had controlled a billion people (*The Economist*, 1994). But under Deng's reform, while millions strove merely to survive, especially in the country's destitute interior provinces, entrepreneurs and cadres in the southern and coastal provinces illegitimately seized hold of the good life with both hands (Gaylord and Levine, 1997).

China's ongoing economic transition has been dramatically successful, but increased productivity has displaced millions of workers (Wong, 1994). Conservative estimates indicate that 260 million of China's nearly 900 million peasants, the world's largest rural population, are no longer needed on farms (Kuhn and Kaye, 1994). As many as 100 million of these expendable workers are on the road in search of jobs in towns and cities. Officially called *liudong renkou*, or "floating population," they comprise one of the largest peacetime migrations in history (Tyson and Tyson, 1995). In the coastal provinces, farm jobs that remain are being filled by desperately poor peasants, from China's interior, willing to work for next to nothing. The pressure of unemployment and personal debt, combined with abuse from venal officials, makes daily life increasingly difficult for growing numbers of Chinese. According to Li Sunmao, a criminal investigator in China's Public Security Bureau, the pressure of such massive rural migration is largely to blame for the growing numbers of new recruits to organized crime groups. Currently, in the richer cities, 70 to 80 percent of arrested criminals are peasants from the countryside (Beck, 1997). Though the statistical picture may be less bleak than in many Western countries, it contrasts sharply with the surface calm of totalitarian control before Deng (see Bakken, 1993).

The opening of China's economy, together with the penetration into the mainland by Hong Kong, Macanese and Taiwanese criminals, has seen some astounding figures come to light. Experts estimate the annual number of new recruits to organized crime groups in China has grown from 100,000 in 1986 to more than half a million in 1994 (Beck, 1997). Today the country faces highway bandits, kidnapping gangs, tomb-robbing gangs, tax receipt forging syndicates (subject to the death penalty under a law passed in 1995), and even "vampire gangs" who bleed their victims and sell the blood to hospitals. The existence of crime groups such as these, has led some observers to compare the current situation in China to that which occurred in Russia in the wake of the breakup of the Soviet Union. Others have suggested that much of the corruption, speculation and disregard for the law that China faces in its headlong rush to development is similar to that confronted by the U.S. in the late 19th century heyday of robber-baron capitalism (Hornick, 1993).

In recent years, a new lexicon of corruption has cropped up in the Chinese popular press. It includes such term as "*pocket-swapping*," in which public assets are transferred to private control, or "sign-flipping," whereby a government agency transforms itself into a private consultancy by merely changing its name and then parlaying its clout into fees (Kaye, 1993). In the view of many Chinese, however, corruption, greed and disorder are an acceptable price to pay for economic and social liberation. According to a lawyer in Beijing, "When the economy grows, crime will grow with it" (Hornick, 1993).

Twenty years ago, the American sociologist William J. Chambliss (1978) reported that, in the United States, the distinction between organized crime, business and government was almost impossible to discern. Field research in the West coast city of Seattle revealed that what was commonly referred to as "organized crime" consisted not just of gangsters but networks of people including police, politicians and ordinary citizens investing in illegal enterprises for a high return on their money. This argument does not in any sense deny the existence of criminal organizations whose purpose is to gain money by providing forbidden goods and services to willing customers. But Chambliss's argument highlights the fact that the people who run the organizations that supply the vices in the major cities of the world are members of the business, political and law enforcement communities and are not simply members of a criminal society.

The same patterns are evident in China today. In Shanghai, for example, the People's Liberation Army is in business with the Public Security Bureau, which has connections to "fixers" who have paid off party officials, who in turn know the right people in various ministries, and so on and so forth.   The powerful make deals with the powerful, no matter where the power comes from. The rackets are seemingly endless. With the right connections it is possible to buy Public Security Bureau vehicle plates and ignore traffic rules. By bribing curators, one can buy priceless art treasures from state museums and smuggle them to Hong Kong. In China today, money and *quanxi* trump the law every time (*The Economist*, 1995).

What began in the early 1980s as a handful of private entrepreneurs and petty crooks operating at the margins of society has now evolved into a complicated web of quasi-legal and illegal associations which implicate party and government officials at every level. The problem has become so acute that, in 1993, the Public Security Ministry was moved to issue a list of "10 No-No's" for police officials. For example: no selling of protection services to dance halls, massage parlors and smuggling rings; no tipping off crooks about police raids in advance; no helping oneself to food or merchandise from shop owners without paying. "Next thing you know, you'll have to remind the police 'no killing, no stealing'," thus complained one disgusted factory manager (Kuhn, 1994).

This is an example of what the Chinese call *hei shehui,* or "black society." By design, it is hidden from view, obscured by secrecy, corrupt officials and the hopelessly blurred distinction between private and public sectors.

"Black society" is an all-encompassing term, from small bands of highwaymen to international heroin syndicates; from gang-controlled cigarette stands on urban street corners to nationwide publishing networks operating outside the state-run monopoly; from local sects rooted in feudalistic superstition to secret societies with thousands of members. As China's state sector becomes progressively hollowed out from corruption and mismanagement, a parallel universe simultaneously expands to fill the void left by the diminishing influence of central authority (Hood, 1992).

Crimes thought to have disappeared following the communist revolution drug use, prostitution, the sale of women and children -- not only have reappeared, but are now widespread. According to Chinese officials, the number of "major criminal cases" has increased tenfold in the past decade, growing forty percent per year since 1985. In Tengzhou, for example, a mid-sized city in Shandong province, officials mobilized 1,000 public security personnel who, over a two-month period in 1991, "broke up 54 human-trafficking rings, captured 165 members and 22 chiefs, and exposed nine bases of operation," according to a provincial radio report. More than 1,000 women and children who had been sold into bondage were rescued. Such criminal organizations, according to similar reports from around the country, have networks stretching across several provinces (Hood, 1992).

Table 5.1: Criminal cases as filed by the police in China, 1981-1995

Year	Homicide	Assault	Robbery	Rape	Fraud	Theft	Total
1981	9,576	21,499	22,266	30,808	18,665	743,105	890,281
1982	9,324	20,298	16,518	35,361	17,707	608,501	748,476
1983*							610,478
1984	9,021	14,526	7,273	44,630	13,479	394,840	514,369
1985	10,440	15,586	8,801	37,712	13,157	431,323	542,005
1986	11,510	18,364	12,124	39121	14,663	425,845	547,115
1987	13,154	21,727	18,775	37,225	14,693	435,235	570,439
1988	15,959	26,639	36,318	34,120	18,857	658,683	827,594
1989	19,590	35,931	72,881	40,999	42,581	1,673,222	1,971,901
1990	21,214	45,200	82,361	47,782	54,719	1,860,793	2,216,997
1991	23,199	57,489	105,132	50,331	60,174	1,922,506	2,365,709
1992	24,132	59,901	125,092	49,829	46,991	1,142,556	1,582,659
1993	25,380	64,595	152,102	47,033	50,644	1,122,105	1,616,879
1994	26,553	67,864	159,253	44,118	57,706	1,133,682	1,660,734
1995	27,356	72,259	164,478	41,823	64,047	1,132,789	1,690,407

*The 1983 statistics are not available.

Sources: The statistics from 1981 to 1987 are from *Zhongguo Falu Nianjian* (China Law Year Book) 1987, p 820; The statistics from 1988 to 1994 are from *Zhongguo Falu Nianjian* 1988, p. 1084; 1989, p. 996; 1990, 942; 1991, p. 861; 1992, 940; 1993, p. 1033; and 1994, p. 1069. The statistics for 1995 is from Ministry of Public Security, "Criminal Cases as Filed by the Police in 1995 and their classification" (1996) 46 *Gongan Yanjiu* (Public Security Studies) 47.

In addition to crime, populist uprisings are also on the increase (Chiang, 1994). Arbitrary tax levies, brigandage, local warlordism and internecine feuds sorely beset China's hinterland (Kaye, 1994a). Yet according to Sinologist Philip Kuhn (1980), grass roots justice is a recurring feature of dynastic endgames in Chinese history. Peasant uprisings date back to as early as the Yellow Turban and Red Eyebrow revolts of the Western Han dynasty nearly 2,000 years ago.

More recent outbreaks include the Eight Trigrams and White Lotus uprisings of the early 19th century, the Christian-inspired Heavenly Kingdom of the Taipings in the 1840s and the Boxer Rebellion of 1900. According to Kuhn, such movements can be understood as the natural reaction of people whose sense of security has been threatened. (Kaye, 1994b).

What is happening in the Chinese countryside today looks all too familiar to Kuhn and other scholars. Historically, secret societies have proliferated during period of rising social tension, endemic corruption, economic dislocation and weakened central authority. According to the French scholar Jean Chesneaux (1965, 1972), secret societies constituted the major organized opposition to Confucian China and led the popular revolts that toppled decaying dynasties throughout the imperial period. Chesneaux's interpretation of "secret societies" is broad, treating White Lotus sectarians, Heaven and Earth Society members, and adherents of a wide array of popular organizations as part of the same general phenomenon: popular opposition to oppression at the hands of either the state or the wealthy and powerful gentry. Secret societies were part of what he called the "anti-society;" an opposition force "whose dissent was better organized, more coherent, and better sustained than that of the bandits, the vagabonds, and the dissident literati" (Chesneaux, 1972:2, quoted in Ownby, 1993).

By the late 1980s, the Chinese state faced a crisis of legitimacy. With the economy seemingly stalled midway between planned and market, between bureaucrats and entrepreneurs, China suffered from some of the worst distortions of the old system without enjoying the full fruits of the new (Baum, 1994). Emotions ran high as reform-related stresses reached new levels. Large segments of the population were deeply frustrated within the severe economic turndown and the constant reports of corruption among party officials even at the highest levels of government. After living for nearly four decades with the fundamental security that was provided by the old system, the challenges and uncertainties of the new one were deeply disturbing to millions of ordinary Chinese. The party knew itself to be perched on the edge of an abyss, and that without change it would be rejected by the people. The challenge, simply put, was whether the CCP remained capable of effective leadership.

An important structural cause of the crisis was the resurgence of the very class divisions that the communists had promised to eradicate in 1949. By the mid-1980s, to be rich was "glorious," to be idealistic was passe. Income gaps visibly widened between rich and poor in the cities as nearly three decades of Maoist-style egalitarianism were swept away by the forces of reform. Well-connected businessmen and cadres thrived while ordinary workers felt increasingly disenfranchised. Even more stark then urban income stratification, however, was the steadily worsening terms of trade between cities and countryside. By the late 1980s, notwithstanding the gains made by farmers earlier in the decade, the official urban-rural income ratio had climbed to 2.2 to 1. According to researchers at the Chinese Academy of Social Sciences, the ratio may have been closer to 4 to 1 once state subsidies provided to urbanites and ad hoc fees levied upon farmers had been taken into account (Kaye, 1993).

Families living on fixed income (still the vast majority in China) found themselves falling hopelessly behind. In 1988, per capita income was but $349, and nearly ten percent of the population were still unable to feed and clothe themselves at a subsistence level (Lull, 1991). Public opinion polls began registering a downturn in popular enthusiasm for reform (Bonavia, 1986). By the end of the decade, China's cities experienced major social unrest as double-digit rates of inflation led to growing levels of frustration, alienation, envy (or what the Chinese call "red-eye disease") and anger. Though Deng had promised the people that reform would not lead to a stratified society, such indeed had become the reality. By late 1988, China's top leaders were deeply concerned about the latent anti-government, anti-reform overtones of the ever increasing demonstrations (Baum, 1994).

In autumn of 1988, the Chinese government launched a highly publicized crackdown on companies engaged in official corruption, tax evasion and currency manipulation. *Renmin Ribao* published two commentaries ((1988a,

1988b) that called on authorities to "resolutely punish 'speculating officials' and to not be soft-hearted in punishing 'speculating officials'." (Zhu, 1991) Other newspapers reported that "such transactions lead to...exploitation of consumers," and that "only by removing these tumors from the national economy can the (economic) reform benefit the state and the people" (Zhu, 1991).

Over the next several months, the campaign struck mainly at smaller, politically less well connected companies. But on July 28, 1989, following the violent military suppression of unarmed students and workers in Tiananmen Square, the Political Bureau adopted a remarkable resolution calling for action against China's largest corporations (Renmin Ribao, 1989a). CITIC, Everbright, China Economic Development Corporation and China Rural Trust and Development Corporation were fined sums totaling more than RMB Y50 million ($6.2 million), and Kanghua, deemed to be "the No.1 Speculating Corporation," was fined for profiteering, currency violations and tax evasion and then closed down (Yang, 1991).

On September 5, the State Council issued an order to close eleven types of corporations, including those that had been established under the leadership of the Central Committee (Renmin Ribao, 1989b). Others were punished by administrative measures. By the end of 1989, over 103,000 companies run by the Central Committee, the PLA, local governments and CCP committees had been closed (Renmin Ribao, 1989b). Within the party, the campaign reportedly netted more than 325,000 offenders in its first 18 months of operation. In 1990, 79,000 party members were expelled. By the spring of 1991 an additional 256,000 members had received lesser degrees of party discipline.

But while the crackdown briefly struck fear within local cadres, the higher ranks of the party, with few exceptions, were left largely unscathed. Official newspapers occasionally railed against the "big monkeys," but, as in the past, those occupying the top rungs of the political ladder were able to avoid judicial scrutiny of their misdeeds. Deng Pufang, Deng Xiaoping's son, for example, was pressured into severing his connections with Kanghua, but was never formally accused of a crime. In the first half of 1992, indictments were handed down in less than one-third of the 48,000 cases of lower-level cadre corruption that were officially investigated, while from 1988 to the spring of 1993, merely five provincial and ministerial-level cadres were convicted of economic crimes (Baum, 1994).

Conclusion

After nearly three decades of numbing austerity and perpetual class struggle under Mao's rule, Deng Xiaoping's market-oriented reforms were like a tonic to an exhausted nation. China's economy rose almost immediately from its lethargy and began to grow at an unprecedented rate. Nevertheless, social change on such a vast scale was unlikely to be entirely smooth sailing. Beginning early in the 1980s, China experienced major conflicts and dilemmas as Deng's reforms gave rise to numerous adverse effects, among them rampant urban inflation and increasing inequality of opportunity. The effects proved to be fertile ground for the re-emergence of retrograde social forms thought to have vanished from modern China. Ample evidence suggests organized crime groups were quick to adapt to China's fast-changing economic and political environment, while law enforcement organizations at all levels were ill equipped and poorly prepared to meet these challenges (Gaylord and Levine, 1997).

In post-Mao China, a fundamental contradiction stems from the commitment to the pursuit of a rapid economic development while simultaneously attempting to preserve a centralized authoritarian state. Within the CCP, profound difference exists on how best to achieve these ends. Liberal reformers favor rapid progress towards a market economy; conservatives favor more cautious steps and the development of a so-called "cage economy," in which private enterprise is confined *within* the parameters of state planning (Lo, 1993). The numerous contradictions inherent within China's emerging "market socialism" have been responsible for much of the nation's turmoil in recent years. Until these contradictions are resolved, economic gangs, corruption and "black society" can be expected to thrive in the space between market and plan.

Dr. Mark Gaylord is an Associate Professor of Sociology at the City University of Hong Kong, where he has taught criminology since 1988 and sociology of law since 1987. His publications include The Criminology of Edwin Sutherland (Transaction Books, 1988), Drugs, Law and the State (Transaction Books, 1992) and Introduction to the Hong Kong Criminal Justice System (Hong Kong University Press, 1994). His research interests are crime, law and social change in East Asia.

Dr. Hualing Fu is a research fellow in the Faculty of Law, the University of Hong Kong where he teaches courses on Chinese criminal and constitutional law. He was an Assistant Professor of Law at the City University of Hong Kong from 1993 to 1997. He received a LL.B. from the Southwestern University of Law and Politics in China, an MA in Criminology from the University of Toronto and a JD from Osgoode Law School, York University.

Notes and References

Bakken, B. (1993), "Crime, Juvenile Delinquency and Deterrence Policy in China," *The Australian Journal of Chinese Affairs* 30 (July): 29-58.

Barlow, H.D. (1994), *Introduction to Criminology.* Boston: Little, Brown.

Baum, R. (1994), *Burying Mao: Chinese Politics in the Age of Deng Xiaoping.* Princeton, NJ: Princeton University Press.

Beck, S. (1997), "Jitters on Chinese Crime," *South China Morning Post,* April 17.

Beirne, P. and James Messerschmidt (1991), *Criminology.* New York: Harcourt Brace Jovanovich.

Block, A. (1983), *East Side-West Side: Organizing Crime in New York, 1930, 1950.* New Brunswick, NJ: Transaction.

Block, A. and W. J. Chambliss (1981), *Organizing Crime.* New York: Elsevier.

Bonavia, D. (1986), "Problems at the Plenum," *Far Eastern Economic Review,* October 16.

Brady, J. P. (1982), *Justice and Politics in People's China.* London: Academic Press.

Cai S. (1964), "Guanyu Tiandihui de giyuan wenti" [On the question of the origin of the Heaven and Earth Society]. *Beijing daxue xuebao* 1:53-64.

Chambliss, W.J. (1978), *On the Take: From Petty Crooks to Presidents.* Bloomington: Indiana University Press.

Chesneaux, J. (1965), *Les Societes Secretes en Chine (19e et 20e siecles)* [Secret Societies in China (Nineteenth and Twentieth Centuries)]. Paris: F. Maspero.

Chesneaux, J. (1972), *Popular Movements and Secret Societies in China, 1840-1950.* Stanford: Stanford University Press.

Chiang Chen-chang (1994), "A Study of Social Conflict in Rural Mainland China," *Issues & Studies* 30(3): 35-50.

Chin Ko-lin (1990), *Chinese Subculture and Criminality: Non-Traditional Crime Groups in America.* New York: Greenwood Press.

Cressey, D. R. (1969), *Theft of the Nation: The Structure and Operations of Organized Crime in America.* New York: Harper and Row.

Dobinson, I. (1993), "Pinning a Tail on the Dragon: The Chinese and International Heroin Trade," *Crime & Delinquency* 39(3): 373-384.

Dubro, A. and Kaplan, D. E. (1986), *Yakuza.* New York: Addison-Wesley.

The Economist. (1994), "The Road from Tiananmen," June 4; (1995), "City of Glitter and Ghosts," December 24-January 6.

Findlay, M. and Chiu Chor-wing (1989), "Sugar Coated Bullets: Corruption and the New Economic Order in China," *Contemporary Crises* 13:145-161.

Gaylord, M. S. and P. Levine, (1997), "The Criminalization of Official Profiteering: Law-making in the People's Republic of China," *International Journal of the Sociology of Law* 25(2): 117-134.

Gong T. (1993), "Corruption and Reform in China: An Analysis of Unintended Consequences," *Crime, Law and Social Change* 19: 311-327.

Hornick, R. (1993), "Limits of Progress," *Time,* May 10.

Kaplan, D., D. Goldberg and Linda Jue (1986), "Enter the Dragon," *San Francisco Focus,* December, 68-79.

Kaye, L. (1993), "Rotten to the Core," *Far Eastern Economic Review,* September 16. (1994a), "Disorder Under Heaven," *Far Eastern Economic Review,* June 9. (1994b), "History Repeats Itself," *Far Eastern Economic Review,* June 9.

Kuhn, A. (1994), "Cops and Robbers," *Far Eastern Economic Review,* June 9.

Kuhn, A. and Lincoln Kaye (1994) "Bursting at the Seams," *Far Eastern Economic Review,* March 10.

Kuhn, P. A. (1980), *Rebellion and Its Enemies in Late Imperial China: Militarization and Social Structure, 1796-1864.* Cambridge, MA: Harvard University Press.

Li, L. and K. J. O'Brien (1996), "Villagers and Popular Resistance in Contemporary China," *Modern China* 22(1): 28-61.

Los, M. (1988), *Communist Ideology, Law, and Crime: A Comparative View of the USSR and Poland.* New York: St. Martin's Press.

Lull, J. (1991), *China Turned On: Television, Reform, and Resistance.* London: Routledge.

Ma, L. E. A. (1990), *Revolutionaries, Monarchists, and Chinatowns: Chinese Politics in the Americas and the 1911 Revolution.* Honolulu: University of Hawaii Press.

McCoy, A. W. (1992), "Heroin as a Global Commodity: A History of Southeast Asia's Opium Trade," in Alfred W. McCoy and Alan A. Block (eds.), *War on Drugs: Studies in the Failure of U.S. Narcotics Policy.* Boulder, Co: Westview Press.

McKenna, J. (1996), "Organized Crime in the Royal Colony of Hong Kong," *Journal of Contemporary Criminal Justice* 12(4): 316-327.

Meaney, C. S. (1991), "Market Reform and Disintegrative Corruption in Urban China," in Richard Baum (ed.), *Reform and Reaction in Post-Mao China.* London: Routledge.

Morgan, W.P. (1960), *Triad Societies in Hong Kong.* Hong Kong: Hong Kong Government Printer.

Murray, D. (1993), "Migration, Protection, and Racketeering: The Spread of the Tiandihui within China," in David Ownby and Mary Somers Heidhues (eds.), *'Secret Societies' Reconsidered: Perspectives on the Social History of Modern South China and Southeast Asia.* Armonk, NY: M.E. Sharpe.

Ownby, D. (1993), "Secret Societies Reconsidered," in David Ownby and Mary Somers Heidhues (eds.), *'Secret Societies' Reconsidered: Perspectives on the Social History of Modern South China and Southeast Asia.* Armonk, NY: M.E. Sharpe.

Pace, D.F. and J.C. Styles, (1975), *Organized Crime: Concepts and Control.* Englewood Cliffs, NJ: Prentice Hall.

Posner, G. L. (1988), *Warlords of Crime.* New York: McGraw Hill.

Potter, G. W. (1994), *Criminal Organizations: Vice, Racketeering, and Politics in an American City.* Prospect Heights, IL: Waveland Press.

Renmin Ribao (People's Daily) (1988), (1988a), September 3; (1988b), October 26. 1989 (1989a), July 29; (1989b) September 6.

Reuter, P. (1983), *Disorganized Crime: The Economy the Visible Hand.* Cambridge: MIT Press.

Seagrave, S. (1985), *The Soong Dynasty.* London: Sidgwick & Jackson.

Tyson, J. and A. Tyson (1995), *Chinese Awakenings: Life Stories from the Unofficial China.* Boulder, CO: Westview Press.

United Nations (1953), Department of Social Relations, *Bulletin on Narcotics* 5, No. 2 (April-June), p.49.

Wong, L. (1994), "China's Urban Migrants: The Public Policy Challenge," *Pacific Affairs* 67(3): 335-355.

Yang, C. (1991), "Corporate Crime Under a Changing Socialist Economic System." Paper presented at the annual meeting of the American Society of Criminology, San Francisco, November 8-11.

Zhang, J. (1980), "Cong guoli gugong bowuyuan diancang Qingdai dang'an tan Tiandihui de yuanliu" (A discussion of the origins of the Heaven and Earth based on Qing archives held in the National Palace Museum). *Gugong jikan* 14(4): 63-91.

Zhang, S. X. and M. S. Gaylord (1996), "Bound for the Golden Mountain: The Social Organization of Chinese Alien Smuggling," *Crime, Law and Social Change* 25: 1-16.

Zhu, S. -li (1991), "Economic Structure and the Crime of Speculation." Paper presented at the Joint Meeting of the Law & Society Association and the Research Committee of Sociology of Law of the International Sociological Association, Amsterdam, June 26-29.

Zweig, D. (1986), "Prosperity and Conflict in Post-Mao China," *China Quarterly* 105:1-18.

Zweig, D. (1989) "Struggling over Land in China: Peasant Resistance after Collectivization, 1966-1986," in Forrest Colburn (ed.), *Everyday Forms of Peasant Resistance*, New York: M.E. Sharpe, 151-174.

Glossary

Danwei - work-units.

Hei shehui - organized crime or "black society"

Gaogan zidi - children and other blood relatives of high level communist party cadres.

Jingji bangui - economic gangs.

Liudong renkou - floating population.

Quanxi - reciprocal exchange relationships.

6 Trends of Organized Crime by *Boryokudan* in Japan

Minoru Yokoyama

Abstract

The Boryokudan, Japanese indigenous groups for organized crime, have inherited some subculture from feudal period gangs. The core their ethics have been composed of Ninkyo-do, a type of chivalrous spirit. Subsequent to Japan's economic growth after World War II several powerful Boryokudans became the Koiki (wide area) -Boryokudan through violence and their immense wealth. They currently operate as profit-oriented organizations similar to private enterprises in a capitalistic country rather than functioning as groups disciplined under the ethics of Ninkyo-do.

The Boryokudan are hierarchically structured, in which a great deal of money based on membership fees are pumped in and up to a godfather. Most members have to perform many illegal activities in order to earn their livelihood as well as to pay the expected membership fee to their boss. The most important source of revenue for the Boryokudan is the sale of stimulant drugs.

For a long time the police were in connivance with the activities of Boryokudan. However, the police have gradually gotten rid of the corrupt influence of Boryokudan. During the economic prosperity of the 1980's the Koiki-Boryokudan committed many violent activities, which became more visible and more intolerable to the population-at-large. Public opinion against the Boryokudan increased. In 1991 the Law to Cope with Boryokudan was enacted. Under this law the police control illegal activities of Boryokudan more severely in cooperation with people.

Key Words: Boryokudan, Koiki, Yakuza, Bakuto, Tekiya

Introduction

Gurentai Yakuza or *Boryokudan* Japanese indigenous organized crime gangs are known as *Yakuza* in foreign countries. The meaning of the term *Yakuza* is a "hooligan" or a "worthless scamp."[1] Members of Japanese organized criminal groups were often described as *Yakuza* in the popular movies after World War II. Therefore, they are still called *Yakuza* by ordinary people. On the other hand, the Japanese government calls these organized crime gangs *Boryokudan*, a term which literally means a violent group. By using this term, instead of *Yakuza*, the government intended to warn ordinary people, who are inclined to sympathize with a hooligan or a worthless scamp, against the organized crime gangs.

The term *Boryokudan* is currently prevalent; all of the mass media use it. However, when we, in Japan, had heated discussions about whether we should enforce the Law to Cope with *Boryokudan* of 1991, the term of *Yakuza* was reconsidered. At that time the organized crime gangs called themselves *Yakuza* and were opposed to being placed as the *Boryokudan* under the jurisdiction of this law. Tadao Nawa (1993:1) -- one of their ideologists, who calls himself a former boss of *Yakuza* -- pointed out that most bosses of *Yakuza* live in the way of *Ninkyo-do*, that is a kind of chivalrous way to beat the strong and to help the weak. Makoto Endo (1992:2), a legal counselor for them, advised them to be *Yakuza* sharing with the ethics of Ninkyo-do.

He also insisted that the Law to Cope with *Boryokudan* was unconstitutional, because the law would invade the right of *Yakuza* to organize a group under the Article 21 of the Constitution. However, they failed to persuade the public.

The Origins of *Boryokudan*
Table 6.1: Development of gangs for organized crime in Japan

Period	Groups and Activities
1603-1867	Outlaws dropped out of the feudal caste system *Bakuto* (gamblers) *Tekiya* (peddlers or stall keepers) Ethics of *Ninkyo-do* (a type of chivalrous spirit)
Meiji Restoration	Modernization of legal system Affiliation with conservative groups
End of World War II	Decline of *Bakuto* and *Tekiya* being parasites with conservative groups (1945)Grunt (street hoodlums) Police are in connivance with *Boryokudan* activities Expansion of territory by violence *Boryokudan* (violent group)
1963	Peaking of the total number of *Boryokudan* members
1964	Strategy to catch to top members Decline of many small-sized *Boryokudan* groups Development of Koiki (wide area)-*Boryokudan* through violence and their immense wealth
1979	The second strategy to catch the top members Domination of the *Koiki-Boryokudan* profit oriented activities: *Yamagachi-gumi, Inagawa-kai* and *Sumiyoshi-kai*
1980s	Increased in-fighting among *Boryokudan* after the death of a godfather of *Yamaguchi-gumi*. Increase in violent intervention in civil conflicts during the economic prosperity The movement by citizens against *Boryokudan* Revelation of some *Boryokudan* bosses being involved in political and economic scandals
1991	Enactment of the Law to Cope with *Boryokudan* Severe police control against the *Boryokudan* during the Economic recession

Historically Japanese indigenous organized crime gangs are categorized into three groups: *Bakuto* (gamblers), *Tekiya* (peddlers or stall keepers) and *Gurentai* (street hoodlums). In the latter part of Edo era (1603-1867) *Bakuto* and *Tekiya* were formed by outlaws, who had dropped out of the feudal caste system under the Tokugawa Shogunate. Towards the end of the Edo era Japan witnessed many desperate poor farmers, who indulged themselves in gambling (Masukawa, 1989: 181). Among them some *Bakuto* and *Tekiya* bosses and henchmen became heroes living in the way of Ninkyo-do. In reality, however, they lived mainly by depriving ordinary people of money. The former did so by gambling, while the latter sold commodities of a bad quality, fraudulently, on the street, at fairs and at festivals.

Since the Meiji Restoration of 1868 Japan's legal system has been modernized, based on examples in western countries. Gambling was defined as a crime under our modern criminal laws. The police, however, did not always control gambling or enforce the relevant laws strictly. *Bakuto* could exist until World War II. Often soliciting idle, rich men, they were prone to pass themselves off with an image of a knight living modestly at the bottom of the society, who did not annoy the ordinary, diligently working people. Ordinary people did not necessarily deny this self-image, because it was created to dramatize the popular *Bakuto* bosses and henchmen who lived during the middle of nineteenth century. For example, prior to 1960, such bosses as Jirocho Shimizu and Chuji Kunisada were heroes in popular songs, storytelling, magazines, dramas and movies.

We still see peddlers or stallkeepers, who participate in fairs and festivals that are held on the street and on the sites of shrines and temples. Their ancestors became unified by their worship of Jin-no[2] and formed *Tekiya* during the Edo era. A *Tekiya* boss demanded "rent" from peddlers or stallkeepers. He also worked as a promoter of a show and as a bookkeeper. Unorganized peddlers or stallkeepers, and entertainers always traveled to join a festival and a fair at various places. Through them *Tekiya* had a wide network in the underworld. The deviant behaviors committed by *Tekiya* were more invisible than those by *Bakuto* were. *Tekiya* also continued to exist, in this way, until World War II.

Economic and political factors contributed to both the survival and to the development of *Bakuto* and *Tekiya* during the period from 1868 to 1945. Japan was being industrialized since the middle of the nineteenth century. During this process, companies, especially those engaged in mining, manufacturing, construction and transportation, needed to employ many laborers at cheap wages. *Bakuto* and *Tekiya* tied up with capitalists and provided the companies with cheap labor forces, which they controlled through their violence. Around the beginning of twentieth century organized labor unions emerged to oppose being exploited by capitalists. Capitalists often employed *Bakuto* and *Tekiya* as strikebreakers to cope with these movements. In addition, as nationalism increased, *Bakuto* and *Tekiya*, believing in *Ninkyo-do*, became more closely affiliated with conservative groups. *Bakuto* and *Tekiya* founded a political right wing association in the Kanto area, including Tokyo, in 1919. The following year those living in the Kansai area also organized a similar association in Osaka; many thousands of them paraded under the protection of police officers

(Ibid., 1989:237). Since then, *Bakuto* and *Tekiya*, as a right wing group have maintained good relations with conservative leaders in the ruling class, who drove people into the World War II under the name of an emperor.

The old authoritarian system, which functioned under the emperor, collapsed after the end of World War II. *Bakuto* and *Tekiya* could not survive by being parasitic with the conservative leaders. They had to make their livelihood by their own ability. During the ensuing chaos many of the old *Bakuto* and *Tekiya* fell from their positions of power. Immediately after the Second World War we experienced an absolute shortage of the necessities of life. We could hardly survive without buying commodities at black-markets which were opened spontaneously at a burnt field in a city. Initially, most black-markets were controlled by the Koreans and the Chinese, the core of whom consisted of the Korean males taken compulsorily to Japan for slave labor during the war. Immediately after the war Japan was placed under the control of the General Headquarters of the Allied Powers (GHQ). They had liberated the oppressed Koreans and the Chinese in Japan. On the other hand, under the direction of GHQ, the traditional authoritarian system of the national police was disorganized and revamped towards democratization. Paradoxically, the Korean and the Chinese could participate in many illegal economic activities without their fearing police regulation. However, relatively soon after these events they were expelled from the black markets by the gang violence of young Japanese -- the core of whom were ex- soldiers. These groups were called *Gurentai*.[3]

The surviving *Bakuto* and *Tekiya* also extended their territory over new black markets by use of violence. Therefore, in terms of resorting to violence, we could not distinguish these groups from *Gurentai*. By 1960 *Bakuto*, *Tekiya* and *Gurentai* merged together and developed into the larger-sized gang group, committed every kind of organized crime by violence or by the threat of violence (White Paper on Police in 1989: 11). This is the reason why the police categorize all of these gang groups as being *Boryokudan*.

Hagen (1986:320) presented the organized crime continuum, which structurally places the ideal type of non-organized crime on the one pole and that of organized crime on the other end. The latter is composed of such properties as being highly organized with:

- a hierarchy, restricted membership and secrecy;
- violence or threats of violence;
- provision of illicit goods in public demand - profit-oriented;
- immunity through law enforcement corruption.

The *Boryokudan* seem to manifest all of these properties. Following is an analysis of the characteristics of *Boryokudan* as a typical organized crime gang.

The Structure of *Boryokudan*

The *Boryokudan* are hierarchically structured; one boss, several lieutenants and many soldiers. Previously, most of the *Boryokudan* were autonomous in their small-sized "territory." However, since 1964 the police have strengthened their control over *Boryokudan* activities. Confronted by ongoing police mass arrests, many small-sized *Boryokudan* groups could hardly maintain their organization. They were absorbed into a powerful, large-sized *Boryokudan*, and became a subordinate *Boryokudan*. The police formally call such a powerful *Boryokudan* the *Koiki* (wide area) -*Boryokudan*. We can currently document three giant *Koiki-Boryokudan* groups: *Yamaguchi-gumi, Inagawa-kai* and *Sumiyoshi-kai*.

Police research documented that there were 5,119 *Boryokudan* groups in 1965, 98.8 percent consisting of less than 100 members (White Paper on Crime in 1964:70). As a result of absorption, of a total of 106,754 *Boryokudan* members in 1979, 21.8 percent were affiliated to the three above-mentioned *Koiki-Boryokudan* groups (White Paper on Police in 1989:17). Then, in 1994 the corresponding percentage increased to 64.8 percent, although the total number of *Boryokudan* members decreased to approximately 81,000 (White Paper on Police in 1995:176). We cannot understand the *Boryokudan* in Japan without analyzing the *Koiki-Boryokudan* groups.

The largest *Boryokudan* is *Yamaguchi-gumi*, with approximately 23,100 affiliated persons in 1992 (White Pager on Police in 1993:36). The *Yamaguchi-gumi* was founded with about 50 members in Kobe Harbor around 1915 (Mizoguchi, 1985:47). Their main job was to provide longshoremen cheaply for their customers. *Yamaguchi-gumi* remained a small-sized local group until World War II. In 1941 Kazuo Taoka became the third president of *Yamaguchi-gumi*. Under Taoka, *Yamaguchi-gumi* developed from a local *Boryokudan* in Kobe to the largest *Koiki-Boryokudan*. Taoka, through his charisma and control, led *Yamaguchi-gumi* as an absolute dictator. In addition, his business ability also contributed to the development of *Yamaguchi-gumi*. First, by their conventional business *Yamaguchi-gumi* has succeeded in accumulating a fund to expand their organization. With the recovery of Japanese trades from the damages during the war *Yamaguchi-gumi* could earn large sums of money by providing laborers at Kobe Harbor, which was one of Japan's large important ports. This success made it possible for Taoka to become a boss in the industry of providing the labor forces at the port. The provision of laborers by *Yamaguchi-gumi* was gradually extended from Kobe Harbor to other main harbors. This extension and expansion was also brought about by violence, or by the threat of violence, which *Yamaguchi-gumi* could exert over small-sized local *Boryokudan* groups. Taoka, with the backing of its aforementioned "rich fund," was associated with many influential politicians. His association with corrupted politicians was another reason why *Yamaguchi-gumi* succeeded in their business. After the success in their conventional business *Yamaguchi-gumi* began to participate in other businesses.

Their most successful business was with popular entertainers in show business, in which *Yamaguchi-gumi* worked as bouncers. *Yamaguchi-gumi*, for example, made a great deal of money from the performances of Hibari Misori, a star singer, whom Taoka treated as his daughter.

Takoa succeeded in adopting successful measures to prevent police roundups. Takoa divided his lieutenants into two groups in 1962: managers of the legal enterprises and directors of the "fighting soldiers" (Ibid. 1985:74). The former were prohibited from having their own soldiers, although they continued to conduct their business by using *Yamaguchi-gumi* violence as their last resort. This specialization by *Yamaguchi-gumi* protected their important sources of revenue from police intervention.

Another element in the development of *Yamaguchi-gumi* was their strong manpower equipped with good weapons purchased by their "rich fund." *Yamaguchi-gumi* behaved very warlike in order to expand their territory. Taoka often dispatched his lieutenants and soldiers to take over territory or to interfere in a fight between local *Boryokudan* groups. As a result, either because of their fear of the strong power of *Yamaguchi-gumi* or so as to take advantage of the latter's power, many local *Boryokudan* groups became subordinates. This was the necessary beginning for *Yamaguchi-gumi* to become *Koiki-Boryokudan*.

Another giant *Koiki-Boryokudan* is *Inagawa-kai* with approximately 7,400 members in 1992. Its founder, Kakuji Inagawa, is a professional gambler, who does not have any criminal career except for a gambling charge in 1965. He became boss in 1949, at the age of 35, at the request of four Yokohama *Gurentai* leaders (Masanobu, 1993: 70). Although they behaved selfishly as *Gurentai* leaders, they were fascinated by the charisma of Inagawa, a professional gambler who lived a well disciplined Ninkyo-do life. Ingawa-kai succeeded in absorbing many *Boryokudan* groups including even the famous old *Bakuto* by winning battles for the concession of gambling, show business, etc. The *Boryokudan* rose to power during the conflict period of 1950-1963 (Huang and Vaughn, 1992:25). During this period there were many aggressive activities of two newly risen *Boryokudan* groups, the *Yamaguchi-gumi* and the *Inagawa-kai*.

Yamaguchi-gumi and *Inagawa-kai* developed into the *Koiki-Boryokudan* under such godfathers as Kazuo, Taoka and Kakuji Inagawa.[4] Each of these groups has a pyramidal, multi-strata power structure headed by a godfather. At the top is a pyramid consisting of a godfather and his top henchmen. These "senior" henchmen function as bosses on the second level; each governs his own *Boryokudan* group in a broad area. A lieutenant manages his *Boryokudan* group on the lower levels for the boss. This characteristic of being "highly structured with hierarchy," as noted by Hagen (1986:320), is documented in their stratified structure.

The second largest *Boryokudan*, founded in 1918 in Tokyo, is *Sumiyoshi-kai* with about 8,000 members in 1992. *Sumiyoshi-kai* took the initiative of uniting old *Bakuto* in the Kanto area, and developed it into the *Koiki-Boryokudan* after World War II. In contrast with *Yamaguchi-gumi* and *Inagawa-kai*, *Sumiyoshi-kai* adopts a conglomerate structure (Iwai, 1986: 227).

Bosses of several top *Boryokudan* groups, which compose the federation, elect the president of *Sumiyoshi-kai*.

The Subculture of *Boryokudan*

Tekiya and *Bakuto* had their subculture transmitted from the Edo era, and as previously noted, were based upon the ethics of *Ninkyo-do*. The latter core was composed of conventional virtues such as Giri (obligation and duty) and ninjo (empathy and humanness). *Ninkyo-do* was expressed symbolically through special rituals and manners. During the period of chaos immediately following World War II the old stable order in the underworld maintained by *Bakuto* and *Tekiya* collapsed.

The newly arisen *Boryokudan* groups developed by using violence unreservedly, which the then weakened police could hardly control. However, as the society became settled, even the newly arisen *Boryokudan* groups began to form their own stable order. They succeeded in creating a subculture likened to the Endo period of *Bakuto* and *Tekiya* for this purpose. The conventional subculture was useful for the *Boryokudan* in order to establish the restricted membership based upon secrecy, to make their members loyal to a boss, and to associate with other *Boryokudan* groups without difficulty.

Bakuto and *Tekiya* utilized an apprenticeship system, which was similar to what had been the system during the Edo era of apprenticing a child to a merchant or to a craftsman. Through the long-term apprenticeship these freshmen became professional gamblers, peddlers or stallkeepers, while learning the ethics, manners, underworld slang and the techniques of their occupation. They were promoted from being a soldier to being a lieutenant and even a boss, according to their achievements even though the position of a boss, in some *Bakuto* and *Tekiya*, was often inherited by his son.[5] The *Boryokudan* took over this apprenticeship system, but recently they have been unable to maintain it as it was. During the first stage of apprenticeship, lasting approximately one year, the freshmen had to participate in such jobs as entertaining guests, answering phone calls, cooking, cleaning and taking care of a boss and his family. At present under the influence of western culture, Japanese youth in general have become too individualistic to endure the above-mentioned apprentice training. In addition, many special conventional manners, occupational techniques, etc. which gamblers, peddlers or stall keepers shared, have disappeared with modernization. Therefore, it has become difficult for the *Boryokudan* to maintain their traditional apprenticeship system.

Freshmen are initiated into formal *Boryokudan* membership after the first stage of apprenticeship. They drink a cup of Sake, a Japanese liquor, swearing absolute loyalty to a boss as his quasi son[6] at the initiation. *Boryokudan* members are bound together under the idea of *Ikka* (a whole family) similar to the Italian Mafia (Kaplan and Dubro, 1986:18).

The *Boryokudan* have inherited the quasi-family structure from *Bakuto* and *Tekiya*. They identify their entity as a shelter for the alienated youth under the Ninkyo-do. Under the idea of *Ikka* a boss and his henchmen are proud of the name of their *Boryokudan* as a quasi-family. If they felt that the name of their *Boryokudan* is being neglected or damaged by another, they would revenge themselves on him or her.[7] In the world of *Boryokudan* subculture the *Boryokudan* members manifest and maintain their *Kao* (face) while displaying their *Otoko-gi* (masculinity).[8] As a result they often resort to violence. Many *Boryokudan* members have a tattoo on their body, signifying their being proud of their masculinity.[9]

In the underworld the *Boryokudan* must associate with others according to the ethics of *Giri*. Through this association they must maintain or elevate their name. When the *Boryokudan* have something to celebrate or to mourn, they hold a ceremony created to show off their name as much as is possible.[10] Those invited by them must attend it with a gift of money. Attendees are ranked by their seating order at the ceremony.

By holding a ceremony the *Boryokudan* can collect a lot of money, which exceeds the costs of the ceremony. This is especially so for high level *Boryokudan*. However, since the police monitor *Boryokudan* activities more severely nowadays, they can hardly hold a conspicuous ceremony in public.

Many *Boryokudan* members manifest a contempt for working diligently.[11] Therefore, they are prone to commit risky activities in order to get large sums of money easily without working hard for many hours. In their role of a conspicuous consumer they enjoy wasting money (short-term hedonism) which is considered to be deviant by most Japanese, especially those of the older generation.[12] This is especially so among newly enlisted *Boryokudan* members. *Boryokudan* members are more materialistic than they were before 1970, when the ethics of *Ninkyo-do* were more respected by them (Hoshino, 1988:16).

The middle-aged *Boryokudan* members, on the other hand, cannot indulge themselves in wasteful consumption any more. They wish to establish their stable financial base at least in order to make their livelihood. They appear to be prone, or more greedy, to pursue the collection of money by fair means or foul, while neglecting the Ninkyo-do (Yokoyama, 1994b: 4). At present the *Boryokudan* role commitment seems to be profit-oriented.

The *Boryokudan* have a code of conduct governing their members, which is similar to that shared by American mobs (Kaplan and Dubro, 1986:141). Usually, the code is composed of several simple "norms." Most of the code demands absolute loyalty to a boss and to honor *Boryokudan* secrecy.   If a *Boryokudan* member violates this code, he is sanctioned. The *Boryokudan* have four kinds of sanctions: lynching, *Yubitsume, Zetsuen* and *Hamon* (Iwai, 1966:163). *Yubitsume* means an amputation of a tip of the fifth finger, which symbolizes offender's expression of atonement. *Zetsuen* means the severing of the quasi-parent-child relationship between a boss and the offender. The offender imposed *Zetsuen* is often allowed to return to his former *Boryokudan* by expressing his atonement after wandering through the underworld. The severest sanction is *Hamon* by which the offender is excommunicated not only by his own *Boryokudan* but also from the whole world of *Boryokudan*.

Offenders who are declared to be under some serious sanction may be killed. *Boryokudan* members are strictly controlled by their boss through these above-mentioned sanctions.

The Economics of *Boryokudan*

  Boryokudan members are obligated to pay their membership fee to their boss. In addition, a boss of the subordinate *Boryokudan* must pay the membership fee to a godfather or to the headquarters of *Koiki-Boryokudan*.

  The "flow" of this massive amount of money to *Koiki-Boryokudan* headquarters is documented in Table 6.2. *Koiki-Boryokudan* also collect large sums of money temporarily by holding a ceremony. A godfather and his lieutenants invest money in the legal money market. They may also create or buy enterprises in areas such as real estate, construction and the financial markets, in which some "secret" lieutenants work as the executives. Should any "troubles" occur, they would appeal to the use of violence or threaten the use of violence of their *Boryokudan*.

**Table 6.2: Monthly flow of membership fee
in a *Koiki* (wide area) *Boryokudan***

Rank	Money
Godfather or headquarters	Y 527,000,000
50 henchmen of first rank	Y 1,500,000 x 50 = 75,000,000
60 henchmen of second rank	Y 1,200,000 x 60 = 72,000,000
250 henchmen of third rank	Y 400,000 x 250 = 100,000,000
550 henchmen of fourth rank	Y 1,250,000 x 550 = 125,000,000
900 henchmen of fifth rank	Y 1,100,000 x 900 = 90,000,000
1,300 henchmen of sixth rank	Y 550,000 x 1,300 = 65,000,000

Note: The high-ranked henchmen are bosses of their own *Boryokudan*, in which they have their own system to pump the membership fee up from their henchmen.
Source: *White Paper on Police in 1993, p.28.*

  It is, however, difficult for the police to control the activities of these "enterprises," partly because their usual activities appear to be legal, and partly because victims who are being taken advantage of due to their weak position and fears do not report any of this to the police. The contemporary growth and development in the *Boryokudan* organization makes it possible for a boss and his high-ranking henchmen to live without directly committing illegal activities. As such they are "immune" from police arrest.

  Police research in February 1989, estimated that the total annual *Boryokudan* revenue throughout Japan amounted to 1,302 billion yen; equal to U.S. $11.3 billion[13] (Table 6.3). Of this, the total legal revenue was 19.7 percent. During the prosperity of the late 1980s the percentages seemed to rise. During this period *Koiki-Boryokudan* succeeded in corrupting even the executives of giant leading companies by using their affluent fund. The tip of the iceberg of such corruption was first revealed in the Tokyo Sagawa Kyubin

Scandal in 1992. In this case *Inagawa-kai* and their affiliated companies succeeded in taking money of over 100 billion yen from the Tokyo Sagawa Kyubin Company, a leading transportation company (Nihon Keizai Newspaper, January, 19, 1992).

Table 6.3: Sources of annual revenue of *Boryokudan* in 1988 (Yen)

Source	Total Annual Revenue	%
Total	**1,302**	**100.0**
Illegal Revenue	**1,045**	**80.3**
Sale of Stimulant Drugs		34.8
Gambling and Bookmaking		16.9
Strong-arm Protection as Bouncers		8.7
Violent Intervention in Civil Conflicts		7.3
Violent Activities against Companies		3.4
Others		9.2
Legal Revenue	**257**	**19.7**
Management of Companies		9.9
Others		9.8

Source: White paper on Police in 1989, p. 46.

On the other hand, without committing some illegal activities, gang fee to their boss. Therefore, over 80 percent of *Boryokudan*'s total revenue come from illegal activities. The *Boryokudan* expanded their activities into the established legitimate economy during the boom of the late 1980s. Of the total of all annual *Boryokudan* revenue, 3.4 percent was earned by their violent activities against legitimate companies and 7.3 percent was "earned" by their violent intervention in civil conflicts. Japanese prefer to use informal mediation rather than turning to the courts and beginning a civil suit. During the late 1980s the *Boryokudan* were often employed as an informal "settler" to resolve a civil conflict quickly by the use of violence or by the threat of use of violence (Yokoyama, 1994b: 7). In such instances even ordinary innocent people were victimized by the *Boryokudan* violence. This was especially so with regard to the violent intervention of *Boryokudan* serving *Jiageya,* a kind of loan shark, which attracted the public's attention. This led to a rise of public opinion against *Boryokudan.*

The Law to Cope with *Boryokudan* was enacted in 1991 with the support of the public (ibid., 1994b: 12-15). The main purpose of the law is to prohibit members of *Shitei-Boryokudan* (the *Boryokudan* which are put under the jurisdiction of the Law to Cope with *Boryokudan*) from committing minor violent, threatening, "demand" behaviors, which was not previously categorized as offenses under any criminal law such as extortion and intimidation.[14]

After the enforcement of the law the violent intervention of *Boryokudan* in civil conflicts seemed to decrease due to both the severe regulation by the police and Japan's economic recession.

A traditional, conventional *Boryokudan* activity is strong-arm protection, as a bouncer. The *Boryokudan* collect money from stores, bars, cabarets, gamehouses[15] etc., in their territory, as a fee for their strong-arm protection. Since the enforcement of the Law to Cope with *Boryokudan* in 1992 the police have encouraged owners and managers of the above-mentioned businesses not to pay this fee to the *Boryokudan*.

Without the cooperation of the owners and managers, the police could not succeed in eradicating these violent, threatening, and "demand" operations. Of related interest, we still see peddlers and stallkeepers on the street, at fairs and at festivals. The police have encouraged them to sever their relations with the *Boryokudan* since 1992.

Gambling is the most important conventional way for *Boryokudan* to earn money illegally. After World War II races were legalized by local governments (e.g. horse racing and bicycle racing) with the role of legal bookmakers. A special bank was authorized to issue the lottery cards. In addition to the races and the lottery, people enjoy various kinds of games such as Pachinko and mahjongg, which are usually played as popular gambling games under the tacit permission of the police. As a result the illegal gambling offered by the *Boryokudan* is less attractive to ordinary people.

Boryokudan members cannot earn much money from gambling as the *Bakuto* did from dice gambling or the *Hanafuda* (card gambling). There are many bosses as well as their high-ranking professional gamblers for playing dice or *Hanafuda*. At present they are very careful about attending gambling gatherings for fear of police arrests. The large-sized gatherings for gambling, presided over by a boss, decreased since the arrest of Kakuji Inagawa in 1965. Gambling and bookmaking are, however, important monetary sources for the lower-ranking gang member (Table 6.3). Since the enforcement of the Law to Cope with *Boryokudan* their financial dependence upon gambling and bookmaking seems to have increased.

Considering both the aforementioned and that people generally, and youth specifically, enjoy a variety of pleasures, which continue to be offered to them legally and competitively by the prospering gaming industry, it is most likely that the usual, illegal, gambling supplied by the *Boryokudan* is likely to wane. It is important to note that Japan does not permit gambling casinos.

Boryokudan's most important income source is the sale of methamphetamine stimulant drugs. During the early 1950s we witnessed the most serious spread of the use of stimulant drugs[16] in which the newly expanding *Boryokudan* sold and distributed them in the black market.[17] During this period of time the Japanese had to work hard in order to earn a very scanty living. Many people, therefore, used stimulant drugs to prevent drowsiness or to recover from tiredness. Japan succeeded in suppressing this "epidemic" for only a few years after its peak in 1954 (Yokoyama, 1991: 6-7). Japan has, however, continued to experience a long-term stimulant drug use "epidemic" since 1970. It is very difficult to produce stimulant drugs in Japan without being noticed by the police. Therefore the *Boryokudan* participate in smuggling stimulant drugs into Japan from several foreign countries such as Taiwan and China.[18] They then distribute and retail it through their under-world network (Tamura, 1992:99). The *Koiki-Boryokudan* network is very sophisticated. The *Boryokudan* make a great deal of profit from stimulant drug sales[19] by monopolizing the market.

Paint thinner and toluene are their other profitable illicit commodities. Japanese youth began to misuse paint thinner, by sniffing it in plastic bags, around 1962 (Yokoyama, 1991:14). Ever since then the police have been unable to eradicate thinner and toluene misuse. Sale of thinner and toluene is strictly regulated in Japan, making it difficult for youth to obtain them for sniffing. The more severe the regulation is, the higher their price is for these youth. The *Boryokudan* fill the market "demand." It is very difficult for the police to suppress these illegal drug sales without a decline in the youth's "demand."

Heroin addiction drew attention in Japan beginning around 1960. Japan has not, however, experienced a serious spread or "contagion" of "hard drugs" such as heroin and cocaine. Colombian cocaine cartels planned to smuggle cocaine into Japan in sophisticated ways during the early 1990s. However, in 1994 only 28 Colombians were arrested on a charge of some offense related to cocaine (White Paper on Police in 1995: 144). The police have yet to reveal whether there is a direct connection between the Colombian cartels and the *Boryokudan*. It is reasonable that such a connection will not develop because of the language barrier, the geographical location and the strict checking of Colombian gangsters and smugglers by the law enforcement agencies such as the police and customs.[20]

Koiki-Boryokudan headquarters declared that they are not involved with illegal drugs. Moreover, Kazuo Taoko, a godfather of the *Yamaguchi-gumi*, became an influential sponsor of the League to Cleanse National Land by Expelling Illicit Drugs movement in 1963. Several famous intellectuals had organized this movement. In reality, *Koiki-Boryokudan* members have actively been involved in illicit drugs in the underworld. For example, the police arrested 6,581 *Boryokudan* members on a charge of some offense covered by the Stimulant Drug Control Law.[21] These included:

Yamaguchi-gumi	Inagawa-kai	Sumiyoshi-kai
2,169	869	949

Source: White Paper on Police in 1991:69

In 1988, by the initiative of the United Nations, the control of illicit traffic in narcotic drugs and psychotropic substances was discussed from an international perspective. In order to ratify a drug control treaty from the UN

Vienna Convention in December 1988, Japan enacted a special law in 1991 to supplement her current drug control laws. This law prescribed the Controlled Delivery as a new method for the control of illicit traffic,[22] and some measures against money laundering. However, even under this law the police cannot uncover the sophisticated *Koiki-Boryokudan* network for smuggling illicit drugs - particularly stimulant drugs nor for the money laundering. Japan shall not succeed in eradicating the dealing in illicit drugs by *Boryokudan* without revealing this network.

Prostitution is yet another illicit "service" provided because of public demand. The Prostitution Prevention Law was enacted in 1956 by the initiative of Christian and female groups (Yokoyama, 1993: 216). Prior to 1956 many *Boryokudan* members, racketeers and/or pimps, exploited professional prostitutes. More recently, many females work as part of call-girl systems (Yokoyama, 1995:57). They got rid of the direct supervision of *Boryokudan*. However, by using a sophisticated way for seduction, *Boryokudan* members often become their pimps as well as their lovers. The police do not know the total amount of money which *Boryokudan* members deprive females, as their disguised lovers. The role of a pimp must be attractive to young, idle, gang members.

Corruption and the Police

Hagen (1986:329) noted the resulting "immunity" from law enforcement action, due to police corruption, as one of the characteristics of a typical organized crime gang. How has the Boryokudan caused corruption? This problem will be analyzed below focusing on the police.

Immediately after World War II the police were de-centralized by the General Headquarters of the Allied Powers in order to democratize their system. The weakened police could not control violent activities of the newly risen *Boryokudan*.

However, under the regime of conservative parties the police resumed a strong power gradually. At that time the police were worried about the leftists' activities for overthrowing the national government then ruled by a conservative party. The *Boryokudan*, successors to *Tekiya* and *Bakuto*, were still affiliated with rightists. Therefore, during a political crisis in 1960, Yoshio Kodama, an influential fixer, planned to organize *Boryokudan* members as guards against leftists protesting the visit of a president of the United States. This was done in order to supplement police power (Masanobu, 1993: 144). In such a political climate the police often overlooked the illegal activities of *Boryokudan*.[23]

The newly risen *Boryokudan* such as *Yamaguchi-gumi* and *Inagawa-kai* expanded their territories through fights. Their fights sometimes occurred in public without being suppressed by the police. The most serious case was the fighting in Bettupu, a tourist city, in 1957.[24] A new article in the Penal Code prohibits gathering with weapons for the purpose of damaging another life, body or property was adopted in 1958 in order to prevent such battles. Its maximum punishment is two years imprisonment. Further criminalization against the

Boryokudan followed in order to prevent their violent activities and to strengthen the regulation against their possession of a gun and a sword under the Firearms and Swords Control Law.

Political tension ceased after 1960. The national government no longer needed the help of *Boryokudan* members as "rightists." On the contrary, it had to respond to the public opinion against violence, especially such visible *Boryokudan* violence as was exerted in Bettupu in 1957.

We saw the second peak of juvenile delinquency during the early 1960s when violent offenses by Japanese youth drew public attention (Yokoyama, 1986:108). The total number of *Boryokudan* members reached a peak in 1963 [25] as they recruited juvenile gang members. People felt the menace of the *Boryokudan* keenly. Then, in 1964 the National Police Agency carried out a strategy against the *Boryokudan* by using all prefectural police forces. By this strategy, called "the strategy to catch the top," the police arrested many bosses and high-ranking gang members.[26] Other purposes of the strategy were to discover *Boryokudan* sources of illegal revenue, to uncover and confiscate their weapons, and to suppress their battles. The illegal power of the *Boryokudan* was weakened by these arrests.

Unfortunately many bosses and gang members arrested in 1964 were discharged from prison by 1970.[27] In order to prevent activities designed to reconstruct their *Boryokudan*, the police started their second strategy to catch the "top" in 1979.[28]

Many small-sized *Boryokudan* could hardly perform their illegal money collecting activities due to the continual police roundups. It is this that led them to fall under the domination of *Koiki-Boryokudan*.

There was an increase in "in-fighting"[29] between *Boryokudan* groups around 1985; shots were often fired. By the late 1980s many citizens embarked in a movement to expel *Boryokudan* from their community. The typical case was the movement by Hamamatsu City citizens against Ichiriki-ikka,[30] a subordinate *Yamaguchi-gumi Boryokudan* (Yokoyama, 1994b: 11). In 1992 the Tokyo Sagawa Kyubin Scandal shocked the public. In addition, the mass media revealed some scandals of leaders of the ruling Liberal Democratic Party were in conspiracy with some *Boryokudan* bosses.[31]

The Liberal Democratic Party lost her political power in 1993, for the first time in 38 years, due to these revelations. The Law to Cope with *Boryokudan* has been enforced since 1992 in order to combat such situations. This law gave the police new ways to control the *Boryokudan*. Isolating themselves from corrupt relationships with the *Boryokudan*, the police earnestly regulate *Boryokudan* illegal activities.[32]

In addition, the Center for Promoting Movement to Expel Violence was established, under this law, in all prefectures.[33] This center, in conjunction with the police, provides counseling for citizens who are anxious about troubles caused by the *Boryokudan*.[34] It also offers rehabilitation assistance to *Boryokudan* members who wish to get rid of his *Boryokudan*. These activities are designed to reduce troubles caused by the *Boryokudan*.

Relationships of the *Boryokudan* with Organized Crime/Global Organized Crime

Although the networks for organized crime have widened internationally these days, the *Boryokudan* have not succeeded in playing an important role in these networks. They have, however, established their links to some foreign gangs for two main purposes: for smuggling stimulant drugs into Japan and for helping to smuggle aliens from Asian countries such as Thailand and China. As for the former, the *Boryokudan* buy the stimulant drug from foreign gangs who govern the process from producing it at the underground factory to smuggling it into Japan. Concerning the latter, the *Boryokudan* help the alien smuggling, which is planned by foreign gangs. During the 1980s they helped gangs in Thailand and in the Philippines who sold woman as prostitutes in Japan (Yokoyama, 1995:57). During the 1990s we drew attention to the activities of the Snake Head, Chinese gangs who specialized in alien smuggling. The Snake Head, in the Fujian area, organize an illegal tour to Japan for Chinese people, who want to smuggle into Japan to make money. In order to receive an excessive fee from the Snake Head, the *Boryokudan* help these smugglers to land in Japan, give refuge to them and find a job for them. Japanese law enforcement agencies are expected to cooperate with the foreign agencies that are concerned with eradicating the international operations of the *Boryokudan*.

Conclusions and Perspectives for the Future

The *Boryokudan* have inherited a subculture from *Bakuto* and *Tekiya*. They have become more profit-oriented recently, and have gradually lost the ethics of Ninkyo-do, with which many ordinary Japanese people sympathized. During the 1980s even innocent citizens were annoyed, or sometimes victimized, by a *Boryokudan* battle or by their violent intervention in civil conflicts. The *Boryokudan* amassed a great deal of money, illegally, through gambling and sale of stimulants. The *Boryokudan*, with support from their affluent funds, expanded their operations geographically - both in the Pacific Rim area as well as in the United States[35] (Huan and Vaughn, 1992: 47).

The Law to Cope with *Boryokudan* was enacted in 1991 in order to counteract the *Boryokudan*, and more specifically, the growing *Koiki-Boryokudan*.

The police are the main agency in Japan for counteracting the *Boryokudan*. The police have gradually gotten rid of the corrupting *Boryokudan*, and their associates, influence. This includes, above all, that of conservative politicians. Recently, the police employ many good graduates of a university as an ordinary police officer.[36] We expect these young officers to counteract activities of the *Boryokudan* due to their being relatively isolated from corruption.

Caveats

- In order to eradicate the *Boryokudan*, not only is the ongoing, strict, police control of their activities necessary, but also equally critical is an ongoing, active cooperation between Japan's citizens (the population at-large) and the police. We can expect this cooperation to be promoted because the police have established good relationships with the populace through their many community activities (Bayley, 1976).

- In addition, people should refrain from demanding illicit products such as stimulant drugs and paint thinner as well as from *Boryokudan* illegal gambling.
- If *Boryokudan* members wish to leave their *Boryokudan*, people should help them to rehabilitate themselves.[37] We expect that the Center for Promoting Movement to Expel Violence function effectively for this purpose.

Finding a job is most important for the former members of *Boryokudan* to rehabilitate themselves. At the end of April 1993, the Council to Cope with Rehabilitation of *Boryokudan* Members was organized in thirty-four prefectures. The police, the publics employ security office, the Center for Promoting Movement to Expel Violence and about two thousand companies joined this council. However, it is not easy for a former *Boryokudan* member to find a good stable job in the economic recession after 1990.

*Professor **Minoru Yokoyama**, completed his B.A in Law and an M.A. in both Criminal Law and Sociology at Chuo University, Tokyo. He is a professor and the former Dean of the Faculty of Law at Kokugakuin University. He is a member of the board of directors and the former 2nd Vice President of the Research Committee for the Sociology of Deviance and Social Control of the International Sociological Association. He is the President of both the Japanese Association of Sociological Criminology and the Tokyo Study Group of Sociological Criminology He has presented numerous papers at national and international conferences and symposia, and has published many articles in professional journals.*

References

Bayley, D. H. (1976), *Forces of Order: Police Behavior in Japan and the United States.* California: University of California Press.

Endo, M. (1992), *Interpretation of a New Law Against Boryokudan* (written in Japanese) 3. Tokyo: Genda i shokan.

Hoshino, K. (1988), "Organized Crime and its Origins in Japan." Paper presented at the 40th Annual Meeting of the American Society of Criminology in Chicago.

Iwai, H. (196 6), "*Yakuza* Groups" [written in Japanese], in K. Ohashi and J. Oyabu (eds.), *Social Pathology*. Seishinshobo, Tokyo. (1986) Organized Crime in Japan, R. Kelly (ed.), *Organized Crime*. Totowa, N J: Rowman & Littlefield.

Kaplan, D. and A. Dubro (1986), *Yakuza*, Massachusetts: Addison -Wesley Publishing Company, Inc.

Masanobu, T. (1993), *Last Gurentai* [written in Japanese] Tokyo: Sanichishobo.

Masukawa, K. (1989), *Japanese History of Gambling* [written in Japanese] Tokyo: Heibonsha.

Mizoguchi, A. (1985), *Document of Yamaguchi-gumi--Blood and Fighting* [written in Japanese]. Tokyo: Sanichishobo.

Nawa, T. (1993), *Live in the Way of Ninkyo-do* [written in Japanese]. Tokyo: Seiunsha.

Tamura, M. (1992), "The *Yakuza* and Amphetamine Abuse in Japan," in H. Traver and M. Gaylord (eds.), *Drugs Law and the State*. Hong Kong: Hong Kong University Press.

Yokoyama, M. (1986), "The Juvenile Justice System in Japan," in M. Brusten, J. Graham, N. Herriger and P. Malinowski (eds.), *Youth Crime, Social Control and Prevention*. Wuppertal, Germany: Centaurus-Verlagsgesellschaft.

Yokoyama, M. (1991), "Development of Japanese Drug Control Laws toward Criminalization," in *Kokugakuin Journal of Law and Politics* 28-3:1-21.

Yokoyama, M. (1993), "Emergence of Anti-Prostitution Law in Japan," *International Journal of Comparative and Applied Criminal Justice*. 17-2:211-218.

Yokoyama, M. (1994a), "Treatment of Prisoners under Rehabilitation Model in Japan," *Kokugakuin Journal of Law and Politics* 32-2:1-24.

Yokoyama, M. (1994b), "Change in Japanese Organized Crime and the Enactment of the Law to Cope with *Boryokudan*in, 1991," Paper presented at the 13th World Congress of Sociology of the International Sociological Association in Bielefeld, Germany.

Yokoyama, M. (1995), "Analysis of Prostitution in Japan," *International Journal of Comparative and Applied Criminal Justice* 19 -1: 47-69.

Notes

[1] There are two explanations for the origin of the term of *Yakuza* (Iwai, 1966:149): (1) the name of a bad set of cards appearing in *Hanafuda, a* conventional card gambling game, and (2) the word which means the obligation to gather in order to serve the feudal lord in case of an emergency. Belief in the former explanation is more prevalent.

[2] *Jin-no* is a Chinese legendary god, who taught people how to farm and how to produce drugs. *Jin-no* was believed to relieve diseases by drugs. *Tekiya* worshipped him as a symbol of Ninkyo-*do* by which they justified their activities. (Iwai, 1966:151). Another reason for their believing in *Jin-no* might be that many members of Tekiya were farmers;

the sale of drugs was their important job. It should be noted that under the influence of Shinto, an indigenous shamanistic and animistic religion, Japanese have had the flexibility to accept foreign gods.

3 We already saw street hoodlums in some large cities before the war. In 1945 one of the hoodlums' groups in a Tokyo district was called *Gurentai*. The term *Gurentai* literally means *foolish companions* (Iwai, 1966:152).

4 Although both Takoa and Inagawa have charisma, Taoka is rational in contrast with Ingawa, who is more of a conventional godfather.

5 For example, a son of Kakuji, Inagawa became the third president after the death of Susumu Ishii. Following the custom of *Bakuto* and *Tekiya* the name of *Boryokudan* is usually adopted by the family name of their boss.

6 A Boryokudan member, through a similar ritual, often establishes a quasi-relative relationship with another member (e.g. quasi-brothers)·

7 Police research in 1993, documented that 63.3% of all respondent *Boryokudan* members were willing to fight in the front, when their *Boryokudan* is involved in a combat with another *Boryokudan* (White Paper on Police in 1993:19).

8 Police research in 1993 affirmed that 79.2% would revenge themselves if they would be shamed in public (Ibid.34).

9 Historically both *Bakuto* and *Tekiya* adopted tattooing to show people their courage, toughness, and masculinity (Kaplan and Dubro, 1986:26). Many *Boryokudan* members continue this practice.

10 The most important ceremonies are the celebration for a boss released from prison, and the funeral for a dead boss.

11 Police research in 1993, documented that 60.3% considered that diligent work was trivial (White Paper on Police in 1993:34).

12 Police research in 1993, noted that 72. 2% affirmed such a life style in which people enjoy themselves in pleasures of the moment without considering their future (Ibid.34).

13 In 1988 the total sum of the general revenue account of Japan's annual national budget was 56,700 billion yen; 2.3% of this is equivalent to the total estimated annual revenue of all *Boryokudan* groups.

14 One example of such a "demand" behavior is the threat of a *Boryokudan* member for money by showing a badge of his *Boryokudan.*

15 In Japan, *Pachinko* (a kind of pinball game) parlors are popular among adults, while many juveniles enjoy themselves at game houses with various computer games machines.

16 At that time the government embarked on a nation-wide campaign against the stimulant drug. It appealed to people not to use the stimulant drug because it was harmful to their health. Since then we have used the words: '*contamination of the stimulant drug*'. Around 1970 western countries heatedly discussed the decriminalization of selected drugs. Although Japan followed this discussion we did not adopt the policy of decriminalization of drugs. We have witnessed, on the contrary, the continual criminalization of all kinds of narcotic and psychotropic substances. (Yokoyama, 1991)

17 At the end of World War II the Japanese armed forces preserved lots of stimulant drugs. Following the post-war chaos these preserved drugs were "drained" out to the black-market. It caused the spread of stimulant drug use for the first time. By 1954 the *Boryokudan* not only sold stimulant drugs in the black market but also produced drugs in underground factories.

18 For 5 years, since 1990, the police confiscated 844 kilograms of stimulant drugs; 50.1%, 20.8% and 5.0% were smuggled from Taiwan, China and Hong Kong. (White Paper on Crime in 1995:271)

19 The retail price of one gram of the stimulant drug is about 10,000 yen (U.S. $87); the corresponding price in Taiwan is 2,000-3,000 yen.

20 In the United States the Colombian cocaine cartels have several cocaine distribution capitals where Colombian gangs operate a network among Colombian immigrants (Hagen, 1986:348). They will not be able to establish such a network, for cocaine distribution, in Japan, with only their own members and the Colombian immigrants; the total number being very small. Moreover, the *Boryokudan* will hesitate to contact them because of the language barriers and the geographical location. The *Boryokudan* who manage to maintain a stimulant drug smuggling network from the neighboring countries, cannot afford to deal with cocaine actively because of their fear of confrontation with the police in the latter's strict arrests and roundups..

21 The total number of offenders of the Stimulant Drug Control Law in 1990 was 15,038. Most of those arrested, excluding *Boryokudan* members, were stimulant drug users. Ever since drug criminalization began in 1973, even the users have been sentenced to imprisonment (Yokoyama 1991:12)

22 Under the prescription on the Controlled Delivery, if there is a police or public prosecutor's request, customs do not confiscate illicit drugs smuggled into our country. Law enforcement agencies can then trace both the place and to whom the drugs are delivered

23 After some serious offenses such as injury and murder were committed, a *Boryokudan* boss would negotiate with the police to make some "soldiers" appear before the police in lieu of the real offenders (Masanobu, 1993:119). These substitute "offenders", returning from their prison incarceration, were promoted in the *Boryokudan* hierarchy.

24 *Ishi i-gumi*, a subordinate *Boryokudan* of *Yamaguchi-gumi*, invaded the territory ruled by *Ida-gumi* in Bettupu. Both fought in order to acquire concessions for the 1957 exposition. First, the boss of Ishi *i-gumi* was shot and seriously injured. Then, *Ishi i-gumi* attacked *Ida-gumi* in revenge. Over 400 *Boryokudan* members gathered to support either *Ishi i-gumi* or *Ida-mugi* (Mizoguchi, 1985:102). Holding pistols and swords they walked around looking for a fight in the center of Bettupu. Their activities were not effectively suppressed by 521 police officers under the direction of the Oita Prefecture Police Headquarters.

25 The total number of *Boryokudan* members increased from 92,860 in 1958 to 184,092 in 1963 (White Paper on Crime in 1964:69).

26 Police arrested Kakuji Inagawa, an *Inagawa-kai* godfather, in 1965, on a charge of gambling at Hakone, which many *Boryokudan* bosses joined. On the other hand, they failed to arrest Kazuo Taoka, a godfather of *Yamaguchi-gumi*.

27 Imprisonment terms are shorter in Japan than they are in the United States (Yokoyama, 1994a: 3). In 1994, of a total of 22,781 newly admitted prisoners, only 12.7% were sentenced to more than 3 years imprisonment (White Paper on Crime in 1995:82).

28 Around 1970 the bosses and their high-ranking gang members, in the large-sized *Boryokudan* groups, became more indirectly involved in criminal activities, because little evidence against them was available to the police. As a result, the police could not repeat the strategy to catch the "top" after 1970.

29 After the death of Kazuo Taoka at the age of 68, in 1981, *Yamaguchi-gumi* was split into two groups through the quarrel about the succession to the position of a godfather. Their hostility reached a peak, in 1985, with 293 cases of documented fights all over the country; over five times as many as the 56 cases in 1981 (White Paper on Police in 1989:2). The *Boryokudan* smuggled in many guns to prepare for fighting.

30 Citizens sued *Ichiriki-ikka* for the prohibition of using a building as an office for the activities of *Boryokudan* members. Although a member of *Ichiriki-ikka* stabbed the legal counselor, a leader of their movement, with a knife, they did not back down. Their law suite drew nation-wide mass media attention. They were supported by public opinion and won their suit, and the *Ichiriki-ikka* were expelled from the building in their community. Notwithstanding this lawsuit, the *Boryokudan* have been tacitly accepted into Japanese society. They maintain offices which display their emblem on the front door. (Kaplan and Kubro, 1986.6)

31 For example, Asahi Newspaper reported one scandal on July 28,1992. According to the report, Shin Kanemaru, the most powerful leader in the Liberal Democratic Party, requested that Susumu Ishii, the second president of *Inagawa-kai*, work to make a group of ultra-rightists stop the campaign against Noboru Takeshita, a candidate for a prime minister.

32 The police received a great deal of information through their ordinary contact with *Boryokudan* members with whom they had personal acquaintance. The enforcement of the Law to Cope with *Boryokudan* may create difficulties for the police to acquire needed informants.

33 The Hiroshima Prefectural Assembly, sensitive to the upsurge of public opinion against the *Boryokudan,* resolved, in 1986, to promote the movement to expel the *Boryokudan* from their prefecture (White Paper on Police in 1989:77). This resolution was followed by the establishment of the "Hiroshima Prefectural Conference to Expel Violence" foundation, August 1987. It received support from the local governments and the police in the Hiroshima Prefecture. Similar organizations were created in many prefectures. The organization was formally authorized as the Center for Promoting Movement to Expel Violence by the Law to Cope with *Boryokudan*. By September 1992, an authorized center existed in all prefectures. In addition to the professional staff , community leaders such as   a legal counselor, a volunteer probation-parole officer and a retired police officer, work as counselors

34 One year after the enactment of the Law to Cope with *Boryokudan*, there were a total number of 8,281 counseling meetings at the Center for Promoting Movement to Expel Violence. (White Paper on Police in 1993:68)

35 The purposes of *Boryodukan* operations are to smuggle in such illicit goods as fire arms and stimulant drugs, to earn money by gambling held for Japanese tourists in foreign countries and to have a refuge to escape to arrests in confrontations with the Japanese police (White Paper on Police in 1992:74). During the late 1980's boom, the *Boryokudan*, posing as Japanese companies, actively invested money in order to buy real estate in foreign countries.

36 The position of a police officer is more highly evaluated among the university students since the economic recession in the early 1990's. Since then many students have failed to pass the examination to be employed as a police officer.

37 It is most important for the former members of *Boryokudan* to find a job in order to rehabilitate themselves. At the end of April, 1993, the Council to Cope with Rehabilitation of *Boryokudan* Members was organized in 34 prefectures. The police, the public employment security office, the Center for Promoting Movement to Expel Violence and about two thousand companies joined this council. However, it is not easy for a former *Boryokudan* member to find a good stable job in the post-1990, economic recession.

7 The Future of Sicilian and Calabrian Organized Crime

Letizia Paoli

Abstract

In order to figure out the future of Sicilian and Calabrian mafia associations, two facets of their action must be distinguished and taken into consideration separately: 1) mafia groups' participation into international illegal markets; 2) the local systems of mafia power.

This paper argues that the position and the degree of involvement of Italy's most powerful mafia coalitions in world illicit exchanges primarily depends on the tendencies of the international political economy, although law enforcement action may exercise a considerable influence in the short term. The power exercised by mafia families in their local communities, on the contrary, is largely the product of the interplay of three collective actors: mafia groups themselves, state institutions and the Italian civil society.

Key Words: Mafia, Illegal markets, Narcotic drugs, "Pentiti", Extortion, Cosa Nostra, 'Ndrangheta, Men of honor

Introduction

Notwithstanding the great variety of proposed definitions, there is a wide consensus in the academic community that organized crime involves a continuing enterprise operating for the production and sale of illegal goods and services (Hagan, 1983). The two major Southern Italian crime consortia - approximately 90 mafia families associated with the Sicilian Cosa Nostra and an approximately equal number of cosche belonging to the Calabrian 'Ndrangheta - may certainly be included into such a definition. Sicilian and Calabrian mafia associations do, however, much more. Mafia groups have imposed their control on a variety of local resources through the monopolization of violence in local contexts since their rise in the 19th century. This represents their major source of income even nowadays, notwithstanding their entrance into international illegal markets. Furthermore, in local contexts long plagued by the absence of an effective state power, mafia families have exercised important functions of social regulation and have long seen their role recognized as being legitimate by wide sectors of the population and by state authorities themselves (Hess, 1970, 1973; Blok, 1974, 1986; Schneiders, 1976; Arlacchi, 1983, 1988; Paoli, 1997).

These two aspects of mafia action need to be kept separated in trying to predict Southern Italian criminal consortia's future trends of development. Whereas mafia actors' role in illegal markets is significantly conditioned by international political economy tendencies, the permanence of the local systems of mafia power will be determined -- as it has been in the past -- largely by the interaction of three collective actors: in addition to the criminal groups themselves, state institutions and the national -- and, specifically, Sicilian and Calabrian -- civil society.

Figure 7.1 Major crime coalitions in Southern Italy

Involvement in Illegal Markets
Past and Present

At least since the Second World War, Sicilian and Calabrian mafia families are active in the production and trade of commodities which were declared illegal by state authorities. They have greatly profited from the expansion of world illegal markets, most notably tobacco and narcotics, which has continued in the post-war World War II period.

Many mafiosi, i.e. the members of the two above-mentioned mafia consortia, as well as other figures of the Italian underworld, began their fortunes through smuggling and black market trading during the last world war, "by selling in difficult times indispensable goods at prices eight-ten times higher than what they had paid for them" (Piselli and Arrighi, 1985; Mangiameli, 1987). Exploiting the experience made on wartime black markets, several mafia associates started to deal in smuggled cigarettes and, to a minor extent, in drugs. The scale of both illicit trades and the degree of involvement of mafia members in the 1950s and 1960s were, however, much more limited than the dimensions reached in the three following decades. The mafia, furthermore, monopolized neither of these activities. In the case of tobacco smuggling, "men of honour" (as mafia affiliates define themselves) either limited themselves to extracting some form of bribe from the underworld characters involved in this activity, or imposed their commercial partnership by exploiting their superior military expertise. As the Guardia di Finanza (Customs Police) noted, "the Sicilian smuggling organizations do not identify with mafia cosche, although some elements of mafia origin can be found among the traffickers" (1971b: 1065).

Their involvement in drug trade was even more limited. It is, however, proved that Cosa Nostra adherents participated in the smuggling of the heroin produced by pharmaceutical industries. In the early 1950s at least 250 kilos of substance produced by the Schiapparelli Corporation were hidden by the director and allegedly sold to Italian-American gangsters working in Milan. The most important among them was Salvatore Lucania, known as Lucky Luciano, who settled in Naples in 1947; instead, the role of Sicilian mafiosi was marginal.

When this channel expired due to a law, passed in 1952, that prohibited the production of all heroin even if for legal purposes, some Sicilian mafiosi organized the shipment to the United States of heroin illegally refined by French traffickers (Comitato provinciale, 1971; CPMS, 1972). Two networks of mafia members, respectively associated to the cosche of Castellammare del Golfo and Alcamo and with those of Salemi and Vita, in the Trapani province, had a leading position in these activities thanks to their connections in the United States.[1] Another trafficking group, targeted by law enforcement action and headed by the two Palermitan brothers Canepa, shipped at least 285 kg of heroin refined by the French traffickers during the 1950s (ibid., see also CPMS, 1976b). Though the turnover was much smaller than in the following decades (as a result of the still limited dimensions of the American heroin demand), considerable profits were made: it is enough to consider that the resale price of heroin was five to six time higher than the purchase prices. In fact, Sicilians would buy a kilogram of heroin for 2.5 million Lira and sell it to the U.S. wholesalers for 12 to 15 million (Guardia di Finanza, 1971b).

The Sicilian participation in the trade of both these illegal commodities underwent a consistent decline as a result of the strong repressive campaign enforced by law enforcement institutions after the explosion of a car-bomb, that killed seven law enforcement officers, in Ciaculli, in the outskirts of Palermo, on June 30th, 1963. Hundreds of mafiosi were arrested and, as a consequence, illicit activities were seriously hampered for almost a decade. Only the few "men of honour" that managed to escape imprisonment or to expatriate continued to be involved in tobacco smuggling, but the control of this commerce shifted to Neapolitan contrabbandieri.

Cosa Nostra families' presence in tobacco trade once again became dominant only during the early 1970s, when two major trials against Cosa Nostra members ended with the acquittal of most of the defendants. In order to

recover their old stake, the Sicilians imposed their protection upon the
Neapolitans who had, throughout the 1960s, acquired a dominant position on
the market. As the "pentito"[2] Antonino Calderone maintains:

> *At the beginning of the 1970s Naples was a little Sicilian*
> *Eldorado, because there was already the cigarette smuggling.*
> *There were also those who worked in drugs, but it was still a*
> *small thing. Instead, cigarettes was one of the biggest sources*
> *of income. Since in Naples the work was good, the Sicilians*
> *put their foot there, ousting the Neapolitans a bit* (CPM,
> 1992b: 316; se also TrPA, 1973).

In order to force them into obedience, several contrabandieri, both
Neapolitan and Palermitan, were ritually affiliated to Cosa Nostra and two Cosa
Nostra families, directly dependent on the Provincial Commission, were created
in Campania (TrPA, 1986). Due to the use of larger ships, which enabled the
transportation of larger quantities of cigarettes, the turnover of this activity grew
rapidly, as the seizures made by the Guardia di Finanza clearly show. Over the
period 1966 to 1973, the kilos of confiscated cigarettes increased more than
2,500 percent. Considerable profits were made: a box of cigarettes cost
approximately 42,000 Lira at the moment of shipping in a Yugoslavian port and
was sold on the retail market in Italy for about 150,000 to 160,000 Lira (Guardia
di Finanza, 1971a and b).

**Table 7.1: Quantities of smuggled tobacco seized by the Guardia di Finanza
over the years 1966-73 in Campania, Apulia, Calabria and Sicily**

1966	1967	1968	1969	1970	1971	1972	1973
13,380	142,252	232,453	276,964	298,622	325,532	305,766	353,317

Source, Commissione Parlamentare d'inchiesta sul fenomeno della mafia in Sicilia (CPMS, 1976b:
522-23).

The real step forward, however, came later, around 1978 with the
entrance in wholesale narcotics trafficking. Though some "men of honour,"
such as the Grado brothers, were already marginally involved in drug dealings
(TrPA, 1986, 6: 993), this step was taken primarily due to Nunzio La Mattina, a
former smuggler affiliated to Cosa Nostra. In fact he exploited his tobacco
smuggling connections in order to import the first huge quantities of morphine
to refine into heroin in Sicilian laboratories (TrPA, 1986: 1885). The police
official Boris Giuliano, later to be killed in a mafia ambush, perceived this trend
as early as 1979:

> *the Sicilian mafia has returned to the international drug*
> *trafficking with a great availability of men and means,*
> *exploiting especially the channels of the widespread tobacco*
> *smuggling networks which are active in Southern Italy and on*
> *the islands, under the iron leadership of the big mafia bosses*
> (TrPA, 1986, 9: 1888).

The trafficking immediately turned out to be big business. The

Palermitan Investigative Judges of the Palermitan maxi-processo estimated that Nunzio La Mattina, first, and then, Antonino Rotolo bought in less than two years about two tons of drugs for an overall price of U.S. $55 million (TrPA, 1986, 9: 1879-80). A division of labour soon followed. Together with Tommaso Spadaro and Giuseppe Savoca, La Mattina and Rotolo took charge of the morphine supply, but "each worked on his own and kept jealously safe the secret of their own organisations." Others took control of the processing of drugs in clandestine laboratories: in the early 1980s, according to Salvatore Contorno, there were at least seven different drug laboratories in Western Sicily (TrPA, 1986, 9). Others, then, were responsible for the transportation and the distribution of drugs in retail markets for the whole organization, the packages of the different families being distinguished through a system of marks. Among this last group, a prominent role was played by the Cuntrera-Caruana family and Giuseppe Bono, chief of the Bolognetta mafia family and a close ally of the Corleonesi. As the judges of the Palermo maxiprocesso put it:

> De facto inside Cosa Nostra autonomous but functionally linked structures have been created; each in charge of the different phases which make up the complex drug trade, whereas the men of honour that do not have operational responsibilities in the trade may financially contribute to it, sharing, to different degrees, in the profits and the risks (TrPA, 1986, 9: 1887).

The turn-over of the overall business is impressive: it has been estimated, on the basis of records of proceedings in Italian and American courts (TrPA, 1982; 1986; Biden, 1980), that between four and five tons of pure heroin were produced each year in the late 1970s by Sicilian laboratories. This quantity, largely exported to the United States, then represented some 30 percent of the total demand of that country. Subtracting the costs of production and transport, this gave a net profit of around 700 or 800 thousand billion Lira (Arlacchi, 1988). The huge profits, which could suddenly be gained with heroin trafficking, have been stressed by several pentiti. Hence, for example, Buscetta recalls that coming back to Palermo in June 1980, "I realized that a great wealth invested more or less all Cosa Nostra members. Stefano Bondate explained to me that this was the consequence of drug trafficking" (TrPA, 1992a: 96).

From the late-1980s, however, the involvement of Sicilian "men of honour" in heroin refining and transcontinental trafficking progressively declined (Ministero dell'Interno, 1993; 1994; 1995). On the contrary, Cosa Nostra associates have increased their presence into cocaine trafficking, importing lots of drugs directly from Latin America or more frequently acquiring cocaine by Colombian distributors in Europe. However, whereas they remain active in the distribution of drugs over the Italian market, several investigators believe that their involvement into transcontinental shipping and the distribution over the overall European market has shrunk over the last decade (Ministero dell'Interno, 1993; 1994; 1995; DEA, 1992; Sabella, 1996).

Only in the late 1960s did Calabrian 'Ndranghetisti began to be systematically involved in tobacco trade, exploiting the strategic advantages associated with their location: Calabrian coasts were less guarded and closer to the markets (Naples and Rome) than the Sicilian shores. Their entry onto the market also reflected a change in Mediterranean smuggling routes. Whereas up to the mid-1960s most smuggling ships were loaded in the free ports of Tanger and Gibraltar and run by Spanish crews, from about the middle of that decade, Yugoslav ports took over most of the traffic and the crews were principally Greek. As a consequence, Apulian and Calabrian landing places became more convenient (Legione Carabinieri di Palermo, 1973). Initially, the 'ndrine simply demanded a tangente in exchange for the authorization to use their territory for cigarette loading and hiding as well as for the guarantee of local police inaction. Soon, however, they entered into partnership with Neapolitan and Calabrian drug traffickers: the massacre of piazza mercato which took place in Locri in 1967 was, in fact, provoked by a "sgarro," an attempted fraud, in the cigarette business (Ciconte, 1996: 44-51; 112-6; Gambino, 1971: 139-45).

The establishment of co-partnerships with the then more advanced traffickers of neighboring regions also promoted the involvement of Calabrian groups into whole-scale narcotics trade, which soon largely substituted the smuggling of cigarettes (CPM, 1993a: 36). Throughout the 1980s some of the major cosche of the province of Reggio Calabria - the groups De-Stefano-Tegano and the Iamonte of Reggio Calabria, the Papalia of Pla and the Calabria of San Luca - were co-partners of the Catanese family of Santapaola in the import by sea of bulk amounts of hashish and heroin from Lebanon and Turkey respectively. These were unloaded in the port of Saline Joniche, in the territory controlled by the Iamonte cosca.

As a result in the early 1990s, the position of the Calabrian cosche was by no means lower than that of the main Sicilian families concerning the contacts with suppliers, working in the upper levels of the national and international distribution network and ramification of exports. From 1989 on a "cartel" of cosche of the Ionic side handled several lots of heroin for a total amount of 500kgs and cargoes of cocaine of up to 300kgs at a time (PrRC, 1993b). Even to a higher degree than Sicilians, Calabrians currently appear to be involved in large imports of cocaine directly from source countries. For example, in the early 1990s a coalition of seven Calabrian mafia families of the Ionian coast - Mazzaferro, Pesce, Ieri, Cataldo, Barbaro, Morabito and Romola - succeeded in importing into Italy at least 11 tons of cocaine in eight different shipments. The last shipment – 5,490 kilos -- was seized in March 1994 on the outskirts of Turin and accounts for the world largest cocaine seizure ever made outside of the areas of production (TrTO, 1994).

Other illegal commodities have, of course, not been neglected, although narcotics trade remains the main source of revenue: arms, money and human beings trying to enter illegally into Italy are currently traded by the major Italian mafia consortia. Money laundering has, in particular, become a necessity, since Cosa Nostra and 'Ndrangheta members have to launder and reinvest the capitals accumulated with drug trafficking. Long unable to "wash" the money themselves, since the criminal expertise which is necessary to carry out sophisticated financial services was seldom available within the clan or to its immediate periphery, mafia affiliates increasingly came in touch with institutions and characters moving in the sphere of economic crime. The financier Michele Sindona certainly laundered Sicilian mafiosi's dirty money from the early 1970s up to the bankruptcy of his American bank, the Franklin National Bank in 1974 (Spero, 1980).[3] Another example is the Banco Ambrosiano which, under the management of Roberto Calvi, progressively took over Sindona's role when the latter decided to leave Italy in the early 1970s and for years laundered and invested drug trafficking proceeds for several Cosa Nostra clans. As Francesco Marino Mannoia, a mafioso now collaborating with the judges, stated, "Salvatore Inzerillo and Stefano Bontade (two leaders of Palermitan Cosa Nostra) had Sindona, the others (i.e. the Corleonesi) had Calvi" (1991). Though it is impossible to make precise calculations, these choices cost mafia members relevant sums of money. Ever more prisoners of the financial "merry-go-round" they had built themselves, both Calvi and Sindona ended up bankrupt. The collapse of Calvi's Banco Ambrosiano, for example, was estimated to involve a one U.S. billion loss and was, up to the early 1990s, the largest bankruptcy in Western banking history (TrMI, 1989; Paoli, 1993; Calabri, 1992; Naylor, 1987).[4]

Thanks to the rapid growth of their economic turnover, however, over the last decade mafia groups have struggled to acquire direct access to the market and to assert their specific advantages deriving from the use of violence even in these fields, as the most recent investigations prove. With such an aim in view, different strategies have been adopted. Occasionally, white-collar criminals have been internally co-opted. More frequently, mafiosi have directly bought front companies, such as banks and financial companies, and given their own children the necessary education to acquire the skills, the official qualification and social contacts so as to directly enter the market. An investigation carried out in 1993 by the Procura della Repubblica of Locri showed, for example, that a "criminal entrepreneur" living in Locri, whose ritual affiliation to the 'Ndrangheta is uncertain, but whose ties to the local cosche were extremely close, successfully laundered huge amounts of money of illicit origin on behalf of major mafia families. Through a network of financial institutions registered in the name of figure-heads based in Pescara, Padua, Ferrara and Milan, Salvatore Filippone made transactions for various billions of rubles and millions of dollars thanks to speculative operations in the Russian Republic and in the former Soviet Republics (TrLO, 1993; see also TrCT, 1995).

Future Trends

Cosa Nostra and 'Ndrangheta's success in illegal markets is subordinated to the rules and trends of economics. In order to foresee their future involvement in illicit trafficking, particularly in the drug market, several variables have to be taken into account:

- closeness to source countries and traffic routes;
- presence in final consumer markets;
- available assets;
- criminal expertise and military potential.

Another crucial resource is represented by the inaction of law enforcement bodies which can be obtained through a variety of means; the corruption of state officers or their direct involvement in illicit deals; intimidations and threats and, in the extreme cases, the physical elimination of the most "dangerous" law enforcement officers. This "resource" represents the main linking element between the two aspects of mafia actions analyzed here. Since, however, it largely depends on the wider relations between mafia associations and the State, it will be analyzed in the second part of this paper.

There are no doubts that Sicilian and Calabrian crime consortia have plenty of the third and fourth resource: that is, money, criminal expertise and arms and explosives. Matters, however, become even more complicated when one considers the first and second variables. As far as the first one is concerned, it is evident that neither Cosa Nostra nor 'Ndrangheta families are close to the areas where narcotics are produced, nor to their traffic routes. The distance from source countries represents the primary factor to explain the expulsion of Cosa Nostra actors from the transcontinental trade of heroin, which had granted them so many profits in the early 1980s. Heroin was originally refined by experts far away from production sources -- in the 1960s and 1970s Marseilles, then by the Sicilians (Lamour and Lamberti, 1974). Since the mid-1980s a process of concentration of the refining phase in source countries has been taking place worldwide: as in other markets, the production of the final product, heroin, and of the semi-manufactured products, morphine and heroin base, tend today to be carried out in developing countries, where production and labor costs are lower (Lewis, 1985: 15). According to the data of the U.S. Bureau of International Narcotic Matters (BINM, 1993; 1992), about 50 percent of the world supply of opium -- estimated in 2,600 metric tons in 1992 -- comes from Myanmar (former Burma) and, to a lesser extent, from the neighboring countries forming the so-called "Golden Triangle" (Thailand, Laos and Myanmar). The other traditional area of opium cultivation is the so-called "Golden Crescent," which includes Afghanistan, Pakistan and Iran: about 30 percent of the opium production -- 1,102 metric tons in 1992 -- allegedly takes place there.[5] Moreover, the criminal actors who are settled next to the production areas often control the transport and the wholesale distribution of narcotics in the final markets. When Italian and U.S. law enforcement agencies successfully disrupted several important networks of heroin import and distribution in the United States -- most notably with the so-called "Pizza Connection" (Alexander, 1986; Blumenthal, 1988) and "Irontower" operations (Stille, 1995: 269-72) -- the gap left by Italian-American traffickers was quickly filled up by Mexican traffickers, who sold the "black tar" heroin cultivated in their country and then, by Chinese traders, who directly imported heroin from the "Golden Triangle" (Thailand, Laos and Myanmar). From the early 1990s

Colombians have also begun to grow the poppy plant themselves and to refine the heroin in Colombia and now allegedly control almost half of the North American heroin market (NNICC, 1995; International Herald Tribune, March 31st, 1997).

In the same way, even as far as the European market is concerned, Sicilian as well as other Italian groups have been active only in the wholesale and middle-level distribution of heroin since the mid-1980s. The importing of the substance has, instead, largely been monopolized by Turkish and Kurdish traffickers who buy heroin or, more frequently, morphine in their homeland from traders coming from the production areas of the so-called "Golden Crescent" (TrMI, 1994; DEA, 1995).

A distinction between Sicilian and Calabrian crime groups must be made as far as the second resource is concerned: namely, their presence in final consumer markets. Given their wider national and international connections and activities, Calabrian mafia families seem to be in a much more advantageous position than the former ones. The most widespread Sicilian foreign branch was in the United States, but this was largely disrupted by law enforcement action in the second half of the 1980s with the two above-mentioned police operations. On the other hand, the external branches of the Calabrian 'Ndrangheta much more extensive. Whereas Cosa Nostra has always opposed, with one exception, the transfer of mafia families outside Sicily in order to maintain the cohesion of the criminal consortium; whole 'Ndrangheta families have settled in Lombardy and Piedmont and have managed to recreate, in several cohesive communities of Calabrian immigrants, the same sort of territorial dominion that they impose on their villages and towns of origin (CPM, 1994a). The larger number of personnel in Northern Italy in the mid-1980s enabled a network of Calabrian mafia families -- Sergi, Papalia, Mazzaferro and Flachi-Trovato -- to assume a leading position within the Milanese underworld. They gained control of the local drug market, which is Italy's largest, ousting the Sicilian mafia. Furthermore, in addition to the cells that are located in Germany as well as in Holland, France and the United States, the 'Ndrangheta has its most developed foreign settlements in Canada and Australia, consisting of several hundreds of affiliates who continue to act in close cooperation with the home seat in Calabria (Paoli, 1993). Starting from the late 1970s an organization of immigrant Calabrian criminals coming from Siderno and other neighboring towns, called the "Siderno Group," has been responsible for the distribution of large amounts of heroin in Europe, North America and Australia (TrRC, 1993). A final proof of the relevance of branches outside the region of origin is given by the fact that the only Sicilian mafia family, which continuously appears to be involved in transcontinental shipments of drugs, is the Cuntrera-Caruana. They originated from Siculiana (AG) in Western Sicily and currently constitute the only Sicilian Cosa Nostra cosca that has permanently moved its home seat outside of the island, to Venezuela, and today it enjoys widespread connections in four continents.

All in all, as far as the drug market is concerned, which represents by far the largest illegal market, the future prospects for Sicilian and Calabrian crime groups' role do not look very bright. Both groups have plenty of money and arms to employ in this enterprise and enjoy the protection and the complicity of several Italian politicians and state officers. But, whereas 'Ndrangheta families are favored by their extensive branches in Northern Italy and abroad, Cosa Nostra cosche appear to be seriously hampered by their limited presence in final markets. Furthermore, both associations are far away from the major areas of production and refinement of narcotic substances. It is, hence, probable that they will be progressively marginalized from international drug trade. On the other hand, they have good chances -- and, particularly, the 'Ndrangheta with its connections in Northern Italy where the largest consumer markets are located -- to maintain a significant role in the national system of narcotics distribution. Even in this respect, however, Sicilian and Calabrian mafia groups will face the growing competition of traffickers coming from North Africa, Turkey, China and Colombia who import drugs directly from production areas in their homelands.

More generally, a likely scenario of the Cosa Nostra and 'Ndrangheta's future involvement in illegal markets cannot be made without taking into account the trends of the world political economy. These trends may favor a criminal group, by enabling it to enter into the most profitable section of an illegal commodity chain of production and/or distribution; or they may determine its expulsion from the trade of a specific illicit commodity. For example, whereas Italian crime groups' involvement in international drug trafficking has been declining since the late 1980s (Ministero dell'Interno, 1995), Sicilians and Calabrian mafia groups have succeeded in penetrating the "wholesale" sector of international arms trafficking during the same years as a result of the "democratization" of the arms market created by the fall of the Soviet Empire and the civil war in Yugoslavia. Due to these two events, and, in particular, to the arms "demands" of the Yugoslavian civil war, a huge illicit arms market was created at the Italian borders. In the past, instead, members of both organizations were largely extraneous to the wholesale section of illegal arms trade. In fact, this section, as also happens in the money or gold market, constitutes only a relatively small appendix of the respective legal market and, therefore, presents extremely selective entry barriers, by requiring from whomever wants to deal in them not only specific skills but also an official professional curriculum as well as contacts in the licit and illicit sections of the market (Naylor, 1995; 1996).

Due to the "liberalization" produced by the two above-mentioned events, Sicilian and Calabrian mafia associates -- or, more frequently, close referents of theirs -- have succeeded in penetrating the "wholesale" sector of international arms trafficking, participating in sizeable and very high-profit yielding transactions and doing business with foreign criminal groups, representatives of economic crime and the political-military machinery of foreign countries (Ministero dell'Interno, 1994 and 1995). Over the last few years, there has been much speculation on the role played by Italian mafia groupings in the diversion of the conventional and nuclear arsenals of the former Soviet Empire onto the illegal section of the market and their sale to a variety of crooks and terrorist groups and states.   Whereas some of these allegations are probably grossly exaggerated, the management of large scale illegal arms transactions by Italian mafiosi and their front-men has been demonstrated in a recent investigation of the Procura della Repubblica di Catania (PrCT, 1995).   The main person under investigation is Felice Cultrera, a Catanese financier who resided for a long time in Marbella, Spain and who is charged not only with laundering money on the account of the mafia boss Nitto Santapaola but also of brokering billion dollar illegal sales of arms to several non-European countries -- ranging from Morocco to Saudi Arabia -- in partnership with famous arms dealers such Adnan Khassogghi and Al Khassar Monzer.

Given the extra-profits resulting from state bans and restrictions on these "desirable" commodities, it is highly probable that Sicilian and Calabrian mafia consortia, as long as there is a demand, will go on trading in illegal goods and services.   Their position and degree of involvement, nonetheless, are heavily conditioned by market trends, which largely escape the control of mafia families and Italian state bodies.   The best example to demonstrate the shaping power of international trends is represented by the case of Apulia.   Up to the 1970s, in fact, this Adriatic region was exempt from any ongoing and "rooted" problem of organized crime. Its development in the past quarter of a century was originally prompted by the decision of the Campanian tobacco smugglers to shift the unloading of cigarette boxes from the frequently patrolled Tyrrhenian waters to the relatively safer Adriatic ones.   Hence, they moved the fast motor boats used to unload cigarette cartons from large ships from the Campanian to the Apulian coast and started to recruit local gangsters as workers.   The colonization of the region by Campanian crime groups enhanced the growth of an autochthonous organized crime.   Throughout the last fifteen years, the illicit activities of Apulian criminal groups and their external financiers have expanded without interruption, favored by the privileged geographical position of the region, which is separated only by a short sea strip from the coasts of Albania, Greece and the former Yugoslavia. From the mid-1980s onwards, the fast motor boats owned by Apulian smugglers have started to be harbored in Albania and in Montenegro, and the cigarette cartons are shipped from the factories directly via land to the Albanian and Montenegrian ports.   Furthermore, as has happened in other regions, the means, the expertise and the contacts gained in the tobacco business have also been exploited in other more profitable trades, such as narcotics and arms trafficking and, more recently, in the smuggling of illegal immigrants.   Whereas this last activity seems to be a particularly promising one (Ministero dell'Interno, 1995).   The Apulian crime groups have, since the late 1980s, also come to hold an important role in international heroin trade, due to the outbreak of civil war in Yugoslavia.   This compelled traffickers to abandon the traditional "Balkan route" (linking Turkey to North European markets through the Balkans) and to develop new alternative routes (NNICC, 1994).   Thanks to its position, Apulia today represents the most "promising" land for illegal business and Apulian traffickers enjoy a relevant competitive advantage over older and more traditional mafia actors located in the other region of the Mezzogiorno.

The Local System of Power
The Functions and the Legitimization of the Mafia

It would be a gross oversimplification to reduce Southern Italian mafia consortia's meaning and danger to their provision of illicit commodities. Throughout their history, Cosa Nostra and 'Ndrangheta mafia groups have done much more than that. Sicilian and Calabrian mafia associations have succeeded in monopolizing a variety of localized resources from the mid-19th century onwards through the control of violence. The management of inland large estates; the agricultural products of the rich coastal areas where intensive agriculture was widespread; the mills and presses for grain, wine and olive oil; orders for construction firms or licenses for the retail sale of automobile fuel are just a few examples of the resources over which mafiosi have exercised their monopolizing claims (Hess, 1973; Arlacchi, 1988 Ciconte, 1992; Paoli, 1997).

By merely pursuing their own self-interest, mafia associates have simultaneously fulfilled functions of social regulation within their local communities plagued by the absence of a strong political authority capable of monopolizing violence. "All in all," Judge Falcone admitted, "the mafia has contributed to that the Sicilian society would not sink into social chaos" (1991: 133). The mafiosi provided protection of life and property against the attacks by thieves or bandits in return for the payment of a tribute. They acted as broker between the local community and the outside world and mediated conflicts within the local society. As Calogero Vizzini, one of the most famous mafia bosses of the first post-war period,[6] said, "In any society there must be some people that adjust situations when they become complicated and usually they are the state officials. But when the state is not there or does not have sufficient force, this is done by private individuals" (Montanelli, (1961) 1973:114)

The mafia chiefs regulated conflicts arising from the failure to respect traditional norms and behaviour as well as those entailing the control of social and economic resources or the competition for honour. In these cases, the mafiosi acted as veritable judges of peace and their intervention insured that the threatened order would be restored. As the writer Stajano noted in his book about Africo, a village originally on the Calabrian Aspromonte slope that subsequently moved nearer to the sea as a result of a landslide:

> *The mafia was rooted in the village, it governed misery and poverty, regulated the contrasts and resolved the quarrels that so often occurred in the peasant world because of the use or abuse of pastures, the violation of boundaries and cattle rustling. The 'Ndrangheta behaved as a government authority, it used violence and diplomacy, threat or the art of compromise* (1979:37).

As guarantor of order and social stability, mafiosi also ensured the repression of common crime. Though occasionally exploited for their own aims, individual bandits and bands of brigands were usually eliminated by mafiosi, both because they represented potential powerful competitors and because their actions challenged the mafia's work of guaranteeing order. This activity lasted well up to the beginning of the last post-war period. Immediately after the end of the war, for example, mafiosi eliminated at least 63 bandits in the province of Caltanissetta alone (Chilanti and Farinella, 1964: 38; see also Mangiameli, 1987). In Sicily the mafia also served as an armed agent of the state in the repression of political deviance, killing unions representatives and members of Left-wing parties during several periods of the island's history (Hess, 1973; Romano, 1963).

By exercising the functions that filled the vacuum left by state bodies, mafia acolytes rendered their power accepted and acknowledged as legitimate by the local communities. That is, it was transformed into authority. Mafia associations, in fact, alternatively responded to the needs and interests of different social classes and enjoyed the support or at least the tolerance of wide sections of the community. As Hobsbawm pointed out in his contribution on the mafia in 1959:

> One cannot say it was imposed on the Sicilians by anyone. In a sense, it grew out of the need of all rural classes, and served the purpose of all in varying degrees. For the weak - the peasants and the miners - it provided at least some guarantees that obligations between them would be kept, some guarantee that the usual degree of oppression would not be habitually exceeded...It might even, on occasions, have provided the framework of revolutionary or defensive organization...For the feudal lords it was a means of safeguarding property and authority: for the rural middle classes a means of gaining it. For all, it provided a means of defence against the foreign exploiter -- the Bourbon or the Piedmontese government -- and a method of national or local self-assertion (1959: 40-1).

Though formally condemning mafia violence and occasionally fiercely repressing it, Italian state institutions since the Unification (1860) usually came to terms with the representatives of mafia power and de facto delegated them the maintenance of public order in the territories under their control. Claiming their power over their homeland and effectively controlling a considerable amount of its human, social and economic resources, mafia associations long set their relationships with state institutions on an equal basis, almost like two sovereign entities and have seen their power recognized as legitimate not only in the eyes of the local public opinion but also by state representatives and officials. A veritable "dual regime" (Sabetti, 1984) was established. As the Parliamentary Anti-Mafia Commission finally acknowledged in 1993:

> in practice, the relationships between institutions and mafia took place, for many years, in the form of relationships

> *between two distinct sovereignties: neither would attack the*
> *other as long as each remained within its own boundaries ...*
> *an attack (by State forces) would be made only in response to*
> *an attack by Cosa Nostra, after which they would go back to*
> *being good neighbours again.*

Such complementarity was strengthened by the perfect inclusion of mafia sodalities into the web of clientelistic relationships through which the central government integrated Southern elites into the national political system and secured their invariable support to the government majorities. In such a system, the clientele run by the capomafia and composed by his mafia consociates as well as by his clients and his blood relatives, represented "the specific application of a more general system. Its peculiarity distinguished itself for the fact that in this case one reached the extreme of the armed menace and the suppression of the antagonist and the opponent" (Romano, 1967: 161).

Since the 1880s the relationship between mafia and politics has always been so deep and intense that numerous scholars believe the mafia phenomenon to consist in the interaction between delinquent structures and political circuits (Pezzino, 1994; Romano, 1963). Given the information disclosed by former mafia members, these positions appear one-sided but it is, nonetheless, true that mafia groups owe much of their long-standing power and impunity to their intermingling with politicians. In fact, in exchange for mobilizing their own clientele as well as for using violence to discourage opposing candidates or to convince uncertain electors, even a hundred years ago the mafiosi managed to obtain all kinds of favours. Moreover, since electoral competition was fierce, the latter were often in a position of advantage and could bargain the conditions to support this or that candidate. One of the first favours expected was protection from judicial investigations: if necessary the political patron was prepared to interfere with the competent police officer or judge, in order to guarantee a mild sentence, the revocation of an "ammonizione," the concession of an arms license, etc. In addition, mafiosi were granted substantial contracts for tax collection and for public works. Occasionally the capomafia himself or more frequently his political patron even obtained the control of the town council thanks to which they could further enlarge their following and consolidate their power.

Although state institutions since the end of the last world war progressively exempted mafiosi from the maintenance of public order, the post-war history of mafia groups cannot be understood without taking into account the complicity of wide sectors of state institutions and the political class. The change of regime and the rise of mass parties were not enough to destroy the clientelistic channels used to obtain political consensus in the South. There was, indeed, a transformation from the traditional vertical clientelism, founded on notables, to a horizontal or bureaucratic one, capable of recruiting interest groups at the mass level though an organization of party officials (Tarrow, 1967; see also Fantozzi, 1993). But in such a system of mass patronage the associates of mafia families secured a role no less important than the one they had played vis-a-vis traditional notables. At the same time, the "occupation" of government by the majority party, the Democrazia Cristiana (DC), and the devolution of huge resources to the enhancement of the industrialization of the South multiplied the possibilities of clientelistic exchange (see Gribaudi, 1980; Chubb, 1982, 1989; Walston, 1988; Tranfaglia, 1994).

Thanks to their political protections in the inland agro-towns as well as in Palermo (though the relative weight of this city has substantially increased during the post-war decades), members of mafia families managed to exert a heavy influence over four basic sectors of the regional economy: the credit market, wholesale markets, the labor market and the construction industry. Most important was this last one which, given the overall weakness of the manufacturing sector, accounted -- and still today accounts -- for a disproportionate share of industrial employment in all the Mezzogiorno. Moreover, leaving aside state financed projects, the construction industry was the only one to expand significantly throughout the second half of the 1950s and all the 1960s; in Palermo and most other Southern cities "the economic miracle" merely consisted in an unprecedented and savage urban expansion that rapidly and drastically changed the face of the city within a decade (Chubb, 1982). By the early 1970s the construction industry in the city of Palermo was almost entirely in the hands of by the mafia:

> "... mafia organizations control completely the building sector in Palermo -- the quarries where aggregates are mined, site clearance firms, cement plants, steel depots for the construction industry, sanitary equipment wholesalers and so on..." (Falcone and Turone, 1982).

When mafiosi did not succeed in getting a subcontract, they imposed at least the payment of a protection tax or the recruitment of a mafia acolyte as a guard (the so-called guardiania).

In the mid-1980s the Sicilian mafia consolidated its control over the assignment of public tenders and began to penetrate itself in a pre-existing system of illegal allocation of public contracts previously dominated exclusively by commercial syndicates, politicians and public officials. As stated in the order for preventive detention against Serafino Morici and four others, issued by the Palermo Court in 1991, starting from about 1985:

> ...the mafia associations no longer limited themselves to a merely parasitic exploitation of economic and entrepreneurial activities, which had taken the concrete form of imposing kickbacks, subcontracts and the hiring of labour, but rather aimed at obtaining complete control and substantial internal conditioning of the entrepreneurial world in the public works sector in Sicily (TrPA, 1991: 8).

With such an aim, the mafia began to establish itself in a pre-existing system of illegal allocation of public contracts previously dominated exclusively by commercial syndicates, politicians and public officials. The assumption of this role was favoured by the gradual concentration of power in the hands of

"Toto" Riina and his closest allies, known as Corleonesi.[7] Whereas in the past each mafia family had been free to impose kickbacks on building contractors working within its territory, the coalition of the Corleonesi gradually succeeded in getting exclusive control on over the handling of the relations with contracting firms operating in the public works sector (ibid.:35). Cosa Nostra's intervention in this field was entrusted to Angelo Siino, an entrepreneur of San Giuseppe Jato who, for many years, acted as "ambassador" of the Corleonesi in the public works sector. Together with some collaborators, Siino managed in the latter part of the decade to impose Corleonesi's influence not only over the entire Palermo province but also on large areas of Sicily. Acting as a unitary organization, Cosa Nostra progressively established a close cooperation with the so-called comitati d'affari, made up of entrepreneurial groups, politicians and public officials, which previously had entirely controlled the whole system of parcelling out tenders from the very moment of planning of the public investment. As another inquiry found out, Cosa Nostra's:

> involvement has over the years progressively increased,
> tending to gain in some sectors total and hierarchical control,
> in others, impinging on the space formerly reserved
> exclusively for business syndicates and in others still,
> developing a kind of co-existence with these same syndicates
> (TrPA, 1993: 32).

It is evident that these pacts between mafiosi and politicians would not have been possible without the support or at least the acquiescence of large parts of the Southern Italian people. There were instances of great collective protest in the 1890's and after the end of both world wars, when peasant mobilized for the elimination of the latifundia (that is, great estates) and the distribution of the land. Nonetheless, these protests, often violently repressed by law enforcement agencies and mafiosi, did not succeed in changing economic and social relationships of power. Consistent strata of the Sicilian and Calabrian population, furthermore, received advantages from mafia system of power whereas the national public opinion, up to the late 1970s, largely ignored the mafia phenomenon.

It is the interplay of these three factors - mafia associations, politicians and state officials and the public opinion - that will decide the length and the manner in which the mafia power will survive. Even in this respect however, the perspectives are not entirely optimistic for Sicilian and Calabrian mafia associations.

The Loss of Legitimization and the Rise of Anti-mafia Movements

A slow process of delegitimation of mafia power has been going on since the end of World War II. This process is the result of the contradictory but undeniable economic and cultural modernization, that has overwhelmed the whole country in the post-war decades, reaching even the most peripheral areas of the Mezzogiorno.

The evolution of the larger social and cultural systems has progressively undermined the mafia subsystem of meaning by which mafia chiefs had long legitimated their power both in face of the local communities and their own acolytes. It is, first of all, the subculture of honour, by which mafia associates have long justified their use of private violence and political authority that has, more and more, come under attack. Likewise, its connected ideal of life, inspired by aristocratic values, of the man that does not dirty his hands with material labours, has been progressively substituted in the minds of the inhabitants by the more trivial pursuit of wealth the primary parameters of man's value and basis of an individual's reputation. The growing emphasis placed by mafia associates on the economic dimension can itself be understood as an attempt to "keep up" with the modernization of the whole country, to fight the threat of being marginalized and to maintain the same social status by adapting to the values that were becoming prevalent, that is, by trading honour for wealth (Arlacchi, 1988).

The cultural evolution, as well as the underlying social and economic developments, has far from proceeded in a steady and linear way. The process of state centralization of violence, for example, to which the decline of the subculture of honour is primarily linked, has made overall a considerable advance throughout the post-war decades and recovered the gap lost in the anomic years following the Allied occupation of the Mezzogiorno in 1943. Nonetheless, this trend has also been marked by considerable steps backward, by moments of carelessness and even shady pacts with illegal centers of power (among which mafia organizations), "owing in part to the fact that what the Italian state accomplishes with one hand it often undermines with the other" (Schneiders, 1994: 240). In the 1970s, for example, when law enforcement attention largely focused on terrorism, state monopoly of violence underwent a serious crisis in mafia areas, which was exploited by the Sicilian mafiosi to make unprecedented attacks against state officials. The same institutions - such as mass parties and unions - that challenged the mafia families' traditional functions of regulation and articulation of interests, gave an ambiguous message. On one hand, in fact, they were the carriers of more universalistic instances of representation. On the other, they often incorporated mafia clienteles and relied on mafia methods, thus, further perpetuating the power of the former and legitimating the latter.

Notwithstanding these inconsistencies, the "enlightened" minority of Sicilians and Calabrians that openly questioned the cultural legacy of their home region and opposed mafia dominion even against their own short-term interests, kept growing. A clear acceleration came about in autumn 1982, when General Carlo Alberto Dalla Chiesa, who had been sent three months to Sicily as prefect of the Palermo province and high commissioner against the mafia, was killed together with his wife and driver in Palermo. This murder came at the end of a three-year period during which more than 15 state officials and politicians had been shot by Cosa Nostra[8] and mafia internecine killings often bloodied Palermo, as if to mark the rise of the Corleonesi hegemony. Two weeks afterwards, the La Torre law, named after the Sicilian Communist leader who had also been killed by the mafia in April 1982, was passed. It introduced the crime of delinquent association of mafia type (art. 416 bis Penal Code) and authorized the seizure and forfeiture of illegally acquired property of those suspected of art. 416 bis (see Turone, 1995). Between 1982 and 1986 nearly 15,000 men were denounced in all Italy for criminal association of mafia type. Four hundred and six were brought to trial by the Palermo investigating magistrates of the anti-mafia pool in the so-called maxi-processo, which was based on the declarations of Tommaso Buscetta and other important mafia turncoats. More than half of the defendants - including several mafia chiefs -- received heavy sentences, which were definitively confirmed by the Supreme Court in January 1992 (TrPA, 1986; (1986), 1992; Chinnici and Santino, 1992).

The state anti-mafia campaign was supported and encouraged by widespread public support. Shocked by the murder of Dalla Chiesa and his young wife, the Palermitani participated in unprecedented public demonstrations, including a spontaneous candlelight procession in honour of his memory. Since then a "protean and multifaceted anti-mafia movement" has developed (Schneiders, 1994). In January 1984, representatives of the city party section and trade unions, responding to other assassinations, formed the so-called Coordinamento Antimafia, whose activities included organizing conferences and demonstrations on behalf of mafia victims. In 1985 Leoluca Orlando, a member of a reformist, left-wing current of the Christian Democratic Party who had taken a clear stance against the mafia, began to serve as mayor. During his administration, which lasted up to 1990, the city hall became a focal point for the condemnation of mafia and its supportive political culture. For the multiplicity of activities that accompanied Palermo's maxi-processo, the mid-1980s were labelled as "Palermo's springtime."

After a period of retreat and disillusionment in the late 1980s, anti-mafia movements recovered energy and vitality in the early 1990s. Following the model of the Associazione commercianti di Capo d'Orlando (ME), which collectively rendered public extortion threats and brought racketeers to stand trials, many anti-racket associations and movements have flourished in Sicily and in the rest of the country (Grasso, 1992). As a result, in 1992, the year of peak activism, denunciations of extorsions rose by 17.6 percent at the national level and by almost 40 percent in Sicily. Gathered in a national net, anti-racket associations have also been able to obtain the creation of a "Fondo di solidarieti per le vittime dell'estorsione" in 1992 to support shopkeepers and entrepreneurs whose activities and properties were damaged as a result of their stance.[9]

The shocking murders committed in rapid succession of the magistrates Giovanni Falcone and Paolo Borsellino also moved large strata of the Sicilian civil society and of the entire country. Demonstrations of an unprecedented dimension took place in Palermo as well as in other parts of Italy: a march organized in memory of Giovanni Falcone thirty days after the Capaci massacre brought to Palermo an estimated 500,000 people. Several anti-mafia initiatives have since then flourished in Palermo (Alajmo, 1994; Schneiders, 1994).

State institutions also reacted to these events with a strong counterattack, which produced the highest peak of anti-mafia activities in the last 30 years. In the summer of 1992 a new anti-mafia act was passed, according to which most mafia chiefs were to be detained in special high security prisons, 7,000 soldiers were sent to Sicily to help civil police forces and anti-mafia investigations were substantially facilitated. Since then, up to early 1994, virtually all mafia bosses, some of whom had been on the hide for decades, were captured and important inquiries concerning the collusion between mafia members and politicians were initiated.

The enactment of a law to protect Justice collaborators and their families, the wide range of provisions foreseen by the law of August, 1992 as well as the successes of law enforcement forces have favoured the growth of the phenomenon of pentitismo, powerfully intensifying the internal tensions and contradictions of mafia associations.   Pentiti (e.g. former organized crime affiliates who decided to cooperate with law enforcement agencies) numbered 1,177 as of June 30, 1996 (Ministero dell'Interno, 1996).   The declarations made by Justice collaborators have been an incentive for broadening and updating of the investigators' body of knowledge on the different facets of Italian organized crime and led to the localization of fugitives and to the beginning of police investigations.

As a result of this process of delegitimation, the spaces of mediation open to politicians and state officials ready to come to terms with the mafia have greatly shrank. Thanks to the greater sensitivity demonstrated by police forces and magistrates in the prosecution of the crimes against the public administration as well as the increased reactivity of the public opinion towards corruption and embezzlement episodes, today the costs and the risks of mediation and protection of mafia interests in political and institutional seats have considerably grown.   These costs have been further increased by the adoption of new legislative instruments and by a higher readiness to grant authorization to investigate against the members of Parliament. ·Since the approval of the Law n. 221/91, "concerning the dismissal of the councils of communes, provinces and other local institutions infiltrated and conditioned by the mafia," more than 80 communal councils have been dismissed in Campania, Apulia, Calabria and Sicily (Ministero dell'Interno, 1994). Furthermore, in the XI legislature (1992-94), dozens of requests of authorization to proceed against single deputies concerning serious crimes such as delinquent association of mafia type, cooperation in murder, extortion and corruption, have been sent to and granted by the Parliament. After the 1994 national elections and the loss of parliamentary immunity, many former deputies (even a former Interior Minister) have been arrested. Accusations of connivance with organized crime have also been addressed to numerous magistrates investigated by their own colleagues and suspended from their duties (Di Lello, 1995; Stille, 1995).

The weakening of popular support and the acceleration of the anti-mafia state action has been favoured by the contemporary wave of investigations targeting corrupt and collusive agreements between politicians and state employees and private entrepreneurs. Starting out with the arrest in February

1992 of the obscure manager of a Milanese public institution, the investigations of the Milanese "Clean Hands" Prosecutors' pool escalated in a few weeks time, bringing to light a widespread system of illegality and corruption (the so-called Tangentopoli). An unexpected domino effect took place, which could not be stopped in time by the already weakened and delegitimated centers of political power and which led to the collapse of the Italian political system. Backed by a strong popular support, the magistrates acquired an unprecedented degree of freedom and power vis-a-vis politicians and were thus able to push forward their investigations and reach the "heart" of the Italian political and economic system (see Magatti, 1996; Della Porta, 1992; Della Porta and Vannucci, 1994).

Without denying motivations of moral order in some, the propagation of their ideas as well as of a nation-wide opposition towards corrupt practices was given impetus by the escalation of costs brought about by the clientelistic system and by the restrictions on an ulterior increase in public debt in the name of welfare programs. The impact of these changes was strongest in Southern Italy that had most intensively relied on state jobs and welfare services (such as civil invalidity pensions and rural unemployment funds) as well as on the endless renewal of financial aid for public intervention (meant to alleviate the tensions and distortions produced by modernization without industrialisation). In the early 1990s public extraordinary intervention for the development of the South came to a brusque halt. The Department and the Agency for the Mezzogiorno, that had taken the place of the Cassa per il Mezzogiorno created in the 1950s, were suppressed starting on May 1st, 1993 and their activities entrusted to a liquidator whose job was to transfer the functions of the suppressed bodies to the agencies of the ordinary state administration. Nor was the interruption of extraordinary funding replaced by the consolidation of ordinary aid programmes for depressed areas of the national territory. "A heavy anti-Southern mortgage," fed by the scarce results produced by thousands of Italian Lira billions spent in the previous decades to stimulate Southern Italian development, long prevented the conversion into law of the bills necessary to regulate the new supportive intervention of ordinary type and to coordinate the action of the different public bodies involved (SVIMEZ, 1995). At the same time, as the politics of extraordinary intervention came to a brusque halt, welfare benefits were also severely cut as a result of the no longer postponable need to reduce the state deficit (see Trigilia, 1994).

The abrupt stop in the early 1990s of these practices greatly affected the fragile basis of consensus of a corrupt and increasingly delegitimated Southern political class. It also had a direct impact upon Cosa Nostra and 'Ndrangheta families from which the control of public tenders market in the late 1980s was not only the primary source of profit in comparison to even the narcotics trade but also a fundamental tool through which to impose a lasting dominion over the social, economic and political life of their communities.

An Open Outcome
To reassert their power and to face the rapid decrease of popular support,

Sicilian mafia chiefs have increasingly relied on brutal force, not only internally, vis-a-vis their own subordinates, but also externally. Whereas the first murders of state men in the early 1980s were largely a manifestation of the newly amassed economic availability (Lodato, 1994; Stille, 1995), the resort to open violence by the Sicilian Cosa Nostra in the early 1990s appear - notwithstanding the impressive modalities and the display of sophisticated war techniques - above all a "desperate" attempt to secure people's support and silence by force and to oblige colluded politicians to respect pacts.

Cosa Nostra leaders appear to be caught in contradictory exigencies. The massacres of 1993[10] were principally aimed at reaffirming the leadership of the detained major Cosa Nostra bosses vis-a-vis their lower-ranking men. In fact, as a result of penitentiary restrictions introduced by the anti-mafia bill in August 1992,[11] mafia bosses could no longer keep in touch with their men outside and exercise their command, whereas low and middle ranking "men of honour" in prison became increasingly restless as they no longer felt adequately protected by the organization's leadership.[12] To reassure Cosa Nostra "people" and to warn their political referents of possible retaliations, mafia bosses launched a terrorist strategy, hoping to induce state institutions to tacitly revise the new detention regulations and to stop judges from using the pentiti's confessions while, at the same time, trying to discredit these in various ways. Such a strategy, however, not only fell short of the expected results (notwithstanding the many attempts of several politicians and state officials to follow such a course) but also produced negative effects on the stance of the public opinion towards the mafia issue and strengthened popular support towards judicial investigations.

Yet, it would be a gross underassessment to consider this gradual loss of legitimization as a steady and irrevocable process. Especially in the Reggio Calabria province mafia families still enjoy a high degree of social consensus and the process leading up to the rejection of the 'Ndrangheta and of its mafia values has so far involved smaller proportions of the population, being much slower than in Sicily. While in this last region anti-mafia demonstrations have become fairly frequent and hundreds of thousands of people participate, it was only in the summer of 1992 that in Calabria for the first time a large array of citizens convened together in Calabria to march against the mafia. While in many respects the support given to the 'Ndrangheta is more "apparent" than real, it being the result of an atmosphere of intimidation and terror that the mafia groups produce, it is also true that in many areas of Calabria "civil society and the public institutions have shown a very weak, uncertain and inadequate opposition which is symptomatic of a weak civil conscience used to decades of mafia arrogance" (TrRC, 1988: 194). Even in Sicily, although a considerable part of the Sicilian society has turned against the nihilistic and cynical components of the cultural heredity of the island, there are still wide areas where fear, passivity and, in some cases open consensus dominate. The magistrates of the Procura della Repubblica di Catania, for example, have recently lamented the fact that still today homicides take place at the presence of several people, in broad daylight, for which no witnesses, not even among the relatives of the victim, can be found (TrCT, 1994: 38).

The reasons for the survival of mafia power do not lie only in the limitations and the contradictions of the process of refusal of mafia values. Mafia associations still have many resources:

- First of all, they have the money amassed over the last thirty years: though much smaller amounts than reported by the press the sums are, nevertheless, consistent. Likewise, notwithstanding the difficulties recently encountered in several economic enterprises particularly by Cosa Nostra families, their control over local resources and the local job market is still relevant today.

- Both mafia consortia continued to possess a huge military force, as the repeated seizures of large arsenals of arms and explosives in both regions proved. Not only do they have access to automatic weapons but also to explosives and military-type weapons (missiles, recoilless cannons, piercing munitions, etc.). In fact, the recent acts of terrorism are undeniable proof of the fact that Cosa Nostra has access to sophisticated explosives and enjoys effective logistic support.

- Notwithstanding the fact that mafia consortia's ramified net of political and institutional connections has begun to be targeted by judicial inquiries, a considerable number of politicians and state officials is still ready to advocate mafia interests. The bulk of this group is represented by members of the political and institutional establishment who have "recycled" themselves in the so-called "Second Republic" and who are subjugated to mafia interests. Their political survival depends, in fact, on the cover-up of their past and present collusive agreements especially from judicial investigations, whereas their physical well being depends on the ability to confute accusations of betrayal by mafia members. Beyond monetary rewards, the identification with mafia interests is for these actors almost total complete.

This web of contacts and alliances was to be exploited in 1993 to launch a separatist project that by creating an independent state in Southern Italy or at least in Sicily, would have enabled mafia associations to exert a tight influence over its political and judicial decision-making (Sabella, 1996). This project went through the first implementation stages and even obtained some promising success. At the election for the renewal of the Catania provincial council in January 1994, a separatist list Sicilia Libera, created by Tullio Cannella acting on the orders of the Corleonesi, gained about nine percent of the consensus. Initiatives to support such a plan were also taken by the bosses of the Calabrian mafia association. The plan, however, came to a sudden halt, as Cosa Nostra and 'Ndrangheta bosses thought their interests could be represented at the national level by the alliance of center-right and right parties that took shape in the late-1993 under the leadership of TV tycoon Silvio Berlusconi and that won the March 1994 national elections. As the Calabrian pentito Cesare Polifroni stated right after the elections:

> In this moment waiting for the politics of the new government is the prevalent attitude. I may say in this respect that there was the order of all the organizations in Sicily, Calabria and Campania to vote either for Berlusconi or for Pannella, with the certainty that they were going to be the winning group. We believe that the new government will dismantle all the repressive legislation and go back to the "free state" (PrRC, 1995:5071).

Despite repeated attempts to discredit pentiti and to reform the anti-mafia legislation, the Berlusconi government, lasting only a few months, did not succeed in satisfying mafia expectations. Nonetheless, the investigations concerning the 1994 elections, initiated by both the Palermo and the Reggio Calabria Procure della Repubblica, clearly demonstrate that the basin of mafia supporters in the political and institutional establishment is constantly fed and renewed by politicians willing to make a "pact with the devil" in order to foster their political career as well as by state officials ready to face the increased risks of mafia cooperation so as to integrate their income with occult rewards and gifts.

- Lastly, although a process of deinstitutionalization is taking place especially within the Sicilian consortium and the decline of mafia subculture is clear, the perpetuation of mafia power is still enhanced on a systemic level by the unaccomplished (and largely not even yet begun) institutionalization of new mechanisms of social regulation that provide effective alternatives to mafia and patronage practices. Nor can such a process be accomplished in a short time. As well as re-writing some basic rules regulating political competition, in fact, which have recently been greatly debated in Italy, this transformation entails the development and assimilation of a new political culture, the implementation of a set of norms that effectively ensure effective market competition and the consolidation of boundaries between the political and the economic sphere.

As long as these steps are not taken, however, there is a persisting tendency to fall back on old mechanisms of social regulation, irrespective of their decreasing legitimation. Whereas the party identified with mass patronage has suddenly fallen in upon itself as a result of the "Clean Hands" investigation, old methods of political aggregation and distribution of resources may be replicated and exploited by new political subjects. Far from undermining the mass support for the machine, the economic crisis, that has been plaguing

Southern Italy since the early 1990s as a consequence of the abrupt stop put to all state programs aimed at promoting economic development, may actually strengthen it. As the supply of available resources shrinks, the role of clientele as intermediary between individual citizens and state resources is enhanced, for people in need are prepared to try all sorts of channels so as to get a job or obtain a state pension. Furthermore, falling back on old practices of corruption and collusion may paradoxically be fostered by the spreading disappointment resulting from the slowness and contradictory nature of the reform process.

Thus, the change, instigated by the judicial investigations, may end up being largely illusory. By focusing on specific events (on which the amount of judicial evidence in more solid), the magistrates may, in the end, succeed only in altering the equilibria within the underworld, favouring specific groups and actors at the expense of others.

Notwithstanding their decreasing legitimation, mafia associations may, in such a context, be able to maintain a significant power for a long while yet. There may be a reduction of the authority enjoyed by capimafia in their areas of settlement as well as new organizational changes to cope with the increased need of secrecy but, as long as they are able to preserve even a small share of the illegal markets turnover and to influence the allocation of local resources, there will always be a pool of youngsters who hope to rapidly make a lot of money ready to enter Cosa Nostra and 'Ndrangheta families. Likewise, as long as the cosche of the two consortia are able to redistribute resources within the local context and to act as intermediaries with politicians, they will have at least a minimal level of consensus within the local population. It will be - and already is - much more fragile than in the past, since it is based only on the constant renewal of favours and exchanges, but such consensus is nonetheless sufficient to exert a lasting influence on the local political competition.

Ultimately, the definitive defeat of mafia associations cannot but take place at the same time as the deep change of the social and cultural system that has long acknowledged and nurtured them.

---

*Dr. **Letizia Paoli** is a researcher in the Department of Criminology of the Max-*

Planck-Institut für auslandisches und inter-nationales Strafrecht in Freiburg, Germany. She recived a Ph.D. at the Department of Political and Social Sciences of the European University Institute in Firenze, Italy, in June 1997, defending a thesis on Sicilian and Calabrian mafia associations. She graduated from the University of Florence under the supervision of Prof. Pino Arlacchi. She was a consultant to the Italian Ministry of the Interior (1992-1995) and to the United Nations Office for Drug Control and Crime Prevention (1997) in Vienna.

References

Alajmo, R., (1994), *Un lenzuolo contro la mafia*, Palermo.

Alexander, S. (1986), *The Pizza Connection: Lawyers, Money. Drugs and Mafia*, London: Weidenfield & Nicholson.

Arlacchi, P. (1983, 1986, 1988), *Mafia Business. The Mafia Ethic and the Spirit of Capitalism*, Oxford: Oxford University Press.

Arlacchi, P. (1988), "Saggio sui mercati illegali," *Rassegna Italiana di Sociologia*, XXIX, 3:403-436.

Arlacchi, P. (1992, 1993), *Men of Dishonor. Inside the Sicilian mafia: An Account of Antonino Calderone*, New York: William Morrow.

Arlacchi, P. (1994), *Addio Cosa Nostra. La vita di Tommaso Buscetta*, Milano: Rizzoli.

Arlacchi, P. (1995), *Il processo. Giulio Andreotti sotto accusa a Palermo*, Milano: Rizzoli.

Biden, J. R. (1982), "The Sicilian Connection: Southwest Asian Heroin en Route to the United States," *Report of Senator J. R. Biden to the U.S. Senate Committee on Foreign Affairs*.

BINM, U.S. Department of State, Bureau of International Narcotics Matters (1993), *International Narcotics Control Strategy Report*, April.

BINM, U.S. Department of State, Bureau of International Narcotics Matters (1992), *International Narcotics Control Strategy Report*, March.

Blok, A. (1974, 1988), *The Mafia of a Sicilian Village, 1860-1960: a Study of Violent Peasant Entrepreneurs*, New York and Oxford: Polity Press.

Blumenthal, R. (1988), *Last Days of the Sicilians. At War with the Mafia. The FBI Assault on the Pizza Connection*, New York: Times Book.

Calabri M. A. (1991), *Le mani della mafia: vent'anni di finanza e politica attraverso la storia del Banco Ambrosiano*, Roma: Edizioni Associate.

Chilanti, F. and M. Farinella (1964), *Rapporto sulla mafia*, Palermo: Flaccovio.

Chinnici, G. and U. Santino (1992), *Gabbie voute. Processi per omicidio a Palermo dal 1983 al maxiprocesso*, Milano: Angeli.

Chubb, J. (1982), *Patronage, Power, and Poverty in Southern Italy. A Tale of Two Cities*, Cambridge: Cambridge University Press.

Chubb, J. (1989), *The Mafia and Politics: the Italian State under Siege*, Ithaca, NY: Cornell University Press.

Ciconte, E. (1992), *'Ndrangheta dall'Unitad oggi*, Bari: Laterza.

Ciconte, E. (1996), *Processo alla 'ndrangheta*, Bari, Laterza.

Comitato provinciale stupefacenti di Roma, (1971), "Relazione del 24 maggio 1971 del dott. Giorgio Staffieri, dirigente la Sezione Narcotici del Comitato provinciale stupefacenti di Roma su mafia, contrabbando di tabacchi e traffico di stupefacenti nella provincia di Roma," in Commissione Parlamentare d'inchiesta sul fenomeno della mafia in Sicilia, ed., *Documentazione allegata alla relazione conclusiva*, doc. XXIII, n. 1/VIII, vol. IV, tomo XIV:1005-13.

Commissione P2, Commissione parlamentare d'inchiesta sulla loggia massonica P2, (1984), *Relazione di maggioranza e Relazioni di minoranza*, Roma, Camera dei Deputati, doc. XXIII, IX Legislatura.

Commissione Sindona, Commissione Parlamentare d'inchiesta sul caso Sindona e sulle responsabilit politiche ed amministrative ad esso eventualmente connesse, (1982a), *Relazione di maggioranza (relatore Azzaro)*, VIII Legislatura, doc. XXIII, n. 2-*sexies*,

Roma, Camera dei Deputati.

1982b, *Relazione di minoranza (relatore Teodori)*, VIII Legislatura, doc. XXIII, n. 2, Roma, Camera dei Deputati.

Cornwell, R., (1983), *God's Banker. An account of life and death of Roberto Calvi*, London, Victor Galleancz.

CPM, Commissione Parlamentare d'inchiesta sul fenomeno della mafia e sulle altre associazioni similari, (1992), *Audizione del collaboratore di giustizia Antonino Calderone*, 11 novembre, XI legislatura.

(1993), *Relazione sui rapporti tra mafia e politica*, doc. XXIII, n.2, XI legislatura, 6 aprile.

(1994a), *Insediamenti e infiltrazioni di soggetti ed organizzazioni di tipo mafioso in aree non tradizionali*, doc. XXIII, n. 11, XI legislatura.

(1994b), *Relazione conclusiva*, doc. XXIII, n. 14, XI legislatura, 18 febbraio.

CPMS, Commissione Parlamentare d'inchiesta sul fenomeno della mafia in Sicilia, 1971, *Relazione sull'indagine riguardante casi di singoli mafiosi*, doc. XXIII, n. 2-*quater*, V legislatura.

(1972), "Sintesi delle conclusioni cui era pervenuto nel corso della V legislatura il comitato per le indagini sui casi dei singoli mafiosi, sul traffico di stupefacenti e sul legame tra fenomeno mafioso e gangsterismo americano', enclosed to Idem, (1976b), *Relazione sul traffico mafioso di tabacchi e stupefacenti nonch sui rapporti tra mafia e gangsterismo italo americano (Relatore: Zuccal)*, doc. XXIII, n. 2, VI legislatura: 447-93.

(1976a), *Relazione conclusiva (Relatore: Carraro)*, doc. XXIII, n. 2, VI legislatura: 1-328.

(1976b), *Relazione sul traffico mafioso di tabacchi e stupefacenti nonch sui rapporti tra mafia e gangsterismo italo americano (Relatore: Zuccal)*, doc. XXIII, n. 2, VI legislatura:329-567.

DEA, Drug Enforcement Administration, (1992), *Cocaine Situation in Europe*, October.

(1995), *Drug Trafficking in Europe*, June.

Della Porta, D., (1992), *Lo scambio occulto. Casi di corruzione politica in Italia*, Bologna, Il Mulino.

Della Porta, D. and A. Vannucci, (1994), *Corruzione politica e amministrazione pubblica. Risorse, meccanismi, attori*, Bologna, Il Mulino.

Di Lello, G., (1994), *Giudici*, Palermo, Sellerio.

Falcone, G., (1991), in cooperation with Marcelle Padovani, *Cose di Cosa Nostra*, Milano, Rizzoli.

Fantozzi, P. (1993), *Politica, clientela e regolazione sociale. Il Mezzogiorno nella questione politica italiana*, Soveria Mannelli, Rubbettino.

Grasso, T. (1992), *Contro il racket. Come opporsi al ricatto mafioso*, Bari-Roma, Laterza.

Gribaudi, G., (1980), *Mediatori, Antropologia del potere democristiano nel Mezzogiorno*, Torino, Rosenberg and Sellier.

Guardia di Finanza, (1971a), "Relazione dell'11 giugno 1971 del maggiore Bernardo Angelozzi del Comando Generale della Guardia di Finanza su mafia e traffico di stupefacenti," in Commissione Parlamentare d'inchiesta sul fenomeno della mafia in Sicilia, ed., *Documentazione allegata alla relazione conclusiva*, doc. XXIII, n. 1/VIII, vol. IV, tomo XIV:1015-32.

(1971b), "Relazione dell'11 giugno 1971 del capitano Pietro Soggiu del Comando Generale della Guardia di Finanza su mafia e contrabbando di tabacchi," in Commissione Parlamentare d'inchiesta sul fenomeno della mafia in Sicilia, ed.,

Documentazione allegata alla relazione conclusiva, doc. XXIII, n. 1/VIII, vol. IV, tomo XIV:1035-1066.

Hagan, F. (1983), "The Organized Crime Continuum: a Further Specification of a New Conceptual Model," *Criminal Justice Review*, 8, Spring:52-57.

Hess, H. (1970, 1973), *Mafia and Mafiosi. The Structure of Power*, Westmead, Saxon House.

Hobsbawn, E. J. (1959, 1974), *Primitive Rebels. Studies in Archaic Forms of Social Movement in the 19th and 20th Centuries*, Manchester, Manchester University Press.

Lamour C. and M. R. Lamberti (1974), *The International Connection. Opium from Growers to Pushers*, New York, Pantheon Books.

Legione Carabinieri di Palermo (1973), Interessi mafiosi nel contrabbando di tabacchi e nel traffico di stupefacenti', in CPMS ed., *Documentazione allegata alla relazione conclusiva*, doc. XXIII, n. 1/VIII, vol. IV, tomo XIV: 1479-1563.

Lewis, R. (1985), "Serious Business: the Global Heroin Economy," in A. Henman, R. Lewis and T. Malyon, *Big Deal. The Politics of the Illicit Drug Business*, London, Pluto Press:5-49.

Lodato, S. (1994), *Quindici anni di mafia. La guerra che lo Stato pu ancora vincere*, Milano, Rizzoli.

Lombard, (1980), *Soldi truccati. I segreti del sistema Sindona*, Milano, Feltrinelli.

Magatti, M. (1996), *Corruzione politica e societ italiana*, Bologna, Il Mulino.

Mangiameli, R. (1987), "La regione in guerra (1943-50)," in M. Aymard and G. Giarrizzo, eds., *La Sicilia*, Torino, Giulio Einaudi Editore:485-601.

Ministero dell'Interno (1993), *Rapporto annuale sul fenomeno della criminalit organizzata per il 1992*, Roma.

Ministero dell'Interno (1994), *Rapporto annuale sul fenomeno della criminalit organizzata per il 1993*, Roma, Camera dei Deputati, doc. XXXVIII-bis, n. 1, XII legislatura.

Ministero dell'Interno (1995), *Rapporto annuale sul fenomeno della criminalit organizzata per il 1994*, Roma.

Ministero dell'Interno (1996), *Relazione semestrale sull'attivit svolta e i risultati conseguiti dalla Direzione Investigativa Antimafia nel secondo semestre del 1995*, Roma.

Montanelli, I. (1961, 1973), *Pantheon minore*, Milano, Mondadori.

Naylor, R. T. (1987), *Hot Money and the Politics of Debt*, New York, Simon & Schuster.

Naylor, R. T. (1995), "Loose Cannons: Cover Commerce and Underground Finance in the Modern Arms Black Market," *Crime, Law and Social Change*, 22:1-57.

Naylor, R. T. (1996), "The Underworld of Gold," *Crime, Law and Social Change*, 25: 191-241.

NNICC, National Narcotics Intelligence Consumers Committee (1993), *The NNICC 1992: the Supply of Illicit Drugs to the United States*, Washington, September.

NNICC, National Narcotics Intelligence Consumers Committee (1994), *The NNICC 1993: the Supply of Illicit Drugs to the United States*, Washington, September.

NNICC, National Narcotics Intelligence Consumers Committee (1995), *The NNICC 1994: the Supply of Illicit Drugs to the United States*, Washington, September.

Pantaleone, M. (1962, 1972), *Mafia e politica 1943-1962. Le radici sociali della mafia e i suoi sviluppi pi recenti*, Torino, Einaudi.

Paoli, L. (1993), "Criminalit organizzata e finanza internazionale," *Rassegna Italiana di Sociologia*, XXXIV, n. 3, luglio-settembre:391-423.

Paoli, L. (1997), *The Pledge of Secrecy. Culture, Structure and Action of Mafia Associations,* Ph.D. Dissertation, European University Institute, Firenze.

182 Letizia Paoli

Pezzino, P. (1994), "Mafia, stato e societ nella Sicilia contemporanea: secoli XIX e XX," in G. Fiandaca and S. Costantino, eds., *La mafia, le mafie*, Bari Laterza:5-31.

Piselli F. and G. Arrighi (1985), "Parentela, clientela e comunit" in P. Bevilacqua and A. Placanica, eds., *La Calabria,* Torino, Einaudi:367-493.

PrCT, Procura della Repubblica di Catania, Direzione Distrettuale Antimafia (1995), *Richiesta per l'applicazione di misure cautelari nei confronti di Cultrera Felice + 8*, 19 marzo.

PrRC, Procura della Repubblica di Reggio Calabria, Direzione Distrettuale Antimafia (1993), *Richiesta di ordini di custodia cautelare in carcere nel procedimento contro Morabito Giuseppe + 161*, 5 novembre.

PrRC, Procura della Repubblica di Reggio Calabria, Direzione Distrettuale Antimafia (1995), *Richiesta di ordini di custodia cautelare in carcere e di contestuale rinvio a giudizio nel procedimento contro Condello Pasquale + 477*, luglio.

PrMI, Procura della Repubblica di Milano (1991), *Profili penali dell'espatrio e della morte di Roberto Calvi nel giugno 1982. Requisitorie definitive del Pubblico Ministero Pierluigi Maria Dell'Osso*, 29 luglio.

PrMI, Procura della Repubblica di Milano (1988), *Requisitoria del Pubblico Ministero dell'istruttoria per la bancarotta del Banco Ambrosiano, Pierluigi Maria Dell'Osso*, 28 luglio.

Romano, S. F. (1963, 1967), *Storia della mafia*, Milano: Sugar.

Sabella, A. (1996), "Interview with dott. Alfonso Sabella, member of the Direzione Distrettuale Antimafia, Procura della Repubblica di Palermo," May.

Schneider J. and P. Schneider (1976), *Culture and Political Economy in Western Sicily*, New York: Academic Press.

Schneider J. and P. Schneider (1994), "Mafia, Antimafia and the Question of Sicilian Culture," *Politics and Society*, 22, 2:237-58.

Spero, J.E. (1980), *The Failure of the Franklin National Bank. Challenge to the International Banking System*, New York: Columbia University Press.

Stajano, C. (1979), *Africo: una storia italiana di governanti e governati, di mafia, di potere e di lotta*, Torino: Einuadi.

Stajano, C. (1991), *Un eroe borghese. Il caso dell'avvocato Giorgio Ambrosoli assassinato dalla mafia politica*, Torino: Einaudi.

Sterling, C. (1994), *Thieves' World*, New York: Simon and Schuster.

Stille, A. (1995), *Excellent Cadavers. The Mafia and the Death of the First Italian Republic*, London: Jonathan Cape.

Svimez, Associazione per lo sviluppo dell'industria nel Mezzogiorno (1995), *Rapporto 1995 sull'economia del Mezzogiorno*, Bologna: Il Mulino.

Tarrow, S. G. (1967), *Peasant Communism in Southern Italy*, New Haven and London: Yale University Press.

Tosches, N. (1986), *Power on Earth*, New York: Arbor House.

Tranfaglia, N. ed. (1994), *Cirillo, Ligato e Lima. Tre storie di mafia e politica*, Bari: Laterza.

TrCT, Tribunale di Catania, Ufficio del Giudice per le Indagini Preliminari (1994), *Ordinanza di custodia cautelare in carcere nei confronti di Cocuzza Antonino + 44*

TrCT, Tribunale di Catania, Ufficio del Giudice per le Indagini Preliminari (1995), *Ordinanza di custodia cautelare in carcere nei confronti di Cannizzo Giovanni, s.d.*

TrLO, Tribunale di Locri (1993), *Ordinanza di custodia cautelare in carcere nei confronti di Filippone Salvatore + 12*, 30 ottobre.

TrMI, Tribunale di Milano (1984, 1986), Ufficio Istruzione Processi Penali, *Sentenza-ordinanza di rinvio a giudizio nei confronti di Michele Sindona*, luglio, published in

Sindona. L'atto di accusa dei giudici di Milano, Roma, Editori Riuniti.

TrMI, Tribunale di Milano (1989), Ufficio Istruzione Processi Penali, *Ordinanza di rinvio a giudizio per la bancarotta del Banco Ambrosiano emessa dai giudici istruttori Antonio Pizzi e Renato Bricchetti*, Milano, 7 aprile.

TrMI, Tribunale di Milano (1994), Ufficio del Giudice per le Indagini Preliminari, *Ordinanza di custodia cautelare in carcere nei confronti di Cirelli Lucia + 16*, 3 giugno.

TrPA, Tribunale di Palermo (1982), Ufficio Istruzione Processi Penali, *Sentenza-ordinanza di rinvio a giudizio nei confronti di Rosario Spatola + 119*, s.d.

TrPA, Tribunale di Palermo (1986), Ufficio Istruzione Processi Penali, *Sentenza-ordinanza di rinvio a giudizio nei confronti di Abbate Giovanni + 706*, novembre.

TrPA, Tribunale di Palermo (1986, 1992), ed., *Mafia: l'atto d'accusa dei giudici di Palermo, estratti da Tribunale di Palermo, Ufficio Istruzione Processi Penali, Sentenza-ordinanza emessa nel procedimento penale contro Abbate Giovanni + 706*, Roma: Editori Riuniti.

TrPA, Tribunale di Palermo (1991), Ufficio del Giudice per le Indagini Preliminari, *Ordinanza di custodia cautelare in carcere nei confronti di Morici Serafino + 4*, 9 luglio.

TrPA, Tribunale di Palermo (1993), Ufficio del Giudice per le Indagini Preliminari, *Ordinanza di custodia cautelare in carcere nei confronti di Riina Salvatore + 24*, 18 maggio.

TrRC, Tribunale di Reggio Calabria (1988), Ufficio Istruzione Processi Penali, *Ordinanza sentenza di rinvio a giudizio contro Albanese Mario + 190*.

TrRC, Tribunale di Reggio Calabria (1993), Ufficio del Giudice per le Indagini Preliminari, *Ordinanza di custodia cautelare in carcere nei confronti di Archin Rocco Carlo + 44*, 8 gennaio.

TrTO, Tribunale di Torino, Ufficio del Giudice per le Indagini Preliminari (1993), *Ordinanza di custodia cautelare in carcere nei confronti di Marando Pasquale + 51*, 15 ottobre.

Turone, G. (1995), *Il delitto di associazione mafiosa*, Milano, Giuffr.

Walston, J. (1988), *The Mafia and Clientelism. Roads to Rome in Post-War Calabria*, London and New York: Routledge.

Notes

[1] The former mostly had contacts with the New York Bonanno family whose chief as well as many of its affiliates originated from Castellammare del Golfo. Bonanno himself travelled to Sicily in 1957 and, though there is no proof, it seems probable that he actually arranged drug trafficking deals (Guardia di Finanza, 1976b). As a matter of fact, in 1952 a trunk containing 5.8 Kg of heroin, ready to be shipped to the United States, was discovered in Alcamo. Between 1951 and 1961 the Salemi squad illegally traded at least 76 Kg of heroin under the leadership of members of American Cosa Nostra families, that financed the shipments (CPMS, 1972:457).

[2] *Pentiti* (literally, repentants) a popular term used for the mafia affiliates who cooperate with law enforcement agencies.

[3] Born in Patti in Sicily, Michele Sindona in the 1960s appeared to be one of the most successful investment bankers of the Italian financial market. However, it turned out that the sources of his money were to a large extent 'dirty' and his methods were often illicit: not only did he extensively bribe to members of the majority party, *Democrazia Cristiana*, but he even resorted to intimidation and murder in order to discourage competitors and to stop law enforcement action (Commissione Sindona, 1982a and b; Commissione P2, 1984; TrMi, (1984) 1986; Tosches, 1986; Lombard, 1980; Stajano, 1991).

[4] Less than two months earlier, on June 18th, the lifeless body of Roberto Calvi, the former President of the *Banco*, had been found dangling beneath Blackfrairs Bridge in London. These two events dramatically concluded the existence of the *Banco Ambrosiano*, which had begun almost a century earlier, in 1896. The *Banco Ambrosiano* was founded by a group of 153 shareholders headed by Catholic priest don Giuseppe Tonini, with the aim of providing an alternative to the large lay banks. Known as 'the priests' bank', the *Banco* flourished and for almost a century it represented the views and the interests of a large part of the Lombard Catholic bourgeoisie. At the end of its life span, in 1982, the bank, which was the largest private banking group in Italy, ran 107 counters and employed more than 4,000 workers. Very close contacts with the Vatican had also developed, so far that after the collapse of the *Banco Ambrosiano*, the Vatican bank, *Istituto per le Opere di Religione (IOR)*, agreed to pay a 250 US $ million 'voluntary contribution' to aid in clearing the *Ambrosiano*'s debts. In 1987 The Milanese prosecutors ordered the arrest of three directors of the *IOR* but the arrest warrants were stopped by the Cassation Court on the grounds of a 'lack of jurisdiction' of the Italian judicial authorities vis-*a-vis* Vatican citizens (PrMI, 1988; 1991; Cornwell, 1983).

[5] It is important to stress, however, that only an estimated 40% of total world opium production (estimate by DEA) is converted into heroin and introduced into the drug markets. Most of the rest - over 60% of raw opium grown on the Asian highlands - is used in the same producing or neighboring countries, where millions of opium smokers currently live. Lastly, a small percentage share is destroyed as a result of eradication programs or is seized by the law-enforcement authorities (NNICC, 1993; 1994; 1995).

[6] For a portrait of Vizzini, see Pantaleone ((1962) 1972:74-94).

[7] This network of Cosa Nostra mafia families, which has dominated Cosa Nostra from the early 1980s onwards, is known as *Corleonesi*, since the leading family, headed up until 1993 by Riina, was that located in Corleone, a town about 50 Kilometers away from Palermo.

[8] In addition to General Dalla Chiesa, the most important victims of mafia violence in

the late 1970s and early 1980s were the following: Cesare Terranova, a magistrate likely to become chief of the Investigating Judges in the Palermo Court (September 25th, 1979); Piersanti Mattarella, President of the Sicilian region (January 6th, 1980); Gaetano Costa, chief prosecutor (August 6th, 1980); Pio La Torre, regional secretary of the Communist Party (April 30th 1982); Rocco Chinnici, Chief of the Palermo Court's Investigating Judges (July 29th, 1983); Antonino Cassar, vice-police Questor (August 6th, 1985). See Lodato (1994) and Stille (1995).

9 On this matter it is important to clarify that the government has not in reality been able to support the diffusion of these initiatives. Notwithstanding the approval in February 1992 of the law creating such a fund, its activation has been delayed by numerous bureaucratic hindrances and its management has been a failure. In the very first year alone, for example, 119 requests have been received by the Committee for the Solidarity fund but, although there have been 9 supporting proposals, no sum has effectively been granted (CPM, 1994b). As a result, in the period 1993-95 a decrease of extortion denounces was registered and this reflects victims' lack of trust towards law enforcement action accompanied by a generalized lack of interest of the public opinion in the problem.

10 In spite of dozens of minor attacks and many foiled attempts, three episodes of this subversive strategy are most important: on May 14, 1993 a car bomb exploded in Via Ruggero Fauro in Rome, aimed at killing a popular TV journalist; two weeks later, on May 27, an even more devastating blast in Via dei Georgofili, in Florence's historical center, seriously damaged some halls of the adjacent *Museo degli Uffizi* and caused the death of 5 persons; lastly, on the night between July 27 and 28, three bombs rapidly exploded one after the other near the Basilica of San Giovanni in Laterano and the ancient church of San Giorgio in Velabro in Rome, and in the gardens of the municipal villa in Via Palestro in Milan. These attacks caused the death of 6 people, wounded many others and seriously damaged the features of several buildings.

11 Art. 41 *bis* of Law 354/75, introduced by the above-mentioned bill, gave the Ministry of Justice the power to suspend the application, for very serious crimes, of the ordinary penitentiary treatment regulations. Likewise, art. 4 *bis* denied the *mafiosi* leaves, measures alternative to detention, and daily release for work. Contacts with the outside world were, thus, abruptly cut and the most dangerous convicts were moved to high security prisons and deprived of the many - small and large - privileges that they used to enjoy in the prisons located in the own sphere of influence.

12 It is enough to say that in the first twelve months of application, thirteen members of mafia groups detained under these special conditions have decided to collaborate with the law-enforcement agencies.

Glossary

Mafia - Up to the early 1980s a major branch of the scientific and popular discourse understood the term mafia as an attitude and behaviour typical of Sicilians, denying a corporate dimension. Since then however, thanks to judicial investigations, it has become clear that organized crime groups lie at the core of the mafia phenomenon. The most structured of these groups is represented by the coalition named Cosa Nostra. By extension the term it used to point out other forms of Southern Italian organized crime, and, specifically, the Calabrian 'ndrangheta and it is, more generically, also employed as a synonym of organized crime.

'Ndrangheta - Association of about 90 mafia families located in Southern Calabria and their ramifications in Northern Italy and foreign countries. The word itself is of Greek origin and, literally, means "the association of the men of honor." More than 3,000 members of 'Ndrangheta families are known to the police.

Men of honor - the expression used by ritually affiliated members of Sicilian and Calabrian mafia families to define themselves.

Illegal Markets - Markets which deal in goods and services declared illegal or restricted by the legal authority of a state.

Extortion - The crime of obtaining money or some other thing of value by violence, intimidation or abuse of authority.

"Pentiti" - A popular term used to indicate the mafia adherents and gangsters that "cooperate with Justice," as the formal expression puts it, that is, report their crimes and experiences in the underworld to policemen and magistrates.

8 The Future of Traditional Organized Crime[1] in the United States

Howard Abadinsky

Abstract

Some observers argue that the American Mafia is down and just about out, primarily as a result of the success of federal law enforcement efforts. Double-digit sentences typically handed down to organized crime figures has led to the demise of "omerta," the much-vaunted code of silence. This assertion, however, is not new--indeed, the demise of the American Mafia has been predicted for decades. But has the time finally come when we can write the Mafia out of America's future? For insight, this paper considers theories that explain both the creation of the phenomenon and its continued existence, and analyzes the results against what is known about contemporary Italian-American organized crime.

Key Words: Anomie, Differential opportunities, Ethnic succession, "hood," Social disorganization, "wannabes," and "wiseguys"

Introduction

The American Mafia is down and just about out, states Reuter (1995), primarily as a result of the success of federal law enforcement and its use of the Racketeer Influenced and Corrupt Organizations (RICO) statute. He points to the double-digit sentences typically handed down to organized crime figures, which has led to the demise of *"omerta"* the much-vaunted code of silence.

Reuter's assertion is not new--indeed, the demise of the American Mafia has been predicted for decades. But has the time finally come when we can write the Mafia out of America's future? For insight, this paper will consider theories that explain both the creation of the phenomenon and its continued existence, beginning with anomie.

Anomie

Building on a concept originated by Durkheim (1951) back in the nineteenth century, Merton (1938) set forth a social and cultural explanation for deviant behavior in the United States wherein organized crime is conceived of as a normal response to pressures exerted on certain persons by the social structure. Merton points to an American preoccupation with economic success—"pathological materialism." It is the goal that is emphasized, not the means that are at best only a secondary consideration. "There may develop a disproportionate, at times, a virtually exclusive stress upon the value of specific goals, involving relatively slight connect with the institutionally appropriate modes of attaining these goals*"* (1938:673).

This being the case, the only factors limiting goal achievement are technical, not moral or legal. According to Merton:

> emphasis on the goals of monetary success and material property leads to dominant concern with technological and social instruments designed to produce the desired result, inasmuch as institutional controls become of secondary importance. In such a situation, innovation [such as organized crime] flourishes as the range of means employed is broadened (1938:673).

Thus, in American society, "the pressure of prestige-bearing success tends to eliminate the effective social constraint over means employed to this end. 'The-ends-justifies-the-means' doctrine becomes a guiding tenet for action when the cultural structure unduly exalts the end and the social organization unduly limits possible recourse to approved means" (1938:681). The activities of earlier American "godfathers," the "robber barons," facilitated by laissez faire capitalism and rampant corruption, exemplifies the spirit that Merton refers to as innovation. Taking advantage of every (legitimate and illegitimate) opportunity, men such as Astor, Carnegie, Gould, Rockefeller, Stanford, and Vanderbilt, became the embodiment of the great American success story. However, the opportunity for economic success is not equally distributed, and the immigrants who followed these men to America found many avenues from "rags to riches" significantly limited if not already closed. Culture conflict, however, provided opportunity for later day adventurers to innovate.

Culture Conflict

Sellin (1938) points out that conduct norms express cultural values of a group, and the content of those norms varies from culture to culture. In a homogeneous society, the conduct norms express the consensus of the group: few people disagree about what is right and wrong. The same is not true of more heterogeneous societies, where disagreements abound about what is right and wrong, what is to be valued, and what is to be demeaned. In a heterogeneous society, laws represent the conduct norms of the dominant group. Whenever immigrants leave one culture for another, they run the risk of culture conflict. While the United States is the quintessential "nation of immigrants," the contemporary movement of refugees and labor across national boundaries provides the elements for worldwide culture conflict.

In the United States culture conflict between earlier and later immigrants created a demand from the latter for goods and services outlawed by the former. This led to the creation of gambling/vice syndicates and the infamous criminal organizations of the Prohibition era (1920-33). Writing several years before Merton, Robinson (1933:16) spoke of an American credo according to which "we dare not or at least will not condemn the criminal's goal, because it is also our goal. We want to keep the goal ourselves and damn the criminal for pursuing it in the only way he knows how."

*The methods which criminals use in attaining our common
goal of wealth may, of course, differ from those which the
noncriminal classes use. But this is to be expected. They are
probably not in a position to employ our methods. We can
think of a variety of reasons why a man without capital or
without education or without industrial skill or without this or
that advantage or handicapped by any one of several factors
which anyone could easily name would be forced to seek the
common goal by means differing from those employed by
another man better situated or endowed* (1933:15-16).

In a capitalist society, socioeconomic differentials relegate persons to an
environment wherein they experience a sense of strain--anomie--as well as
differential association (Sutherland 1972).   In the environment that has
traditionally spawned organized crime, this strain is intense. Conditions of
severe deprivation are coupled with readily available success models that are
innovative: for example, racketeers and drug dealers. However, learning the
techniques of sophisticated criminality also requires the proper environment--
ecological niches or enclaves -- the "hood" -- where delinquent/criminal
subcultures flourish and this education is available.

The enclave is characterized as a place where:

*various types of people tend to seek out others like themselves
and live close together. Located within these distinctive
clusters are specialized commercial enterprises and
institutions that support the inhabitants' special ways of
life...Each distinctive group, along with its stores and
institutions, occupies a geographic area that becomes
intimately associated with the group. Through this linkage,
areas acquire symbolic qualities that include their place
names and social histories. Each place, both as a geographic
entity and as a space with social meaning, also tends to be an
object of residents' attachments and an important component
of their identities.* (Abrahamson, 1996:1).

*The enclave has some characteristics of a subculture, in which
a group of people shares common traditions and values that
are ordinarily maintained by a high rate of interaction within
the group* (Abrahamson 1996:3).

Subcultures and Social Disorganization

Instead of conforming to conventional norms, through differential
association some persons organize their behavior according to the norms of a
delinquent or criminal group to which they belong or with which they identify.
In certain areas--enclaves with strong traditions of OC--young persons stand a
greater chance of being exposed to criminal norms. In these areas, Kobrin
(1966) points out, persons exhibiting criminal norms are often well integrated

into the community, and such areas are the breeding ground for entrants into organized crime.

Central to the issue of culture versus subculture are norms, "group-held prescriptions for or prohibitions against certain conduct" (Wolfgang and Ferracuti 1967:113). Norms are general rules about how to behave and expectations that are predictive of behavior. The vast majority of a society, which provides rewards or punishments for conformity or violation, approves these rules and expectations. "The 'delinquent subculture' is characterized principally by conduct that reflects values antithetical to the surrounding culture" (Wolfgang and Ferracuti 1967:110). Subcultural theory explains criminal behavior as learned; the subcultural delinquent has learned values that are deviant: Ideas about society lead to criminal behavior. A number of studies indicate that delinquent youth hold values that differ markedly from non-delinquents. Indeed, they may view their criminal behavior as morally wrong, but this is not the controlling attitude. Being right or wrong in terms of the wider society is simply not a guidepost for behavior. Non-conventional behavior--the ability to fight, to win at gambling--is admired (Elliott, Huizinga, and Ageton 1985).

Shaw and McKay, sociologists at the University of Chicago, used that city as a "laboratory" for their study of patterns of criminality during the 1920s and 1930s. They found that certain clearly identifiable neighborhoods maintained a high level of criminality over many decades despite changes in ethnic composition. Such neighborhoods are characterized by attitudes and values that are conducive to delinquency and crime, particularly organized crime:

> The presence of a large number of adult criminals in certain areas means that children there are in contact with crime as a career and with a criminal way of life, symbolized by organized crime. In this type of organization can be seen the delegation of authority, the division of labor, the specialization of function, and all the other characteristics common to well-organized business institutions wherever found...

> The heavy concentration of delinquency in certain areas means that the boys living in these areas are in contact not only with individuals who engage in proscribed activity but also with groups that sanction such behavior and exert pressure upon their members to conform to group standards. (1972:72, 174)

A disruption of the social order is associated with high rates of delinquency in a community, the result of a breakdown in mechanisms of social control. In many U.S. cities around the turn of the century, the combined interactive effects of industrialization, immigration and urbanization disrupted the social order. Deviant traditions developed and competed with conventional norms; in some communities, deviant norms won out. Once established, these norms took root in areas which, according to Shaw and McKay, were characterized by attitudes and values, which are conducive to delinquency and crime, a subculture of crime. The attitudes and values, as well as the techniques of organized criminality are transmitted culturally:

> Delinquent boys in these areas have contact not only with other delinquents who are their contemporaries but also with older offenders, who in turn had contact with delinquents preceding them, and so on back to the earliest history of the neighborhood. This contact means that the traditions of delinquency can be and are transmitted down through successive generations of boys, in much the dame way that language and other social forms are transmitted" (1972: 174).

Back in the 1920s, Landesco (1968) found that organized crime in Chicago could be explained by the prevalence of social disorganization in the wider society (during the period of Prohibition), and the distinct social organization of urban slums from which members of OC emerge.

> Once a set of cultural values is created and established--either because of economic factors or intellectual or moral transformations--they tend to become autonomous in their impact. From that point on, they can influence human relations independently of their original sources. And since they are, as a rule, accepted uncritically and through the most inadvertent process of socialization, they are regarded as normal and inevitable within each cultural system (Saney 1986:35).

In other words, the roots and culture of particular neighborhoods explain why gangsters come from clearly delineated areas "where the gang tradition is old" (Landesco 1968: 207), and where adolescents, through differential association, can absorb the attitudes and skills necessary to enter the world of adult organized crime.

In order for an organized crime group to survive, it must have "an institutionalized process for inducting new members and inculcating them with the values and ways of behaving of the social system" (Cressey 1969:263). Cressey notes (1969:236) that "in some neighborhoods all three of the essential ingredients of an effective recruiting process are in operation: inspiring aspiration for membership, training for membership and selection for membership." In his research, Suttles (1968) refers to areas from which members of organized crime have typically emerged as defended neighborhoods: recognized ecological niches whose inhabitants form cohesive groupings and seal themselves off through the efforts of delinquent gangs, restrictive covenants, and a forbidding reputation. Such neighborhoods have traditionally provided the recruiting grounds that ensure the continuity of traditional OC.

In such communities, notes Kobrin (1966:156), the conventional and criminal value systems are highly integrated. Leaders of organized criminal enterprises "frequently maintain membership in such conventional institutions of their local communities as churches, fraternal and mutual benefit societies, and political parties." Formal and informal political, economic, and religious ties provide both illegitimate and legitimate opportunities. These leaders are able to control violent and delinquent behavior in their domain--they are effective instruments of social control. "Everyone," particularly would-be miscreants, "knows" not to "mess around" in certain neighborhoods. And those who do not "know" have suffered serious consequences--selling drugs in one Chicago suburb, for example, resulted in mutilated corpses. In the Italian area of New York's Greenwich Village, "street corner boys" enforced the social order--made sure the streets were safe. And their self-appointed role was backed by the formidable reputation of the neighborhood's organized crime figures. For this, neighborhood residents reciprocated by providing "wiseguys" with a safe haven (Tricarico 1984).

Pileggi (1985: 37-38) describes a *defended neighborhood* in Brooklyn:

In Brownsville-East New York wiseguys *were more than accepted--they were protected. Even the legitimate members of the community--the merchants, teachers, phone repairmen, garbage collectors, bus depot dispatchers, housewives, and old-timers sunning themselves along the Conduit Drive--all seemed to keep an eye out to protect their local hoods. The majority of the residents, even those not directly related by birth or marriage to wiseguys, had certainly known the local rogues most of their lives. There was the nodding familiarity of neighborhood. In the area it was impossible to betray old friends, even those old friends who had grown up to be racketeers.*

The extraordinary insularity of these old-world mob-controlled sections, whether Brownsville-East New York, the South Side of Chicago, or Federal Hill in Providence, Rhode Island, unquestionably helped to nurture the mob.

Recruitment into OC is made viable because "in the type of community under discussion boys may more or less realistically recognize the potentialities for personal progress in the local society through success in delinquency. In a general way, therefore, delinquent activity in these areas constitutes a training ground for the acquisition of skill in the use of violence, concealment of offense, evasion of detention and arrest, and the purchase of immunity from punishment" (Kobrin 1966:156).

Lombardo points out that prospective members of OC "typically come from communities which share collective representations and moral sentiments which allow them to recognize the pursuit of a career in the underworld as a legitimate way of life" (1979:18; 1994). Young men from these areas dress in a certain style – "gangster chic" – and congregate in social clubs and nightspots where they are able to associate with the men who have already been allowed entry into "*the life.*" They are ready --eager -- show their mettle by accepting assignments from "goodfellas." Even those who have moved to suburban locations--if they accept the "wiseguy" credo--gravitate back to the "*hood.*" In Chicago this phenomenon has been referred to as the "*suburbanization of the Mob*": young men who have known only middle-class economic conditions becoming part of organized crime. Like the member of an outlaw motorcycle club, these young men are attracted to a lifestyle, not necessarily by the potential financial rewards offered by organized crime. For example, Salvatore ("Solly D.") DeLaurentis (b. 1938), who was raised in the Taylor Street neighborhood in Chicago, aspired to be a "gangster"--a term he uses to describe himself--since his earliest days. His family moved out to suburban Lake County, and Solly D. found himself cut off from his career path: Lake County lacked the critical mass of older criminals and their young associates/ "wanabes." So DeLaurentis gradually made connections back in the old neighborhood and eventually became a member of the Outfit's notorious "Rocky Infelice crew."[2]

Even senior members of the Outfit who reside in suburban locations, frequent the restaurants, nightspots, and social clubs back in the 'hood. James D. Antonio ("Jimmy D."), the ranking member of the Grand Avenue crew, resided in suburban Skokie. But until his death in 1993 from an auto accident, the 65-year-old operated a storefront social club in the Grand Avenue neighborhood which even sponsored a boys baseball team (O'Brien 1993).

According to Spergel (1964), in such communities life in organized crime is considered acceptable and therefore a legitimate avenue of aspiration for young persons. While these communities provide an appropriate learning environment for the acquisition of values and skills associated with the performance of criminal roles, integration into OC requires selection and tutelage in the process of acquiring recognition--and only a select few are given recognition by those who control admission. Entry into organized crime is characterized by *differential opportunity*.

Differential Opportunity

In agreement with Merton, Cloward and Ohlin (1960:107) note that American preoccupation with economic success, coupled with socioeconomic stratification, relegates many persons to an environment wherein they experience strain:

> *Many lower-class male adolescents experience extreme deprivation born of the certainty that their position in the economic structure is relatively fixed and immutable--a desperation made all the more poignant by their exposure to a cultural ideology in which failure to orient oneself upward is regarded as a moral defect and failure to become mobile as proof of it.*

Conditions of severe deprivation with extremely limited access to ladders of legitimate success result in collective adaptations in the form of delinquent subcultures. Anomie alone, note Cloward and Ohlin, is not sufficient to explain participation in organized crime: what is necessary is cultural transmission (Shaw and McKay) through differential association (Sutherland). However, Cloward and Ohlin point out that illegitimate opportunity for success, like legitimate opportunity, is not equally distributed throughout society (1960:145): "Having decided that he 'can't make it legitimately,' he cannot simply choose from an array of illegitimate means, all equally available to him." In other words, access to criminal ladders of success is no more freely available than are noncriminal alternatives:

> *Only those neighborhoods in which crime flourishes as a stable, indigenous institution are fertile learning environments for the young. Because these environments afford integration of different age-levels of offender, selected young people are exposed to "differential association" through which tutelage is provided and criminal values and skills are acquired. To be prepared for the role may not, however, ensure that the individual will ever discharge it. One important limitation is that more youngsters are recruited into these patterns of differential association than the adult criminal structure can possibly absorb. Since there is a surplus of contenders for these elite positions, criteria and mechanisms of selection must be evolved. Hence a certain proportion of those who aspire may not be permitted to engage in the behavior for which they have prepared themselves.* (Cloward and Ohlin 1960: 148)

The future of traditional organized crime is dependent on having a surplus of contenders.

Ethnic Succession

During the decades following World War II, organized crime (OC) underwent considerable change. It became increasingly clear that OC was dominated mainly by Italians--the Irish, except for small pockets in New York and Boston, were no longer involved. And while the sons of Jewish immigrants played a vital role in organized crime, by the third generation the Jews had moved out.

The pool of available candidates for membership in organized crime dwindled among the Irish and the Jews. In Italian communities it remained adequate enough; the large-scale organizations needed to profit from Prohibition were no longer necessary. In Chicago, for example, during the height of Prohibition, Al Capone is reputed to have employed 700 gunmen for an organization that involved thousands of persons (McPhaul 1970), while contemporary estimates of the size of the Chicago Outfit have ranged only as high as one hundred and thirty.[3] The largest of the crime families, Genovese, is estimated to have no more than 400 members. (These core members, however, have associates and the total number of criminal actors participating directly or indirectly in a crime group's enterprises is many times the size of the core membership at any given time.)

Bell (1964) refers to crime as an American way of life, "a queer ladder of social mobility." He points out that the "jungle quality of the American business community, particularly at the turn of the century, was reflected in the mode of 'business' practiced by the coarse gangster elements, most of them from new immigrant families, who were 'getting ahead' just as Horatio Alger had urged" (1964: 116). Ianni (1974:13-14) notes that this "queer ladder" had organized crime as the first few rungs:

> The Irish came first, and early in this century they dominated crime as well as big-city political machines. As they came to control the political machinery of large cities they won wealth, power and respectability through subsequent control of construction, trucking, public utilities and the waterfront. By the 1920s and the period of prohibition and speculation in the money markets and real estate, the Irish were succeeded in organized crime by the Jews, and Arnold Rothstein, Lepke Buchalter and Gurrah Shapiro dominated gambling and labor racketeering for over a decade. The Jews quickly moved into the world of business and the professions as more legitimate avenues to economic and social mobility. The Italians came next...

According to this thesis, each successive immigrant group experiences strain to which some members react by *innovating* in accord with a tradition that had been established by earlier unscrupulous entrepreneurs such as the "robber barons." Ethnic succession results when a group experiences success in crime and legitimate opportunities thereby become more readily available. "Strain" subsides, and the group moves out of organized crime, creating an opportunity for the succeeding immigrant group. According to this thesis, persons involved in organized crime are not committed to a deviant subculture, but are merely using available--albeit illegal--opportunity to achieve economic success.

Ianni (1972:193) describes the "Lupollos," the Italian OC Family he studied, whose core members are all related by blood or marriage. In the fourth generation, "only four out of twenty-seven males are involved in the family business organization. The rest are doctors, lawyers, college teachers, or run their own businesses." He states that "the Italians are leaving or being pushed out of organized crime [and] they are being replaced by the next wave of migrants to the city: blacks and Puerto Ricans." (While the succession may not have been obvious to Ianni when he was conducting his research in New York during the early 1970s, today we would have to add other ethnic groups-- Chinese, Colombians, Dominicans, Jamaicans, Mexicans, Nigerians, Russians.) According to the ethnic succession thesis, involvement in organized crime is simply a rational response to economic conditions.

Other theorists reject this one-dimensional view; organized crime, they argue, provides important psychic rewards, and meaningful social structures.

Young Italian-American males from middle-class circumstances continue to be drawn by the allure of Cosa Nostra--a romantization of the mob kept alive in certain neighborhoods and reinforced by media representations.[4] Being "connected" brings prestige and in the social environment inhabited by "wiseguys"--bars, restaurants, night clubs--a privileged status is evident. The "wannabe" outlaw is socialized into an exciting world where he eagerly adopts the attitude, behavior pattern, and even the clothing styles exemplified by "wiseguys."

Lupsha (1981) argues that despite Ianni's limited findings, Italian OC figures who have gained economic status are not leaving organized crime and, in many instances, their progeny have followed them into "the life." This view certainly has some empirical support--there are dozens of contemporary OC members whose children have followed them into "the life." An example is the rise of a notorious gang of Italian-American hoodlums in the Pleasant Avenue section of Harlem, a syndicate stronghold, dubbed the "Purple Gang," apparently after the murderous Detroit (Jewish) mob of Prohibition days. They have been used as "muscle" and executioners in many gangland murders, and their reputation for violence has made them very useful to the leadership of traditional organized crime. In his study of some members of the Purple Gang, Lupsha (1983) found that they tend to have been born between 1946 and 1951, third-generation Italian-Americans who are related by blood and marriage. While they come from the Pleasant Avenue neighborhood in Harlem, most reside in the Bronx or suburban Westchester County. "They are now, like man New York suburbanite businessmen, commuters to the old neighborhood for work, money, and visiting rather than residents" (1983:76). Many Purple Gang members have been "made" --inducted into membership of traditional OC Families in New York. Similar groups have been identified as part of other OC Families. In 1992, the head of an enforcement crew in the Bonanno family, Thomas ("Tommy Karate") Pitera, then 37-years of age, was accused of dealing drugs, torturing victims, and killing seven people. The martial arts devotee, owner of a Brooklyn bar and disco, had *no prior criminal record* (Lubasch 1992). After a seven-week trial, Pitera was convicted of six murders and sentenced to life without parole.

Entry into organized crime, states Lupsha (1981: 22), is not based on blocked aspirations, that is, anomie or strain. Rather it "is a rational choice, rooted in one perverse aspect of our values; namely, that only 'suckers' work, and that in our society, one is at liberty to take 'suckers' and seek easy money." In fact, the term for a member of traditional OC, "*wiseguy*," exemplifies such an attitude. Pileggi (1985:20) offers Paul ("Paulie") Vario, a powerful caporegime in the Lucchese crime Family, as an example. A Lucchese Family associate is talking:

> *Paulie was always asking me for stolen credit cards whenever he and his wife, Phyllis, were going out for the night. Paulie called stolen credit cards "Muldoons," and he always said that liquor tastes better on a Muldoon. The fact that a guy*

*like Paul Vario, a capo in the Lucchese crime family, would
even consider going out on a social occasion with his wife and
run the risk of getting caught using a stolen credit card might
surprise some people. But if you knew wiseguys you would
know right away that the best part of the night for Paulie
came from the fact that he was getting over on somebody.*

With a great deal of insight, Pileggi (1985: 36) captures the "wiseguy"
attitude toward society:

*They lived in an environment awash in crime, and those who
did not partake were simply viewed as prey. To live otherwise
was foolish. Anyone who stood waiting his turn on the
American pay line was beneath contempt.*

According to this view, OC comprises a deviant subculture to which
members have a *commitment* that is not mitigated by the absence of strain. As
one Gambino crime Family member told a reporter: "[W]e don't want to be part
of your world. We don't want to belong to country clubs" (Brenner 1990:181).
Benjamin ("Lefty") Ruggiero of the Bonanno Family explained: "As a wiseguy
you can lie, you can cheat, you can steal, you can kill people--legitimately. You
can do any goddamn thing you want, and nobody can say anything about it.
Who wouldn't want to be a wiseguy?" (Pistone 1987:330).

But while such young men appear to enjoy playing the wiseguy role--
often outfitted with large pinkie rings and gold chains--many are neither bright
nor tough, although some do have a college education. The long neighborhood-
based apprenticeships through which OC chooses the cream of the "wannabes"
are history. Those accepted into membership are often not the street-smart,
stand-up kids of yesteryear, but social failures and potential informants quick to
play "I've got a secret"--turn on their closest associates to avoid incarceration.
As one knowledgeable Chicago detective explains, the Outfit lacks "quality
control." In fact, he notes, the lack of adequate resources for violence has
caused a greater reliance on nonmember associates and even outlaw bikers to
carry out murders.

In New York, however, young men raised in comfortable middle-class
circumstances have advanced into organized crime in a most violent way. Roy
DeMeo of Brooklyn, a second-generation American of Neapolitan heritage,
became a loanshark while still in his teens. His uncle was a star prosecutor in
the Brooklyn District Attorney's office. But at age thirty-two, in order to protect
an extortion scheme run with his partner, a member of the Gambino Family,
Roy committed his first murder--a solo job using a silencer-equipped pistol. He
subsequently put together a crew of active criminals from the (middle-class)
Canarsie section of Brooklyn. Their initial murder victim, a car dealer who was
testifying against them before a Brooklyn grand jury, was kidnapped, stabbed
repeatedly, and dismembered. The medical examiner that handled the case, Dr.
Dominic DiMaio, did not know that his cousin Roy DeMeo -- his branch of the
family spelled the name differently -- was responsible for the murder. DeMeo
was initiated into the Gambino Family, and his crew eventually killed an

estimated 75 persons -- most of the bodies were never found (Mustain and Capeci 1992).

A recent development affecting ethnic succession in OC is the arrival of relatively large numbers of southern Italian immigrants--often mafiosi fleeing enemies or Italian government crackdowns-- into the New York metropolitan area—"*zips*"--who have both reinforced existing crime Families and formed their own groups for independent operations, particularly in drugs.

There has been a "shakeout" in traditional organized crime. The government has skimmed off the leadership of an earlier--arguably more adept but clearly--more senior generation. They have been replaced by younger men, often better educated--some with college--but who lack the traditional long-term street internships that permit careful screening for membership. Some have moved too quickly into leadership positions, filling vacuums left by government prosecution.

This younger generation is impelled not by strain but by a "romanticization of the mob" and sociopathy. Gambino Family *caporegime* Joe ("Piney") Armone noted this in an FBI-taped conversation with his boss Paul Castellano: "But you know Paul, I think some guys just take so much pleasure from breaking heads that they'd almost rather not get paid" (quoted in O'Brien and Kurins 1991). Smarter and deadlier, with discipline and loyalty in doubt-- this is the future of traditional organized crime.

Conclusion

While "strain" can help explain why some persons in disadvantaged groups become involved in organized crime, it fails to provide a satisfying explanation for the continued existence of traditional organized crime. In other words, while poverty and limited economic opportunity can certainly impel one toward innovative activities, they do not explain why middle-class youngsters become involved in organized crime. Instead, we need to look for explanations in subcultural theory and sociopathy. This would appear to be the case with members of Italian-American organized crime whose strong subcultural orientations have belied changes in their economic status. The future of an organized crime group can be assessed according to the strength of their ties-- loyalty--to a criminal subculture, separating the "wiseguy" from the ruthless businessman. Persons committed to financial success--not a criminal lifestyle-- are likely to exit organized crime in the following generation.

Howard Abadinsky, Ph.D., is professor of criminal justice and sociology at Saint Xavier University in Chicago. He was a parole officer for the state of New York for fifteen years, and an inspector for the Cook County Sheriff's Office for eight years. Professor Abadinsky has a Ph.D. from New York University and is the author of a number of books, including three on organized crime: The American Mafia: An Oral History (Praeger 1981). The Criminal Elite (Greenwood 1983) and Organized Crime, 5th ed. (Nelson-Hall 1997). He served as a consultant to President Ronald Reagan's Commission on Organized Crime and is the founder of the International Association for the Study of Organized Crime.

References

Abadinsky, H. (1997), *Organized Crime*, 5th ed, Chicago: Nelson-Hall.

Bell, D. (1964), *The End of Ideology*, Glencoe, IL: Free Press.

Brenner, M. (1990), "Prime Time Godfather," *Vanity Fair* (May): 109-19, 176-81.

Cloward, R. A. and Lloyd E. O. (1960), *Delinquency and Opportunity*, New York: Free Press.

Cressey, D. (1969), *Theft of the Nation*, New York: Harper and Row.

Durkheim, E. (1951), *Suicide*, New York: Free Press.

Ianni, F. A. J. (1974), *The Black Mafia: Ethnic Succession in Organized Crime*, New York: Simon and Schuster.

Ianni, F. A. J. (1972) *A Family Business: Kinship and Social Control in Organized Crime*, New York: Russell Sage Foundation.

Kobrin, S. (1966), "The Conflict of Values in Delinquency Areas." pages 151-60 in R. Giallombardo (ed), *Juvenile Delinquency: A Book of Readings*, New York: Wiley.

Landesco, J. (1968), *Organized Crime in Chicago*, Chicago: University of Chicago Press.

Lombardo, R. M. (1994), "The Organized Crime Neighborhoods of Chicago," in R. J. Kelly, K. -L. Chin, and R. Schatzberg, (eds.), *Handbook of Organized Crime in the United States*, Westport, CT: Greenwood pp. 169-87.

Kelly, R. J. (1979), "Organized Crime and the Concept of Community." Department of Sociology, University of Illinois at Chicago.

Lubasch, (1992a) "Death Penalty Sought at Trial in Brooklyn." *New York Time*, April 14:16.

Lupsha, P. (1983), "Networks Versus Networking: Analysis of an Organized Crime Group" in G. P. Waldo (ed.), *Career Criminals*, Beverly Hills, CA: Sage pp. 59-87.

Lupsha, P. (1981), "Individual Choice, Material Culture, and Organized Crime." *Criminology* 19: 3-24.

McPhaul, J. (1970), *Johnny Torrio: First of the Gang Lords*. New Rochelle, NY: Arlington House.

Merton, R. (1938), "Social Structure and Anomie." *American Sociological Review*, 3:672-82.

Mustain, G. and Capeci, J. (1992), *Murder Machine: A True Story of Murder. Madness, and the Mafia*. New York: Franklin Watts.

O'Brien, J. (1993), "James J. D'Antonio, 65, Mob Driver." *Chicago Tribune* (December 15): Sec. 2:11.

O'Brien, J. F. and Kurins, A. (1991), *Boss of Bosses: The FBI and Paul Castellano*, New York: Dell.

Pileggi, N. (1985), *Wiseguy: Life in a Mafia Family*. New York: Pocket Books.

Pistone, J. D. (1987), *Donnie Brasco: My Undercover Life in the Mafia*. New York: New American Library.

Potter, G. (1994), *Criminal Organizations: Vice. Racketeering, and Politics in an American City*. Prospect Heights, IL: Waveland.

Reuter, P. (1995), "The Decline of the American Mafia." *The Public Interest* 120 (Summer): 89-99. 1983 *Disorganized Crime*. Cambridge, MA: MIT Press.

Robinson, L. N. (1933), "Social Values and Mercenary Crime." in E. D. MacDougal (ed.), *Crime for Profit: A Symposium on Mercenary Crime*, Boston: Stratford Company pp. 13-31.

Saney, P. (1986), *Crime and Culture in America*. Westport, CT: Greenwood.

Sellin. T. (1938), *Culture Conflict and Crime*. New York: Social Science Research Council.

Shaw, C. and McKay, H. D. (1972), *Juvenile Delinquency and Urban Areas*. Chicago: University of Chicago Press.

Spergel, I. (1964), *Racketville. Slumtown, and Haulberg*. Chicago: University of Chicago Press.

Sutherland, E. H. (1972), *Edwin H. Sutherland: On Analyzing Crime*, K. Schuessler, (ed.) Chicago: University of Chicago Press.

Suttles, G. D. (1968), *The Social Order of the Slum*. Chicago: University of Chicago Press.

Tricarico, D. (1984), *The Italians of Greenwich Village*. Staten Island, NY: Center for Migration Studies of New York.

Wolfgang, M. E. and Fercutti, F. (1967), *The Subculture of Violence: Toward an Integrated Theory in Criminology*, London: Tavistock.

Notes

1 Organized crime has been the subject of definitional debates. For a discussion of the definition of organized crime, see Abadinsky (1997).

2 Rocco Ernest Infelice (b. 1922), a former paratroop combat veteran with an expensive home in suburban River Forest and a vacation residence in Fort Lauderdale, Florida, had extensive connections in suburban law enforcement and politics. He expanded "Outfit" control over gambling and marginal businesses--bars with sex shows, for example--in the suburbs through intimidation and murder. He is currently serving a 63-year sentence for racketeering and murder conspiracy.

3 Various law enforcement and journalistic sources.

4 The book (Pileggi 1994) and motion picture *Casino*, depicted the violent activities of Tony Spilotro (played by Joe Pesci). Spilotro's father was the owner of a small but successful restaurant -- in an OC neighborhood-- and Tony's older brother became a dentist and Air Force officer.

9 Organized Crime in the United States: Some Current Trends

Robert J. Kelly

Abstract

The American Mafia, La Cosa Nostra, has been under concerted law enforcement attack but it cannot be described as destroyed. As the economic conditions and socio-political environments that nurtured the Mafia have changed, it has transformed and re-defined itself. Other ethnic groups, referred to as 'nontraditional' organized crime, are rising in the ethnic enclaves and ghettos of new immigrant communities. The essay examines the processes of decline and re-alignment within La Cosa Nostra and sketches the structures and dynamics of Chinese extortion rings.

Key Words: Corruption, La Cosa Nostra, Mafia, RICO.

Introduction

At the 50th Anniversary Assembly of the United Nations in October 1996, President Bill Clinton made a short, trenchant speech that not only reconceptualized foreign policy but redefined forms of crime as threats to national security previously thought to be domestic law enforcement problems.[1] The speech was an unclassified version of Presidential Decision Directive 42 (PDD42) which acknowledged the growing danger posed by international organized crime and which outlined a series of initiatives authorized by the President to combat a crime problem that constitutes a serious threat to U.S. citizens and other nations around the world. The initiatives are designed to counter the growing nexus among narcotics traffickers and other international criminals fostered by development in international communications, the end of the Cold War, and the exponential growth of economic market forces in many countries.

My topic concerns organized crime in the United States and this means paying attention to La Cosa Nostra, the American Mafia, which remains the most important organized crime threat in the United States. After examining LCN's status, I will turn to other migrant and ethnic groups that have emerged as criminal competitors in recent years of Cosa Nostra within America.

Although weakened in the past twenty-five years, La Cosa Nostra has not been eliminated; instead, it has been joined by a variety of increasingly powerful domestic and international organized criminal networks operating in the United States. Criminal organizations (particularly those from China and Latin America -- Triads and Drug Cartels) are taking advantage of the increases in immigration into the United States for cover, concealment, and recruitment into criminal activities. For example, aliens mainly from China smuggled by boat

Table 9.1: Ethnic/international organized crime groups

Ethnic group	Origins	Groups	Illicit activities	North American locales	Notable characteristics
Chinese (Tongs, Triads, street gangs)	17th century China	Wa, 14X	Gambling, extortion, Drug trafficking, robbery, prostitution, murder, arms dealing, racketeering	California, New York	Tongs and street gangs posses many characteristics of OC groups
Japanese Yakuza	7th century Japan	Yamaguchi Gumi	Weapons trafficking (to Japan) methamphetamine (trafficking to Japan), murder, gambling, extortion, bookmaking	California, Hawaii	All Yakuza groups are highly structured/hierarchical. Legitimate activities include banking and real estate. Estimated annual revenue is $32 billion
Colombian drug traffickers	Colombia has a long history of social banditry	Medellin and Cali cartels	Cocaine trafficking	New York area, Miami, Los Angeles, Houston	Complex infrastructures; estimate: employs about 24,000
Vietnamese gangs	Arrival of immigrants in U.S. in 1970s	Born to Kill	Extortion, prostitution, Auto thefts, arson, gambling, armed robbery	Chicago, New Orleans, Houston, Washington DC, Los Angeles, Boston	Not a major problem compared to other ethnic organized crime groups
Jamaican Posses	Kingston, Jamaica. Came to U.S. in mid-1970s	Shower Posse Spangler Posse	Cocaine (crack distribution), firearms trafficking, money laundering, fraud, robbery, kidnapping, murder, auto theft	NY, Miami, Los Angeles, San Francisco, Detroit, Philadelphia, Dallas, Washington DC, Chicago, Houston	One of the most violent OC groups in the United States
Russian Mafia	Émigrés arrived in large numbers in the 1970s	Odessa, Malina, Organiz-atsiya	Marketing illegal goods (drugs, weapons, stolen cars) extortion, forgery, loan sharking, racketeering, gasoline bootlegging	New York, New Jersey, Philadelphia, Los Angeles, Chicago, Baltimore, Dallas, Cleveland, Phoenix, Toronto	Perestroika reforms coupled with economic mayhem fueled a tremendous growth in new forms of organized crime

Sources: Compiled from - U.S. Comptroller-General (1989) *Non-traditional Organized Crime*, Washington DC: US General Accounting Office; Ko-lin Chin, Jeffrey Fagan and Robert J. Kelley (1994) *Gangs and Social Order in Chinatown*. Washington, DC: National Institute of Justice. Unpublished Final Report

pay exorbitant passage fees and cannot work at regular jobs; thus, they are exploited by unscrupulous employers or become active in vice activities such as prostitution, the drug trade or other aspects of the illegal economy. In this way, victims become criminals themselves (Table 9.1).

La Cosa Nostra: Decline or Re-Alignment?

Over the past decade the prosecution and conviction of 21 of the 25 "crime family" bosses in the American La Cosa Nostra (LCN) or Mafia and a decline in the membership of the five major New York City "crime families," as Cosa Nostra groups are sometimes described, from 3,000 in the 1970s to 1,200 today, represents an unprecedented aggressive and sophisticated anti-crime effort directed by the FBI that resulted in many convictions and defections of members which weakened Mafia control in various vice industries and markets.

Table 9.2: Major Cosa Nostra trials and outcomes 1980s and 1990

Year	Name	Age	Alleged Role	Offense	Outcomes
1985	Gennaro Langella	47	Underboss of Colombo group in New York City	Perjury, obstruction of justice	10 years prison, $15,000 fine
1986	Matthew Lanniello Benjamin Cohen (and 6 others)	65 66	No mention of organized crime in indictment	Skimming from NYC bars, restaurants	6 years 5 years
1986	Michael Franzese (and four others)	35	Son of "captain" in Colombo group	Racketeering and tax conspiracy	10 years plus $15 million fine forfeit
1986	Gennaro Anguilo (and four others)	67	Underboss of New England (Partriarce) group	Racketeering, gambling, loansharking, murder	45 years prison $120,000 fine
1986	Anthony Spilotro and eight others	47	Overseer of Las Vegas operations for Chicago group	Conspiracy, racketeering in Las Vegas burglary ring	Mistrial (found murdered 2 days before retrial)
1986	Paul Castellano, Anthony Gaggi, Ronald Ustica, Henry Borelli	72 60 41 37	Leader and members of Gambino crime group in New York	Car theft, conspiracy, and murder (Ustica and Borelli)	Castellano killed during trial, Gaggi 5 ears, others lif in prison
1986	Matthew Ianniello Benjamin Cohen (and 4 others)	65 66	"Captain" and associates in Genovese group	Racketeering, Fraud, extortion in garbage collection	14 years prison, 5 years prison, 5 years prison
1986	Anthony, Joseph and Vincent Colombo	41 39 35	Members of Colombo group in New York City	Racketeering, Conspiracy, Narcotics	14 years prison, 5 years prison, 5 years prison
1986	Santo Trafficante	71	Leader of Florida group	Racketeering, gambling	Mistrial
1986	Joseph Bonanno	81	Retired boss of Bonanno group	Contempt for refusal to testify	14 months jail

1986	Carmine & Alphonse Persico, Gennaro Langella (and seven others)	53 33 47	Head of Colombo crime group and associates in New York City	Labor and construction racketeering, extortion	39 years prison, 12 years prison, 65 years prison
1986	Paul Vario	73	Counselor in NYC Lucchese group	Extortion at JFK Airport	6 years prison $25,000 fine
1986	Cahng An-lo (and seven others)	30s	Leader & members of the United Bamboo Chinese gang in New York	Narcotics distribution, murder	25 years prison
1987	Paul Castellano, Anthony Salerno, Anthony Corrallo, Gennaro Langella, Philip Rastelli (and four others)	72 75 73 48 69	"Commission" trial of leaders of Gambino, Genovese, Lucchese, Colombo, Bonanno groups in New York	Racketeering, conspiracy, loansharking, labor bribery, extortion in construction	Castellano murdered during trial, other leaders each received 100 years in prison
1987	Philip Rastelli (and seven others)	69	Leader of Bonanno group in New York	Labor racketeering in moving industry	12 years prison
1987	Ilario Zannino	67	Underboss in New England group	Gambling, loansharking	30 years prison
1987	John Gotti, Armand and Aniello Dellacroce (and six others)	64 46	"Pizza Connection" Turkey - Sicily - Brazil - New York drug importation via pizzerias	Narcotics distribution, conspiracy	Each received 45 years prison and $1.1 million fine
1987	Nicodemo Scarfo	58	Boss of Philadelphia group	Extortion from developers, narcotics distribution	14 years prison acquitted
1988	Carlos Lehder	38	A Medellin Cartel Leader	Drug smuggling, conspiracy	2 consecutive life terms, plus 135 years prison
1989	Loren Piccarreto	38	Head of Rochester, NY crime group	Gambling and extortion	7 years prison
1989	Nicodemo Scarfo (and seven others)	59	Boss of Philadelphia group	Murder	Life in prison (overturned on appeal, due to prosecutorial misconduct)
1989	Nicodemo Scarfo, Philip Leonetti, (and 13 others)	59 36	Boss of Philadelphia group	Racketeering, murder, extortion, narcotics, gambling	55 years prison, 45 years prison
1990	John Gotti	49	Boss of Gambino crime family in New York	Assault	Acquitted
1990	Rayful Edmond	25	Head of Washington D.C. cocaine ring	Drug trafficking	3 life terms

1990	Matthew Ianniello	70	Captain in Genovese group	Racketeering, extortion	5 years prison
1990	Charles Porter, Louis Raucci	58 61	Underboss and member of Pittsburgh group	Racketeering, narcotics, tax violations	28 years prison
1991	Raymond Patriarca, Jr.	47	Leader of New England group	Racketeering	8 years prison
1991	Nicholas Bianco	59	Boss of Patriarca (New England group)	Racketeering	11 years
1992	Joseph Russo (and four others)	58	Counselor in New England Group	Kidnapping, extortion, murder	16 years
1992	Victor Orena	58	Acting boss of Colombo family	Racketeering, murder, Loan-sharking, Conspiracy	Life in prison
1992	Thomas Pitera	37	Soldier in Bonanno group	Six drug-related murders	Life in prison
1992	John Gotti	51	Boss of Gambino group in New York	Five murders, including that of Paul Castellano	Life in prison
1993	Michael Tacetta, Michael Perna	46 50	Head of Lucchese group in New Jersey	Racketeering and murder conspiracy	30 years prison
1993	Thomas Gambino	64	Captain in Gambino group	Racketeering, gambling loansharking	5 years prison
1993	Johnny Eng	36	Head of Flying Dragons in New York's Chinatown	Racketeering, heroin trafficking	24 years prison, $3.5 million fine
1993	Salvatore Lambardi (and six others)	54	Captain in Genovese group in New Jersey	Racketeering, extortion, gambling	22 years prison, $175,000 fine
1993	John Riggi	69	Boss of New Jersey crime group	Murder conspiracy	7 years prison begins after current sentence
1993	Gregory Scarpa, Sr.	65	Captain in Colombo crime group in New York	Murder conspiracy	10 years prison (Scarpa was terminally ill)
1994	John and Joseph Gambino	53 47	Members of Gambino crime group	Racketeering, narcotic, trafficking	15 years prison
1994	Joseph Loveti	44	Former chapter leader of Pagans motorcycle gang	Trafficking in methampheta-mines	22 years prison
1994	Salvatore Avellino, Jr.	58	Associate of Lucchese group on Long Island	Racketeering and murder conspiracy	10 years prison plus 21 years probation
1994	Leonard Falzone	59	Enforcer in Buffalo crime group	Racketeering and loansharking	5 years prison

Source: Based on Jay S. Albanese (1996) *Organized Crime in America*, 3rd ed. Cincinnati, OH: Anderson Publishing Co.

Table 9.2 documents some of the most significant trials involving key figures in La Cosa Nostra crime families and it reflects the outcomes of concerted law enforcement efforts. The table also reflects the power of the draconian sentences, fines and forfeitures of wealth for convicted offenders. RICO's effectiveness has been enhanced by the use of immunity statutes for witness evidence, and the Witness Security Program, which affords government witnesses and their immediate families' protection against threats to their lives.

By 1988, nineteen crime family bosses, thirteen underbosses, and some forty "captains" (lower-level leaders) had been convicted.[2] Figures 9.1 and 9.2 depict the types of structures and models of relational networks creating channels of interaction and bonds of cohesion among members. Whether the crime family is corporate-like (and in some of its activities, it probably is), or built around clientelist personalistic connections is not particularly important from a prosecutional standpoint.

Table 9.2 documents, in terms of the positions, offenses, and sentences of principal offenders, that many of the cases of racketeering convictions involved the infiltration of legitimate businesses through extortionate activities. The average sentence exceeded 25 years - quite severe, especially when one considers the average age of convicted and sentenced offenders: 62 plus. Even with parole eligibility it is likely that a new leadership will emerge among the crime families. Though many of the cases and offenders are located in the New York area, other parts of the country have been affected as well and attest to the national scope of La Cosa Nostra.

An unintended (and undesirable) consequence of the successes of the government against the LCN may be that younger, more aggressive leaders will emerge who are prepared to use violence more freely to achieve the top and to intimidate informers and competitors. Yet another outcome has to do with more sophistication as criminals react to law enforcement effectiveness. To the degree that law enforcement becomes more efficient, criminal technologies and operations will shift to more secure venues and markets - at least that is what may be hypothesized as a future development within markets. But even with its loosened grip on racketeering enterprises in legal markets (trucking, construction, waste disposal, gambling), the LCN remains resilient and functionally viable.

The LCN is a serious problem for other reasons as well: it has successfully penetrated the American legitimate economy and politics; it is not focused only within a particular ethnic community, as are the Chinese, African-Americans, Vietnamese and Russians; rather, it permeates many sectors. One of the greatest concerns of law enforcement still is the LCN's infiltration of labor unions. At present, even after numerous and vigorous investigations and prosecutions, the LCN controls or has influence in more than one hundred labor unions at local and national levels. Its presence is felt particularly in the construction industry, as well as in the gaming, restaurants, and transportation industries. Clearly, the LCN has shown itself to be a very entrenched, adaptable, criminally diverse group.[4]

Figure 9.1: An organized crime family

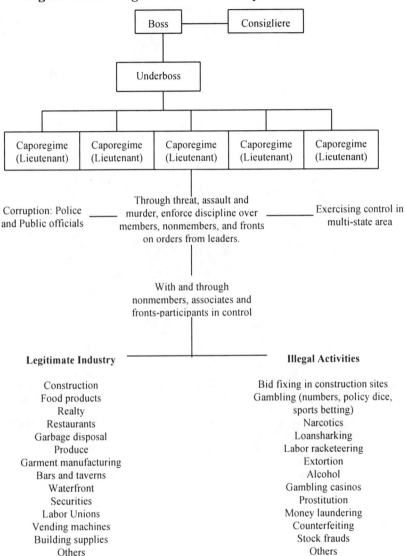

Boss —— Consigliere

Underboss

| Caporegime (Lieutenant) | Caporegime (Lieutenant) | Caporegime (Lieutenant) | Caporegime (Lieutenant) | Caporegime (Lieutenant) |

Corruption: Police and Public officials —— Through threat, assault and murder, enforce discipline over members, nonmembers, and fronts on orders from leaders. —— Exercising control in multi-state area

With and through nonmembers, associates and fronts-participants in control

Legitimate Industry

Construction
Food products
Realty
Restaurants
Garbage disposal
Produce
Garment manufacturing
Bars and taverns
Waterfront
Securities
Labor Unions
Vending machines
Building supplies
Others

Illegal Activities

Bid fixing in construction sites
Gambling (numbers, policy dice, sports betting)
Narcotics
Loansharking
Labor racketeering
Extortion
Alcohol
Gambling casinos
Prostitution
Money laundering
Counterfeiting
Stock frauds
Others

Sources: Task Force on Organized Crime, 1967, 9; A

Figure 9.2: Patron-client network of
Italian-American organized crime

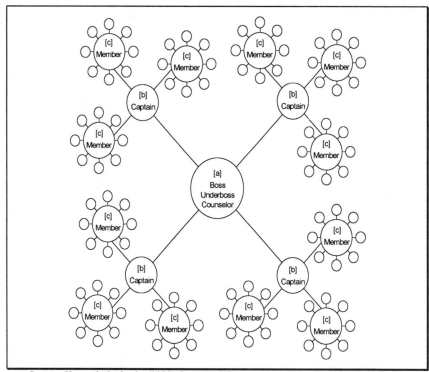

Source: Howard Abadinsky (1990) Organized Crime 3rd ed. Chicago: Nelson-Hall, p. 29

(a) At the center of each organized crime unit (famiglia: Family) is the boss (capo).
(b) He is assisted by an underboss (sottocapo) and a counselor (consigliere).
(c) Surrounding the boss are his clients, the captains (capiregime).
     Orbiting around each captain are his clients, the lowest-ranking members who
     have been initiated into the Family (soldati, 'made guys'). The members act as
     patrons to nonmember clients. Each unit is tied to other Families throughout the
     country by the capo whosesovereignty is recognized by the other bosses.

The development of crime-fighting technologies did produce a great
weight of resources in law enforcement's favor, but this has encouraged
illusions that need to be dispelled. For example, it is dubious to rely on the
number of crime bosses imprisoned as a measure of effective crime control
when it seems pretty clear that removing a boss does little to impede criminal
operations.

Table 9.3: Cities where families of La Cosa Nostra are alleged to exist

City	State
Boston-Providence	Massachusetts, Rhode Island
Buffalo	New York
Chicago	Illinois
Cleveland	Ohio
Detroit	Michigan
Los Angeles	California
New York (5)	New York
New Orleans	Louisiana
Philadelphia	Pennsylvania
San Francisco	California
Tampa	Florida
San Jose	California
Denver-Pueblo (Inactive)	Colorado
Kansas City	Missouri
Pittsburgh	Pennsylvania
Milwaukee (See Boston)	Wisconsin
St. Louis	Missouri
Pittston-Cranston-Wilkes-Barre	Pennsylvania
Tucson	Arizona
Rockford	Illinois
Madison	Wisconsin
Elizabeth-Newark	New Jersey
Springfield	Illinois

Source: FBI (1980)

Despite a rash of convictions over the past twenty years, the LCN has shown a resilience and vitality rarely acknowledged by law enforcement officials. With leadership changes occurring frequently since RICO convictions have intensified, one would expect major succession crises in the organized underworld. Apparently they have not materialized; the death of a boss or his conviction has not meant as much to crime family entrepreneurs well positioned in their rackets and businesses. The very grassroots nature of the LCN crime families with thousands of mob figures and associates means that the American Mafia is still alive and thriving but doing so more cautiously. Everyone is keeping their heads down after the conviction of John Gotti, the head of the Gambino Crime Family, which the Department of Justice has called the most powerful crime family in the United States. The imprisonment of leaders in the late 1980s, which many commentators hailed as "The Twilight of the God-fathers," has not been the crushing blow to street rackets in loansharking, gambling, extortion, cargo theft, credit card fraud and drug trafficking; the backbone of the crime families, its lowest-ranking members and non-member associates, are the real, everyday, criminal masterminds: they still have a grip on illegal and legal industries.

Figure 9.3 International structure of the Helmer Herrera-Buitrago cocaine distribution organization in New York City

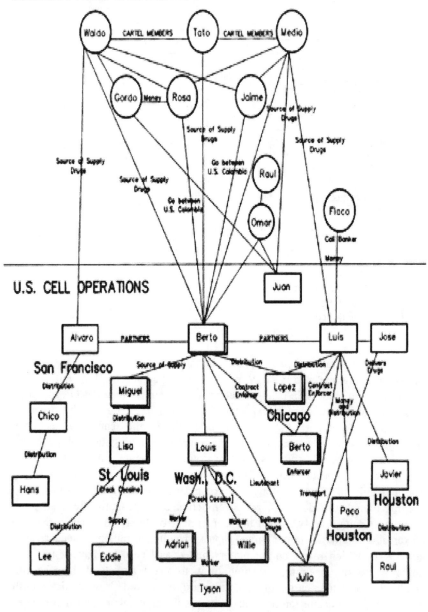

Several factors have emerged since the passage of RICO legislation in the early 1970s that have had an impact on LCN activities and structure.

- First, the structure of urban politics and policing has been altered. The principal original asset of the Mafia, built during the Prohibition Era, was its connections with, and manipulations of urban political machines. Those associations with mayors and local politicians helped the Mafia develop proprietary interests to centralized police corruption, which enhanced its power over the police. But since the 1960s and 1970s the old political machines have disappeared; cities in which Mafia crime families operate are mostly governed by broad civic and economic coalitions with strong federal involvement in local government financing so that local corruption must be more sophisticated and above all must be less pervasive and naked. Also, the flight of white ethnic communities has dispersed some of the Mafia's principal markets and recruitment pools.

- Secondly, relationships between Mafiosi and African-Americans, Latinos and others in local communities have been often abrasive and not of the kind that encourages trust. This is not meant to imply that the LCN lost or lacks the capacity to corrupt. It is engaged in the corruption of political figures if only because campaigns are very expensive and politicians are vulnerable, attractive targets for corruption. The evidence of LCN involvement in political fundraising has been a continuous scandal among many urban politicians locally and nationally. The thesis of the "Twilight of the Godfathers" may be interesting reading but scarcely accurate as a description of the underworld. Corruption has changed as have LCN criminal operations: because they don't compete on the street with African-Americans or Latinos in drug trafficking there is less need for the LCN to compromise an entire police force -- only key components that might jeopardize their rackets need to be approached.

- Third, local police agencies have become more professional - if not more honest -- and the expansion of federal law enforcement agencies with concurrent local jurisdiction and a strong interest in making corruption cases has inhibited and jeopardized the traditional relationships between Mafiosi and police. At best, local police might sell political protection but

Figure 9.4 Modern Triad structure

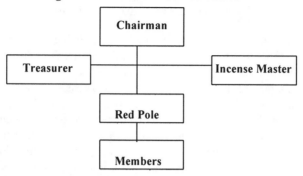

Source: Robert Kelly, et al Final Report, NIJ, Dept. of Justice, Washington D.C. (1994).

even that is problematic because they are wary of gangsters who often seek relief from federal prosecution by making deals with prosecutors and offering up their local protectors and partners within the police forces.[5]

- Fourth, better federal law enforcement necessitates LCN re-organization. The FBI has gotten out of its pinstripe suits and taken to the streets in long-term undercover operations. The federal judiciary armed with RICO has imposed life sentences without parole that amount to death sentences, and the bond of silence that solidified crime families - the vaunted loyalty through "omerta" - has been shattered by the Witness Security Program that protects informants.

Still, with all the induced crisis and turmoil, the LCN continues to retain residual power. The Mafia may be in retreat on all sides except one. Its one important activity, major commercial business conspiracies where criminals infiltrate the legitimate sector through extortion, intimidation, and violence, has not substantially subsided: The conspiracies in waste hauling, trucking, construction, restaurants and food industries are long-lived and relatively unabated. In short, the Mafia has not disappeared but like a chameleon, it re-configured itself. The danger may be that law enforcement may slacken its tenacity, and become somewhat complacent with its successes and lose its vigilant edge. Resources and energy may turn to other threats and new problems such as terrorism and the emergence of new organized crime groups. Indeed, there are signs of a diminution of state and federal efforts at the Justice Department and in local jurisdictions where intelligence units and state-level crime commissions have been disbanded.[6]

The Future of Organized Crime

Organized crime has not disappeared from American cities. While the Mafia may live off its vaunted reputation, new ethnic gangs from Latin America, East Asia and Eastern Europe have become wealthy through their control of large-scale illicit drug distribution systems.

They are also effective extortionists in their own communities. Whether the new groups will take on Mafia-like styles and capabilities can only be conjecture at this point. So far while the Colombian cocaine traffickers and the Chinese groups organized and managed by Tongs (versions of Hong Kong Triads) have exhibited some Mafia-type entrepreneurial abilities, neither have branched out into other activities in the United States. They have not been able or have not chosen to diversify as widely as has the Mafia, into mainstream political and social institutions outside their own communities. Most of all, from the standpoint of reputation, the major Tongs and drug cartels lack the reputation of Mafia families.

The structures of Triads and Tongs (see Figures 9.4 and 9.5) will be seen to contain functional roles of activity and behavior similar to those in Cosa Nostra families. But their development and evolution is culturally and ecologically determined -- that is, the positions are defined by the particular task environments which the crime groups are situated in and the historical contingencies that each cultural group experienced. Likewise, in Figures 9.6 and 9.7, which illustrate the organizational structure of the Yakuza, their structures of criminal formation are similar to Mafia groups, Triads and Tongs. Hierarchy, a division of criminal labor, and power accumulating at the top of the administrative pyramid are characteristic features of these groups. Despite different cultures and different political and social histories, crime organizations are similar to legitimate business firms. Both make adjustments to their milieu in order to survive while attempting to manipulate that environment to make it more amenable to their operations.

The insularity of the Chinese community is similar to that of the Colombians. One would think that the huge revenues of cocaine trafficking would enable Colombian drug dealers to take on Mafia-type capabilities. But that has not happened. Unlike their Mafia counterparts of the 1920s and 1930s, Colombians have not branched out into other activities in the United States. And neither have the Chinese. Drug traffickers in Colombia have greatly broadened their base of legal and illegal activities, which contrasts sharply with their reserve and secretiveness in the United States. The difference is probably attributable to the possibilities for systemic corruption. In Colombia the success of the drug cartels has been built on the political influence they brought along with their willingness to intimidate law enforcement. That influence and power permitted the Medellin and Cali cartels to invest with impunity in agricultural land and local media.[7]

In the United States that sort of protection/corruption has not been available or exploited by the Colombians. The key members of the cartels have not developed connections to political machines and personalities nor created an

Figure 9.5: Typical organizational structure of Tong-affiliated and non-affiliated gangs

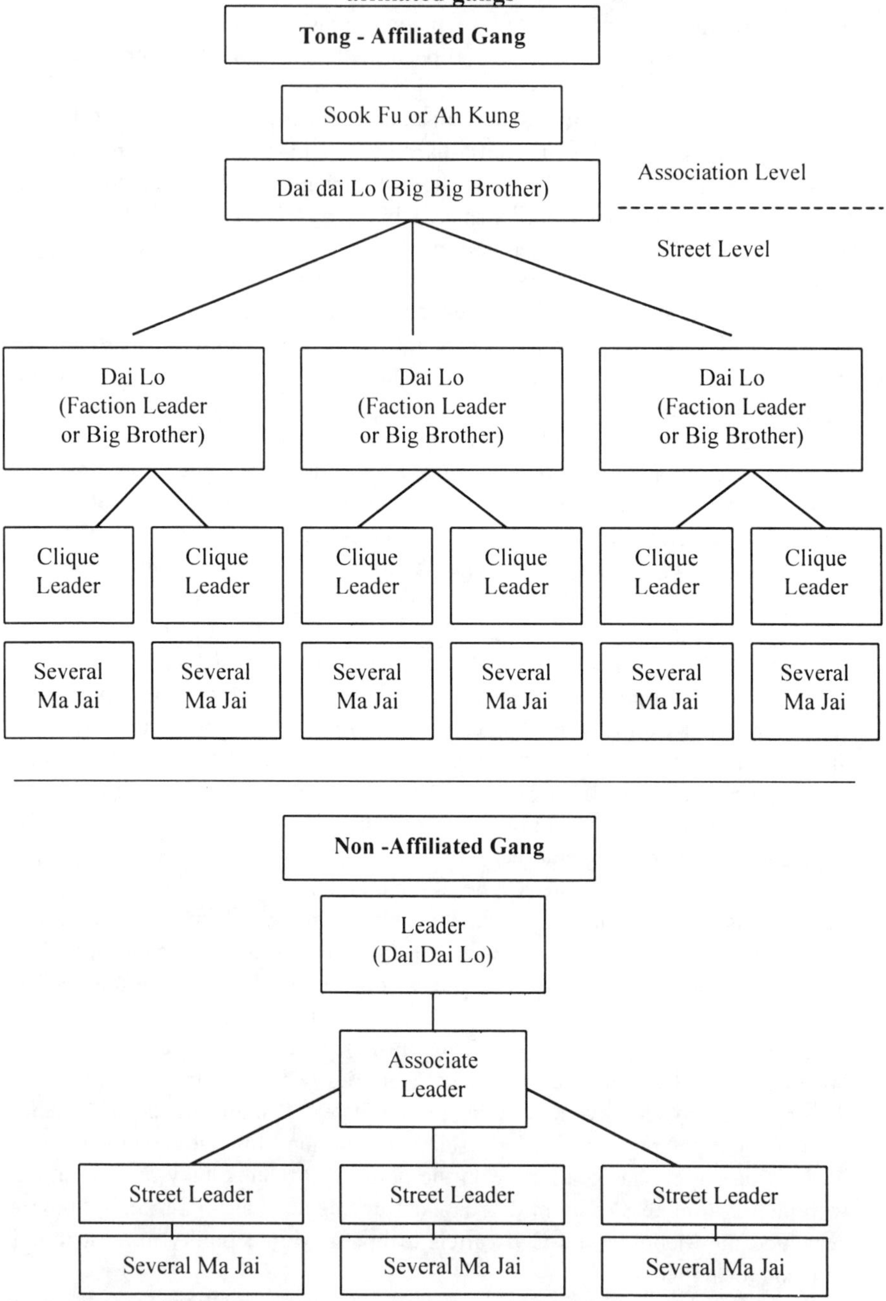

Source: Chin et. al. Gangs and Social Order. 1994.

Figure 9.6: Structure of Sumiyoshi-rengo criminal organization (gambling syndicate)

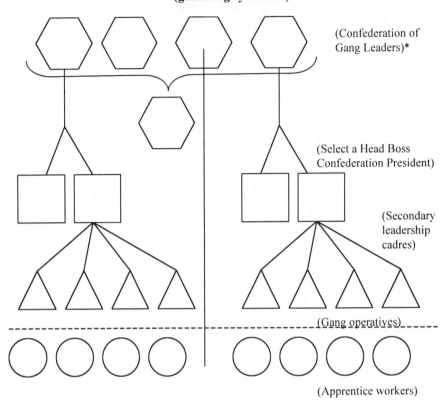

(Confederation of Gang Leaders)*

(Select a Head Boss Confederation President)

(Secondary leadership cadres)

(Gang operatives)

(Apprentice workers)

* Each individual gang leader maintains control over his own organization
Source: Hioaki Iwai, "Organized crime in Japan" in Robert J. Kelly, (ed.) Organized Crime: A Global Perspective, NJ: Rowman & Littlefield, (1986). p 227

intricate base for expanded operations as the early LCN members did six decades ago. However, the vice activities of Mafia overlords in gambling, prostitution, and illegal alcohol distribution were not as stigmatized publicly as drug dealing. Gamblers and bootleggers could and did become public figures such as Frank Costello, Samuel Bronfman and Joseph Kennedy; where in contrast drug dealers are rewarded for discretion and low profiles. Moreover, wholesale drug dealing is not a retail business and does not require long-term, continuous police protection. In addition, drug trafficking is inherently treacherous and prolonged exposure can be quite dangerous. For these and other reasons, Colombian traffickers have not planted themselves in the social soil and diversified their activities through their wealth to create the criminogenic conditions necessary to produce a Mafia type criminal structure.

Figure 9.7: Structure of Yamaguchi-gumi criminal organization
(vice syndicate)

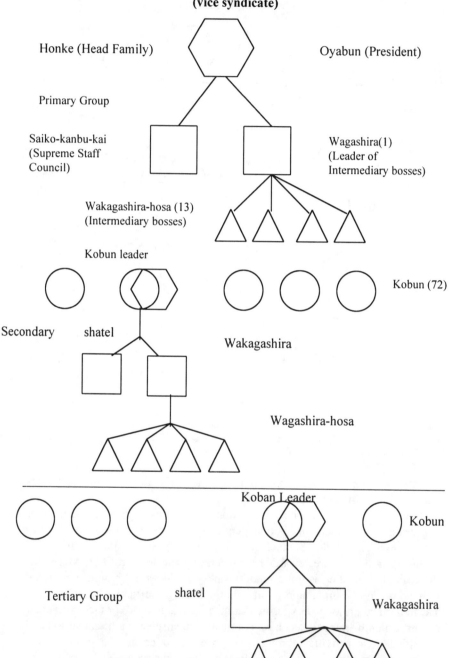

Source: Hioaki Iwai, "Organized crime in Japan" in Robert J. Kelly, (ed.) Organized Crime: A global Perspective, NJ: Rowman & Littlefield, (1986). p 226

Table 9.4 compares selected organized crime groups using a number of key parameters.

Table 9.4: A comparison of ethnic/international groups as organized crime groups

Group Type	Corruption	Violence	Continuity	Multiple Criminal Enterprises	Structure	Involving Legitimate Businesses	Sophistication	Discipline	Bonding
Chinese Tongs and Triads	*	*	*	*	*	*	*	*	*
Japanese Yakuza	*	*	*	*	*	*	*	*	*
Colombian (drug) cartels	*	*	*		*		*		
Vietnamese gangs	*	*		*	*			*	*
Jamaican Posses	*	*		*	*	*	*		
Russian Mafia	*	*	*	*	*	*	*		

Source: Based on definitional criteria from M. Maltz (1985), "Towards Defining Organized Crime" in H. Alexander and G. Caiden (eds.) The Politics and Economics of Organized Crime, Lexington, MA: D.C. Heath

The situation with the Chinese is somewhat different.[8] Chinese gangs have been effective extortionists in their own communities able to intimidate small (and sometimes large) businesses. And with the expansion of these communities with new migration - both legal and illegal - conditions for crime have increased. An important factor that contributes to the crime, primarily extortionate crime, is the general suspicion of the police who are viewed as culturally alien. It must be said that police departments in the United States have recognized this problem but their modest recruiting efforts in attracting ethnic Chinese into police work have produced little success in Asian communities.

Extortion Racketeering in Chinatown: A Case Study

To illustrate the point about new forms of organized crime in the United States, I want to present some data on a study conducted in New York City's Chinatown. The research began in 1989 and concluded in 1994 (see Kelly, Chin and Fagan, 1994). It was driven by questions that focused on the extent of gang extortion in the Chinese communities of the United States; on its principal victims, and on the severity of extortionate crime in the commercial sector.

The research effort was based on first-hand accounts collected from street gang members, gang victims, community leaders, law enforcement authorities, and hundreds of business people within New York City's Chinatown.[9] The research focused on extortion of businesses within the community and revealed the pervasiveness of crime and the general fear that gangs and their Tong sponsors instilled in the community. In more than six hundred interviews it became clear that the economic vitality of the community had been sapped, and lawlessness was perceived as widespread, which made a mockery of law enforcement presence.

The study also uncovered the brutal realities of life in an ethnic ghetto insulated from the larger society. Gangs functioned in many instances as "equalizers" within an environment filled with individual and group conflicts where social, political and economic issues were not mediated or resolved in the courts. Chinatown's informal economy, the underground world of illegal immigrants and illegal businesses seems to require gangs as both providers and protectors of illegal services. Organized crime in this setting was nothing less than a pathological manifestation of a closed community isolated from the mainstream. The data collected below provide some sense of the nature of the institutional problems within a community where "organized crime" has transformed the community into a criminal supermarket.

Table 9.5 provides information on the sample victim population studied. The New York City Police believe that gangs extort 90% of Chinatown businesses. It was this startling claim that motivated the research.[10] How valid is it?

Table 9.5 shows personal and business attributes of the respondents. Most are male, in their mid-forties, immigrants from Hong Kong. In terms of education, most completed 12 years or more of school and most respondents resided in the U.S.A. for at least 16 years. A typical subject could be described as a relatively well educated Cantonese male from Hong Kong who had lived in the U.S.A. for more than 10 years.

The businesses in the study sample were mostly restaurants, retail food stores and goods stores (shoes, videos, beauty shops, etc.). Most businesses were relatively new (8 years on average); and most were restaurants. (As with other organized crime extortion rackets, businesses with high volume cash flow are attractive to extortionists.)

With regard to the severity of gang extortion Table 9.6 indicates that forced sales and "extortion" (a.k.a. "Lucky Money") are the most prevalent forms of gang extortion. Sixty-nine percent of businesses reported one of the 4 types listed here.

Table 9.6 documents the prevalence of extortion by type with forced sales being the most common (51%). We speculated that businesses were less likely to resist demands for overpriced goods because it was culturally acceptable - a matter of "face" (a cultural precedent one could construe as "honor" or "dignity") to buy something than to simply turn money over to street thugs.

Table 9.5: Respondents' personal and business characteristics

Personal	N	%	Business	N	%
Sex			**Type of business**		
Male	472	78	Restaurant	211	3
Female	131	22	Retail food store	130	22
			Retail nonfood store	108	18
Age			Service	117	19
Mean	43		Factory	36	6
Median	42				
Mode	41		**Location**		
			Manhattan's Chinatown	335	56
Country of Origin			Queens' Chinatown	129	21
Hong Kong	624	54	Brooklyn's Chinatown	42	7
Taiwan	104	17	Manhattan non-Chinatown	34	6
China	85	14	Queens' non-Chinatown	22	4
Others	89	15	Brooklyn non-Chinatown	41	7
Ethnicity			**Age of Firm**		
Cantonese	332	56	Mean	8	
Fukinese	44	7	Median	5	
Chiu Chao/Hakka	29	5	Mode	3	
Taiwanese	44	7			
Shanghainese	45	8	**Size of Firm**		
Other Chinese	73	12	Very small	55	9
Others	28	5	Small	172	29
			Medium	253	43
Education			Large	111	19
No Schooling	8	1			
6 grade or less	55	9	**Sole owner of Business?**		
7 to 9 grade	68	12	Yes	283	48
10 to 12 grade	198	33	No	305	52
College	230	39			
Graduate School	34	6	**Also own the Property ?**		
			Yes	80	14
Number of years in the U.S.			No	508	86
Mean	16				
Median	14				
Mode	10				

Table 9.6: Lifetime prevalence of gang extortion (N=603)

Type of victimization	% Attempted	% Completed
Protection	22	11
Extortion	41	27
Forced Sales	51	41
Theft of foods / services	17	16
All 4 types	69	55

Table 9.7 documents the incidence of extortion by type. Most victims of protection demands paid monthly; "lucky money" extortionate activities occurred infrequently either four times a year (54%) or once a year (39%). Although forced sales were the most prevalent type of gang extortion, its victims were exploited only once or twice yearly. In sum, extortion victim encounters with perpetrators varies by type of extortion.

Table 9.7: Frequency of completed gang extortion (%)

	Protection	Extortion	Selling Items	Theft of Goods or Services
Number	70	156	246	94
2-3 times a week	0	0	0	8
Weekly	16	1	0	4
Bi-Weekly	0	1	0	12
Monthly	42	5	0	6
Several times a year	0	0	5	23
Quarterly	6	54	26	27
Semi-Annually	5	0	27	0
Annually	9	39	41	15
Once/Lump sum payment	22	0	0	5
Annual Frequency				
Mean*	14	5	2	17
Median	3	2	2	7
Mode	12	3	1	3

* The annual mean, median, and mode are approximate figures calculated from the frequency presented above.

The Costs of Extortion

Contrary to law enforcement allegations and claims about the amount of extortion paid, we found discrepancies between police estimates and victim reports. On the average, as Table 9.8 indicates, victims paid $129 for each protection payment, $75 for each "lucky money" payment, $51 for forced sales and a loss of $119 worth of goods or services. The typical payment was $100 for protection with a yearly average of $1,294, $20 for "lucky money" ($313 yearly), $50 for forced sales ($117 yearly), and $30 for theft of goods and services ($1,532 yearly).

Table 9.8: Financial costs of gang extortion

Per Incident

	Protection	Extortion	Selling Items	Theft of Goods or Services
Number	70	156	246	94
Minimum	$3	$2	$5	$1
Maximum	1,000	1,300	200	3,000
Mean	129	75	51	119
Median	65	30	40	45
Mode	100	20	50	30

Per Year

	Total	Protection	Extortion	Selling Items	Theft of Goods or Services
Minimum	$3	$5	$3	$5	$4
Maximum	31,220	12,000	9,100	1,250	31,200
Mean	688	1,294	313	117	1,532
Median	20	480	90	80	210
Mode	50	100	20	30	210

The annual cost of all types summated (regardless of the type of extortion) was $688. Relative to other costs of doing business, extortion is not significant in strictly financial terms when factored into the cluster of other costs including rent, taxes, insurance, employee salaries, commercial certificates, etc. (This may partially explain why victims do not readily report extortion demands and threats to the police.)

Reactions to Extortion

This consideration leads to questions about how the victims of extortion typically react. The media and the police often characterize Chinese business people as powerless, frightened victims cowered into silence, who are reluctant to talk to the police much less testify in a trial against a gang member.

Police claim, rather defensively, that Chinese immigrants are unwilling to report crimes to authorities. In fact, Chinese business people comply with criminal extortionate demands but also resist them; they report crimes to the police and they do not - all of this depends on their perceptions of the criminal justice system and their adaptations to gang victimization. The study examined why business people often hesitated to report extortion to the police and compared these rates with national data from the National Crime Victim Survey (NCS).

Table 9.9 illustrates the results. Only 4% if those intimidated into Forced Sales reported the event to the authorities. The overall-reporting rate was 20%, which is substantially lower than the reporting rate for all personal crimes.

Again the question is why do Chinese business owners seem reluctant to contact the police? It was found that most victims do not consider the crime important enough. Others claimed that the police could not or would not do anything and some feared gang reprisals. The most significant predictor of crime reporting behavior was the seriousness of the extortion: the more money demanded or the credibility of threats of violence prompted police contacts by victims.

Other reasons affecting police reporting came into play For one, they themselves may be operating businesses illegally (without proper certification and insurance), or they may be employing illegal aliens; or receiving stolen goods and so on.

Table 9.9:Reasons for not reporting extortion to police by type of gang victimization

	NCVS Personal Robbery	Protection	Extortion	Forced Sales	Theft of Goods and Services
Number of Victims	1,149,710*	130	245	308	103
Report rate	50	24	18	4	16
Number of reasons stated for not reporting	714,480	126	312	354	120
Object recovered/ offender unsuccessful	19	13	13	5	
Lack of proof/ in-surance would not cover/unable to recover property	14	16	22	18	22
Police ineffective inefficient or blasted	11	9	7	1	6
Private of personal matter	9	3			
Police would not want to be bothered	8	4	8	3	1
Fear of reprisal	7	21	6	6	19
Too inconvenient or time-consuming	7	5	7	2	2
Reported to another official	7				
Not aware crime occurred until later	1				
Crime not important enough	1	23	28	29	34
It's a way to generate luck		2	4	1	
This is expected in Chinatown		4	1	1	1
Will report if it happens often		2	2		2
I can handle it myself			2	4	12
We need the items anyway				3	
See it as gift giving				9	
See it as an ordinary sale				9	
Other reasons	15	2	1	7	3

* Number of Victimization. Reasons for not reporting are in %

But though extortion is not as pernicious as law enforcement authorities would have us believe, it does make a significant impact on the community in the way the business sector reacts. Many business people indicated that they took precautions to hide their identities as owners by hiring managers and even white employees. (Gang extortion against non-Chinese businesses is virtually non-existent). Business practices (hours, locations) were changed in order to avoid gang approaches. Security measures on the premises were improved and strengthened.

Merchants said they would like to see tough enforcement measures. The Tongs themselves are fully aware of the gang extortion problem and leaders of the Tongs claim (somewhat hypocritically) that the problem is long-standing and that they are helpless in dealing with it. In fact, they indirectly benefit from gang intimidation in that out of exasperation some of the bigger, more lucrative businesses "donate" money to the Tongs and ethnic associations believing that they will provide a protective cloak against gang harassment. Storeowners will often display a certificate of Tong membership, which seems to work.[11]

The problem is serious enough so much so that extortion has become institutionalized and "normalized" within the community; it is integrated into the typical routines and customs of the community where business owners, police and community leaders take it for granted - meaning it is so endemic to community life that it has become tolerable and customary.

In the victim survey, when asked if they thought police were prejudiced against Asians, almost three-quarters (74%) said yes. Merchants questioned police impartiality and others thought that the police did not take their complaints seriously so they didn't bother to report them.

Table 9.10 documents that of all of the personal attributes of extortion victims; subjects who had more education and English proficiency were less likely to be targeted by gang extortionists. Extortionists' "sociology" is thus shrewd: education and language proficiency are construed as evidence of assimilation and familiarity with American culture and presumably are equated with knowledge and willingness to summon and report threats to the police.

Extortionists

The research work on the street gangs engaged in extortion targeted a sample of 62 male subjects (including 8 female subjects who associated with male gang members) who were either active or former members of New York City's Chinese gangs. They were recruited through contacts with former gang members who are now business people and a Chinese journalist concerned with street gang activity.

The sample accomplished most of the goals of getting a representative sample: included were low-level members, and faction and street leaders of most of the key gangs in Chinatown. This aspect of the study followed the 2-year field investigation of businesses victimized by the gangs. Experienced Chinese field workers who spoke fluent Cantonese/Mandarin and English conducted all interviews.

Our task here was to look at the characteristics of the gangs and their criminal activities in the Chinese community.

Table 9.10: Association between subjects' selected personal/business characteristics and attempted extortion (N=603)

Percentage of subjects who have experienced attempted extortion = 69

Personal		Business	
Sex		Type of Business	
Male	69	Restaurant	84***
Female	68	Retail food store	75
		Retail nonfood store	65
Country of origin		Service	47
Hong Kong	71	Factory	47
Taiwan	65		
China	71	**Location**	
Other	65	Manhattan's Chinatown	72*
		Queens' Chinatown	59
Education		Brooklyn's Chinatown	76
No schooling	75*	Manhattan non-Chinatown	79
6 grade or less	80	Queens non-Chinatown	55
7 to 9 grade	72	Brooklyn non-Chinatown	71
10 to 12 grade	72		
College	67	**Sole owner of Business?**	
Graduate school	47	Yes	64*
		No	74
English Proficiency		**Estimated Profitability**	
Poor	80***	Good	75*
Average	75	Average	67
Fluent	60	Poor	61
Affiliation with community organization?		**Chinatown Zone**	
Yes	69	Vietnamese zone	58**
No	69	Italian zone	80
		On Leong zone	77
		Hip sing zone	70
		Tung On zone	82
		Fukinese zone	76
		Other core zone	59
		Outskirts	29

* p < .05; ** p < .01; *** p < .001

Gang Violence

Table 9.11: Frequency and participation rates in criminal activities (N=62)

Self-Reported Criminal Activities	At least Once	Regular : Three or More times	Frequent: Twelve or More times
	%	%	%
Individual Acts:			
Prior Year			
Violence			
Assault	96		67
Robbery	82	70	54
Shooting	52	33	5
Victimization of Business			
Theft of goods / services	97	93	87
Protection	90	88	78
Extortion	86	82	61
Selling Items	68	53	22
Drug Use			
Alcohol	94	91	73
Marijuana	52	37	21
Crack	10	3	
Cocaine	10	3	2
Heroin	8	2	
Drug Sale	17 (a)	(b)	(b)
	At least a few	**At least some**	**Most**
How many members were actively involves in the following activities?			
Fighting	100%	97%	71%
Extortion (c)	100	95	68
Guarding gambling houses	97	83	62
Gambling	96	81	52
Drug use	81	54	12
Drug sale	72	47	8

(a) Ever involved in drug sale.
(b) Item not asked
(c) The word "extortion" here denotes all four kinds of gang victimization of business owners mentioned above.

Violence outside the gangs against non-gang victims was relatively rare. And in extortion events the rate seems quite low. Our data from the business survey suggested that actual violence as opposed to threats was quite low. Of the 603 subjects in our study, only 2 reported being physically assaulted for resisting gang demands.

But as Table 9.11 documents most gang respondents (96%) admitted that they have been involved in violent crime. Gang members not only mug people in the streets of Chinatown but rob stores, gambling dens, and massage parlors (prostitute houses). The links with the Tongs (Figure 9.4) are unlike those that exist between Mafia/LCN crime families and Italian-American adolescent street gangs. Some Tong members were involved in organized crime activities and served as criminal "power brokers" or "middlemen" knitting together Tongs and gangs. The criminal partnerships were not necessarily permanent. The Tong members were in alliance with affiliated gang bosses but these "Uncles" were not usually prominent Tong officials but behind the scenes operators.

In comparison to Latino and African-American street gangs, Chinese gangs seem less involved in drug use and drug selling; but do use alcohol excessively. The Tongs are not a Chinese "mafia," nor does it seem that a criminal confederation linking Triads, Tongs and street gangs together exists. Much of the organized crime (drug trafficking, alien smuggling, gambling) is entrepreneurial and localized - not tied to national or international criminal entities. The gang is an economic enterprise for its members and a source of local prestige.

Conclusions

What the study suggests is that:

1. A lack of substantial connections between the police and the ethnic community. The fact that police estimates are so inaccurate concerning the extent of extortion suggests that the community is very vulnerable to other criminal activities as well.

2. The results also indicate that the Chinese community is distrustful or suspicious of law enforcement and police anti-crime activities in particular.

3. Chinatown is for the most part a community in which criminal activities thrive. Extortion is but a small but telling indicator of this community condition.

4. If the police are ineffective and largely disconnected with the community, then private police and criminal groups that can provide stability and security will hold power in Chinatown - not legitimate law enforcement authorities.

5. The survey data suggest that extortionists are not completely isolated in the ghetto. Their tactics are sensitive to the potentiality of police interventions and their sociology of likely victims reflects insight and knowledge into the psychology of their victims, their "Americanization" and its implications in terms of cooperation with law enforcement authorities.

6. It is also clear that many Chinese business people believe that the police are alienated or indifferent to their problems.

Will more ethnic Chinese police change that perception? Perhaps, but no one knows. What exists in Chinatown is a crime structure within the business sector that spills over into the social life of the community at large.

It is not more or less complex than Mafia -LCN extortion racketeering but distinctively different; it is crime that is well adjusted to the historical, economic and cultural conditions and dynamics of the community it inhabits - or preys upon.

The utility of this research may lay in its descriptive narrative and analyses. From it, enforcement might be able to develop anticipatory prediction models of extortion and organized crime based on the vulnerability and susceptibilities of certain types of commercial enterprises.

Another conclusion to be tentatively drawn from the study is that law enforcement has an idea about the nature of the crime structures in Chinatown, but they have failed to define appropriate responses to it because the community, and its crime victims, seem ambivalent and in conflict over anti-crime solutions and the police as crime fighters.

Though business people indicate that they favor the eradication of the street gangs and criminal elements within the Tongs, at the same time they do not hesitate to use them: for illegal goods and services; to discourage business competition; and as source of cheap, illegal labor. Thus, the community and the victims have not and can not clearly define a collective attitude. Many of the victims are in criminal partnerships with the street gangs and Tongs. In many respects this ambivalence toward organized crime prevalent in the Chinese community was widespread in the larger society decades earlier where crime preyed upon society but also served it and fed its illicit appetites.

Robert J. Kelly, Ph. D., is *Broeklundian Professor of Social Science at Brooklyn College and The Graduate School and University Center of the City University of New York.*

He has served as a consultant to numerous foreign, federal, state and local governments on issues concerning organized crime, terrorism and extremist politics.

Current research interests include a longitudinal study on remedial teaching technologies in higher educational institutions sponsored by the US Department of Education, and a study of illegal Chinese immigrants in the United States for the National Science Foundation.

Recent publications include Hate Crimes: the Politics of Global Polarization (Southern Illinois University Press); The Upperworld and the Underworld: Racketeering Penetrations of Legitimate Business (Plenum Publishing Co.); African-American Organized Crime: A Social History (Rutgers University Press).

Notes and References

[1] President William J. Clinton. "U.S. Initiatives Against International Organized Crime" at the 50th Anniversary Assembly of the United Nations. New York City, October 22, 1995.

[2] James B. Jacobs (1994). *Busting the Mob: United States v. Cosa Nostra.* NY: New York, University Press.

[3] President's Commission on Law Enforcement and Administration of Justice (1967). *Task Force Report: Organized Crime.* Washington, DC: U.S. Government Printing Office, p. 9; Howard Abadinsky (1990) Organized Crime 3rd ed. Chicago: Nelson-Hall, p. 29.

[4] President's Commission on Organized Crime (1986) *The Edge: Organized Crime, Business, Labor Unions Interim Report,* March. Washington, DC: U.S. Government Printing Office; New York State Organized Crime Task Force (1989) *Corruption and Racketeering in the New York City Construction Industry. Final Report,* December. White Plains, NY.

[5] Merry Morash and David Hale (1987). "Unusual Crime or Crime as Usual?" in Timothy Bynum, (ed.) *Organized Crime in America: Concepts and Controversies.* Monsey, NY: Criminal Justice Press; Michael Franzese (1992). *Quitting the Mob.* NY: Harper Collins; Frank Rogano and Selwyne Roab (1994). *Mob Lawyer,* NY: Charles Scribner's Sons; Herbert Edelhertz and Thomas Overcast (1993). *The Business of Organized Crime.* Loomis, CA: Palmer Press.

[6] Charles H. Rogovin and Frederick Martens. "The American Mafia is Alive and Kicking." Paper presented at the "13th Annual Symposium on International Economic Crime." Cambridge University (UK), September, 1995.

[7] Rens Lee, III (1992). "Colombia's Cocaine Syndicates" in A.W. McCoy and A. Black, (eds.) *War on Drugs: Studies in the Failure of U.S. Narcotics Policy.* San Francisco, CA: Westview Press.

[8] Robert J. Kelly, Ko-lin Chin and Jeffrey Fagan (1994). "Gangs and Serial Order in Chinatown in the New York Metropolitan Area" Final Report National Institute of Justice, U.S. Department of Justice, Washington, DC.

[9] Ko-lin Chin (1996). *Chinatown Gangs: Extortion, Enterprise and Ethnicity.* NY: Oxford University Press.

[10] Based in field interviews with members of the 5th Precinct, New York City Police Department, 1994.

[11] Personal Interviews and communications with Tong Association members.

10 Organized Crime in Israel

Menachem Amir

Abstract

The paper charts the study of organized crime in Israel as it is reflected in media investigatory reporting, and in academic research. The history of the study of organized crime in Israel is continually and constantly characterized by debates between police, academicians and media about the definition, nature of and reaction to organized crime in Israel. The nature of organized crime reflects the second most important characteristics of the Israeli society (the first one being security): — that of waves of immigrants who also enter the crime scene including organized crime. Organized crime in Israel has therefore the nature of ethnic succession, *the last one is that of the Russian immigrants. Their involvement in crime and organized* crime *is now depicted.*

Key Words: Organized crime, Immigration, Media, Structure of organized crime groups, Organized crime commissions.

The Israeli Approach to Organized Crime

The events, which are happening in Israel, resemble that of many other places in the Western world, especially in the US. First, as elsewhere there are interim semantic squabbles about the definition of organized crime, which identify largely the failure to clarify the distinction between *professional organized criminality* and *organized crime*. Organized crime is one type of organized criminality. Organized criminality contains most of the characteristics of organized crime such as duration, continuity, rationality (division of labor, hierarchy). However, it lacks the monopolization aspect of organized crime, i.e., the drive to gain exclusivity over markets or territories [for definitions, see Abadinsky, 1990; Maltz, 1985; Bersten, 1990]. Organized criminality can develop into organized crime, but does not necessarily do so.

A second tendency, evident in Israel, as elsewhere, is the erroneous identification of the concept of "organized crime" with that of the Italian-American Mafia. Thus, if the elements of American Mafia, were not observed or assumed, the existence of organized crime was then denied, and its observed characteristics were called "serious (see Shamgar, 1971 for Israel or, CRI Report 1988 for Holland.) criminality," "professional criminality," or other terms that denote organized criminality.

Third, organized crime was often looked upon as an ethnic phenomenon, especially in societies that absorb immigrant-ethnic groups (Bell, 1970; Homer, 1974; Ianni, 1984; for a rebuttal, see Lupsha, 1981 and Lupsha, 1983). In Israel too, organized crime (in Israel -termed the "underworld") was conceived mainly as one avenue of acculturation and upward mobility into the host society.

The fourth feature in the debate over organized crime in Israel is the refusal of the country's authorities, mainly the police, to admit the existence of organized crime in Israel. For a while they were successful in this strategy of denial since they control the access to information about crime in Israel. Thus, as in other places, it was the media, mainly newspaper investigating reportage, with the help of some academics that raised the issues related to the existence of organized crime, and maintained public awareness to this type of crime.

The Media and Commission Era of Organized Crime in Israel

This paper will discuss the phenomenon of organized crime in Israel as it developed historically since the establishment of the State in 1948. But unfortunately, as we shall see later, only at the end of the 1970s did academics and some police officers who studied in the USA start to study organized crime. Until then the existence and some of the characteristics of this type of crime could be revealed only through the media which gained its information from the police. In Israel, close relationships exist between the police, the media and between them and academicians who also had close relationships with "police sources." Therefore, it was and still is, possible to rely on the media as a reliable but not full source for studying certain aspects of crime and organized crime, as it was the case also in the U.S. (e.g., Landesco, 1969). To use the media, and the commissions that studied organized crime in Israel is therefore not only the main source of information but also a method, albeit with some problems to fully understand the phenomena of organized crime in Israel.

In the 1960s organized criminality emerged as a serious criminal problem in Israel. This was so especially because of the reports about robberies, burglaries, the emerging industry for the sale of stolen goods, and the smuggling of highly taxed goods. It involved some persons "known to the police," who led groups of Israeli-born young men, or whose parents immigrated to Israel, mainly from Muslim culture countries (Israeli Police Annual Reports, 1964, 1969).

In April-June 1971, Mr. Ran Kislev, the main investigative reporter from *Ha'aretz,* the most prestigious newspaper in Israel, published a series of reports on organized crime in Israel, using Puzo's (1969) book, *The Godfather,* as a model to analyze the data he has gathered mostly from police sources.

In these reports, the situation in Israel was compared to the Italian-American model of the Mafia, as portrayed in *The Godfather.* The main organizational characteristics were of local "godfathers" who controlled protection rackets, carting and hauling of goods, and enforced settlements of disputes. Internal disciplinary violence, and "underworld" (the euphemism to denote organized crime in Israel) killings were reported. These occurred because of violation of gang codes, akin to the *"omerta"* principle, or because of not sharing criminal proceeds, or as retaliation for violating the rules of leaders, and entering unauthorized relations with other gangs. External violence was also reported due to rivalries and competitions in the illicit markets. There were also various kinds of corruptive relationships between organized crime and local politicians and local, city, administrators and licensing inspectors.

Because of these newspaper reports, and the real increase (as portrayed in police annual reports) in organized criminality, the then State Attorney General, Shamgar, published a report based on his investigation of organized crime. This report, the "Shamgar Report" (1971) was based on police data and was analyzed according to Cressey's model of Italian-American organized crime, as published in his *The Theft of a Nation* (Cressey, 1969). That is, a comparison was made between the Israeli scene and that of a syndicated type of organized crime in the USA The Report concluded that organized criminality exists in Israel but not organized crime. By making this a comparison it was easy to dismiss the existence of organized crime in Israel, mainly because the Report could not prove the corruption of government officials, especially within the legislative and the judicial branches.

In August 1972 another series of investigating newspaper articles, by the same reporter, appeared (again in *Ha'aretz*) on developments in organized crime in Israel. It portrayed, based on police reports, the increase in demand for "hard drugs," mainly hashish but also heroin, that led to the development of sophisticated and violent drug trafficking networks. Drugs were smuggled from Turkey, Europe or the Far East. There was also an increase in drug-related crimes, mainly burglaries, and the spread of protection rackets. They were accompanied with internal and external (competition type) of violence. (For an analysis of violence in organized crime, see Amir, 1995 and full bibliography there.)

In August 1973, still another series of investigating reporting on organized crime appeared in *Ha'aretz*. The author of this article assisted the reporter in analyzing the data. The existence and scope of local organized crime groups was revealed and their leaders were identified. Violent rivalries between groups, were described, as well as dispute resolutions and agreements over territories. The report mentioned the failure of Jewish organized crime groups from abroad (mainly France) to muscle themselves into the organized crime enterprises in Israel (e.g., protection, illegal gambling, and drug distribution.). It also noted organized involvement of certain groups in banks and diamond robberies; warehouse burglaries for financing drug importation and dealings were noted. Cases of operating legitimate businesses by organized crime leaders and alleged corruption of police and city government personnel were described. The reportage purposely dodged a clear definition of organized crime in order to avoid a debate over such definition, which could have been used by the authorities to lessen the severity of the situation, which the articles wanted to portray. However, the characteristics of organized crime were given offhand, such as rationality in organization and operation, systematic violence, corruption, and the attempts to monopolize the illegal markets.

Between 1973 and 1977 the media, mainly the newspapers, continued, although sporadically, to describe the phenomena of organized crime. Until the mid 1980s, the subject of organized crime was taught only at the Hebrew University in the Institute of Criminology (mainly for Masters' students and police officers), and since then in another university. Actual study of organized crime was conducted only at the Hebrew University. Although organized crime did not become a public issue, its related offshoots, such as drug use and only occasionally trafficking or protection were highlighted when overt violence was involved. Corruption was very local and hidden. All these prevented organized crime from becoming a recognized "social problem" requiring a planned policy to deal with it. The Minister of Police and the police publicly denied the existence of organized crime even when the fact of its presence was presented to them. But covertly they bowed to public pressure to study the phenomenon. Indeed, the police had organized an internal police commission, headed by the commander of investigation in Tel Aviv and known as "The Buchner Commission" in 1976 to "study serious crime."

This Report again confirmed all the newspaper and academic descriptions and analyses of organized crime. However, it added more data on the following: organized import of "tainted" (black) money for laundering; organized thievery of agricultural products, machinery and of livestock, by both Jewish and Arab groups; organized fencing of stolen building materials, gold, and electrical appliances. It also alluded again to corruptive arrangements between leading crime figures and local officials including those of the regulative agencies and the police.

From the description of certain organized crime groups and their criminal activities, we can learn about the social background of most of the members of these groups. Some are Israeli-born from the non-European ethnic groups, and were involved in organized criminality since the establishment of the State, in 1948. Until the 1950s they were engaged in black marketing, fencing and extortion that developed into protection rackets. Other members are second and third generation of immigrants mainly from Muslim countries (e.g., North Africa or Iraq). This fact of continuity and durability of organization and activities led to theorizing in the US and continued in Israel, of organized crime being an ethnic and immigration phenomena (Abadinsky 1990: 53–58, as a summary and bibliography), rather than taking an economic perspective (e.g., Ianni and Ianni, 1980; Schelling, 1971; Smith, 1982). The latter can be applied to the Israeli scene, in which its centralized and bureaucratized controlled economy becomes the main context for explaining organized crime activities.

The importance of the Buchner internal report was in its recommendations (mainly in the intelligence area); one of which resulted in the establishment of a special unit, termed "the Unit for the Investigation of Serious Crime." This unit has been responsible for the investigation of organized criminality, and what only some of the members of the unit dared to call "organized crime." Some of the committee members were students of organized crime in Israel and abroad, but yielded to the pressures of the Israeli National Police Headquarters to avoid the use of the term and concept "organized crime." Also, the intelligence department of the police was ordered to focus and target its investigation on people and activities that were considered to be connected with "serious crimes."

Continuous investigative reports by the media, helped by criminologists, led in 1978, to the formation of a "State Commission for the Study of Crime in Israel," known as the "Shimron Commission" (1978) with the mandate to focus on "serious crime" and organized crime. The commission consisted of a former Attorney General as the Head of the Commission, and former Directors of the Secret Service, the Customs Department, and the Income Tax Services.[1]

The general mandate to study "Crime in Israel" led to the study of such issues as petty criminality and prison conditions, while organized crime received only relatively only minor attention.

The Commission's Report described the general patterns of crime and the trends toward seriousness in terms of frequencies and types. It confirmed what was already known and went on to describe the operations of organized groups in the areas of protection rackets, smuggling, fencing, gambling, loan-sharking, trafficking, distribution and dealing in drugs, the infiltration into and operation of legitimate businesses. Violence within and between organized crime groups and against witnesses was also mentioned.

Special attention was given to an essential aspect of organized crime, namely corruption. On this issue, the Shimron Commission criticized the 1971 "Shamgar Report" for the denial of the existence of organized crime in Israel, by virtue of not finding cases of corruption in the legislature and judiciary systems, and only a small number of cases of police corruption among low-ranking policemen or among local politicians.

In contrast to the "Shamgar Report," the Shimron Commission reported the existence of corruption not only on the local level, but also on the national level. Corruption existed in the form of "social relations" and "mutual help" between prominent businessmen, national political leaders and high-ranking military officers. While no direct bribery was disclosed, the report suggested the existence of political patronage, albeit local, in the form of contribution of money by certain organized crime persons to political parties, or the bringing of voters to ballot booths in exchange for licenses in businesses and other favors.

While this report refrained from a clear formal definition of organized crime, it enumerated its main features, as suggested by Cressey (1969, 1972) and the definition given by the scientific advisor to the Commission. The Report stated (1978:19) that: "Israel's criminal code does not contain a category of 'organized crime' type of crime, but that of 'criminal conspiracy.'" Because the data does not reveal that there is organized crime on the national level, and the scientific advisor of the Commission suggested that the syndicated model does not exist in Israel together with the fact that this model is not the only organizational type of organized crime, it was possible for the Commission to declare the "existence of a 'special' Israeli version of organized crime." The importance of this statement lies in that the criminological definition of organized crime, was taken more seriously, and received the attention of law enforcement and the judiciary. Thus, the Commission's report includes a lengthy subsection report of what is known theoretically and empirically about the organization and activities of organized crime. The purpose of the report was that the authorities would know the indicators, the warning signs of organized crime, and its future directions, hoping to be able to guide the authorities in what to do organizationally and operationally to combat organized crime.

The scientific section of the report explained the syndicate, the "Godfather," and the network types of organized crime (Albini, 1971; Homer, 1974; Lupsha, 1983). The absence of a syndicated type was explained by the smallness of the country which did not allow the development of such a large-scale criminal organization; the non-corruptibility of the legislative, judicial, and most of the executive branches (particularly administration and law enforcement). All these factors hinder the development of some conditions necessary for syndicate crime (i.e., the monopolization of markets on a national scale, large-scale diversification of economic activities, and serious infiltration into major legitimate businesses (see Cressey, 1969, 1973).

However, on the local level in some businesses located mainly in the Tel-Aviv area, where there were attempts at monopolization or control over territories (e.g., protection, sale of music and video, often pirated cassettes, and drug distribution), we find also groups that diversified their illegal businesses (drug distribution, extortion, debt collection, theft and sale of stolen goods and non-official gambling). There is local level infiltration (by investment) and participation in or owning legitimate businesses, such as restaurants, clothing outlets, small food processing plants, etc.

Local groups, Israeli and Arabs, separately and together, also forged an ad hoc cooperation for the importation of drugs and other contraband goods, or in settling disputes in underworld courts. The Report recommended the strengthening of the special unit that was established to combat "serious crimes," and the intelligence units that attended to such crimes. A more extensive use of income tax regulations as a weapon against known organized crime figures was also recommended. This, as part of the "war of attrition" against leaders of organized crime groups.

Since the appearance of the Shimron Commission in 1978 till the end of the 1980s, organized crime became again a "non-issue" to the public. As is so typical in Israel, other "more burning" issues of survival and security override every other problem. Problems such as organized crime appear and disappear from the public arena after they receive short-lived attention by the media, the Knesset (Parliament) or academia (examples include school violence, violence against women, or child abuse). Only the "drug scene," mainly the "demand side" and there mainly the consumption of drugs by youth, received constant public, official and academic attention (see annotated bibliography by Shore, 1990).

Thus, when murders in the "underworld" occur, usually around drug dealing and control of distribution, or because of rivalries and competition in the protection rackets, or when names of known leaders of organized crime appear in the media, then for a few days organized crime becomes a media event for public attention. In these occasional reports it is also revealed that the known and traditional activities of organized crime continue and even expand, mainly in the "drug scene," contraband, extortion and large-scale theft of business and warehouse burglaries.   However, newly emerging phenomena was the appearance of organized crime and organized criminality among Israeli Arabs, mainly in the area of drug smuggling and trafficking, organized automobile theft for stripping of parts, or large scale theft of agriculture material and products. Jewish and Arab groups were found to cooperate around criminal activities such as drug importation and trafficking, or fencing of stolen goods (Private communication, 1972).

Another aspect of organized crime theft, mentioned relatively often, was the connection between Israeli organized crime groups and their comrades abroad, mainly in Europe (e.g., Holland, England, Germany and Turkey). Israeli criminals who left Israel formed groups that were involved in organized crime activities in their host countries (i.e. drug distribution, extortion, prostitution or gambling).   They also established connections, or strengthening of former connections with their friends (often who became accomplices) in Israel.   The main cooperative enterprises are in trafficking in smuggled drugs (heroin, cocaine, PCP, and other illicit drugs) and the smuggling of other (mostly highly taxed) electronic goods.

According to the police another relatively new type of organized criminality emerged in the 1970s and the 1980s was the counterfeiting of money, mainly U.S. dollars and sometimes Jordanian dinars, or other foreign currencies.

The Scientific Era

The only academic research on organized crime in Israel appeared after three years of research (Amir, 1986).   The study was on organized crime activities among the Georgian Jews who immigrated to Israel from the Republic of Georgia (or Gruzia in the former USSR).   These new immigrants arrived by the thousands during the mid-1970s.   The media and the police repeatedly reported during 1980–1982 that "special" types of criminals were found among the Georgian Jews.   They were engaged in "big and serious" crimes, which they had also practiced in Georgia, or were connected with organized crime groups, these through protection, or corruption of officials for their private enterprises. What became a hallmark of their specialty was their control, by the use of violence, of carting and hauling services in the air and seaports.   They used this position for large-scale theft of passengers' luggage, as well as from cargo planes and anchored ships.   Also reported were grand scale theft from warehouses, sophisticated frauds of religious objects, diamonds, counterfeiting of money and documents (driving licenses, professional degrees, etc.) and large-scale fencing operation and smuggling.

It was decided to study this group firstly because of its reputation in the media, which led to stigmatizing the whole group.   Second, they did reveal some new types of crimes, e.g., counterfeiting of money and forging documents, or increasing the magnitude of known crimes.   It was also learned that this group had become a specifically targeted group by the police. Moreover, it was possible to gain, relatively easy, access to police intelligence data. For the first time the total or sole reliance on media reports, leaked by the police, was abandoned, and another research approach was adopted, that of an ethnographic-anthropological method, i.e., to interview those who were in contact with Georgian organized crime (offenders, police, community leaders, personnel in agencies who are in contact with Georgian Jews). The anthropological approach was employed by comparing their "way of life," including their involvement in crime there (mainly contraband, corruption, theft from government agencies) in their culture of origin (Georgia). The study looked at the changes that certain groups within this community underwent in Israel, which, together with their original normative system, favored their immediate entrance and persistence into organized criminality and organized crime.

Based on the literature on the necessary conditions for the development and continuity of organized crime among social ethnic groups (Abadinsky, 1990; Cressey, 1969, 1971; Reuter, 1983), the following explanations were offered:

- Social and religious solidarity and cohesiveness.
- A sense of isolation and rejection from the Israeli society, of being marginal and isolated, even ecologically, from the social domains of the so-called absorbing society.
- Cultural customs and traditions that favor evasion of the law, the demand for conspicuous consumption, disdain toward "honest" work.
- The economic, partly criminal tradition learned and adopted in communist Georgia — e.g., corruptive relationships with social control agencies, extensive involvement in the illicit sub-economy (especially in contraband, grand theft of government property, and general evasion and violation of the law whenever possible).

The exploitation of the nature and structure of the Israeli political economy (e.g., the highly centralized and regulated Israeli economy, the scarcity of goods because of high taxation, the perception of a weak social control system (the police or criminal justice apparatus).

For a long time, from a social control perspective, it was impossible to penetrate this group because of their special language, mainly family — nuclear or extended — members were accepted to the group, and because of their strong adherence to the code of "omerta" with brutal punishment awaiting violators.

Each group was led by a strong leader, often with experience in crime in Georgia, and with some expertise in crime showing their economic acumen mainly in frauds and other economic crimes. Networks or groups cooperate with each other in some ventures like fencing or counterfeiting of documents or money.

The reaction by the authorities towards these groups was conducted by

employing two strategies:
- by conducting a "war of attrition" against leaders and members (i.e., arrests after long undercover work, and by the use of income tax prosecution);
- by removing them from working in sites that were used for their criminal activities.

Two years ago the author of this study on the criminality of some Georgian groups conducted an informal follow-up of this group. It was found that the "war" against Georgian organized crime was partly successful, in the sense that some members of the group left the country. But some continue their criminal activities where they chose to reside, and also keep criminal relations with their brethren who remain in Israel (e.g., contraband of goods, drugs, laundering money, or distributing counterfeit money in Europe which was produced in Israel).

The Georgian Jews' organized crime changed their criminal activities and became, therefore, less observed and received less attention by the media. Most of the money gained by criminal activities was invested in housing and in legitimate businesses such as jewelry and food stores. A second generation of Georgian organized crime does not exist. Those whose fathers were involved in crime, either "went legitimate" or were still involved in fencing of stolen or contraband goods. The groups that were involved in counterfeiting of money were either arrested, or left the country. The forgeries of documents still persist serving the needs of the new wave of Russian immigrants who arrived at the end of the 1980s. Unlike the "native" organized crime, Georgian organized crime almost did not have any inroads to local politics, although in one town (Ashdod) they constitute a sizable minority group. In the places where they concentrated, they were able to corrupt some city inspectors or local city officials.

The New Era

A new phase in the existence of organized crime in Israel emerged with the arrival, between 1988–1995, of about 650,000 immigrants from Russia and other states of the former Soviet Union. The criminal aspects of this immigration such as shoplifting, fraud, and loan sharking were noted immediately in the media. It focused on the fact that many immigrants arriving with forged documents that either falsified their Jewish status for the sake of receiving preferential treatment as immigrant Jews, and forged certificates about professional status to qualify for high-skilled positions. Also repeatedly reported in the media was the relatively large number of women, some very young, that were engaged in prostitution. Some of them became prostitutes in Israel because of being destitute, and some were already "working the streets" in Russia. The tabloid sections of the evening and weekend newspapers were saturated with ads of "newly arrived Russian girls." Reporters in the newspaper repeatedly wrote, quoting police officials, about organized groups that import the girls, set them up in bordellos and "massage parlors" that are controlled by natives or jointly with Russian men. Also, the girls were exploited and controlled by extortion, and violence, by gangs, which have their bases in Russia.

The media also reported other aspects of the criminality of the Russian immigration; forgeries of documents, including any document which the immigrants need; extortion of Russians by other immigrants, loansharking with violence, even death for recalcitrant debtors, shoplifting by poor and destitute men and women, of "heavy drinking" including driving while intoxicated by Russian newcomers who use forged driver licenses. While these and other accusations were reported and discussed in various social circles, the authorities said nothing publicly or officially to dispel or confirm these dark attributes of the new wave of immigration. This stemmed from the desire to prevent a negative stigma for all Russian new immigrants, who came to Israel because of the "Law of Return" (i.e., the right of every Jew to become an Israeli citizen immediately upon his arrival). It was also deemed politically unwise to enrage them, lest they would not join the existing ruling party.

Both the police and the probation services refused to react publicly to media reports about the increase in representation of Russian youth in juvenile crime. They argued that such impressionistic media reports were not confirmed by the official juvenile crime statistics, although they later (1995, 1996) admitted the increase in juvenile crime activities and group crime among Russian gangs. They countered that the reports about the existence of Russian youth gangs that were involved in drugs, extortion, group violence and group rapes were exaggerated, although such groups do exist (estimated at two or three in every major city or place where Russian immigrants are concentrated). Since 1995, in interviews, even in class lectures, police officials report the growing numbers of well-organized Russian youth gangs.

The author of this chapter started to investigate Russian immigrant organized crime. Interviews were conducted with policemen "who know," with newspaper reporters, with some of those in the agencies who work with the Russian immigrants, including youth corner groups. I was able to read some internal police reports on the problem of Russian criminality. What follows is the beginning of a more extensive study on the problem of organized criminality and organized crime among the new immigrants from Russia. There is no attempt at this stage to assess the scope and magnitude of this phenomenon which according to some informants changes toward alarming proportions (with violence or fraud), but to learn if there is something new in organized crime in Israel, that did not exist prior to their arrival. At this stage, we can furnish only a preliminary picture, that confirms some of the information in the police internal reports.

At the outset, it should be mentioned that the higher echelon of the police denied publicly and in an interview with me, the allegations and accusation of serious organized crime activities of the Russians. They did confirm the existence "of identified criminals...who have formed organized gangs that are active in various areas of crime through the use of violence," and "there is serious organized criminality among them." It is not, however, yet of a serious social-criminal problem. It did not change for them their assertion that "in Israel no organized crime exists as it is defined or understood in the U.S. or Italy." This was not acknowledged even in the latest publication of the Israeli police magazine, *Mar'ot* (1994) which published part of an internal report, until now secret, on Russian crime, which was presented in 1993 in Paris at a conference on Russian international organized crime.

Besides the local and international "native" organized crime and the organized crime activities in the smuggling of foreign laborers (which will be discussed later), three types of Russian immigrant organized crimes can be discerned (often overlapping but analytically reported for the sake of discussion).

The "natural" type of organized crime, the conditions of absorption, the real or imagined sense of deprivation of opportunities, the need for immediate resources (money, brokerage services with the authorities) have created organized services to supply these, and other needs. Some of the people who organized or became members of these groups have experience in crime and organized crime in Russia. This type is the natural, but "queer" (a-la Bell, 1961) ladder of economic, racial (and political) entrance into the absorbing society. In the beginning, and up until now, they operated alongside the native Israeli and Arab organized crime. Lately, it is observed that individual and groups of Russian "Mafiosi" entered into relationships with local native criminals (individual groups arranged importing and distribution of drugs, extortion, fencing of stolen goods and operations of illegal gambling, and forging of documents. Such internal and external violence exist (Amir, 1995). This type also uses juveniles (individuals and groups) in their activities. These types of organized crime activities are often confused in the media with "general" criminality like, shoplifting, violence in the family, the increased use of alcohol and drunken driving.

The second type is the "local international" type. The criminal activities of local Russian groups are organized and "supervised" by groups based in Russia (mainly from the big cities like Moscow, St. Petersburg, or places in the Caucasian and Muslim Republics). Most noted is the illegal transportation of women, placing them in massage parlors and other types of ill-famed houses, overseeing the management of these establishments, collecting the revenues and sending some of it to Russia. Other types of activities of these groups are the importation of drugs (including heroin or cocaine), forging of documents including I.D. cards and counterfeiting of money. Later it was reported (allegedly based on police data) of the entrance of these groups (with moneys and "soldiers" or "muscle men") to the growing illegal gambling, with the attempt to control, by extortion, or by forced partnership, or by investments, these illegal gambling casinos. Also, defrauding innocent immigrants of the "absorption package" (the official support of about $50,000 – $70,000) that each new immigrant receives from the government, and other types of fraudulent schemes.

Much violence is observed in these activities, internal or external (Amir,

1995), such as maiming or killing of prostitutes, of rivals, bombing or setting fires. Also noted is some corruption of those who can interfere or facilitate these illegal activities (i.e. issuing Israeli I.D. cards). The police are also investigating the investment of some of the illegal proceeds in legitimate businesses.

The third "high" type of Russian immigrants' organized crime concentrate on investing in Israel large sums of money in banks, in real estate and businesses, from proceeds of (mainly) illegal and legitimate money. Again, this money came from Russian organized groups in Russia or Europe. As said, Israel is considered a "safe haven" for investing money because of "no questions asked" in the banks of the sources of the money. Top Russian Mafiosi from Russia, Europe and the United States, convened in Israel three times between 1993-1994 to decide upon the policies of investments or resettling disputes. The outside groups have representatives in Israel who made connections with Israeli businessmen, lawyers, and local and national politicians.

It should be noted that the first and second types are organized around "existing ties" i.e., according to the areas in former Russian Republics, i.e., Russia, Ukraine or the Republics. The third type consists mainly from Russia (Moscow and St. Petersburg). Also, as police authorities informed me, even in Russia groups became a target for intensive investigation (of first and second "types" of Russian organized crime).

Gangs of juvenile Russian immigrants also operate in the organized crime scene. In some cities and municipalities, these gangs (whose leaders often have criminal records and gang participation already in Russia) have attempted to control extortion in their locale or enter the drug market as distributors and pushers. Sometimes older people (up to 30 years old) guide these groups of 14-17 year olds.

Among Russian youthful gangs two tendencies were revealed vis-a-vis local native-street-corner groups. First, conflicts and violent clashes between Russians and native groups over territories ("Turfs"), or from conflicts emanating from a sense of being looked down upon and abused by the Israeli youth groups (and the whole Israeli society). It also became a clash between two ethnic groups, since still most of the Israeli delinquent groups are from "oriental-sepharadim" (Muslim) background. The second trend, which is just beginning, but which can be expected to develop, is a reverse trend — that of cooperation between the ethnic groups — the Russians get drugs from the native Israeli groups for consumption and for sale or the Russians will fence stolen goods for the "natives."

Local "native" organized crime still persists in the "drug scene" (mainly importation and distribution), extortion, illegal gambling, fencing of stolen goods, car theft (sometimes with Arabs from Israel and Palestinians from the West Bank and Gaza), the smuggling of everything that is in demand into Israel, loan sharking and more. Israeli Arab organized crime also continues to operate in the areas of car theft (in cooperation with Palestinians -- in Gaza and the West

Bank -- in smuggling drugs from Lebanon and Egypt) in the theft of Israeli (and Arab) agricultural products and tools (often sold to Arab farmers in Israel and the West Bank and Gaza).

The main explanation given for Russian organized crime in Israel is that of alien imported conspiracy, i.e., that some of the immigrants brought with them their criminal code, and the general, often openly expressed, disregard for Israel's laws. They do not perceive the Israeli criminal justice system as a deterrent factor. This is a result, as the police reports state, of "lighter" punishments, shorter detention periods, the possibility of bail, the length of time between arrest and trial, that enable people to change identity and/or leave Israel. The systems of law enforcement and criminal justice are deemed weak, inefficient, and at the same time incorruptible.

It was also found that the relative failure of the interrogation by the police to illicit confession. The suspects admit that it was never as violent as in Russia. The Russian criminals usually do not admit to charges placed against them, do not turn in their friends — another aspect of the criminal code the immigrants brought with them to Israel.

A conference on Russian Crime in Israel was conducted by the police and attended by Russian officials in January 1995. It was also revealed that leaders of organized crime from Russia and other Eastern European countries have convened in Israel to discuss business. Also, that Russian organized crime groups from Russia and elsewhere, and local Russian groups, already invested criminal proceeds in legitimate business, real estate, and in the banks. This, since Israel is considered a safe haven because of the lack of control on investment in banks. Thus, the laundering of money is quite simple and easy. It was suggested and reported in the media (and in a meeting in which I participated) that between 2.5 to 4 billion dollars have been invested in banks and about 600 million in real estate.

Organizationally, the Russian criminal groups that were identified (about eleven) are organized as in Russia around "funds," which are mutual aid financial organizations. Becoming a member of the groups is recognized by the ritual of accepting him to the "fund" where he invests money on a regular basis. Criminals can operate independently, but when their individual criminal activities may conflict with that of a criminal group, then, either he joins the "fund" or is punished (they or their families). This arrangement was transplanted to Israel from Russia. At the head of the fund there is always a leader, who heads a group with a division of labor, according to expertise. There is much violence between groups and within groups, but there is also arrangements of disputes, resolutions by "sit-downs" between leaders of groups.

From interviews conducted with people who know the scene, it seems that only recently, (i.e., three years after the described phenomenon was observed) the law enforcement and criminal justice agencies (mainly the state prosecution apparatus) are paying special attention, in high echelon police staff meetings and at cabinet meetings, to the phenomena of organized crime and organized criminality of the Russian immigrant groups. Thus, by strengthening intelligence activities, sharing information with law enforcement agencies abroad was possible. Also, by changing the basic first constitutional "law of return" that allows anyone acknowledged to be Jewish to become an Israeli citizen instantly upon his arrival.   The law does allow the prevention of criminals and those ill with communicative diseases from entering the country. Furthermore, by initiating some special laws, mainly those that lead to better control on immigration (authenticity of certificates and documents), on the investment of money to control the laundering of crime money and the arrangements to deport the first 11 of about 35 known "leaders" of groups, some of them known already as "Mafiosi" in Russia and who have established lucrative businesses (mainly of import-export) with moneys which were brought from Russia. Leaders of Russian local groups have told police investigators that they are reconsidering remaining in Israel. They say that Israel is too small anyway for big business and it is hard to evade the police. Indeed, as of October 1996, some leaders had already left the country and withdrew their bank investments.

Social programs are needed to prevent the creation of "reservoirs" for organized crimes. It means the prevention of waywardness and delinquency of Russian youth and others, especially among imputed "vulnerable" groups who already clashed with the law.

For young adults this requires the creation of legitimate opportunities into social and economic skills (work, recreation, and participation in social and cultural activities).   And on the basis of intelligence, "weed" programs or "attrition" wars, i.e., the prosecution of leaders and soldiers, especially on non-Jews, including legal arrangements of deportation (i.e., some changes of the "law of return," or using the income tax as a weapon against organized criminals on various types of war against organized crime, see Homer, 1974). In each type of activity of organized criminals there should be special programs of prevention and deterrence (i.e., aggressive policing and prosecution) also as part of the effort to destabilize the market or by decriminalization of certain types of behavior (gambling, drugs).

In sum, it means:
- a war against organized criminals, their organizations and against demand and supply markets;
- some of the indexes of success in the war against organized crime in Israel are:
  1. the prevention of new recruits in Israel and abroad for organized crime,
  2. the stoppage of immigration of known criminals,
  3. fostering of the process of social, economic and cultural absorption to prevent the entrance into organized crime groups,
  4. the entrenchment of organized crime groups in these markets, and disappearance of second generation organized criminals.

In Israel, as in any organized society, every new wave of immigrants contributed its share to the "organized underworld." Some groups, however, bestow to this more growth than others do. In other groups, their immanence in organized crime has faded away, as in the case of the Georgian organized crime group.

The Russians are entering the Israeli crime scenes with vigor, including such areas as drugs, counterfeiting, fraud schemes and organized crime. Their sheer numbers is an important factor, as well as the tradition of criminality that some of them brought over. The existence of many new immigrants who try so hard to build their economic future, create an "internal market" for the operations of organized criminality and organized crime, for example, extortion, supply of usurious money, brokerage with the government (national and local) agencies and their services.

The Future

The history of immigrant-absorbing nations documents for us as was the case in the USA (Abadinsky, 1990) or Australia (McCoy, 1986) that organized crime seems to be an unavoidable aspect of immigration due to the attempts of individuals and groups to enter the absorbing economy and society. If the situation that leads to its operation (e.g., lack of legitimate means to enter the social and economic mainstream of the absorbing society) continues, organized crime will flourish and entrench itself as part of the criminal but also the legitimate economic system. However, with social and economic structural changes, and with better control systems, such development can be avoided, and organized crime will remain a small part of the crime phenomenon of Israel. Its serious aspects (mainly of violence, corruption and entrance into legitimate economic markets and the social scene) may be either weakened by the absorption processes into the legitimate economic and social system, as it was in the United States (Abadinsky, 1990), or as was shown by the experience of the Georgian organized crime in Israel, or because of the vigorous policies against leaders and criminal markets. It is also possible that Russian organized crime will become a strong force in criminal markets because of its penchant for violence, corruption, its sophistication, expertise and organizational and economic acumen.

Much research is still needed on the phenomenon of Russian organized crime in Israel.

- First, the demographic aspects. We must possess knowledge about those who immigrate to Israel, as to whether they have had experience in crime and especially in organized crime, in their country of origin.
- Second, the organizational aspects such as recruitment and apprenticeship, division of labor, leadership and command aspects, specialization in crime and relationships with other Russians and "native" organized criminality and organized crime.

- Third, the line of specialized activities and attempts to control criminal, plus legal enterprises, on "turf's."
- Fourth, the "upper world," its corruptibility, and its legal reaction (police, prosecution) or the supply of resources with opportunities to exit from criminal careers, and their effectiveness.
- Lastly, research about organized crime is limited to the police (mostly by the author's students) and by the author of this paper alone. Recently, the police requested a report on Russian organized crime from me to be incorporated in the "Police Strategic Planning" for the 21st Century. Funds were allocated to the study of certain aspects of crime by Russian immigrants (and Ethiopian immigrants, too), mainly of youth (e.g., the formation of gangs and their activities). These grants allow Master and Ph.D students to conduct studies on organized crime in general and not only on immigrants' role and place in this criminal phenomena.

Prof. **Menachem Amir** *received his Ph. D. at the University of Pennsylvania. He is a member of the permanent faculty of The Institute of Criminology, at the Hebrew University, Jerusalem, Israel and has served as its director. He specializes in and writes about the mafia, juvenile delinquency and victimology, and is currently concentrating his work on organized crime national and international), on police and police issues. He conducts research for the Israeli*

government in the areas of police violence, community policing and undercover police work. He has been a consultant for various Israeli government Ministerial Committees; has published widely, and has served as a member of the editorial boards of: Violence, Aggression and Terrorism and The International Journal of the Addictions (Substance Use and Misuse). His most recent book is Force and Control: Police Violence Patterns and Issues. He is co-editor of the first two volumes of The Uncertainty Series: Organized Crime: Uncertainties and Dilemmas, and Police, Security and Democracy. Prof. Air has lectured at various universities throughout the world (Sweden, Finland, Australia, Canada, USA, South Africa, and The Netherlands). He is married to a feminist and womens' studies medical sociologist and Prof. of Social Work, father to two daughters and a grandfather to two grandchildren.

References

Abadinsky, H. (1990), *Organized Crime,* Chicago: Nelson Hall.

Albini, J., "Organized Crime in Israel and the U.S.A.," (Part I) *Crossroads: Trends and Issues in Contemporary Society* (1978): 119–142.

Amir, M. (1986), "Organized Crime among Georgian Jews in Israel," in R. Kelly (ed.) *Organized Crime in Global Perspectives,* Lanahn MD: Littlefield Adams Pub., 172–192.

Amir, M. (1987), "Organized Crime: Theoretical Perspectives," in E. Shimron, *The Commission to the Study of Crime in Israel,* Ministry of Justice (Hebrew).

Amir, M. (1994), "Organized Crime: The Discourse about the Concept," *Plilim* (Criminality), 4: 189–221 (Hebrew).

Amir, M. (1995), "Violence in Organized Crime," *European Journal of Crime and Crime Prevention,* 44:1–17.

Anderson, A. (1994), "The Red Mafia: A Legacy of Communism," in E.L.L (ed.) *Economic Reform in Russia,* The Hoover Institution Press.

Bell, D. (1961), "Crime as an American Way of Life: A Queer Ladder of Social Mobility," in D. Bell, *The End of Ideology,* Glencoe, The Free Press, ch.7.

Bersten, M. (1990), "Defining Organized Crime in Australia and the USA," *Australia and New Zealand Journal of Criminology,* 23:39–59.

Buchner, A. (1986), *Organized Criminality in Israel: A Police Internal Committee Report,* Israeli Police.

Cressey, D. (1969), *Theft of a Nation,* New York: Harper and Row.

Cressey, D. (1972), *Criminal Organizations,* New York: Harper.

CRI Report (May 1988), *Georganiseer Crimilitet en Enterregiunale Groehs Criminoliterit.* Holland, Den Haag.

Homer, F. (1974), *Guns and Garlic: Myths and Realities of Organized Crime,* West Lafeyette: Purdue University Press.

Ianni, F. (1984), *Black Mafia: Ethnic Succession in Organized Crime,* New York: Simon and Schuster.

Ianni, F., and Ianni, F. (1980), "Organized Crime: A Social and Economic Perspective," in G. Newman (ed.) *Crime and Deviance,* Thousand Oaks, CA: Sage:274–313.

Israel Police Annual Reports (1964, 1969), "Introductory Remarks, Chief of Police," Jerusalem: Israel Government Priniting Office.

Kislev, R. (April-June 1971), "Organized Crime in Israel," *Ha'aretz.*

Landesco, J. (1968), *Organized Crime in Chicago,* Chicago: University of Chicago Press.

Lupsha, P. (1981), "Individual Choice, Material Culture and Organized Crime," *Criminology* 19: 3–24.

Lupsha, P. (1983), "Networks vs. Networking: Analysis of Organized Crime Groups," in G. Waldo (ed.), *Career Criminals,* Sage:59–87.

Maltz, M. (1985), "Toward Defining Organized 'Crime'," in H. Alexander and G. Coiden (eds.) *The Politic and Economics of Organized Crime,* Lexington, D.C., Heath:21–35.

McCoy, A. (1986), "Organized Crime in Australia: An Unknown History," In R. Kelly (ed.) *Organized Crime: A Global Perspective,* Lanahn MD: Littlefield Adams:231–226.

Private Communication (1972), Head of Israel Police Intelligence.

Puzo, M. (1969), *The Godfather,* New York: Fawcett.

Reuter, P. (1983), *Disorganized Crime: The Economics of Visible Hand,* Cambridge MA: MIT Press.

Schelling, T. (1976), "What is the Business of Organized Crime" in F. Ianni and E.R. Ianni (eds.) *The Crime Society: Organized Crime and Corruption in America,* New York: Meridan Book:69–83.

Serio, J. (1992), "The Soviet Union: Disorganization and Organized Crime," *Criminal Organizations,* 6: 3–7.

Serio, J. (1993), "Organized Crime in the Former Soviet Union: New Directions," *C.J. International* 9: 15–17.

Shamgar, M. (1971), "Attorney General Report on Newspaper Reports on Organized Crime," Ministry of Justice (Hebrew).

Shelley, L. (1994), "Post Soviet Organized Crime," *Criminal Organizations* 9: 14–22.

Shimron, E. (1987), *The Commission to Study Crime in Israel,* Ministry of Justice.

Share D. (ed.) (1990), *Addiction, Prevention and Treatment,* Jerusalem. Szold Institute (Hebrew).

Smith, D., Jr. (1982), "Paragon, Pariahs and Pirates: A Spectrum Base Theory of Enterprise," *Crime and Delinquency,* 26: 358–386.

Sterling, C. (1994), *Thieves' World: The Threat of the New Global Network of Organized Crime,* New York: Simon and Schuster.

Vaksberg, A. (1991), *The Soviet Mafia,* New York: St. Martin's Press.

Valentine, A. (August-Sept. 1973), "Organized Crime in Israel," *Ha'aretz.*

Volobuev, A. (1989), "Soviet Union — Combatting Organized Crime," *C.J. International* 5: 11–15

Notes

[1] Mr. Shimron was a former Attorney General of the State of Israel.

[2] According to some estimates made by political leaders, up to twenty percent or more of this immigration wave was not Jewish.

11 Organized Crime: An Austrian Perspective

Maximilian Edelbacher

Abstract

Organized crime is the primary challenge to the contemporary world, especially so in Europe. An enormous change has taken place in Europe since 1989, when the "Iron Curtain" fell. Austria's geographical position in the center of Europe and her new role as a member of the European Community brings with it new responsibilities to combat organized crime. Austria is of interest to newly developed OC gangs because of their "money laundering" activities as well as Austria becoming a base for OC operational activities. Austria's new role brings with it the responsibility for combating OC by creating and sharing new needed ideas and counterstrategies.

Key Words: Corruption, Greed, Harmonization of laws, "Money laundering", Organized crime.

Introduction

Austria, a relatively small country with an area of 84,000 km, is located in the heart of Europe. Less than ten percent of its eight million inhabitants - 850,000 -are foreigners. Austria's capital, Vienna, is situated in the eastern part of the country and has a population of nearly two million, 350,000 of which are foreigners.

Austria is a Democratic Republic, which includes several political parties. Her National Assembly currently consists of five larger parties. Austria was liberated in 1945 and in 1955 Austria once again became an independent state. Since then, Austria has become the tenth wealthiest country in the world and has achieved a high rate of economic growth, placing it among the "best" in Europe. The unemployment rate is relatively low and the majority of Austrians are materially well off. Table 11.1 documents relevant unemployment rate data.

Table 11.1: Unemployment rates in Austria

Year	Unemployed	Men	Women	%
1985	139,447	84,155	55,292	4.8
1990	165,795	89,032	76,762	5.4
1995	215,716	120,004	95,712	6.6
1996	301,983			7.4

Source: Burgstaller, J., et al, Die Arbeitsmarktservice Osterreich, 1995

Table 11.2: Selected gross national product data

Year	Nominal	Real
1991	1923.53	1486.36
1992	2047.25	1516.69
1993	2124.07	1522.22
1994	2262.92	1568.60

*Sources: Volksswirtschaftliches   Buro   der   Oesterreichen
Nationalbank, 4.7.1996, Volkswirtschaftlichen Büros of the Austrian
Federal Bank and is based on the year 1983. The amounts are in
billions of Austrian Schilling.*

Austria, and especially Vienna, are the gateways to the East. Austria, as a member of the European Community since January 1st, 1995 (the Treaty of Schengen 1992), is obligated to achieving the European standard for border control. Austria aims to reach the level of the European standard by the end of the year 1997.

There are more than 380 million people in Europe. The largest countries are Germany, France, Italy, Poland, Spain, Sweden, Turkey and The United Kingdom. The European Community will have to integrate between 300,000 to 600,000 immigrants, every year, over the next few years, including 250,000 from the former East Bloc. Approximately 15 million foreigners settled in the European Community between 1980 to 1992; 45 percent of them came from Africa, Asia, Latin America and Turkey. A United Nations survey, from 1993, documents that approximately twenty million Eastern Europeans want to immigrate to the European Community. The target countries in the European Community, for these people from the East, are Germany and Austria. Since the in 1989 the biggest migration since post-World War II (1945) began after the "fall of the Iron Curtain." According to Russian estimates, 1.5 to 2 million citizens are ready to emigrate for economic reasons. An additional 5 to 6 millions are "considering" emigration. These are the large demographic challenges that also have an impact on organized crime (Holyst, 1995). Table 11.3 summarizes major reasons for the current emigrations.

Table 11.3: Main reasons for the increasing migration movement

- No noticeable improvement in the economic situation.
- The wish for a better social living conditions.
- Political instability and fear of the future.
- More crimes of violence (an increase in murders, robberies and blackmail.
- The increasing destruction of the environment and the resulting restriction of living space.
- Political tensions, e.g. civil wars.
- Violations of human rights by totalitarian and dictatorial regimes.
- The population explosion in the developing countries; approximately 1.4 billion people will live in developed areas as opposed to approximately 6 billion people in underdeveloped areas in the year 2010.

Source: Edelbacher, 1996

As a result of these factors and processes it is reasonable to anticipate the following changes or outcomes: (Edelbacher, 1995)

- A high proportion of crime, committed by foreigners, due mostly to the great mobility of the criminals.
- A higher proportion of foreigners among criminals.
- An increase in types of organized crime.
- An increase in violent crime.

The Nature and Extent of Organized Crime in Europe and in Austria

Organized crime was not a topic of discussion in Europe, until relatively recently, although the phenomena of organized crime has existed for centuries in Italy. It is worth noting that crime has approximately doubled in Europe during the last forty years. In Austria the figures for registered criminal acts have doubled during the last twenty years.

Table 11.4: Selected Austrian crime statistics and rates for solving crimes

Year	Amount	%
1975	245,374	47
1985	377,517	45
1995	490,539	42

Source: Aahs, Polizeiliche Kriminalstatistik, 1996,1997

The problem of *quantity* is not considered to be Austria's main problem, as her crime rate has doubled. The crime's *quality* is considered to be more dangerous. According to the Director General of Public Security, Mag. Michael Sika, the proportion of organized crime is approximately thirty percent of Austria's overall crime rate (Sika, 1992).

Table 11.5: Crime committed by foreigners

Year	%
1975	8
1985	12
1995	20
1996	22

Source: Aahs, Polizeiliche Kriminalstatistik, 1996, 1997

Table 11.6: Organized crime

Year	%
1994	20
1995	25
1996	30

Source: Sika, 1991 and 1992

The existence of organized crime was denied by senior political leaders and policy makers in most European countries until the late 1970s when "Organized Crime" was related to as a cancer:

It cannot be openly seen, but it grows and can soon endanger the whole society. It grows slowly but continuously and when the symptoms come out - it is almost too late to react - fighting organized crime is therefore extremely difficult and sometimes it seems useless. It is like fighting a tornado, a hurricane or the great floods (Marvo, 1996).

Organized crime is currently Europe's number one challenge. It is difficult to estimate the extent of organized crime in Europe. It is known that the general economic, social and political conditions are the basis for the growth of organized crime structures. If these conditions become worse, organized crime groups can and do penetrate and expand. The history of the "Italian Mafia" and the now growing "Russian Mafia" are examples.

Definition of Organized Crime

Defining "organized crime" is itself a problem. Although there is no definition that is accepted by all Europeans the definitions used by Interpol, Bundeskriminalamt Wiesbaden and the Dutch are the most popular ones.

Interpol defines organized crime as follows:

Organized crime comprises systematically prepared and planned committing of serious criminal acts which were committed in a longer, undefined period of time by more than three accomplices united in hierarchy and job division and organized criminal association in which the methods of violence, various types of intimidation corruption and other influences are used, with the view to secure the development of criminal activities in order to gain financial profits and powers.

This definition of OC focuses on the use of violence or corruption to achieve quick profit. The following elements are critical and "symptomatic":

- The existence of a criminal association or group.
- A criminal activity is carried out in an entrepreneurial way.
- The basic goal of the group is to achieve profit with illegal activities.
- The group uses violence or corruption to achieve its goals.

The *Bundeskriminalamt Wiesbaden's* definition of organized crime (Dormann et al, 1990) is:

organized crime is the profit and power-oriented systematic commission of crimes which are considerable importance individually or collectively if more than two persons involved cooperate for a longer or an indefinite period:

- *by using business or business-like structures,*
- *by using violence or other means suitable for intimidation,*
- *by exerting influence on politics, media, public*

administration, judicature or economy.

In The Netherlands, Criminal Intelligence Units (CIU's) deal with organized crime in a different way from the traditional forms of serious crime (van der Heijden, 1996).

Crime analysts filled in a structured questionnaire on every active criminal group. A criminal group was defined as the cooperation of two or more people who are involved in crimes, which in view of their impact or their frequency or the organized framework within which they are committed, represent a serious violation of the legal order. The questionnaires that were completed were processed at the national Criminal Intelligence Division (CRI). In the analysis of the answers, a number of characteristics were used as selection criteria, in order to establish the organizational degree of groups. The following eight criteria were applied:

- The group has a hierarchic system of leaders and subordinates, with a more or less fixed division of tasks between core members.
- The group has an internal system of sanctions, such as intimidation, acts of violence and sometimes even liquidations.
- The group concentrates on acquiring income from different forms of crime, depending on the profitable opportunities involved in more than one type of serious crime.
- The group has criminal contacts with the world of trade and industry and/or with government agencies (corruption).
- The group launders criminal earnings by investments in legal enterprises, real estate, or in movable property or by foreign exchange.
- Business enterprises are used as a front.
- The core members have been acting jointly for over three years.
- The group uses intimidation, acts of violence and sometimes even liquidations against competitors within the criminal world.

In the analysis of the data, the degree of organization of a criminal group is determined simply by counting the characteristics. As more characteristics are present, a higher the degree of criminal organization is posited. The designation "organized" is given to groups, which complied with six or more of the eight criteria. The "at least six out of eight formula" takes into account both the diversity of organized crime and the fact that the police in the early stages of the investigation process usually do not have complete knowledge of all the existing and necessary features.

All definitions of OC point to one important main theme or trend: *Organized crime is greed driven.* This is not simply a theoretical issue. It is important to know the attributes and indicators of organized crime in order to carry out effective practical efforts to combat OC. Table 11.7 summarizes a paradigm of such indicators that were developed by the working group "Judicature/police" in Germany (Geiger, 1992).

Table 11.7: Indicators for assessing the existence of "Organized Crime"

Planning/preparation of the crime
   Accurate planning
   Hired labor
   Large investment

Utilization of the spoils
   Highly profit-oriented
   Backflow into legal economic cycle
   Money laundering measures

Existence of a criminal network
   Supraregional
   National
   International

Conspiratorial criminal behavior
   Counter-observation
   Complete voluntary isolation
   Code names

Group structure
   Hierarchical set-up
   Dependent and authoritative relationship between several suspects of a crime
   Internal sanction system

Help for gang members by
   Escape aid
   Providing lawyers
   Threats to intimidate people involved in trials
   Nontraceability of witnesses
   Silence of the persons involved
   Testimonies of witnesses for the defense
   False testimony
   Taking care of prisoners
   Looking after the relatives
   Readmission into the "scene" after release from prison

Corruption
   Inducing dependence (e.g. by sex, gambling)
   Bribery
   Corruption

Efforts to create monopolies
   Control of certain sections of nightlife
   Offering "protection" against payment

Public relations
   Manipulating the press for the gangs' benefit

Source: Geiger, 1992, Polizei-Jurischen Rundschau, Nos. 3 and 4

Fields of Criminal Activities in Europe

Practical experience shows that the following fields of crime are mainly relevant to organized crime structures in Europe (Edelbacher, 1997):

Trade in Human Beings

Since the opening of the borders to the East, subsequent to the fall of the "Iron Curtain," two main movements continue to influence Europe. One movement of humans is from the East to the West; the other one is from the South to the North. Africa is the poorest continent. Millions of black Africans come mainly to France, Italy, Portugal, Netherlands and The United Kingdom, but they are present in all other countries of Europe as well. Many of these poor people are smuggled into Europe by professional organizations.

Drug Trafficking

This is the second major crime-problem for Europeans. In addition to heroin, which is smuggled from Asia to Europe, the South American cartels provide the European market with tons of cocaine. The smuggling, growth, development, distribution and use of hashish, marijuana and synthetic drugs are also growing problems in Europe.

Environmental Crime

Environmental crime is an ongoing challenge that has become more and more important. Nobody really has any idea how much damage is caused to Europe and to the world by professional criminals, who dispose of "problematical materials," such as nuclear waste, which is an expensive matter for the industrial producers.

Trafficking in Arms

Trafficking in arms is becoming an enormous danger for the democratic countries again following the former communist countries' extensive reduction in their military forces. The war in former Yugoslavia has shown that trafficking in arms is very often connected with drug trafficking.

Illegal Car Trafficking

Subsequent to the fall of the "Iron Curtain" more than one million cars are being stolen every year in Europe. Illegal car trafficking is a new booming criminal profession. Stolen cars are mainly brought to Russia, Poland and the Ukraine. The cars are primarily stolen in the United Kingdom, Germany, France and Italy.

Extortion of Protection Fees and Protection Racket

Extortion, through protection fees and protection rackets are increasing, with the advent of many ethnic minorities settling into and establishing themselves in European cities. These victims are the new owners of restaurants, bars and nightclubs. Many of these restaurants are now owned by Chinese, Italian and Turkish minorities and they are the potential victims.

Prostitution and Gambling

Prostitution and gambling are the traditional fields of operation for organized crime groups. Since many poor women want to come to the richer part of Europe, prostitution has become a growing problem. Illegal gambling, a "drug" for many people, is also booming.

Art Thefts, "Trick Thefts" and Professional Burglaries

Property offenses continue as arenas of interest and activity for European criminal groups. For more than thirty years, professional gangs from former-Yugoslavia, Poland, Rumania and Russia have broken into houses, dealt in stolen art and have "picked pockets."

International Financial Fraud, Money Laundering, Computer Crime and White-Collar Crime

The Western world is increasingly confronted with "money laundering," computer crime, international financial fraud and white-collar crime, because organized crime groups are increasingly involved in these activities. For example, check fraud and credit card fraud are especially well organized all over the world.

Corruption and Bribery

It is axiomatic that "Organized Crime" is not possible without the phenomena of corruption and bribery. These fields of crime grow dramatically, as ethics become less important worldwide.

Active Criminal Groups in Europe

Organized crime groups such as the "Russian Mafia," the South American "Cocaine Cartels," the Chinese "Triads," the "Cosa Nostra," the "Camorra," the "'Ndrangheta" and other mafia organizations, the Nigerian organizations and the Japanese "Yakuza" are creating serious crime problems worldwide generally and in Europe specifically.

Fields of Crime and Criminal Groups in Austria

The "crime scene" in Austria is somewhat different notwithstanding the "money laundering" activities of the Russians and the Italians within Austria's borders.

Crimes of Violence, Murder Cases, Extortion/Protection Fees

The number of murders is relatively small in Austria compared to other countries. There were 168 attempted and actual killings in Austria, in 1995, including 69 in Vienna. Three murder cases were associated with OC in 1995 and 1996.

Extortion via "protection fees," from Yugoslavian and Turkish bars and restaurants is "quite common." For example, there are about 1,800 restaurants, bars and nightclubs in Vienna; approximately 500 of these belong to former Yugoslavians, about 300 belong to Chinese and approximately 220 brothels and "bars" belong partly to organized gangs.

Property Offenses, (e.g. stolen car trafficking, burglary, pick pocketing, art thefts)

These phenomena exist in Austria as they do throughout Europe. Crime has doubled in Austria during the last twenty years; this being primarily due to property offenses.

Financial Fraud and "Money Laundering"

Austrian bank laws guarantee bank secrecy for accounts. Large amounts of money are transferred to Austria by Russians and Italian OC because of the availability of these anonymous accounts. Austria, and Vienna in particular, is an "interesting financial center" since the opening of the Eastern borders.

Crimes Involving Narcotic Drugs

Whereas Austria was always a transit country for drug dealers, drug use has been on the increase since the 1960s - especially the use of heroin and cocaine.

Prostitution and Gambling

The "market" has changed since the borders to the East were opened. Vienna itself has approximately 150 brothels and 100 bars where girls, mainly from the eastern neighboring countries, work. Organizations dealing with the smuggling of people often bring these women to Austria and Germany on the pretext of offering them legal employment. All too often, during the trip, these women are grossly abused and made irrevocably dependent so that it is very difficult for the police to create enough confidence during their patrols to convince these victims to testify against their procurers and against the smugglers. Gambling has also become very international in Austria since the fall of the "Iron Curtain."

Criminal Groups

Austrian criminals continue to be strongly represented in the "classical criminal domains" such as procuring and gambling. Additional fields of activity are bank robbery, burglary, handling of stolen goods, fraud and forgery. There are, in addition, so-called "joint ventures" with criminals from neighboring eastern countries. Operationally, Austria mainly has problems with gangs from former Yugoslavia and Poland, who are responsible for a number of burglaries; gangs from Turkey and Iran, who are involved in drug dealing on a higher level, and Nigerian gangs, who are active as drug dealers and in fraud.

Measures to Combat Organized Crime

Fighting organized crime in Europe is especially difficult because of the variety of laws, penal codes and penal procedure codes. Individualism always was the strength and the weakness of Europe. Even now, in the age of the growing European Community, the individualism of the individual members of the EC creates daily problems.

Security problems are changing in contemporary Europe. During the 1970s, Europe was confronted with the "plague" of terrorism; in the 1980s the new problem was the increase of drug trafficking and in the 1990s primary problem number is organized crime.

Organizational, Technical, Educational and Legal Measures
Organization

When new problems arise the first measures taken all over Europe are very similar. Law enforcement agencies established new units against terrorism, drug-associated crimes and organized crime between the 1970s and the 1990s. These initial organizational measures were the first responses made by the responsible officials.

New forms of police cooperation have been developed in the European Community. One of the principle ideas was to create the EUROPOL. Europol is designed to be a special instrument in the fight against drug trafficking. This police force will be a more efficient instrument than the Interpol.

Police President Meetings

Austria initiated a new form of cooperation between police chiefs. The police presidents of Berlin, Bratislava, Budapest, Munich, Prague and Vienna meet on a regular basis and discuss all of their important security problems.

Technical Measures

New technical measures have improved the possibilities of the executive forces to fight crime in addition to the new organizational measures. The development of technologies is an enormous support in combating organized crime. Computer technologies help to analyze crime structures, records of persons and enterprises. Computer data includes an assimilation of personal history, case files, related court documents and public documents.

Education

All of these new methods need a "modern and educated police officer," who is more of a technocrat than being the traditional investigator. Although interview - technology is still very important, in order to more effectively fight organized crime, it is necessary to improve new modern concepts, strategies and techniques. Therefore education on the one hand, and a new profile of police officers on the other hand, are the most important issues.

The Middle European Police Academy

The Middle European Police Academy was founded in 1992. Eight members participate in this educational idea: Austria, the Czech Republic, Germany, Hungary, Poland, The Slovak Republic, Slovenia and Switzerland. Senior officers from these countries attend the academy in Vienna between February and May. The uniqueness of this Police Academy is that the participant "students" travel around and are taught in all member countries. Members of the Police Academy have been successful in several instances; two murder cases and the biggest post office robbery in Austria's crime history could be solved by them.

Legal Measures

All of these new, ongoing changes will, by necessity, be based on fundamental judicial considerations. Therefore, new laws are being discussed intensively in all European countries.

The Penal Code Measures:

In some countries provisions were set in the field of criminal legislation with which the state tries to prosecute different kinds of organized criminal activities. These measures help prevent organized crime activities such as: criminal association, criminal conspiracy, "money laundering" and extortion.

The Procedural Measures:

Special measures such as wire taping, secret police cooperation, apparent purchase of objects, apparent bribery, eavesdropping in private places by use of technical devices, access to the computer system of banks or any other legal persons engaged in financial or other economic activity are necessary in the penal procedure.

International Initiatives to Counter "Money Laundering"

Organized crime, almost without exception, exists and perpetuates itself for the purpose of making money. The concept of greed, and the power that money - in vast quantities - assures, is integral to most manifestations of serious organized crime.

Contemporary organized crime syndicates have adopted the same structures and *modus operandi* as legitimate businesses. The "laundering" of the proceeds of criminal activities through the financial system is vital to the success of criminal operations.

In addition to putting the soundness and stability of the financial system in jeopardy, "money laundering" permits organized crime to take root and extend its influence over different regions of the world. This enormous flood of criminal proceeds involves considerable risk of corruption for administration, judicial authorities and political parties, as well as private institutions and constitutes a danger to stability of democracies. European countries have taken part in various international initiatives, which have been undertaken in order to combat "money laundering."   These included, for example, the Vienna Convention, December 1988; the Basle Statement of Principles, December 1988; the Strasbourg Convention, of 1980 with the first recommendation of the Committee of Ministers and the Financial Action Task Force (FATF) formed in 1989 by the Group of Seven (Plywaczewski, 1996).

The Vienna Convention

The United Nations Convention against Illicit Traffic in Narcotic Drugs and Psychotropic Substances, December 1988, ratified by over sixty countries, adopted a number of key proposals (Plywaczewski, 1996). Specifically, it:

- creates an obligation to criminalize the laundering of money derived from drug trafficking.
- deals with international co-operation, thereby facilitating cross-border investigations into money laundering.
- enables extradition between signatory states in "money laundering" cases.
- sets up principles to facilitate co-operative administrative investigations.
- sets forth the principle that banking secrecy should not interfere with criminal investigations in the context of international co-operation.

The Basle Statement of Principles 1988

The Basle Statement of principles was issued by the Basle Committee on Banking Regulations and Supervisory Practices in December 1988 (Plywaczewsky, 1996). It signaled the agreement by the representatives of the Centralbanks and supervisory authorities of the Group of Ten countries to the danger posed by "money launderers," to the stability of the banking system world-wide, and of the need for an international set of principles, to overcome differences in the practical implementation of supervisory regimes in each member country. The basic policies and procedures outlined in the Statement of principles included:

- the need for effective procedures to identify customers.
- compliance with laws and regulations pertaining to financial transactions and refusal to assist transaction which appear to be associated with "money laundering."
- co-operation with law enforcement agencies.

These basic concerns, expressed by the Basle Committee, are particularly important for countries in which the financial services industry is being established in an expanding market economy:

- public confidence in the new range of services offered by financial institutions is an important requisite to the growth of these institutions, and
- without effective money laundering legislation, international business with financial institutions in these countries will be significantly hampered by the risks of exposure to 'money laundering' by financial institutions in countries complying with strict money laundering regulations.

The Strasbourg Convention

The Council of Europe, in a Recommendation of the Committee of

Ministers in 1980, was the first to warn the international community of the dangers which "dirty money" in financial systems represents to democracy and to the rule of law.

The Council's approach was to consider not only "laundering" of drug proceeds as a crime but also to criminalize the proceeds derived from all kinds of offenses (Plywaczewsky, 1996).

The Underlying Idea is That the Criminals Should Not Be Permitted to Profit From Their Crime.

The work of the Council in the field of "money laundering" is action-oriented. Several international conferences on the subject were held in the 1980s and inspired the work on an international Convention on *"Laundering, Search Seizure and Confiscation of the Proceeds from Crime"* (Strasbourg Convention).

The Financial Action Task Force (FATF)

The Financial Action Task Force was formed in 1989 by the Group of 7 of major industrial nations and the President of the Commission of the European Communities, to assess the results of co-operation already undertaken in order to prevent utilization of the banking system for "money laundering" purposes, and to consider additional preventive measures in this field, especially the adoption of the legal and regulatory systems to enhance multilateral judicial assistance. There are 40 measures recommended by the FAFT for adoption by countries combating "money laundering." These measures include a general framework, improvement of national legal systems to combat "money laundering" and strengthening of international co-operation (Plywaczewski, 1996).

Comparing Various Anti-Organized Crime Measures

It is rather difficult, if not almost impossible to compare the various anti-organized crime measures, which are undertaken by European states. The traditional measures used are mainly written down in the penal codes and penal procedure-codes of the European states. As organized crime became more and more of a problem, several states introduced different measures to fight organized crime. Since organized crime is the primary challenge in Italy and Russia, focusing on these countries as examples may show which measures dealing with the phenomena of OC were set by these countries. In Austria, where organized crime is not such an issue as it is in Italy and Russia, "money laundering" continues to pose a problem.

Italy

Italy has been burdened with the problem of organized crime for decades. Since Organized Crime is Italy's primary problem, Italy has reacted dramatically in the fight against it. The measures of the Italian parliament and government are therefore the most interesting ones, in comparison to those of other European countries (Santini, 1996).

Italy introduced 114 laws regarding organized crime, directly or indirectly, between 1982 and 1992. All these laws are connected with terrible crimes that shocked people, both locally and internationally, and are considered to be the response to an "emergency situation"; which means that they are answers to the criminal challenge and are not part of a coherent law enforcement program.

The most significant provisions are: the measures taken against "money laundering," the provision for mafioso who collaborate with law enforcement officials, the so called "*pentiti*" (repenters), the revision of the procedure code for the treatment of mafioso, the creation of the DIA (Direzione Investigativa Antimafia: Antimafia Investigating Administration), the DNA (Direzione Nazionale Antimafia or Superprocura (National Antimafia Administration), the integration of criminal association of the mafia type, that includes those that interfere with the right to vote. One of the candidates for the position of Superprocuratore (General Attorney) was Giovanni Falcone, who was assassinated alongside his wife and three bodyguards on May 23rd, 1992, while driving on the highway that connects Palermo's airport, Punta Raisi, to Palermo (the Capaci massacre).

After the Capaci massacre and the massacre of Via D'Amelio, in which Judge Paolo Borsellino and five of his bodyguards were assassinated on July 19th, 1992, new emergency measures called "urgent modifications to the new Penal Proceedings Code and actions against organized crime of the mafia type" were taken.

The new law introduced further protective measures for "*pentiti*," arranged severe prison terms for mafioso, preventive measures regarding patrimonies and includes two clauses regarding elections. The first criteria used to qualify a mafia crime is intimidation; for example, to hinder or deny the right to vote or to obtain votes. The second regulation punishes the "political-mafia exchange;" when a member of the mafia promises to obtain votes for a politician in exchange for money. The original form of the law included the promise to obtain concessions, authorizations, contracts, public financing, or any means of gaining illegal profits.

Although the regulative framework that began taking shape during the last decades was fairly chaotic, nonetheless, a few fundamental principles were created.

The first was the "double track regime." The penal Code Procedure was applied to common criminals and not to mafioso, for which different prison treatment was expected.

The second principle concerns the legislation that rewards mafioso who collaborate with justice. Introduced for terrorists, it has been greatly expanded since then.

The third principle stipulated that a person being investigated as a mafioso had to prove the legitimate origin of goods and moneys in his possession -- however the Constitutional Court in Italy declared this unconstitutional in February 1994.

Organized Crime of the mafia type has existed since the nineteenth century but only since a law was passed in 1982 is association with the mafia recognized as a crime. It is only with the help of this law that "mafia enterprises" can be touched.

Despite the fact that responsive measures, such as laws by decree, are almost always taken after a terrible crime i.e. murder of an important person, massacres, etc., Italy is the most successful country in Europe in its fight against the mafia. This might be due to the fact that the mafia and accompanying problems are handled as top priority (Santini, 1996).

Russia

The second most dangerous criminal phenomenon is the organized crime in Russia (Gilinsky, 1996). Organized crime constantly expands spheres of influence. Crime organizations are interested in access to state structures, determining the rate of economy and policy. It is impossible to single out any one reason for the extremely serious and total crisis currently affecting Russian Society. One cause may be the lack of a democratic tradition -- the centuries long tradition of despotism under the regime of the "Tsars."

In October 1917, the Russian society attempted to build utopia. In 1988 Gorbachev's *Perestroika* was a necessary attempt to save the power structures through reforms. His reforms turned out to be of a radical nature, but were not satisfactory. All symptoms of the socio-economic catastrophe remained untreated. Corruption has taken on a monumental nature in all organs of power and establishments; the militarization of economy and politics continues. The contrast between the poor majority and the "new Russian rich minority" is a source of very real social conflict.

Organized crime, primarily in form of gangsterism, existed in Russia even after 1917. In 1930s, a peculiar well-organized association of "thieves in law" was established. Contemporary organized crime is enterpreneurship in the form of economic enterprises, criminal syndicates and criminal industry. Consequently the Russian society is confronted with the criminalization of business in combination with economization and politicization of the crime.

In Russia, anti-organized crime measures are primarily established by legislation. In the criminal legislation, the most severe measures of punishment for "ganging" were provided firstly in the Criminal Code 1922, i.e. deprivation of freedom for three to fifteen years, or execution with confiscation of property. The struggle with "thieves in law" was conducted on an illegal basis. The penitentiary administration has used camps of archipelago GULAG. The number of "thieves in law" was reduced drastically in a bloody war. Unfortunately, they couldn't be liquidated.

Radical attempts to fight the new forms of organized crime in Russia were undertaken in 1983 under Yuri Andropov and in 1990 under Gorbachev's "Perestroika." But at the end of the 1980s and beginning of the 1990s, the Russian society had to realize the economic, social and political danger of organized crime. Organized criminal communities have been able to become established through corruption of power structures and legislative measures appear to be insufficient counteractions. However, a new Criminal Code will be passed through the Parliament in 1997. According to Yakov Gilinsky, (1996) the difficulties in finding real and successful counter measures against organized crime have to be seen in the light of Russia's economic, social and political crisis and instability, not to mention a total corruption of federal and regional power structures; for example the police and courts.

Austria

For more than twenty years the phenomena of organized crime was denied in Austria, although practical experience showed that organized crime existed. The current Austrian law recognizes the term "organized crime" only in the Security Police Act (Edelbacher, 1996).

In the third part, article 16, section, 1 subparagraph 2 of the Security Police Act the term "general danger" is described:

> *General danger exists (1) in the event of a dangerous attack*
> *(sec.2 and 3) or (2) as soon as three or more persons get*
> *together with the intention of repeatedly committing criminal*
> *acts punishable by the court (gang or organized crime).*

The Code of Criminal Procedure and the Criminal Code do not define the term "organized crime" at all. In article 278 Criminal Code - formation of gangs the term "organized crime" is used but not defined (Edelbacher, 1996).

After Austria was criticized heavily by the United States and the European Community measures against money laundering were introduced in the banking law and in the penal code in 1994.

The European Council

According to the European Council many measures, proposed by the European Council, were introduced on the national level of different European countries (Csonka, 1996). Drug trafficking and money laundering are the two main fields of interest in Europe.

It is impossible to elaborate a final evaluation of the various anti-organized crime measures. The example of Italy shows, that there is some hope to overcome the phenomena of organized crime; the Russian situation doesn't let one hope. All other European countries are more or less in a similar situation. In some countries (for example: Austria, France, Germany, United Kingdom) the extent of organized crime is not so extreme and there is hope of being successful in the fight against organized crime. In other countries, however, chances for success are slimmer.

Proposed Measures to Combat Organized Crime

Economic, social and political measures are more important than the legal ones in order to combat organized crime. When a person does not find legal means, he will resort to illegal, including criminal means. There are a number of contradictions in today's society which merit consideration; the most relevant are the following:

- Contradiction between legality and reality.
- Contradiction between the opacity of the financial system and the fight against laundering.
- Contradiction between capitalist restructuring and development policies (Santino, 1996).

In our contemporary world 23 percent of the world's population consumes 80 percent of the resources. If the explanation for the growth of the illegal economy and the diffusion of criminal groups of the mafia type is to be searched for among the characteristics of contemporary society, effective anticrime policies must be connected with the profound mutation and radical choices that have an effect on cultural goals and social relationships.

The Secretary-General of the United Nations Boutros-Boutros-Ghali told the World Ministerial Conference on Organized Transnational Crime in Naples at its opening meeting:

> *Powerful international criminal groups now work outside national or international law. They include traffickers in drugs, money laundering, the illegal trade in arms - including trade in nuclear materials - and the smuggling of precious metals and other commodities. These criminal elements exploit both the new liberal international economic order and the different approach and practices of states. Some criminal "empires" are richer than many poor states. These problems demand a concerted, global response* (Santino, 1996).

Organized crime has become predominantly *transnational* in character, but law enforcement worldwide remains predominantly local and national. In a declaration and Global Action Plan, Ministers of Justice and the Interior of most countries of the world who took part in the Naples (Italy) Conference in November 1994, urged states to move swiftly to counter a rapidly globalizing movement of inter-linked organized crime groups and their spread into new spheres of activity. The Plan reflects agreement that if organized crime is not stopped in time, it will undermine political structures, endanger international peace and development and threaten not only emerging democracies but also well established ones. It calls for improved data gathering and analysis, anti-corruption safeguards, special investigative units and implementation of existing measures directed against loopholes that allow trans-border criminals to circumvent justice.

Although much has been done by governments to make an impact on organized crime, efforts are hampered by lack of knowledge, common orientation and international operation. This new approach against organized crime must work alongside an increase in proactive methods. It requires the involvement of the public to provide the solution, but it is clear that crime cannot be tackled successfully unless others sectors of society are also involved.

Today, success will be achieved by the use of a multinational and multidisciplinary approach which uses preventive as well as control measures applied by the Criminal Justice systems and governments, utilizing the knowledge and resources of industry and science. The motto for this approach should be "it concerns us all, let's tackle it together." (Marvo, 1996; Santino, 1996)

According to past resolutions and decisions of the United Nations, member states should intensify their efforts to combat organized crime at the national level more effectively. This includes considering the following measures, if it is thought necessary, in their respective systems; subject to safeguards and maintenance of basic rights under ordinary legal procedures and in conformity with international human right standards. Table 11.8 summarizes selected forms of counterstrategies against organized crime: (Edelbacher, 1996)

Table 11.8: Counterstrategies to combat organized crime
Short-term and Medium-term Counter-Strategies
- An honest policy: many politicians attack the phenomena of organized crime aggressively, but without any real action.
- Harmonization of legislation in Europe.
- Modernizing national criminal laws and procedures.
- Organizational changes of police and law enforcement agencies.
- The strengthening of law enforcement authorities - professionalism.
- Improvement of analytical and communication abilities of law enforcement agencies.
- Modern and efficient technical equipment for law enforcement agencies - education.
- The use of prevention strategies and not only setting of repressive measures.
- The establishment of national institutions-national crime authorities or commissions.
- The review or adoption of laws relating to taxation, the abuse of bank secrecy and gambling houses.
- Establishing multilateral agreements on police cooperation.
- Intensifying international cooperation.
- Multilateral co-operation and regional co-operation.
- Better cooperation between different institutions and agencies within each country.
- Sensitizing the population to organized crime.

Long-term Counter-Strategies
- Analysis of the social, economic and politic development of the European economic area.
- Analysis of the migration movements.
- Development of aid programs for the poor regions of the world.
- Cooperation with the international organizations such as the United Nations in planning and developing aid programs.

Conclusions

As was previously noted, Europe is currently confronted with two phenomena of Organized Crime. On the one hand there is the traditional organized crime, the classic Italian gangs of Mafia, 'Ndrangheta and Camorra, or the gangs from former Yugoslavia and from Poland. On the other hand, Europe is challenged by new forms of organized crime from the former communist countries, especially from Russia. In addition to these forms of crime many traditional gangs from former Yugoslavia or from Poland are very active in Europe. And furthermore Europe has to confront criminal gangs from Africa, South America and Asia. Some of them are integrated in "joint ventures" with gangs from the European countries. Many criminals from Germany, Austria, France or the United Kingdom deal with these international gang groups and make a lot of money.

The primary areas of activity of organized crime gangs are trafficking of human beings, drugs, weapons (especially when the war was going on in former Yugoslavia), stolen cars from Western Europe to Russia, Poland and the Ukraine, prostitution and gambling- the traditional areas of organized crime activities- as well as environmental crime, international financial crime, such as crimes against banks and insurance companies, credit card and check fraud, "money laundering," computer crime and white collar crime.

The fifteen members of the European Community are not homogenous. There are significant differences between the poor members and the rich members of the Community. It is very difficult to predict or to anticipate EC's future political, sociological and economical development and their critical dimensions. A most serious problem will be the rising unemployment rate in the different European countries.

Organized crime is based on greed and cannot exist without corruption. If we cannot overcome the growing differences between poverty and wealth, the new capitalism, we cannot defeat organized crime. Developments in the rest of the world are very strongly connected to these questions. Consider, for example:

- Can we overcome the world problems of poverty in Africa, South America and Asia?
- How will the future development in the world influence the political, sociological and economical situation in Europe?

We don't know, for example, how many refugees will come to Europe in the future. If Europe wants to fight organized crime much more effectively, forms of international police cooperation have to be improved. The different laws in the European countries have to be harmonized. Special legal options should be introduced into the penal and procedure codes in order to help law enforcement agencies.

To conclude, briefly, you, the reader are asked to consider that the main issues involved in combating contemporary organized crime efficiently are:

- Harmonization of laws of the European countries.
- More legal power to law enforcement agencies.

- International cooperation in the judicial, law enforcement and scientific fields.
- International education of law enforcement agencies and agents, state attorneys and judges (Edelbacher, 1996).

---

*Mag. **Maximilian Edelbacher** completed his degree in jurisprudence at the University of Vienna, worked as a foreign affairs expert in a banking institution, was a legal expert for the Austrian Federal Police, worked at the Viennese Major Crime Bureau (burglary, fraud, forgery and prostitution), headed their homicide squad and became Chief of the Bureau in 1988. He is involved in the training of criminal investigators and executives for the Austrian Federal Police, is a lecturer for the Middle European Police Academy and at the Vienna University of Economics and Business Administration. He has published numerous technical articles on policing and crime, 3 volumes on Applied Criminology (1995) and the Viennese Criminal Chronicle (1993).*

References

Aahs, A., (March 1996 and March 1997), Bundesministerium für Inneres, Abteilung II/16, (Statistical data from the Ministry of Interior) *Polizeiliche Kriminalstatistik.*

Burgstaller, J., Flink, H., Meier, E., and Schmitzberger, F. (1995), *Die Arbeitsmarktlage 1995,* (The situation of the working-market in Austria) Arbeitsmarktservice Österreich.

Csonka, P. (November/December 1996), "Council of Europe, Organized Crime: A World Perspective," paper presented at the Yokohama Conference on Organized Crime.

Dormann, U., Koch. K-F., Risch, H. and Vahlenkamp, W. (1990), "Organisierte Kriminalitat-wie groß ist die Gefahr?" (Organized Crime -how great is the danger?) *BKA-Forschungsreihe,* Bundeskriminalamt Wiesbaden.

Edelbacher, M. (January/February 1997), Third International Police Executive Symposium, Summary of the European Chapter.

Edelbacher, M. (March 1996), "International Issues of Crime and Social Control," lecture presented to the Academy of Criminal Justice Sciences, Las Vegas, U.S.

Edelbacher, M. (March 1996), "Organized Crime in Austria - Vienna, the Gateway to the East," lecture presented at the Academy of Criminal Justice Sciences, Las Vegas, U.S.

Edelbacher, M., and the members of the European chapter. (November/December 1996), The Yokohama Conference on Organized Crime.

Edelbacher, M. (June 1995), "Serie Angewandte Kriminalistik, Schutz vor Kriminalitat" (Safety against Crime) Verlag Staatssicherheit, Wien, page 7.

Geiger, E. (1992), "Organisierte Kriminalitat - eine Herausforderung für Justiz, Polizei und Verwaltungsbehorden," (Organized Crime a Challenge for Justice, Police and Administration), *Der Polizei-Juristischen Rundschau,* Nos 3 and 4.

Gilinsky, Y. (November/December 1996), "Organized Crime : The Russian and World Perspective," paper presented at the Yokohama Conference on Organized Crime.

Holyst, B. (1995), "Die neuen Richtungen in der Entwicklun der organisierten Kriminalitat in Osteuropa," (The New Development of Organized Crime in Eastern Europe) *MEPA-Lehrbrief des Bundesministeriums für Inneres,* 34:2.

Marvo, D. (November/December 1996), "Organized Crime: A World Perspective and the View from Slovenia," paper presented to the Yokohama Conference on Organized Crime.

Plywaczewski, E. W. (November/December 1996), "Organized Crime: A World Perspective," paper presented at the Yokohama Conference on Organized Crime.

Santina, U. (November/December 1996) "Law Enforcement in Italy and Europe against the Mafia and Organized Crime," paper presented at the Yokohama Conference on Organized Crime.

Mag.Schüller (1996), Volkswirtschaftliches Büro der Oesterreichischen Nationalbank, Information per Fax vom 4.7., Information from the Federal Bank of Austria.

Sika, M. (1992), Die unsichtbare Gefahr, Vortrag beim Kuratorium Sicheres Österreich, Litschau 1991, und Die Bekimpfung der organisierten Kriminalitt, Vortrag beim Kuratorium Sicheres Österreich in Salzburg.

van der Heijden, T. (November/December 1996), "Combating Organized Crime in The Netherlands," paper presented to the Yokohama Conference on Organized Crime.

12 African-American Organized Crime: Racial Servitude and Mutiny

Robert J. Kelly

Abstract

To think about La Cosa Nostra as the "core" of organized crime in the United States today, naturally leads to the consideration of peripheral forms of the phenomenon - namely, minority, or "non-traditional" organized crime. This paper offers some reflections on specific forms of "non-traditional" organized crime, African-American groups, and their prospects for growth.

Apart from drug trafficking, it is argued that political mobility within the minority community is a pre-requisite for the growth and stability of traditional organized crime activities.

Key Words: Cosa Nostra, Mafia, Policy, Syndicate, Crime networks, "Minority middlemen," Ethnic succession, Jamaican Posses, Crips and Bloods.

Introduction

A decade ago, in the Report of the President's Commission on Organized Crime (The Impact: Organized Crime Today) scant attention was devoted to African-American organized criminality. The Report refers fleetingly to radical political prison groups such as the Black Guerrilla Army (which existed in California's prison system more than twenty years ago), that were presumably active in the 1980s and also linked to the Black Liberation Army which carried out armed robberies and the murders of policemen (President's Commission 1986:79). When considering that numerous witnesses provided the Commission with extensive testimony that large-scale sophisticated heroin trafficking networks existed in African-American communities managed by African-Americans the lack of attention to this phenomenon was indeed puzzling. The testimony suggested a highly structured level of organization but still no coherent statement was contained in the Report as to the status of these criminal activities (President's Commission 1985: 194-245).[1]

Ignoring African-American organized crime is not unique to the President's Commission. In an otherwise well-informed overview at a symposium on organized crime control, the FBI Assistant Director of Investigation referred to "non-traditional" organized crime groups including "the outlaw motorcycle gangs, Mexican and Colombian narcotics cartels and oriental organized crime gangs" (Revell, 1986:6). There was no mention of African-American organized crime.

Despite the meltdown of the American Mafia brought on by vigorous prosecutions and mounting evidence that organized crime is not limited to the operation of La Cosa Nostra and its crime families, "Italian geography"[2] still dominates official and public thinking. The concession the President's Commission *Final Report* made concerning non-Italian organized crime was its recognition that Asian, Central and South American groups were playing significant roles in drug trafficking and minor extortion rackets in their ethnic communities (Albanese, 1987). This is especially interesting in view of the fact that official agencies have for some time abandoned alien conspiracy theories for the most part and have embraced the view that organized crime is an integral part of the social system and not limited to La Cosa Nostra. Still, the fixation with Mafia - a legacy perhaps from the Kefauver days and the emphasis placed on it by numerous official and academic studies, persist in the thinking and work of law enforcement agencies.[3]

Academic treatments of organized crime, among other social groups in American society, seem no less blind than official inquiries. In a widely used text, Abadinsky describes African-American organized crime as a phenomenon that emerged well after World War II. He confidently claims that:

> *heroin provided the vehicle by which black criminal operators*
> *were able to enter the ranks of organized crime. Resistance*
> *from already established Mafia entrepreneurs proved futile;*
> *emerging black criminal organizations revealed a willingness*
> *to use violence on a scale that neutralized otherwise*
> *formidable opposition (1985:155).*

This passage betrays a lack of familiarity with a body of literature that illustrates convincingly the existence of African-American organized criminality decades before World War II (Schatzberg, 1993; Schatzberg and Kelly, 1996). To focus just on gambling in Harlem since the 1920s, the policy rackets had been widespread among poor African-Americans where numbers gambling functioned as a substitute for the legitimate financial institutions that were conspicuously absent in impoverished communities.

Apart from their chief purpose to generate as much money as possible, Light shows that numbers gambling banks operated as alternatives or substitute savings and credit institutions and as sources of ready capital in the African-American community (1977). In addition, a usury industry sprung up to service the clientele of the numbers game. This species of an illegal appended enterprise may have broadened the scope of numbers gambling beyond the needs of the minority community and took on a life of its own (Lesieur and Shelley, 1987). The extent to which numbers was an integral part of the African-American economy is indicated by Redding who characterized the pervasiveness of number gambling as "...the fever (that) has struck all classes and conditions of Men" (1934:542).

Numbers was a chance, however slim, for poor African-Americans to suddenly realize a windfall of cash by investing as little as a penny, nickel or a dime. For the operators of the policy game, risks were minimal and profits very sizable -- even with the overhead of police corruption, protection payoffs, salaries for workers, commissions and the like.

Before the Schultz gang (a white criminal enterprise operating in the boroughs of Manhattan and the Bronx in New York City) seized much of the Harlem policy racket and consolidated its control, numbers was not a criminal monopoly or cartel operation. It consisted of numerous independent bankers who conducted the game, each for themselves, each providing the requisite operating capital and each taking the profits (Nelli, 1976:Ch. 8). Initially, the policy rackets were led by gambling "barons" who were unsettled by the intrusions of white gangs. Politics and political influence with corrupted officials was a major tool in the process of confrontation between the community-based African-American operators and the alien white gangs. The two elements of struggle in the underworld of Harlem in the 1920s and 30s, violence and political clout, enabled Schultz to win the keys of the policy kingdom. But it was a success story soaked in blood, as were so many of his criminal enterprises. Mitgang reported that there were forty murders and six kidnappings as a result of the policy gambling war in New York City in the early 1930s (1963:204).

African-American Organized Crime: Field Studies in the '70s

In 1974, Ianni's study of burgeoning organized criminal networks in Harlem found that "while there are characteristic patterns of organization with the various networks we observed there is no overall pattern that ties the networks together (1974:104)." There was in effect no "Mafia" or syndicate structure among these minority criminal groups. They did not evolve around a common code of behavior or rules governing relationships between and among various groups; the protection they paid to operate in illicit goods and services was not of a magnitude that would have significant political impact and there were no examples of networks influencing an election, delivering a vote, funding a political candidate, or dabbling in union affairs. The scale of corruption was modest, highly localized, and tied to the particular criminal activity involved.

But why suppose that organized crime that does not fit the pattern of a Mafia is not "organized?" The structure of African-American organized criminality may indeed vary from its white counterparts and its scale may be modest by Cosa Nostra standards, but these aspects in themselves suggest a continuum of organized criminality ranging along several axes of size, division of labor, normative operating procedures and power to influence the external constraints impinging upon their operations (Kelly, 1987).

Because the Cosa Nostra/Mafia model may not apply neatly to African-American organized crime should not require that most descriptive theories of indigenous origins be abandoned. In fact, Ianni's refinements of the ethnic succession theory and its application to the data he compiled on Harlem and other minority communities seem especially pertinent.

As Myrdal pointed out in 1944 concerning African-American organized crime: there was indeed an African-American "underworld." To it belong, not only petty thieves and racketeers, prostitutes and pimps, bootleggers, dope addicts, and so on, but also a number of "big shots" organizing and controlling crime, vice, and racketeering, as well as other more innocent forms of illegal activity such as gambling - particularly the "policy," or the "numbers," game. The underworld has, therefore, an upper class and a middle class as well as a lower class. The shady upper class is composed mainly of the "policy kings." They are the most important members of the underworld from the point of view of their numbers, their wealth and their power. The policy game started in the Negro Community and has a long history. This game caught on quickly among African-Americans because one may bet as little as a penny, and the rewards are high if one wins (as much as 600 to 1). In a community where most of the people are either on relief or in the lowest income brackets such rewards must appear exceptionally alluring. During most of its history the policy racket in the African-American community has been monopolized by African-Americans.

At the time of his study more than two decades ago, Ianni was able to describe the pre-conditions in Harlem, through the "ethnic succession" and social systems theory that could explain how the bases for organized criminal groups within Myrdal's black underworld could emerge.

For African American and Hispanic ghetto dwellers one of their most important problems - one that confronted white ethnic immigrants decades earlier -- was how to escape poverty through socially approved means, when these means were virtually closed. This problem is resolved to some extent by crime activities. For most ghetto dwellers the provision of illegal goods and services or the illegal provision of licit goods and services is tolerated widely because it is not seen as intrinsically evil or socially disruptive. Poverty provides its own moral climate for organized criminality in the ghetto with the exception, perhaps, of drug peddling. And even here, escape from the bondage of poverty provides emotional pressure and an acceptable context for wide-spread drug use. It is then the pervasive persistent poverty of the ghetto and its collective despair that is at the basis of recruitment into criminal networks.

African-Americans involved in ghetto crime enterprises and networks are driven by aims no different than those that motivated Irish, Jewish and Italian criminals that preceded them: assimilation into, and accommodation by, the larger American society. Apart from the seething poverty, the cultural and structural forces that shaped the growth and evolution of white ethnic organized criminality may not apply or be relevant to African-Americans and Hispanics. There does not appear to be a cultural ethos and cohesive kinship system among some African-Americans that produced a high degree of organizational development in criminal syndicates which was characteristic of Italians. Certainly, African-American criminal networks would be expected to respond to their own subcultural imperatives. And they may substitute in place of kinship and extended family solidarity, peer relationships formed in street gangs, and ties forged in prison. Also, strengthened by a common sense of victimization in a racist society, that very process of social rejection and stigma itself may constitute the catalyst necessary to produce and sustain an enduring cohesive criminal enterprise.

A decade after Ianni's field studies in the African-American ghettos of New York City and New Jersey, testimony was presented to the Senate Judiciary Committee in 1983 by the New York City Police Department, which described African-American organized crime as divisible into two main groups - that of American, native-born blacks and Jamaican-based religious cultists, the Rastafarians. Until then, African-Americans had been described as more or less confined to roles within La Cosa Nostra which dominated the ghetto gambling rackets and drug trafficking. In the 1970s there seems to have been a rupture between African-American criminals and their former La Cosa Nostra patrons and employers. Several major narcotics' groups, established and operated exclusively by African-Americans appeared in the ghettos. Eventually they either dissolved or were broken up by drug enforcement Task Forces and the police. Some law enforcement officials speculated that gambling profits and those derived from other enterprises such as loan-sharking and fencing in stolen goods, were the capitalization instruments for autonomous drug ventures. The African-American drug rings developed their own international sources of supply, importing methods, processing procedures, and distribution outlets. As with their white counterparts, the huge profits earned in narcotics appear to have been funneled into legitimate businesses in the ghettos.

In the 1960s and 1970s some of the larger, more powerful drug syndicates, those of Frank Matthews, LeRoy (Nicky) Barnes, and Charles Lucas, spread out beyond the ghetto. The level of sophistication and scope of trafficking varied, of course, and some, such as the Lucas organization, showed that it was competitive with Cosa Nostra groups.

In its international smuggling operations, the Lucas syndicate employed relatives as a hedge against security breeches. Participation in the drug trade was not restricted to wholesaling but sought control from source bases from Indochina to street level sales in American African-American ghettos. All the trademarks of astute organization characteristic of La Cosa Nostra operations were apparent in the Lucas group: personnel were selected because they were trustworthy, not merely because of some sentimental friendship or childhood attachment; a division of labor among personnel existed such that participants knew only what was necessary in order for them to function; and state of the art technologies in transport, processing and packaging were extensively deployed.

In other densely populated urban areas, such as Chicago, where African-Americans are at the bottom of the economic ladder, organized criminal groups are active. One known as the Royal Family, consisted of former inmates from Stateville Penitentiary who deliberately modeled themselves on the fictitious Coreleone family in Puzo's novel, *The Godfather* (Abadinsky, 1985:Ch 10). However, the Royal Family would not dare challenge the white Chicago syndicate ("The Outfit") but allied itself with it, working principally as low-level enforcers.

According to Abadinsky, the largest and probably most powerful African-American organized criminal group in the Chicago area more than a decade ago was the El Rukns, a group that openly and contemptuously defied

"The Outfit."[4]   El Rukns were suspected of narcotics dealing and assorted shakedowns in the African-American communities. It evolved out of a street gang, the Blackstone Rangers, and had participated actively in local political campaigns. With guile and cunning it petitioned for status as a nonprofit charity organization when its key leaders were under indictment or imprisoned. It may not be as outrageous as it sounds when a notorious gang of toughened street youths, now adult, engaging in serious crime, also does socially useful work within the ghetto among the impoverished. Mafia organizations have often done the same thing; they simultaneously exploited and helped, always to their advantage.

This brief chronology suggests questions about African-Americans organizing themselves into powerful criminal groups as others have done when poverty and oppression were acute and painful. The criminal organizations that did emerge in numbers, prostitution and drug peddling were feeble by comparison with today's groups, and were easily overwhelmed by powerful white gangsters (Kobler, 1971; Peterson 1983).

The rise of African-American organized crime groups in the Post-World War II era seems to have run astride with the rise of African-American political consciousness, with the awakening of political and social militancy. The data show that major African-American drug traffickers surfaced at approximately the same time, the early and mid-sixties, when militant political pressures were mounted for jobs, educational reform, fair housing and a greater share of political power. Apparently, a combination of factors coalesced, some with unanticipated consequences, that produced both legitimate and illegitimate opportunity structures. In the wake of sweeping racially motivated reforms, greater control over communities was gained and as political strength grew, criminal elements were able to take advantage of the correlative declines of white power and influence within the ghetto crime scene. Thus, African-Americans seemed more able then at any other time to wrest the ghetto from bondage to white syndicates and become less dependent upon La Cosa Nostra political and police influence; that enabled them to independently bargain with whites who were increasingly unable to operate freely in the racial ghettos.

In this arena of rising racial power on the one hand, and deflation of power on the other, the Civil Rights Movement appears to have set in motion social and economic mobility and at the same time inadvertently diminish the power of white crime groups that had dominated African-American criminals. As the ghettos developed their new found strength and accumulated political punch, the political agent, the operator, the political machine functionary, with connections in the "administration" or City Hall, appeared on the scene. As the emancipatory movement of the Civil Rights Movement achieved success, the African-American ghettos became more politically assertive and economically more viable. A host of new actors arose: the "minority middlemen," the ghetto power brokers, (those equally comfortable in the official world of government and business as in the ghetto shadows of opportunism and crime, where favors are arranged and deals made); these individuals assumed prominent roles in social, economic and political affairs.

The ghetto underworld is not a homogeneous, monolithic structure of power and influence wielded only by African-Americans - perhaps it never was. Since the late sixties in New York City, and in urban areas in New Jersey, Maryland, Washington, DC, Florida, California and in Toronto, Canada, the Rastafarians have engaged principally in marijuana and cocaine smuggling on a comparatively large scale. A close-knit group centered on a religious ideology with political overtones that deifies Ethiopia's former emperor, Haile Selassie, the "Rastas" have achieved something of a détente with white organized crime families and other African-American criminal groups over criminal turfs and territories. The "Rastas" have gained control over the criminal economy (temporarily, at least) in the West Indian and Jamaican communities. Whether they are hierarchically organized with ascending positions from boss downward to the street worker, is not known. As with other ghetto-bound criminal groups, it is likely that a system of patron/client relations exists which is viable as an operational strategy in such fluid settings. What they have are the two organizational factors that all durable criminal enterprises must possess: a capability and reputation for violence and criminogenic assets including resources to corrupt and neutralize law enforcement control agencies.

Culture and Ethnicity

Among other things the rather controversial theory of ethnic succession proposes are that illegal enterprises are domestic in origin rather than imported. The *form* and *shape* they take is related to the cultural styles of the participants. While Albini did not work out the details, he advanced the same idea by emphasizing the spectrum of ethnic and racial minorities in the United States engaged in organized crime at one time or another (1971). Ianni and Albini would describe the ethnic diversity of criminals as a consequence of structurally engendered poverty and disadvantages rather than some sort of social group cultural proclivity. Both Ianni's and Albini's arguments appear to rest upon the anomie theory of deviance which suggests in its broadest formulations that when legitimate avenues of social and economic mobility are blocked, those frustrated by discriminatory obstacles seek out deviant or criminal ways to advance socially and economically. While such theoretical considerations appear to be necessary in an explanation of the genesis of organized criminality, they have not proven sufficient. Over the past thirty years, the predominance of Italian-Americans in organized crime even after they have largely overcome institutional discrimination has encouraged an unfortunate blurring between the specific features of Italo-American criminal enterprise and the general problem of organized crime. The one has been made to appear synonymous with other and the persistence of Italians in organized crime in a major way has not been satisfactorily explained.

At the other extreme, some critics of the cultural interpretation of organized crime developed analyses that de-emphasized explicit references to cultural or ethnic heritage as a structural factor of criminal activities (Becker,

1968; Schelling, 1971; Rubin, 1973). Ethnicity and culture from this perspective are largely extraneous to the conduct of criminal activity. However, the argument that organized crime is part of the social system of the United States and that the socio-cultural characteristics of participant groups are not especially relevant to criminal activities, seems to miss important features of the phenomenon. Quite the contrary, culture shapes values and informs behavior.

Ianni's ethnographic study of African-American and Cuban organized crime networks sought to show precisely this: that the phenomenon of organized crime is not unique to Italian-American experience and that it has a logic of its own manifesting itself among other groups when they are poised to exploit the criminal opportunities American society thrusts upon them. And, above all, it seems clear that the style of illegal activities is affected by the cultural and ethnic characteristics of the participants to a degree that seems to defy analysis.

African-American Organized Crime Within the Ghetto

The socio-cultural characteristics of provider subgroups are important factors affecting the manner in which minority vice industries are structured to meet consumer demands. Empirical studies and field work on marijuana distribution networks in New York indicated that retail-level traffickers were sensitive to the real or imagined racial and cultural backgrounds of those with whom they chose to do business (Kelly, 1987). Today in African-American communities where a large underclass exists, where unemployment is high and despair deep, crack cocaine is to the young ghetto gangster what illegal liquor was to the white ethnic gangsters more than half a century ago.

Three classes of criminals created the crack epidemic. One was composed of anonymous kitchen chemists and drug traffickers in the United States who used rudimentary science and marketing savvy to help hundreds of small-time criminals set up operations. Another group consisted of indigenous crime organizations, common in most medium and large American cities, who seized local markets from smaller operators. The third group were gangs on both coasts who franchised crack operations into every corner of the country using African-Americans and Latinos as their subordinates.

Every large urban African-American ghetto has criminal organizations operating in its midst. Some of these gangs are large, some small. A local African-American usually leads these criminal enterprises; some examples illustrate the organizational patterns.

In the Washington Heights section of Manhattan, New York, Dominican drug gangs employed up to 100 people in the city's first big crack market. The Renkers posse operated a huge portion of the crack trade in Brooklyn, New York employing fifty workers selling crack in the Bedford-Stuyvesant, Crown Heights, and Flatbush ghetto sections of the borough. The Renkers have branched out to Philadelphia, Baltimore and Washington, D.C.

In many minority urban ghettos crack cocaine is the currency of the informal economy. The gangs that developed around it reflect the dynamics of the trafficking systems that have emerged. In these respects modern minority criminal groups have little structural resemblance to La Cosa Nostra crime families. Still, these groups are no less dangerous nor are they likely to be short-lived or only drug-dependent; the gangs may thrive beyond the demand for crack by transforming themselves to meet the illegal market conditions of other commodities in demand. Crack could enable minority groups to generate essential criminogenic assets (the use of violence and the availability and distributions of illegal commodities). Once established, these groups might explore other criminal opportunities in much the same way that the earlier criminal groups, including Cosa Nostra, emerged to serve the demand for illicit alcohol.

Detroit's Chambers Brothers

Growing disillusionment with the failure of criminal justice control policies over the last fifteen years has prompted scholars and others to observe inner-city hustlers and dealers firsthand. Though approaching the subject from different angles, they have arrived at remarkably similar conclusions. Adler (1996) traces the fortunes of two African-American brothers, Billy Joe and Larry Chambers who rose from a backwater town in the Arkansas Delta to run the largest crack operation in Detroit, Michigan. In personality, the brothers could not be more different: the bantam-sized Billy Joe was a rambunctious womanizer, obsessed with Cadillacs and parties, while Larry was a stern vegetarian, yoga practitioner, and voracious reader unfailingly polite even as he readied to do violence, which was often. While Billy Joe contented himself with running a half-dozen crack houses, Larry took over an entire apartment building and turned it into a state-of-the-art crack empire, with fliers advertising his drugs, quality control procedures, and a job hotline. The brothers became folk heroes for street kids and even some adults.

The twisted entrepreneurship of the Chambers brothers began in Arkansas's Lee County, the sixth poorest county in the nation. Nearly half of its African-American children were described in official surveys as malnourished or undernourished, and only one in five African-American adults had graduated from high school. By the early 1980s, blue-collar work had all but disappeared from the region and racial prejudice was so strong that African-American adults were still afraid to register to vote. So, like countless young people before them, the Chambers brothers headed north.

The situation there was no less bleak. On Detroit's Lower East Side, where they lived, life had once centered on "Old Jeff," the Chrysler assembly plant of Jefferson Avenue. But the auto company had been forced to slash its workforce during the recession of the late 1970s, and by 1982 more than 50 percent of the city's young African-Americans were unemployed. Crack cocaine, when it spread, supplied the job opportunities once provided by the auto industry.

The crack-cocaine operation founded in 1983 by the Chambers brothers evolved in just a few years to some 200 crack houses that employed up to 500 people mostly teenagers recruited from their hometown in Arkansas. In 1988, during a drug conspiracy case against 14 members of the Chambers brothers gang, authorities said that the Chambers network "once supplied half the city's crack"[5] with profits amounting to one million dollars a week.

Adler does not sentimentalize the brothers; as criminals they must be held accountable for their actions. At the same time, he points out that for many young people, crack distribution was a rational career choice, a reaction to the devastating consequences of the Regan-Bush era's domestic spending policies for inner-city residents, and a reaction to the collapse of opportunity during the 1980s for those at the bottom of the economic heap -- especially poor African-Americans.

The Crips and Bloods: The Black-lash

As minority gangs developed and spread in the mid-1980s the United States was caught in a pincer movement. The Los Angeles street gangs moved east, and the Jamaican posses moved west from the East coast. Between them by the end of the decade they had introduced much of the rest of the country to crack.

The chief Los Angeles gangs have been identified as the Crips (approximately 30,000 strong now) and the Bloods (about 9,000); the gangs consists primarily of Latinos and African-Americans. Their expansion to other parts of the country took off in 1986 and since then they have expanded into the Northwest and Midwest.[6] In 1991, the Justice Department placed the Crips and Bloods in 32 states and 113 cities. Some experts think that Los Angeles-based gangs now control up to 30 percent of the crack trade.[7] Neither gang is rigidly hierarchical. Both are broken into loosely affiliated neighborhood groups called "sets," each with 30 to 100 members. Many gang members initially left Southern California to evade police while others simply spread to other areas by setting up branch operations in places where friends or family were located.

Compared with Los Angeles, many cities have been easy pickings, especially for "rollers" or "O.G.s" -- (Original Gangsters) and other criminal entrepreneurs in their twenties who have established a connection with Colombian suppliers. Crips and Bloods are reflections of a demographic bulge where their members tend to be in the most criminally prone age cohorts - adolescence to adulthood. Coupled with the exceeding high unemployment rate among young males (36 percent), the conditions for the rapid expansion of African-American crime are present.

In communities that are severely depressed economically, crime is often seen as an attractive alternative, if not the only one, to prolonged deprivation. However, the crime that emerges is not in the least beneficial to these communities. Generally, illicitly earned income among gang members, primarily drug money, is not recirculated in the community, banked, invested in commercial enterprises, or used to capitalize commercial activities that benefit the community as a whole. Instead, income is typically used for personal luxury items or reabsorbed by the drug economy whose infrastructure lies outside the community of the consumers it exploits. Unlike the policy rackets of years ago,

Table 12.1: Southern California Crips sets: Los Angeles and San Diego

52 Hoover	Neighborhood Crips	98 Main Streets	Ghost Town Crips	East Coast 118
59 Hoover	Broadway 112	Broadway 52	Playboy Style	East Coast 97
74 Hoover	Ruthless Posse Crips	West Coast Crips	Grape Street Crips	East Coast 89
83 Hoover	5 Deuce Crips	Front Street	102 Budlong Gangsters	East Coast 69
92 Hoover	Pocker Hood	Back Street	99 Mafia	East Coast 62
107 Hoover	Bahala Na-Barkada	Raymond Crips	Lanatna Block	83 Main Streets
112 Hoover	Linda Vista Crips	Shotgun Crips	Gear Gang Crips	94 Main Street
Rollin' 30	Santana Blocks Rollin' 90's	Rollin' 20 Crips	105 Underground	Water Gate
Rollin' 40	Venice Shoreling Gangsters	Front Hood	106 Playboy Style	Marvin Crips
Rollin' 60	Playboy Gangsters	P.J. Watts	Insanes	94 Hoover
Nutty Blocks	Watts Baby Coc Crips	Kelly Park Crips	Kitchen Crips	8- Tray Gangsters
East Coast 1	East Coast 190	Schoolyard Cs	Inglewood Village Crips	357
East Coast 59	Schoolyard Crips	Compton Crips	Tiny Oriental Crips	

Note: Street Names are usually pronounced not as numbers but as separate words (e.g. Five-Deuce Hoover, Eight Tray Gangsters, Broadway One-twelve, East Coast six-Deuce, and so forth). The rolling numbers are pronounced as seen Rollin' Sixties.

Source: Compiled from: Leon Bing, Do or Die (New York: Harper Collins, 1991); William B. Sanders, Gangbangs and Drive-bys (New York: Aldine De Grutyer, 1994); District Attorney's Office, Gangs, Crime and Violence in Los Angeles (Los Angeles, Office of the District Attorney, May, 1992): Kody Scott, Monster: The Autobiography of an L.A. Gang Member Sanyika Shakur, A.K.A. Monster Kody Scott (New York: The Atlantic Monthly Press, 1993); and personal interviews.

Table 12.2: Southern California Bloods sets: Los Angeles and San Diego

Athens Park	Black P. Stones	Bounty Hunters
8-9 Families	Inglewood Families	Swans
West Side Pirus	Ludas Park Pirus	Rolling Twenties
Outlaw Twenties	Miller Gangsters	B-Bop Warts
Treetop Pirus	Holly-Hood Pirus	Denver Lanes
Pablos	Five-Deuce Villians	Pasadena Devil Lanes
Fruit Town	Lime Hood	*Kompton Fruit Town
Van Ness Gangsters	* Skottsdale Pirus	Ujima Village Bloods
* Karson Pirus	* Kabbage Patch Pirus	Six-Deuce Brims
Nine-Deuce Bishops	Sirkle-Sity Pirus	Five-Nine Brims
Pomona Island Pirus	Mid-Sity Gangsters	*Senter Park Pirus
Compton Pirus	Northside Blood	Skyline Pirus
Lincoln Park Pirus	Little Africa Pirus	Eastside Pirus
Bell Haven	* Sirkle Sity	Thirty-Seventh Street
Bounty Hunters	Bounty Hunters	Fruit Town
Neighborhood Pirus	Avenue Pirus	Krenshaw Mafia
5/9 Brim Pirus		

* Note that the capital letter C has been changed to letter S or K

Source: Compiled from: Leon Bing, Do or Die (New York: Harper Collins, 1991); William B. Sanders, Gangbangs and Drive-bys (New York: Aldine De Grutyer, 1994); District Attorney's Office, Gangs, Crime and Violence in Los Angeles (Los Angeles, Office of the District Attorney, May, 1992): Kody Scott, Monster: The Autobiography of an L.A. Gang Member Sanyika Shakur, A.K.A. Monster Kody Scott (New York: The Atlantic Monthly Press, 1993); and personal interviews.

drug money flows out of the community and is drained off by large non-community based syndicates.[8]

Los Angeles's Gangs as a Revolutionary Lumpen-Proletariat

As the study of street gangs is developing into a vast cottage industry, little has actually been written about Los Angeles's destructive gang culture. The first generation of African-American street gangs emerged as a defensive response to confrontations in the schools and streets with whites during the late 1940s. Until the 1970s these gangs tended to be defined mainly by school-based turf rather than by microscopically drawn neighborhood territories. Besides defending African-American teenagers from racist attacks these early gangs were also the unwitting architects of social space in new and usually hostile settings.

Another factor in gang formation was the decimation of the Black Panthers that led directly or indirectly to a recrudescence of gangs two decades ago. For example, "Crippin," that most extraordinary gang phenomenon, was a bastard offspring of the Panther's former charisma, which filled the void when law enforcement groups crushed the Panthers across the country. The street legends about the Crips agree on certain particulars: the first "set" incubated in the social wasteland caused by the clearance of a community for an urban freeway. Radical urban renewal which ignored neighborhood life was traumatizing and destructive in Los Angeles. One legend has it that "Crips" stands for *"Continuous Revolution in Progress."* However apocryphal this may be, it best describes the phenomenal spread of Crip sets across the ghetto between 1970 and 1972. And under incessant pressure other independent gangs federated as the red-handkerchief Bloods. The Bloods have been primarily a defensive reaction-formation to the aggressive appearance of the Crips.

This was not merely a gang revival in Los Angeles but instead a radical permutation of gang culture. The Crips inherited the Panther aura of fearlessness and transmitted the ideology of armed vanguardism. "Crippin" often represents an escalation of intra-ghetto violence to "Clockwork Orange" levels (murder as a status symbol). They have also blended a penchant for ultra-violence with an overweening ambition to dominate the entire ghetto. The Crips achieved, like the El Rukns in Chicago, a "managerial revolution" in gang existence. If they began as a teenage substitute for the fallen Panthers, they evolved through the 70s into a hybrid of teen cult and proto-Mafia.

In 1972 at the height of Crip hysteria a city-sponsored conference gave a platform to the gangs, which produced a document of their grievances. To the astonishment of officials, the "mad dogs" outlined an eloquent and coherent set of demands: jobs, housing, better schools, recreation facilities and community control of local institutions. It was a bravura demonstration that gang youth, however trapped in their own delusionary spirals of vendetta and self-destruction, clearly understood that they were the children of deferred dreams and defeated ambitions. Young African-Americans have seen their labor-market options virtually collapse as the factory and truck driving jobs that gave their fathers and older brothers a modicum of dignity, replaced by imports or relocated to white areas far out of the galactic spiral-arms of the Los Angeles megalopolis. The deteriorating labor-market for these young males may be a major reason the counter-economy of drug dealing and youth crime has spread like a virus through many economically fragile African-American communities.

The tacit expendability of African-American and Hispanic youths can be directly measured by the steady drainage of resources (with minimum outcry from elected officials, it should be noted). Job alternatives for gang members have been almost nonexistent, despite widespread recognition that jobs are the most potent deterrents to crime. The school system meanwhile has been traveling backwards at high speed. At the state level the educational system has been in steep decline.

The specific genius of the Crips has been their ability to insert themselves into a leading circuit of the international drug trade. Through crack cocaine they have discovered a vocation for the ghetto in the new world city economies. Peddling the imported, high-profit rock to a bipolar market of final consumers, including rich whites and poor street people, the Crips have become "lumpen" capitalists as well as outlaw proletarians.

In an age of *narco-imperialism* they resemble modern analogues of the "gunpowder states" of West Africa, those selfish, rogue chieftains who were middlemen in the eighteenth century slave trade, prospering while the rest of Africa bled. In contemporary jargon of the marketplace, the cocaine and crack trades are stunning examples of what economists call "flexible accumulation." The rules of the game are to combine maximum financial control with interchangeable deployment of producers and sellers across variable markets.

The appearance of crack has given the Crips subculture a terrible, almost irresistible allure. There is little reason to believe that the crack economy of the new gang culture will stop growing, whatever the scales of repression, or stay confined to African-American ghettos. Although the epicenters remain in the ghetto zones of hard-core youth unemployment, the gang mystique has spread into middle-class African-American areas where parents are close to panic or vigilantism in fear for their own children.

Conclusions and Projections

It is widely taken for granted that corruption of public officials and law enforcement is a key prerequisite for organized criminal activities. Political bosses and political machines, to be successful, must be able to guarantee some police protection to those who provide illicit goods and services in demand. In other respects, the head of a political machine must be able to arrange variances and liquor licenses for the right people. And he (or she) must be able to close their eyes to all kinds of infractions and illegalities (Krase and La Cerra, 1987).

Although the avenues of corruption have been assiduously nurtured and sustained by whites, the growing political and economic autonomy of the African-American community suggests that rackets and political organization are, or will be, major continuing elements of slum life. While African-

American criminals may find it difficult to ingratiate themselves into the kinds of social relationships with white politicians that offer protection, it is not difficult to imagine how African-American politicians operating from powerful political machines will provide services and favors for those on the periphery of the legal and the illegal.

The economic roles of "legitimate" and "illegitimate" business run parallel in the ghetto. Both forms are concerned with the provision of goods and services for which there is a public demand. The relevant difference between the provisioning of licit and illicit goods and services is small as shown in gambling and the traffic in consumer goods. In terms of social status, the legitimate business groups in the ghetto and the criminal groups are poles apart, yet status itself does not fully determine behavior and the interrelation between groups. Functions modify these relationships in social settings where the informal economy is as large as the formal economy.

"Just as the political machine performs services for legitimate business, so it operates to perform not dissimilar services for illegitimate business, vice, crime and rackets."[9] Minority politicians asserting themselves in the ghetto are likely to organize in terms of their perceptions of their functions and their own survival needs and in this regard they will resemble their white colleagues. For both the legitimate and illegitimate sectors within the ghetto, the political machine has a similar function. Above all, it must satisfy the needs of its clientele and constituencies for an operating environment that enables criminal and non-criminal alike to meet economic demands without interference from the government. Whether a political machine turns a blind eye to crime, or vigorously attacks it, depends on the relative economic and political strength of the client or the protagonist. As far as market demands for goods and services are inadequately met by the legitimate sector, an alternative illegal sector will develop to fulfill them.

It would seem impossible to map out in a scientifically rational manner what a society free of organized crime might look like because "Organized Crime" is an expression of the impossibility of reconstructing complex social systems by rationalist, scientifically inspired methods. If one examines the factors that are conducive to organized crime - cultural and social conflicts of interests, the fetishism of material wealth, the inadequacies and corruptibility of social control institutions, most notably the police and criminal justice agencies - all these are at work in present day society and likely to be present in a scientifically constructed social utopia. In the case of African-Americans, the aspirations to radically reformulate the racial equation, to improve economic opportunities of ghetto residents, and to reform community institutions has largely succeeded in creating a massive social mobility, but at the same time that African-Americans have managed to achieve some modicum of control over the social chaos, the political and economic structures of their communities have become infected with the irrationality of the environments in which they are situated. The leading cause of death among African-American males between the ages of 14 and 25 years is homicide; drug addiction in the poorer inner-cities is rampant, and out-of-wedlock birth among African-American teenage women is at historic highs. Who can fathom, much less analyze, such a destructive delirium?

The questions remain and may be addressed together. Much has been written on the origins and causes of organized crime as this concept is ordinarily understood - as, in effect, a form of conspirational, parasitic crime emerging in the impoverished ghettos of minority communities. But little has been done really on the community conditions conducive to its disappearance. In short, the analyses which describe its appearance implicitly suggests the conditions which may lead to its diminution and eradication. In spite of the complacency and inertia of American society to radically restructure itself and its political policies short of a national emergency, what can be hoped for are:

- better, more powerful organized crime suppression strategies, and
- continued research into the problem that informs public understanding.

Unquestionably, government knowledge of organized crime has greatly improved over the past decades since the sensational Valachi hearings where the identity of La Cosa Nostra was first revealed. Since then, with the enactment of the RICO laws, changes in the investigative tool kits and technologies of investigative agencies, the creation of immunity statutes, and the implementation of the Witness Security Program, it is apparent that law enforcement authorities possess a more comprehensive picture of the activities of organized crime groups. While aggressive law enforcement measures should be adopted and implemented, one of the keys to controlling the organized crime and the gang problem in African-American communities may lie with the cultivation of community cooperation including neighborhood groups, schools, social welfare agencies, and business - (the latter are often victimized by gangs engaged in extortion activities). A standard law enforcement approach has been to attack gang leaders and other influential criminals. The attempt to eradicate organized crime in African-American communities by focusing solely on the gangs while neglecting the moral and financial support structure could prove futile as a policy. Eliminating gang leaders seems to have little impact because in the aftermath of a succession crisis they can and have quickly regrouped.

An anti-crime policy that promises a greater impact has to do with improving police and community relations. Tensions between law enforcement authorities and community residents are harmful to both. There are several channels through which relations can be facilitated. One of these represents a major shift in urban policing that has occurred with the implementation of "community policing." A cardinal tenet of community policy is that a new relationship between police and neighborhoods is required if the quality of residential and commercial life is to be protected or improved. The concept perceives the community as an agent and partner in promoting security rather than as a passive audience. This notion is in contrast to the traditional concept of policing that measures successes chiefly through response times, the number of calls handled, and detection rates for serious crimes. To the extent that cooperative strategies can enhance the capacities of neighborhoods to defend themselves against predatory crime -- a fundamental characteristic of organized criminality -- reducing crime in a collective, concertive way affords psychological protection against the weaning influences of the criminal milieu by destroying the viability of its infrastructure. Moreover, reducing crime and it disruptive effects on community ties eliminates the largest and most devastating obstacle to economic development in many poor neighborhoods. And where businesses can develop, they encourage further growth and help create a community's cohesiveness and identity and strengthen its capacities to resist crime.

The other facet in an anti-organized crime strategy is in the area of research work in structural analysis. Law enforcement interventions could benefit from more refinement and applications of "network analysis" of the kind that Ianni proposed more than twenty years ago. Future research might take on the task of getting beyond the metaphoric use of the "network" concept and aim to define it more sharply, distinguishing types of networks and empirically operationalizing their dimensions and dynamics. Many questions remain unanswered concerning the explanatory variables that figure into the mobilization processes operating among gangs. Networks would appear to be one of the important elements explaining the how and why of gang involvement. Personal, neighborhood-bound networks could also be considered an intervening variable, since this structural variable may clarify the step from individual willingness to participate, whereas cultural variables (such as values, attitudes, availability and experience) may better explain the development of an underlying motivational structure to take part in criminal activities.

Robert J. Kelly, Ph. D., is Broeklundian Professor of Social Science at Brooklyn College and The Graduate School and University Center of The City University  *of New York. He has served as a consultant to numerous foreign, federal, state and local governments on issues concerning organized crime, terrorism and extremist politics. Current research interests include a longitudinal study on remedial teaching technologies in higher educational institutions sponsored by the U.S. Department of Education, and a study of illegal Chinese immigrants in the United States for the National Science Foundation. Recent publications include Hate Crimes: the Politics of Global Polarization (Southern Illinois University Press); The Upperworld and the Underworld: Racketeering Penetrations of Legitimate Business (Plenum Publishing Co.); African-American Organized Crime: A Social History (Rutgers University Press).*

References

Abadinsky, H. (1985), *Organized Crime*, 2nd ed. Chicago: Nelson-Hall.

Adler, W. M. (1996), *Land of Opportunity: One Family's Quest for the American Dream in the Age of Crack*. NY: Atlantic Monthly Press.

Albanese, J. S. (1987), "Government Perceptions of Organized Crime: The Presidential Commission," 1967 and 1987 (Paper presented to the 39th Annual Meeting of the American Society of Criminology, Montreal, Canada, Nov. 13th).

Albini, J. (1971), *The American Mafia: Genesis of a Legend*. New York: Appleton-Century Crafts.

Becker, G. S. (1968), "Crime and Punishment: An Economic Approach," *Journal of Political Economy* 76:169-217.

Block, A. (1983), *East Side - West Side: Organizing Crime in New York, 1930-1950*. New Brunswick, New Jersey: Transaction Books.

Dubro, J. (1985), *Mob Rule: Inside the Canadian Mafia*. Toronto: A Totem Books.

Ianni, F. A. J. (1974), *'Black Mafia': Ethnic Succession in Organized Crime*. New York: Simon & Schuster.

Kelly, R. J. (ed.) (1986), *Organized Crime: A Global Perspective*. Totowa, New Jersey: Rowman & Littlefield, Publishers.

Kelly, R. J. (1987), "Field Research among Deviants: A Consideration of Some Methodological Recommendations." *Deviant Behavior* 3:219-228.

Kobler, J. (1971), *Capone: the Life and World of Al Capone*. Greenwich, CT: Fawcett Publishers.

Krase, J. and C. La Cerra (1987), "Ethnicity and Machine Politics: The Madison Club of Brooklyn" City University of New York, unpublished manuscript.

Lesieur, H. R. and J. R. Shelley (1987), "Illegal Appended Enterprises: Selling the Lives," *Social Problems* (June), Vol. 34, No. 3:249-260.

Light, I. (1977), "The Ethnic Vice Industry, 1880-1944," *American Sociological Review*, Vol. 42 (June):464-479.

Light, I. (1977b), "Numbers Gambling Among Blacks: A Financial Institution," *American Sociological Review*, Vol. 42 (December):892-904.

Merton, R. K. (1957), *Social Theory and Social Structure*, Rev. ed. New York: Free Press:192-294.

Mitgang, H. (1963), *The Man Who Rode the Tiger: The Life and Times of Judge Samuel Seabury*. New York: J. B. Lippincott Company.

Myrdal, G. (1944), *An American Dilemma*. New York: Harper & Row.

Nelli, H. S. (1976), *The Business of Crime: Italians and Syndicate Crime in the United States*. New York: Oxford University Press.

Petersen, V. (1983), The *Mob: 200 Years of Organized Crime in New York*. Ottawa, IL: Green Hill Publishers.

Pileggi, N. (1986), "The Mob and the Machine," *New York Magazine* (May 5):36-41.

President's Commission on Organized Crime (April, 1986), *The Impact: Organized Crime Today*. Washington, DC: U.S. Government Printing Office.

President's Commission on Organized Crime (Feb. 20- 27, 1985), *Organized Crime and Heroin Trafficking*, Record of Hearing V Miami, Florida. Washington, D.C.: U.S. Government Printing Office.

Report on Organized Crime in New York City (1983). Testimony of the Police Department, City of New York (July 11) before United States Senate Committee on the Judiciary.

Revell, O. B. (Sept. 25-26, 1986), "The Many Faces of Organized Crime" papers presented to Major Issues in Organized Crime Control: Symposium Proceedings, NIJ, Langely, Virginia.

Rubin, P. E. (1973), "The Economic Theory of the Criminal Firm" in S. Rottenberg (ed.) *The Economies of Crime and Punishment.* Washington, D.C.: Cesseicen Enterprises Institute.

Redding, J. S. (December 1934), "Playing the Numbers," *The North American Review*: 533-542.

Schatzberg, R. (1993), *Black Organized Crime: 1920-1930.* New York: Garland Publishing Co.

Schatzberg, R. and R. J. Kelly (1996), *African-American Organized Crime: A Social History.* New York: Garland Publishing Co.

Schelling, T. C. (1971), "What is the business of organized crime?" *Journal of Public Law*, 20:71-84.

Judge Samuel Seabury (March 28, 1932), *In the Matter of the Investigation of the Magistrates' Courts in the First Judicial Department and the Magistrates Thereof, and of Attorneys-at-Law Practicing in Said Courts.* Supreme Court, Appellate Division, First Judicial Department. Final report, 256 pp.

Notes

[1] According to the testimony of LeRoy 'Nicky' Barnes a 'Council' of narcotics traffickers was formed in Harlem. Its prime purpose was to pool criminal capital for more lucrative wholesale buys. The Council also provided other services to its members. It made available economic instruments that could be collectively shared: money launderers, attorneys, loans and pharmaceutical supplies. While each Council member retained control over his own organization, each had access to automobiles for transporting drugs and cash; numerous milling houses for processing and packaging; safe drops for street dealers; and more enforcement muscle otherwise unavailable in the absence of syndication. (Testimony of LeRoy 'Nicky' Barnes, *Record of Hearing V.* Miami, Florida, Feb. 20-21, 1985).

[2] The term is Jimmy Breslin's. It refers, as James Dubro points out in his *Mob Rule: Inside the Canadian Mafia*, to the practice of gathering information with no discernible purpose other than the information itself. According to Breslin: 'This is practiced by the FBI, and many police intelligence units and newspapers and magazines. 'Italian geography' is the keeping of information on gangsters: the price they pay for clothes, the restaurants in which they eat, the news of all relatives out to the fifth cousins, their home address and their visible daily movements. All this information is neatly filed and continually added to. This data is never used for anything; still the process goes on until the death of the individual concerned. But Italian geography keeps many people busy and collecting salaries, and is considered a commendable occupation.' See, Jimmy Breslin (1968) *The Gang That Couldn't Shoot Straight.* New York: Viking Press, p. 171. Another devastating critique of the pre-occupation with the Mafia may be found in Frederick Martens, (1985), 'Media Magic, Mafia Mania.' *Federal Probation*, June, pp. 60-68.

[3] 'Mafia' is not a secret society in the ordinary sense of the phrase at all. Unlike the Masons, the Knights of Columbus or the Knights of Pythias, it has no president, no general initiation (there is some question as to initiations), nor dues, elections or by-

laws, except unwritten ones. Its cohesiveness is guaranteed by family relationships which go back over generations and an uncodified ideology captured in the phrase 'Honore e Famiglia.' J. Albini, (1971). *The American Mafia*; F.A.J. Ianni 'The Mafia and the Web of Kinship.' *The Public Interest*, No. 22 (Winter, 1971).

4 Reuter may be correct in his estimation that the Mafia may be no more than a 'paper tiger' with a fierce reputation when it comes to defending some of its criminal prerogatives. Not everyone is easily intimidated by its daunting name and legend. When New York Crime families threatened some of Frank Matthews's drug dealers he retorted angrily that 'touch one of my people and I'll load my men into cars and we'll drive down to Mulberry Street ..and shoot every wop we see.' (Messick, 1979: 27, quoted in Abadinsky, 1985). Similarly, in Chicago, the leader of the El Rukns, a black gang, was summoned before the leadership of 'The Outfit' (the Cosa Nostra family in Chicago) and was warned to confine his drug operations to certain areas or else. Fort, the head of the Black syndicate was not intimidated and decisively countered by burning down the restaurant where the meeting took place the very next day. 'The Outfit' was then told to get out of the South Side of Chicago or be carried out (Abadinsky, 1985: Ch. 10).

5 *Detroit News.* 13 October 1988, B 3

6 Witkin, op. cit.

7 Witkin, op. cit., p. 51.

8 Harold D. Lasswell and Jeremiah McKenna, 1972. *The Impact of Organized Crime on an Inner City Community.* Their project was designed to gauge the effects of how organized crime interacts with the inner city community of Bedford-Stuyvesant in New York City. The research also analyzed the economic impact that drugs and the numbers racket had upon that Brooklyn Community. The authors report that drugs and the numbers racket impacted the community negatively.

9 Merton, *Social Structure*, 132.

Glossary

La Cosa Nostra - literally "this thing of ours," the term was aired publicly in 1963 by Joseph Valachi, a Mafia soldier in the Genovese Crime Family. Valachi revealed how Mafia insiders referred to the cluster of crime families making up the American Mafia.

Crips and Bloods - California based African-American street gangs engaged in a range of criminal activities including crack cocaine distribution.

Jamaican Posses - organized crime gangs of black criminals from the Caribbean island of Jamaica. They are known for their violence and sophisticated drug trafficking.

Ethnic Succession - a process where one ethnic group replaces another prominent in organized crime activities. The change in the ethnic composition of minorities in organized crime is usually attributed to wholesale group and cultural assimilation, and socio-economic mobility.

Syndicate - a term describing the organization of criminal enterprises; sometimes used synonymously with Mafia.

Policy - a form of numbers gambling still prevalent in the African-American communities.

The Outfit - the name of the Italian-dominated mob based in Chicago, Illinois.

Minority Middlemen - members of minority groups with organized crime ties who are also active in legitimate politics and business.

Part III
Selected Topics

13 The Global Sex Trade: Human Beings as the Ultimate Commodity

Sarah L. Shannon

Abstract

Commercial sexual exploitation of women and children has become a worldwide phenomenon. To an increasing extent, transnational criminal organizations engage in this highly lucrative business. The facts surrounding the global sex trade are repulsive. If effective counter measures are to be created, a detailed understanding of these very facts is required. Therefore, some of the distinctive features, geographical aspects and emerging trends of this flesh market are discussed in this study. A brief consideration of global responses to the problem concludes the examination.

Key Words*:* Trafficking, prostitution, sexual exploitation, pedophile, forced labor.

Introduction

Traditionally, organized crime has been seen as involvement in the supply of illicit goods and services. Usually, these are assumed to be products such as liquor during prohibition, and heroin, cocaine and other drugs in the current era. Yet organized crime has also interested itself in commercial sexual exploitation and control of such activity continues to be a major source of profits for these gangs. In recent years, the scale of this industry has increased tremendously. Trafficking in women and children is now a global problem of immense proportions. Yet internationally organized prostitution is not a problem that can be singularly understood. Journalist Chris Lyttleton puts it well:

> *The general perspectives that poverty and/or gender roles are uniform social texts that foster prostitution do not explain regional and individual variation nor do they account for the multiplicity of engagements, premises and strategies that fall under this rubric.*[1]

Therefore, this analysis seeks to illuminate some of these complexities first by acknowledging the global sex trade as the insidious widespread occurrence it has become and also by highlighting its regional manifestations, distinctive features and some of its current trends.

Definition

The international sex industry involves the trafficking and exploitation of persons for the purpose of forced prostitution or other forms of sexual enslavement. Commercial sexual exploitation is defined as the use of a person for sexual purposes in exchange for money or other compensation between customer, intermediary, pimp or organization which profits from the exploited for these purposes. The World Congress against the Sexual Exploitation of

Children specified three main forms of the sexual use of persons:[2]

- *Prostitution* - To engage or offer the services of a person to perform sex acts for money or other recompense.
- *Trafficking and sale of persons for sexual purposes* - To transfer persons from one party to another for commercial sexual purposes in exchange for money or other recompense (such transporting can be interstate or transnational).
- *Pornography* - To create, distribute, use or otherwise participate in material which portrays persons in a sexual context. For example, the depiction may include the victim's involvement in explicit sexual actions or the exhibition of the victim's genitals in order to provide sexual gratification for the user.

These three categories are necessarily linked. The trafficking of humans usually implies voluntary or forced involvement in prostitution while the trade in children often involves the production of pornographic materials. These ingredients are essential elements of an appalling and booming industry that is easily accessible to those willing to sell and use other people's bodies. The international sex trade is a business that buys, sells and in other ways treats its victims as sexual and economic commodities rather than human beings.

Scale of the Activity

The world's sex market is a multibillion-dollar industry, which pervades both developing and developed countries.[3] Although the vast majority of its victims are women and girls, the market does include a growing number of boys. The situation is confusing because of a lack of reliable statistics. Nevertheless, it is estimated that each year more than one million children are forced into prostitution, trafficked for sexual purposes or used in child pornography.[4] The numbers for women must be at least as high. While exact global figures are impossible to determine, certain assessments do exist for specific geographical regions. Although these are approximations rather than specific numbers, they provide a broad indication of the scale of the problem.

Children

The term child usually refers to one under the age of eighteen.[5] Victims of the child sex industry are primarily 13 to 15 years old. However, such activity most definitely involves younger victims; reports of boys and girls aged 6 and 7 are increasingly common.[6] Table 13.1 documents estimates of child sexual exploitation from around the world.

Table 13.1: International estimates of child sexual exploitation

- 100,000-300,000 child prostitutes working in the United States[7]
- 300,000 children involved in the sex industry in Thailand[8]
- 30,000 children involved in the sex industry in Sri Lanka[9]
- over 650,000 children working in the sex industry in the

Philippines[10]
- 400,000 children active in the sex industry in India[11]
- 200,000 child prostitutes working in Brazil[12]
- as many as 500,000 child prostitutes thought to be working in Peru[13]
- 2,000 child prostitutes working in San Jose, Costa Rica are exploited annually by foriegners.[14]
- A 500% increase in prostitution among children aged 8-13 between 1986-1993 in Bogota Colombia.[15] (Central and South America face significant problems due to the prevalence of street children in these areas; many such youngsters turn to prostitution for survival.)[16]
- The global profit from child trafficking and sexual exploitation is estimated at $5 billion annually, with the United States spending nearly $1 billion of that.[17]
- According to the Bundeskriminalmt (BKA) in Germany, more than 1,000 boys are trafficked into Western Europe annually by organized criminal groups.[18]

Women
Table 13.2 documents estimations of female sexual exploitation from different regions of the globe.

Table 13.2: International female sexual exploitation
- Over 100,000 women are involved in the Japanese sex industry. Most are Filipino and Thai.[19] It is estimated that 40,000-50,000 Thai women reside illegally in Japan where they work as prostitutes.[20]
- More than 40,000 Burmese women and girls are sold into prostitution each year.[21] There are approximately 334,000 illegal Burmese immigrants living in Thailand who provide labor for the construction and sex industries.[22]
- 50,000 women from The Dominican Republic are working abroad in the sex industry.[23]
- 19,000-25,000 foreign prostitutes are presently working in Italy.[24]
- Of the 2,000 foreign prostitutes working in Belgium, 200-300 are victims of trafficking schemes.[25]
- In Russia, trafficking in women yields $7 billion annually.[26]
- In the past three years, Israel has deported almost 1,500 Russian and Ukrainian women who were victims of the sex industry in that country.[27]
- Israeli police calculate approximately 25,000 monetary transactions for sex on a daily basis.[28]
- Italian police report that women forced into prostitution in

Italy are murdered at least once a month.[29]

- The International Organization for Migration estimates that 500,000 women are trafficked into Western Europe each year.[30]

More detailed statistics are widely unavailable. Clearly, the need for reliable worldwide estimates is pressing. What we can be sure of however, is that the international sex industry is a global phenomenon of alarming proportion. The problem is even more ominous because it has become increasingly transnational.

Actors

Who runs this business? The circumstances and occurrences of sexual exploitation vary. Women and children may be victims of small-time entrepreneurs or large organized criminal networks. Perpetrators range from novices to amateurs to professionals. Generally speaking however, transnational criminal groups are heavily involved in the international sex slave business. Organized crime may engage in trafficking on its own or may involve itself in joint ventures with individuals who are not formally members of criminal organizations. Structured criminal groups can provide smuggling services or ensure a cover for such illegal entrepreneurs.[31] Furthermore, it is easier for established criminal organizations to operate across borders because of their links to one another and their skill and experience in circumventing national authorities. For example, the Japanese Yakuza controls the sex trade of Southeast Asia and has been tied to American contacts on the West Coast.[32] There are connections between trafficking groups in America and Thailand and child pornography rings in America and Western Europe.[33] European victims may be traded by Russian Mafia gangs operating out of Germany, where Polish, Czech, and Slovak girls have traveled to look for work.[34] In "Imprisoned Prostitutes," Paul Kaihla describes the activities of Asian gangs operating in Canada.[35] He identifies two Chinese groups, the Dai Huen Jai and the Big Circle boys, which help run the network of brothels in cities like Toronto, Vancouver and Calgary.

The sex industry is a highly lucrative business; the supply must be maintained. Consequently, Yakuza or Triad members typically recruit females in big cities such as Bangkok or Manila, they furnish them with fake passports. Kaihla cites an example in which "a gang associate based in Hong Kong had provided false passports to smuggle about twenty girls into Canada -- and then put them on display at the hotel for various brothel keepers."[36] The gang members also prey on poor families from rural areas, trying to persuade them to sell their daughters.

Organized crime syndicates often operate prostitution schemes in conjunction with other forms of criminal activity such as drug dealing or alien smuggling. For example, a Japanese Yakuza gang may conduct a gambling operation or sell *shabu* (crystal methamphetamine) from a massage parlor.[37] The Ravna Gora in the former Yugoslavia, known primarily for arms smuggling, also traffic in women and children (male and female).[38] Similarly, "in Russia, women have become a favorite commodity of the criminal class along with such illicit trade as smuggling enriched uranium and cocaine."[39] In one instance, an investigator for the Global Survival Network focusing on organized crime's involvement in wildlife smuggling realized that, "a group trading tiger bones and skins to Chinese and Japanese buyers had developed a sideline in supplying sex clubs abroad with Russian women."[40]

Even if many victims are trafficked with the help of organized crime, this is only part of the picture. In addition to criminal organizations, there are a number of other players whose involvement makes the industry possible. Additional participants include:

- intermediaries such as pimps, procurers, brothel owners, and translators.
- parents and family members who sell their youngsters into prostitution.
- Such sales are particularly common in cultures where a female child is either not valued at all or regarded as a burden to the family.
- authorities who release jailed victims back to pimps or criminal networks.[41] In many cases local police are simply insensitive to the plight of escaped victims and hence release the girls back to the pimps and brothel owners. This happens especially when the trafficked women are foreign, partly because authorities are often indifferent to a non-native's plight.[42] In some cases, authorities are so corrupt that the pimps use them to get the girls back, even once they have returned home. Police may go to a home and threaten the family with jail unless they repay the pimp for the girl's value.[43]
- customers such as Western businessmen who take 'sex tours' to Southeast Asia or other locations in which sex with children is known to be available.[44]
- governments that are nonchalant or negligent regarding their protection of victims.
- For example, the Japanese government refuses to provide medical care to prostitutes who are sick or injured.[45] Perhaps the most serious example of hostility towards prostitutes and treatment of them as criminals rather than victims occurs in Burma. According to the April 5, 1993 issue of the *Chicago Tribune*, twenty-five Burmese women were kidnapped and sold into forced prostitution in Thailand. Thai police eventually rescued these women who, upon being found HIV positive, were immediately deported back to Burma. Once back home, Burmese health officials injected the women with cyanide in order to help prevent the spread of the virus. Reportedly, the Burmese government customarily executes females who return from Thailand infected with AIDS.[46] A similar degree of governmental indifference to this type of

activity is exemplified by the Belgian Dutroux case discussed
below.

- pedophiles who seek an outlet for their perversion.

- Recent reports have targeted German, Swiss, Swedish,
  American and Scandinavian pedophiles who operate in India,
  Sri Lanka and Thailand.[47] However, Western Europe is newly
  aware of threats to its own children's security, in part due to
  the pedophile activity brought to light by the Belgian Dutroux
  scandal.[48]

The Dutroux case is a particularly gruesome example of the degree to
which pedophilic perversion can develop and of the failure of a government to
protect its most innocent citizens. In August 1995, Paul Marchal's 17-year-old
daughter An disappeared, along with her best friend, Eefje Lambricks. Police
told the distraught father not to worry, that An had probably met a nice boy and
was off somewhere enjoying his company. Ignoring evidence that suggested
otherwise, the police continued to display total indifference. When Marchal
took matters into his own hands, searching for his daughter along with the
parents of Melissa Russo and Julie Lejeune, who had also disappeared that
summer, authorities were perturbed. In January 1996, the chief of police in
Bruges, Luc van Tirgham, wrote Marchal a letter asking him to stop arousing
public attention and to quit bothering police. Yet because of Marchal's publicity
campaign and unrelenting efforts, Marc Dutroux, a convicted child molester and
rapist, was finally arrested on August 13, 1996. Two adolescent girls who had
disappeared earlier that year were found alive in captivity in his basement. The
remains of four other girls (including An and Eefje) were discovered buried in
the backyards of Dutroux's other home and that of his business associate,
Bernard Weinstein. All had been raped; two had starved to death. Additionally,
police found hard core child pornography videos in Dutroux's home. What
made the case so awful, however, were not just the simple facts of the girls'
sufferings. This horror was infinitely compounded by evidence which suggests
that authorities knew about Dutroux's activities and ignored the warnings of an
informer, even as the girls were being held hostage. Furthermore, there is some
evidence that Dutroux actually received protection from police, in part because
of his ties to important businessmen and government officials. Three days after
the arrest of Dutroux, a prominent businessman named Jean-Michel Nihoul was
also arrested in connection with the affair. Police confiscated 300 videos from
his home, some reportedly showing high society figures engaged in violent
sexual acts with children. Indeed, it was never any secret that Nihoul hosted
Gatsby-like parties, attended by distinguished doctors, lawyers and government
officials, during which sexual orgies and "carnality shows" were common.
Specific links between the Dutroux case and the Belgian government have yet to
be proven. However, one thing is certain: had the authorities acted promptly
and properly, the lives of the known Dutroux victims could have been spared.

DistinctiveFeatures

"Sex tourism" is a term that had to be invented to describe an industry which is inextricably linked to tourism itself.   Yet there is a particularly causal relationship between it and child sexual exploitation.   The UN's Rights of the Child document defines the term as: "Tourism organized to facilitate, directly or indirectly, a commercial sexual relationship."[49]   For certain developing areas of the world, the illicit can provide allure and bring in money when the country fails to entice visitors in other ways.   How many people are aware of the existence of beaches, areas and resorts created exclusively for the sex tourist? Thailand, Brazil, the Dominican Republic and Sri Lanka are all known destinations for such tourists, in part because laws are so lax in these countries.[50] Countries like Cambodia, China, Laos, Burma and Vietnam are also common destinations.[51]   Consumers include men from Europe, Japan, North America, Australia and the Middle East.[52]   Travel agencies sell tours to vacationers with the understanding that the renting of sexual partners is part of the package of services offered.[53]   For example, in 1992 a Swiss travel agency was forced to close because it arranged sex tours in developing countries.[54]   Australian police report:

> In recent months, a joint Child Exploitation Unit/Australian operation uncovered a number of prominent male offenders involved with an international boys' association who were traveling to both Thailand and the Philippines and having sexual relations with Asian boys, the same age as those normally committed to their care in the youth organization...Given the low cost of labor generally in Asia, a holiday for an average Australian tourist can be very cheap...Unfortunately, what has emerged in the tourist boom is the black market for children to become prostitutes and be at the whim and call of wealthy westerners.[55]

Representative Joseph Kennedy II stated in his Keynote Address to the Symposium on Forced Labor, The Prostitution of Children:

> Sex tours from Europe and the US supply a significant portion of the demand for child prostitutes throughout the world. Recently an Austrian airline even used a cartoon drawing of a child in a sexually explicit pose to sell sex tours...Many U.S. travel agencies set up sex tours for thousands of Americans every year. These package tours include airline, hotel, transportation and a choice of escorts for the duration of the tour. The tours take travelers to far-off destinations like Bangkok, where Thai police recently arrested eighteen underage girls servicing seventeen men per night. Seventeen of the eighteen girls tested HIV positive.[56]

Although Thailand is probably the most notorious of the countries in which child prostitution is rampant, there are many other examples of the same phenomenon.   For example, the beaches of Boca Chica and Sosua in the Dominican Republic[57] and the western state of Goa in India[58] are havens for pedophiles and tourists seeking the sexual company of children.   Dorianne Beyer reports in "Child Prostitution in Latin America"[59] that both Costa Rica and the Dominican Republic provide children for sex as part of sex tour packages. She says, "the interaction between foreign tourists and child prostitution is particularly pronounced."[60] Thus, it can be said that tourism is a distinctive feature of the global sex industry.

What is most distinctive and important about this form of transnational criminal activity however, is its cost in human misery. While financial crime and drug trafficking may undermine economic and even political systems, and something like arts and antiquities smuggling is unfortunate, the international sex trade is particularly repulsive. In the address mentioned above, Joseph Kennedy labeled it, "the most denigrating, dehumanizing of all crimes that can possibly be imagined."[61] Unlike other forms of international criminal activity, the global sex trade is not so much an assault on political or economic systems; rather, it is an attack on humanity because its basis is the use and abuse of human beings. In denying its victims the freedom and dignity normally associated with even the most primitive existence, the sex industry becomes fundamentally different from other global criminal activities. In this sphere alone are women and children seen exclusively as commodities of economic value.

Supply and Demand

The market for the global sex industry is demand driven. The supply can be either voluntary or involuntary but it is continuous because the demand never diminishes. There are always pedophiles in search of an outlet for their perversion, men who prefer unnatural expressions of their sexuality over normal, mutually consenting interactions, and criminals willing to overlook other people's humanity in order to make a lot of money. Beyond these observations, there are at least two other elements that provide for the continuation and proliferation of this industry: poverty and cultural attitudes.

Poverty

One of the root causes of sexual exploitation is poverty, which is often sadly compounded by family disintegration.[62] Certain socioeconomic conditions of an area or individual are more conducive to this type of activity than others. For instance, often a girl is sold into prostitution by a family struggling to support itself, either for the quick cash or because the offending family member feels that even prostitution is better than the almost certain starvation the child would face were she to remain at home.[63] Aaron Sachs, author of "Child Prostitution in the Developing World," explains, "many parents can hardly feed themselves and find it nearly impossible to refuse a cash payment in exchange for one of their daughters…"[64] He continues:

> No story is more wrenching than that of a prostitute who has been deceived or forced by violence into her trade. But it is perhaps even more tragic, and more significant for society, when parents who have no other criminal dealings knowingly offer their children to sex traffickers. Such decisions signal a raw desperation in the countryside.[65]

Alternatively, the victim is often lured into sexual bondage through the false promise of a job. Young people from rural areas are frequently offered jobs in big cities with the promise that they will be able to send money home to help their families. They then end up facing debt bondage, confinement, forced labor, rape, prostitution and related physical and mental abuses. Many are never heard from again.[66] An example of the employment scheme occurs in the U.S. The Japanese Yakuza is reportedly very active in job scams in California, which advertise singing and acting jobs in Japan to susceptible young American women.[67] Thus, whether due to familial sale or the hope of a job, women and children can find themselves in peril. It is no coincidence that the majority of the victims who are involved in the sex trade are also victims of poor economic situations.

Cultural Attitudes

Many societies in the world still regard women and children as second class citizens. Such remaining discriminatory attitudes cannot be overlooked as a reason for the continued sexual exploitation of women and children for commercial purposes. Certain persistent cultural beliefs define males as superior and women as inferior human beings. Furthermore, women often are seen not only as inferior, but are also viewed as entities whose purpose is to fulfill and please men, sexually and otherwise.[68]

In addition to patriarchal societies, which are inherently oppressive towards those deemed less valuable, traditional religious beliefs can contribute to sexual exploitation.[69] For example, in strict Roman Catholic countries, religious dogma may create an atmosphere of shame, secrecy and guilt. Females, who have been less than pure, even if involuntarily, are forever tainted. Indeed, Bolivia's laws against pre and extramarital sex apply even to the divorced and widowed. Once a woman is seen as "dirty" or "bad," it follows that her use and abuse by men is condoned by the rest of society. The concept of rape no longer exists for such females; there are no laws to protect them.[70]

Another example of distorted religious beliefs contributing to sexual exploitation is that of the Hindu Devadasi tradition in India. Here ritual dictates the choosing of a young girl to be deified and sent to a temple to become a "sex goddess."[71] Aaron Sachs comments on this custom explaining, "believers... have been dedicating their daughters to a religiously sanctioned life of prostitution for well over a millenium."[72] Additionally, many Indian men believe that having sex with pre-adolescent virgins will cure sexually transmitted diseases.[73] Sadly, this seems to be a rather common belief. Vitit Muntarbhorn, Rapporteur-General for the World Congress against the Sexual Exploitation of Children notes:

> The demand factor is also linked with...the old fixation that by
> having sex with a virgin girl, one can rejuvenate oneself, and
> the newer fixation that by having sex with the young, one can
> protect oneself from HIV/AIDS.[74]

This accounts for the increased occurrences of girls as young as six being raped, prostituted, and infected with sexually transmitted diseases.

Techniques - How does this happen?

There are three main methods of procuring victims for supply in the sex trade: sale by family, the promise of work and kidnapping.[75]

- *Sale by Family* [76]

As previously mentioned, victims are sometimes sold into prostitution by their families. This happens most often with young girls. Usually it is a father or uncle who sends a youngster to work in this manner in order to help support the family. Dr. Duong Quynh Hoa, director of a children's hospital in Ho Chi Min City Vietnam, comments on this:

> '*It's always the father...never the mother...One father came with his twelve year old daughter...she was bleeding from her wounds and as torn as if she had just given birth. He told [me], 'We've earned $300, so it's enough. She can stop...*'[77]
> When another man brought his eleven year old girl in for treatment, Dr. Hoa asked him why he would sell his daughter for sex. He responded, '*We are very poor, and this is a good age to do it...she is still too young to get pregnant.*'[78]

Sometimes the victim is simply sold to a pimp or brothel owner in a single transaction and is never heard from again. However, it may also be that the victim is sent to work the streets during the day and is expected to return home each night with a certain amount of money to avoid a beating.[79] Normally, those victims who are exploited by organized crime syndicates are owned by the people who control their lives; they rarely regain contact with their families.

- *Promise of Work* [80]

As mentioned above, women sometimes get caught in the sex trade because of deceptive employment opportunities. They may be promised jobs as waitresses, sales clerks, dancers, singers, or housemaids. In some cases they are given fake contracts to sign and in many instances their transportation is arranged and initially paid for, although they must repay that debt through work. Upon arrival in the new city or country they may be met by an unfamiliar person who informs them that their contract was bought and that they are now owned by someone else and are expected to perform a different service. Often there is no explanation at all; girls are simply beaten into submission and locked inside a brothel. One 1993 report notes a case in which, '...a number of captives burned to death when a fire broke out in their brothel and they could not escape because they were chained to their beds.'[81] Women in similar conditions may not be given any food and little water for weeks until their resistance is broken. Passports, money and clothes are all taken away.[82] In such situations it is extraordinarily difficult to escape.

In other cases however, immigrant women are sometimes aware of the situation in which they will find themselves upon arrival in a foreign country.[83] Females may actually choose this option, sending the money they make from selling their bodies back home to parents or children. In certain societies, lawful employment yields such a pathetic salary that prostitution seems a welcome choice.[84] Yet such decisions on the part of women and girls who feel they have no other viable alternatives should not condone the practice of trafficking in desperate women. Often these women return to their original countries severely depressed or with other serious mental disturbances, if they are even able to return home at all.[85] Their perceived solutions to real economic troubles are not without significant ramifications.

- *Kidnapping* [86]
    Perhaps the easiest way to transfer women from one country to another is simply to kidnap them. Kidnapping is the most indiscriminate form of procuring women in the sense that this tactic is not a function of poverty. Victims come from every class and economic status and organized crime is heavily involved.[87] For example, gangs kidnap women from countries such as Burma, Laos, Vietnam and China and take them to Thailand where they are forced into prostitution.[88] Such activities are not unique to Asia. Teenagers are frequently taken from Paris and other large European cities to be sold to Arab and African customers.[89] The daughter of a Dutch count, for example, was kidnapped in Brussels and transported to Zaire for forced prostitution.[90] Moreover, kidnapped women usually suffer the worst abuses because there are no ties back to the family or homeland.[91] No one knows where they are or what they are doing. They are frequently strangers in very strange lands and their lives have little, if any value.

What about escape?
    One point remains when considering the question, "how does this happen," and that is the question of escape. What keeps the victims in these awful situations? Why do they not flee? The answer is depressingly simple: they cannot. Victims are often beaten well and regularly, locked in a room, and even chained to a bed or post.[92] In "Saving the Children," Ellen Lukas reports that children in brothels in Bombay are sometimes held in cages.[93] Due to physical abuse, constant exposure to numerous sexually transmitted diseases, and inadequate food and clothing, they are recurrently sick; pimps and brothels do not provide much medical care. Furthermore, even if they could escape the premises, how would they run? There is no money for food and clothing much less a bus or train ticket. When victims are trafficked to other countries, they face unfamiliar surroundings and cannot speak the language. They confront unsympathetic law enforcement authorities who return them to their previous bondage while governments look the other way.[94] What are the prospects for a child who must contend with such obstacles? The situation quickly becomes hopeless.

Geographical Activities
    The sex industry is a worldwide phenomenon. Although the problem is sometimes viewed as primarily Asian, that region no longer has a monopoly on the sex trade. It may be true that third world states are more afflicted but the problem exists even in the most industrialized nations. Though commercial

sexual exploitation is global however, there are national and regional variations. For example, in countries like Thailand and the Philippines, which are known for their activity in the sex trade, there are obviously a higher number of massage parlors, go-go clubs, sleazy hotels and brothels.[95] India is known to be the new destination for pedophiles, due in part to its lax laws and the supposed lower incidence of AIDS,[96] while Sri Lanka is heavily involved in child sexual exploitation, especially with boys.[97] Perhaps the easiest way to understand the global dimensions of the sex trade is to identify trafficking routes. This next section is divided under separate headings for women and children although identification of trafficking in one group does not negate similar involvement with the other.

Table 13.3: Trafficking routes - women

ASIA FROM:	TO:
Burma	Japan, Thailand [98]
Philippines	Japan (in largest part)[99], China, the Middle East [100]
Thailand	The rest of Southeast Asia, especially Japan[101]
China, Laos, Vietnam	Thailand and Burma[102]
CENTRAL AND SOUTH AMERICA FROM:	TO:
Dominican Republic	Haiti, Panama, Puerto Rico, Venezuela, Austria, Germany, Italy, Spain, Switzerland, the Netherlands, Greece[103]
Brazil, Peru, Colombia, Argentina	Western Europe (similar to states identified from Dominican Republic)
CENTRAL AND EAST EUROPEAN COUNTRIES FROM:	TO:
Czech Republic, Hungary,* Switzerland, Slovakia	Austria (in largest part), Belgium the Netherlands, Germany[104]
Hungary and the Czech Republic are often preferred shipment routes into Western Europe. Both are also used as the main trafficking routes for children out of Romania, a country that has a large number of orphaned infants who are easy prey for organized criminal networks and pedophiles.[105]	
Serbia, Ukraine, Russia, Poland, Romania	Western Europe[106]
Former Soviet Union	Macao, Dubai, Germany, Israel, United States,[107] Japan, Thailand,[108] Australia, Italy, China, Turkey[109]
Albania and Nigeria	Italy[110]

Table 13.4: Trafficking routes – children

ASIA	
FROM:	TO:
Nepal, Bangladesh	India[111]
Bhutan, Bangladesh, Nepal, India, Sri Lanka	Pakistan[112]
Bangladesh, India	United Arab Emirates, Oman, Cyprus, Middle East[113]
Thailand, Philippines, South Korea, Sri Lanka	Western Europe[114]
Cambodia	Thailand, Malaysia[115]
NOTE: One-fourth of those persons exploiting children for sex in Asia is American military or businessmen. [116]	
AFRICA	
FROM:	TO:
Sudan	Libya[117]
TO AND FROM:	
India and Sri Lanka	
Cambodia, China, Laos, Burma, Thailand and Vietnam[118]	
United States and Western Europe[119]	

OTHER:

- Both Latin America and Eastern Europe supply Western Europe with children for the sex trade. Germany, Portugal and the Netherlands lead the European Union in the filming of pornographic videos of children.[120]

- Romania provides most of the boys working in the gay section of Amsterdam (the Paardenstraat) although Slovakia, Poland and the Czech Republic also supply young males to Holland for work in the sex trade.[121]

Table 13.5: Countries facing significant child prostitution problems domestically

AFRICA
Senegal, Zimbabwe, Sudan, Kenya, Libya, Algeria, Ghana, Mauritania,* Namibia, Cote d'Ivoire, Burkina Faso[122]   *increase in foreign pedophile activity and number of boy victims.[123]
EUROPE
France, Belgium, Russia,[124] Czech Republic,[125] Germany[126]
ASIA
See above "To and From" section
CENTRAL AND SOUTH AMERICA
Argentina, Bolivia, Brazil, Chile, Colombia, Ecuador, Mexico, Peru,* Costa Rica.[127]   *many registered "adult" prostitutes are believed to be minors who obtained false Ids.[128]
NORTH AMERICA
The United States[129]   One report indicates that the criminal groups that control them sometimes tattoo victims of child prostitution in the U.S. [130]

History and Trends

Sadly, neither the sale of people nor the sale of flesh is a new phenomenon. Such activity has been around since civilizations began. As Gaines Post says in Ancient Roman Ideas of Law: "from St. Augustine on, Christian theologians went so far as to admit that some laws of the state were good, even when they seemed contrary to the moral commands of God."[131] Prostitution fell under this category. Post cites Nicholas of Lire (early 1300's) who said that the state must legalize prostitution to ensure the male libido would not "cause anarchy and destroy the public welfare."[132] Obviously, it would be impossible to trace a history of where and when the human body was first seen as a commodity, or women were first deemed second class citizens, or children were first exploited by a misguided society for forced labor. Human beings have always violated others. Nevertheless, the sex industry is in a process of constant change and adaptation. Hence, the most recent trends in the sex trade are discussed next.

TRENDS
Women

One of the most notable new happenings in The trafficking of women is that it is no longer primarily confined to females from developing countries. Although Brazil, Thailand and the Philippines continue to supply the most significant numbers of migrant women who are forced into prostitution, the transportation of women from Eastern to Western Europe has increased rapidly.[133] Political upheaval, economic disruption and social dislocation give impetus to the rise of organized criminal activity. Thus, it is not difficult to see how recent events in Eastern Europe and the former Soviet Union could spur the development of new supply centers and routes for trafficking in women. For the European markets, it is easier and cheaper to transfer women from countries in Central and Eastern Europe than to get women from Third World nations; the former are closer and the opening of borders often abolishes old visa restrictions.[134] For example, neither Denmark nor Italy requires visas.[135] We increasingly see women from the more eastern European countries being trafficked to Western Europe. Beyond this generalization, it is possible to list a few specific trends:

- Between 200,000-500,000 women work in the illicit sex trade of the European Union.[136]
- 75 percent of German prostitutes are foreign; 80 percent of prostitutes working in Milan are foreign. Of approximately 20,000 foreign prostitutes working in Italy, about 2,000 are victims of trafficking schemes.[137]
- There has been significant growth in activity of trafficking from Nigeria and Albania to Western Europe, especially Italy, where nearly three-quarters of foreign prostitutes work in street prostitution. (Turin reportedly has a high number of Nigerian prostitutes.)[138]
- There is significant growth in trafficking of women from the

Dominican Republic to Western Europe, especially upper Austria.[139]

Hungary, Slovakia and the Czech Republic have become the most important Eastern European sending countries for Austria. A new method is for pimps to drive Czech girls across the border to Vienna in the morning and then transport them back at night after a full day's work.[140] The following chart supports these listed trends: [141]

Table 13.6: Prostitution in Vienna

VIENNA, AUSTRIA			
	1990	**1994**	**1995**
Registered Prostitutes	800		670
Unregistered Prostitutes	2,800		4,300
# trafficking cases	50	316	
# convictions	19	49	

Source: Phil Williams, Major Trends in Transnational Organized Crime

Children

- Traffickers and pimps who addict children as young as 8 years old to inhalants[142] (glue, paint, benzene gum) in order to maintain complete control over their lives. This trend was first seen in Chile but is common in many Latin American countries.
- The "Sanky Panky" boys of the beach sex resorts in the Dominican Republic[143] These 13 to 18 year olds will become a visitor's annual partner, sometimes establishing a relationship that lasts for years. Often the foreign sex tourist supports the boy throughout the year, even though he only sees the youngster once or twice annually. Occasionally both parties form bonds that go beyond the shared sexual activities.
- The prevalence of increasingly younger victims.[144]
- The spread of AIDS (as well as other sexually transmitted disease) has contributed to this trend because of the belief that the likelihood of infection is less if with a younger partner.[145]
- Utilizing the accessibility of cyberspace as a vehicle for child pornography and victimization.[146] In the Western world especially, there is a large and growing black market for child pornography in videos and magazines. America is the world's leading producer of pornography, creating as many as 150 new films a week.[147] The technology provided by computers and the anonymity of the Internet allow for easy creation and distribution of such materials. For example, the French company Minitel, an on-line provider accessed via telephone,

is suspected of providing children for sexual services.[148] In the US, a child pornography ring using America Online was recently discovered.[149] Finally, the Internet's World Sex Guide advertises that in Cambodia, "a six year old is available for $3."[150]

Videos and Snuff Films

Under this section of trends in child pornography it would be remiss not to mention the increasing existence of "snuff" films involving children (a pornographic video in which the victim is actually killed on screen.). Often the children are drugged, both to minimize the physical pain of what is being done to them and to make their small bodies more pliant and accessible.[151] The youngsters, who are most often kidnapped, may be bound, gagged, beaten, burned and hooded.[152] Pedophiles seem to prefer boys to girls, and victims as young as possible.[153]

Brian Freemantle's *The Octopus* describes the ease with which pornographic and snuff videos can be made.[154] In Western Europe at least, original videos from the United States, the Netherlands or Germany are copied by wiring VCRs together. Such copying yields millions of tax free dollars a year. Ironically, British tax law exacts far harsher penalties for this activity than do British anti-obscenity regulations. The following are some examples of the degree to which human perversion can go.

Freemantle reports that in 1994 a Swiss man was charged with making and starring in a film in which he tried to kill a 14-month old girl. The same man was also charged with attempting to bring children from Romania into Switzerland for the creation of a snuff film. Freemantle's book also tells the story of a 19-year-old British boy who confessed to witnessing the filming of twelve men successively raping and then killing an adolescent boy. After his confession, the young informer was attacked and subsequently disappeared. This account was part of an investigation by Scotland Yard's Obscene Publications Squad, codenamed Operation Orchid. The inquiry began after the murder of a 14-year-old boy named Jason Swift, which was traced to a pedophile ring known as the Lambs to the Slaughter group. Swift was paid about $35 to participate in a homosexual orgy in London during which he was drugged with Valium and eventually strangled. Although the video was never found, Operation Orchid detectives were told that a copy of the violent affair circulated in Amsterdam.

One final note: these videos seem to exhibit increasing amounts of brutality and extreme perversion.[155] It may be safe to assume that this trend towards severe depravity is more universal than not. For instance, during the Dutroux investigation, police found a letter in Weinstein's house that is thought to be a request from a satanic cult for girls to use as human sacrifices.[156]

Impediments to the Global Sex Trade

Global responses to the problem are grossly inadequate. Prostitution remains both legal and generally accepted in most of Europe. Pimps, brothel owners and traffickers are more often tolerated than prosecuted.[157] Few countries have adopted extra-territorial criminal laws, which would allow them to prosecute their nationals for crimes committed abroad. Germany, Australia and New Zealand are three nations that have passed such laws, though only regarding child sexual exploitation.[158] While a number of international conferences and conventions have sought to deal with the worldwide sex trade, rarely are programs actually planned and implemented. The International Program on the Elimination of Child Labor (IPEC), established 1992, is one of the exceptions.[159] IPEC programs are effected in participating countries with the help of the ILO. Presently, IPEC supports anti-child prostitution programs in Thailand and the Philippines. Clearly this is an insufficient effort. Conferences and conventions are not enough; they have accomplished little thus far. It is important that government officials, authorities, and experts from around the globe congregate to share information and plan strategies but such meetings should be followed by strong and effective action. A few specific examples of attempts to combat this global problem are detailed in Table 13.7.

Interestingly, it seems that the most direct and effective countermeasures are taken by non-governmental organizations that are formed specifically to combat child sexual exploitation. For example, the group ECPAT, mentioned above, was originally, "an *ad-hoc* coalition of church people and social workers,"[160] who realized the enormity of the problem in countries such as Thailand, Philippines, Sri Lanka, Taiwan, India and Korea. They turned to UNICEF for help but were told that child prostitution was not within the mandate of the UN.[161] Under the leadership of a pastor from New Zealand named Ron O'Grady, the group determined to persevere alone. In the end they succeeded, for the World Congress against the Sexual Exploitation of Children, which is probably the most comprehensive undertaking to date, came about due to ECPAT's efforts.

A second example of a non-governmental organization formed solely to address the needs of exploited children is the Development and Education Program for Daughters and Communities (DEP), established 1989.[162] This program operates in Chiang Mai, Thailand, the northernmost province bordering on Myanmar. The DEP focuses on preventing at-risk girls from becoming involved in the sex industry.

These two NGOs exemplify the type of efforts that can make a difference in the fight against child sexual exploitation, as well as forced prostitution in general. Yet their work alone cannot begin to adequately address the problem. In "International Perspectives and Child Prostitution in Asia," Vitit Muntarbhorn spoke about the then upcoming World Congress against the Sexual Exploitation of Children: "it is expected that the Congress will adopt a strategic Plan of Action to counter child prostitution with realizable goals to be achieved in a fixed timeframe."[163] Such phrasing is far too lenient. When exactly will governments and international organizations like the UN ensure that steps are taken to diminish the enormity of the flesh trade? Even Ron O'Grady, former director of ECPAT, acknowledges that there is nothing to guarantee that the decisions and goals of the World Congress will be implemented.[164] Additionally,

Table 13.7: Efforts at combating the local sex trade

WHEN	WHAT	PURPOSE
1930	Forced Labor Convention[165]	Aims at eliminating compulsory labor "of all forms"
1949	Convention on the Suppression and Traffic in Persons and of Exploitation of Prostitution of Others[166]	Aims specifically at the perpetrators of prostitution
1979	UN Convention on the Elimination of All Forms of Discrimination Against Women[167]	Encourages states to enact legislation to suppress the trafficking and "exploitative prostitution" of women
1985	World Tourism Organization adopts the Tourism Bill of Rights and Tourist Code[168]	Advises both travel agencies and tourists to avoid being involved in the sex business
1987	African Charter on the Rights of the Child[169]	Advocates against child sexual exploitation
1989	UN Convention on the Rights of the Child[170] (Article 34)	Encourages states to take "all appropriate measures to prevent the exploitative use of children in unlawful sexual practices."
1990	Agreement between Thailand, the Philippines, South Korea, Sri Lanka, Taiwan, the United Kingdom, Germany, France, Switzerland, the United States[171]	Agree to cooperate on action against pedophiles
1991	Establishment of ECPAT[172] (End Child Prostitution in Asian Tourism)	Had been able to mobilize action at the international level
1992	Adoption of the Program of Action for the Prevention of the Sale of Children, Child Prostitution and Child Pornography by the UN Commission on Human Rights[173]	A multifaceted approach which advocates improved law enforcement and cooperation between agencies
1994	Criminal Justice and Public Order Act[174] (Great Britain)	Stipulates that DNA samples are to be taken from all convicted sex offenders and stored at a national database
1994	Child Sex Abuse Prevention Act[175]	Specifically addresses: "Transportation and Travel with Intent to Engage in a Sexual Act with a Juvenile."

it is clear from the above information that efforts to fight the global sex trade have been directed almost exclusively against child sexual exploitation. Important as this is, there is no excuse for ignoring the sufferings of females who are no longer considered minors. Their plight is no less serious.

In truth, there are no significant impediments to this type of criminal activity. Certain countries may try to address the problem as it exists within national borders but the sex trade is not a domestic affliction; it is a global disease. Thus, an individual state's efforts to combat whatever part of it happens only on its own soil can never be effective. Transnational organized trafficking could be prevented if the international community were to take collective measures. One possibility would be the creation of an international law enforcement agency set up to combat such global crime. At the very least it is necessary to exact harsher penalties under an international agreement designed specifically for this purpose. However, belief in such action presumes that the world realizes the severity, danger and tragedy of the global sex trade. Unfortunately, such a presumption remains a naively hopeful notion.

Sarah L. Shannon - A graduate of Penn State University, in 1996, with a BA in French Language and Culture -as Valedictorian of my French class- I am presently completing a masters in Public and International Affairs at the University of Pittsburgh. My interest and specialization area is International Security Studies. I work for Dr. Williams at the Ridgway Center for International Security Studies at the university, which is great because I am so intrigued by the research being done here. He introduced me to an area I knew nothing about and it is now my focus too.

I am a Court Appointed Special Advocate in the Juvenile Court system, where I investigate and testify on cases of abused and neglected children for the judge. I help at an after school program for inner-city Afro-American children, which is run in conjunction with a soup kitchen in one of the poorest districts of the city. I LOVE my kids there and am unabashedly emotionally attached. Nights and weekends I waitress so that I can pay for school, but it's not so much like work because I have the best time with all my friends at the restaurant. And none of this would mean anything to me without my family, who are the greatest people I have ever known. They are what keep me laughing and this is good, because it's my favorite hobby.

Notes and References

[1] Chris Lyttleton, "The good people of Isan: commercial sex in northeast Thailand," *The Australian Journal of Anthropology*. Fall 1994, v5, n3, p 257.

[2] Background Document for the World Congress against Sexual Exploitation of Children. UNICEF and ECPAT, NGO group for the Convention on the Rights of the Child, p 2-3. (http://www.acapa.org.za/back.html).

[3] Forced Labor: The Prostitution of Children. U.S. Department of Labor, Bureau of International Labor Affairs, 1996. Contact the International Child Labor Study Office, Room S-1308, 200 Constitution Avenue, NW, Washington, DC 20210 for copies of this report. Telephone (202) 208-4843.

[4] Background Document for the World Congress Against Sexual Exploitation of Children, op. cit., p 1 and UN Reports that Children in Sex Work at High Risk of HIV Infection. Stockholm, Sweden, August 28, 1996. (http://www.casa-alianza.org/stockh5.html).

[5] Forced Labor, op. cit., p 9.

[6] ibid, references and examples throughout entire document.

[7] ibid, p 2.

[8] ibid.

[9] Carol Aloysius. "Is our Paradise Islands becoming a haven for pedophiles?" August 25, 1996, p 1 (http://www.lanka.net/lakehouse/anclweb/observr/weekl/features/25fea06.html)

[10] Phil Williams "Major Trends in Transnational Organized Crime." Paper prepared for UN Crime Prevention and Criminal Justice Division, 1997, p 7.

[11] Rahul Bedi. India: Bid to Protect Children as Sex Tourism Spreads. March 19, 1996, p 1. (http://www.alternatives.com/crime/INDCHILD.HTML).

[12] Forced Labor, op. cit., p 32.

[13] ibid.

[14] ibid.

[15] ibid.

[16] ibid p 26, 38.

[17] Brian Freemantle. *Europe in the Grip of Organised Crime* Orion, London, 1995, p 125.

[18] ibid, p 140

[19] Matsui Yayori. "Eliminating Trafficking in Asian Women," p 1 (http://www.alternatives.com/crime/ASIAWOM.HTML)

[20] Phil Williams, op. cit., p 5.

[21] Youngik Yoon. 'International Sexual Slavery,' p 2. (http://law.touro.edu/AboutTLC/journals/internationallawrev/vol16/part7.html).

[22] Phil Williams, op. cit., p 3.

[23] 'Trafficking in Women from the Dominican Republic for Sexual Exploitation,' June, 1996, International Organization of Migration, Migration Information Programme (http://www.iom.ch)

[24] 'Trafficking in Women to Italy for Sexual Exploitation,' June 1996. International Organization of Migration, Migration Information Programme (http://www.iom.ch)

[25] Phil Williams, op. cit., p 6

[26] Victoria Pope. 'Trafficking in Women. Procuring Russians for sex abroad - even in America.' *US News and World Report*, April 7, 1997, p 42.

[27] Michael Specter. 'Traffickers' New Cargo: Naive Slavic Women.' *New York Times*, January 11, 1998, p 1.

[28] ibid, p 6

[29] ibid

[30] ibid

[31] Vincenzo Ruggiero. *Organized and Corporate Crime in Europe*. Dartmouth Publishing Company, Aldershot, 1996, p 140.

[32] Youngik Yoon, op. cit., p 4

[33] Forced Labor, op. cit., p 26

[34] Brian Freemantle, op. cit., p 137

[35] Paul Kaihla. 'Imprisoned prostitutes: the gangs run lucrative brothels.' *Maclean's* March 25, 1991, v104, n12, p 24.

[36] ibid

[37] Christopher Seymour. *Yakuza Diary: doing time in the Japanese Underworld*. Atlantic Monthly Press, New York, 1996.

[38] Brian Freemantle, op. cit., p 137

[39] Victoria Pope, op. cit., p 42

[40] ibid

[41] Youngik Yoon, op. cit., p 10 and Forced Labor, op. cit., p 24

[42] Youngik Yoon, op. cit., p 5

[43] ibid, p 3

[44] Forced Labor, many references throughout document, op. cit.

[45] 'Plight of Burmese Detailed.' Burma News Network, November 12, 1996, p 1 (http://www-uvi.eunet.fr/asia/euro-burma/fbc/nov1/a'18nov96-4.html)

[46] Youngik Yoon, op. cit., p 2; Forced Labor, op. cit., p 22 makes similar assertions about the Burmese government's mistreatment of prostitutes

[47] Forced Labor, op. cit., p 22, 25, 26, and Rahul Bedi, op. cit., p 1

[48] Timothy W. Ryback. 'Four Girls Abducted, Raped, Murdered. A Country on Trial.' *New York Times Magazine*, February 23, 1997, p 42-48.

[49] United Nations Commission on Human Rights, Rights of the Child. Report of the working group on its second session, p 19 (http://www.unhcr.ch/refworld/un/chr/chr96/thematic/1996-101.html).

[50] Dick Ward. 'Child Victimization is a Global Problem.' *Criminal Justice International*, November-December, 1996, p 4.

[51] Forced Labor, op. cit., p 22

[52] ibid.

[53] Forced Labor, op. cit., p 25, 31, 39 - sex tourism is an issue discussed in many parts of this document.

[54] ibid, p 25.

[55] ibid, p 27.

[56] ibid, p 4.

[57] ibid, p 36.

[58] Carol Aloysius, op. cit., p 1 and Rahul Bedi, op. cit., p 1.

[59] Forced Labor, op. cit., p 32-40.

[60] ibid, p 39.

[61] Forced Labor, op. cit., Keynote Address, p 1.

[62] ibid, p 3, 11, 13, and UN Commission on Human Rights, Rights of the Child report, op. cit., p 5-6.

[63] Youngik Yoon, op. cit., p 3.

[64] Aaron Sachs. 'The Last Commodity: Child Prostitution in the Developing World.' *World Watch*, July-August 1994, v7, n4.

[65] ibid.

[66] 'Plight of Burmese Women Detailed,' op. cit., p 1.

[67] Youngik Yoon, op. cit., p 4.

[68] Forced Labor, op. cit., p 33.

[69] ibid, p 34-35.

[70] ibid, p 35.

[71] ibid, p 12-13, 21.

[72] Aaron Sachs, op. cit., p 5.

[73] Rahul Bedi, op. cit., p 2.

[74] World Congress against Commercial Sexual Exploitation of Children. August 27-31, 1996, Stockholm, Sweden, The Report of the Rapporteur-General Professor Vitit Muntarbhorn, p 7.

[75] Youngik Yoon, op. cit., p 2-4.

[76] ibid, p 3.

[77] 'The International Sex Market in Children.' WIN News, Spring 1993, v19, n2, p 51.

[78] ibid.

[79] Forced Labor, op. cit., p 39.

[80] Youngik Yoon, op. cit., p 4 and Brian Freemantle, op. cit., chapter 12.

[81] Youngik Yoon, op. cit., p 3.

[82] ibid, p 4.

[83] Phil Williams, op. cit., p 5.

[84] ibid.

[85] Matsui Yayori, op. cit., p 1 and Youngik Yoon, op. cit., p 4.

[86] Youngik Yoon, op. cit., p 2.

[87] ibid, p 1.

[88] ibid, p 2.

[89] ibid.

[90] ibid.

[91] ibid, p 2-3.

[92] ibid, p 3.

[93] Ellen Lukas. 'Saving the Children.' National Review, Dec 23, 1996, v48, n24, p 2.

[94] ibid, p 5.

[95] Rahul Bedi, op. cit., p 1.

[96] ibid.

[97] Carol Aloysius, op. cit., p 1.

[98] 'Plight of Burmese Women Detailed,' op. cit.

[99] Matsui Yayori, op. cit., p 1.

[100] Youngik Yoon, op. cit., p 4.

[101] Matsui Yayori, op. cit., p 1.

[102] Youngik Yoon, op. cit., p 2, 4.

[103] 'Trafficking in Women from the Dominican Republic for Sexual Exploitation,' op. cit.

[104] 'Trafficking and Prostitution: The Growing Exploitation of Migrant Women from Central and Eastern Europe,' May 1995 and 'Trafficking in Women to Austria for Sexual Exploitation,' June 1996. Both from the International Organization of Migration, Migration Information Programme (http://www/iom/ch).

[105] Brian Freemantle, op. cit., p 137.

[106] 'Growing Exploitation of Migrant Women from Central and Eastern Europe,' op. cit.

[107] Victoria Pope, op. cit., p 38.

[108] Michael Specter, op. cit., p 6.

[109] Victoria Dunaeva. 'Selling Souls.' The Russian, October 1997, p 36.

[110] 'Trafficking in Women to Italy for Sexual Exploitation,' op. cit.

[111] Forced Labor, op. cit., p 23.

[112] ibid, p 24.

[113] 'The international sex market in children.' WIN News, Spring, 1993, v19, n2, p 51.

[114] Brian Freemantle, op. cit., p 125.

[115] 'Virgin Territory.' The Economist, March 2, 1996, v338, n7955, p 2.

[116] Forced Labor, op. cit., p 4.
[117] 'The Flourishing Business of Slavery.' *The Economist*, September 21, 1996, v340, n7984, p 43.
[118] Forced Labor, op. cit., p 22.
[119] ibid, p 26.
[120] Freemantle, op. cit., p 125.
[121] ibid, p 140.
[122] Forced Labor, op. cit., p 24.
[123] Phil Williams, op. cit., p 7.
[124] Forced Labor, op. cit., p 24-25.
[125] Brian Freemantle, op. cit., p 137, 140.
[126] ibid p 136.
[127] Forced Labor, op. cit., p 32-40.
[128] ibid, p 32.
[129] Forced Labor, p 41-49 and Brian Freemantle, op. cit., chapters 11-12.
[130] Forced Labor, op. cit., p 26.
[131] Philip P. Wiener. *Dictionary of the History of Ideas.* Charles Scribners Sons, New York, Vol. 2, p 688.
[132] ibid.
[133] 'Growing Exploitation in Migrant Women from Central and Eastern Europe,' op. cit.
[134] ibid
[135] Phil Williams, op. cit., p 5.
[136] ibid.
[137] ibid, p 5-6.
[138] "Growing Exploitation of Migrant Women from Central and Eastern Europe," op. cit.
[139] "Trafficking in Women to Austria for Sexual Exploitation," op. cit. and "Trafficking in Women from the Dominican Republic for Sexual Exploitation," op. cit.
[140] "Trafficking in Women to Austria for Sexual Exploitation," op. cit.
[141] created from data provided in Phil Williams paper, op. cit., p 6.
[142] Forced Labor, op. cit., p 35-36.
[143] ibid, p 36.
[144] see: Forced Labor report, Brian Freemantle (chapters 11-12), Rahul Bedi article, Carol Aloysius article, all previously cited.
[145] Rahul Bedi, op. cit., p 2 and Aron Sachs, op. cit., p 4.
[146] Brian Freemantle, p 140-144, op. cit. and 'Child Pornography: An International Perspective,' p 5-7. (http://www.acapa.org.za/P/porn.html).
[147] Eric Schlosser, 'The Business of Porn.' *US News and World Report*, February 10, 1997, p 43-50.
[148] Forced Labor, op. cit., p 24.
[149] ibid, p 4.
[150] 'Virgin Territory,' op. cit., p 1.
[151] Brian Freemantle, op. cit., p 123.
[152] ibid, p 129.
[153] ibid, p 126.
[154] ibid, p 128.
[155] ibid, p 129.
[156] Timothy Ryback, op. cit., p 45.
[157] 'Europe: the East to West traffic in Women,' *WIN News,* Summer 1993, v 19, n3, p 6.
[158] Forced Labor, op. cit., p 25, 27.
[159] ibid, p 56-62.
[160] Ellen Lukas, op. cit., p 2.
[161] ibid.

[162] Forced Labor, op. cit., p 63, 68-70.
[163] ibid, p 20.
[164] Ellen Lukas, op. cit., p 4.
[165] ibid, p 55.
[166] ibid, p 111-122.
[167] ibid, p 122.
[168] ibid, p 55.
[169] ibid, p 19.
[170] ibid, p 9, 123-151.
[171] Brian Freemantle, op.cit., p 125.
[172] Forced Labor, op.cit., p 20.
[173] ibid, p 15-17.
[174] Brian Freemantle, op.cit., p 127.
[175] Forced Labor, op. cit.

In dwelling, live close to the ground.
In thinking, keep to the simple.
In conflict, be fair and generous.
In governing, don't try to control.
In work, do what you enjoy.
In family life, be completely present.
When you are content to be simply yourself
and don't compare or compete,
everybody will respect you.
--From: Tao te ching - #8.
New English Version by Stephen Mitchell.

14   Art and Antiques Theft

Lauren L. Bernick

Abstract

This chapter examines the growing illicit trade in art, antiquities and cultural property. Although art theft and the plundering of archeological treasures has occurred for centuries, elements within the changing international environment and the increasing demand of art have contributed to the current proliferation of the market. New to the illicit art market are international networks, which smuggle art objects into the museums and auctions houses of developed countries by targeting museums, archeological sites and churches worldwide. The networks either are organizations dedicated solely to the theft of art or are already established transnational criminal organizations which have found art theft profitable. Traditional transnational criminal organizations, such as the Italian Mafia and Colombian drug cartels, use stolen art to facilitate other illicit transactions, thus linking art crime to money laundering and drug dealing. The connivance of the licit art world and government officials presents an additional challenge to international law enforcement agencies in stopping the flow of stolen art across international borders.

Key Words: Antiquities, art theft, cultural property, illicit art trade, smuggling

Introduction

Transnational organized crime occurs across international borders, violating domestic regulations and international conventions. The professional networks involved in this type of crime participate in and facilitate various illegal activities, with smuggling or trafficking constituting a major part of many criminal endeavors. The organized trafficking of commodities is generally regarded as dealing in illicit goods but it also trades licit good and regulated goods obtained illicitly. Art crime encompasses both illicit goods and licit goods smuggled illicitly. Possession of artwork in of itself is usually not illegal. Purchasing and selling of stolen, illegally excavated or illegally exported art, however, is criminal. Transnational crime includes art and antiquities theft because the transporting of stolen objects spans national borders and criminal syndicates are deeply involved in the illicit trade.

Have you ever questioned how ancient antiquities originating from Africa and Asia are transported to Western museums and art houses? Do the ancient antiquities auctioned for thousands or even millions of dollars in auction houses like Sotheby's and Christies' elicit some level of curiosity regarding the manner by which the Houses obtained such art works? Most of the art and antiquities are traded and transported legally, but recently the trade in illicitly excavated and exported art has grown to a level usually accepted as one of the largest illegal commodities on the global market. A combination of actors and economic and political factors has changed the features of art theft. Art is no longer stolen solely for art's sake. Today's art trade functions within the context of markets, profitability, the duality of actors and international criminal networks. The new emphasis involves a spectrum of actors - ranging from individual entrepreneurs to elaborate criminal networks. The successful sale of the art now depends on various actors, their connivance or corruption and criminal networks.

The growing global demand for art and artifacts in economically developed countries has significantly stimulated the illicit trade in art, especially the exporting of art items from less developed countries. Art theft and the looting of archeological sites have occurred for centuries. Plundering of a nation's cultural property has a long history, spanning all regions on the globe. Today, four key areas in the trade and smuggling of illicit art need to be examined. New to plundering is the concept of protecting a country's history and its antiquities through international conventions and the cooperation by international enforcement agencies, non-governmental bodies and governments themselves. The antiquities are often considered to be cultural and heritage property by the source country. This can cause diplomatic tensions between countries seeking the repatriation of artifacts and the countries in which the artifacts were sold. Secondly, connivance and corruption among government officials, auction houses, museums and dealers produces another current trend. Without the tacit approval or the willingness to 'look the other way' of these participants, the smugglers would face greater challenges and resistance in transporting and selling the illicit art. Third, although smuggled art usually proceeds from amateurs burglarizing poorly guarded churches or local looters illegally excavating archeological sites, internationally connected and professional networks' participation in the illicit art trade has grown. The criminal syndicates involved in art smuggling are either groups for which the trafficking of illicitly obtained art constitute one area of their illegal activities or networks specifically created to facilitate the smuggling of art. The involvement of transnational criminal organizations and the violence of their actions demonstrate an even more disturbing aspect of the international network trend. Finally, as can be expected with the growing involvement of criminal organizations, art and antiquities theft connects to other criminal markets. Law enforcement agents have frequently reported links between stolen art and money laundering and drug deals.

Obviously, these issues affect many countries and organizations. Turkey, China and Mali have voiced concerns over the quantities of their cultural items smuggled into the international art market and sold abroad. Countries view looting of their cultural property as tantamount to destroying pages of their history. International organizations such as UNESCO and INTERPOL have attempted to address the problem. States and officials concerned with the rise of transnational criminal organizations share the same concerns. Law enforcement agencies now find their paths crossing more frequently as the criminal markets become more committed and interdependent. Obviously, all of these issues affect the art community as the lines between illicit and licit grow blurred. Some private organizations and auction houses, however, do attempt to combat art theft in cooperation with law enforcement agencies and in accordance with international conventions.

Definitions

The field of art crime encompasses a variety of illegal activities: art theft, fraud, forgeries, fakes and vandalism. The first four categories fit easily with the illicit trade and smuggling of art and the transnational criminal organizations which facilitate the illicit art trade. Vandalism is conducted by individuals with personal or political reasons and does not usually involve organizations. It often occurs not as a direct goal of the person vandalizing but accidentally: thieves working for criminal syndicates can inadvertently damage the art work in the process of the theft. Brief definitions of the art theft terms used in this article are listed below.

- *Art* - within the context of the illicit trade of art, is generally understood to be paintings, prints and drawings and includes antiquities.
- *Antiquities*- objects usually looted from archeological sites and graves which are valuable because of their age and history.
- *Cultural Property*- property of great significance to a country's history and culture. This includes art, antiquities, archeological sites and discoveries, buildings and immovable property. For purposes of this article, though, cultural property will refer primarily to art, antiquities and archeological objects.
- *Art theft* - theft of fine , including paintings, photographs, prints, drawings and sculptures; decorative arts; icons and antiquities, usually achieved through burglaries or robberies from private or public collections or looting.
- *Fakes* – "works of art made to resemble existing ones."[1]
- *Forgeries* – "pieces that are passed off as original works by known artists."[2]

- *Art fraud* – "which includes but is not limited to the production and sale of counterfeit art, is made possible by a trust essential to art world transactions."[3]
- *Looting* - illegal excavation of archeological sites.

Art theft is primarily reported to Interpol and to national law enforcement agencies such as the Federal Bureau of Investigation (FBI) in the United States and a private foundation, the International Foundation on Art Research (IFAR). The Art Loss Register (ALR) provides an international database documenting stolen art. Art and antiquities smuggling is the illicit transporting of stolen art, antiquities and artifacts (whether the pieces are authentic or forgeries) or of pieces that are being exported illegally to be sold in the international art market. The smuggling proceeds from the illegal exportation of art works and continues with shipment through one or more transit countries, and the transportation of the pieces to their final destination and potential buyers.

State Sponsored Art Theft vs Organized Art Crime
Warfare and Colonialism

Historically, the looting of a nation's cultural property during wartime was quite common. Napoleon's forces plundered art and antiquities from the nations he conquered in Europe and from Egypt. In this century, the SS stole from churches, palaces, private homes, and museums. Czarist palaces in Russia, according to Russian claims, were looted of more than 200,000 art treasures.[4] Indeed, it appears that the "Germans had planned their looting of Soviet museums and palaces from the beginning of the war, even designating an expert in the Leningrad collections to choose which pieces to steal after the invasion."[5] Estimates suggest that 2.5 million art objects were confiscated by the Soviets from Germany after the war, making many of the pieces doubly confiscated as the Nazis had plundered works from France, the Netherlands, Poland and from Hungarian Jews.[6] The ramifications are still felt in current debates over property rights and repatriation of art confiscated during World War II by the Nazis and the Soviets. In February 1997, Russia and Germany agreed to discuss repatriation of certain items. Later, President Yeltsin made a symbolic gesture to Chancellor Kohl by returning works from the treasures which were looted.[7] Post World War II conflicts also contributed to international plundering. The struggle between China's Communists and Nationalists allowed for many art treasures to be taken by Chiang Kai-chek to Taiwan. Today, "mainland Chinese Communist regard Chiang Kai-chek as a thief; contemporary Taiwanese nationalists believe they are safeguarding their people's cultural heritage."[8] During the 1969 Biafran war in Nigeria, numerous Benin bronzes and sculptures were looted and placed on the international illicit art market.[9] Most recently, Iraq looted approximately 17,000 pieces from Kuwait during the 1990 Gulf War.[10] These pieces were subsequently repatriated after Iraq's defeat.

Nations also lost many of their cultural treasures during occupation by outside powers. Obviously, European colonialists looted antiquities from their colonies in Africa and India. During the 19th century, "British expeditionary forces in Africa looted gold artifacts from the Ashanti and important masks and sculptures from Benin City."[11] The Japanese stole artifacts from Korea during their occupation and annexation of that country in 1910. In 1997, Egypt's Supreme Council for Antiquities "sent experts to the Sinai Peninsula to investigate allegations that Israelis hauled away archeological treasures when occupying the area in 1967-1982."[12]

The Change and Proliferation of Art Crime

Although, individual smugglers and the acts of looting by governments -- whether during peacetime or war play a role in smuggling -- primary consideration in this article is given to transnational syndicates. It is important, however, to acknowledge and understand the effect of government corruption and connivance on the illicit art trade. Art theft supported by transnational criminal organizations and international networks, as opposed to state-sponsored art theft, is a more recent phenomenon that has flourished in today's international environment of weaker states, more porous borders, greater demand for art and stronger linkages among criminal markets. The illicit trade in art and cultural property revolve around markets and profits. In this sense, it is similar to other illicitly traded commodities such as drugs, weapons of mass destruction or fauna and flora trafficking. Markets and transnational criminal organizations differentiate art theft from state-sponsored plundering. Historically, pillaging during warfare or colonialism was for the political and economic gain of the state and the regime in power. Current art crime promotes economic gain and facilitates the functioning of additional criminal markets for transnational criminal organizations and networks.

Stolen art and antiquities are predominantly transported across multiple borders through established networks, "suggesting that organized crime, or at least criminal organization, is involved in the international trade in stolen art."[13] Although the global reach of art and antiquities smuggling is massive and increasing at an alarming rate, little information exists regarding the organizations responsible for the illicit trafficking of art and antiquities. Sources frequently mention, but do not document, the participation of transnational criminal organizations. The Italian Mafia, both in America and Italy, has been cited in the smuggling of art and antiquities. Art sources and enforcement agencies emphasize the involvement of the Camorra Mafiosi group. Colombian drug cartels, especially the Cali cartel, have also used the illicit trade in art as part of their criminal activities. Law enforcement agents also find stolen art in drug raids thus demonstrating an additional link between art smuggling and drug smuggling. Furthermore, it appears that transnational syndicates with the sole purpose of smuggling art have developed recently and are growing in size, capacity and frequency.

Market Context and Implications

Art theft encompasses a diversity of products today as it has in the past. Smuggled items include paintings, artifacts, statues (from small pieces to over life-sized pieces), sculptures, gold, icons, vases and even ancient books. In the past, actual building were plundered as is evident in the ancient Egyptian collections found in many museums. The actors and participants involved in the illicit trade in art have changed dramatically. At the initial stages of art theft, amateurs and professional thieves begin the smuggling process. Local looters, known as *trombali* in Italy and *haqueros* in South America, plunder tombs and archeological sites. Smuggling networks and transnational criminal organizations are either involved in the hiring of thieves or looters for specific pre-ordered thefts or the purchasing of the stolen pieces to sell on the illicit art market. These groups sell the art to auction houses, art dealers, museums and individual buyers. Law enforcement agencies and international organizations combating art theft such as Interpol, Customs agencies, UNESCO and the International Foundation for Art Research complete the list of main actors involved in either the efforts promote or contain the illicit trade in art.

Crucial to the success of the illicit trafficking of art are the pervasive dynamics of connivance and corruption. Unlike some other markets, art theft has the unique characteristic of blurring the illicit and licit markets and actors. Museums, auction houses and dealers who primarily deal with the licit market will sometimes buy illicit works, not necessarily knowingly, but without actively researching the source of the piece. Corruption, present in the art arena, is perhaps more prevalent in the government and enforcement arenas, but is not entirely restricted to the public sector. Bribery of border patrols, customs official, security guards in museums and archeological sites, and auctioneers, serves to facilitate the trafficking of looted and stolen art.

Moreover, the opportunities for theft in the art world are numerous. Tombs, churches and archeological sites tend to have little if any security. Private homes and smaller museums are often poorly protected and provide easy access. The nature of many art works themselves also facilitates the operation of this illicit market. Rolled-up paintings can be hidden easily and many smaller antiquities can be covered with materials that make them appear new or fake.

With the growth in international art theft, a trend has emerged linking the illicit trade in art and antiquities with other illicit markets. The involvement of the Colombian Cali cartel illustrates the connection between drug trafficking and art trafficking. There have been documented cases in which stolen art has been used as a means of exchange in drug deals. The marrying of art theft and money laundering, offer another link between criminal markets.

Actors

The smuggling of art and antiquities is propelled by a whole spectrum of actors: individuals and grave robbers; museums and auction houses; drug cartels; the Italian Mafia; bribed government officials, especially border inspectors; and most recently international syndicates solely for the illicit trafficking of art and antiquities. The actors in the illicit trade of art and antiquities - schematized in Figure 14.1 -- can be divided into four main groups and a sub-group on the periphery:

Figure 14.1: Smuggling art and antiquities: Actors

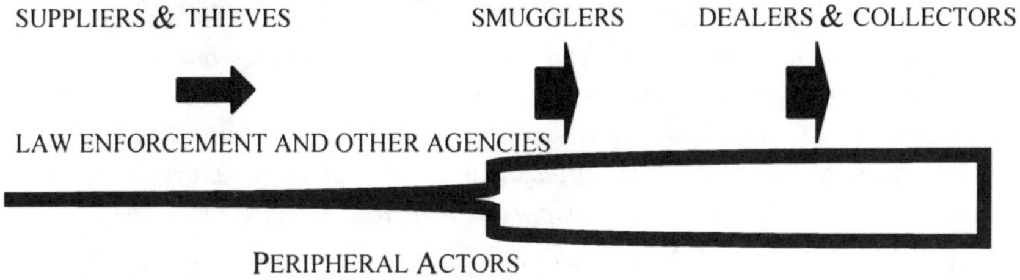

SUPPLIERS & THIEVES   SMUGGLERS   DEALERS & COLLECTORS

LAW ENFORCEMENT AND OTHER AGENCIES

PERIPHERAL ACTORS

Suppliers/thieves

This group primarily consists of individual grave robbers and can be considered to constitute disorganized crime supplying the art and antiquities for the organized aspect of the illicit trade. Local villagers are responsible for the theft or looting of art, especially with antiquities and not-so-famous art, found often in poorly guarded churches. The example of the 1987 looting of a Moche tomb in Sipan, Peru by *huaqueros*, illustrates the role of villagers in art and antiquities smuggling. The looters who unearthed unparalleled riches in the tomb had been looters since childhood, with the skills of the trade having been passed down from generation to generation. After obtaining the treasures, the looters quickly sold them on the local black market or to individual smugglers who had clients abroad, not obtaining anywhere near the sum that the pieces would finally sell for on the international art market. In Turkey, for example, smugglers paid a farmer who found a Hellenistic statue the equivalent of $7,400 - it went on sale in New York for $540,000.[14] The looters, however, receive pay for a single item in excess of the average salary, providing incentive to steal art object despite the punishment of incarceration or the death penalty they may face if apprehended. Two thieves in Iraq "confessed to selling two 5,000 year-old Sumerian statues they illegally dug up from a mound in southern Iraq from about 100 million dinars (approximately $100,000): a huge sum considering the average monthly salary of a civil servant is 3,500 dinars."[15]

In some cases, thefts are pre-ordered by dealers and collectors. In China, instances of *"stealing to order"* have occurred where a looter shows photographs of art available in a poorly guarded museum to a prospective buyer, steals the selected item and arranges for its transportation out of China.[16] As the difficulty rises in obtaining a work of art, so does the likelihood that the thieves will be professional and closely tied to networks of art and antiquity smugglers. The professionals can either work by themselves or as a part of the larger organization. Whichever the case, difficulties in distances encourage organization that can overcome them.

Smugglers

Smugglers act as the intermediaries between the thieves and the dealers, transporting the art pieces from the supplier country through various jurisdictions to reach its final destination. Smugglers need various skills, connections and knowledge of the art world. The tools of the smuggler include:

> *connections to organized crime, access to thieves and looters, relationships with the licit art trade (auction houses, museums, private collectors those who are innocent and those willing to forego questions - connivance); art and antiquities expertise, large reserves of cash and transportation; storage facilities; knowledge of import/export law; access to top lawyers; and access to corrupt government officials.*[17]

Corruption becomes evident at this level with border inspectors and customs officials accepting bribes from smugglers. In numerous cases, members of the diplomatic corps have participated in smuggling. Muayad Demerijii, head of Iraq's Antiquities Department, asserts that people outside Iraq finance illegal excavations. Mr. Demerijii reported in an interview to Reuters that "we have the proof that some of the workers in the diplomatic corps and the United Nations are purchasing antiquities and trying to smuggle them."[18] Even considering the political origin of these allegations, they simply cannot be dismissed. Past experience suggests they could have a real basis.

Although smugglers usually are part of a network, they are not always part of a cohesive group. Often the smuggler is one individual who uses contacts in other countries to help facilitate the shipment of goods. However, in some instances, the smugglers are members of an organized criminal group, which is involved in other criminal activity. In the past, stolen art was simply used as status symbols. Now, the Italian Mafia uses art and antiquities as an investment and as merchandise to exchange for drugs and arms.[19] The art theft unit in Italy located 27 paintings in Kingston, Jamaica stolen from Italian museums, to be used in a drug deal as a means of exchange.[20] In Turkey, smugglers belong to a cartel, described as the Turkish Mafia, and are comprised primarily of Kurds and Syriacs. The gangs often employ middlemen to buy the artifacts from the looters then transport the pieces to Istanbul.[21] These gangs were apparently involved in smuggling the Lydian Hoard, the valuable silver Byzantine treasure, and nearly two thousand Greek coins out of Turkey in 1970. These two gangs are also involved in the smuggling of heroin.

Pervasiveness of transnational criminal organizations and networks

The impact of transnational criminal organizations is most strongly felt in the stealing and smuggling of art and antiquities. The syndicates involved in art and antiquity smuggling are either criminal organizations, such as the Italian Mafia, or organizations created for the sole purpose of art and antiquity smuggling. Examples of prominent networks involved in smuggling art works include the Italian Camorra and Sicilian Mafia, the Colombian Cali cartel, Russian transnational criminal organizations and an antique dealer group in

Turin. The involvement of Chinese gangs in smuggling large art works, in particular life size statues, and showing photos of the art to prospective buyers for ordering has also been documented.[22] The State Bureau of Cultural Relics (SBCR) and the Ministry of Public Security have noted a rise in involvement in the illicit art trade by institutional and professional criminal groups.[23]

Members of criminal networks also engage in felony vandalism, which is the "unintentional damaging of art by thieves in the course of stealing."[24] In Turkey, transnational criminal organizations, such as the Syriac Turks and Kurds, both belonging to the Turkish Mafia, have gained prominence and power in the smuggling of antiquities, creating violent compebetween the gangs. In several cases, violence between competing gangs has been reported. The "smugglers sought to maintain their control of the illicit antiquities trade by murdering competitors and members of their organization who have deserted to rival gangs or cooperated with law enforcement agencies."[25]

According to Russian police general Vasily Fedoshechencko, Western Europe now has 40 groups smuggling cultural and historical valuables out of Russia.[26] Table 14.1 demonstrates the pervasiveness of transnational criminal organizations and the art which the syndicates have stolen. Obviously, this list is not comprehensive but is meant as an illustration providing some of the most prominent examples of network involvement in the illicit art market.

Dealers/collectors

Wealthy individuals, auction houses and museums collect and buy the stolen art and antiquities, whether knowingly or unknowingly. To avoid any culpability if an artwork was stolen, museums and auctions houses often do not question the art's origins and exportation. Many directors or dealers hold the belief that obtaining art and building a collection are more important than securing the legality of the origin or provenance of the art. Thomas Hoving, when he was director of the Metropolitan Museum of Art, "voiced the position that scandal about unethical acquisitions will pass, but a museum's collection will endure."[27] Smaller dealers and private collectors are often more willing to trade on the black market, although both are susceptible to buying art works which they think have been legally acquired, but which have been obtained through illicit means. Early in 1987, a joint effort by the Italian carabinieri and French officials cracked an international organization financed by a consortium of Turino antique dealers.[28] Increasingly, dealers purchase illegally exported objects and knowingly contribute to the trade in illicit art.

Actors on the Periphery

All groups interact with and rely on actors on the periphery of the illicit art trade. These actors usually are disorganized and are not members of any criminal group. They are primarily the museum guards, government officials, border patrols and customs officers, who either are bribed by smugglers or simply ignore the art pieces leaving their museums or countries. Although they are not active participants, with their tacit connivance or susceptibility to bribes,

Table 14.1:[29] Stolen art and transnational organized crime

NETWORK	LOCATION	PROMINENCE	STOLEN ART
Sicilian Mafia group (links between Sicilian group and its American counterpart)	California and Sicily	1961	paintings, later held for ransom
Union Corse	Southern France and Corsica	1960s	several paintings, including works by Cezanne
Bonnano family Mafia group	United States - the East Coast	late 1960s and early 1970s	antiques
Napoli Camorra Mafia group	Naples, Italy	early 1970s	Caravaggio's Nativity painting stolen from a church in Palermo
The David Swetnam network	California and Peru	1987	Smuggled treasures looted from the Sipan tomb in Peru through his own network
Syriacs and Kurds, groups of the Turkish Mafia	Turkey and Greece	late 1960s through 1980s	Lydian horde
Turin antique dealers	Italy and France	1984-1987	International gang financed by the Turin dealers plundered over 200 French chateaux
Chinese gangs	China	1989 - 1990	Artifacts tombs and statues 1,000 years old
Cali Cartel	Colombia	1994	Rubens, Picasso (later determined to be a forgery) and Reynolds

the peripheral actors provide a valuable service to thieves and smugglers by facilitating the theft and transportation of illicitly obtained art objects. Figure 14.2 schematizes the techniques and modalities used in the illicit art trade.

Locate the Target and Assess the Suitability

The first step in the process of the trade in illicit art and antiquities is locating the target. Thieves locate valuable art to steal then determine the suitability and accessibility of their target. Smugglers obtain stolen art from

Figure 14.2: Techniques and modalities used in the illicit art trade

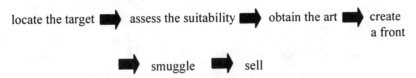

locate the target ➡ assess the suitability ➡ obtain the art ➡ create a front

➡ smuggle ➡ sell

thefts of archeological digs, and burglaries of private homes and collections, museums and most often churches, which have the least security. In Turkey, transnational criminal organizations have "purchased and distributed aerial surveys of ancient sites specially prepared for them by retired military officers" to locate sites containing valuable antiquities.[30]

The majority of targets, whether museums, private homes or archeological sites are chosen because of their poor security. Sites and tombs often do not have guards at all. Churches lack sufficient if any security systems. Museums also fall victim to burglaries that could have been prevented with proper security. In 1992, there were four major thefts from Greek museums: one museum was practically emptied of its treasures on the watchmen's only night off, for which the museum had no alternate guard.[31]

Art thefts in the United States are most likely to be from private homes and galleries, which usually have weaker security systems. However, the proportion of galleries to museums is greater and the likelihood of galleries reporting thefts is greater. Churches constitute the most frequent victims of art theft abroad. In 1990, 3,269 objects were taken from 562 churches in Italy alone.[32] Between 1983 and 1986, IFAR reported that, internationally, churches, private and unknown sources were burglarized the most. In the U.S., art is predominantly stolen from galleries and private homes. More recently, the Art Loss Register (ALR) has determined the "victims" (ie. sources) of art theft between 1991 and 1996, in the United States. They are ranked according to the frequency of burglaries. Unfortunately, updated information on the sources of art theft worldwide is not available.

Obtain the Art

Thefts of art can range from simple burglaries to burglaries and robberies that require special skills and established networks. Professional art thieves have the skills to break alarm systems and the networks to sell the art, although, in many instances, breaking an elaborate alarm system is unnecessary because such a system does not exist. Recently, the British Museum has been successfully targeted by thieves because of its poor security. Often, members of the museum staff themselves steal pieces. One worker reported that "the staff was never searched when leaving, even if they were carrying suitcases, admitting that the workers all knew that objects routinely disappeared as 'souvenirs'."[33] The looting of antiquities involves a greater range of people,

Figure 14.3: ALR categories of theft victims 1991-1996

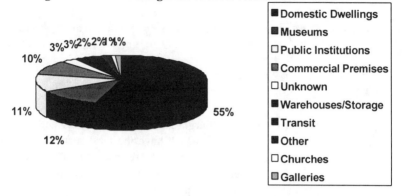

Source: ALS News – Newsletter of the Art loss Register – Issues 6, February, 1997, p. 4.

beginning with the actual grave robber and the cemetery guards who are bribed.

Create a Front

Legitimate fronts are often used to facilitate the sale of smuggled art and antiquities. Thieves pose as a variety of people ranging from potential customers to museum workmen or employees to gain access to artwork. The thief who stole the Mona Lisa disguised himself as a construction worker employed by the Louvre; the thieves who robbed Boston's Gardner Museum in 1990 posed as police officers, telling the museum guards that a disturbance was reported.[34] The Caravaggio Conspiracy, an undercover investigation conducted by the journalist Peter Watson in 1979 in an attempt to recover the stolen Caravaggio painting, Nativity of Christ, demonstrates the importance of fronts in the illicit trade of art. By using the front of a credible art dealer, Mr. Watson was able to contact the smugglers. For their part, the Italian smugglers used their import business in New York to conceal their smuggling, while the thief used his roles as a priest and diplomat to smuggle art across borders.[35]

Smuggle

Thieves employ various measures to hide smuggled art and antiquities, either as a means to avoid suspiby law enforcement agents or to avoid paying bribes to border patrols and inspectors. Paintings are cut from frames, rolled up and are covered with a water-soluble surface paint that can later be washed off without harming the original work. Antiquities are covered with material to make them resemble modern reproductions and artifacts can be broken into pieces to simulate lower value and then reassembled at the final destination.[36] Art has been smuggled out of Italy via boat and plane, packed in crates or in suitcases with false bottoms, or in the Caravaggio Conspiracy case, paintings were wrapped around table legs, covered with cardboard and placed in a container holding many other pieces of furniture.[37] In the past, illegally excavated antiquities were smuggled out of Turkey through American military bases. Now, smugglers ship the "antiquities in officially sealed truck containers through Bulgaria to galleries in Munich."[38] Demonstrating the significance of the peripheral actors, Bulgarian officials are bribed to permit the transportation of the antiquities to Munich, where the pieces are sold on the international market.

Movement of the stolen art is also key to successful smuggling and the eventual sale. Mobility helps avoid law enforcement agents and decreases the likelihood that the stolen art will be recognized in a different city or country. Cases of smuggled art show that mobility is extremely important and is often "circuitous."[39] A painting by Renoir, stolen in Paris, was smuggled to New York City, then sent to Boston on consignment, shipped to Canada and back to Paris, finally settling in New York City again; a man smuggling an Indian statuette was arrested and reported that he belong to an international organization that smuggled art from India and Nepal to the U.S., either directly or through Switzerland; and in 1978, Boston's Museum of Fine Arts discovered that one of its Egyptian wall paintings was looted from a tomb in 1973, trucked to Libya, smuggled to London and then to the U.S.[40]

Sell

Once the art pieces or antiquities have been smuggled into the buyer country, they must be sold. In some cases, specific works of art will be sold prior to the theft. The demand not only leads to the specific targeting of current popular works but in some cases collectors have directly sponsored thieves on expeditions to acquire certain pieces.[41] However, most often smugglers and thieves present themselves to dealers, collectors and curators, either illegitimate or legitimate, using fronts to sell the art. Frequently, buyers, whether individuals or from auction houses or museums, fail to investigate the origin of the pieces. Although most buyers do not directly participate in the smuggling, their complacency in verifying origin allows smuggling to continue.

Distinctive Features

Five aspects of art and antiquities smuggling explains the difficulty in curbing the illicit art trade and differentiate it from other smuggling activities. These features, schematized in Figure 14.4, are:

Figure 14.4: Distinctive features of art and antiquities smuggling

●   LICIT V. ILLICIT

    ●   CORRUPTION

        ●   LINKS TO OTHER CRIMINAL MARKETS

           ●   MOBILITY AND EVIDENCE

               ●   CULTURAL AND SOCIETAL ATTITUDES

Licit v. Illicit - Connivance

Illicit trade in art and antiquities requires interaction among legitimate and illegitimate actors.[41]   Smugglers and dealers frequently maintain fronts which give buyers the appearance of legitimacy. Auction houses often fail to inquire into the legality of an artwork piece and then proceed to auction the piece to buyers who are buying the piece legitimately. Evidence exists showing that antiquities looted from Angkor Wat in Cambodia have ended in Hong Kong, "where the artifacts disappear into a semi-legitimate antiquities market that counts unwary international museums among its prime customers."[42] Legitimate antiquities dealers maintain high ethics in refusing to buy artifacts that have been stolen. However, legitimacy is eroded when the dealers accept pieces that have been on the market for a lengthy duration or in the possession of private collectors, even if these pieces were originally stolen.[43] Other dealers will not buy artifacts from monuments but will buy looted artifacts illegally excavated and exported. An auction house primarily carries legitimate art but is open to accepting pieces illegally exported or sold. In art and antiquities trade, the distinction between licit and illicit, legitimate and illegitimate is frequently blurred.

Corruption

Corruption has been evident in the bribing of museum guards or border officials and in the past, these actors were the primary ones accused of corruption.   More recent evidence, however, suggests that the reach of corruption extends to museum directors, auction houses and diplomats working as smugglers. In February 1997, a key employee of Sotheby's Italian auction house was caught in London offering to smuggle paintings out of Italy. This public discovery sent shock waves through the art community and questioned the level of corruption present in what was viewed as the licit art market. But Sotheby's and auction house are not the only actors to possess corrupt individuals. In 1996, an Arizona museum director was "indicted for illegally trafficking his institution's artifacts, while a New Mexican museum board member stands similarly charged."[44] Storage rooms provide insiders with more accessible means to steal and sale pieces of an institution's collection. Between 1979 and 1989, 57.8 percent of all thefts from public collection in France were from storage spaces, with no signs of forced entry.[45]

Links to Other Criminal Markets

Many cases point to drug dealers and drug cartels' involvement in the smuggling of stolen art and antiquities. The channels used to smuggle drugs are also used to smuggle art. Stolen art and art smuggling can also provide additional financial security for drug cartels. A cocaine producer "who had bought gold pieces looted from the Sipan tomb reportedly sold them off whenever he had a shipment of cocaine confiscated by law-enforcement agents."[46]   Stolen art is also used as collateral for drug deals.   Authorities worldwide agree on the involvement of the Italian Mafia in the theft of

Caravaggio's 1609 Nativity, stolen in 1969. British investigators believe that the painting, worth about $50 million today, has been used by the Mafia for security in drug deals.[47] It is "easier to transport across international boundaries than cash and it is also more difficult for law-enforcement agents to trace than is the flow of money."[48]

Art theft is also used as a means to launder money for drug cartels, as seen in the DEA's 1994 "Operation Dinero." The investigation into Cali's money laundering operations resulted in numerous arrests and the seizure of cocaine, cash, property and three paintings. The paintings were attributed to Rubens, Reynolds and Picasso, although the Picasso was later determined to be a forgery. Prior to the seizure, a member of the Cali cartel met with an undercover agent and said "that he had two paintings supposedly valued at approximately $9 million which he wished to have delivered to the agents in Atlanta for consignment. Selling the paintings would launder the money which had been used to buy them."[49] Profits from drug deals are used to buy artwork. As explained in an issue of Art Intelligence, a typical drug, money laundering and art purchasing operation begins with the drug dealer using money from the drug transaction to purchase art. The painting is then passed on to an art dealer for resale for the same price. The art dealer "furnishes the drug dealer with documents that show a 50 to 100 percent profit from the sale of the art, which account for the drug dealer's extra cash from his drug deal."[50] Laundering money through the illicit art trade is not confirmed to drug cartels or other TCOs. Japanese chave reportedly used art to launder money and avoid paying taxes.[51]

Mobility and Collecting Evidence

Smuggling art and antiquities requires smugglers and networks to move the stolen goods quickly out of the country. Although transshipment is frequent, with the stolen art spending only a brief amount of time in one place, the whole smuggling process can last years, depending on the notoriety of the art and its value. The frequency of movement impedes law enforcement agencies from interdicting the illicit goods and facilitates its sale. Moving the stolen art from its originating area, especially with obscure pieces, decreases the chances that the buyer will realize that the art is illicit.

Not only does the mobility of artwork hinder the collection of evidence but so does the risk in obtaining the evidence itself. Law enforcement agencies must walk a fine line in their investigation. The final goal in recovering the art is not to use it solely for evidence against the smugglers - as is the case with narcotics interdiction. The goal is to return the art intact. The law enforcement agents must avoid inadvertently causing the painting's destruction by smugglers disposing the incriminating evidence.

Cultural and Societal Attitudes

Cultural and societal attitudes surround the illicit trade in antiquities and create a barrier that is very difficult for law enforcement agencies to overcome.

Most looters and the officials who are easily bribed share the sentiment that such trade and smuggling is justified. These people consider that it is better to make some money selling the artifacts instead of the artifacts remaining in the ground. The antiquities provide the looters with a paycheck that is often greatly needed. Many looters also view archeologists as smugglers and the equivalent of international collectors. Other cultures view their artifacts differently from the international art market. Many Africans do not share the western that older is more authentic, original and therefore more valuable. The "objects of interest to Western collectors are considered important by African primarily for the functions they serve in rituals, and a new object can function as well as an old one."[52]

Geographic Scope and Scale
It is sometimes claimed that art and antiquities smuggling is third only to the global smuggling of arms and narcotics, in terms of total volume. Art theft has been estimated at anywhere from $2 to $6 billion per year.[53] Estimates suggest that $200 million worth of antiquities are smuggled out of Turkey yearly, primarily taken from burial sites and ancient cities.[54] The government of the People's Republic of China estimates that 40,000 tombs were robbed in 1989 and 1990, and gangs managed to smuggle out huge statues 1,000 years old or more.[55] Italy recorded 230,00 art thefts from 1970 to 1990; British losses were estimated at $1.5 billion a year; and the Czech Republic said it was losing about 10 percent of its national patrimony per year to theft and smuggling.[56] Figure 14.5 schematizes supply aspects of illicit art and antiquities.

Figure 14.5: Geographic scope and scale: supply

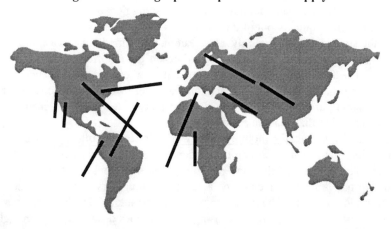

Supply
A country's supply of art and antiquities obviously affects the scope of the quantity looted. Porous borders, such as Italy's especially with the unification of Europe, and countries with weak border controls, such as Russia,

provide the best geographic location for supply and transshipment. Countries with many noted and valuable paintings such as Italy and France supply much of the market's art pieces. Russia, Poland and many of the eastern European countries supply icons, especially because of the accessibility to the churches which house such art. Countries rich with antiquities and artifacts are also targeted for supply. African and South American artifacts are also in great demand and smuggled often. Trends in the demand of the art market, affecting the popularity of items affects regions that are targeted. In the countries supplying the art, politicians, police officers and custom agents accept bribes or ignore the activities of smugglers.[57]

Demand
    Demand stems from wealthy individuals, museums, and members of the drug trafficking organizations who often purchase smuggled art for their own private status symbols. The collectors, dealers, museum curators, and scholars hope to acquire the rarest and finest art and antiquities. These people buy stolen art and antiquities from dealers and smugglers. Auction houses sometimes unknowingly buy stolen, counterfeit or smuggled art. Most art pieces and antiquities are smuggled to clients in Europe, the United States and Japan. Europe also offers a point of transshipment for art destined for the United States. Figure 14.6 schematizes art demand aspects.

Figure 14.6: Geographic scope and scale: demand

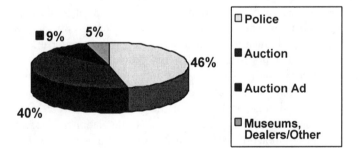

    Stolen art is a global phenomenon, originating with higher intensity from Italy, France, Russia and other eastern European countries, particularly the Czech Republic, Poland and Bulgaria. For example, although art theft in Poland is diminishing, every year between 1,200 and 1,300 art objects are reported stolen mostly from places of worship and since 1990, it is estimated that more than 70,000 items of Czech cultural heritage have been stolen, also from places of worship, and shipped abroad.[58] Poland is also a transit route for religious art smuggled out of Russia. Bulgaria suffers greatly from the smuggling of its cultural property. Police have seized 40,000 items worth millions of dollars from smugglers. However, officials estimate "that this is no more than 20 percent of the items smuggled out Bulgaria."[59] In Italy, international smugglers, often based in Switzerland, illegally export art from Italy to sale on the global market.[60] In Turkey, organized criminal gangs employ middlemen to buy artifacts and antiquities from the looters.[61] Many of Turkey's antiquities are smuggled through Bulgaria to Germany and Switzerland. Switzerland is a "country that is generally regarded as the world center for the smuggling and laundering of art and antiquities because of its lax customs laws."[62]

Stolen artifacts and antiquities stem predominantly from the host countries and regions of Turkey, Italy, Latin America, Africa, China, and the American Southwest. Looting of Native American burial sites has increased dramatically as the demand for such artifacts has grown. Theft of Native American artifacts usually occurs either in museums or at archeological sites, which are unpopulated and unpatrolled.[63] Today, the looting of such artifacts has grown into a highly organized and clandestine business which, according to the FBI, contains groups who employ looters, politicians, and employees of museums and galleries, and whose tentacles reach into the overseas market in Japan and Germany supplied by international smugglers.[64]

Looted artifacts from Angkor Wat in Cambodia cross the 500-mile border along jungle trails, usually with the help of corrupt police, and are sold to Bangkok dealers or directly to dealers overseas.[65] African artifacts such as statues and masks have grown recently in the illicit trade of artifacts. To avoid interdiction and seizure of the African artifacts, which are prohibited from export because of national patrimony laws, dealers use diplomats and airline personnel to smuggle them.[66] The illicit export and trade of Chinese antiquities exploded in the 1980s after travel bans on foreigners were lifted, smuggling networks were created and corruption of border control officials was established. The transit points were and continue to be Hong Kong and Macao. Dealers in Hong Kong sell the artifacts to collectors in the west or Japan.

In Africa, recent political upheavals have provided opportunity for the illicit trade in art to flourish. Nigerian artifacts, among the most valued antiquities on the global market, are being smuggled out of Nigeria at an alarming rate. In 1996 alone, at least 8 of the 30 museums were looted in Nigeria and more than 230 objects were stolen.[67] Ife-Ile National Museum has been a favorite target. Tlooted the Ife-Ile Museum three times between 1993 to 1997.[68] The number of art thefts in South Africa has also grown, coinciding with its new government and re-entry into the international community. One museum official described the steep increase in thefts as a "hemorrhaging" and explained the demand as originating from a renewed interest in South Africa and in acquiring its antiquities. Gillian Berning, president of the South African Museum Association, said that "organized crime syndicates are supplying an increasing international demand for the items, placing the country's cultural heritage under serious threat."[69] Countries devastated by war, such as Rwanda, Angola, Burundi and the Democratic Republic of the Congo, have also seen a growth in the number of their artifacts being plundered. South Africa provides a major transshipment point off the continent for stolen objects from these countries.

Table 14.2 presents examples of illegally excavated sites and art stolen from a variety of locations.

Table 14.2:[70] Selected locations of illegally excavated sites and stolen art

Country	Site	Artwork
Bulgaria	Churches	An estimated 385 icons stolen in 1992.
Cambodia	Angkor Wat	Various statues.
China	Over 40,000 sites	Ancient tombs plundered. A 1,000-year-old Buddha valued at $2.5 million, 177 antiquities valued at $15 million and 256 antiquities worth $95 million were seized at border crossings.
Greece	Church in Siatista	In 1992, several icons and a Bible were stolen.
Italy	Various tombs and cemeteries	Etruscan tombs plundered by tombali looters.
Iraq	Various sites	An estimated 4,00 items were stolen from museums during the Gulf War.
Mali	Thail site	Various antiquities.
Netherlands	Museum in Amsterdam	20 paintings by van Gogh stolen in 1991.
Nigeria	Ile-Ife National Museum Niger State Museum; National Museum, Esie; National Museum, Oron; Ife-Ile National Museum.	In 1993, several bronze heads and others in terracotta. In 1996, respectively: Objects valued over $46,000 were stolen; thieves drugged museum guards and stole one of the largest collections of famous stone sculptures; 36 objects stolen; 34 objects stolen.
Norway	Oslo museum	Edvard Munch's "The Scream" in 1994.
Pakistan	Knational Museum	In 1993, 17 bronze statuettes.
Russia	St. Petersburg	A gold and amethyst statue by Dali and 12 icons dating back to the 16th century (these were recovered).
Turkey	Anavarza site in 1992 Public Library in Amasya Byazit	Two marble tombstones and the capital of a column. In 1992, 17 ancient Arabic manuscripts.
USA	Gardner Museum	In 1990, paintings by Vermeer, Rembrandt, Degas and Manet.

Transportation and smuggling routes are varied but the majority of art finds its final destination in London, the United States and Japan. In Europe, the flow moves from Eastern European countries into the Western European Countries. Switzerland constitutes a major destination point for art from Eastern Europe, Italy, Greece and France. In Switzerland, "a work can come out of a bonded free-port warehouse in Zurich or Geneva with clear legal title to the possessor after 5 years; in Liechtenstein and the Cayman Islands, the term is seven days."[71] The trafficking of art from Russia follows a few routes, flowing either into the Baltics and Finland; into Poland and Germany; or into the Caucuses, Central Asia, Turkey and Iran and Afghanistan.[72] From Turkey and Greece, the art flows into Bulgaria and Germany. In May 1997, Israeli authorities probed an art theft ring stemming from a dealer in Paris to Tel Aviv.[73] From Cambodia, art reaches the international market through Thailand. In China, art is smuggled from the north into the south, where it is sold easily by dealers in Hong Kong. In Africa, the majority of works are smuggled out of Nigeria by road into the West Africa sub-region and to Europe, predominantly Britain, the Netherlands and Spain.[74] Artifacts are also being smuggled directly to the Untied States. Objects plundered from east African countries follow smuggling routes into South Africa, which provides a gateway for shipment abroad.

Notable Cases
Sipan Treasure
The Sipan treasure, looted from a 1,500-year-old Moche civilization tomb in northern Peru, is often heralded as "the richest tomb ever excavated archaeologically in the Western Hemisphere."[75] In February 1987, huaqueros, local looters, unearthed an amazing mass of artifacts after digging in the pyramids for three months. The artifacts included gold beads (90 percent pure), gold and silver ornaments, masks, ancient carvings, peanut-shaped beads and animal figurines. The smuggling of the Sipan treasures demonstrates the types of international networks in place to smuggle artifacts and the disparity in prices looters are paid and the amount the collection eventually nets.

After the huaqueros gathered the artifacts, they sold them to a local dealer who then sold them to the California antiquities dealer David Swetnam. Swetnam smuggled the objects to the United States through connections in the international illicit art market. After hearing of the Sipan discovery, Swetnam convinced several Americans to invest $80,000 to purchase some artifacts; by not using his own money, Swetnam reduced some of his personal risk.[76] Swetnam then contacted Fred Drew, a retired American diplomat living in Lima, who had connections to local dealers and was well know for smuggling artifacts from Peru. In the past, Drew had "used tourist, airplane personnel and even nuns to carry his antiquities form Lima to the United States."[77] Because of increasing risk, however, the artifacts would be moved via London with the help of an expeditor, who reportedly had connections to the Medellin drug cartel. Swetnam mailed Drew's payment in "cashier checks in amounts of $9,999, just under the $10,000 limit that banks must report to international-tax and customs inspectors."[78]

Drew and his partner shipped the treasures to England, stored them there, and later sent the objects to the United States. Swetnam hired a partner, Michael Kelley, to smuggle the goods from London to California. Kelley told Swetnam that United States customs agents would not be suspicious because Kelley would tell the agents that the objects were the possession of his recently deceased British father who had collected the artifacts while traveling in the

1920s, prior to the passage of Peru's cultural property law of 1929.[79] Following the second successful shipment of the treasure, estimated around $150,000, Kelly reported the smuggling operation to United States Customs officials after feeling used by Swetnam and fearing his own vulnerability in the operation. Kelly's cooperation in recording conversations with Swetnam provided the evidence for a raid on Swetnam's home and the residences of several collectors, resulting in the seizure of nearly 2,000 pieces (most of which were not actually from the Sipan tomb). Swetnam was the only one convicted of conspiracy, smuggling, and customs violation. He was the "first person ever incarcerated for smuggling pre-Columbian antiquities."[80] Although some of the Sipan treasured was returned to Peru, mostly pieces in the possession of Swetnam, a United States judge ruled in favor of a dealer who unwittingly purchased artifacts from Swetnam, allowing the dealer to keep the antiquities seized from him.

Turkey's Decadrachm Hoard and the Lydian Hoard: Smuggled Antiquities

The illicit trade in Turkey's antiquities has grown in recent years with criminal organizations taking control of the smuggling. However, two collections, the Decadrachm and Lydian Hoards, stolen in 1984 and 1966 respectively, are widely known and have repercussions for impeding the current illicit trade in antiquities worldwide. Both demonstrate the years over which items are smuggled; how "reputable" museums are involved; and the difficulty in repatriating objects once they have been on the international market for some time. The smuggling of the Decadrachm Hoard illustrates the numerous sales and people involved and the escalating prices as the artifacts are sold to more discriminating and prestigious dealers and collectors. The Lydian case set a precedent for the repatriation of cultural property.

The Lydian Hoard consisted of silver and gold artifacts 2,600 years old from the Lydia region in Turkey. In 1984, New York's Metropolitan Museum of Art exhibited a bowel, which the Turkish government claimed originated from excavation in Lydia and had been illegally exported out of Turkey on to the international art black market. To prove the origin, excavators, who had originally unearthed the treasure, identified the pieces in the Metropolitan as the pieces they dug up - and some of the pieces confiscated from the looters matched the pieces exhibited by the museum.[81] After the treasure of over 300 artifacts was plundered in 1966, authorities were able to recover some objects left behind and arrest and prosecute the looters. However, most of the hoard had already been smuggled out of the country. Antiques dealer Ali Bayirlar sold the hoard to international dealers George Zacos of Switzerland and John Klejman of New York, who sold it to the Metropolitan between 1966 and 1970 for $1.5 million. The museum made no formal announcement of the purchase and provided no information of the collection in its public catalogue.[82] Once Turkey verified the artifacts, a controversy erupted over ownership of the hoard. Turkey claimed the hoard as cultural patrimony and the Metropolitan lobbied the state legislature to pass a law protecting the museum's right to the collection.[83] Eventually, in 1993, after the involvement of both the Turkish and United States governments, the hoard was repatriated to Turkey. The "return ended a 25-year effort to recover the material and a six-year legal struggle with the Metropolitan."[84]

The Decadrachm Hoard, consisting of nearly 2,000 ancient Greek silver coins, including some decadrachm, was uncovered by 3 local looters in 1984, using a metal detector. Prior to the discovery of the Decadrachm Hoard, "only 13 decadrachms were known to exist. The last one to be sold had been auctioned in 1974 for $270,00."[85] A Turkish smuggling network bought the coins from the looters in Istanbul for $692,00, smuggled them to a Munich based dealer who bought the hoard for $1,335 million and sold them to an international network, known as the OKS Partners, for $2.7 million. The three partners in the American company "believed that because the coins had been legally exported from Germany, they would hold title to them, overlooking the fact that the coins had been illegally exported from Turkey to Germany and had been sold by a cartel that did not hold legal title to them."[86] The OKS Partners began selling the hoard in 1987 to international dealers, including a dealer in Switzerland who purchased 60 coins, including three decadrachms, for a sum in excess of $1 million; this dealer then sold most of the coins to the Numismatic Fine Arts Gallery, who advertised the coins in a sales catalogue for auction in 1988.[87] Hearing of an auction catalogue advertising coins from Turkey, the Turkish government investigated and was able through its lawyers to achieve the repatriation of ten coins. In addition to those ten coins, Turkey has recovered nine other coins. As for the other remaining coins, "either OKS will return them voluntarily, or the courts will decide who gets them."[88]

Impediments and Methods for Combating Art Theft
UNESCO and Cultural Property Convention

The United Nations Educational, Scientific and Cultural Organization, UNESCO, promotes the international acceptance of the definition of cultural property. It also promotes acceptance of the Recommendation on the Means of Prohibiting and Preventing the Illicit Export, Import and Transfer of Ownership of Cultural Property, developed in1970, which outlines general principles to ensure the protection of cultural property. UNESCO defines cultural property as movable and immovable property of great importance to the cultural heritage of a country. The general principles of the convention are to ensure the protection of cultural property; regulate the import of cultural property; and prevent the illicit transfer of cultural property. Parties to the Convention "agree to prohibit the import of, and to recover and return to the source nation, any cultural Property stolen from a museum or a religious or a secular public monument or similar institution in another State Party to this Convention…provided that such property is documented as pertaining to the inventory of that institution."[89]

Law Enforcement and Other Agencies

Law enforcement agencies are the front line in stopping art and antiquities smuggling. Many countries have separate squads within their agencies for the interdiction of illicitly traded art. The FBI and the Custom Service have officials dedicated to art crime. The French Ministry of Interior has about 30 officers specializing in art crime.[90] In 1968, Italy created the Comando Carabinieri Tutela Partimonio Artistico to investigate art crimes. By 1992, the Italian art squad had "120 members and a computerized data base of 200,00 stolen objects."[91] Between 1970 and 1987, the squad arrested 2,500 suspects and recovered 112,00 works of art.[92]

International enforcement agencies, such as the International Criminal Police Organization (INTERPOL), and joint operations between enforcement groups in neighbouring countries play a significant role in combating art and antiquities smuggling. INTERPOL "circulates only that information about cultural objects which have been reported to member police forces, as stolen or as property found in suspicious circumstances."[93] In the United States, the Federal Bureau of Investigation (FBI), Drug Enforcement Administration (DEA) and Customs control comprise the enforcement agencies responsible for fighting the illicit art trade. In the 1980s, the FBI started the National Stolen Art File (NSAF) to record information about stolen art and updates the entries every six months.[94] Private foundations play a role in educating the public, collectors and law enforcement agencies on what constitutes stolen art and artifacts.

The Getty Information Institute provides another impediment for art and antiquity smuggling - primarily through the dispersion of information. The Getty Art History Information Program has launched an international initiative to establish documentation standards for the protection of cultural objects. UNESCO, the Council of Europe, and the International Council of Museum (ICOM) have all recognized the importance of this initiative and have lent their support to the project. ICOM distributes publications to the many actors in the art community and together with UNESCO, organized the first workshops for museum officials, police and customs agents on illicit traffic.[95] The institute also promotes the G7 Multimedia Access to World Cultural Heritage project. The goal of the project is open and diverse access to information about cultural heritage.

The Art Loss Register (ALR) offers another means of curbing the illicit trade in art and antiquities smuggling by documenting stolen art and cooperating with law enforcement agencies, auction houses and insurance companies in tracking stolen art. ALR is an international computerized database of stolen art, operating out of London, New York and Perth, Australia, with offices in European cities. ALR has assisted in the recovery of 700 items valued at $25 million in 1995 alone. This success stems in most part from law enforcement agents referring to the Register. Agencies which use the Register regularly include: Interpol, the FBI, Carabinieri, Scotland Yard, Geneva Police, the Garda in Dublin and the Dutch Police, with the BKA in Germany and the French Police also beginning to use the service.[96] According to ALR, police play the biggest role in the recovering of stolen art, followed closely by catalogue screening prior to auction, having a recovery rate of 46 percent and 40 percent

respectively. Figure 14.7 summarizes sources of recoveries of stolen art, 1991-
1995.

Figure 14.7: Sources of recoveries of stolen art: 1991-1995

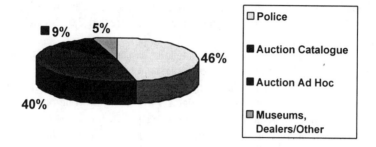

Summary

As the involvement of transnational criminal organizations and the
linkages between the illicit trade in art and other criminal markets grow, the
international community concerned with art theft and loss of cultural property
will face formidable challenges in combating art crime. Combating art theft
must focus on various fronts and requires the cooperation of many actors and
institutions. For the initial steps in the battle against art theft, countries need to
evaluate the perverseness of government corruption, the weakness of their
borders and their domestic regulations on illegal exportation of art objects and
repatriation of such objects to their country of origin. The art community,
primarily museums, auction houses and dealers, should increase security
systems, address connivance and cooperate more thoroughly with law
enforcement agencies. Law enforcement agencies need to look beyond the
traditional methods of enforcement and address the corruption within their own
agencies and governments. Whatever actions are undertaken, all actors
concerned with the illicit art trade must understand its new dynamics and the
proliferation of transnational criminal organizations which are increasingly
coming to dominate the trade.

The data on transnational criminal organizations' involvement in art and
antiquities smuggling points to large unresolved issues. Further research and
better data is needed to gain a better understanding of the transnational criminal
organizations involved. Which networks are currently involved and do these
networks cooperate with each other? What is the extent of their connection to
the licit aspect of the art world? How strong are the links to other criminal
markets?

One fact remains constant and will continue to conceivably affect art and
antiquities in the future. The international environment provides a plethora of
opportunities for the illicit art trade. Demand for antiquities and other art
objects increasingly dwarfs the licit supply, raising prices on art to arguably
obscene amounts and providing ample motives for all participants to maintain

and expand their involvement. Porous borders, weaker states, economically distressed regions and greater international interdependence facilitate the trafficking. Most significant however, is the proliferation of transnational networks globally and their international presence stimulates and facilitates numerous criminal endeavors. These organizations, with their resources, connections and ability to evade law enforcement agencies, will continue to control the illicit art trade and will permeate the licit art world. The art community, law enforcement agencies and governments, however, must look inward and not simply blame outside forces. To successfully fight art and antiquities theft and smuggling, corruption and connivance must be eliminated from the licit realm.

Lauren L. Bernick, University of Pittsburgh, Ridgway Center for International Security Studies, recently completed her first year of law school at the University of Pittsburgh School of Law. She will study Chinese law in Beijing, China this summer and will subsequently work in a small law firm in Michigan.

Ms. Bernick received a Bachelor of Arts in International Relations with a focus on U.S. foreign policy from Mount Holyoke College in 1994 and completed a Masters in Public and International Affairs from the Graduate School of Public and International Affairs at the University of Pittsburgh in 1997. While pursuing her degree in international affairs and a certificate in international security studies, Ms. Bernick interned for the U.S. Department of State in the U.S. mission to the Organization of Economic Cooperation and Development under the auspices of the American Embassy in Paris. Most recently, she completed an independent study on foreign direct investment in the ASEAN-5 countries. As a student of Dr. Williams, Ms. Bernick contributed to the formation of a web-site on Transnational Organized Crime and interned at the Ridgway Center for International Security Studies. This article developed from an independent study under the supervision of Dr. Williams. Ms. Bernick thanks Dr. Williams for all of his input, advice and patience and takes full responsibility for any shortcomings in the article.

Notes and References

[1] Conklin, John E. *Art Crime,* (Westport, Connecticut: Praeger), 1994, p. 48.

[2] Conklin, John E. *Art Crime,* p. 48.

[3] Conklin, John E. *Art Crime,* p. 87.

[4] *Art Intelligence,* Fall 1993 Issue, p. 1. This is a quarterly newsletter published by Robert E. Spiel Associate, Inc.

[5] Conklin, John E. *Art Crime,* p. 219.

[6] Akinsha, Konstantin and Kozlov, Grigorii. *Beautiful Loot: The Soviet Plunder of Europe's Art Treasures.* (New York: Random House), 1995, p. 1.

[7] Beeston, Richard. 'Yeltsin shrugs off Duma to give Kohl looted work of art'. Museum Security Network, April 16, 1997, p. 13. According to the article, the disputed works include French Impressionism masterpieces and the Schliemann collection of gold artifacts from ancient Troy. Museum Security Network is an internet website, located at: http://www.xs4all.nl/~securma/artcrime6.html#4

[8] Conklin, John E. *Art Crime,* p. 224.

[9] Middlemas, Keith. *The Double Market: Art Theft and Art Thieves.* (Hampshire, England: Saxon House), 1975, p. 207.

[10] Conklin, John E. *Art Crime,* p. 224.

[11] Conklin, John E. *Art Crime,* p. 217.

[12] United Press International, March 4, 1997. Posted on page 4 of the Museum Security Network artcrime site.

[13] Conklin, John E. *Art Crime,* p. 185.

[14] Rose, Mark and Acar, Ozgen. 'Turkey's War in the Illicit Antiquities Trade'. *Archeology,* March/April, 1995, p. 45.

[15] Reuter, February 26, 1997. 'Iraq Battles Against Archaeological Theft'. Cited from the Museum Security Network art crime site, p. 6.

[16] *Art Intelligence,* Spring 1995 Issue, p. 1.

[17] Middlemas, Keith. *The Double Market: Art Theft and Art Thieves,* p. 81.

[18] *Reuters,* February 26, 1997. 'Iraq Battles Against Archaeological Theft', p. 6.

[19] Stille, Alexander. 'Art Thieves Bleed Italy of Its Heritage'. *The New York Times,* August 2, 1992, p. H27.

[20] Stille, Alexander. 'Art Thieves Bleed Italy of Its Heritage', p. H27.

[21] Conklin, John E. *Art Crime,* p. 208.

[22] WuDunn, Sheryl. 'China is Fighting for Its Soul: Its Looted Antiques'. *The New York Times,* Tuesday, December 8, 1992, p. 18.

[23] Murphy, J. David. 'Stealing China's Past: The People's Republic Reports a Hemorrhage of Artifacts'. *Archeology,* November/December, 1995, p. 69.

[24] Conklin, John E. *Art Crime,* p. 228.

[25] Conklin, John E. *Art Crime,* p. 209.

[26] Museum Security Network. Russia Police: Art Smuggling Grows, Thursday, 17 April, 1997, p. 10 on the art crime website.

[27] Conklin, John E. *Art Crime,* p. 191.

[28] Suro, Robert. 'Going Undercover for Art's Sake'. *The New York Times Magazine,* December, 1987, p. 50.

[29] Data was compiled from a variety of sources cited in this article.

[30] Conklin, John E. *Art Crime,* p. 208.

[31] *Art Intelligence,* Winter 1993-1994 Issue, p. 2.

32 Stille, Alexander. 'Art Thieves Bleed Italy of Its Heritage', p. H27.
33 Harlow, John and Leake, Jonathon. 'Foreign gangs raid 'soft touch' British Museum', Museum Security Network, April 27, 1997, p. 4.
34 Conklin, John E. *Art Crime*, p. 177.
35 Conklin, John E. *Art Crime*, p. 181.
36 Conklin, John E. *Art Crime*, p. 204.
37 Conklin, John E. *Art Crime*, p. 205.
38 Conklin, John E. *Art Crime*, p. 208.
39 Conklin, John E. *Art Crime*, p. 202.
40 Conklin, John E. *Art Crime*, p. 102-103.
41 Conklin, John E. *Art Crime*, p. 13
42 Boyd, Alan. 'The Raiders of Angkor Wat'. *World Press Review*, November 1994, v41, n11, p. 48.
43 Conklin, John E. *Art Crime*, p. 196.
44 *Art Intelligence*, Fall 1996, p. 1.
45 Walsh, James. 'It's a Steal', p. 88.
46 Conklin, John E. *Art Crime*, p. 184.
47 Walsh, James. 'It's a Steal'. *Time*, November 25, 1991, v. 138, issue 21, p. 86.
48 Conklin, John E. *Art Crime*, p. 184.
49 *IFARreports*, 'DEA Operation Nets 3 Pictures', December 1995, p. 7.
50 *Art Intelligence*, Summer 1994 Issue, p. 2.
51 Conklin, John E. *Art Crime*, p. 91.
52 Conklin, John E. *Art Crime*, p. 215.
53 *IFARreports*, 'DEA Operation Nets 3 Pictures', December 1995, p. 6.
54 Doxey, John. 'Stemming the Flow - Turkey's Fight Against the Illegal Importation of Its Antiquities'. *The Middle East*, July-August 1996, n. 258, p. 35.
55 WuDunn, Sheryl. 'China is Fighting for Its Soul: Its Looted Antiquities', p. A6.
56 Blumenthal, Ralph. 'Museums Getting Together to Track Stolen Art: *The New York Times*, Tuesday, July 1996, p. C13/
57 Conklin, John E. *Art Crime*, p. 188.
58 *The Warsaw Voice* - Crime, September 24, 1995, no. 39, p. 1.
59 *The Associated Press*, 'Bulgaria an El Dorado for Treasure Smugglers'.
60 Conklin, John E. *Art Crime*, p. 205.
61 Conklin, John E. *Art Crime*, p. 208.
62 Conklin, John E. *Art Crime*, p. 211.
63 *Art Intelligence*, Fall 1996, p. 1.
64 Conklin, John E. *Art Crime*, p. 159.
65 Boyd, Alan. 'The Raiders of Angkor Wat', p. 48.
66 Conklin, John E. *Art Crime*, p. 215.
67 Mbachu, Dulue. 'Museum thieves steal Nigeria's heritage'. Reuter News Service, cited from the Museum Security Network Artcrime website, June 22, 1997, p. 12. Younge, Gary. 'Stealing beauty from Africa'. The Museum Security Network Artcrime website, May 23, 1997, p. 10.
68 Mbachu, Dulue. 'Museum thieves steal Nigeria's heritage'. Reuter News Service, cited from the Museum Security Network Artcrime website, June 22, 1997, p. 12.
69 Barnes, Lindsay. 'Thieves rob South Africa of its cultural heritage'. Distributed via Africa News Online, cited from the Museum Security Network Artcrime website, May 26, 1997, p. 12.
70 Data compiled from the various articles cited in these endnotes, with the Museum Security Network Artcrime page and the article, 'The Illicit Traffic of Cultural Property

Throughout the World', ICOM, providing the majority of the data. 'The Illicit Traffic of Cultural Property throughout the World' was obtained from the ICOM website at http://www.icom.organization/ICOM/traffic.html, p.1-5.

71 Walsh, James. 'It's a Steal', p. 87.

72 According to Mr. Ianvov, the chief detective of the art and weapons crime unit in St. Petersburg, cited in Possehl, Suzanne. 'Russian Art Objects Vanishing to the West in Smugglers' Bags' *The New York Times*, Wednesday, March 17, 1993, p. 20.

73 'Israeli police probe art theft ring', May 11, 1997, Museum Security Network, p. 12.

74 Mbachu, Dulue. 'Museum thieves steal Nigeria's heritage'. Reuter News Service, cited from the Museum Security Network Artcrime website, June 22, 1997, p. 12.

75 Leary, *The New York Times* , 1988:A8

76 Conklin, John E. *Art Crime*, p. 212.

77 Kirkpatrick, Sidney D. *Lords of Sipan: A Tale of Pre-Inca Tombs, Archeology and Crime*. (New York: William Morrow and Company, Inc.), 1992, p. 75.

78 Kirkpatrick, Sidney D. *Lords of Sipan: A Tale of Pre-Inca Tombs, Archeology and Crime*, p. 75.

79 Conklin, John E. *Art Crime*, p. 213.

80 Conklin, John E. *Art Crime*, p. 214.

81 Conklin, John E. *Art Crime*, p. 213.

82 Rose, Mark and Acar, Ozgen. 'Turkey's War in the Illicit Antiquities Trade', p. 46.

83 Conklin, John E. *Art Crime*, p. 212.

84 Rose, Mark and Acar, Ozgen. 'Turkey's War in the Illicit Antiquities Trade', p. 46.

85 Rose, Mark and Acar, Ozgen. 'Turkey's War in the Illicit Antiquities Trade', p. 52.

86 Conklin, John E. *Art Crime*, p. 209.

87 Rose, Mark and Acar, Ozgen. 'Turkey's War in the Illicit Antiquities Trade', p. 52.

88 Rose, Mark and Acar, Ozgen. 'Turkey's War in the Illicit Antiquities Trade', p. 52.

89 Getty Information Institute Website. 'Protecting Cultural Objects Through International Documentation Standards: Background', p. 1. The site is located at: http://www.gii.getty.edu/gii/pco/part1/part105.htm

90 Conklin, John E. *Art Crime*, p. 276.

91 Stille, Alexander. 'Art Thieves Bleed Italy of Its Heritage', p. H27.

92 Suro, Robert. 'Going Undercover for Art's Sake', p. 50.

93 Getty Information Institute Website. 'Protecting Cultural Objects Through International Documentation Standards: Background', p. 1.

94 Conklin, John E. *Art Crime*, p. 5.

95 Getty Information Institute Website. 'Protecting Cultural Objects Through International Documentation Standards: Background,', p. 1.

96 *The Art Loss Register*, 1995 Review, p. 3.

15 Money Laundering

David Hess, Kenneth Myers,
Michele Gideon, Sal E. Gomez,
and John Daly

Abstract

Money laundering is reviewed in terms of its objectives, methods, instruments, institutions of money laundering and various money laundering opportunities, identifying vulnerable institutions and countries.

Keywords: Money Laundering, La Cosa Nostra, La 'Ndrangheta, Camorra, Sacra Corona Unita

Introduction

According to Margaret S. Beare, vulnerable businesses and financial institutions include: deposit-taking institutions, currency exchange houses, the securities industry, the insurance industry, real estate firms, the incorporation and operation of companies, the gold market/precious gems/jewelry stores, casino operations, the travel industry, the luxury goods industry.[1] As exhaustive as the list is, it is still not complete. But what Ms. Beare's list does demonstrate is that almost nothing is sacred when it comes to the laundering of illicit proceeds.

In order to present the range of opportunities for money laundering, this chapter is divided into four sections, beginning with a brief discussion of the objectives of money laundering. For descriptive purposes, the next two sections will explore the methods, instruments, and institutions of money laundering. The final section addresses the countries in which criminal organizations choose to launder proceeds. These sections develop what is, in effect, a list of money laundering opportunities. It will identify vulnerable institutions and countries. There are considerable incentives for criminal organizations to use these institutions and countries to launder proceeds. Not all opportunities are grasped, however, and one of the most important tasks of the subsequent analysis is to identify which opportunities are exploited and which are not.

Objectives

To help understand the money laundering process, it is important to have a full grasp of the main objectives and the extensive process employed by criminal organizations. Criminal organizations may engage in money laundering to achieve any one or all of the following objectives: concealing the origin of funds, repatriation of profits, and removing money from possible seizure by law enforcement officials. A definition of money laundering, encompassing these objectives, is:

the process whereby proceeds, reasonably believed to have been derived from criminal activity, are transported, transferred, transformed, converted or intermingled with legitimate funds, for the purpose of concealing or disguising the true nature, source, disposition, movement or ownership of those proceeds.[2]

This definition includes the three main phases of money laundering: *placement, layering*, and *integration*. According to the Financial Crimes Enforcement Network's report *Trends in Money Laundering*, the definitions of the three phases of money laundering are as follows:

- *placement:* the physical disposal of the bulk cash profits that are the result of criminal activity.
- *layering:* the piling on of layers of complex financial transactions to separate the proceeds from their illicit sources.
- *integration:* the provision of legitimate-looking explanations for the appearance of wealth by providing investments in the legitimate economy.[3]

Ernesto Savona further enhances the understanding of the money laundering process by distinguishing between its *dimension* and its *cycle*. He argues that the dimension or *"laundering method preferre,"* can be either local, national, or international depending upon the level at which the money laundering activity operates. The cycle is the extent to which the laundering transgresses through the phases of placement, layering, and integration. Progressing through all three would be considered a full cycle.[4] Criminal organizations employ a number of different methods, mechanisms and instruments in order to achieve the objectives of money laundering.[5] The method, instruments and mechanisms of money laundering are the subjects of the following two sections.

Methods and Instruments

A money laundering *method* is the actual technique for laundering money. The *instruments* the criminal organizations choose to employ in money laundering vary including hard currency, insurance policies, electronic money transfers, and precious materials.[6]

- *Electronic Funds Transfers:* Usually, there are no requirements for bank-to-bank transfers. It is therefore possible for a bank outside the United States to transfer funds to a U.S. bank and then draw upon those funds by check or credit. Consequently, the electronic transfer is a ready instrument for laundering. The usual scheme involves depositing illicit funds into one bank and then transferring these funds to another, via many other countries. Only top bank personnel are able to avoid the bank's internal control mechanisms. Therefore, the use of professionals is still needed to launder money through the more traditional electronic funds transfer system.

- *Cyberbanking:* Cyberbanking provides more opportunity for criminal organizations to enter the international financial system. As of now, "smart cards" can be filled in person or by phone with an unlimited amount of cash. They can be used as a money-laundering instrument due to their complete anonymity for making small or large purchases. Since there is no registration of every transaction, such as in credit card transactions, tracing the money will be virtually impossible. The use of smart cards will make currency smuggling easier by eliminating the bulkiness of the transport. Banking over the Internet is already creating more money laundering methods for criminals and greater challenges for law enforcement officials. Previously, money-launderers relied upon professional money brokers. Now, however, it is possible to make a number of financial transactions from your personal computer, without the interference of a professional.

- *Bulk Transfers:* Although there are new and innovative ways to launder money, the more traditional method of bulk transfers still serves the objectives of criminal organizations, most notably, repatriation of illicit funds. Covertly smuggling large amounts of cash across borders seems to be regaining its popularity as a result of the strong anti-money laundering measures enacted in many nations and financial institutions. Criminal organizations have matured their methods of currency smuggling by *"purchasing businesses engaged in the shipment of goods and hiding 'dirty money' inside the product."*[7] More traditional methods, which are still in use, include physically moving money across borders or smuggling the currency by cargo, by air, by sea, or by land. Money has even been smuggled out of the United States through the U.S. Postal Service.[8] It is also shipped inside such items as refrigerators, televisions, and dishwashers.

- *Bank infiltration:* Criminal organizations infiltrate banks so they may have control over the business in which the banks engage. Only top bank employees are capable of getting around regulations, therefore infiltration may be easier and more efficient than trusting a professional banker. Usually, bank infiltration is accomplished by the appointment of organized criminals to the bank's board of directors or through the purchase of stock.

- *Prime Bank Guarantees:* This laundering method involves the issuance of uncovered guarantees, serving as the instrument, which move in the place of the "dirty money."

Institutions

In addition to the methods and instruments identified above, it is necessary to identify the institutions through which money is laundered. Ernesto Savona has labeled these institutions mechanisms, a term that encompasses financial and non-financial institutions.

The Financial Sector

There are several methods for money laundering with banks and financial institutions serving as mechanisms. They include:

- *Banks:* Many money laundering activities occur in banks. Banks and bank personnel may accept illicit funds as legitimate deposits, facilitate electronic transfers serving to clean money and accept small deposits that will not attract regulatory attention. These are just a few methods of money laundering which take place in banks.
- *Safe Havens*: Organized criminals deposit their drug profits in countries where there are no reporting laws or lax regulation. The Caymans Islands, Aruba, Austria[9] and Uruguay[10] are some of the Mafia's favorite safe havens. Offshore banking institutions "offer attractive opportunities for the transfer and secretion of funds in places where they are relatively safe from identification and seizure by law enforcement."[11]
- *Brokerage Firms*: Organizations may also launder money through purchasing legitimate stocks and bonds or by entering the foreign currency market. The nature of the securities industry makes it vulnerable to money-launderers. It is international in nature, business is conducted by electronic transfer, and the liquidity of securities is extremely attractive to money-launderers. Many times, the brokers will disregard the source of capital because they normally work on commission in a highly competitive market. They sometimes become knowing participants in the scheme, usually charging exorbitant fees. Another incentive to launder through the securities market is that it is very easy to layer funds. Transactions take place nearly instantaneously and a series of transactions is not unusual. Hence determining the licit from illicit transactions in the securities sector has posed great difficulty for law enforcement officials.[12]

The Non-Financial Sector

Businesses and industries are also used as mechanisms to launder money. They include:

- *Front Companies:* Criminal organizations create front and shell companies and they exploit vulnerable industries.

However, at this point, it is important to distinguish between knowledgeable and unknowledgeable participants. Front companies are set up by criminal organizations with or without the knowledge of the company. Knowing front companies include those that are set up by the criminal organizations themselves, or that receive a payment for their services. For example, phony export or import companies are frequently used as a cover for the transfer of funds. An alternative includes legitimate firms over- and under-invoicing merchandise, which is shipped out of the country and resold. Criminal organizations also buy certain companies because their products may be constructed to smuggle large amounts of cash internationally. A New Jersey firm, Reno International, produced fiberglass rolls with compartments that could hold up to $700,000.[13] Restaurants provide opportunities to launder money due to the leeway given in providing a service at self-determined prices. There are many more examples of front companies which are not covered in this section.

- *Casinos:* Although it is acknowledged that casinos are a prime target for money-launderers due to their lack of regulations, the large cash flows and the currency exchange, many in the business contend that they are not a primary means of laundering money. However, because of their cash base, they do offer considerable opportunities.
- *The tourist industry:* Organized crime groups launder money through investing in hotels and tourist complexes. Countries rarely turn down investment funds and often do not subject the origin of these funds to any serious scrutiny.[14]
- *Insurance companies:* The insurance industry is extremely vulnerable to money-launderers. Organized criminals pay cash to independent insurance brokers, who are not responsible for reporting suspicious activity. The insurance companies are responsible for reporting the suspicious activity, but are still under-regulated. Criminals buy single premium insurance bonds and then cash the policy at a discount. The huge penalties are not relevant to the launderer because a large portion of the initial purchase is returned as a legitimate check from an insurance company.[15]
- *Real Estate Industry:* Investment in real estate still remains a prominent money laundering technique. Criminal organizations invest in real estate with the expectation that structural improvements on existing buildings will be made or new structures will be built. If the work is actually undertaken, it rarely costs the reported amount.

- *Joint Ventures:* Criminal organizations target failing businesses and currency poor countries in which to invest. For these businesses and countries, the infusion of cash is essential--so few questions are asked.
- *Bureaux de change*: These facilities are not as regulated as banks and exchange large volumes of currency each day, including U.S. dollars. They therefore provide ample opportunity for criminal organizations to launder proceeds.

Opportunities:

Criminal organizations have a number of venues through which "dirty money" can be laundered. However, there are a few incentives which make one country more attractive than another to a possible launderer and make the country vulnerable to money laundering. They are:

- *Anti-Money Laundering Legislation.* The opportunity for money laundering depends upon a country's anti-money laundering legislation or lack thereof. Many countries do not have any money laundering legislation. In those countries, for all intents and purposes, laundering of illicit funds is completely legal. Other countries have money-laundering legislation but lack the resources or the will to enforce the legislation.
- *Reporting Requirements: Lack* of reporting laws provides an incentive for laundering. If the government does not require banks and other financial or non-financial institutions to report suspicious activity, the risk of detection decreases.
- *Bank Secrecy Practices:* Another incentive is if, and to what degree, bank secrecy practices are adhered to. Bank secrecy laws promote the activity of money laundering because they ensure that the identity of the customer will not be revealed.
- *Currency Controls:* Currency controls are another indicator of a country's vulnerability to money laundering. Lack of control signals that the government is not monitoring the amount of money being exchanged which lessens the risk of detection.
- *Extradition Laws: Another* incentive provided by countries is the lack of extradition laws. Without extradition laws, criminals are provided a safe haven which they can avoid prosecution in other countries.

In summary, criminal organizations have a number of low-risk opportunities to launder money in certain countries. The following table and descriptive list provide an overview of the scope of geographical locations, which are attractive to potential money-launderers.

Table 15.1: Geographical locations potentially attractive to money-launderers

Country	No money laundering legislation	No Reporting requirements	No Currency Controls	Bank Secrecy Protection
Austria				X
Cyprus				X
Luxembourg			X	
Switzerland			X	X
Turkey		X	X	
Argentina	X	X		
Brazil	X			X
Uruguay	X		X	X
Antigua				X
Aruba				X
Cayman Islands				X
Canada		X	X	
Hong Kong			X	
Thailand	X	X	X	X

Western Europe

As a result of the breaking down of borders in Western Europe, organized crime groups have been able to take advantage of the lack of coordination of controls. While the organized criminals have been freed of borders, law enforcement officials are still encountering informational and legal barriers. As the European Community struggles to establish common regulations, links have been forged between the Italian Mafiosi, Colombian drug cartels and criminal groups from Eastern Europe and Russia.[16]

- *Italy:* Although Italy has the proper regulations and legislation in place, money laundering still occurs through the financial and non-financial sectors. Due to the prominence of the Italian Mafiosi, the banking system in Italy is especially vulnerable to infiltration. The Mafiosi have been known to appoint members to the boards of banks, thus controlling the banks' activities.

- *Germany:* It has been reported that over $50 million was laundered through German banks after it was transferred from Moscow to Cobourg and then to Milan.[17] This has been discovered during the 1996 law enforcement investigation into money laundering, code-name "*cheque to cheque.*" Although the banking system is regulated, regulations are circumvented by bankers and participating in the schemes. Germany lacks currency controls, which has attracted currency smuggling across its borders.

- *Great Britain:* As a major financial system, the British banking system is vulnerable to money laundering activities. Due to the numerous financial transactions and the speed in which they are conducted, advanced financial systems are attractive to money-launderers because they present a forum for easy layering of funds. There is concern that the Russian Mafia activity has increased its activity in the United Kingdom, especially through the financial institutions and front companies.[18]

- *Austria:* Bank secrecy laws remain the most adhered to in Europe, even surpassing Switzerland. Austria has become an offshore banking center in the heart of Europe. Chinese and Turkish "criminal gangs" also deposit money in the Austrian banking system.[19]

- *France:* Although the French have some of the toughest anti-money laundering legislation, including asset seizure laws, France is still a venue for money laundering, mostly through real estate investment and investment in the tourist industry. The French Riviera has been a popular real estate investment front for money-launderers. Illicit proceeds enter the French banking system through its elaborate branch system throughout the French Caribbean.

- *Switzerland:* Switzerland is known for its discreet banking practices. Therefore, it has traditionally been a safe haven for criminal proceeds. Switzerland also lacks controls on the amount of currency that may be brought into or out of the country. This combination has kept Switzerland a prime target for money-launderers, despite the government's effort to curb the activity.

- *Luxembourg:* Luxembourg is a major banking system and is reportedly used more for layering and integration rather than being the initial point of entry for illicit funds. Banking secrecy is not as strictly adhered to as in other countries, but there are no exchange controls.[20]

- *Turkey:* Money laundering was completely legal in Turkey until November 1996. Anti-money laundering legislation was passed, but the regulations for implementation of the new law have not yet been developed. Therefore, money laundering in Turkey still remains as an international concern. To further encourage this activity, Turkey has no controls on currency, generous reporting laws and no laws regulating the non-financial institutions. It therefore provides the greatest opportunities for potential money-launderers.

- *Cyprus:* Although Cyprus has strong bank regulations and

reporting laws, Cyprus continues to be a venue for money laundering. The activity mostly takes place in the offshore companies and banks. The INCSR voices concern that money is transferred for branch banks back to the host banks located in Turkey.[21]

Latin America

Historically, Latin American countries have been attractive to organized crime groups. Easy access to the Caribbean makes it convenient for money-launderers. Many Latin American countries have lax extradition laws which provide money-launderers safe havens from prosecution in other countries. Furthermore, the weak financial systems starving for capital do nothing to dissuade potential money-launderers.

- *Mexico:* Mexico's proximity to the United States makes it an attractive venue for money laundering. Mexico passed anti-money laundering legislation in May 1996, but it is unclear whether or not the legislation will actually be implemented. Both the financial and non-financial systems are utilized to clean money in Mexico. The INCSR states, "Mexico has become the money laundering haven of choice for initial placement of U.S. drug cash into the world's financial system."[22] Furthermore, an official of the Mexican Government has voiced concerns that their banks are being used as laundering centers via the Internet. "Internet is already a route for unlimited, unobstructed transactions in which the banks will be mere intermediaries."[23]
- *Colombia:* Due to the prominence of the Colombian drug cartels, Colombia is an obvious location for money laundering. The lack of bank regulations further encourages money-laundering activities.
- *Venezuela:* As a neighboring country of Colombia, drug cartels look to Venezuela for money laundering services. Although Venezuela's financial system is quite advanced, most money laundering takes place in the non-financial sector: exchange houses, casinos, and real estate.[24]
- *Argentina:* Money laundering is only considered illegal in Argentina when the activity is directly linked to drugs. Although general anti-money laundering legislation and reporting requirements are under consideration, Argentina has instituted no such measures and the officials lack the resources, both political and financial, to combat the activity.[25]
- *Brazil:* Money laundering is legal in Brazil. Organized crime groups own more than 200 Brazilian businesses through which "dirty money" is laundered. These knowing and

unknowing front companies include: bakeries, construction companies, motels, transportation companies (including air-taxi and freight) and insurance companies. The criminal organizations buy the fiscally weak companies to provide a filter through which a large amount of dirty capital flows and is subsequently legitimized.[26]

- *Panama:* Panama provides ample opportunity for money laundering activities. Currency smuggling and front companies are the most common forms of money laundering in Panama, encouraged by the tax-free zone.
- *Costa Rica:* Criminal organizations are investing in the tourist industry and real estate. The Costa Rican banking system was recently liberalized which promotes money laundering through financial institutions.[27]
- *Nicaragua:* Although the United States government has placed no priority on Nicaragua as a money laundering center, it has been reported that there is wide-spread money laundering activity in the country. Casinos, banks and trading companies are the mechanisms employed to launder illicit funds.[28]
- *Uruguay:* Money Laundering is legal in Uruguay. There are no regulations controlling the flow of currency. Bank secrecy can only be broken with a court order, an option which is rarely taken.

The Caribbean

The Caribbean has been known for its offshore banks, which are not regulated.

- *Aruba:* The International Narcotics Control Strategy Report of March 1996 (INCSR) has ranked Aruba in the "high priority" category which reflects the amount of money laundering activity the U.S. government believes to take place in Aruba. Although Aruba has all of the necessary anti-money laundering legislation in place and bank reporting requirements, money laundering is prevalent. Since Aruba has many casinos, resorts and offshore banking facilities, it is believed that the government lacks the will to enforce the existing legislation.[29]
- *Cayman Islands:* The Cayman Islands remain one of the leading offshore banking centers in the world. There are no reporting laws and bank secrecy is strictly adhered to. Another incentive which the Cayman Islands provides to money-launderers is the number of shell companies and the ease in which they can be created. The INCSR estimates over 26,000 in existence, none of which can be appropriately

monitored due to lack of government resources.[30]

- *Antigua:* Antigua has a number of offshore banking institutions, which adhere to stringent banking secrecy practices. Antigua also provides ample opportunity for money laundering through its extensive casino industry.

Canada

Canada has been ranked as a "high priority" country in the INCSR. Canada lacks stringent legislation to "monitor currency and monetary transactions"[31] and has no mandatory reporting laws. Organized criminals, take advantage of the lack of controls which has led Canada to be another money laundering center. The main arteries for laundering illicit proceeds in Canada are banks and currency exchange houses. The proximity of Canada to the United States also provides incentives to smuggle currency across the border.

Russia

As a state in transition, Russia faces uncertain times with hardly any controls on capital movement, an under-developed financial market with little regulation, and law enforcement that lacks either the capability or the will to appropriately handle the growing organized crime problem. "Police forces, lacking sufficient training and modern technology, have been no match for these increasingly sophisticated and violent networks. Many cops, demoralized by their meager pay and loss of prestige, succumb to corruption."[32] Therefore, Russia is an attractive market for money laundering and other criminal activities. Anti-money laundering legislation came into effect in September 1996, but it is not yet clear as to whether or not it will be enforced. Infiltration of banking institutions is also a serious problem in Russia. Out of 1800 banking institutions, the Mafia controls 700.[33]

Central & Eastern Europe:

Organized crime groups are taking advantage of states in transition. Russian and Italian crime groups have been "taking advantage of the political and economic transition in central and eastern Europe to establish new bases for money laundering and for transnational criminal activities like drugs, arms, and alien smuggling."[34] Such countries include:

- *Hungary:* There is a danger that Hungary may become a center for money laundering. It is an economy in transition, and is therefore vulnerable to criminal infiltration. There is "lax regulation on banking, gambling, insurance, and free trade of hard currency."[35]
- *Czech Republic:* Many organized crime groups have been competing for influence in the Czech Republic. Criminal organizations are attracted to this currency-starved country and have invested in joint ventures in the Czech Republic.

Nigeria

With the growth and dissemination of Nigerian organized crime, Nigeria has become an active area for money laundering, even though its financial system is not yet fully developed. Imports illegally bought abroad are sold in Nigeria or neighboring countries. The Nigerians then place the money into the Nigerian financial system.[36]

Asia

Extreme financial development and economic growth coupled with the proximity of drug production centers has made Asia vulnerable to money laundering. There are a few extreme cases that promote money laundering through their financial systems. For instance:

- Thailand: Thailand is one of the most attractive venues for money laundering in Asia. Thailand has one of the fastest growing economic systems. It also has an offshore banking system to accommodate foreign investment in the region. Money laundering is completely legal in Thailand. Furthermore, there are no reporting laws, strong adherence to bank secrecy practices, no control over the flow of currency, and no legislation controlling non-financial institutions.[37] With this combination of money laundering incentives, Thailand is very attractive for money laundering.
- Singapore: Singapore has been ranked a "high priority" country by the International Narcotics Control Strategy Report due to the strength of the financial system and the size of its foreign exchange market.[38]
- Hong Kong: Since Hong Kong has one of the most advanced international financial systems and is located near drug producing countries in Asia, it is an obvious target for money-launderers. Hong Kong lacks both currency controls and controls on non-financial institutions. Therefore, bureau de exchange houses are the most popular method of money laundering.[39]

Banks and governments, by failing to provide ample legislation and reporting practices, provide ample opportunities for money laundering. Criminal organizations may take advantage of these opportunities through employing one or a combination of money laundering methods and instruments, such as electronic transfers or currency exchange. The preceding sections provided an overview of the methods, institutions and opportunities money launders have available to them. The following four sections will outline the organization and activities of the four Italian Mafiosi, thereby making it possible to determine which of the available opportunities have been grasped and which have not.

The Neapolitan Camorra

Introduction

The Neapolitan Camorra has been an influential part of Italy's history since the sixteenth century. Throughout the four centuries of its existence, the Camorra has been one of the leading organized crime families in Italy. In the early 1990s many scholars and experts on organized crime considered the Camorra the strongest and most influential crime family in Italy. Today, the Camorra has lost power relative to the Sicilian Mafia, the 'Ndrangheta, and the Sacra Corona Unita. Fighting between clans and penitents or "turncoats" have greatly affected the Camorra's overall power. The reports of the Camorra's ultimate demise may be premature since it continues to play an active role domestically and internationally.

History

The Camorra, also known as the Neapolitan Mafia, the Naples Mafia, the Neapolitan Camorra, and the Campagnia Mafia, is the oldest of the Italian organized crime groups. It was established during the first Spanish reign of Naples and Sicily from 1504 to 1707. The original Camorra organization "was a mix of invading Spaniards and Neapolitans, and it was based on rules and codes of an earlier Spanish criminal society called the 'Garduna.' "[40]

The Camorra actually gave rise to the Sicilian Mafia during the second Spanish invasion from 1738 to 1860. Although the Sicilian Mafia grew into the most powerful criminal organization in Italy and the world, the Camorra was the most powerful criminal organization in Italy for most of the 18th and 19th centuries.[41]

The Camorra has experienced a turbulent history. More specifically, the membership and strength of this organization has fluctuated greatly. In certain periods it has had a large membership and has exerted great influence within Naples and Italy, while at other times its membership has been quite small and the Camorra has exerted little power within Naples or Italy.

Although its power, influence, and membership has historically fluctuated and although there are several smaller organized crime groups operating out of Naples, the Camorra is considered by many to be "the queen of Neapolitan organized crime."[42]

Composition

Organizational Structure

- Fragmented and widespread
- Number of different gangs, clans or families within Camorra
- The Camorra has a horizontal organizational structure. More specifically, there is not a hierarchical structure. According to Judge Giuseppe de Gennaro, the "Neapolitan Mafia has a 'fragmented' and widespread structure, made up of a number of gangs which easily band together and then split up, sometimes peacefully, but more often after bloody wars."[43]

Leadership
  - No overarching hierarchy for Camorra.
  - No recognized leader for the entire Camorra.
  - Groups, clans and families within Camorra have their own leadership.
  - Leaders within clans are extremely young.

Although the Camorra does not have one ultimate leader, the respective clans that make up the Camorra have their own leaders and leadership structure. Within the Camorra the most influential families or clans are the Alfieri family, the Contini family, the Casalesi clan, and the Autiero clan.

Thus, the Neapolitan Camorra is not based on a hierarchy but a loose confederation of families, clans, or gangs. The Camorra clans are very individualistic and very independent and only come together when the situation merits it.[44] This organizational structure has definite ramifications for the operations and influence of the Camorra. Because of this structure, the Camorra does not have an overarching leader or boss -- a "boss of bosses." This particular organizational style has "so far prevented the Camorra from having influential and recognized leaders."[45]

Strength
  - Families/Clans/Groups (Not comprehensive)
  - Alfieri Family
  - Contini Family
  - Casalesi Clan
  - Autiero Clan
  - Frattamaggiore Clan
  - Sant Animo
  - 6,700 members

There are many clans within the Camorra organization. In fact, there are 111 clans or families consisting of approximately 6,700 members. The number of members and groups within the Camorra has increased since 1993. In 1993 the Camorra had approximately 107 clans and nearly 6,000 members while in 1996, only three years later, the Camorra has approximately 111 clans and 6,700 members.[46]

Aside from the actual members of the Camorra, there are several thousands associates of the Camorra crime group. In particular, in 1993, the Camorra had approximately "1,000 flankers and 50,000-60,000 people directly involved."[47] The meaning of the term "flankers" is not defined. Referring to the context in which this term was used, flankers probably refers to those individuals who work indirectly for the Camorra.

Disposition
    The Camorra's base of operations is in the Campagnia region of Naples, Italy. Aside from its base of operations within Italy, the Camorra has a transnational, global presence. It has operations in Russia, Central and South

America, the United States, Canada, and Europe. In addition, there is a strong possibility that the Camorra has operations in Africa and Asia.

Areas of Influence
Italy

The Camorra's main base of operations is within Italy. In particular, the Camorra is based in the Campagnia region of Naples, Italy. Within Campagnia, the Camorra has shown an adroit ability to corrupt public officials. Campagnia has the highest number of administrators removed from office -- a total of 64 -- for committing acts contrary to the Constitution. In fact, the corruption in Campagnia has become endemic; "32 town councils out of 75 have been dissolved because of Mafia influence."[48] The problem of corruption has not been restricted to Campagnia's political sector. Campagnia also has the highest number of magistrates under criminal investigation for corruption. In the final analysis, the ability of the Camorra to influence the political and economic sectors "flashes an all-out warning signal."[49]

The Camorra is also entrenched in many areas throughout the Italian peninsula. In particular, the Camorra has extensively corrupted public officials in Molise and the Marches. These two Italian cities serve as the Camorra's center for the illegal traffic of arms, drugs, and even nuclear material. In addition, the Camorra has infiltrated Valdarno and Figline. The specific operations in these two areas have not been identified, but Italian officials have confirmed that Camorra clans are operating in both of these areas.[50]

In addition to the previously mentioned areas, the Camorra has also "plundered businesses and real estate enterprises in Turin, in Piedmont, and even in Val d'Aosta... [it] is also making incursions into the Bologna suburbs and the industrial enclave of Modena, Reggio, Emilia, Carpi, Sassuolo, and Faenza..."[51]

Thus, the Camorra has certainly been an influential organization within the Italian borders. The Camorra's influence and operations, however, also span the globe. These operations are discussed below.

Foreign/International Areas of Influence

- Spain   Drug Trafficking
- Czech Republic   Drug/Arms/Nuclear Materials
                              Trafficking, Money Laundering
- Germany   Drug Trafficking
- France   Drug trafficking, Money Laundering
- Belgium   Drug Trafficking
- Austria   Money Laundering
- Former Yugoslavia   Arms trafficking
- Romania   Drug/Arm/Automobile Trafficking
- The Netherlands   Drug Trafficking

Spain
    The Camorra has extensive bases of operation in Europe.   These operations ostensibly include drug trafficking, weapons or arms trafficking, nuclear materials smuggling, and the laundering of illicit funds. Within Spain, the Camorra is reported to have a base of operations for the transport of drugs -- primarily cocaine -- from Colombia.[52] Thus, the Camorra has allied with the Colombian cartels -- the Cali Cartel, in particular -- to transport drugs to the European continent.

Germany
    The Camorra's drug trafficking links to Europe are also evident in Germany. As in Spain, the Camorra is reported to have a base of operations in Germany. Within Germany the Camorra has operational links with German organized crime elements, primarily for the transport of illicit drugs.[53] Other than working with German organized crime groups, the Camorra is reported to be running a drug distribution network in conjunction with the Russian Mafia and the Chinese Mafia.[54]
    In addition to the Camorra presence in Germany the other Italian organized crime groups, primarily the Sicilian Mafia and the 'Ndrangheta, and the Russian Mafia have bases of operations in Germany. There may be a strategic alliance between the other Italian organized crime groups and the Russian Mafia in Germany.

France
    France has not been immune to the penetration of the Camorra. In France, the Camorra is involved in drug and money laundering operations. According to Liliana Ferraro, Italian Director of Criminal Affairs, "[m]afiosi -- mostly from the Camorra group -- have taken refuge [in] a number of regions [in France]."[55] In France, especially on the Cote d'Azur, the Camorra is making major property/real estate and capital investments to serve as money laundering fronts.

Belgium and The Netherlands
    In Belgium and the Netherlands the Camorra is involved in the trafficking of cocaine. In these two regions the influence of the Italian Mafiosi, including the Camorra, is not as influential as the Chinese organized crime triads, like the 14K, Tai Huen Chai, and Ah Kong. Nevertheless, Belgium and the Netherlands are additional bases of operations for the Camorra and the other Italian organized crime groups.

Czech Republic and Former Yugoslavia
    The Camorra is also operating in the Czech Republic and the Former Yugoslavia, primarily in Croatia. Within these two areas, the Camorra is ostensibly involved in arms trafficking, drug trafficking, nuclear materials smuggling, and money laundering operations. In the Czech Republic the

Camorra is principally involved in the dealing of drugs, arms, and nuclear materials.[56] In addition, the Camorra has established an alliance with some Russian crime groups. More specifically, the "Italian and Russian Mafiosi set up a joint venture in Prague, with the Italians providing the brains (specialists in laundering drugs money) and the Russians providing the muscles (Afghanistan veterans as killers)."[57]

Romania

The Camorra has also penetrated this former Warsaw Pact country. In Romania, it is suspected that the Camorra is primarily involved in drug, arms, and automobile trafficking.[58] The Camorra is most likely pursuing these operations with the assistance of Russian organized crime groups.

Austria

The Italian organized crime groups almost certainly use Austria as a base of operations for their money laundering operations. Although no specific sources have been uncovered that corroborate a definitive link between the Camorra and Austria, it is highly suspected that the Camorra uses Austria to launder a portion of its illicit proceeds.

Latin America
Central America

- Nicaragua-Money Laundering
- Guatemala-Money Laundering

South America
"Golden Diamond"

- Peru-Drug Trafficking
- Colombia-Drug Trafficking, Money Laundering
- Venezuela-Drug Trafficking, Money Laundering
- Brazil-Drug Trafficking, Money Laundering

Like the European continent, the Camorra has operations in Latin America, both South and Central America. The Camorra's operations in South America are discussed first, followed by its operations in Central America.

South America
Colombia and Venezuela

The Camorra has extensive connections with the Colombian Cartels, primarily the Cali Cartel and the Venezuela drug organizations. The Camorra's drug operations with these two countries were established in the late 1980s by Umberto Ammaturo, a boss of one of the Neapolitan Camorra clans, who was "allegedly responsible for the [Camorra's] connections with the Colombia [n], Peruvian, and Venezuelan drug cartels."[59] Apparently, the Camorra transports drugs produced in Colombia, Venezuela, and the Golden Diamond (Bolivia, Colombian, and Peru), via Brazil, to European consumer countries, including

Spain, France, Germany, Belgium, and the Netherlands.

Brazil

Aside from being used as a transit state for the drugs produced in Colombia, Peru, and Bolivia, Brazil is an important center for the Camorra's money laundering activities. More specifically, the Camorra has used Brazil "to set up [its money laundering] 'businesses.' "[60]

In particular, the Camorra members in Brazil receive drugs from other South American countries and ship them to Europe as part of the "*Spaghetti Connection.*" The Spaghetti Connection is a reference to the Camorra's Brazilian money laundering operation. The Camorra has set up a chain of Italian restaurants in Brazil to launder their drug proceeds. One of the specific Camorra-Brazilian restaurants involved in the Spaghetti Connection is the Baroni-Fasoli Restaurant located on Jangadeiros Street, in the Ipanema district of Brazil.[61]

The Camorra also has connections to two organized crime groups in Brazil, the Jacare Phalange and the Red Company.[62] There is very little information on the Jacare Phalange other than that it is a medium-sized gang involved in drug trafficking. There is more information on the Red Company. The Red Company is a "criminal organization in Rio de Janeiro that is responsible for kidnapping, bank robberies, auto theft, and narcotics trafficking in major Brazilian cities...[which] is believed to have set up improvised labs to refine the [cocaine] paste in some of the shantytowns...in Petropolis and Teresopolis."[63]

Peru

As previously mentioned, the Camorra transports drugs produced in Colombia and Peru via Brazil to the European continent. Consequently, the Camorra has established links with Peruvian drug traffickers. In particular, the Camorra has established relations with the drug gang headed by Reynaldo Rodriguez Lopez, known by the police as "El Pardino" – "The Godfather."[64]

Central America
Nicaragua

Nicaragua is a money-laundering center for the Italian organized crime groups, including the Camorra. The Italian organized crime groups, including the Camorra, are "operating and 'laundering money' in Nicaragua through all sorts of financial institutions and, at least, one gambling house (casino)."[65] In addition, the Italian organized crime groups follow particular economic schemes in Nicaragua, including banking and nonbanking systems, the renting of property with an option to purchase, invoicing, and trade companies.

Guatemala

Guatemala used to be one of the major Central American countries involved in the laundering of illicit funds. This country's operations have been primarily taken over by Nicaragua. However, there is still a strong possibility that the Italian organized crime groups, including the Camorra, are laundering money in Guatemala.[66]

Russia

The Russian Mafia and the Camorra have recently established a cooperative counterfeiting relationship -- an operation linked to the laundering of money. The Camorra apparently has been counterfeiting money primarily for Russia, but many of these counterfeit dollars are penetrating the fragile and unregulated economies of Eastern Europe.

The process of counterfeiting dollars for the Russian mafias is described in the following passage. "A $1 bill is immersed in particular acid and, using sophisticated technologies, is reprinted as a $100 bill... Bills counterfeited in this manner are invading all the Eastern European countries, Russia in first place."[67]

The large-scale availability of these counterfeit dollars in Russia and Eastern Europe creates possibilities that are then exploited "to develop other criminal activities: banking networks for the recycling of 'dirty money'; the purchase of chemical industries intended for the production of synthetic drugs; the purchase of arms and arms factories; the organization of international prostitution and white slavery from Eastern European countries."[68]

The Camorra is also producing counterfeit goods and products on a large-scale basis. Most of these counterfeit goods are making their way to Russia and the Eastern European markets. These goods include "[h]andbags, dresses, fabrics, perfumes, pharmaceutical products, shoes, and detergents." The counterfeiting done for the Russians and East Europeans also includes: "credit instruments, certified checks to bearer, travelers checks, credit cards, postal canceling stamps, manufacturers' certificates, stamps and passports of every nationality."[69]

In exchange for these counterfeit dollars and goods, the Camorra receives "synthetic drugs (which the Russians now produce on a large scale), prostitution including juvenile prostitution, arms, atomic material, everything."[70] The Russian mafia also provides the Camorra with "highly sophisticated technological equipment stolen from Army depots and with heavy and light weapons, radar apparatus, ground-to-air missiles, and uranium."[71]

The United States

The Camorra's operations and influence within the United States do not appear to be as sizable as that of the other Italian mafia groups, particularly the Sicilian Mafia and the 'Ndrangheta. The Camorra, however, does operate small-scale drug trafficking operations in the United States. These operations usually occur with the assistance of the Sicilian Mafia or the 'Ndrangheta or both.

The Camorra's involvement in drug trafficking in the United States was substantiated by Operation Onig -- an operation undertaken by Italian authorities and the United States Federal Bureau of Investigation in 1994. Operation Onig "smashed a drug trafficking operation controlled by a cartel made up of the [Sicilian] Mafia, the 'Ndrangheta [Calabrian Mafia] and the Camorra [Neapolitan Mafia]."

While the Camorra was involved in the trafficking of cocaine to the United States, it appears that the Camorra was and continues to be a relatively minor player in the Italian cocaine trade in America

Areas of Interest

"Areas of Interest" are defined as those regions within Italy or foreign countries that the Camorra has shown interest in establishing operations.
- Italy
  - Continued penetration of Northern Italy
  - Turin

- Foreign Countries/Regions
  - Estonia and the Baltic Countries
  - Asia

Activities
- Money Laundering
- Contraband cigarette trade
- Arms/Weapons Trafficking
- Nuclear Material Trafficking
- Counterfeit money and commercial goods
- Gambling
- Prostitution
- Loan Sharking
- Usury
- European Union Fraud*
- Waste Management*

Most of the above activities of the Camorra have already been mentioned in the "Areas of Influence" section. However, two of these activities have not been explained: European Union fraud and waste management. They are both covered briefly below.

European Union Fraud

The Camorra has been involved in many fraud operations of the European Union. The most notable example, however, is the 1993 Camorra sugar-fraud incident. The Camorra bought 4,000 tons of sugar from two refineries in Rotterdam, destined for Croatia and Slovenia. Once the shipment of sugar entered Yugoslavia, the trucks carrying the sugar changed directions and headed back to Italy. In France, the Camorra removed the customs seals and headed to Northern Italy. Once in Italy, the sugar was sold on the black market at a price between the world and the European Union rates.[72]

Waste Management
The Italian mafia groups, including the Camorra, have recently become involved in waste management. This type of operation involves the use of bribes to win orders for the disposal of waste -- including, in many instances, toxic waste. After winning the contract or order the "waste is either disposed of in Italy itself or in developing and threshold countries 'for considerably lower costs' and in an improper way."[73] The mafias then offer the services of specialized firms that clean up the environmental damage caused by the illegal and improper waste disposal.

Connections
Domestic
- Sicilian Mafia
- 'Ndrangheta
- Politicians and Judges -- Campagnia region

International
South America
- Colombia   -- Drug Cartels (Cali Cartel)
- Peru   -- Drug Traffickers
- Venezuela   -- Drug Trafficking gangs
- Brazil
    Red Company
    Jacare Phalange

Europe
- Spain
    Colombian Cartels (Cali Cartel)

- Germany
    German Organized Crime groups
    Russian mafia
    Chinese mafia

- Czech Republic/Former Yugoslavia
    Russian Organized Crime
    Romania-- Russian Organized Crime
    Austria -- Businessmen

- Russia
    Russian Organized Crime
    Russian bankers/businessmen

Peculiarities
The Camorra, like the other Italian organized crime groups, is involved in

illicit money making operations. Money is the end game for the Camorra. One activity, though, that the Camorra appears quite willing and able to participate in is nuclear materials smuggling. There have been many operations, primarily with the Russian mafiya, that include the transfer of nuclear materials. This component of the Camorra's operations offers interesting and frightening policy implications.

The Camorra is also highly involved in corrupting public officials, politicians and judges, in Campagnia and the adjoining areas. While corruption may not be unique to the Camorra, the level of corruption attained by the Camorra is definitely impressive. This corruption indeed assists the Camorra's illegal operations and activities within Italy.

Vulnerabilities

In the late 1980 and the early 1990 the Camorra was regarded by many as the most influential Italian organized crime group in Italy. In fact, many experts believed that the Camorra was largely underestimated. The power and the influence of the Camorra vis-a-vis the other crime groups, however, have decreased over the last several years. The faltering of the Camorra's power is largely the result of two factors: penitents and the Camorra's organizational flux.

Penitents, or turncoats, have hit the Camorra hard. Many Camorra members have turned state's evidence which, in turn, has jeopardized many of the Camorra's operations and has thus marginalized its overall power and influence within Italy. The "[Camorra] clans have been decimated by the hundreds of 'turncoats'...."[74]

One penitent, in particular, has greatly undermined the operations and power of the Camorra. Carmine Alfieri, the former undisputed head of the Camorra, was recently arrested and has turned state's evidence. His arrest has apparently lead to the weakening of the Camorra.[75]

The rise in the number of turncoats within the Camorra clans has led to a situation where there is a power vacuum. This vacuum has been filled by young clan members who "have no hesitation in resorting to the use of guns in their efforts to reach the top of the organization."[76] Thus, it appears that there is mounting tension and considerable in fighting between the clans of the Camorra. This in-fighting could further undermine the power of the Camorra.

Summary

The Camorra is the oldest of the Italian organized crime groups (IOCGs). It has been an influential actor in Italy for more than three centuries. Penitents and internecine conflict have recently affected the power and efficacy of the Camorra. Nevertheless, the Camorra is still heavily involved in a widespread number of illicit operations in Italy and throughout the world.

The Camorra is involved in money laundering activities in Europe, Central America, South America, and Russia. The money laundering activities practiced by the Camorra make use of restaurants (Brazil), real estate and capital investments (France), and gambling houses or casinos (Nicaragua).

The Sicilian Mafia (aka) *La Cosa Nostra*
Introduction
Although there are four major Italian organized crime groups operating throughout the world the term "mafia" is used when discussing any and all of them. While each group must be reviewed independently. However, because the term Mafia is used so frequently it is important to discuss its origins.

Numerous stories stating the origin of the term MAFIA exist. It is safe to say that there is no one authoritative and precise recording of the Mafia's origin or definition of the term itself. Stories date as far back as 1282 with the French invasion of Sicily and the resistance motto of "Morte Alla Francia Italia Anela:" "Death to the French is Italy's Cry."[77]

Some claim the term MAFIA stems from the "archaic French word 'maufer' god of evil" or that it is an acronym for "Mazzini Autroizza Furti Incendi Avvelenamenti" regarding the Italian patriot Giuseppe Mazzini.[78]

Historians tend to credit another Italian patriot, Giuseppe Garibaldi, with the start of the Mafia. While liberating Sicily, Garibaldi was joined by gangs of young peasants known as "Picciotti" who hid in caves known as "maha" and were referred to as "squadri della mafia." Shortly after Italian unification the Picciotti "took over [Sicily]." An 1865 dispatch cites it by name as a "criminal secret society."[79]

In the United States (U.S.) the term La Cosa Nostra (Our Thing) is often synonymous with Italian organized crime, particularly the New York Mafia or Mob. The Sicilian Mafia shares the name of La Cosa Nostra (LCN) with the American Mafia. The fact that these two organizations have a common name is not coincidental. The two organizations share a long history and ancestry which is discussed in greater detail below.

Topics addressed in this paper include the Sicilian LCN's history, relationship with the American LCN, areas of operations, organizational structure, connections with other criminal groups and activities, as well as the LCN's peculiarities and vulnerabilities.

History
Like the term Mafia the origins and history of the LCN are subject to debate. Nonetheless, it is generally believed that the Sicilian Mafia came into existence during Spain's second occupation of Sicily circa 1738-1860. Leaders of the Camorra, Italy's first crime group and most powerful criminal organization during the 18th and 19th centuries formed the Cosa Nostra.[80]

As alluded to above, Italian patriot Giuseppe Mazzini is sometimes noted as the Sicilian Mafia's founder. In 1831, Mazzini established the Young Italy Society. "The articles of organization for the Young Italy Society were drawn from tenets of the Camorra and later became the basis of the Sicilian Mafia organization."[81] This criminal organization made its initial wealth by offering estate owners protection. With Palermo under its control the Cosa Nostra quickly expanded its influence throughout Sicily.

In 1878 "a prestigious Mafiosi, Giuseppe Esposito, from Palermo was the first known Sicilian Mafia member to emigrate to the United States."[82] It was not an entrepreneurial spirit that brought Esposito to the United States. He was fleeing Sicily where he had murdered several people including a Sicilian leader. Giuseppe Esposito initially arrived in New York but quickly relocated to New Orleans, which had a large Sicilian migrant community.

In 1881, Esposito was arrested in New Orleans and extradited to Italy where he was wanted. Joseph Macheca, a first generation American of Sicilian descendent, became the Cosa Nostra's new boss. Macheca continued to recruit Sicilians into the organization. Giuseppe Esposito passed the Sicilian Mafia's torch to a new generation in a new world and Joseph Macheca carried it forward.

Benito Mussolini's rise to power and campaign to eliminate the Sicilian Mafia resulted in a mass migration of Mafia members to the U.S. "Some of the more notorious individuals that arrived in the United States at this time were Carlos Gambino, Stefano Maggadino, Joe Profaci, Joe Magliocco, Mike Coppola, and Salvatore Maranzano. They joined earlier Sicilian arrivals, such as Joe Bonanno (1915) and Lucky [Salvatore] Luciano (1907)."[83]

Eventually, conflict between the Sicilian Cosa Nostra and American Cosa Nostra erupted into what was called the Castellammarese War. This conflict lasted for three years and concluded in 1931 with Salvatore Maranzano of the Sicilian faction the victor. However, several months later, Lucky Luciano and Vito Genovese arranged for Maranzano's killing. Luciano attempted to expand the American Cosa Nostra and sever relations with the Sicilians. Initially it appeared that he was successful in severing relations but as discussed below in fact he was not.

Composition
Organizational Structure: Hierarchical
In 1974 the Royal Canadian Mounted Police (RCMP) uncovered the Cosa Nostra's organizational structure while monitoring a conversation. During this conversation, Montreal Mafia leader Paul Violi and a partially identified visitor from Sicily detailed the "Sicilian Mafia's tight hierarchical structure."[84]

Details provided by Tommaso Buscetta and other Mafia members turned informants allowed Italian authorities to envision the LCN's structure. The informants illustrated an organization that was "global, unitary, rigidly regimented, and vertically structured, governed from the top down."[85] The recent rash of Cosa Nostra members who have become informants has resulted in the Sicilian Mafia "reorganizing itself into small cells to limit the risk of betrayal."[86]

Tradition is a vital element in the composition of the LCN. As discussed above, the Sicilian Mafia consists of a hierarchical structure. Titles are provided to individuals in the organization. The following titles are commonly used in the American LCN and there is no reason to believe that the Sicilian Mafia does not use them as well.[87]

Capo di Tutti capi	Boss of Bosses
Capo Crimini	Super Boss
Consigliere	Trusted Advisor; Counsellor
Sotto Capo/Capo Bastone	Underboss
Contabile	Financial Advisor
Caporegime/Capodecina	Lieutenants; Captains
Sgarrista	High Soldier
Picciotto	Low Soldier; Buttons
Giovane D'Honore	Associates

Leadership

Don Calogero Vizzini
Luciano Leggio
Salvatore "Toto" Riina

The most recently recognized leader of the Cosa Nostra is Toto Riina. Riina has also been referred to as "the Beast" and "Corto." Riina is serving a life sentence for "the killings in 1985 of two senior police officials."[88] Riina was also tried for the 1992 murder of Judge Giovanni Falcone. Information regarding the Cosa Nostra's current leadership is vague. However, it does not appear that Riina has been replaced as supreme leader of the LCN.[89] Salvatore Riina was Luciano Leggio's "chief proconsul and designated heir."[90]

Some would argue that the title of Capo di Tutti capi would historically be synonymous with the name Luciano Leggio. In 1944, at nineteen years of age Leggio joined the LCN. It can be said that he joined the LCN on the "ground floor" in post World War Two Italy. With Mussolini out of the way the Cosa Nostra quickly established its reign on Sicily and recognized Don Calogero Vizzini as the Capo di Tutti capi. Vizzini once stated, "when I die the Mafia dies."[91] Luciano Leggio had a notorious reputation and a penchant for killing; he was not about to let the Mafia die. It took several years but Leggio managed to exploit the heroin trade and ruthlessly killed to secure his position as the Capo di Tutti capi.

Strength

Italy's largest criminal organization

Families	161
Clans	27
Members	5,700

As mentioned above there are four crime groups operating out of Italy. The Cosa Nostra is not the only organized crime group found in Italy, or on Sicily for that matter. However, the "Cosa Nostra is the largest and most powerful of four main criminal gangs. It operates in more than 40 countries, including all the Americas and throughout drug producing countries of Asia."[92] The Sicilian Mafia consists of approximately 161 families with 5,700 members. These families are arranged into approximately twenty-seven clans. It is important to recognize that it is the LCN's international reach and connection with other criminal organizations- rather than simply the number of members- that gives it much of its strength. A comprehensive list of the Cosa Nostra's clans can be found in Claire Starlings' book *Octopus, The Long Reach of the International Sicilian Mafia.*

Disposition

The Sicilian Cosa Nostra is truly an international organization with bases of operations around the globe. Discussed below are areas where the Sicilian Mafia's operations are well documented, illustrating its significant sphere of influence.

Areas of Influence:
Italy

The Sicilian Cosa Nostra possesses considerable influence in Sicily where it was originally established approximately 200 years ago. Undoubtedly, the LCN's "strength comes from below, consisting of absolute territorial control over many areas of Sicily and consequently of the activities that go on there."[93]

The LCN has also established itself in northern Italian cities. During the 1970s a small number of heroin laboratories were established in the vicinity of Milan. This location allowed French chemists easier access to processing laboratories.[94] More recently, there are some indications that money-laundering opportunities are attracting the Cosa Nostra to Northern Italy.

United States

As previously discussed the LCN has historically possessed influence in the United States. In 1984, 35 alleged members of the Sicilian Mafia were indicted in connection with the "Pizza Connection." The Pizza Connection consisted of an LCN network of pizza shops throughout the U.S. used as fronts to traffic heroin and undoubtedly launders money.

The Pizza Connection was uncovered in 1977 when investigators discovered that a rather insignificant pizzeria on Virginia Beach was spending "around $5,000 a month on phone calls to hundreds of pizzerias throughout the United States, as well as Milan, Palermo and Caracas."[95] As investigators pursued this case it was revealed that the "Sicilian Mafia was importing massive amounts of heroin into the United States."[96]

Further evidence of the Sicilian Mafia's influence and activities in the U.S. is that, as of 1987, the Federal Bureau of Investigation (FBI) and the Drug Enforcement Administration (DEA) had confirmed information revealing the presence of "over 25 Sicilian Mafia 'members' in the United States."[97]

Venezuela

Venezuela offered a charmed life to Sicily's Men of Honor. There were no big drug busts in its sunlit capital, Caracas, during the 1960s, 1970s, or 1980s. Indeed, nothing untoward has ever happened to the Sicilian Mafia in Venezuela.[98]

This South American country offered the Cosa Nostra various advantages. Geographically it provided the Sicilian Mafia quick access to offshore banking institutions in the Caribbean and short lines of communications to Colombia's cocaine cartels. Venezuela's relatively healthy economy allowed for the establishment of front organizations ranging from cattle to construction. These fronts were undoubtedly used for money laundering and drug trafficking activities.

Perhaps what made Venezuela most attractive to the LCN was the ease with which official documents and citizenship could be obtained. It was not difficult to "buy a complete new identity from some obliging petty functionary for $500...as 'naturalized' citizens, they could not be extradited under Venezuelan law."[99]

One could argue that Venezuela is the LCN's clearing house for the Americas. The LCN has used Venezuela as a way station for drug trafficking and "80 percent of the cocaine leaving Colombia now passes through Venezuela."[100]

Canada

The LCN's activities in Canada date back to the end of the Second World War when Joe Bonanno established operations in Montreal. This operation was akin to the American Cosa Nostra. The Canadian LCN, like its American cousin engaged the Sicilians in violent conflict. Montreal's boss, Paul Violi, was killed in 1978 during these hostilities. With Violi's death "Montreal was now the Sicilian Mafia's northern gateway to the United States."[101] Montreal was used by the Sicilians to launder money and more importantly it secured a north-south corridor for drug trafficking into the United States. Recent reports have not revealed significant information regarding the Sicilian Mafia's activities in Canada.

Brazil

Sao Paulo is quickly becoming a haven for the Cosa Nostra. According to a Brazilian report "50 Mafia kingpins are living in the country, 27 of them in Sao Paulo."[102] Moreover, it has been reported that Sicilian Mafia members "control or have small numbers of shares in at least 200 Brazilian enterprises."[103]

Business establishments that are about to declare bankruptcy are identified and targeted for either partial or complete take-over. Unfortunately, some legitimate businessmen become unknowing accomplices of the Cosa Nostra. Undoubtedly, these businesses are exploited by the Cosa Nostra for money laundering and to mask drug trafficking activities.

Areas of Interest
Central America (Nicaragua, Guatemala, Costa Rica)

The region of Central America, particularly Nicaragua, is proving to be lucrative for the Cosa Nostra. Recent reports revealed that Nicaraguan financial institutions and a gambling establishment are being exploited for money laundering activities.[104]

Similar activities have transpired in Guatemala and Costa Rica in the past. These countries are good locations to conduct such operations since their law enforcement communities are not very sensitive to money laundering activities.

Romania

A 1994 Romanian intelligence report states that criminal organizations from various countries including Italy are establishing "bridgeheads ...and have become involved in trafficking armaments, ammunition, drugs and automobiles."[105] The Cosa Nostra and other Italian crime groups are specifically mentioned in the report.

The report goes on to claim that the violent behavior of organized crime groups may result in people confusing criminal behavior for terrorism. Sadly, this illustrates the level of violence these criminals are willing to execute to accomplish their goals.

Germany

A recent Federal Criminal Office (BKA) of Germany report stated "the BKA is much concerned about the constant rise in the number of foreigners involved in organized crime, whose proportion rose from 50.6 percent in 1991 to 63.6 percent last year."[106] The report claims that almost six percent of foreign criminals come from Italy.

German authorities also believe that the majority of individuals in foreign criminal activities "had links with criminal organizations such as the...Sicilian Mafia,"[107] and others.

Antigua

U.S. and Caribbean law enforcement agencies believe that the island of Antigua is a site employed by the Sicilian Mafia for money laundering. More importantly, however, officials believe that this is also the location where Russian organized crime groups meet with Italian and Colombian organized crime groups.

The preceding paragraphs mentioned only a few countries and areas of the world in which the Cosa Nostra is active and exerts influence. Law enforcement officials believe that through its international connections regarding money laundering and drug trafficking the Cosa Nostra is active in over 40 countries.

Activities

The Sicilian Mafia actively engages in numerous illegal activities. The following is a partial list.

Significant
- Murder
- Drug Trafficking
- Money Laundering
- Arms Trafficking
- Kidnapping
- Extortion

Minor
- Prostitution
- Bribery
- Auto Theft
- Influence Peddling
- Blackmail

Of all the activities in which the Cosa Nostra is involved, money laundering, drug trafficking and influence peddling appear to be most prevalent. The LCN cannot efficiently carry out all these activities by itself. Therefore, connections with other criminal organizations, legitimate, and illegitimate, businesses are required.

Connections

The Cosa Nostra spends a considerable amount of time and energy in establishing domestic and international connections to fulfill or execute the activities listed above. The LCN has established connections with the following groups or institutions.

Domestic
- Other Italian Organized Crime Groups
- Italian Political Leaders
- Italian Bankers

International
- Colombian Cartels
- Russian Organized Crime Groups
- American LCN
- Moroccan Drug Dealers
- International Bankers

A result of "Operation Onig" in 1994 was the uncovering of a drug ring consisting of three Italian organized crime groups. The three groups involved were the Cosa Nostra, the Camorra and the Ndrangheta. This ring was operating in both Italy and the United States. This is particularly interesting because the American LCN was excluded.[108]

Although the Cosa Nostra launders money in numerous locations around the world it must establish positive relations with Sicilian and other Italian bankers to launder large sums of money domestically.

Until very recently the Sicilian Mafia was always sure to have its political cronies in positions of authority. These political puppets allowed the Cosa Nostra to operate throughout Sicily with carte blanche. Furthermore, many of these individuals were in positions to guarantee the LCN construction contracts and other apparently legitimate business opportunities to mask illegal activities.

The Cosa Nostra has had a long profitable relationship with the cocaine cartels of Colombia. "Operation Green Ice," in 1992, "provided firm evidence of growing cooperation and operational links between the Cali Cartel and the Sicilian Mafia."[109] A more recent report indicates that the Cosa Nostra is diversifying it contacts in Colombia. "Operation Dinero" revealed the "international networks between the Colombian gangs based in the Cauca valley, (aka, the Cali cartel) and the Sicilian Mafia."[110]

The fall of the Soviet Union gave rise to a vast new area of operation for the Cosa Nostra. Numerous reports discuss the growing ties between the LCN and Russia's organized crime groups. As mentioned earlier some Russian-Sicilian meetings take place on Antigua. Reports from the former Soviet Union as recent as June 1996 discuss links between former officials and the Sicilian Mafia regarding drug trafficking.[111] Interestingly the Russians are also cooperating with the American LCN.[112]

The relationship and activities of the American LCN and the Sicilian LCN have already been discussed.

The Cosa Nostra's network extends to Morocco. A February 1996 Moroccan Interior Ministry Statement discussed the relationship between the Sicilian Mafia and a Moroccan drug ring. The report identified a Moroccan by the name of Mohamed Mahjour, alias Allouche, as "the ringleader of a drug-smuggling network to Italy, where he had good links with the Sicilian Mafia."[113]

Undoubtedly, one of the Cosa Nostra's most lucrative activities is money laundering. The LCN launders money in various parts of the world. It takes advantage of offshore Caribbean banking systems as well as the banks of Switzerland and developing Central American countries. As noted above the Sicilian Mafia exploited the casinos in Nicaragua and other reports have discussed the exploitation of casinos in Monte Carlo, Monaco.[114]

Peculiarities
- Established Heroin Market Niche
- Planned Casino Losses to Launder Money
- Relationship with Colombians
- Use of Sea Lines of Communications to Ferry Drugs
- Growing Interest in Waste Disposal

It appears that the Cosa Nostra's drug of preference is heroin. This was the narcotic that brought the Cosa Nostra's initial fortune.

Two reports on money laundering, one regarding Nicaragua and the other Monte Carlo both state that Cosa Nostra couriers purposely lose large amounts of money at designated casinos to launder money. These casinos are more than likely LCN run and operated.

The Cosa Nostra has also established a long a profitable relationship with Colombian cocaine cartels. Furthermore, the Sicilian Mafia is exploiting its access to the sea-lanes of the Mediterranean to ferry drugs between East and West Europe.[115] Reports indicate that drugs are transferred onto "cutters and yachts belonging to the Sicilian Mafia in the central part of the Mediterranean Sea." These vessels then dock in various ports of Western and Eastern Europe where the drugs are passed on to the local markets.

It now appears that the Cosa Nostra is expanding its involvement in "legitimate" businesses. "The management of waste, according to many experts, is one of the new frontiers of the Mafia economy."[116] The LCN is most likely interested in this venture for money laundering activities.

Vulnerabilities
- Increasing of defectors
- Increasing expenditures
- Domestic Rivals
- International Rivals

Fortunately for law enforcement communities, more and more members are choosing to leave the LCN and cooperate with authorities. Historically, the LCN has been a "secret society par excellence; the initiation ceremony involves pricking a finger of the novitiate who lets the blood fall on the picture of a sacred image which is then ignited and burnt in his hand. He is then informed that he is 'a man of honour' for life."[117]

The murders of Judges Falcone and Borsillino resulted in the introduction of a new law "encouraging former members to give evidence against the syndicate."[118] Since the introduction of this law 750 Mafia members have decided to cooperate with authorities. It is not clear if all 750 individuals were members of the LCN specifically. Nonetheless, the important issue is that the Mafia's "code of silence" is breaking down.

This hemorrhaging of members will hamper the Cosa Nostra's activities and increase its vulnerabilities to law enforcement's operations in the future.

Increased monetary expenditures are starting to take their toll on the Cosa Nostra according to a 1995 report stating that "there are indications,...based on investigative reports, that the Cosa Nostra is currently in serious financial difficulty, thereby confirming that it has been weakened as a result of the decisive actions taken by the anticrime agencies."[119]

The "Stidda" (star), an emerging Sicilian organized crime group is engaged in violent conflict with the Cosa Nostra according to an Italian news report. The report claims that "the Stidda and the Cosa Nostra have been involved in a bloody clan war in southern Sicily."[120]

Emerging Nigerian criminal organizations may pose a threat to the Cosa Nostra's heroin niche and relationship with the Colombian cartels.

They [Nigerians] have developed an alliance of sorts with the
Colombians based on product exchange. In several instances

Nigerian trafficking organizations have supplied heroin to the Colombians in return for cocaine. This has helped the Colombians to develop their own heroin market while also offering opportunities for the Nigerians to sell cocaine in Western Europe.[121]

This relationship may be a business threat to the Cosa Nostra because it is very similar to its own relationship with the Colombians. The Nigerians also represent additional competition for profits in Western Europe.

Summary

The Sicilian Cosa Nostra has a long, nefarious history, at one time ruling Sicily and its citizens. It is a worldwide organization with links to other criminally oriented organizations.

Today, the LCN has suffered various setbacks mostly resulting from informants and tougher measures instituted by Italian and international law enforcement agencies.

These efforts have caused the Cosa Nostra to increase its expenditures while decreasing its revenues. Furthermore, the Sicilian Mafia is now being challenged by upstart criminal organizations such as the Stidda on Sicily, which was once undisputed Cosa Nostra territory.

At the international level, the Cosa Nostra's ties with the Colombian cartels may be weakening. It appears that the Cosa Nostra now faces challenges from African organized crime groups in Western European drug sales.

However, the Cosa Nostra's effects on the international community cannot be dismissed. Although it seems that the LCN may be losing its edge, its involvement in money laundering activities is still significant. The Sicilian Mafia's recent interest in waste management is not the result of environmental concerns. More than likely it is just another avenue to launder money.

The fall of the Soviet Union and the emergence of Russian organized crime elements have given the Cosa Nostra another area of the world to exploit.

The Sicilian Mafia will remain at the forefront of international criminal activity well into the twenty-first century. After all, this very same organization survived Spanish occupation, Benito Mussolini's purges and most recently the *"maxi-trials."*

A dated map[122] continues to be important because it depicts the Sicilian Mafia's whereabouts in the United States and illustrates the notion that the Sicilian Mafia does maintain contact with American organized crime.

'Ndrangheta
Introduction

The 'Ndrangheta is one of the four main Italian organized crime groups (IOCGs). It has largely been overshadowed by the Sicilian Cosa Nostra and only recently has the 'Ndrangheta been recognized as a national and international criminal force.

From its traditional base in southern Calabria, the 'Ndrangheta has spread throughout Italy, North and South America, Europe, and Australia. The 'Ndrangheta or the Calabrian Mafia family is usually referred to by the following words in Calabrian dialect, 'ndrina or fibbia. Known as "The Honored Society," Fibbia, Santa, or the Calabrian Mafia, the 'Ndrangheta's composition is based upon blood relationships and inter-marriages. Each group is named after its village, or after a family leader.

Contemporary official figures have cited the 'Ndrangheta groups as numbering 159 with about 6,000 members and 9,000 affiliates. The 'Ndrangheta began as a covert, rural organization in the late 19th century. Its main activities are extortion, kidnapping, usury, drug trafficking, and arms trafficking. The recent emergence of this criminal organization internationally is due to the drug trade and Italian law enforcement's preoccupation with the Sicilian Cosa Nostra.

History

Based in southern Italy (Calabria region), the 'Ndrangheta was formed in the mid 1800s as a defense mechanism for impoverished rural peasants against their aristocratic landlords. The region of Calabria has a frail economic fabric and lacks significant industrial resources. The name 'Ndrangheta comes from the Greek word *andragaqos*, which means a courageous and brave man. This organized crime group has been largely overshadowed by the Sicilian Cosa Nostra and only recently emerged as a group whose strength has begun to equal that of the Sicilian Cosa Nostra.

The 'Ndrangheta, like the Sicilian Cosa Nostra, has crime groups operating in North America. Members of these Calabrian crime groups emigrated to Canada and the United States, and were discovered running a "black hand" intimidation scheme in Pennsylvanian mining towns in 1906. After World War II, the 'Ndrangheta shifted its focus from banditry to extortion, kidnapping and drug trafficking.

The 'Ndrangheta was primarily focused on extortion and kidnapping until the 1970s. Although, extortion still constitutes one of the most substantial sources of illegal earnings for the 'Ndrangehta, profits earned from extortions and kidnappings allowed the organization to diversify into the drug trade and public contracts. With the money from ransoms, the mafia bosses could buy construction equipment to compete for government public contracts and buy large amounts of drugs to get into the wholesale drug trade. It was during the 1970s that the 'Ndrangheta branched into the drug trade and took on an international focus.[122] As a result of its international drug trade, the 'Ndrangheta has become involved across the world and is becoming a major international criminal force.

Composition
Organizational Structure: Vertical

The 'Ndrangheta is believed to be organized vertically. This structure of organization gives power to one individual or commission and it filters down as in a pyramid structure. The Calabrian mafia family's nucleus is usually made up of a blood family, around which a network of natural and artificial relationships develops. The real strength of the family depends on the dimensions of the core, the one or two biological families and their networks of artificial kinships that are at the core of the group. An analysis of the internal composition reveals that the more powerful groups tend to have no less than three brothers.

A greater number of brothers within a group usually means that this group has spower, because groups built around a single individual have an inherent fragility, and tend to decline and disappear quickly.[123]

In order to strengthen the cohesion of the inner nucleus of groups, the practice of intermarriage between first cousins is strongly encouraged. The rationale for the support of blood relationships is that it discourages turncoats. To abandon the 'Ndrangheta, would not only be repudiating a way of life and the environment in which one was brought up, but also betraying one's own father, brother, uncle, or cousin.

The success of this relationship is evident in the statistics of government informers. Out of more than 700 collaborators for the Italian Police to date, Calabrian state witnesses only account for ten percent compared with fifty percent for the Sicilians. The bosses and other 'Ndrangheta members often live without outward signs of wealth or power. The 'Ndrangheta organization has also split into two levels: the "*maggiore*" (senior level) and the "*minore*" (junior level). This places a barrier between low-level common crimes and higher-level political and white-collar crimes.[124]

Leadership

Until recently it was believed that only in the late 1980's did the 'Ndrangheta develop a hierarchy to establish control of its organization. Previously, the Calabrian mafia was less effective because it lacked a mechanism for internal conflict regulation. It was not until the end of the Second Mafia War (1986-1991), that the 'Ndrangheta adopted an organizational model similar to that of the Provincial Commission of the Sicilian Cosa Nostra. A Commission was established to fix territorial boundaries of each group. Furthermore, instead of families taking action against each other any conflict between groups was to be brought to the attention of the Commission. The establishment of a Commission led to a steady decline in killings amongst criminal families in the Calabrian region.[125]

It was also believed that the 'Ndrangheta group operated independently from each other and did not have a hierarchical system to control all the groups. But, according to the Italian police and state witnesses, the myth of absolute autonomy and self-sufficiency by the Calabrian mafia and its declared horizontal structure are factitious. Accounts and testimonies point to the fact that there has always been some form of high level management, though not as strong and powerful as the Provincial Commission of the Sicilian Cosa Nostra. It now appears, therefore, that the Commission that established after the Second Mafia War did not mark the end of a traditional set-up and the beginning of a new one, but rather resulted from the refinement of organizational modules that previously had been rudimentary.

Strength

The strength of the 'Ndrangheta lies in its blood relationships and is reinforced by an extensive use of rituals, symbols, and a distinctive slang. The 'Ndrangheta is seeking links to the Italian political world in order to better control its territory. The crime syndicate is believed to have some 15,000 members and affiliates in Italy. These members are divided up into 160 groups. It has expanded into other countries along with emigration. Because the core families have blood relationships, the members of the 'Ndrangheta abroad adhere to the same normative and organizational structure as their brethren in Calabria.[126]

Disposition
Areas of Influence
Italy

The 'Ndrangheta operates primarily in Reggio de Calabria, which is located in southern Italy. For over 100 years, the 'Ndrangheta has used southern Italy as its base of operations. It developed its power base due to poor economic conditions and lack of natural resources. The 'Ndrangheta is particularly adept in its ability to corrupt public officials and gain the majority of government contracts in southern Italy. The 'Ndrangheta, like the Sicilian Cosa Nostra, is seeking links to the Italian political world in order to better control its territory.[127] There is also a strong presence in northern Italy, especially Milan. The 'Ndrangheta has been using Northern Italian cities to re-invest some of its laundered money and use this area for drug and arms trafficking into the heart of Europe.

Germany

A strong presence of the 'Ndrangheta is located in Germany. The Calabrian mafia has been found operating in the states of Baden-Wuerttemberg, Bavaria, Hesse, and Nordrein-Westphalia. It is involved in car thefts and smuggling, cocaine and heroin trafficking, and robberies. The 'Ndrangheta also uses Germany to launder and reinvest its money by operating a number of small and medium businesses and tourist establishments--restaurants, pizzerias, ice-cream shops, and garages, etc.[128]

Australia

The 'Ndrangheta has had historical ties with Australia and Canada. The 'Ndrangheta has been operating in Australia since the early twentieth century, and it was estimated in 1964 that there were 700 members of the group active in the country. In the following decades, the Calabrian mafia became involved in frauds, heroin and cocaine drug trafficking, extortion, control of prostitution, arms smuggling, and established a monopoly of cannabis production in

Australia. The Calabrian groups operating in Australia have a close tie with their brethren in Italy.

Australian police forces have found several copies of codes containing the rituals, written in Italian, for the admission to this secret, criminal society.[129] The Australian Crime Authority reported that the 'Ndrangheta is a national network held together by family relationships, lifelong friendships, and mutual interest. The 'Ndrangheta is providing help and expertise to member criminals in Australia. Its principal activity is commercial cannabis cultivation and money laundering, but a minority of its members are involved with heroin, cocaine, and extortion.[130]

Canada

In Canada, the 'Ndrangheta has been operating in certain cities since the 1950s. Groups have been identified in Toronto, Hamilton, and Ottawa and are currently involved in drug and arms trafficking and money laundering.[131] There is believed to be a board of control that coordinates the activities of the Calabrian families within Canada, and connects them with the U.S. and Australian sectors of the Sicilian Cosa Nostra, and of the 'Ndrangheta itself. The 'Ndrangheta is believed to be using Canada to launder money because there are no Canadian laws that are similar to the U.S. racketeering and money laundering offenses.[132]

Colombia

There is a credible link between the Colombians and the 'Ndrangheta in drug trafficking. In 1994, pure cocaine worth over 300 billion lire was seized from several warehouses in Turin, in what was the largest anti-drug operation ever carried out in Italy against the South American drug-traffickers linked to the 'Ndrangheta. These crime groups had discovered a new way to transport vast quantities of cocaine to Italy by ship and long-haul vehicle. The primary distribution area was to be central Italy and eastern Europe. The amount of cocaine seized indicates that there is a definite link with the Colombians. Without this link, such a large amount of cocaine would certainly not have been sent.[133]

Brazil

The 'Ndrangheta has been linked to the Cali cartel in Colombia in international drug trafficking. Both these organizations have been using Brazil as a transshipment point for cocaine smuggling. This discovery was a result of two years of investigation by police from five countries. It led to more than fifty arrests and the confiscation of seven metric tons of cocaine. The investigation began in July 1994, when police arrested 43 Mafia members during the largest cocaine seizure in Europe: five metric tons hidden inside a shoe shipment. The container arrived at the Port of Genoa and was taken by truck to Turin. The investigation was handled by Brazilian Federal Police intelligence agents, and Swiss, American, and Bolivian policemen.

Investigations show that prior to this record cocaine seizure in Turin, three other ships loaded with cocaine left the port of Santos, San Paulo, with the destination, Italy. These investigations also show that the cocaine was destined for U.S. and European markets, and that a faction of the Calabrian mafia that had begun to operate outside Italy had ordered it from the Cali cartel.[134] Following a split among the Italian mafia organizations, some families came to Brazil and others to Venezuela where, according to Interpol, they continued to administer their illegal businesses.

The most powerful family came to live in Copacabana, Rio de Janerio. Investigations and police interviews with members of these criminal groups detail how they moved the cocaine from South America to Italy. The Cali cartel would buy drugs from Bolivian laboratories. Brazil was used as a corridor to send this cocaine to Europe embedded within large amounts of Brazilian exports. Cocaine was hidden among animal hides to be exported to the General Tenemus company in Lugano, Switzerland. The consignment was supposed to be detoured in the Port of Genoa, where the 'Ndrangheta members were expecting it and where it was to be distributed throughout Europe.[135]

The United States

The 'Ndrangheta and other Italian Mafia organizations have been linked to the United States. In *"Operation Onig,"* Italian police and the FBI made some 100 arrests in both countries and destroyed a drug trafficking operation controlled by a cartel made up of the Cosa Nostra, 'Ndrangheta, and the Camorra. This operation was dedicated to the memory of Judge Paolo Falcone, and it demonstrated that the 'Ndrangheta today constitutes one of the largest criminal organizations in the world. In the United States, these organizations established a cartel of drug traffickers by uniting their respective forces without asking the permission of anyone, especially the mafia in America.[136]

Investigators from the Italian Central Anti-Crime nucleus and the FBI came to the conclusion that these criminal groups exported heroin in exchange for cocaine. These two law enforcement groups concluded two distinct facts as a result of this operation. One, in Italy, heroin refineries are continuing to work at full speed and their management has been assigned to the 'Ndrangheta. Second, also in Italy, big business for these organizations is constituted by cocaine, which has flooded the drug markets and for which demand continues to grow.[137]

Argentina

The 'Ndrangheta has taken advantage of the lax banking laws in Latin America. A recent operation by the Italian and Argentine police forces led to the arrest of over sixty people involved in a money laundering scheme operated by the 'Ndrangheta in Argentina. *"Operation Hidros"* revealed how the 'Ndrangheta used banks in Argentina to buy Primary Bank Guarantees (PBGs) that were worth over three million dollars and the money was reinvested in northern Italy in legitimate businesses. This operation began as a result of the arrest of Giacomo Lauro, a high-ranking member of the 'Ndrangheta, in 1992. The investigation also revealed that the 'Ndrangheta not only used banks in Argentina, but also in England, Germany and Hungary.[138]

Areas of Interest

The 'Ndrangheta is actively working to strengthen its area of influence in Russia and Eastern Europe. Due to the fact that the majority of its profits comes from the drug trade, the 'Ndrangheta is trying to establish itself as the supplier of heroin and cocaine in Europe and the United States. The 'Ndrangheta is also believed to be trying to establish links with Asian mafia groups, especially the Chinese Triads and the Japanese Yakuza.

Activities
Significant Activities

The 'Ndrangheta is involved in extortion, drug trafficking, money laundering, kidnappings, arms trafficking and public contracts.

Extortion is one of the main activities for the 'Ndrangheta. It continues to constitute one of the most substantial sources of illegal earnings and a major source of revenue for the lower ranks of the Calabrian mafia. Extortion allows the 'Ndrangheta to control its territory and is a visible tribute to its power.

According to the Advocate General of the Reggio Calabria, each and every business activity in town and in the province of Calabria is subjected to the extortion racket. These include industrial plants, commercial businesses, farms, etc. The bribe may be represented by payment in money or the hiring of non-existent personnel. It may also take the form of compulsory participation in the public works that the extorted company has been contracted.[139]

The 'Ndrangheta is now the leader in Italy for heroin trading. It has replaced the Cosa Nostra's control of this trade and the heroin trade has directly led to the expansion of the 'Ndrangheta. 'Ndrangheta groups have established effective links with the Asians and Turkish criminal organizations to plan, buy and ship heroin. The distribution of cocaine throughout Italy has also been the domain of the 'Ndrangheta.

The Calabrian mafia groups have emerged as significant cocaine traffickers in Italy in the past few years. The 'Ndrangheta has allegedly imported eleven metric tons of cocaine into Italy over a 3 year period. It is also involved in cannabis cultivation and smuggling. Cannabis is imported from Morocco to be distributed or it is cultivated in greenhouses or farms in southern Italy.[140]

"*Operation Riace*" was conducted by the Italian Anti-drug Bureau and it exposed some of the international links the 'Ndrangheta is using to get illegal drugs into Italy. It discovered channels for heroin and cocaine traffic from northern to southern Italy through a network linking Verona, Padua, Ferrar, Reggio Calabria, Turin, Milan and foreign countries. The drug arrivals for the 'Ndrangheta were primarily heroin and hashish from Pakistan and Thailand via

Moscow, or by sea via the Suez Canal or Turkey. The barter transactions would take place in small retail stores that sold electric household appliances, candy and fabrics. The cocaine came from Colombia along the usual sea routes (Gibraltar or Great Britain) or via Moscow and the Balkan countries. The money would than be deposited in Swiss banks and then transferred to the Arab Emirates and subsequently reinvested in the acquisition of new quantities of drugs.[141]

Money laundering is done within Italy and internationally to take advantage of lax money laundering laws in certain countries. During the 1970s, the 'Ndrangheta used local credit institutions that operated in the Calabrian region to launder money. In the past decade, the 'Ndrangheta has been able to diversify its channels of money laundering, exploiting non-banking financial institutions and foreign intermediaries.[142]

The 'Ndrangheta has used some of its "dirty money" in legitimate businesses, such as public works. The 'Ndrangheta used Argentina's national bank to launder money by buying primary bank guarantees. The Argentine press reported from Italy that the Calabrian mafia laundered 3 billion dollars of drug and arms money through banks in Latin America, Britain, Germany, Hungary and tax havens such as the Cayman Islands. They quoted Italian police saying the money was laundered by depositing it in foreign banks, then using it as collateral for bank loans from Italian finance houses.[143]

Kidnappings have long been an activity that the 'Ndrangheta used to make money. Through kidnappings for ransoms, the 'Ndrangheta accumulated the monetary funds which allowed it to start into public works and the wholesale drug trade. Kidnappings have declined in part because of negative public reaction toward these actions and laws enacted by the Italian government to freeze the assets of a kidnapped person.[144]

Arms' smuggling is sometimes done in conjunction with other Italian criminal organizations. Due to the central location in the Mediterranean of the 'Ndrangheta, the trading of arms has its benefits. The fighting in former Yugoslavia and the arms embargo in place has created an illegal market for weapons. Due to Calabrian ties in northern Italy, weapons were purchased from Switzerland or from traders in Eastern Europe and sent to former Yugoslavia or to the arsenals of Calabrian groups in Southern Italy. The 'Ndrangheta and the Sacra Corona have used northern Italy and the Balkans in their smuggling of arms between Italy and the Balkan coast.[145]

Public works is a legal sphere where the Calabrian mafia launders its dirty capital. The revenues gained from extortion and kidnappings allowed the Calabrian mafia to buy construction equipment necessary to compete in government contracts. By controlling public contracts, the 'Ndrangheta has increased its power in the Calabrian region economically and politically.[146]

Connections

The 'Ndrangheta families have established connections with numerous domestic and international sources. These criminal groups have provided the 'Ndrangheta with the means and resources to operate with success.

Domestic
- Camorra
- La Cosa Nostra
- Sacra Corona Unita
- Politicians - Calabrian Region

International
Latin and South America
- Brazil   - Drug Traffickers
- Colombia   - Drug Cartels(Cali Cartel)
- Argentina   - Money Laundering
- Nicaragua   - Casinos/Money Laundering

Europe
- Germany   - Drugs/Money Laundering
- Switzerland   - Money Laundering/Drugs Trafficking
- Russia   - Drugs/Money Laundering

North America and Asia
- United States   - Drugs/Money Laundering
- Canada   - Money Laundering
- Australia   - Drugs

Peculiarities

There are two striking characteristics of the 'Ndrangheta. One is its use of the Free Mason's Society. It had been theorized that the 'Ndrangheta crime groups were not able to extend themselves within Calabria until they were able to infiltrate regional politics. They accomplished this by making good use of the formidable vehicle of Freemasonry. According to DIA (Anti-Mafia Investigative Directorate), the Masonic lodges are allegedly an important loop in connecting the Mafia with politics. The power of the 'Ndrangheta groups is enhanced because Freemasonry gives them contact with politicians and members of the public administration, who typically are Freemasons. This is how the 'Ndrangheta gains influence to acquire public contracts in the Calabrian region. It is significant that one-third of all Italian southern Masons come from Calabria. There are twice as many Masons in Calabria as there are in Sicily and six times as many as in Campania.[147]

The other characteristic is the use of women by the 'Ndrangheta. The group structure of the 'Ndrangheta gives an influential role to women. Recent investigations have shown that women belonging to 'Ndrangheta groups are assigned the duty of keeper of the values and the continuity of the family. In the past fifteen years, the wives and sisters of 'Ndrangheta bosses have started to take up a function which is less extraneous to male illicit activities. Women have been assigned to supervise of the organization of rackets, to maintain contact with fugitives, to work with the imprisoned bosses and transmitting their orders to lower ranking members. In addition, they provide logistic support during kidnappings and have become the official owners of family property.[148]

Vulnerability

The recent and fast-paced expansion of the 'Ndrangheta due to drug trafficking has created some problems. Various groups are beginning to fight amongst themselves for territory and resources in the lucrative drug business. Another vulnerability is the increased number of turncoats who have become state witnesses. The importance of state witnesses in the 'Ndrangheta hierarchy is also rising and this is offering the Italian police an effective way of combating Calabrian organized crime. Consequently, increased prosecution by the Italian government and police could become destabilizing factors for the 'Ndrangheta.

The 'Ndrangheta flourished in the early 1990s due to the belief that it was a vertical organization that had serious conflicts amongst the groups within the 'Ndrangheta. This is no longer the case. The Italian government and police have seriously begun to target the 'Ndrangheta and believe that its stature is now the same as the Sicilian Cosa Nostra. This intense focus could hamper its ability to operate within Italy and the rest of the world.[149]

Summary

The 'Ndrangheta began as a rural based criminal organization over a hundred years ago. Its original activities of kidnapping and extortion have evolved over the past twenty years to international activities such as drug trafficking, arms smuggling and money laundering. With the end of their civil war in 1991 and the establishment of a Commission and a stronger hierarchy, the 'Ndrangheta has become an international criminal force equaling that of the Sicilian Cosa Nostra. The strength of the Calabrian mafia is due in part to its close-knit groups of blood relatives. The number of state witnesses against the 'Ndrangheta, although rising, is still low in comparison to the other Italian criminal groups. The strength of the 'Ndrangheta is further enhanced by its control of the Calabrian region through Freemasonry and public contracts. The base it has developed in Italy permitted the 'Ndrangheta to expand its operations internationally. The Calabrian groups operating outside Italy and the links with other criminal organizations are continuing to grow and the lack of international coordination necessary to combat the illicit wealth of the 'Ndrangheta has only made this criminal group a stronger international power. It will continue to be a major criminal force until Italy and other nations recognize the threat that this organized crime group poses.

La Sacra Corona Unita (SCU)
(The United Holy Crown)

Introduction

Increased criminal activity in the Italian region of Apulia at the heel of the Italian boot is a recent revelation as to the expanded power of organized crime in southeast Italy. Apulia is a region open to all the Italian Mafias and, consequently it is extremely dangerous. After years of mafia activity, Apulia has absorbed the mafia mentality of the Calabrian 'Ndrangheta and the Neopolitan Camorra i.e. there is little hesitation to use violence. Subsequently, after years of this influence, the Sacra Corona Unita has evolved into a new and separate mafia group made up of what were once small tributaries to the other organizations. The SCU has become a powerful organization of autonomously acting groups, infiltrating Apulia between the end of the 1970s and the beginning of the 1980s. The region has always been a transit area for refugees and goods from Eastern Europe and the Middle East, but more recently it has become a center for weapons, drug trafficking, and cigarette smuggling.[150]

In the cities and the small towns of Apulia and on their peripheries, the local gangster organizations exercise control over the territory in the mafia tradition of exploiting the native population. All the illicit trafficking that is conducted through these towns has created a demand by the citizens for drugs, explosives and arms.

Mafia turncoat, Salvatore Annacondia, explained in a letter to magistrates and investigators the disturbing level of corruption between gangsters and politicians in Apulia including the "shaded area" of collusion between clans and the highest levels of government. Annacondia recounted the illicit affairs of the mafia from Apulia; he especially confirmed the connections from the SCU to the Cosa Nostra, 'Ndrangheta, and Camorra.[151]

A brief history of the Sacra Corona Unita is followed by an analysis of its composition and disposition, SCU activities, the peculiarities of the group, and its vulnerabilities. The SCU's money laundering activities are also highlighted.

History

Giuseppe Rogoli allegedly founded the SCU on Christmas 1983 while he was in jail in Lecce (a town in the region of Apulia). Rogoli, a native of Mesagne, and life long criminal is currently serving a life sentence for the murder of a tobacco storeowner in Giovinazzo in the province of Bari. From jail, Rogoli, like many other mafia leaders, maintains control of the organization.[152] Guido Ruotolo, an expert on the activities of the SCU, suggests in his book *La Quarta Mafia*, there is evidence of the discovery of the SCU some months before December. On October 5, 1983, an informant, Vittorio Curci, confided to a magistrate in Bari that Curci assisted in a strange ceremony of affiliation to a secret association at a home in Acquaviva delle Fonti. The leader of the ceremony was Romano Oronzo, an enforcer for the Rogoli gang, and the "baptized," Giovanni Dalena. From that point Dalena advanced his career rapidly and from 1987 with the blessing of Rogoli, Dalena headed the clan in Bari known as "La Rosa," maintaining relations with the Fidanzati family, for the trafficking of cocaine.[153]

To head the SCU, Rogoli appointed Antonio Dodaro as his right hand man. In a letter in April 1986 Rogoli wrote to Dodaro, "...you are boss of the bosses and you must give account to me and no other man in the world."[154]

Composition
Organizational structure

The SCU is organized horizontally with a series of autonomous clans, but the clans are accountable to the common interests of the organization. The table shows the locations of the groups in the different principalities in Apulia, followed by the clan family name, membership, and connections to other Italian mafia groups. Here is an example of the structure of some of the clans of the Sacra Corona Unita:

**Table 15.2: Selected structural aspects of some of the
clans of the Sacra Corona Unita[155]**

LOCATION	CLAN/FAMILY NAME	# OF MEMBERS	CONNECTIONS
Province of Foggia	Rizzi-Morretti	101	Camorra (Nco)
Foggia	Laviano	8	Camorra (Nuova famiglia)
Cerignola and Periphery	Caputo-Ferraro	62	Camorra (Nco)
Fasano and Periphery	D'Onofrio-Sabatelli	22	Nuova Sacra Corona Unita
Province of Brindisi-Lecce and part of the Province of Taranto	Donatiello-Buccarella-Rogoli (Nuova Sacra Corona Unita)	62	'Ndrangheta and Camorra
Trani-Bisceglie	Annacondia	52	Camorra and Nuova SCU
Bari-Bisceglie	Capriati	26	Catania Mafia
Province of South Bari	"La Rosa"	49	ther groups from Apuli
Bari and the villages of the Belt	Parisi	81	Other groups from Apulia
Monopoli	Muolo	26	'Ndrangheta
Province of Lecce	De Tommasi (Nuova SCU)	26	'Ndrangheta

Leadership

Due to homicides of anti-mafia Judges Borsellino and Falcone in 1992 there has been a significant crack down in mafia activity. General outrage and indignation by the Italian people after the murders of the judges created a synergy against the medieval style mafia. Many of the significant leaders of the mafia including the SCU are now serving long jail sentences.

On June 6, 1995 it was reported that federal police had captured Giovanni

Dalena, aged 35, in Bahia, Brazil. A member of the La Rosa family, and the third ranking man in the Sacra Corona Unita, Dalena had been sought by Interpol for the past 12 years. Dalena is accused by Italian police of heading over 200 Mafiosi linked to the Neapolitan, Sicilian, and Calabrian Mafias. He is also charged with committing over 30 crimes, including 20 murders, as well as narcotics trafficking, extortion, arms smuggling, illegal gambling, and prostitution. His wife, Maria Teresa, is imprisoned in Spain, also accused of involvement with the mafia. Dalena had already been convicted in Italy and sentenced to 13 years in connection with trials involving 180 persons linked to the mafia. He had escaped after two years to Madrid where he was jailed, and again he escaped, and was finally arrested in Brazil.[156]

Another significant arrest in 1995 was that of Angelo Clemente, who had been convicted in his absence of murder and mafia association. Arrested in a farmhouse south of Rome, Clemente was identified by police as boss of the SCU.[157]

Strength
According to data given by the observatory on the European Phenomena, the SCU is comprised of 47 clans and 1561 members (last counted in May 1996.)[158]

Disposition
Area of Influence
The Sacra Corona Unita's area of influence is the Italian region of Apulia in southeast Italy at the heel of the Italian boot. The cities of dominion are Taranto, Brindisi, Bari, Lecce and Salento. Salento is the epicenter of the organization.

Area of Interest
The SCU has its greatest stake in Albania, Croatia and Greece. For Italy and Albania the stretch of Adriatic, that separates the two countries, has become a strategic transfer area for criminals. The unlawful activity that used to go the overland route or "Balkan route" through the former Yugoslavia into Western Europe has been splintered because of the civil war in the former Yugoslavia. Consequently, because of the cease-fire, the U.N. peacekeeping mission, and the surveillance associated with this mission, the former Yugoslavia has become extremely difficult to traverse for travelers and criminals alike. Many areas that were open and free to pass are closed; checkpoints must now be observed. Consequently, most criminal activity originating in Eastern Europe, Southeast and Southwest Asia, must now journey through the Adriatic stretch by boat or ship adding time and possibility of interdiction.

Bonded TIR (Transport International Routier) trucks concealing southwest Asian heroin and driven by Turkish traffickers, used to cross the Balkan route. Now, because of the disruption of that passage the trafficking activity has moved north and south of the conflict area. Southwest Asian heroin shipments concealed aboard TIR trucks, buses, and private vehicle often cross Italy's northeast border with Austria and Slovenia. Additionally, to the south, heroin smugglers take full advantage of new maritime links across the Adriatic Sea by transporting narcotics to southern Italy aboard speedboats and ferries from the coast of Albania and Croatia.[159] Once in Italy the trucks proceed to various distribution points. Certain points in Croatia reportedly harbor "Mafia" sponsored speedboats capable of smuggling contraband to the Italian coast in a couple of hours. Heroin smuggling over this southerly variation of the Balkan route has mushroomed according to Italian officials.[160]

Bari and Brindisi, two important Italian port cities on the Adriatic, have become important illicit activity reception areas due to the conflict in the former Yugoslavia. Indeed, this conflict has empowered the SCU to a level of mafia eminence that it would not have otherwise achieved.

Activities
Significant activities
- Refugee Smuggling (Albania)
- Drug trafficking
- Cigarette Smuggling
- Weapons Smuggling
- Prostitution of Albanian women

Refugee smuggling has always been done on a large scale between Albania and Italy. Now, though, the developed routes across the Adriatic Sea make it easy for any smuggler who does not want to risk the Balkan route because of increased surveillance.

In 1990, some 60 percent of the illicit drugs reaching Italy and Austria came overland via Yugoslavia. This has fallen dramatically because of the aforementioned obstacles. Instead, supplies now travel from Turkey via Greece and Albania, or Romania and Hungary.[161]

The role of the Albanian gangs is particularly important and it has been estimated that 70 percent of the drugs reaching Germany and Switzerland have come via Albania. Criminal groupings in Albania have forged mutually lucrative alliances with the Sicilian mafia and especially the Sacra Corona Unita. As the Balkan highway closed, the sea routes that had been developed to smuggle refugees became conduits for heroin.[162]

Cigarette smuggling has also become a major source of revenue for the SCU. The smuggling is done on speedboats that can cross the Adriatic in a few hours. Each boat has space for 250 cases. According to Marcello Orlandini, journalist for *Ouotidiano*, the take for each load of cigarettes is about 3 million lire (U.S. $20,000) gross and 14 million net profit after expenses (U.S. $9,300).[163]

Cocaine trafficking has emerged in Albania, with South American cocaine being shipped directly through Greece to Albania and from there to Western Europe especially Italy.[164] Albania has become a focus for international trade in stolen cars and weapons, largely as Albanian drug gangs look to reinvest their earnings and diversify. In the absence of effective regional law enforcement, and given both the Albanian gangs' wealth and their apparently good relations with the ruling Democratic Party, there is little Albania's neighbor, Italy, can do in response.[165]   As the Albanian gangs continue to proliferate, the SCU has been there to support them in joint venture opportunities such as the trade of weapons for drugs.

Rai Uno (Italian television station) and the entire press in the Apennines have been writing lately about the frightening transfer of arms between the Italian Apulian region, Montenegro, and Albania. The direct impetus for this campaign was the capture in the port of Brindisi of a large group of arms smugglers from Italy, Montenegro, and Albania.

It was announced in 1995 by the Italian media that members of the SCU are in collusion with the Montenegro authorities, and the police prefects in Brinidisi. Italian TV believes that the illegal arms are shipped on speedboats to Albania and Montenegro and from there are distributed to the Bosnian Serbs.[166]

Minor Activities
- Money laundering
- Auto Theft
- Extortion
- Bribery
- Political Corruption

It has been difficult to trace the money laundering activity of the SCU. Because the four mafias work in close cooperation, one would suspect that the more powerful groups launder money for the lesser crime families, which have not infiltrated the banking system to the same extent.   This seems to be especially true with the SCU, which is the smallest of the Italian mafia groups. Still, there have been traces of SCU infiltration into the Italian banking system. On a wiretap conducted on July 18, 1994, Pasquale Ciola who assumed *de facto* control of the Cassa Rurale and the Artigiana Bank of Ostuni was caught on the telephone plotting with a mafia boss Claudio Locatelli in a venture to take over the Cassa Rurale in Cellino Sammarco.   Ciola reacted that he wanted nothing to do with that particular bank because he thought it was in the control of the SCU and did not want to acquire a "dirty" bank. This is only circumstantial evidence but it does show that the SCU has managed to get into or is seeking to enter the Italian banking system.[167]

Cassa Rurale Artigiana di Ostuni where deposits doubled in the space of a few months ended up in the investigator's net.   In the Brindisi bank, a small group of bank directors and officials worked at a Japanese pace without ever leaving their positions ungarrisoned.   This was a disturbing signal, in that insurance companies indemnify credit institutions for losses resulting from internal fraud only on condition that the bank's officials take uninterrupted holidays lasting at least 15 days.[168]

Connections

The SCU being a relative neophyte has had to develop certain strategic alliances to sustain its growth as a mafia power. Some analysts have suggested that the essence of a strategic alliance is cooperation to exchange technology, and goods and services across national borders, an exchange that can be accomplished through informal agreements, joint ventures and minority equity alliances.[169] The SCU has capitalized on strategic alliances both domestic and international.

Domestic

The SCU maintains close ties with all the Italian mafia groups. The main reason for this is that as the most recently established groups the SCU lacks the resources and the networks to conduct independent business on its own.

The SCU maintains close co-operation with the Cosa Nostra, 'Ndrangheta, and the Camorra. With the SCU's strategic position on the Adriatic Sea it provides these other mafia groups with services they would not be able to provide for themselves e.g. access to cities along the Adriatic, especially Brindisi and Bari, two major import areas for a plethora of smuggling activity.

Government connections are also a big part of SCU operations in south Italy. In December 1991 the minister of Finance, Rino Formica, declared war against the cigarette giant Phillip Morris. The ministry said that Phillip Morris was doing business with smugglers and suspended the sale of Phillip Morris cigarettes i.e. Marlboro, Merit, and Muratti. The market for these products, however, remained large, and promises great opportunities for the SCU.[170]

The smugglers sold these high demand cigarettes on the black market for over us $6 a pack and a river of contraband cigarettes began to flood into the region.[171]

Subsequently, police told a news conference in the city of Bari that Rino Formica had been arrested on suspicion of corruption, as part of a probe into the funding of health care in the southern Apulia region. Formica a socialist, and native of Bari, was charged with corruption and illegal financing of political parties, offenses at the heart of the then 3 year old Tangentopoli (Bribesville) political scandal that has toppled Italy's old guard.[172]

International
(1) Formal

The SCU's main international link is with Albania. The Albanians benefit not only from their links with Italian criminals but also their connections within their own region. Their sphere of influence extends from Kosovo and the country mountainous north what has been called the "Balkan Medellin"[173] to the Macedonian border town of Gostivar, and Vratnica, the Serbian settlements of Veliki Trnovac and Blastica.[174] In Macedonia, for example, the ethnically Albanian party for Democratic Prosperity is widely seen as a front for the Albanian gangs.[175]

(2) Informal

There is increasing evidence that the Italian mafia organizations Camorra and SCU are running a drug distribution network in Germany with the help of the Chinese and Russian mafias.

A newspaper quotes a customs spokesperson from Bari as saying, "heroin, cocaine and other drugs are arriving from Albania by the ton and they are distributed in Germany because of a high profit margin."[176]

Investigation by police and reports showed the SCU has links to the Colombia cocaine cartels, as well as Russian and Southeast and Southwest Asian organized groups.[177]

In another report, police have arrested a mafia member who two years ago escaped from Italy and who was living in Bahia, Brazil, Filipo Abaddo.[178] Here is evidence of a connection or previous safe haven in Brazil. Both Abaddo and Dalena were captured and extradited from the same area of Brazil.

It is suspected that Italian mafia organizations are investing in the former Soviet Union. The Italian-Albanian joint venture, Trans Adriatic Import-Export, was suspected of illegal trafficking as a result of the arrest of an Italian related to the company.[179]

Peculiarities

The SCU resembles a holy mystical organization. Informer Cosimo Capodieci said the SCU used the Crown (Corona) because it resembles the rosary typically used in the Catholic Church to reenact the stations of the cross, and United (unita) because it was necessary to be connected metaphorically to one another, similar to the links of a chain.

Romano Oronzo commissioned a design work to signify the Sacra Corona Unita. He wanted a triangle (sign of the Holy Trinity), the face of Jesus, a dove, the world, the eyes of Romano Oronzo, and a hand that catches a thunderbolt.

Oronzo said he felt dispatched by God to help the world. In the design he asked for the presence of America, Italy, and Sicily designed with various colors, and three islands of the Bermuda Triangle.[180]

There are also peculiar characteristics of Apulian crime with regard to the role of women. Although the prevailing culture considers women second class, women are given powerful roles in the SCU structure. The sister of Giosue Rizzi, one of the SCU bosses, has been given responsibility for maintaining the import and export of drugs from South America. In addition, Domenica Biondi, wife of Giuseppe Rogoli, a woman of few scruples and temper of steel, has been given the role of overseeing the permanence of the hierarchy.[181] The SCU, in this sense, does not discriminate against women in a culture that typically does.

Vulnerabilities

As in any law enforcement operation the number one priority of law enforcement officials should be to seize assets. The Italian authorities have tried to co-operate with the Macedonian police, most notably in the "Macedonia" operation in Skopje, which took place 1994-1995, as well as stepup naval patrols in the Adriatic. All this has yet to show any real results. The coastlines are long and the gangs are increasingly powerful.[182]

Summary

Italy has taken significant measures to debilitate organized crime. In the past, wire-tapping was illegal. Today, however wire taps and other means of surveillance are employed by law enforcement agencies. Laws also are in effect that permit Italian law enforcement officials to confiscate criminal assets. Without capital to influence politicians and bankers, the crime groups will no longer have the leverage they once enjoyed to infiltrate and manipulate the all important checks and balances so vital to Italy's governmental structure.

Italy's battle against the SCU will weaken the Apulian economy because of a significantly reduced cash flow. In the long run, Apulia will only benefit after the weakening of organized crime. The region will have the opportunity to develop a viable market and to utilize its natural resources to maintain stabilized growth while eradicating the stigma of being a crime ridden profligate region.

Conclusions
Opportunities Exploited

To launder illicit proceeds, the IOCGs use any combination of methods and are not strictly limited to one specific geographical area. In fact, as the chapter, *Money Laundering*, demonstrates, criminal organizations are provided a number of opportunities. Countries without anti-money laundering legislation, reporting laws, and currency controls attract and promote money-laundering activities. Banks which adhere to strict secrecy or client confidentiality practices invite money-launderers to do business in their banks. Beyond government and banking controls, criminal organizations are free to operate laundering activities in the non-financial sector with little deterrence.

In the four organizations outlined above, we have identified a number of money laundering opportunities taken and the methods employed by the Italian Mafias. These are summarized in tabular form below.

Camorra

As the table demonstrates, the Camorra exploits opportunities provided by governments, which lack anti-money laundering legislation and maintain bank secrecy. Since Brazil has no money laundering legislation, the Camorra is actively cleaning illicit proceeds in that country. The "*Spaghetti Connection*" is the Camorra's scheme to launder money through a chain of restaurants in Brazil.[183] In regards to bank secrecy practices, Austria has become the Camorra's depository of choice. Austria has also served as a base for the Camorra's criminal activities in Europe.[184]

The Camorra has not limited itself to laundering proceeds solely through inviting countries and offshore banking institutions. The Camorra has resorted to using unknowing front companies in the United States. Reynolds Tobacco

Table 15.3: Money laundering opportunities taken by four Italian Mafias

Country Status	Camorra	Cosa Nostra	'Ndrangheta	Sacra Corona
No Legislation	X	X		
No Reporting Laws			X	
No Currency Controls		X	X	
Bank Secrecy	X	X	X	
Other	X		X	X

was an unknowing participant in a Camorra money-laundering scheme which bought Camel cigarettes through a phony export company.[185] The Camorra then exported the goods and sold the cigarettes at a huge discount in other countries, thus cleaning the money. Furthermore, the Camorra has also invested in European countries with so-called stringent anti-money laundering regulations. The Camorra launders money through capital investments and real estate investment in southern France, specifically, the Cote d'Azure.

The Camorra has been reported to be laundering money in several Central American countries, including Costa Rica, Guatemala, and Nicaragua. Historically, the Camorra used Costa Rica and Guatemala as money laundering centers. This connection has not been substantiated, however, in the recent literature. Recent reports have identified Nicaragua as the leading Central American money-laundering center for the Camorra. In Nicaragua, the Camorra has made use of casinos to launder illicit funds.

La Cosa Nostra

La Cosa Nostra, like the Camorra, have taken advantage of the lack of anti-money laundering legislation in Brazil and has developed extensive money laundering operations there. The Cosa Nostra has taken over businesses in Brazil that were about to declare bankruptcy and used them to launder money. La Cosa Nostra also exploits the offshore banking centers, and is believed to be operating in Antigua, with the Russian mafia, to launder money.

La Cosa Nostra has taken advantage of the opportunities to launder illicit proceeds through Venezuelan banks and exchange houses. La Cosa Nostra accomplishes this by employing the front company method of money laundering. It sets up front companies in Venezuela to assist in laundering money in the Caribbean.

Recent reports indicate that the LCN is now engaged in waste disposal ventures. Undoubtedly this is just another money laundering front. It strongly appears as if the LCN is attempting to "corner" the money laundering market, which will enable it to sustain positive revenues while divorcing itself from the less savory aspects of organized crime. This is not to say that the Cosa Nostra will cease and desist from its criminal activities.

'Ndrangheta

The 'Ndrangheta exploits the lack of anti-money laundering legislation, reporting requirements, and currency exchange controls as well as bank secrecy practices. Since Argentina has no mandatory reporting laws and bank secrecy can only be broken through a court order, the 'Ndrangheta has been able to launder money through prime bank guarantees in excess of three million dollars.[186] Although Switzerland and Austria are not physically located "offshore," for all intents and purposes, due to their strict bank secrecy practices, Swiss and Austrian banks are offshore facilities. The 'Ndrangheta has deposited money in these banking systems to launder illicit proceeds. The 'Ndrangheta has also taken advantage of Canada's lack of control over currency.

Although Germany has strong anti-money laundering legislation and reporting laws, these only apply to the financial sector. The 'Ndrangheta has taken advantage of Germany's non-financial sector by laundering and reinvesting money through German tourist industries, restaurants, and garages.[187] There are no controls on the amount of currency which can be brought into and out of Germany. Therefore, the money is easily repatriated to Italy once it is laundered.

Australia has some of the strictest money laundering legislation and yet, laundering still takes place. The 'Ndrangheta launders money in Australia due to its ethnic ties to the region and the extent of its criminal activities there.

Sacra Corona Unita

Increased rigor in implementing existing anti-money laundering legislation and banking regulations, along with successful "sting" operations, has lessened criminal confidence in laundering through the Italian banking system.[188] Therefore the Sacra Corona has resorted too less traditional methods of laundering through banking institutions. Bank infiltration has been widely reported and it is feared the Sacra Corona has infiltrated the Cassa Rurale di Ostuni and also the Cassa Rurale di Cellino Sammarco.[189] Through bank infiltration, the SCU has developed a means of circumventing Italy's stringent banking legislation, reporting laws, currency controls, and bank secrecy. Italy's 1994 comprehensive money laundering law is fully consistent with the Financial Action Task Force Forty Recommendation and the European Union Money Laundering Directive.[190] Evidently, though, there are still bank officials willing to risk their positions for financial gain. Alternatively, these officials could be pressured into processing the organization's proceeds out of fear. Whatever the case, money laundering is continuing.

Combined Operations

In addition to the specific organizational money laundering activities noted above, this report has discovered some venues at which more than one of the Mafias have actively laundered illicit proceeds. For instance:

- Due to its proximity to Italy and its bank secrecy practices, *Austria* is one of the favorite places for the IOCGs to launder their money.
- All of the IOCGs, including the Cosa Nostra, the Camorra, the Sacra Corona and the 'Ndrangheta, use *Nicaraguan* financial institutions, casinos and trading companies to launder "dirty money." $3.5 to $6 billion was reported to be laundered through Nicaragua by the Cosa Nostra alone in the early 1990s.[191] In Nicaragua, the preferred method of laundering is casinos. The Mafias hired a courier to "lose" large amounts of money in the mafia-controlled casino.[192]
- *Switzerland* served as the *"bank for dirty money"* in a drug trafficking ring which included the Italian Mafias (the 'Ndrangheta and the Camorra) the United Arab Emigrates, the Colombian drug cartels and the Russian mafia.[193]
- Money from a drug ring which included the Italian mafia based in Brazil and Bolivian and Colombian drug cartels was laundered through banks in Uruguay.[194]
- Although it is unclear which Italian Mafia group participated, the Italian and Albanian Mafias have joined together to launder illicit proceeds. The Italian-Albanian joint venture, Trans Adriatic Import-Export, was suspected of illegal trafficking as a result of the arrest of an Italian related to the company.[195] It was also reported that the Russian and IOCGs set up a joint venture in money laundering and drug smuggling.[196]

Domestic and International Links

The IOCGs are working together in certain areas and activities in the world. Cocaine trafficking with the Cali cartels is an example. The Colombians are responsible for delivery of the cocaine and the Italians are responsible for its distribution in Europe. The IOCGs have utilized Central and South America for drug trafficking and money laundering. With the end of the Soviet Union, the IOCGs also have taken advantage of the new opportunities in the newly independent states. They are working with the Russian mafiya in drugs, arms, and nuclear material trafficking and money laundering.

The Cosa Nostra, 'Ndrangheta, and the Camorra were discovered to be trafficking cocaine to the United States. The significance of this discovery was that it demonstrated that the IOCGs are powerful enough to operate in another continent and not need the assistance of the indigenous criminal organizations. The 'Ndrangheta, Camorra, and the Sacra Corona Unita have also benefited from the close scrutiny that the Italian police have placed on the Cosa Nostra. It provided a window of opportunity for these groups to solidify their gains and influence in Italy and make international connections. The IOCGs have exploited the laxity of money laundering laws in certain areas of the world and are placing their "dirty money" in legitimate and illegitimate businesses.

Opportunities NOT Exploited

Before concluding, it is important to mention what our research has not found. For instance, although the Caribbean is a known money-laundering center, we have found very little evidence or specific examples of Italian laundering practices in the region. In open source material, there are often vague references to money laundering activities that do not name specific organizations or the methods they employ. Following are what appear to be a few glaring examples of the opportunities not exploited by IOCGs--at least, according to open source research.

Asia

After an extensive study of the money laundering activities of the IOCGs, it was a surprise to learn that Asia was not being better utilized. In regards to money laundering opportunities, Thailand provides every incentive for this illicit activity. Money laundering is completely legal, and there are no reporting laws or controls on the amount of currency flowing in or out of Thailand. Furthermore, there are no money laundering regulations for the non-financial sector. Thailand has an offshore banking system which will provide services under the banking secrecy practices. Finding no evidence of laundering through Thailand could mean that the system is so unregulated that laundering is not acknowledged or that Thailand is only used by local or regional organized crime groups.

The 'Ndrangheta has operations in Australia and does receive heroin from Thailand. If the 'Ndrangheta is working with other organized crime groups throughout the world, it may have connections to the Japanese Yakuza or the Chinese Triads. Heroin from Southeast Asia is controlled by organized crime but no documentation linking the Asian mafia groups with the 'Ndrangheta has been found in open sources. The 'Ndrangheta is also in Canada, where there is a significant Asian mafia presence. This would also be an environment where the Asian mafia and the 'Ndrangheta could collaborate on certain activities.

Canada

There has been speculation that the Cosa Nostra is in Canada. However, our references to Italian mafia involvement in Canada have been general and historic references, not specifically naming the Cosa Nostra. Therefore, the report cannot conclude, due to lack of definitive evidence, that the Cosa Nostra is in Canada, although there are strong suspicions.

In sum, the open-source literature suggests that not all the opportunities for money laundering, identified in the earlier section, have been grasped. There is no evidence, for example, that the IOCGs have even used the Internet to launder money even though it creates opportunities for easy layering and placement. Since this is a new technology with many unknown security implications, however, open source material may not be the most effective method of researching its possible exploitation for money laundering purposes. Indeed, since all the conclusions of this analysis were drawn from open-source material, the objectives of this project will not be fully served until the final comparison is made with closed source materials.

David Hess, MPIA, University of Pittsburgh, Ridgway Center for International Security Studies.

Kenneth Myers, MPIA, University of Pittsburgh, Ridgway Center for International Security Studies.

Michele Gideon, MPIA, University of Pittsburgh, Ridgway Center for International Security Studies.

Sal E. Gomez, MPIA, University of Pittsburgh, Ridgway Center for International Security Studies.

John A. Daly is a second year, dual-degree, graduate student at the University of Pittsburgh. He studies international affairs and business at the School of Public and International Affairs and the Katz School of Business. He will be studying Eastern European business practices this summer at the Czech Management Center outside Prague. His last study in Europe was at the University of Trento in North Italy. There he researched subjects in European Union Law, Italian History, and Comparative Politics for one year. He worked last summer for the Organization for Security and Co-operation in Europe as a registration and election monitor for the 1997 Municipal Elections in Bosnia-Herzegovina.

References

Trends in Organized Crime, Transnational Organized Crime, Thieves World and *Octopus* by Claire Sterling.

Hot Money and the Politics of Debt by R.T. Naylor.

Notes

[1] Margaret S. Beare (1995), "Money Laundering: A Preferred Law Enforcement Target for the 1990s," *Contemporary Issues in Organized Crime*, edited by Jay Albanese, Criminal Justice Press.

[2] Police Review, (1990) quoted in Nigel South, "On Cooling Hot Money: Transatlantic Trends in Money Laundering," *Criminal Organizations*

[3] As reported by Ernesto Savona (1993) in "Mafia Money Laundering Versus Italian Legislation," *European Journal on Criminal Policy and Research*, Vol. 1, No. 3, page 33.

[4] Ibid., page 34.

[5] Savona (1996), "European Money Trails," *Transnational Organized Crime*, Winter (forthcoming).

[6] Ibid.

[7] Financial Action Task Force on Money Laundering, *FATF-VII Report on Money Laundering Typologies*, June 28, 1996, page 5.

[8] John J. Fialka (April 7, 1996), "Drug Dealers Export Billions of Dollars to Evade Laws," *The Wall Street Journal*, page A4.

[9] "Bank Secrecy Laws Aid Mafia Money Laundering," (May 10, 1995) FBIS.

[10] "Italian Mafia Narcotics, Arms Dealer Arrested in Rio," (May 18, 1995) FBIS.

[11] Phil Williams, "Money Laundering," *Criminal Organizations* (forthcoming) page 11.

[12] Financial Action Task Force on Money Laundering (June 28, 1996), *FATF-VII Report on Money Laundering Typologies*, pages 7-8.

[13] Clifford Krauss and Douglas Frants (October 30, 1995), "Cali Drug Cartel Using U.S. Business to Launder Cash," *New York Times*, page A1.

[14] John Follain (September 17, 1996), "Border-Free Europe Helps Mafia Bosses-France," Reuter European Community Report.

[15] FATF *Report on Money Laundering*, page 7.

[16] Follain, September 17, 1996.

[17] "First Evidence: German Bank Involved in International Money Laundering," (October 27, 1996) FBIS.

[18] "Russian Mafia Reportedly Increasing Presence in UK, Europe," (May 26, 1996) FBIS.

[19] "Bank Secrecy Laws Aid Mafia Money Laundering-Crime Fighter Workshop Viewed," (May 5, 1995) FBIS.

[20] *International Narcotics Control Strategy Report* (March 1996), U.S. Department of

State, Bureau for International Narcotics and Law Enforcement Affairs, Washington, DC, pp. 562-563.

[21] Ibid., p. 543.

[22] Ibid., p. 565.

[23] "Mexico: Official Predicts Money-Laundering Invasion," (September 6, 1996) FBIS.

[24] INCSR, p. 595.

[25] Ibid., p. 528.

[26] "Advantages Country Offers to Organized Crime Analyzed," (December 10, 1995) FBIS.

[27] INCSR, p. 541.

[28] "Indications of 'Mafia-Like' Organizations Detailed," (January 18, 1995) FBIS.

[29] INCSR, pp. 528-529.

[30] Ibid., p. 537.

[31] Edison Stewart (August 28, 1996), "New Laws Studied to Fight Organized Criminals," Toronto Star, page A5.

[32] Michael J. Jordan (May 7, 1996), "FBI Takes a Nibble Out of Crime in East Europe," The Christian Science Monitor, page 1.

[33] "Italy: Anti-Money Laundering Agreement Signed with Russia," (August 2, 199) FBIS.

[34] David Carey, Director DCI Crime and Narcotics Center (January 31, 1996), Prepared Statement before the House International Relations Committee on International Organized Crime.

[35] "Hungary: Police Fear Spread of Organized Crime, Money Laundering," (March 25, 1996) FBIS.

[36] Ibid., p. 571.

[37] INCSR, pp. 591-592.

[38] Ibid., pp. 582-583.

[39] Ibid., pp. 553-554.

[40] McWeeney, Sean M. (February 1987), "The Sicilian Mafia and Its Impact on the United States," FBI Law Enforcement Bulletin, p. 1.

[41] Ibid., p.1.

[42] "Mafia Money Laundering Practices Explained," (7 July 1994), FBIS Report.

[43] Gennaro, G. de (Winter 1995), "The Influence of Mafia Type Organisations on Government, Business and Industry," Trends in Organized Crime, Vol. 1, No. 2, p. 38, FBIS Report.

[44] "World Atlas of Criminal Organizations Noted: The Atlas of Crime and Extortion," (February 16, 1994) La Republica, , FBIS Report.

[45] Gennero, p. 39.

[46] d'Antona, Enzo, "Mafia's 'Financial Crisis' Reported," (November 19, 1995) Il Mondo, FBIS Report.

[47] "World Atlas of Criminal Organizations Noted," (16 February 1994), FBIS Report.

[48] Gennaro, p.37.

[49] "Camorra Said More Extensive Than Other Mafias," (8 December 1993) Il Massagero, FBIS Report.

[50] Mariotti, Cristina (26 January 1994), "It is Cinisello, But It Seems Like Alcamo," Rome Espresso, , FBIS Report.

[51] "Mafia Money Laundering Practices Explained."

[52] MacKenzie, Eduardo (12 January 1993), "Drug Cartel Links to European Mafias Discussed," *El Espectador*, FBIS Report.

[53] "Germany: BKA Says Fall in Organized Crime 'Rather Unlikely," (17 June 1996) *Munich Focus*, FBIS Report.

[54] "Former Minister: Mafia Sending Arms to Serbia," (28 May 1995) *Berlin DDP/AND*, FBIS Report.

[55] Heuze, Richard (16 March 1994), "Justice Official on Anti-Mafia Cooperation with France," *Le Figaro*, FBIS Report.

[56] Sramkova, Marina (3 May 1995), "Russian Mafia 'Bosses' Penetrate Legal Economic Structures," *enni Telegraf*, FBIS Report -- EEU-95-090.

[57] Zoon, Cees (1 February 1994), "Mafia Exploits East European Drugs Market," *De Volkskrant*, FBIS Report.

[58] "Dangers of Terrorist Groups Cited," (11 November 1994) *Bucharest Evenimentul Zilei*, FBIS Report.

[59] Lombardi, Renato (18 May 1993), "Activities of International Mafia Groups Surveyed," *O Estado de Sao Paulo*, FBIS Report.

[60] ibid.

[61] "Rio Becomes Center for Italian Mafia, Colombians," (18 May 1993), FBIS Report.

[62] ibid.

[63] Lombardi, FBIS Report.

[64] "Italian Prosecutors Investigating Peruvian Drug Gangs' Links to 'Camorra,'" (23 February 1994) *El Comerci*, FBIS Report.

[65] Orozco, Roberto B. (11 November 1995), "Indications of 'Mafia-Like' Organizations Detailed," *La Prensa*, , FBIS Report.

[66] ibid.

[67] "Camorra Dollars Arrive; How Organized Crime Moves in Economic Fabric," (21 April 1995) *Rome Confcommercio*, FBIS Report.

[68] ibid.

[69] ibid.

[70] ibid.

[71] "Mafia Money Laundering Practices Explained."

[72] "Police Smash Mafia-led Sugar Fraud Scam," (28 September 1993) *Paris AFP*, FBIS Report.

[73] Guensche, Karl-Ludwig (05 July 1996,), "Germany: BND Notes Russian, Italian Mafia's Modern Methods," *Berlin Die Welt*, FBIS Report.

[74] Faenza, Vito (4 December 1996), "Italy: Minister Moves 180 Detectives to Naples to Fight Camorra," *Rome L'Unital*, FBIS Report.

[75] "Interior Minister Reports to Committee on Organized Crime," (22 October 1995) *Rome Il Giornale*, FBIS Report.

[76] ibid.

[77] Internet Abstract; Lamothe and Nicaso (1995), *The Global Mafia, The New World Order or Organized Crime*, , Toronto: Macmillan.

[78] Claire Sterling (1990), *Octopus* W.W. Norton & Company, New York, London, pp. 46-47.

[79] Ibid.

[80] Sean M. McWeeney (February 1987), "The Sicilian Mafia and Its Impact on the United States," *FBI Law Enforcement Bulletin*, p.1.

[81] Ibid.

[82] Ibid, p.2

[83] Ibid, p.4.

[84] Sterling, p. 133.

[85] Ibid, p. 282.

[86] *Agence France Presse,* (February 20, 1995),   Information provided by Italian Magistrate Pier Luigi Vigna at a conference in Catania Sicily.

[87] http://home.earthlink.net/~donellio/LaCosaNostra/lacosanostra2.html#hierarchy

[88] *Agence France Presse,* February 20, 1995.

[89] "Falcone Murder Trial Opens As Police Make More Mafia Arrests," (February 21, 1995) *Agence France Presse*.

[90] Sterling, p. 306.

[91] Ibid., p. 63.

[92] Brian Sullivan (May 1996), "International Organized Crime: A growing National Security Threat," *Strategic Forum, Institute for National Strategic Studies,* No.74, p. 2.

[93] Alison Jamieson (January 1993), "Collaboration, New Legal and Judicial Procedures for Countering Terrorism," *Conflict Studies,* No. 257, p. 4.

[94] Sean M. McWeeney (February 1987), "The Sicilian Mafia and Its Impact on the United States," *FBI Law Enforcement Bulletin*, p. 4.

[95] Sterling, p. 181.

[96] McWeeney, p. 6.

[97] Ibid., pp. 6-7.

[98] Sterling, p. 130.

[99] Ibid., p. 135.

[100] Ibid., p. 131.

[101] Ibid., p. 135.

[102] Joel Guimaraes (December 10, 1995), "Advantages Country Offers to Organized Crime Analyzed," FBIS Report.

[103] Ibid.

[104] Roberto Orozco (January 18, 1995), "Indications of 'Mafia Like' Organizations Detailed," *La Prensa* FBIS Report.

[105] "Dangers of Terrorist Groups Cited," (November 19, 1994) FBIS Daily Report, EEU-94-228.

[106] "Interior Minister Manfred Kanther Report to the Cabinet Meeting Last," (June 12, 1996) FBIS document.

[107] Ibid.

[108] "Campaign Mounted Against Drug Traffickers in Italy, U.S. --News Conference Held on Operation," (JPRS-TDD-94-041-L) September 15, 1994.

[109] Roy Godson and Williams J. Olson (Jan/Feb. 1995), "International Organized Crime," *Society*, 32:18-29, p.27.

[110] "Time to Reassess the Results of the War Against Drugs in the Andes," (February 2, 1995) *Latin America Newsletters*.

[111] "Russia: Large-Scale Drug Operations, Mafia Viewed," Moscow ZAVTRA, FBIS-TDD-96-024-L.

[112] "Russian, Other Eastern Mafia Activities Reported," Hamburg, DER SPIEGEL, FBIS-WEU-95-074.

[113] "Morocco: Interior Ministry Statement on Dismantling of Drug Networks," Rabat RTM Television, FBIS-TDD-96-008-L.

[114] "Money Laundering Allegations Under Probe At Monaco Casino" (March 7, 1995), *Los Angeles Times, Business; Part D,* Orange County Edition. p.7

[115] "Russia: Large-Scale Drug Operations, Mafia Viewed," Moscow ZAVTRA, FBIS-TDD-96-024-L.

[116] "Mafia's 'Financial Crisis' Reported," (September, 1995) *Il Mundo,* FBIS-TDD-95-035-L.

[117] Jamieson, p. 4.

[118] *Agence France Presse,* February 20, 1995.

[119] "Mafia's 'Financial Crisis' Reported," (September, 1995) *Il Mundo,* FBIS-TDD-95-035-L.

[120] "Falcone Murder Trial Opens as Police Make More Mafia Arrests," (February 21, 1995) *Agence France Presse.*

[121] Williams, Phil (Winter 95), "Transnational Criminal Organizations: Strategic Alliances," *Washington Quarterly* 18; p. 65.

[122] Italian Organized Crime Groups, http://www.alternatives.com/crime/italmaf.html, p. 2

[123] L, Paoli (1994-3), "An underestimated criminal Phenomenon," *European Journal of Crime, Criminal Law, and Criminal Justice,* p. 215.

[124] Italian Organized Crime Groups, http://www.alternatives.com/crime/italmaf.html, p. 2

[125] L. Paoli, p. 218.

[126] "Calabrian Mafia network -- up to 15,000 members," (April 11, 1995) *Agence France Presse.*

[127] "Italy sounds warning over second mafia," (April 11, 1995) *Reuters North American Wire.*

[128] L. Paoli (1994-3), "An underestimated criminal Phenomenon," *European Journal of Crime, Criminal Law, and Criminal Justice,* p. 228.

[129] Ibid., p. 229.

[130] "NCA report shows ethnic criminal links," (December 3, 1996) *The Sydney Morning Herald.*

[131] L. Paoli, P. 229.

[132] "Florida trial ordered for four Metro-area men," (January 22, 1996) *The Toronto Star.*

[133] "Country's Most Important Drug Seizure Detailed," (9 March 1994) Rome RAI Uno Television Network.

[134] "Antinarcotics Operation Tocaia Described," (May 22, 1995) Rio de Janerio Rede Globo Television, FBIS.

[135] Ibid

[136] "Results of Joint Anti-Drug Operation Announced," (Sept. 15, 1994) Rome RAI Due Television Network, FBIS

[137] "Results of Joint Anti-Drug Operation Announced," (Sept, 15, 1994) Rome RAI Due Television Network, FBIS.

138 "Italia: investigan a la Argentina en un caso de lavado de dinero," (10 May 1996) http://www.clarin.ciom.ar /diario/96-05-10/mafias.html.

[139] L. Paoli, P. 221.

[140] *Drug Trafficking in the Mediterranean Littoral* (March 1996), Drug Enforcement Agency, p. 60.

[141] "Drug Traders Redistribute Trafficking Patterns," (27 Oct 1993) *IL MESSAGGERO*, p. 14.

[142] L. Paoli, p. 223.

[143] "Italian mafia may have used Argentine national bank," (May 10,1996) *Reuters World Service*.

[144] L. Paoli, p. 222.

[145] "Mafia-Waffenlager in Mailand ausgehoben," (March 30, 1996) Germany Live, http://www.germany-live.de.

[146] L. Paoli, p. 224.

[147] "'Ndrangheta Reportedly Collaborating," (6 January 1994) *Turin LA STAMPA*, FBIS, p.11.

[148] L. Paoli, p. 216.

[149] "DIA: 'Ndrangheta has wrenched drug trade control from mafia," (April 11, 1995) *Rome ANSAMAIL*, FBIS.

[150] Guido Ruotolo (1994), *La Quarta Mafia*, Napoli: Tullio Pironti, 26-41.

[151] Ibid.

Glossary

Money laundering - A definition of money laundering, encompassing these objectives, is 'the process whereby proceeds, reasonably believed to have been derived from criminal activity, are transported, transferred, transformed, converted or intermingled with legitimate funds, for the purpose of concealing or disguising the true nature, source, disposition, movement or ownership of those proceeds.

Placement - the physical disposal of the bulk cash profits that are the result of criminal activity.

Layering - the piling on of layers of complex financial transactions to separate the proceeds from their illicit sources.

Integration - the provision of legitimate-looking explanations for the appearance of wealth by providing investments in the legitimate economy.

La Cosa Nostra - Sicilian based organized crime group composed of 161 families, 27 clans, and 5700 members. The Cosa Nostra is organized into a hierarchical structure.

'Ndrangheta - Calabrian based organized crime group composed of 160 families and 6,000 members. The 'Ndrangheta is organized into a hierarchical structure.

Camorra - Naples based organized crime group composed of 111 clans and 6700 members. The Camorra has a horizontal organizational structure based on a number of different gangs.

Sacra Corona Unita - Apulia based organized crime group consi'sting' of 47 clans and 1561 members. The Sacra Corona Unita has a horizontal structure with a series of autonomous clans.

16 State (Organized) Crime, Its Control, Unintended Consequences, and Suggestions for Future Research

Jeffrey Ian Ross

Abstract

This article analyses the concept of state crime as a form of state organized crime, focuses on its control, posits a number of areas where control can have a number of unintended consequences, and then suggests how to advance the controlling state crime agenda.

Key Words: State crime, Political crime, Human rights violations, Political corruption

Introduction

During the 1980s, due to a what might be described as a frustration with theoretical explanations about interest articulation and representation and policy development and implementation (e.g., Evans, Rueschemeyer and Skocpol, 1985; Jessop, 1990), the role of the state has become an increasing concern among a growing number of Political Scientists, Sociologists and Criminologists.[1] Although research on this so-called "state theory" has primarily focused on the importance of government bureaucracies in setting the agendas for social welfare and defense issues, some analysts and activists, however, have taken this discussion one step further by suggesting that not only can the state be a victim, punisher, or mediator of crime, but it can also be identified as an initiator. By extension, not only can the state perpetrate crimes domestically, but it can also commit them against a foreign country.

Consequently, the term "*state crime*" has recently entered the social scientific lexicon. Accompanying this development is the acknowledgment that the greatest impediments to the study of state crime are definitional, conceptual, theoretical and methodological in nature, the design and implementation of practical methods to combat this type of behavior, and the provision of adequate resources to accomplish this task (Ross, 1995c).

Indeed, state crime lies at the crossroads of a variety of different academic literature: human rights, political violence, political crime, public administration and policy, and political corruption. This is both an asset and liability to studying this phenomenon. It can draw on this diverse literature, but those unaccustomed to the term may have an initial aversion to its use because it does not so easily fit the conceptual rigidity that some topics or disciplines develop.

Despite some researchers' difficulty and eloquent argument against the use of the term state crime (e.g., Sharkansky, 1995), and considerable variability in how state crimes are defined (Barak, 1991; Ross, 1995c; Kauzlarich and Kramer, 1998), there is also consensus among experts with respect to which actions should be labeled state crimes. State crime, as defined here, is limited to cover-ups, disinformation, unaccountability, corruption, violation of a domestic and/or international law, but also those practices that although they fall short of being officially declared illegalities, are perceived by the majority of the population as illegal or socially harmful. This definition recognizes that legal systems are slow to enact legislation, highly normative, and often reflect elite, if not class, or nonpluralistic interests (Ross, 1995c: 4-6).[2]

State-organized crime, in particular, has been identified as a unique type of state crime. In fact, Chambliss (1989) circumscribes this concept by suggesting that "state-organized crime does not include criminal acts that benefit only individual office holders...unless such acts violate existing criminal law and are official policy" (p. 184). Nevertheless, under this domain he includes certain historical examples of state collusion in piracy, smuggling, arms smuggling, assassinations, and murder focuses primarily on American complicity in these acts. As Friedrichs (1995: 72) so clearly points out:

> [a]s *with much other white collar crime, however, the lines between individual and organizational benefit cannot always be so easily drawn. I would also argue that rarely is this type of activity organized in the figurative sense of the term. Albeit it can be argued that because the perpetrator is an organization, then all things being equal, state crime is, albeit a rarely acknowledged form of organized crime* (e.g., Tilly, 1985).

Friedrichs adds that state-organized crime:

> *can be carried out on all government levels, not simply on the federal level, but on the state and local level as well, down to improper actions of municipal policemen. State-organized crime on the federal level will generally have more pernicious and far reaching consequences than will state-organized crime on the state and local level, simply because the federal government has extraordinary resources and its actions impact on far more people nationally and internationally* (1995: 72-73).

Over time, a number of practices to control state crimes (organized or not) have been articulated and analyzed. Not only will these be outlined, but building on Newtonian physics, because each action inevitably produces a reaction, I also look at the unintended effects of these controls. Finally, I review a series of areas that might be pursued that would improve our ability to control state crime.

The Context of Control
Introduction

In general, although most state crimes go undetected, when they do come to public attention, state crimes are usually perceived as *scandals* (Markovitz and Silverstein, 1988) and/or *crises* of legitimization (Habermas, 1975). In the main,

there are four principal outcomes to these crises of legitimacy or scandals:
- external control initiatives,
- internal resistance,
- public relations, and
- internal control initiatives.

These processes may operate independently or in concert and may be ordered along a continuum of "tangible" (e.g., firing a corrupt police officer/s) versus "symbolic" actions (e.g., press conferences) (e.g., Gusfield, 1963; Edelman, 1964: 1971). The distinction between tangible and symbolic actions is difficult because tangible actions carry with them symbolic benefits as well (e.g., Wilson, 1973).

Too often, attempts by the government or outsiders to control state crime result in additional state criminality in the form of cover-ups and obstruction of justice. Controls that are initiated from inside state agencies should carry more weight than will those implemented from outside. And those controls directed against individuals will be more effective than those involving the entire organization (Ross, 1995a; 1995b).

Nevertheless, the most relevant outcome is control (Gibbs, 1989). Not only do many constituencies believe that state crime should be controlled, several academics, policymakers, and activists have articulated a series of controls that have or should be used.

The next step in this domain is to examine the methods that public and private organizations have used to control state crime caused by individual countries and their respective criminogenic agencies,[3] but realize that controlling state crime can have unintended consequences.

Types of Control

In any government organization, the principle of control arises from the need for members to perform their duties in accordance with some set of standards. These are generally outlined in policy manuals, disciplinary codes, professional rules of conduct, reinforced by ethics guidelines, and bounded by constitutional, administrative and criminal law. Such control should be an ongoing process, not simply a response to some specific wrongdoing.

With respect to the academic research, control is often discussed in research on public administration and policy. Individuals have advanced lists of factors believed to be important in controlling particular government agencies or "deviant" actions perpetrated or engaged in by government departments or the persons who work for them. Additionally, the notion of controlling government agencies is covered by studies that develop typologies, analyze reform, review discretion, and study deviance.

In general, there are seven dimensions/dichotomies of control:
- internal/external,
- domestic/foreign,
- inclusive/exclusive,

- formal/informal,
- state driven/public-initiated,
- violent/non-violent, and
- legal/illegal.

Not only are these controls complimentary, one must recognize that there are no hard and fast demarcations between each dimension/dichotomy. Decisions to use a particular control depend on the context. The decision to rely on a particular control is bounded by the perceptions of community interest and resources. In many instances the general population is indifferent to governmental wrongdoing.

First, control mechanisms may be either internal or external. Internal controls (those implemented inside a bureaucracy) include hiring policies and practices, training, supervision, hierarchy, disciplinary codes, policy manuals, collective agreements, internal review boards, and intra-agency competition. External controls (those administered outside a bureaucracy under question) include external review boards, legislation, and extra-agency competition. Both kinds of control may include powers of review or sanction.

Second, also embedded in this discussion, is a tension between controls initiated inside a country (domestic) versus those implemented from beyond the state's borders (foreign). In many situations, it is not possible to implement controls inside a particular country, but foreign controls suffer from problems connected to a state's sovereignty. In the modern era, according to diplomatic norms and buttressed by international law, states are protected against unlawful intrusion into their own affairs. Thus, part of the solution to securing change in a country's questionable affairs lies in reforming international law and processes, such as the International Court of Justice (e.g., Yarnold, 1995).

Third, control may also differ on an inclusivity/exclusivity dimension. According to Marx (1988), "civilian review boards in the United States, for example, deal single-mindedly with police; legislatures, on the other hand, regulate the police as part of a larger mandate to regulate governmental processes generally."

Fourth, internal and external types of control may be further classified as "institutional/formal" (e.g., legislation, legislative oversight, congressional committees, courts, advisory boards, review boards, ombudsmen, ethics committees, commissions of inquiry, governmental regulation, monetary appropriations, prosecutors, inter-agency competition, etc.), and, "informal" (e.g., public opinion, media attention, public protest, educational activities, lobbying, critical international attention, etc.).

The former is bureaucratic solutions, while the latter are more unstructured and spontaneous. Informal controls are often the last resort for citizens and usually have some influence on other forms of control. Conterminously, these control mechanisms (both formal and informal) can be ordered along a continuum from low-intensity (e.g., letters sent to elected officials) to high-intensity (e.g., riots, armed attacks, assassinations). In sum, institutional controls are primarily conventional and legislated, whereas informal controls are mostly unconventional and nonlegislated.

Fifth, controls can also be divided into state-driven or public-initiated mechanisms. Typically, either public complaints against the government or the state's own fear of losing legitimacy will motivate the government to engage in what appears to be controls against state crimes. State-driven mechanisms include a number of diverse processes. For example, Gill (1995) and Sharkansky (1995) mention judicial or legislative commissions of inquiry that were instituted when there was some suspicion of wrongdoing, (i.e. state crime). These inquiries typically produced reports that made a series of recommendations and occasionally forced the resignations of those under investigation, the restructuring of criminogenic organizations; or, the adoption of new policies. Others, such as Friedrichs (1995), Ross (1995d), and Yarnold (1995) refer to the use of criminal and military trials, and in some cases convictions of a number of "civil servants" (e.g., U.S. Army's Lt. William Calley, and Panama's Manuel Noriega, etc.), who committed state crimes. Clear guidelines or policies, concerning contentious actions which may lead to criminal activities, is another alternative that state criminogenic agencies may adopt (e.g., Menzies, 1995).

Another state-driven mechanism to improve control is training of state actors, in the general discipline of philosophy with a particular emphasis in ethics and morality (e.g., Menzies, 1995). Victimization studies of citizens affected by state crimes may help them prevent possible acts of state crime or deal with acts of state crime before they become more severe (e.g., Menzies). Special agencies, supervisory bodies, or social auditors, could monitor state criminogenic actors (e.g., Gill, 1995; Menzies, 1995). Moreover, building on the Madisonian framework (e.g., *Federalist* 10), criminogenic organizations should serve several masters, not only one (e.g., Gill, 1995; Menzies, 1995). Finally, in some, but not all cases, international law has served as a symbolic motivator to countries that engage in state crimes to change their contentious behaviors (e.g., Molina, 1995) and is one of many tools in the state's arsenal to control other state crimes.

Sixth, since the creation of the modern state, the burden for control has traditionally been left to the public administration itself, with occasional input from citizens and organized nonstate actors. When actions by the public have been taken, they are either violent or nonviolent, and either legal or illegal. On the violent side of the continuum we see such behaviors as oppositional political terrorism, guerrilla warfare, assassination, and collective violence. On the nonviolent end of the spectrum, we have "Publicity ... and access to files of state" criminogenic agencies (Gill, 1985).

Seventh is the distinction between legal and illegal methods of control. In some cases, actors (i.e., individuals or groups) have broken into the offices of state criminogenic organizations and stolen materials that would prove the state was illegally interfering with their group (e.g., Gill, 1995). Others suggest legal nonviolent actions. These behaviors include forming alliances with other nonstate groups. Tunnell, for example, documented how North American Labor has become allies with environmental organizations. This activism can extend to boycotting the products and services of corporations that have benefited from state crimes (e.g., Tunnell, 1995); supporting opponents (e.g., activists, politicians, candidates) who are capable or advocate controlling state crimes (e.g., Tunnell, 1995); launching civil suits against governments and corporations that have profited from state crimes (e.g., Tunnell, 1995); and, Social Defense and civil disobedience are alternative mechanisms to control state crime (e.g., Martin, 1995). However, some responses (e.g., protest, secession of regions from states which may contain a dominant minority in the total state) can be both violent and nonviolent depending on the immediate conditions (e.g., Friedrichs, 1995).

Most democracies are bound by constitutions, the rule of law and, in the majority of cases, a separation of powers and systems of checks and balances among the executive, legislative and judicial branches of government. These notions were outlined by the framers of the American Constitution which was developed in part through a careful reading and interpretation of political theory and the British and French Constitutions as they existed at that time. It is believed that these legal mechanisms will provide a large measure of control over state crimes. A number of other methods have been instituted in democracies, including political competition (in the form of political parties, interest groups, and social movements) which minimizes and in some cases control state crimes. In other states, controls include the reform of public administration, making sure the public administration is paid the prevailing wage if not a higher one for their work, and temporal limits on the time public officials can be in power.

Most state criminogenic agencies in advanced industrialized countries are subject to the previously mentioned types of control. The relative influence of these mechanisms, however, varies with the state criminogenic agencies, units in these organizations, state agents, and the many different actions the state agents engage in.

Additionally, a discussion of controls must be context-specific to be meaningful. Gill, for example, suggests that "effective control and oversight require some mechanism at each level. It does not specify that any particular institutional form will be universally superior; such mechanisms must be rooted within their own culture" (Gill, 1995). He adds, "elegant structures of control and oversight may be erected but may be worthless if those responsible for them see their role as providing no more than a modicum of public reassurance that previous problem-areas of government are under control" (Gill, 1995).

The Adverse Effects of Controls or the Irony of Controlling State Crime

Controls on state criminogenic agencies and practices can have unintended and undesirable effects. This realization is not necessarily new. Merton (1936), for example, suggested that "deliberate social action often produces alternative or additional results to those intended, because of ignorance, error, habit and the imperious immediacy of interest." In particular, controls may lead to unplanned censure of activist politicians by more powerful governmental forces. Additionally, when governments produce reports of inquiries, occasionally some portions are considered to be so secret, preventing full exposure (e.g., Sharkansky: 1995). Moreover, sometimes the internal inquiries "have narrow terms of reference" which prevents the revelation of contentious issues that the general populace considers to be state crimes, or prevents those found culpable to ultimately be held responsible (e.g., Gill: 1995). Both governmental commissions and the reports they produce, give critics of the state (e.g., activists) and victims of state crimes the impression that the government examine their crimes, but it is often interpreted simply as a symbolic gesture if the whole report cannot be released (e.g., Lipsky, 1968; Platt, 1970).

Occasionally trials and convictions of state criminals are "widely criticized [for] deflecting attention from the far more substantial crimes of those higher in the chain of command" (Friedrichs, 1995). Although launching complaints with official bodies is an oft-recommended policy, one should be sensitive to the policies and practices that state criminogenic agencies themselves have established for resolution. Some of these institutional follow-ups may have undesirable consequences especially when the complaint is unfounded. Some of these effects include punishing the wrong person, unjustly singling out an individual, and damaging a person's career, and the toils this can take on his/her health (physical and psychological) and family life (e.g., Cabrera, 1995). Ironically, this practice may encourage unaccountability in some segments of the public bureaucracy.

Rejection of "judgments of an international judiciary concerning [a country's] military actions, even if it supports an international court with more limited jurisdiction" is another unintended effect (Friedrichs, 1995:67-68). This is the frequently cited frustration with international law exemplified when, in 1986, the United States was accused of placing mines in the Managuan harbor. Moreover, broadly based recruitment of individuals from sectors of the community who are traditional victims of state crime into the government or public bureaucracy is not a panacea. Conflicts will develop when "people's self-imposed conformity in the face of some perceived organizational 'dominant ideology'" (Gill, 1995: 97).

Although mass media exposure of state crimes is an essential component of the process of control, its involvement may be circumscribed. For example, the media are generally owned by large corporations that are ideologically aligned with the state or lack the resources (e.g., access or ability) to provide informed analysis of state transgressions (e.g., Tunnell, 1995). The problem is not circumvented with the alternative media because it is simply too underfinanced or does not have a large enough readership/viewership to inform enough members of the public (e.g., Tunnell, 1995).

Better training of government actors (especially the coercive agents) can be seen as an improvement (e.g., Menzies, 1995), but it is not clear in what areas and how we should educate and retrain these individuals. Alternatively, professionalism (in terms of pressures for higher or specialized education and training, the development of professional organizations/associations, etc) is advocated by many pro government organizations and the criminogenic state actors themselves, but this mechanism is criticized as investing the police, military, or national security, etc., organizations with too much power to identify what they define as the important factors for the mission of their organization and the policing of breaches of conduct. Unfortunately, professionalism can isolate the criminogenic organization from public control.

Where control is located in order to maximize its effectiveness is often debated. Local democratic control, which is often advocated, is problematic, as Menzies [1995] argues, because it might lead to a "tyranny of the majority" and may ignore the more subtle ways by which state criminals carry out their activities. Moreover, while some states have implemented legislation to protect whistleblowers, as Gill states, "the main hazard faced by civil servants everywhere has been the variety of internal administrative 'punishments' that might be inflicted upon them" (1995: 98). Finally, formal methods of control are resource intensive (e.g., time consuming) and the result is a powerful motivation to remain silent (e.g., Hurwitz, 1995).

Perhaps Martin (1995) provided the most radical critique of the problems with controlling state crime. He generally suggested that reforms are often piecemeal, and what we need is simply the dismantling of the state as we currently know and experience it. The point of the above discussions is that we must trace the implications of the controls we implement for they may have consequences that were unintended and actually frustrate our ability to control state crime.

Conclusion or How to Advance the Controlling State Crime Agenda
Introduction

How can we advance the controlling state crime agenda?   Three suggestions are put forward: improve and expand research, construct better theory and engage in praxis.

Research

We need to examine, in more detail, the methods that public and private organizations have used to control state crime in individual countries. One way to achieve this is by compiling an extensive set of case studies written by a number of country experts, and attempts to control state crime. This data provides the raw material for a more sophisticated comparative treatment of controlling state crime.

1. Case Studies

A systematic analysis of state crime in and by individual states provides a contextual approach to the subject of state crime. By seeing how states compare against each other we have a base line from which we can observe what facilitates and deters states crimes in particular settings. One of the important ways to examine controls is by compiling case studies written by country experts, who analyze attempts to control state crime. These efforts provide the raw material for a sophisticated theoretical treatment of controlling state crime and possibly aid those intent upon controlling, minimizing or reducing the frequency and intensity of state crime.

2. Evidence Marshaled

Researchers should not be content to simply use anecdotal, hearsay, or undocumented evidence. Instead they should analyze empirical data. By this it is meant that the marshaling of historical examples, case studies and statistics where appropriate. Each analysis should include a brief historical treatment of the subject however the bulk of the discussion should covers the past thirty-eight years (i.e., since 1960), a period coterminous with what some authors label the post-industrial phase (Ingelhart, 1977).

3. Case Selection Criteria

Cases should be selected based on economic and political-ideological grounds, rather than on a geographical rationale. This strategy also recognizes the centrality of political and economic forces in the commission and control of state crime. In practice, analysts should begin by systematically analyzing advanced industrialized democracies, as they are most amenable to investigation because of the relative openness of their governmental bureaucracies.

The next logical step should be a systematic investigation of controlling state crime in lesser-developed contexts using the same carefully documented sources and style of investigation used in this project. This may involve an analysis of controlling state crime in Caribbean, Central American, South American, Middle Eastern, African, and Asian states. Many of these countries were or are client states of the larger advanced industrialized countries.

Finally, we need to examine the process and outcomes of controlling state crime in the Communist or formerly Communist countries, also known as second world, or transitional contexts. Because of the changing nature of these countries they should be tackled last in order to take into account the processes and mechanisms put in place by these embryonic new governments to control their citizens and states.

Only the most frequent types of state crime occurring in a variety of states experiencing a high level of state crimes should be reviewed. There should be a systematic effort to include a wide variety of cases, not only those ones that are the most readily available. This precaution would add some generalizability to the findings. A comparative approach requires adequate rationale for the selection of different cases or processes. Contributions should also demonstrate historical depth; research needs to deal with events and mechanisms that are connected to overt and covert causes, which may otherwise be overlooked. The genesis of these state crimes as well as the success or failure, if any, of solutions implemented to control such crimes should also be integral components of this proposed research agenda.

Theory Development

So far, the majority of work both on the causes and control of state crime has been in the structural theoretical tradition. Clearly the psychological and public administration/policy theories have to be examined. Applying psychological and public administration/policy theories which examine individual level processes at the individual and group level can shed light on the problems and opportunities inherent in controlling state crime.

Praxis

Perhaps, more important than theory construction and empirical research should be in the area of policy development, particularly the implementation and evaluation of programs and methods to control state crime. Evaluation is a "powerful tool for planning, developing and managing...[governmental] programs. As an objective means of documenting success, identifying problems and guiding refinements, program evaluation is important to a variety of stakeholders" (Przybylski, 1995: 4). In the main, there are two types of evaluation: process and impact/outcome. The former is:

> *systematic observation of a program's implementation and activities. The focus is on internal dynamics and how actual operations are organized and carried out. In process evaluations, the aim is to discover what actually is happening and how that compares with what was planed or expected* (Przybylski, 1995:4).

In the latter, we:

> *attempt to discover outcomes and to attribute them to the program, rather than outside influences. In other words, impact evaluations aim to provide stakeholders information that clearly confirms that the program (or specific activities) does or does not work* (Przybylski, 1995: 4-5).

There is a considerable need to utilize available, viable usable process and outcome assessment criteria that would measure success, failure, boomerang effects, and process that are simply irrelevant.

While multifactor analysis should be utilized, most research uses linear "cause and effect" paradigms that arguably are best suited for studying simpler phenomenon. Since state (organized) crime is dynamic and complex, the study of state crime could profit by using the newer Artificial Science paradigms (i.e., chaos, uncertainty, complexity etc. theories) and their artificial neural network tools (Buscema, 1998).

Summary

In sum, controlling state crime is a collective process requiring the good will and patience of many individuals and organizations in different disciplines, professional groups and countries. Research and policy development in this area is a herculean task. Assembling research priorities and worthwhile policy initiatives is difficult at best. Having analysts sing from the same sheet or music is hard given vagaries in disciplines, professions, training, and languages. The accumulation of information, however, should be perceived not as an end in itself, but a continuation in the battle to combat state crimes and preserve democracy.

Jeffrey Ian Ross, *Ph.D. has conducted research, written and lectured on national security, political violence, political crime, violent crime, and policing for over a decade. His work has appeared in many academic journals and books as well as in popular magazines. Dr. Ross is the editor of Controlling State Crime: An Introduction (Garland Publishing, 1995), Violence in Canada: Sociopolitical Perspectives (Oxford University Press, 1995), Cutting the Edge: Current Perspectives in Critical and Radical Criminology (Praeger, 1998); and State Crime: A Comparative Study of Control in Seven Advanced Industrial Democracies (Harrow and Heston, forthcoming); and the author of Police Violence as a Social Problem (Gordon and Breach, 1998) and The Dynamics of Political Crime (Sage, forthcoming). He received his Ph.D. from the University of Colorado.*

References

Almond, G. (1956). "Comparative Political Systems," *Journal of Politics* Vol. 18, August, pp. 391-409.

Barak, Gregg. (ed.) (1991), *Crimes By the Capitalist State: An Introduction to State Criminality*. Albany: State University of New York Press.

Buscema, Massimo P. (1998). "Artificial Neural Networks and Complex Social Systems," *Substance Use and Misuse*, Vol.1. 'Theory, Vol. 2. 'Methodology', Vol. 3. 'Applications.'

Cabrera, Natasha. (1995). "Control and Prevention of Crimes Committed by State Supported Educational Institutions," in Jeffrey Ian Ross (ed.) *Controlling State Crime*. New York: Garland Publishing, pp. 163-206.

Chambliss, William. (1989), "State Organized Crime." *Criminology* Vol. 27, No. 2, pp. 183-208.

Edelman, Murray. (1964), *The Symbolic Uses of Politics*. Urbana: University of Illinois Press.

Evans, Peter B., Dietrich Rueschemeyer, and Theda Skocpol (eds.). (1995), *Bringing the State Back*. Cambridge, Eng: Cambridge University Press.

Friedrichs, David O. (1995), "State Crime or Governmental Crime: Making Sense of the Conceptual Confusion," in Jeffrey Ian Ross (ed.) *Controlling State Crime*. New York: Garland Publishing, pp. 53-80.

Gibbs, Jack. (1989), *Control: Sociology's Central Notion*. Urbana: University of Illinois Press.

Gill, Pete. (1995), "Controlling State Crimes by National Security Agencies," in Jeffrey Ian Ross (ed.) *Controlling State Crime*. New York: Garland Publishing, pp. 81-114.

Gusfield, Joseph. (1963), *Symbolic Crusade: Status Politics and the American Temperance Movement*. Urbana, IL: University of Illinois Press.

Habermas, Jurgen. (1975), *Legitimation Crisis*. Boston: Beacon.

Hurwitz, Leon. (1995), "International State-Sponsored Organizations to Control State Crime: The European Convention on Human Rights," in Jeffrey Ian Ross (ed.) *Controlling State Crime*. New York: Garland Publishing, pp. 283-316.

Ingelhart, Ronald. (1977), *Silent Revolution: Changing Values and Political Styles among Western Publics*. Princeton: Princeton University Press.

Kauzlarich, David and Ronaid C. Kramer. (1998), *Crimes of the Nuclear State*. Boston: Northeastern University Press.

Lipsky, Michael. (1968), *On the Politics of Riot Commissions*. Madison, WI: Institute for Research on Poverty, University of Wisconsin.

Markovitz, Andre S. and Mark Silverstein (ed.) (1988), *The Politics of Scandal*. New York: Holmes and Meire.

Martin, Brian. (1995), "Eliminating State Crime by Abolishing the State," in Jeffrey Ian Ross (ed.) *Controlling State Crime*. New York: Garland Publishing, pp. 389-419.

Marx, Gary. T. (1988), *Undercover: Police Surveillance in America*. Berkeley: University of California Press.

Menzies, Ken. (1995), "State Crime by the Police and Its Control," in Jeffrey Ian Ross (ed.) *Controlling State Crime*. New York: Garland Publishing, pp. 141-162.

Merton, Robert K. (1936), "Unanticipated Consequences of Purposive Social Action," *American Sociological Review* Vol. 1, 894-904.

Molina, Luis F. (1995), "Can States Commit Crimes? The Limits of Formal International

Law," in Jeffrey Ian Ross (ed.), *Controlling State Crime.* New York: Garland Publishing, pp. 349-388.

Platt, Anthony (ed.) (1970), *The Politics of Riot Commissions, 1917-1970* New York: Collier.

Przybylski, Roger (1995), "Evaluation as an Important Tool in Criminal Justice Planning" *The Compiler* Summer, pp. 4-17.

Ross, Jeffrey Ian. (1995a), "Confronting Community Policing: Minimizing Community Policing as Public Relations," in Peter C. Kratcoski and Duane Dukes (eds.) *Issues in Community Policing.* Cincinnati, OH: Anderson Publishing, pp. 243-259.

Ross, Jeffrey Ian. (1995b), "A Process Model of Public Police Violence in Advanced Industrialized Democracies," *Criminal Justice Policy Review* Vol. 17, No. 2, pp. 67-90.

Ross, Jeffrey Ian (ed.) (1995c), *Controlling State Crime.* New York: Garland Publishing.

Ross, Jeffrey Ian. (1995d.), "Controlling State Crimes by the Military," in Jeffrey Ian Ross (ed.) *Controlling State Crime.* New York: Garland Publishing, pp. 115-139.

Sharkansky, Ira. (1995), "A State Action May be Nasty But Is Not Likely to Be a Crime," in Jeffrey Ian Ross (ed.) *Controlling State Crime.* New York: Garland Publishing, pp. 35-52.

Tilly, Charles. (1985), "War Making and State Making as Organized Crime," in Peter B. Evans, Dietrich Rueschemeyer, and Theda Skocpol (eds.) *Bringing the State Back In.* Cambridge, Eng: Cambridge University Press, pp. 169-191.

Tunnell, Kenneth D. (1995), "Crimes of the Capitalist State Against Labor" in Jeffrey Ian Ross (ed.) *Controlling State Crime.* New York: Garland Publishing, pp. 207-235.

Yarnold, Barbara M. (1995), "A New Role for the International Court of Justice: Adjudicator of International and State Transnational Crimes," in Jeffrey Ian Ross (ed.) *Controlling State Crime.* New York: Garland Publishing, pp. 317-348.

Wilson, James Q. (1973), *Political Organizations.* New York: Basic Books.

Notes

1 Including, but not limited to academics, policymakers, politicians and activists.

2 This definition does not suggest that violation of democratic norms and values are unethical, but there is ample evidence of government agencies, groups in those organizations, and individuals who work for the government who violate criminal, civil, and international law.

3 There is some appreciation that not only can states be domestic contributors to crime but they can also be transnational criminals (Chambliss, 1989). Many of the advanced industrialized countries have supported and also exploited lesser developed countries. This phenomenon usually characterized by 'dependency theory' has led a number of development and dependency theorists to suggest that what the advanced industrialized countries are doing is a subtle form of state crime.

Part IV
Reactions of
Criminal Justice

"What is past is prologue,"
William Shakespeare,
The Tempest

17 The Future of Narco-Terrorism: Colombia – a Case Study

Peter A. Lupsha and Sung-Kwon Cho

Abstract

Using Colombia as a case study, narco-terrorism, *is defined and described noting the necessary "actors" - in both the criminal and legitimate communities, including the State; conditions for its initiation and continuation, variations in actions and reactions, types and predictions about its future within the context of organized crime and transnational organized crime.*

Key Words: Narco-terrorism, Narco-violence, Narco-dominance, Narco-dialogue, Narco-dollars, Co-location, State capacity, Organized crime/transnational organized crime, State- symbiotic relationships.

Introduction

In order to understand the future of narco-terrorism we must heed Shakespeare's admonition. The surest guidance to the future is that it will build upon the incremental escalation of violence etched in the blood and bone of our recent past.

The key difference between narco-terrorism and other forms of terrorist violence is that it is economic. It is business-based, rooted in economic evaluations of contract, conduct, risk and threat. narco-terrorism is not an ideational commitment to political redress or to revolutionary change.

While there are a variety of types and degrees of narco-terrorism, all are based on a business paradigm. Regrettably most of the analysts who have written about it have simply taken ideational terrorism frameworks and have applied them to the narco-violence situation. Works such as Richard Clutterbuck's (1990) speak of *"Terrorism, Drugs and Crime,"* and how European civil society should react to them, but make only passing mention of narco-terrorism. Clutterbuck recognizes that - narco terrorism is based in business or corporate relationships, but fails to develop the paradigm. Instead, he focuses on the traditional frameworks and models of terrorism. Others, such as Schmid (1985), place narco-terrorism under the rubric of "criminal terrorism." Thus, they stress the criminal predicate and law enforcement's response and responsibility rather than the economic exchange nature of the acts. More recent studies, which understand the interjurisdictional nature of this problem, such as Nadelmann (1993) or Friman (1996) stress the internationalization of law enforcement and US foreign policy initiatives and imperatives. They recognize that the future of narco-terrorism and responses to it must be interjurisdictional. They fail to note, however, the ways in which inherent corporate-business nature of this issue color and often mislead that response.

There are a number of reasons for this. First, there is an unwillingness to recognize that the criminality of narco-terrorism is both organized and corporate-business based. Or more importantly, that it is commonly a reaction to previous implicit understandings between the political system and organized criminal community, which is noted in the literature.

Second, there is the problem of definition. The term narco-terrorism was "coined" by Peruvian President, Belaunde Terry. He used the term "*narcoterrorismo*" in 1983 to refer to attacks on the counter-narcotics police by Sendero Luminoso insurgents. By 1986, the term was commonly used in Peru and Colombia to refer to relationships between the drug traffickers and guerrillas. By May of 1987 it had become part of common speech and U.S. News and World Report, headlined "*narco-terrorism*" in a cover report.

As Lupsha (1996) points out, insurgents of both the right and left frequently turn to the illicit drug industry as source of income via taxation, extortion or security support. But epistemically speaking, this was a poor beginning for scholars.

The term came to stress the linkages between insurgent terror, guerrillas and drug trafficking entrepreneurs. A criminal label was immediately stuck on the act, and colored by adjectives such as "heinous" and "cowardly." Such adjectives and images are at times factually correct. But too frequently these kinds of adjectives present the mindset of the State. State actors in these circumstances are looking for rationalizations to present to the global media and policy community for the lack of state's capacity to enforce law or have territorial integrity or control over their land area. Thus, narco-terrorism frequently becomes a politicized synonym for insurgent guerrillas being somehow involved in drug cultivation or processing operations controlled by drug traffickers- usually through informal taxation (extortion) or protection (security).

It is a useful image for governments seeking moneys, support, and modern military equipment, and who know that "drug trafficking" is a "hot button" to push with United States policymakers. It is not, however, an accurate or useful definition of narco-terrorism.

Never mentioned, whether by ignorance or deception, is the fact that these nation-states and their regime agents frequently have interactions, transactions and ongoing dialogues with both insurgent guerrilla organizations and organized drug trafficking entrepreneurs. It is disruption in the equilibrium of these understandings between the criminal and political community that frequently results in true narco-terrorism. Narco-terrorism refers to acts of violence and terror against persons and property --frequently agents of the State or media influentials--in order to further the political, economic, and social agendas of drug traffickers by intimidating or coercing governments, their agents, individuals, groups or elite populations to influence and change their behaviors and policies. This definition is the centerpiece of what follows. But first we need to isolate some other "smoke and mirrors" misconceptions that make it difficult to discuss this topic.

One important misconception is the problem of State capacity or lack thereof. The lack of state capacity, i.e. the ability to make it's official will felt, especially over vast areas of geographic territory as in Bolivia Colombia and Peru, or in "denied" urban areas such as Brazil's shantytowns, or entire cities or regions of narco-dominance, such as the cities and regions around Cali or Medellin Colombia, is one key reason for the confusion and, at times active deception, that often surrounds this concept. No regime or state agent willingly enjoys acknowledging that they, the government, do not control their own territory.

They therefore, chose to stress one major point of conceptual confusion group. Namely that ideological and political insurgents ("terrorists" from the regime's perspective), drug cultivators and the agents of international trafficking corporations frequently are co-located in geographic areas of the country that the government does not control. *Co-location* is not empirical evidence of interaction. The typical State spokesman response is simply an example of the "*post hoc ergo propter hoc*" (i.e. "After this, therefore, because of this") fallacy. As Lupsha (1989) has documented, co-location empirically increases the probability that interaction may take place. In fact, we now have decades of data, from a number of countries around the globe, which support the assertion that in areas of co-location insurgents tend to tax cultivation and processing, as well as, provide protection to production (laboratory) areas in return for cash and arms. The ongoing muddled question, needing an empirical answer, is whether insurgents have extended such interactions into actually taking over production and trafficking from the frequently law enforcement fragmented drug trafficking entrepreneurs? (Lupsha, 1987) Although this is an important and interesting question for which we need better answers, none of this is *narco-terrorism*.

The argument being presented in this paper is that "true" narco-terrorism tends to occur, when empirically certain normative value structures, "rules of the game," between the state and organized crime are broken and the equilibrium of perceived "shared understandings" between organized crime and the State are thrown out of balance.

Some readers may strongly disagree, or may even fail to see this conceptualization. It is a different paradigm. Or, they may choose to deny that in many nation-states there is a nexus of rules and understandings between organized criminal and legitimate regime and political communities. They may also deny that regularized dialogues and exchange relationships, rules, roles, bargaining. Boundaries and mutual payoffs occur regularly and are understood by the experienced players of the game (Kaplan and Dubro, 1986). Anyone who has lived with or studied organized crime and the State over time, particularly in less developed nation-states, knows that this is correct. Given the different perspective which we are presenting, we ask you, the reader, to allow us to press our argument before extending it into the future.

We are arguing that when the unwritten exchange "contracts" between organized crime and State is broken, for some reason, or are in disequilibria, violence in the form of terror is likely to occur. In the case of transnational organized crime groups - such as the major drug trafficking entrepreneurs - narco-terrorism will result. The bottom line too often ignored by both students of criminology and international relations, after global oil, and perhaps on a par with gold, diamonds, tobacco and arms, illicit drugs are one of the key drivers of the global hard currency economy (Williams, 1995). This is especially so for the developing world. In order to better understand how the interaction between drug trafficking and the State leads to narco-terrorism, we will closely examine one of the best documented and most empirically detailed cases of narco-terrorism, its evolution and its effects: Colombia.

Colombia: A Case Study

Drug trafficking began to take-off in Colombia after the 1972 fall of the Allende government in Chile, the establishment of a military regime there and the accompanying crackdown on drug trafficking. The result was that Chilean-based drug chemists and entrepreneurs, who were associated with Cuban trafficking organizations, scattered around the globe, but especially to Bolivia and to Colombia.

The growth of the Colombian cocaine industry was mostly ignored by the international system until the late 1970's when it began to clearly affect the United States. Marijuana, grown and exported from Colombia, was one of the main drugs of choice for the American consumer from the early 1970's on. By the mid-1970's this was beginning to be followed and supplanted by cocaine. Any narco-terror, however, was small scale, individually focused and primarily directed to problems of "Platt or plum" (i.e. "take the money or the lead") with police or other agents of the State, or used for internal (inter-group) discipline and control.

This situation began to change in December 1981 with the kidnapping of Martha Nieces Ocher Vasquez, sister of Jorge Ochoa, the leader of the Ochoa clan within the Medellin "cartel," by the M-19 guerrilla group. As Castle (1987) notes, this event galvanized the Ochoa's who called a meeting of major drug traffickers at their Las Margaritas estate. While these various drug entrepreneurs had been loosely aligned in the past, they all had faced the threat of kidnapping and extortion by the guerrillas. They had another common bond, they were all threatened by an extradition treaty between Colombia and the United States, which had been ratified in 1980 but had not as yet been enforced.

The result of this meeting was the formation of MAS (*Muertea Secuestradores*) "Death to Kidnappers" organization. It took out full page advertisements in the major Colombian dailies, and even air-dropped leaflets over major soccer stadiums, offering rewards and promising death to all kidnappers unless they stopped threatening Colombia's businessmen and ranchers. Soon bodies branded with a cross, the mark of MAS, began to appear dumped on church steps and university campuses as the advertisements had foretold. This direct action by these drug entrepreneurs not only put them in touch with the government which shared their concerns about the guerrillas and kidnapping, but also with the guerrillas who needed money and arms and controlled "liberated" territories suitable for airstrips, cultivation and as drug laboratory sites.

By the time Martha Ochoa gained her freedom, MAS had accomplished four major, but likely unforeseen, goals:

- It impressed the Colombian public and elites with its ability to get things done. Efficiency and justice, even curbside justice, being a rare commodity in Colombia.
- It had strengthened the working relationships among various regional drug trafficking organizations.
- It had created contact points and potential alliances with both the government and its agencies, particularly the military.
- It established similar contact points with the guerrillas.

Prior to this time, the traffickers' relations with the government had primarily been economic via banking and investments and political via gifts and campaign contributions. The economic clout of these "narco-businessmen" in Colombia was real and impressive. The vast influx of narco-dollars from marijuana and cocaine trafficking allowed it, alone among the South American nations, to escape the debt crisis that engulfed the region at that time. Narco-dollars so flooded Colombia - affecting the black-market hard currency exchange rates - that by 1976 the National Bank was forced to establish the "*ventanilla siniestra*" (the left-handed window) to legally convert narco-dollars into pesos. As Lupsha (1981) reported, from 1976 to 1979 narco-dollars ranged from 14 to 20 percent of Colombia's money supply. Thus, it is not surprising that Colombian governments of this period preferred to view illicit drugs as one of the United State's domestic problems and not one that should concern Colombia very much.

This position changed in 1984, when Colombian Justice Minister Rodrigo Lara Bonilla was assassinated shortly after he had authorized the raid on the Tranquillandia laboratory complex. The government immediately announced they would begin to implement the extradition treaty and to extradite Colombians wanted by the United States for drug trafficking.

What is less known outside of Colombia about the Tranquillandia complex is that it was a direct outgrowth of relationships among traffickers and others begun with MAS. It was a corporate joint venture by Pablo Escobar, Evaristo Porras of Leticia, Gonzalo Rodriquez Gacha, who had made his money in emerald smuggling, and the Ochoa clan. It was protected by the FARC guerrilla organization that taxed production and provided physical security. Also less known, is the fact that these millionaire "*narco-businessmen*," who were making major contributions to the economic and political communities, believed this was a safe investment. They thought they had established claims on the political system, and particularly on Justice Minister Lara Bonilla and others who had received their campaign contributions and whom they had helped elect. Colombian drug traffickers had invested in Colombian politics, politicians and campaigns since the early 1970's. They believed that they had established a working relationship with the regime, particularly with those political figures whom they dined, gifted, and met with, as well as, contributed to. In Justice Minister Lara's case, Evaristo Porras, a trafficker and community leader in Leticia was the contact-man for the group. At the same time Pablo Escobar had been elected to the Colombian Congress as "Alternate Congressman" from Medellin.

After the election, however, confidence in Minister Lara Bonilla began to sag among the illicit drug industrialists. The US Embassy and the media were "puffing up" and magnifying the Justice Minister as being a strong friend of the United States and its counter-drug efforts. More importantly, he appeared to enjoy their praise and attention. In response to rumors and a sense that Lara was untrustworthy, the drug traffickers tried direct dialogue. When that approach failed, they sent him a message. On February 24, 1984 they assassinated his assistant, a lawyer named Eduardo Gonzalez. But the message was misinterpreted. Rather than intimidating Lara, it drove him closer to the US Embassy and to his taking a hard line.

Eddy (1988) reported that Justice Minister Lara had told narco-entrepreneur and political contributor Evaristo Porras, in referring to Pablo Escobar and Gonzalo Rodriguez Gacha, "so now the birds are firing at the guns." But at this time the drug traffickers viewed themselves as being almost legitimate businessmen and not criminals or "birds" shooting, or to be shot at.

The day before the Tranquillandia raid, which only six key Colombian government officials were supposed to know about, the narco-entrepreneurs still wanted to deal and negotiate with the key representatives of the political system. They sent four representatives to the home of Colonel Jamie Ramirez, who was in charge of the Tanquillandia operation for Minister Lara. He happened to be away for the weekend, but his brother, a retired National Police major, received them. Eddy (1988) reports the following conversation. "Listen...just tell him we have 400 million pesos (approximately $3,000,000) for him which we will deposit anywhere he wants if he just stays put."

Colonel Ramirez, a soldier at heart, would march forward following orders. Justice Minister Lara Bonilla, impressed with US satellite technology, apparent power and courting, chose to ignore the murder of his assistant and misread the likely response from these "birds." He ordered the Tranquillandia raids, which remain one of the greatest successes in the "War on Drugs." It destroyed over 12 tons of cocaine and millions of dollars in narco-investment, labor and effort.

Seven weeks later, narco-terrorism officially began in Colombia. The drug-entrepreneurs retaliated for the perceived breech of faith and catastrophic loss of money, product and production. They assassinated the Colombian Justice Minister, Rodrigo Lara Bonilla on April 30, 1984.

If the past implicit understandings, implied contracts and the "rules of the game" could be broken by the government and its Justice Minister, who appeared to prefer doing the work of the United States in Colombia, then from the narco-entrepreneur's perspective he was just another unfaithful collaborator whose death could be sanctioned. To them this was business. From the government's perspective this was narco-terrorism.

During the crackdown on the cocaine industry, which followed the assassination, the narco-entrepreneurs would once again sit down with the government and its representatives in order to seek some negotiated settlement. Less than a month after the murder, the leaders of the drug cartels who had fled to Panama were meeting with the Colombian Attorney General, Carlos Jimenez Gomez, a recent ex-president, Lopez Michelson and members of the Colombian economic-political oligarchy. At these meetings the "*narco-businessmen*" presented the government with a memorandum outlining their portfolio. According to Arango and Childs (1984) they employed thousands of Colombians and claimed to have an annual income of $2 billion -much of which "is fed into the Colombian economy."

Such "*narco-dialogues*" between the "narco-industrialists" and the government continued in every presidential administration, liberal or conservative, since then. In fact, as Lupsha (1996) reminded Colombians, by the late 1980's the "Cartels" had become a major "*gremio*" (interest group) with which the government had to negotiate. Clawson *and* Lee (1996) interviewed Joaquin Vallejo, "official" liaison between the government and the Medellin Cartel in 1988 and 1989. Vallejo stated that, "they have much money, but they are not free men. They are capable of anything, even retirement, provided that they can get their freedom."

Between periods of narco-dialogue, and primarily due to international pressure the United States and its drug enforcement agencies, Colombia attempted to crack down on the trafficking organizations. Raids, crop eradication, seizures, arrests, and most importantly extradition, and the threat of extradition to the United States, were the major weapons.

At times as we shall see the cartels even cooperated in this. For example, they handed over Carlos Lehder Rivas to the government because of his drug use, violence and threatening erratic behaviors. But more typically the result of any crackdowns was, in the main, an increase in narco-terrorism against the government and those who sought to impose extradition on these narco-entrepreneurs. Indeed, it is possible to map and chart the fluctuations and shifts in *narco-terror* in Colombia as the dance of negotiation and narco-dialogue and U.S. pressure and government crackdowns occurred. As Sung-Kwon Cho (1995) notes the relationship between dialogue and repression, and the rise and fall in narco-terrorism evolved in distinct and observable periods.

Period I - March 1983 - September 1985.

Background: The narco-entrepreneurs appeared to perceive a violation of historic understandings with the government and its contributions to the economy as a U.S. counter-narcotics pressure on the young administration of President Belisario Betancur.

- **Gov. Action**: 3/84. Planning and implementation of the Tranquillandia Complex raid.
- **Dt. Reaction**: 4/84. Justice Minister Lara Bonilla is assassinated.
- **Gov. Reaction**: 5/84. Threat of implementation of the Extradition treaty, and the offer of narco-dialogue.
- **Gov. Action**: 11/84. Government rejection of narco-dialogue under strong US pressure.
- **Dt. Reaction**: 11/84. The bombing of US Embassy. (1 killed; 5 wounded).
- **Gov. Action**: 12/84-9/85. Renewed narco-dialogue. Extraditions are delayed or put on hold.
- **Dt. Reaction**: *narco-terror* subsides. The only acts of terror are against specific judges involved in drug trials who do not respond to warnings or offers of money.

Period II: Sept. 1985- Aug. 1986.

Background: In late 1984 U.S. independent efforts and pressure results in the arrests of Jorge Ochoa and Gilberto Rodriguez Orejuela by the Spanish government while on vacation with their wives. In September they went before a Spanish court hearing regarding their extradition to the United States. The court, however, rejected the testimony of U.S. drug informant Barry Seal relating to their involvement in drug trafficking via Nicaragua and refused extradition.

- **Gov Action**: Colombia asked for and received extradition of Ochoa on charges of "falsification of a public document" and that of Gilberto Rodriguez Orejuela on other minor domestic charges.
- **Dt Action**: 9/85. (1) Alicides Arizmendi, Director of La Picota prison (Bogota) murdered. He had foiled the escape of Juan Ramon Matta Ballesteros, who was critical to the Nicaragua charges pending against Ochoa. After his death the escape was successfully accomplished. (2) The traffickers negotiated a deal with M-19 guerrillas to destroy the court evidence and files against them in Colombia. They had obviously learned from the experience in Spain that files could be fatal. (3) 11/85. The M-19 attacks and occupies the Palace of Justice and the Supreme Court of Colombia.
- **Gov. Reaction**: The army responds to the Court occupation with maximum force. The guerrillas and the all members of

Colombia's Supreme Court are killed, the building set on fire, and all drug files and records destroyed. Any collaboration between the narco-entrepreneurs and the M-19 leadership in the raid was not exposed at the time, and according to Castillo (1991) it is still a matter of debate. Whether it was the M-19 or the Army that was assisting the narco-industrialists, their end was served.

- **Dt Action**: 11/85. The books are cleared on Col. Jaime Ramirez, who led the Tranquillandia raid. He is murdered while on an outing with his family outside Bogota.
- **Gov. Reaction**: None.
- **Dt Action**: 2/86. US Government informant Barry Seal, who testified in Spain against Ochoa, is assassinated in Baton Rouge, Louisiana.
- **Gov. Reaction**. None.

At this time the Colombian government was still focused on the guerrilla's actions. Elements of the government were also engaged in narco-dialogue with the traffickers and seeking their assistance in setting up and arming paramilitary self-defense groups in the countryside to fight the guerrillas. Medina (1994) notes that El Mexicano, Jose Gonzalo Rodriguez Gacha, head of the military wing of the Medellin Cartel, was close to the army leadership in the Magdelana Medio and was increasingly hostile to the left-wing FARC guerrilla demands and taxes on the cartel. Once again the drug industrialist's appeared to believe that they were playing within the government and are within the system's "rules of the game."

Period III: July 1986-August 1989.

- **Dt Actions**: The courts, judicial system, judges and extradition remained the main threats facing the cocaine industry in Colombia. As Luis Canon (1994) tells us: "Better a tomb in Colombia, than a jail cell in the United States" remained the "Extraditable's" motto. By the summer of 1986 they thought that they had it intimidated. One after another, three newly appointed Supreme Court Justices resigned after receiving death threats. Their replacement, Justice Hernando Baquero Bordo, refused to resign and was assassinated. More than 48 lower court judges and magistrates met the same fate during the summer of 1986. Lawyers, who once looked to a court appointment as an upward career move, now literally ran from the opportunity.
- **Gov. Action and Reaction**: 8/96. A new government, that of Virgilio Barco Vargas, comes to power. The new President declares a "hard-line" on drug trafficking and narco-violence.
- **Dt. Actions**: 9/86. Officials of Avianca Airlines, supported by the new government and under U.S. pressure to stop the

use of their aircraft for transporting drugs, and who are cooperating with U.S. drug enforcement agencies, are assassinated.

- **Gov. Action**: The outgoing Justice Minister Enrique Parejo Gonzalez, Lara Bonilla's replacement, calls for a renewed implementation of the extradition treaty. Shortly thereafter, the Barco administration appoints him Ambassador to Hungary in order the remove him from the threat of *narco-terror*. The new administration then introduces legislation to implement a new "second" extradition policy.

- **Dt Reaction**. 12/86. (1) Guillermo Cano Isaza, Director of El Espectador, one of Colombia's leading newspapers, who supported and editorialized the new extradition policy, is assassinated. (2) 1/13/87. An assassination attempt is carried out in Budapest on the former Justice Minister, now Ambassador to Hungary, but it only wounds him.

- **Gov. Reaction**. 12/86-1/87. The government declares a "new" war on drug traffickers.

- **Dt Action**. 2/87. The narco-interests successfully buy off the "war" by handing Carlos Lehder to the government for extradition to the United States. His erratic behavior was a major problem for them. Also, he had never been a "member" of the Medellin group and more reliable associates had surpassed his abilities as transport coordinator. Given his public posturing and drug-induced violence, he was a major liability. The action also made points for the drug "germio" (interest group) by reducing the U.S. pressure on the government. All sides had been given something to "crow" about.

- **Gov. Reaction**. 2/87. The narco-dialogue is reinstated. Elements of the army support the drug cartel's aid to paramilitary self-defense groups and the narco-businessman's war against FARC guerrillas and its political arm, the Union Patriotica (UP) political party and its candidates.

- **Dt Actions**. 2/87-5/89. (1) More than 100 UP political candidates and leftists across Colombia are assassinated. (2) The paramilitary self-defense groups funded by the drug traffickers, and which are assisted by the military, engage in mass killings of peasants, labor organizers and reformers across the country. Over 300 die. (3) 3/88: Violence between the Cali and the Medellin Cartels increases. (4) 9/88-5/89. Medellin cartel leadership, particularly the Ochea family, who are concerned about the increasing violence, make repeated offers for a negotiated settlement and the reintegration of themselves and their wealth into the Colombia community.

- **Gov. Actions**: (1) 5/89-8/89 As the political campaign for the 1990 Presidential election heats up, the government is under increasing US pressure to attack the Medellin Cartel, and is under international human rights group pressure to investigate the peasant killings and to disarm the self-defense organizations.   (2) Behind the scenes, governmental supporters of the less violent, more business-like, Cali Cartel, urge crackdowns on the more violent elements within the Medellin group - Gonzalo Rodreiguez Gacha and Pablo Escobar. DAS Director Miguel Maza forms Special Elite Police Units to lead in this attack.
- **Dt. Reaction**: 5/89. They order a car bomb attack on Major General Miguel Maza Marquez, Director of DAS, the National Police Agency. (4 killed and 50 Wounded.)
- **Gov. Reaction**: 5/89. Major special police operations seek to capture Medellin cartel leadership.
- **Dt. Reaction**: 6/89. They use "plata o plomo" to buy off most operations.
- **Dt. Actions**: 7/89. Rodriguez Gacha and Pablo Escobar received intelligence that the Cali organization is supplying the DAS and the government with information about them and their operations. They believe that Liberal Party Presidential candidate Luis Carlos Galan Sarmiento intends to crackdown on them; perhaps with the support of Cali. So in a bold step, they order Liberal Party Presidential candidate, Luis Carlos Galan, assassinated at a televised campaign rally.
- **Gov. Reaction**: 8/89. Now total war is declared on the Medellin Cartel.
- **Dt. Actions**: 1) 8-9/89. Full-scale *narco-terror* begins. The cartel launches a series of dynamite attacks on both of the major political party headquarters, leading banks, and El Espectador newspaper. (11 killed. 132 wounded.) (2) 9-10/89. There are continued attacks and assassinations of newspaper staffs and offices, especially El Espectador, radio stations, reporters, media personalities, court and police officials across Colombia. (7 killed. 108 wounded.) (3) 11/89. An Avianca airliner, believed to be carrying Cali cartel members, is bombed. (107 killed.) (4) 12/89. The DAS headquarters in Bogota is car bombed. (63 killed. 600 wounded.) (5) The kidnapping of members of elite families in Bogota begins. This is the first time *narco-terror* is directed against the social and economic elite in the capitol city.
- **Gov Reactions**: 12/89. Militarization of the fight against narco-*terror* increases. international assistance is sought. And

with outside help, eventually Medellin Cartel leader Gonzalo
Rodriquez Gacha and his son are hunted down and killed.

- **Dt. Reactions** 1/90. Pablo Escobar escalates Cartel violence
  against the State and continues kidnapping members of the
  Colombian elite, including family members of the ex-
  Presidents.
- **Gov. Action**: 1-2/90. A "Committee of Notables" from the
  elite is organized to create a new narco-dialogue with the
  traffickers.
- **Dt. Reactions**: 3/90. The narco-entrepreneurs respond to this
  effort at mediation by ordering the assassinations of the Union
  Patriotica and M-19 Presidential Candidates. They appear to
  have seen this as an act of patriotism and sign of good faith to
  the Church and to the conservative sectors of Colombian
  society. These acts backfire, however, as human rights groups
  and media pressure causes the dialogue with the "Notables" to
  be canceled.
- **Dt Actions**: 4-8/90. (1) Kidnapping of the elite are increased.
  (2) Car bombings are resumed and *narco-terror* is extended to
  include shopping centers and the mass public. narco-terrorism
  is ratcheted up another notch.
- **Dt Reactions**: The Ochoa family patriarch writes to President
  Barco and pleads for dialogue, and an alternative settlement
  for his sons whom he says "had been led astray by Escobar."
- **Gov. Reaction**: 8/90. A new President, Cesar Gaviria, is
  elected and with the support of the elite calls for narco-
  dialogue. He also promises a debate to abolish the extradition
  treaty.
- **Gov. Actions**. 9/90-6/91. Active "narco-dialogue" on ending
  extradition begins in earnest, with full government support
- **Dt Reactions**. 12/90-4/91. (1) The Ochoa brothers and their
  associates begin to turn themselves in to the government. (2)
  The main Plaza de Toros La Macarena is bombed (18 killed.
  128 wounded).
- **Gov. Reaction**. 6/91. The National Legislature approves the
  abolition of the extradition treaty.
- **Dt Reaction**. 6/91. Pablo Escobar surrenders to a country-club
  prison that he helped design and pay for.

In August 1992, Pablo Escobar was forced to walk out of his prison to
deal with conflicts within his organization, as well as the threat of his rivals in
Cali. This escalates between December 1992 and May of 1993 into a short
reign of *narco-terror* and violence, particularly car bombs in Bogota (44 killed,
326 wounded), and against the police (167 killed). But with public opinion,
Cali's "*narco-businessmen,*" and the government aligned against him, Escobar is
isolated. Direct pressure is placed on his family who is forced to leave

Colombia. They are shunted, driven and frequently refused entry, around the world, until their only alternative is to return home to Medellin. In December 1993, Pablo Escobar, violating his own rules, seeks to talk to his own children and calls them on a cellular telephone. His location is pinpointed. He is found and killed by the elite Search Bloc police. That evening cheers of joy ring-out across the city, and street parties and parades occur in most of the middle-class and wealthier areas of Medellin. Citizens can go out at night for the first time in over a year. There is mourning over the death of "El Patron" in the slums of Medellin. Narco-terrorism appeared to be ended in Colombia. But in 1996, as the Colombian legislature raised the issues of extradition and passed legislation on asset confiscation - in response to "narco-corruption" debates - specific and sporadic use of car bombs once more returned. What is the future of *narco-terror* in Colombia? From this analysis, we can see that it will turn on extradition, the absence of dialogue and will be put down once it directly effects Colombia's ruling oligarchy, capitol city and the elite.

What can we learn about the future of *narco-terrorism* in America from this case study?

- That drug traffickers often see their interactions with the State and its agents in exchange, bargaining, norm and contract terms. Thus, any miscommunication, or perceived code and norm violations can lead to acts of *narco-terror*.
- That once begun *narco-terror* will both escalate in magnitude and in scope. In Colombia it moved from specific targeted individual attacks, to discriminate attacks on government representatives, judicial officials and media spokesmen, to more indiscriminate attacks on the elite and the mass public.
- That *narco-terrorism* will also escalate in terms of techniques and methodologies. In Colombia it went from individual firearm use, to machine guns and grenades, to dynamite bombs, to car bombs and even to altimeter bombs against commercial aircraft. By 1992 the Cali group sought to acquire 500 lb. Bombs from Nicaragua in order to attack Pablo Escobar's prison. And Escobar sought SAM missiles from the Cuban government to thwart this effort. We can expect this continued escalation of lethality to continue in the future.
- What is the safest way to limit and avoid occurrences of narco-terrorism in the future?
- One must make sure that there is always a clear and large area of separation between the State, its agents, and any involvement and complicity with narcotics traffickers or transnational crime. It is when symbiotic relationships are formed between organized crime and the State, and when *narco-dollarization* and political corruption are hidden or

ignored, that *narco-terror*ism can confront the State as it did in Colombia.

***Peter A. Lupsha**, Ph. D., is Senior Research Scholar at the Latin American Institute, University of New Mexico and Professor Emeritus of Political Science.*

***Sung-Kwon Cho** was a Ph.D. student of Professor Lupsha. He is currently a university professor of Latin American Studies in Seoul, South Korea.*

References

Aeango, J. and Child, J. (1984), *Narcotrafico Imperio de la Cocaina*. Medellin: Editorial Percepcion.

Castillo, F. (1987), *Los Jinentes de la Cocaine*. Bogota: Editorial Documentos Periodisticos.

(1991) *La Coca Nostra*. Bogota: Editorial Docomentos Periodisticos.

Canon, L.M. (1994), *El Patron: Vida y Muerte de Pablo Escobar*. Bogota: Planeta Colombian Editorial S.A.

Clawson, P.L. and Lee, R.W. III, The *Andean Cocaine Industry*. New York: St. Martin's Press.

Clutterbuck, R. (1990), *Terrorism, Drugs and Crime in Europe after 1992*. London: Rouledge, Chapman and Hall, Inc.

Eddy, P. (1988), *The Cocaine Wars*: New York: W.W.Norton *and* Co.

Friman, R. H. (1996), *NarcoDiplomacy: Exporting the U.S. War on Drugs*. Ithica, NY: Cornell University Press.

Kaplan, D. and Dubro, A., (1986) *Yakuza*. Redding, MASS: Addison-Wesley

Lupsha, P.A. (1981), "Drug Trafficking: Mexico and Colombia in Comparative Perspective". *Journal of International Affairs*. 35: (Spring/Summer) 95-116

(1987), "Organized Crime: Rationale Choice, not Ethnic Group Behavior: A Macro Perspective" Paper presented at the Am Soc. Criminology, Montreal, Nov. (1989) 'Towards and Etiology of Drug Trafficking and Insurgent Relations: The Phenomenon of *narco-terror*ism' *International Journal of Comparative and Applied Criminal Justice*, 13:2 Fall 61-75

(1996) "La Guerra Contra Drogas esta Muerta, Viva la Guerra vs. Transnacional Criminalidad Orgsanizadad" in A. Guaqueta and F. Thoumi, *La Vision Estadounidense del la Problema de Las Drogs*. Bogota: Universidad de Los Andes.

Medina, A.R. (1994), *Magdalena Medio: Luchas Sociales y violaciones a los derechos humanos 1980-1992*. Bogota: Corporacion Avre.

Nadelmann, E.A. (1993), *Cops Across Borders: The Internationalization of U.S. Criminal Law Enforcement*. University Park, PA.: Pennsylvania State University Press.

Savonna, E. (1996) "European Money Trials" *Transnational Organized Crime* 2:4, 1-21

Schmid, A.P. (1985), *Political Terrorism: A Research Guide to Concepts and Theories*. New Brunswick: Transaction Publishers.

Sung, K. C. (1995), *Narco-terrorism and the State in Colombia*. Ph.D. Dissertation, University of New Mexico, Albuquerque, N.M. (See: Ann Arbor: University of Michigan Dissertation Abstracts).

Williams, P. (1995) "The New Threat: Transnational Criminal Organizations and International Security," *Criminal Organization*. 9:3 and 4, 316.

18 The Globalization of Crime and Criminal Justice: Prospects and Problems

David Nelken*

Abstract

This chapter offers an analysis of the ways in which processes of globalization may be affecting developments in crime and in criminal justice. It first identifies the competing fears which revolve around, on the one hand, the alleged rise of transnational organized crime and, on the other, the alleged dangers of transnational policing. After distinguishing various problems associated with different aspects of globalization it goes on to suggest the need for caution in thinking that strengthening transnational policing is a necessary or sufficient response to these problems.

Key words - Globalization, Criminal justice, Transnational crime, Organized crime

Introduction

Law is both the most local and the most universal or globalized of cultural phenomena. Its role as a bearer of globalization was seen in the past in the spread of Roman law and can be detected now in the emergence of a new *Lex mercatoria* for international business transactions or in the attempt to extend human rights law. But some forms of law, it could be argued, do seem to travel better than others. In particular criminal law is often treated as very much a quintessential part of national sovereignty and it is not without significance that the European Union[1] has moved with extreme caution in urging harmonization in this area of law.

- Are criminal law and criminal justice really immune from the processes of globalization or are they also being affected?
- Should this be encouraged or discouraged?
- And how far are transitional crime and the fear of such crime pushing such developments?

These are rather large questions and in this chapter I cannot offer anything more than an introduction to some of the issues being raised in a rapidly growing though as yet unsynthesized literature. I shall begin by evoking the fears, which focus either on the spread or on the response to transnational crime as examples of the type of problems associated with the globalization of crime. I shall then state something about the meaning of globalization and the various ways the phenomenon can be related to crime and criminal justice.

Finally I shall consider more carefully the claim that organized crime is globalizing, drawing on my empirical research into organized frauds against the subsidies programs of the European Union. I should say that it is not my intention in this chapter to debunk concern over the spread of organized crime as no more than a new "moral panic." If only it were that simple! Descriptions of the growth of this type of crime can be exaggerated, as can descriptions of the threat posed by the organization of police efforts to deal with it.[2] But calling for caution is unlikely by itself to have much influence over rapidly evolving events. What needs to be carefully questioned is the single mindedness of policy making which claims to rely on an allegedly irrefutable logic: since crime now knows no frontiers, it follows that systems of criminal justice can no longer afford to be based on the nation state but must do their best to form a common front. Instead, I shall try to show why the relationship between globalization, crime and criminal justice is a lot more complex than this thought captures.

Two opposite fears

It is possible to detect two types of anxiety in current writing about the globalization of crime. The first of these stems from the argument that globalization is a process out of control, or even beyond control, which is creating enormous opportunities for business and organized crime which locally based criminal justice systems are struggling to keep up with and perhaps are always destined to be behind. The old - new category of *'transitional crime'* is taken to embrace a wide variety of threatening behaviors including terrorism, espionage including industrial espionage, drugs and arms trafficking, the international wholesaling of pornography and prostitution, smuggling and trade in people and body parts, counterfeiting, crimes related to computer technology, international fraud and other financial crimes, tax evasion, theft of art, antiques and other precious items, crimes against the environment, trade in endangered species, and internationally coordinated racial violence.

What is more, much of this transnational crime is assumed (rightly) to be organized by foreign criminal enterprises such as the Sicilian Mafia, the Colombian drug cartels, the Yakuza in Japan, the Chinese and Taiwanese Triads, or sophisticated fraudster networks In Nigeria. Increasingly, attention is also being paid to the challenge represented by the Mafias of Russia and other countries in Eastern Europe who are seen as amongst the main beneficiaries of the break up of the former Soviet Union, the run down of the Red army, the privatization programs or foreign investments and aid payments and so on.

As is confirmed by the recent redeployment in Britain of the secret services to carry out intelligence against them, organized criminals have slipped easily into the slot of public enemy number one, which was previously reserved for the anti-democratic menace of communism. And this is even truer of the United States. As Louise Shelley, an influential American expert on organized crime argues: the world is now facing a new non-state based form of authoritarianism which subjects people to coercion, corrupts law, privatizes weak states for its own goals, and threatens those journalists - and criminologists - who try to expose it.[3] Her conclusion (these arguments always arrive at the same one) is that "the legal institutions of the world are still bounded to the nation- state but the forces of coercion are transnational; existing state based legal systems therefore cannot protect citizens from the new authoritarian threat provided by organized crime."[4] According to this view the globalization of crime thrives on the inability of the criminal law to globalize. And the European Union is the best illustration of this. As another American writer put it:

> crooks were the last item on the European agenda in 1990. Engrossed in plans to make money, economic leaders had given scarcely a thought to the opportunity for criminals to do likewise - no common police academy or training existed, each country had its own laws on extradition, rights of asylum, hot pursuit, exchange of police and intelligence information, undercover agents, controlled drug deliveries, all terms for drug traffickers, money laundering or phone taps (Sterling 1994: 90).[5]

But there are also mirror image fears. The claim here is that police forces are in fact using these fears about transnational crime to forge alliances which are not democratically accountable. America has long been in the lead here in exporting abroad its war against drugs and terrorism but in Europe this is also well illustrated by the Inter-state or TREVI or EUROPOL policing agreements; the European Commission itself only has observer status, the European Parliament still less say. Criminal Justice is thus globalizing along with everything else (and in same way) and efforts at transnational police action represent a real danger to democratic structures which themselves presuppose the national state. As one author claims, "it is by looking at the enforcement practices of the law enforcement enterprise that we can best come to understand the political form of the emergent transnational world system" (Sheptycki 1996: 64)[6] or, as Rosa Luxembourg is alleged to have said, "the police are the one true International." What is more, powers and techniques which are demanded or taken in order to deal with the threat of menacing forms of organized crime often end up being used against more low level or local forms of criminality. Insofar as borders are defended the focus is often on keeping out those immigrants who in the present economic climate are once again assumed to be surplus to requirements: thus Illegal immigration is now included alongside drugs and terrorism as one of the three major threat against which what is increasingly being called *Fortress Europe* needs to be defended. For these commentators on transnational policing the solution is often worse than the problem - not only because it is symmetrically authoritarian- but also because there is ample evidence that unaccountable policing can itself involve illegality or engage in crime in its own account (Nadelmann).

So far the differences between systems and the obstacles to international collaboration are as significant as the moves to common forms of policing and punishment. But even if progress to a unified order of international criminal law is so slow, or perhaps just because it is so slow, we should also note that measures taken to deal with transnational criminality by *individual* nation-states already have serious implications for civil liberties. If INTERPOL is said to have files on 130,000 people of whom 80,000 are drug offenders; researchers quote the police in Britain alone as claiming to have records on the 60 percent of Colombians living in London who they say are involved in the drug trade (as many as 42,000 out of a total of 70,000).[8] An intelligence agent was recently quoted In the Sunday Times as saying –

> *We are one of the very few countries in the world to have legislation that allows us to work very aggressively overseas...We take the view that stealing money from a crook is a good thing and if it's from an account in a foreign country who cares? We are hardly likely to be sued, and there are no fingerprints to lead back to us.*[9] (according to the report these remarks allegedly met with the approval of a leading London legal academic).

The 1992 decision of the American Supreme Court in the *Alvarez Machain* case seemed to authorize state kidnapping of a drug dealer from Mexico. In the same year in the *Chinoy* decision the English courts refused to look at illegalities which had allegedly occurred In the gathering of evidence in France. In sum, whatever globalization may or may not be doing to crime, talk about globalization is increasingly serving as a means by which national criminal justice systems seek to augment their resources and legitimate themselves.

How far can discussions about globalization help us to place these fears about organized crime and transitional enforcement in some wider context so as to give us a better grasp on what is happening? Certainly there have been other periods, such as the early years of this century: which witnessed widespread levels of concern about international drug traffic - though it is worth remembering that Britain, and even more Holland, were then counted amongst the countries accused of profiting from the trade. This and other campaigns against foreign threats were accompanied by a level of xenophobia and fear of immigration even more severe than that being witnessed today. What difference does globalization make? Certainly it would be important if we could show that organized criminals engaged in transnational crimes were simply responding to the pressures and opportunities which were reshaping legal and illegal enterprise alike. For if we were to treat globalization as the real villain of the piece, we could hardly assume that transnational policing could provide the answer. It could certainly do little to offset the many other effects of globalization on levels of crime in different countries and cities. Rather than setting the secret services on the trails of the Mr. Big's of organized crime, the challenge we would face would be better analyzed as having to do with the political choice whether to regulate or deregulate globalization processes more generally (together with the problem of whether and how such regulation could be made effective).

Understanding Globalization

But what exactly is meant by globalization? Is it just the latest jargon phrase wheeled out so as to describe a series of otherwise unrelated matters or is it the magical key to making the connections which otherwise are so hard to find when living through a period of rapid change? The term is now being used in a variety of academic disciplines.

This chapter will focus only a little about some of the definitions, aspects and theories of globalization which I have gleaned from the literature's of sociology and management science.[10] Because it is rare to find much specific reference to crime and criminal justice in these discussions our task will be to tease out the implications of globalization for our subject (as well as to consider how developments in crime and criminal justice and criminology may themselves affect globalization.).

In a recent social science text with this title, Malcolm Walters defines globalization as "a social process in which the constraints of geography on social and cultural arrangements recede and in which people become increasingly aware that they are receding" (Walters 1995:3). Thus globalization has both objective and subjective elements. However, though Walters tends to see these as going together it will sometimes be useful for our purposes to distinguish them. Starting from a concern with criminal justice we might want to ask- does globalization really destroy the local basis for allocating blame? There are good reasons to believe that one of the functions of criminal justice could be to create a sense of group solidarity, which is independent of wider economic developments.

Anthony Giddens - a leading British social theorist- similarly defines globalization as "the intensification of social relations which link distant localities in such a way that local happenings are shaped by events occurring miles away and vice versa."[12] What this means, for our argument, is that what happens in a local neighborhood of a city, including of course its levels of crime, is increasingly likely to be influenced by factors such as world money and commodity markets which operate at an indefinite distance from the neighborhood itself.

For Giddens globalization should be treated as part of the process of modernization *(not postmodernization)* a secular trend through which time and space come to be separated from a person's location or the cycles of the seasons. It represents a further stage in the lifting out of social relations from local contexts of interaction and their restructuring across time and space through symbolic tokens such as money media and expert systems. Those who live in modern times trust their societies and lives to be guided by such impersonal flows of expertise so that to know what to do it is necessary to have to resort to constantly changing forms of knowledge (in the jargon without which sociology would become too user-friendly this is known as *"time-space distanciation,"* *"disemebedding"* and *"reflexivity"*). Each of these changes in the relationship of the individual to her social world has potential implications for crime and its control. A recent attempt to draw conclusions for criminology (Bottoms and

Wiles 1996)[13] shows how Giddens' analysis can explain the increasing difficulty of reinforcing outer boundaries of cultural and legal systems. What replaces these boundaries is our drawing on expert systems so as to create bubbles of security in defined areas of housing and shopping malls which have to be fortified against the risks posed by those members of the population who have been displaced from the economy by processes of globalization change.

Globalization has manifold economic, political and cultural aspects and there is predictable disagreement about which of these is driving the others.[14] As compared to what are described as more culturalist approaches other authors lay more stress on economic factors.

Wallerstein argues that the world capitalist system has always integrated not by nation- states but by global commercial and manufacturing relationships which determine which countries belong to the core, semi periphery or periphery of this systems.[15] In these terms, changes in the dependent nation state system, world military order, and the international division of labor and trading relationships can all be expected to have consequences for the type and levels of crime. Another leading writer stresses the importance of transnational global companies, the transnational capitalist class and the cultural ideology of consumerism and focuses in particular on what he calls the "their transnational practices" which characterize globalization.[16] These practices, which originate with non - state actors and cross state borders, involve among others major capitalist institutions, globalizing bureaucrats, executives of transnational companies, and professional and consumerist elites in the first and third world. From a criminological perspective it would certainly be relevant to examine how the spread of consumerist ideology increases expectations without necessarily providing the income to satisfy them.

A similar stress on political economy, though without the Marxist flavor, is found in the management science literature.[17] It argues that the increasing integration of the world economy is an objective trend which can be measured by descriptive indicators such as price and interest rates convergence. Economic actors increasingly have to take greater account of the way their action in one nation- state influences their action in another. The State loses influence because political action is increasingly dominated by world financial and real goods markets and governments encounter particular difficulties in pursuing policies of regulation, which are out of line with other countries. New forms of interdependence also pose governments with other problems such as how to tax information flows (though no doubt they will find out how to do so one day). In part as a reaction to these difficulties there is an increasing number of regional groupings, not only the European Union (EU) or North Atlantic Free Trade Area (NAFTA) but also the International Monetary Fund (IMF) which has grown in membership from 44 to 178 countries. This literature is especially useful when we come to consider the globalization of organized crime as an aspect of how and why legitimate businesses are integrating worldwide.

Where is globalization leading? What would a fully globalization society look like? Walters[18] tells us it would exhibit a high level of differentiation and multicentricity and there would be no tight set of cultural preferences and prescriptions.   Insofar as culture is unified it will be extremely abstract, expressing tolerance for diversity and Individual choice.   Importantly, for the future of criminal justice, we are told that territoriality will disappear as an organizing principle for social and cultural life. But looking that far ahead is not all that convincing. We would do better to concentrate on trying to clarify our ideas about what is happening now to crime and criminal justice as it is shaped by or tries to resist these trends.

Globalization and Crime

In trying to apply theories of globalization it is all too easy to go from the sublime to the meticulous.   On the one hand, we have sweeping futuristic visions, on the other hand we have all too concrete descriptions of what is happening on the ground in police cooperation or the emergence of new forms of transnational crime, with only an impoverished account of how this relates to wider social changes.   We lack a middle-range theory which makes developments in crime and criminal justice central to its concerns.

But is it even plausible to expect to find one theory, which would successfully explain all types of crime, linked to globalization from genocide to insider trading to computer "hacking" - and which could also succinctly explain the common denominator of globalizing moral panics from pedophillia to political corruption?   Current developments in Belgium, where leading politicians are alleged to have helped prevent investigation of a pedophilia ring, suggest that there can be surprising and disturbing links between such apparently unrelated crimes.   What we can do is at least try to provide a framework which could help us to sort out the various relationships between globalization and developments in crime and criminal justice (M. Levi and D. Nelken, 1996).

Which should be the axis of such a framework? One important distinction to bear in mind is that between increasing homogenization and increasing interdependence (of other kinds). On the one hand, there is the phenomenon of the globalization village (which we can call *homogenization)* in which up to 800 million of the world's population can be found watching an American super bowl game on television whilst eating pizza and drinking coca cola- or the scene In Nani Moretti's film *Dear Diary* where an Italian devotee of soap opera desperately shouts at some American tourists visiting the Etna volcano to find out what has happened In the latest installments of his favorite soap which had been broadcast In the United States- but not yet In Italy.   The spread of American films, television series and novels which feature (particular) images of crime and criminal justice illustrate this sort of globalization.

On the other hand, there is the *interdependence* vividly illustrated by the Chernobyl nuclear disaster or the way a military coup in Nigeria affects the price of oil in Rotterdam and brings about a collapse of prices on the Tokyo Stock exchange. In the sphere of crime we could consider the part played by organized crime pyramid frauds in the recent collapse of order in Albania, in

1996, or the multiple consequences of reckless or fraudulent speculation by merchant banks or other players on the commodities markets in the early 1960s.

Globalization may further either or both of these processes. What is important is to see is that interdependence does not necessarily presume or produce homogeneity[19] -as sociologists of modernity from Durkheim to Luhmann have emphasized, it thrives on difference and differentiation. But there is also a further distinction which needs to be made which is obscured in many discussion of globalization which describe growing interdependence. It is often unclear whether such interdependence is something planned as a *strategy* of integration (for example under the impetus of multinationals such as MacDonalds), or whether it is rather (by definition) a process which is beyond control, as in the way money flows to where it can obtain the best return. Of course both of these processes may sometimes be relevant for different purposes but all this needs careful sorting out. To allow this we need a framework which helps us to see how globalizing processes may involve homogenization and integration in varying degrees.

One final note of caution. We must not assume that developments in crime and criminal justice are merely a *consequence* of globalization; they may also, as already noted, be one of the *causes* of whether or not people feel part of a global order. Notoriously, criminal law functions by creating boundaries between insiders - the members of the "moral community" threatened by the "other" ...the outsiders. By responding to real or constructed threats it helps define enemies or create scapegoats.[20] Whilst this will often, and perhaps typically, tighten the definition of who can count as an insider, attempts to extend the reach of the law, as for example through the creation of the International War Crimes tribunals, or in legislation aimed at dealing with "sex tourists" who victimize children abroad, may also broaden this definition of who counts as an offender or a victim. In addition, discourse about crime, like that about victims, is itself one of most universalizing of current ideologies -after the alleged death of merely political ideologies. As its influence spreads, criminology, like other types of expertise can also be seen as a bearer of globalization, though it puts one in mind of Beck's remark that expertise secures its survival as much through its failure as its success.[21]

Globalization may even *constitute* and not simply cause or facilitate crime. Typically this will be when it increases the levels of criminalization of certain types of behavior, which not long before had been considered as acceptable, or at least containable, within acceptable limits, especially as long as they were confined to local insiders. One interpretation of the move to legislate against a crime which is aptly named "insider trading," which accompanied the so called "big bang" liberalization of the London stock exchange, is in terms of the need to ensure predictability and trust in the globalized City of London once it was opened up to outsiders. As Clarke puts it:

> *it would have perplexed leading members of these institutions*
> *up to the end of the 1950's to be told they were doing anything*
> *reprehensible in acting on such information. It was precisely*

> *because of access to such information that one was part of the*
> *city, and one was part of the city in the clear expectation of*
> *making a considerable amount of money.*[22]

Similarly, it is not easy to decide how much the campaigns against political corruption of the 1990s merely reflect an increase in such misbehavior In the 1980s or also the effects of globalization in making such conduct more "costly" or increasing the centrality of penal law as a political resource.[23]

Table 18.1 sets out the four cells of the framework which I have been outlining, with some illustrative examples (many more could of course be added) showing how increasing globalization interdependence may influence or be influenced by crime and criminal justice. It allows us to draw a number of lessons for the currently popular claim that the crucial threat which globalization represents is the way it facilitates the integration of organized crime (to which the only answer is a similar response by the international forces of order).

In the first place, and most importantly, it suggests the complexity of teasing out the connections between crime and globalization. While some forms of crime result from processes of integration, others belong more to homogenizing processes; some aspects of globalization cannot be fitted into either of these categories. Criminal justice or other agencies need to be aware of this variety; even more, their responses are themselves part of the phenomenon that needs to be understood.

More specifically, the table shows us why an exclusive focus on the threat of transnational criminals fails to capture many of the other ways that globalization may affect opportunities for crime. As cell 3 suggests many of the problems caused by globalization have nothing to do with deliberate integration by organized criminals but result from the differential effects of globalization on different countries, cities or parts of cities which governments cannot or will not attempt to control. From a criminological point of view the drive to economic integration can, and often will, lead to social and anomic disintegration. It will therefore be of small help to integrate at the level of criminal justice responses whilst leaving the underlying causes untouched. The disintegrative effects of economic integration may even be exacerbated by some of the homogenizing globalization processes, which affect criminal justice (as can be seen in cell 1). It is enough to think of the way the rehabilitative approach to punishment fell widely out of favor in Europe and the United States in the 1970s just at the same time as the welfare state faced fiscal pressures because of changes in global competitiveness and oil prices.

We also need to question the assumption that there is an inverse relationship between the problem posed by organized crime and success in achieving agreement on the harmonization of national systems of criminal law and enforcement. The table reminds us that some homogenization of criminal justice (the increasing adoption of the accusatorial model for example) is already taking place as a result of globalization, despite the alleged dependence of criminal law on the nation state and local culture. But a comparison of cells 2

Figure 18.1: Crime, criminal justice and two aspects of globalizing processes of interdependence

← I N T E G R A T I O N →

1. High homogenization, Low integration Global spread of criminal techniques e.g. car ramming and strategies of control, e.g. technological methods of surveillance; Developments and fashions in criminal justice e.g. the decline of rehabilitation, fixed sentencing community policing, local crime prevention, 'victim's rights', mediation, (the re-integrative shaming approach in criminology) Global spread of images of crime (Miami Vice) and criminal justice (PerryMason). Influence of (American) criminology and the Anglo- American concept of 'criminal justice'	H O M O G
2. High integration, High homogenization Greater flows of illegal trade e.g. in pornography, drugs etc. as well as more opportunities for financial crime, as part of increased legal trading; New criminal laws to fight counterfeiting, to protect new information property rights, regulate financial markets, computer 'hacking', the use of the Internet etc. Development of international criminal law, creation of war crimes tribunals, international and regional policing agreements e.g. *Schengen*	E N I Z

3. Low integration. Low homogenization	4. High integration. Low homogenization	
Local differences in types and levels of crime in countries, cities (and parts of cities) in the core semi periphery, and periphery of the 'world system' which result from market and technology driven changes in the flows of trade, information, and people. Other effects of the 'hollowing out' of the State and of 'localization ' as a reaction to (or aspect of) globalization.	*Pax Mafioso-* strategic agreements between organized crime groups exploiting national differences in law and sentencing. The export of hot money, arms, dangerous waste, unsafe products and working practices by state/organized/ business criminals. Competition for 'hot money and money laundering, growth of tax havens Pax Americana- American foreign crime policy in Latin America and elsewhere. Fortress Europe: *TREVI, EUROPOL*: IMF and world bank pressures on developing countries.	I T I O N

and 4 should again remind us of the limits of law as a response, whether uniform or not. It is true that organized crime is able to organize strategically, to exploit differences in the economic and legal order; just as these differences are exploited and reinforced also by legitimate business in its "forum shopping" for favorable legal systems and the way it puts pressure on weak states to soften regulatory regimes. But organized and economic crime has also benefited from the opportunities opened up by increasing homogenization of the world economic and legal order (including the enormous increase in the issue of bonds consequent on the internationalization of the banking system). Greater harmonization of legal procedures and penalties (even apart from the conceptual difficulties this raises) will do little as such to change the balance of incentives which lead to the world-wide distribution of crime even if it may help in the processing of the few who are apprehended. And, in practice, integration of enforcement efforts usually tends to involve subordination rather than homogenization, as in the way the United States attempts to enforce its priorities in South America.

The dialectic between crime and control will not be understood as long as we stick to the idea that the forces of order are waging a losing war against an insidious foreign enemy. Increasing certain sorts of control efforts may even act as an incentive to criminal action, as in the case of drugs and other illegal products and activities in which organized crime specializes. Insofar as crime and control can, for some purposes, be separated, this will depend on our ability to distinguish the dynamics of criminal behavior and of changes in criminal justice, which are highlighted in each of the 4 cells.

- How far do crime and control evolve by following the same or different logics?
- What are the organizational and inter-organizational challenges which each face?
- How far is it true that organized crime strategies reflect a strictly economic logic whereas the growth of international policing responds to more political considerations at both national and international levels?
- And what are the implications of any such differences?

Trend: Tactic or Trope?

Before concluding this brief, and necessarily over simplified, overview of the relationships between globalization and criminal justice there is one further reflection that can be drawn from the social science literature. This warns us to be wary of taking globalization to be something inevitable. There is certainly some evidence to justify talking about globalization as a current trend, just as it made sense - a generation ago- to talk about the economic and cultural convergence between nations that would inevitably eventually be produced through their common reliance on modern technology. But, as that counter-example shows, historical inevitability is not so easily discerned (the move towards market systems in the former communist states may be more attributable to their failure to keep up in the technological battle). Presupposing the inevitability of globalization is itself a loaded description of current developments. Insofar as globalization is to be defined not simply or always as a process out of control, but also as a strategy or *tactic* which is followed by determinate economic and political actors, there will almost always be some room for alternative strategies and resistance.

The progress of globalization is thus not determined simply by the extension of new technologies in communication and transportation but is also the result of social and political action, including decisions (and non decisions) by governments about regulating and deregulating the national and international economy. Talking about globalization *as if* it were inevitable is itself often a tactic for gaining resources, for favoring one or other policy choice - or what is often the same thing-making an alliance with one or other national or international actor or set of actors. It is precisely not the case that "global economic interaction poses an identical legal and law enforcement dilemma for industrialized and newly industrializing nations- opening their borders, economy and society to the free exchange of people, capital and goods, without sacrificing domestic order and protection of the international interests of their citizens."[24]

Even allegedly global environmental problems do not have the same costs for all, just as some countries or groups pay a higher price for trying to deal with them.[25] In particular there are likely to be systematic differences in judgments of globalization from the perspective of members of countries in the semi -periphery or periphery of the capitalist world system - as they experience its effects as packaged by the IMF and the world bank in its curious mixture of economic liberalism and human rights.

This point is often lost sight of because of the way talk about globalization has become a trope or metaphor which carries arguments over all or any obstacle. Take, for our own topic, the following quotation from the same article published in an allegedly radical criminological journal. "Economic and social change," we are told:

> is apparent across the face of a transformed globe, reshaped by technological winds blowing across the globalization landscape as forcefully and as steadily as the Trade winds carried explorers and colonists to reshape the New World. Virtually every institution within industrialized and newly industrializing economies is undergoing rapid evolution to keep pace with the speed of technologically induced social and political change save one, law and law enforcement.[26]

With this type of metaphoric reasoning it is no surprise to find that our author later assumes, rather than demonstrates, the happy arrival of global consensus when he asserts blandly that organized crime (his concern is the Chinese and Taiwanese variety), "imperils the attainment of international objectives like political harmony and economic advancement through free trade" (Myers: 213).

Less scholarly (even less scholarly), though more widely read accounts of organized crime -- which one suspects may influence or echo even more closely some levels of official thinking -- make regular resort to questionable metaphors rather than sober evidence. Crime, we are told, "skids out of control around the globe" (Sterling op. cit.:38). In particular the European Union "faces an uncontrollable invasion of migrants from every direction" and, in 1992, "every kind of criminal was riding in on this human tide" (ibid., 39.) so that "Western Europe lay like a vast open city under murderous criminal bombardment" (ibid., 41). Even what purports to be evidence in such accounts is far from meeting minimum requirements, as in the claim that "crime is the fastest growing industry in Britain" or the fatuous assertion that Holland, "an island of civility on a turbulent continent, has more crimes per capita than the United States" (ibid., 38). Nobody had told our author (an American living in Europe) - assuming she is in good faith- that it is the high level of bicycle theft in that country which so biases its crime statistics.

The Strategy and Culture of Organized Criminals

The exaggerations of those trying to grab our attention with metaphors should not be taken as an excuse to conclude that there is nothing to be worried about regarding organized crime or that globalization is irrelevant to its strategies. But if we are to take seriously both the fears mentioned at the outset of this chapter what can be done about the real threat of organized crime other than entrust the police and the intelligence services with ever increasing (and uncontrollable) powers?

The first step must be to understand more about the strategies of organized criminals.[27] The management science literature, for example, explains the advantages of globalization integration for business multinationals in terms which can apply equally well to organized crime. Thus we read of alliances, protection from competition, economies of scale, the securing of stable supplies and markets, assistance in diversification and bringing products to market, the possibilities of taking advantage of expertise and local knowledge, the reduction of risks, the financing of large scale projects and the acquisition of technology.[28] The opportunities which globalization has opened up for organized crime also reflect the extent to which such crime enterprises have integrated not only with other organized crime groups but also with legitimate and semi-legitimate international business. For example only 5% of the more than 175 billion dollars a day of international transactions is connected to flows of world trade directly.[29] The remainder is made up of capital on the look out for short term liquid or semi-liquid speculative investments. This total has grown enormously as a result of the internationalization of banks and holding companies since the 1960s, the elimination of restrictions and controls on foreign investments and currency swaps, and the impact of electronic technology on the individual national capital markets. As important as the globalization of markets or the technological marvels of electronic money transfer is the development of privileged territories where transactions of huge dimensions can take place without any form of regulation and control - the tax havens and Eurodollar markets at the intersections of main routes of legal and illegal trade. In order to recycle their illegal profits organized criminals have thus increasingly established relationships with the institutions and locations harboring homeless capital and bought themselves into systems of offshore banks and holding companies.

But the dirty money derived from illegal activity is only a minor part of all the "hot money" ready to move from one end of the globe to the other at the smallest change in interest rates, legal regulations, economic policies or political regimes. There are two other main sources of hot money apart from that produced from illegal transactions. A second source is the profit produced in the underground or informal economy, which runs at 10 to 15 percent of gross product in developed countries. This money, made by those otherwise law abiding, cannot be declared because it is the result of transactions organized to avoid paying tax. It needs to flow out of the country until it can reappear safely. A third source of hot money is so called "flight capital" leaving indebted countries in the third world. In the period 1973-1981, for example, multinational bank managers came to depend on the volume not the quality of loans extended without deposits. Highly placed members of foreign governments spent the loans on public works, armaments and luxurious consumer goods but a large part returned to Western countries in the form of illegally exported capital often deposited with the very banks that gave the credits in the first place. The shortsighted complicity of the largest banks in the world revealed itself as shortsighted when countries began defaulting. But when the banks curbed the credit flow to the developing world from 1981 the problem grew worse as frightened members of the meddle classes began expatriating their savings; something like 200 billion dollars was allegedly transferred between 1976 to 1985 to the U.S. and the tax havens of Europe, Asia and Caribbean, leaving their own countries without foreign exchange reserves.

In some parts of the world the destinies of legal and illegal commerce now seem to be fatally intertwined. One chapter of a recent biography of Pablo Escobar (the former Colombian drug baron) begins:

> *Every morning, on the fifth floor of the north Bogota headquarters of one of Colombia's biggest financial and industrial conglomerates there arrives a fax from its main office in the United States. The fax gives the daily US dollar price of cocaine on the streets of New York. Immediately the information is keyed into a computer performance chart. Two parallel lines run across the middle of the graph. When the price spikes through the upper line, it indicates a supply blockage. The scarcity of cocaine in New York means a scarcity of US dollars in Colombia. The company's domestic sales are damaged When the price bursts through the lower tine it heralds the presence of a major new cocaine supplier and a spate of killings and informant -related seizures until the supply drops back to normal levels. In the meantime with US dollars flooding to Colombia, it is a good moment to buy them cheaply. According to a technician who worked for the conglomerate, the chart was installed in 1986.*[30]

Earnings from the illegal drug trade in Colombia are said to be the same as that from legal exports and to have helped to save the economy from debt-related torment, hyperinflation and economic stagnation, which affected so many other countries in South America in the 1980s.[31]

Even in the most developed Western countries there is a blurring of legal and illegal commerce as in the arms trade,[32] and this as often sustained as attacked by the police and intelligence services. A good example is provided by the collapse of the Bank of Commerce and Credit International (Passas).[33] The BCCI grew to be the world's 7th largest private bank with assets of $23 billion and operations in 72 countries.

The criminal enterprises it helped fund included smuggling, drug trafficking, money laundering, illegal arms trade, transfer of nuclear technology, public corruption and capital flight, illegal ownership of U.S. banks, financing of terrorism, frauds against depositors, and the methods adopted ranged from false accounting to the use of violence.

The bank's main beneficiaries were 3,000 powerful customers who included the Colombian drug lords, ruthless dictators such as Duvaller, Somoza, Saddam Hussein, Marcos and Noriega. But the uses made of the bank by the CIA and other Western secret services also played an important part in postponing its hour of reckoning. As Passas argues:

> in order to better understand and fight organized international crime groups, one has to explore their links with legitlmate organizations and (Western and other) government policies that provide crime facilitative conditions and/or create demands such as those fulfilled by BCCI. BCCI reflects and is deeply rooted in the world's structural problems and conflicts (Passas 1996:245).

There are ever more reports of research findings which illustrate the increasing overlap between organized crime, corporate crime, and ordinary business.[34] But whilst it is essential to explore the full extent of symbiosis between legitimate business and organized crime I am uneasy about the temptation in some parts simply to *equate* business and organized crime or to treat organized crime as no more than a special form of capitalist enterprise.[35] It seems to me that, for all the similarities in strategy, there are also significant differences in culture, differences which could perhaps be exploited in seeking to contain the threat posed by this form of criminality. Interviews carried out under my guidance with members of organized crime groups in Italy who are involved in defrauding the European Union, for example, show that there is an uneasy relationship between the locally based organized criminals and the more cosmopolitan legal and accounting experts on whom they have increasingly to rely.[36]

Subtle differences persist in philosophy between organized criminals and businessmen (notwithstanding the now widely accepted accounts of the affinity between approaches of the New Mafia and that of business entrepreneurs).[37] The following extract from a longer interview with two members of the Mafia responsible for organizing European Union fraud in Sicily reveals, amongst other things, a fatalistic zero-sum approach to life which is, in some ways, far from the capitalistic ethic.

The interview was carried out at the height of the judges' attack on corruption in Italy. Asked whether the judges' campaign was bad for business the senior of the two men replied:

> *all the screaming and excitement can never go on for very long - still less can it cause any permanent damage except to those who allow themselves to be frightened. You stop your activities for a moment and wait while the crows scream and get all excited. Then everything returns as it was before. No-one (nothing) can fundamentally upset (the order of) the forest: trees may dry up and die but other ones just the same will take their place, animals die, but others are born. Things can change their position and form but always remain essentially the same.*[38]

Q But the world, the larger society in which we live, isn't actually a forest, and man is not only an animal...

A1 *Man can be any of the things you want but in the end he remains nothing other than an animal. He can wear any type of clothes imaginable, and non imaginable, but under these clothes the only concrete, real and true thing is his body which needs to eat, drink, piss, fuck, kill, defend itself, work, steal, win, dominate and command.*

Q And, above all, love

A1 *Why, do you think that he who kills is unable also to love? It all depends what values we associate we give to love and what rules or concepts we relate it to. Love comes in infinite forms and substance!*

A2 *These ways of talking don't do any one any good. Everyone has their own way of thinking about this subject. Everyone loves and behaves according to his own lights. In the end it is always the strongest who triumphs*

Q It depends what you mean by "the strongest"... in any case Don..., (as you conceded) when the crows shout and get excited you do need to stay a little quieter and therefore you will be suffering losses. How do you make up for or at least limit these losses?

A1 *You always want to understand, to discover. Don't let your brain overwork or your stomach will complain of hunger.*

Q There are those who are satisfied by meat and others who are only sated by thoughts and discoveries. You can give me to eat the food that is best suited to my digestion...

A1 *You really are the son of... a really good woman!*[39] *Well, we always get to know much in advance if the crows are about to start their screeching. We have men who are predisposed for this role, planted in the appropriate positions. We invest* *major capital expenditures so as to maintain these special observers who are above suspicion. We always know to stop in time, before the rumpus starts.*

And so we are able to freeze every activity in time, and destroy any path that might lead to us. In those cases where it is necessary we also set in motion maneuvers or the investigators off the entire apparatuses aimed at throwing scent.

A2 *Sometimes one is also obliged to throw someone or something to the crows so as to quiet them down.*

A1 *But nothing is decided on the spur of the moment. I've less hasty decisions are taken the more one can be certain that the world will carry on going as it always has.*

Q Doesn't the very use of the word "truffa" (fraud/ swindle) bother you?

A1 *And why on earth should it? It is a "truffa." But watch out, my boy, not everything that you think of as wrong really is so. It all depends, as I said before, on which rules you follow. For you the EEC is a legal and good system, for me it is itself nothing other than a "truffa." A real fraud just because it is so accepted and well defended... but come and visit me one day and we will speak at greater length about this. Real honesty is so rare as to be almost Utopian. On this earth perhaps only one man has ever succeeded in being really honest - and we put him on the Cross.*

Meanwhile we all go to Mass and listen to the words of men who swindle and mislead us.... Have you ever asked yourself why we and the Church keep going trying always not to step on each others toes. This is because at bottom we are both systems which, with different rules and rites, seek similar or even identical goals. But let's not speak any more about this now, otherwise you would be capable of wearying me with questions until tomorrow morning...

Q You pursue power and wealth, but it seems to me that you never get the chance to relax and enjoy its fruits because you are always obliged to fight to hold on to it and to defend yourselves from everyone and everything. You have to watch out both for institutionalized legality and your own many internal enemies. So doesn't it all seem without any sense?

Al But *this is just what life is! All systems are forced to fight to survive and to defend themselves continuously. Man's only choice is whether to be essentially the hunter or the prey. All this is natural. And perhaps we (Cosa Nostra) are the most quintissentially natural of all systems...*

A2 *It is not easy to change a system. And it would in any case be useless and unproductive to try because no system could ever be really and deeply different from what came before. Revolutions only change the form of things but the substance always remains the same. So it is better to continue with what there has always been. Why waste energy uselessly?*

Interviews with members of the Camorra based organized crime groups in the Campagna region of Italy also provide equivocal evidence of the effects of globalization on the culture of organized criminals. Here is a member of the New Camorra confirming the changes brought about over the past few years.

A *...The old Camorra had difficulty in getting beyond regional boundaries, and rarely went beyond national frontiers. Its links were with local politicians, together with a very few national politicians and Euro-parliamentarians. It preferred to concern itself with matters that happened in its own backyard, in the political locality: contraband, prostitution, (protection) rackets, extortion, the "pizzo,"[40] illegal gaming, illegal football pools, betting as well as other similar "businesses" and enterprises of various kinds. The New Camorra, on the other hand, has preferred to modernize itself, to turn itself into a full-scale industry, and to organize at national and (even) international level. As a result its "connections" have grown considerably both in number and sophistication. Our mode of operating nowadays is surgical, almost scientific.*

On the other hand, listen to these comments by an accountant compromised into working for the Camorra - the only hopeful signs in his generally bleak picture of the dominance of this crime group in his part of Italy.

A *...The children of those entrepreneurs who rely on this fraudulent way of running their business are beginning to rebel against their parents. These young people **all** come from studying at the University where they have had the chance to acquire an approach to business which is ethically correct, and relies on management skills. -They have been made aware of the (rules of the) market, of market equilibrium at both national and international level. Furthermore, all of them, even if some more than others, having had experience of industries In the North (of Italy), have had the chance to come across their way of doing things and so come to understand that the way things are done where they grew up is completely mistaken. They feel humiliated both personally and in their role as businessmen. That is the reason therefore why, when they take over the reins of their father's business, they rebel against the compromises with organized crime to which their*

*fathers have sunk. But this rebellion is enclosed for the time
being within the walls of the home. Word of it never comes
out. It is within the family that the young are fighting to
change things, even at the price of being killed. I myself have
many times been a witness to bitter family arguments in the
homes of my industrialist friends. And I have seen the force,
the courage and the determination of these young people.
They choose to fight these battles out in the privacy of the
home so as not to undermine the image of a united family in
the eyes of acquaintances and the larger community.*

It is thus worth remembering that globalization may help undermine the opportunities for some crimes as well as increase them. European Union fraud, like many other of the activities of organized crime in fact thrives on protective legislation rather than on globalized market freedom- in this case the common agricultural policy which is explicitly designed to keep out competition from food producing nations outside the European Union.

Think Global, Act Local?

I have no pretensions in this chapter to offer any worked out solutions to the new challenges of transnational crime. My task has been the more modest one of trying to clarify what is at stake and warn against over simple remedies. Relying on increased police enforcement alone is likely to be illusory.[41] Though there is much more to be done in seeking to reconcile the values of accountability and effectiveness in reshaping the role of the police at the national and international level. But if we are not just to leave the battle against organized crime to the police there may be a need for more rather than less local action. The slogan of "thinking globalization and acting locally" adopted by the Green movement has had deserved success in raising ecological consciousness about the wider implications of local action for the fate of common resources. There may be a need for similar consciousness - raising in order to see the links between organized crime and the financial and other choices made by businesses, banks and ordinary consumers of illicit services.[42] What could also repay further investigation is the extent to which organized criminals have ultimately a home -oriented culture. Should we even say that organized crime "acts globalization but thinks locally?"

458   David Nelken

After taking a degree in history and law and a doctorate in criminology at
*Cambridge University **David Nelken** taught at Cambridge University (1974-*
1976) , Edinburgh University (1976-1984) and University College London
(1984-1990) before moving to the University of Macerata in Italy where he is
Distinguished Professor of Sociology and Head of Department. He continues to

teach in the autumn in the UK where he is
Distinguished Research Professor of Law
at Cardiff Law School, Wales and
Honorary Visiting Professor of Law at
University College, London. He has held
various overseas visiting appointments: in
Spring 1996 he taught a course on
comparative criminal justice as Pro-
Seminar Visiting European Professor at
the Boalt Hall Law School, University of
California, Berkeley and in Spring 1998
will be teaching as Visiting Professor in
the Department of Sociology, New York
University.

David Nelken's work in criminology lies in
the areas of social and legal theory, white
- collar and organized crime, criminal justice and comparative criminology. He
is active on the editorial boards of numerous criminological, criminal law,
socio-legal, and political science journals in Italy, the UK and the U.S. - and is
joint general editor of the Dartmouth International Library of Criminology,
Criminal Justice and Penology. His book The Limits of the Legal Process: A
Study of Landlords, Law and Crime, Academic Press 1983, received the 1985
American Sociological Association (Criminology section) Distinguished Scholar
Award. Recent publications include The Futures of Criminology, Sage 1994;
The European Yearbook of Sociology of Law, Giuffr 1994 (with Alberto
Febbrajo); White- Collar Crime, Dartmouth 1994; Globalisation, Legal Culture
and Diversity, Sage 1995; Law as Communication, Dartmouth 1996; The
Corruption of Politics and the Politics of Corruption, Blackwell 1996 (with
Mike Levi); Comparing Legal Cultures, Dartmouth 1997; Issues in Comparative
Criminology, Dartmouth 1997 (with Piers Beirne); and The Centre- Left in
Power: Italian Politics 1996, Westview Press 1997 (with Roberto D'Alimonte).

Practical involvements include serving as a panel member in the Childrens'
Hearings Juvenile Court system in Edinburgh (1979-1984), Trustee of the
Church of England Council on Social Aid in London, and acting as consultant to
the Secure Cities research, policy and training programme of the Emilia-
Romagna Regional government in Italy (1994 continuing). He is married (to an
Italian Judge) and has 4 children.

Notes and References

* This paper is based on a lecture originally given at University College, London which was published in Michal Freeman (ed.) *Law and Public Opinion at the End of the Twentieth Century* (Legal Problems Series, Volume 50), Oxford University Press, Oxford, 1997.

1 N. Passas and D. Nelken 'The Legal Response to Agricultural Fraud In the European Community: A Comparative Study' In Corruption and Reform 6 1991: 237-266, and N. Passas and D. Nelken 'The thin line between legitimate and criminal enterprises: Subsidy Frauds in the European Community (with N.Passas) in *Crime, Law and Social Change* 19 1993: pp. 223-243

2 K G. Robertson 'Practical police cooperation in Europe: the intelligence dimension', In M. Anderson and M. Den Boer (eds.) op. Cit. *Policing across National Boundaries*, Pintcr 1994: 106- 120 at 117 'the conspiracy theorists of European policing arc wrong when they see a vast surveillance State, for the reality is that a true intelligence system is not an easy monster to produce but is one of the rarest of creatures'

3 L Shelley ' Transnational Organized Crime: the New Authoritarianism', paper presented at the Law and Society Conference, Glasgow 13, July19 96

4 Shelley op cit.: 3

5 C Sterling *Thieves' World* Simon and Schuster 1994

6 L.W.E. Sheptycki 'Law enforcement, Justice and Democracy In the Transnational Arena: Reflections on the War on Drugs', *International. Journal of Sociology of Law* 1996 24 61-75): See also L.W.E. Sheptycki 'Transnational Policing and the Makings of a Postmodern State,' *British Journal of Criminology* 199.5: 61.3; 11. Nadelmann *Cops across Borders* Penn State Press 199.3; M. Anderson and M. Den Boer (eds.) op. cit. 1994, M. Anderson et. al *Policing the European Union*. Clarendon Press 1995, C. Fijnaut and G. Marx Undercover: Police Surveillance in Comparative Perspective Kluwer 1995

7 The current politics of exclusion of immigrants to the European community is the subject of a large literature which I can not hope to summarize here, but there is much still to be studied about the relationship between this pattern of exclusion and internal forms of exclusionary social control.

8 see Sheptycki 1996 op.cit·

9 *Sunday Times* 17 / 11/ 1996

10 Others which could be consulted include anthropology, economics and social ecology.

11 Walter *Globalisation,* Routledge 1995

12 A Giddens *Consequences of Modernity* Polity 1990: 64 and cf. A. Giddens *Modernity and Self Identity* Polity Press 1991

13 A Bottoms and P. Wiles 'Crime and insecurity in the City' in C. Finjaut· J. Goetals, T. Peters and L. Walgrave (eds.) *Changes in Society. Crime and Criminal Justice in Europe* Volume I, Kluwer 1 996

14 see M. Featherstone (ed.) *Global Culture* Sagc 1990

15 I. Wallersteln *The Capitalist World- Economy* Cambrldge University Press 1979; for another attempt to situate globalization in historical perspective see also R. Robertson, *Globalization, Social -Theory and Global Culture* Sage 1992

[16] L Sklair *The Sociology of the Globalization System* Harvester Wheatsheaf 1991

[17] see the entries on globalization in M. Warner (ed.) *International Encyclopedia of Business and Management* Routledge 1 996

[18] Op Cit fn 11

[19] See S. Yearley *Sociology, Environmentalism and Globalization,* 1996:23

[20] C. F. J O'Neill 'Aids as a globalization panic,' In Featherstone 1990 op. cit: 329-342

[21] U. Beck *The Risk Society: -Towards a New Modernity* Sage 1992

[22] M Clarke, *Business Crime: It's Nature and Control* Oxford, Polity Press 1990: 162

[23] See e g D. della Porta and Y. Meny (eds.) *Corruzionc e Democrazia: Sette paesi a confronto* Liguori 1995; D. Nelken and M. Levi 'Introduction' In M. Levi and D. Nelken (eds.) *The Politics of Corruption and the Corruption of Politics* Blackwell 1996 and A. Garapon and. Salas (eds.) *La Re'publique Penalis6e* Hachette 1996

[24] W. H. Myers III 'The emerging threat of transnational organized crime from the East' 11 *Crime Law and Social Change* 24: 181-222 1996 at 182.

[25] See Yearley op. cit. fn. 19

[26] W.H. Myers III 1996 op. cit. note 24 at 182

[27] There is no space here to expound on the many differences between organized crime groups. But it is at least worth noting that describing organized crime as a new authoritarian menace to the democratic State fails to bring out the contrast between organized crime groups, or strategies, which aspire to military control over a territory (offering or exacting protection) and those, on the other hand, which thrive on the collusion of complicit or weak States which allow them to accumulate wealth (for example through international frauds or drug smuggling) without drawing attention to their criminal activities.

[28] see M Warner (ed.) *International Encyclopedia of Business and Management* *Routledge* 1996

[29] P. Arlacchl 'Corruption, Organized Crime and Money Laundering World Wide' In M. Punch et. al. *Coping with Corruption in a Borderless World,* Kluwer 1993: 89-104. The best discussion of these matters is still R. T. Naylor *Hot Money* and the *Politics of Debt* Simon and Schuster 1987

[30] S. *Strong Whitewash* Pan Books 1996

[31] ibid

[32] R.T. Naylor 'Loose Cannons: Covert Commerce and Underground Finance in the Modern Arms Market,' *Crime. Law and Social Change* 22 1995: 1-57

[33] N Passas ' BCCI *Crime. Law and Social Change* 23 1996

[34] see e. G. N. Passas and D. Nelken 1992 op. cit. note 1; P. Van Duyne 'Implications of Cross- border crime risks in an Open Europe', *Crime, Law and Soclal Change* 20 1993: 99-111, and P. Van Duyne and A. A. Block 'Organized Cross- Atlantic Crime: Racketeering in Fuels' *Crime.Law and Social Change* 22 1995 127-147

[35] D Gambetta *The Sicilian Mafia: the Business of Private Protection* Oxford Unlversity Press 1993; V. Ruggiero *Organized Crime and Corporate Crime* in Europe Aldershot, Dartmouth 1996: cf. 11. Nelken 'White - Collar Crime', in M. Maguire, R. Morgan and R. Reiner (eds.) *Oxford Handbook of Criminology* 2nd edition (forthcoming)

[36] The following extracts are taken from D. Nelson 'Inflated Claims:Organized Crime and European Union Fraud' forthcoming in A. Febbrajo,: D. Nelken; V. Olgiati (eds). *European Yearbook of Sociology of Law* Giuffre 1997

[37] 3 P. Arlacchi (1985) *Mafia Business* Oxford Unlversity Press

[38] This is the well known thesis of il Gattopardo by Lampedusa

39 3A way of saying 'you son of a whore (= you son of a bitch) which implies friendly recognition that the other is smart but also perhaps too smart.

40 the '*pizzo*' Is the widespread practice of demanding a rake off or 'cut' from all business activities in areas under control and/or subject to the threats or blandishments of organized crime.

41 see G Farrell, K. Manshur and M. Tullis 'Cocalne and Heroin in Europe 1983-93: A Cross- national Comparison of Trafficking and Prices' *British Journal of Criminology* .36: 2 1996: 255-281 at 279 'the implications of this analysis for increasing the effectiveness of European law enforcement are not encouraging. The balance of evidence suggests increasing enforcement will impact only marginally upon prices due to rapidly diminishing marginal returns '

42 see M. Levl 'Pecunla non olet: Cleansing the Money - Launderers from the Temple,' *Crime. Law and Social Change* 16: 217- .302 1991, who notes the difficult policy issues involved

Part V
Appendices

Appendix 1 - The Most Critical Unresolved Issue Associated with Contemporary Organized Crime

Issues of longevity and *replicability* are critical in efforts to both understand and attack organized crime. Longevity is important in weighing the danger posed by a criminal organization: the longer an organization has been in existence, the deeper are its roots and the greater is its potential to integrate into the fabric of a society. The existence of organized crime, as opposed to criminals devoid of an overarching structure, creates and atmosphere conducive to criminal activity. The organization serves as a catalyst, facilitating criminal operations by even nominally or unaffiliated criminals. It does this by offering such services as access to information, arbitration and fencing, specialized implements such as firearms and vehicles, and connections to public officials and persons in legitimate business. The existence of recognized (by other) criminal organizations permits joint planning and activities that are transnational. As in the legitimate world of business, there is greater confidence in dealing with a corporate entity than with individuals, and longevity enhances this confidence.

Despite the importance of this issue, there has been little in the literature on how criminal organizations are able to continue beyond the lives of their current membership.

- How do they successfully recruit new members?
- Is the pool from which members are drawn increasing or decreasing?
- How does this affect the quality of new recruits?

In the absence of a strategy to address these issues, law enforcement efforts against criminal organizations are often either random or focused on headhunting --- investigating and prosecuting the leadership -- while the organization

Howard Abadinsky, Ph. D.

The most critical unresolved issue concerning organized crime, I believe, is its symbiotic relationship to corruption.

Organized crime in its most potent form - syndicated crime - cannot exist without corruption. But today, corruption has reached epidemic proportions. The vast amount of money being paid to governmental and other officials around the world has made a mockery of the law and justice because it allows those entrusted to enforce the law, to look the other way. Thus, if the law and Criminal Justice system can be neutralized by corruption, its effectiveness against criminals is also neutralized. The industrial world has taken the first steps to fight corruption by taking action against the officials accepting bribes. This is only the beginning. If syndicated crime is to be fought successfully, the fight must begin with curbing corruption.

This is, in my opinion, the most serious contemporary concern associated with organized crime.

Joseph Albini, Ph.D., Ph.D., Professor (emeritus) of Criminology, Department of Sociology, Wayne State University, Detroit, Michigan, is the author of The American Mafia: Genesis of a Legend and a renowned expert on organized crime.

The most significant aspect, and the biggest challenge, currently facing the field in the study of and the theory of Organized Crime (national and international) is that of corruption of authority. I mean by that type of corruption as being a principal -anchor- concept
- which organizes the relationship(s) between the "state" [actually social and political conditions] and the emergence, development, growth and expansion even <u>beyond</u> state borders, or conversely,
- the weakening of organized crime [by a state's counter-measure(s) against Organized Crime]

In the study of the relationships between society -state and Organized Crime, we may find answers to other important questions about specific structures and operations of different OC groups ...in different locales or in the international arena.

Menachem Amir, Ph. D

To me, the most critical issue is that we academics, and the police and government policy people STILL tend to think about organized crime in very stereotyped ways---still in a mafia-type version. Now, for certain, that perspective includes other "ethnics" such as Russians, Asians, etc., but we are still not thinking about the *process* by which criminals commit their criminal acts---therefore we still do not include business leaders, corporate leaders, political entrepreneurs who may operate in monopolistic environments, use corruption and criminal advantages, recruit new criminal co-conspirators and continue to perpetuate an array of frauds and schemes upon citizens. In some cases, when these international operations are brought to light and it is clear that multi-millions of resources have been stolen via an on-going criminal operation, the sanction is laughable. The issue is that these international criminal operators do not fit any perceived crime profile. Hence, we must broaden our view of what is or is not organized crime.

Margaret E. Beare, Ph.D., Director, Nathanson Centre for the Study of Organized Crime and Corruption, is a Professor at the Osgoode Hall Law School, North York, Toronto, Canada, President of the International Organization of Organized Crime Associations and an expert on Canadian organized crime and corruption.

In the USA a key issue seems to be the regulation of organized crime through the evolving sanctioning tools, such as RICO, that have emerged from legal reforms within anti-organized crime legislation. The extent to which these conspiracy prosecutions may threaten the civil rights of the accused through their sweeping application is a matter of serious concern that has not been taken up by scholars and others. These matters have been the subject of harangues by defense attorneys defending mobsters whose motives, because of their affiliations with their clients, are dubious.

Another issue that persists concerns political corruption. It is taken for granted that OC can not flourish, or even exist, without political support. The questions are:

- What institutions can develop anti-political corruption attitudes in the public?
- How can we create a social movement---or regenerate such public collective actions against the political-criminal nexus?
- To what extent can government create opportunities against such a nexus?
- How can the cultural ambivalence towards organized crime, which seems to generate hostility towards law enforcement among some segments of the public, be reversed?

Robert Kelly, Ph. D.

An issue that deserves inquiry is the rapidly-declining importance of **organized crime** investigations by local, state and federal law enforcement in the United States. While there appears to be much rhetoric associated with the "war against organized crime," the evidence does not support this political posturing. Beginning with the elimination of the U.S. Organized Crime Strike Forces, the subsequent dissolution of the Pennsylvania Crime Commission and the New Mexico's Governor's Crime Prevention Commission, and the reduction in organized crime investigative resources in New Jersey, California and New York, we are experiencing morbidity in our professed desire to contain the growth or organized crime. Much of this "neglect" - more likely a pattern of conscious dismantling - is being attributed to a reduction in government spending. To the contrary, it would appear that this pattern is directly related to the investigation of politically-sensitive issues -- illegal campaign financing by nefarious persons and organizations. A systematic investigation into the reason(s) behind this phenomenon and aroused public concern about the rape of organized crime fighting resources by what appears to be "corrupt political entities" should be pursued.

Frederick T. Martens, Executive Director (Ret.), Pennsylvania Crime Commission

---

Unresolved critical issues associated with contemporary organized crime include:
- What, if at all, is the difference now between white collar and organized crime?
- How far are organized criminals acting in accordance with the capitalist ethos?
- Can they be fought without the use of police methods which abandon respect for civil liberties?

David Nelken, Ph. D.

Without doubt the most compelling development in organized crime at the end of the Twentieth Century is the trend toward the development of transnational organized crime groups and the suggestion that these groups are beginning to collaborate and cooperate in a systematic manner to facilitate the delivery of illicit goods and services on an international scale. While organized crime scholars have thus far been quite careful in their description of this phenomenon, a real danger of a reconstructed and rehabilitated "alien conspiracy theory" of organized crime as a replacement for the discredited "Mafia" model of years past, emanating from the news media and the state lurks as an imminent danger.

Both the state and the media have clear interests in promoting a conspiracy model of organized crime. Such a model explains the inability of governments to eradicate criminal syndicates, without raising issues of corruption. The media often replicates state doctrine and adds its own touch of sensationalism and exaggeration in an attempt to attract viewers and readers. The danger is that the real issues of transnational crime will be transformed into a comic book caricature resembling James Bonds' SPECTRE. or SMERSH, or more likely Maxwell Smart's CHAOS, headed by a series of cunning and powerful Dr. Moriartys or Fu Manchus.

The fact is that despite the internationalization of crime, little has changed in organization of syndicates. They are still rather informal, loosely structured, open, flexible organizations highly reactive to changes in the political and economic environments. The internationalization of organized crime has not resulted from some master plan by arch-criminals.

It is simply a reflection of the reactive, flexible nature of crime syndicates which has allowed them to respond to technological advancements in communications and transportation; to market adaptations resulting from the internationalization of investment capital, financial services and banking; to the internationalization of manufacturing and increased segmentation and fragmentation of production; and, to the increased emphasis on unrestricted trade across borders.

Organized crime syndicates are still rooted in local conditions, shielded by local corruption, and limited by local markets. The European Union weakens borders and encourages the free flow of people and goods. Russian, Italian, Rumanian, British and Corsican syndicates simply respond to the new reality. It is not the Malina or the Mafia which created these opportunities, it is the state and multinational corporations. Nigerian drug traffickers are not responsible for the enormous recent increase in international trade or heightened flow of people across borders. They merely take advantage of the situation. When they collaborate with Asian heroin producers it does not signify the birth of a new international criminal order it merely reflects the same types of arrangements that are occurring in the business community at large.

Poppy growers can now market their products over a wider arena. Nigerian smugglers have a mechanism in place to efficiently take advantage of new technologies and opportunities.

Collaboration is as natural as a compact between U.S. car manufacturers and parts producers in Brazil or Mexico. But the fact remains that the Nigerian syndicates are firmly rooted in economic inequality and pervasive patterns of corruption that are distinctly Nigerian.

The major issue is not collaboration between and among organized crime groups, but increased political corruption brought on by greater rewards from international commerce and weakened central governments whose powers have been surpassed and often usurped by multinational corporations. National sovereignty is not threatened by Colombian cartels, Southeast Asian warlords, Russian criminal entrepreneurs, or Zambian cattle poachers. It is threatened by pervasive and growing corruption and the increasing irrelevance of individual states in an international economy.

Organized crime has not changed very much from the system of patron-client relations described by Albini; which operates within the context of illicit entrepreneurship described by Smith; and, which is facilitated by the businessmen, law enforcement officials and politicians of Chambliss' crime networks. Organized crime syndicates are still localized, fragmented, and highly ephemeral entities. The only difference is that the world has changed and organized crime has adapted.

Gary W. Potter, Ph. D., is a professor of police studies at Eastern Kentucky University. He has written several books [Criminal Organizations; The Porn Merchant and The City and the Syndicate] and journal articles on organized crime, drug trafficking, and political corruption. His recent research interests have focused on organized crime in rural settings and on the social construction of crime.

Its changing nature and the failure of observers and analysts to look beyond traditional perpetrators and victims.

We are too often locked into easy and fashionable paradigms. These are temporarily comforting until we accumulate information, which contradicts our prior held beliefs. We should be prepared for organizational change in terms of tactics, partnerships, and resources.

This will have an affect on generic organized and state-organized crime .

In order to be aware and to pay attention-which are quite different-we need to consider and to pinpoint:

- what are the necessary conditions which will make this possible (policies, type of staff and their training, necessary institutional/non institutional, formal and informal support systems, community roles, etc.) and
- those conditions which are likely to interfere or prevent the needed awareness, paying attention and the relevant actions?

Jeffrey Ian Ross, Ph. D.

Although there are many issues relating to organized crime that need to be resolved, I would argue that there are four that deserve particular attention: structure of the organizations, corruption as a technique of organized crime, the strategy against criminal organizations, and the idea of legitimization as a key component of strategy.

- The issue of structure centers on the importance of networks.

There has been a tendency in the literature to equate organized crime with formal hierarchy and to see anything that fell short of this as somehow lacking in essential characteristics. This is an understandable but regrettable result of the preoccupation with the Mafia and with "godfather" type figures. In fact, the most important organizational structure for organized crime is probably network-based. Networks are a superior form of organization to most others since they are adaptable, resilient and can be reconstituted after suffering serious damage. They are also a very modern type of structure and many traditionally hierarchical companies have moved to networks to provide dynamism and innovation. Organized crime has been in this position for a long time. Networks allow them to cross borders and also facilitate links with and support from legitimate political and economic power structures

- The linkages between organized crime and governments or financial institutions in the licit world are underpinned by corruption. Yet this is an area that has been neglected. All commentators on organized crime genuflect to the importance of corruption as a strategy; yet few examine the points of vulnerability in the state apparatus and the patterns and networks of corruption relationships that flow into and exploit these vulnerabilities. Conversely, many commentators on corruption treat this as generic problem and do not look at specific forms it takes when connected to organized crime. The relationship between organized crime and corruption needs to be elucidated much more fully than hitherto if effective counter-measures are to be initiated.

- This leads to the third issue - the importance of a strategic international response to transnational organized crime. What strategy should the international community and national governments adopt in the struggle against organized crime? What are the objectives of this strategy? Should the overall aim be destruction or, if this is unobtainable, should it be containment? Moreover, if we accept that it is containment are there some kinds of configuration of power that we can live with much more easily than others (for example, a larger number of small groups rather than a small number of large groups which concentrate political and economic power and can undermine the legitimate authority of governments)?

- A tactical issue within this is whether governments can and should provide incentives for members of criminal organizations to leave the business and go legitimate. This is something that is particularly relevant in relation to Russia where there might actually be a process of growing legitimization anyway. This makes some sense, given that many of Russia's most enterprising entrepreneurs have been criminal. Amnesties on criminal money and amnesties on membership in criminal organizations, if combined with increasingly strong law enforcement and harsh penalties could do something to change the incentive structure for criminals. This could be done either overtly or tacitly. If criminals are to be transformed into licit businessmen, however, it is critical that they leave their patterns of criminal behavior behind - especially the resort to violence and corruption. Consequently, a scheme like this would have to include careful monitoring and the imposition of strong penalties in the event of a reversion to previous habits and behavior patterns. For all its shortcomings, in combination with more traditional law enforcement techniques, such an approach might prove effective

Phil Williams, Ph. D.

The typical gang for organized crime in Japan is the *Boryokudan* - known as "Yakuza." We have recently witnessed the growth of *Koiki*(wide area)-*Boryokudan*. After the enforcement of the Law to Cope with Boryokudan in 1992 many small-sized Boryokudan groups have become subordinates of three giant Koiki-Boryokudan organizations, because they cannot maintain their activities against the severer control by the police. Therefore, the most critical unresolved issue concerns the way to dissolve the Koiki-Boryokudan. The police should at least endeavor to suppress illegal activities of Boryokudan by using all available legal means, especially those authorized under the Law to Cope with Boryokudan.

Reflecting on the phenomenon of globalization, the activities of gangs for organized crime have also become internationalized. The international activities of Boryokudan remain still limited when compared with foreign gangs. However, the Boryokudan have contacts with some organized crime gangs in East Asian countries. For example, gangs which produce stimulant drugs illicitly in Taiwan, and the *Snake Head*, that is, Chinese gangs which transport illegal aliens. In order to stop the development of the transnational activities of Boryokudan, law enforcement agencies in Japan should cooperate with those in the foreign countries concerned. They need, at the very least, to exchange information about the activities of organized crime gangs in their territory.

Minoru Yokoyama, Ph. D.

Appendix 2 - An Exclusive Resource Inventory on Organized Crime

Frederick T. Martens

The ability to inquire of and obtain information about organized and economic crime, as well as public corruption is limited only by one's imagination. The foregoing inventory of resources has been assembled as a means of "opening up doors" for the inquiring mind. It is not, nor was it intended to be, all-inclusive. Quite to the contrary, it is an exclusive inventory -- one that draws upon unconventional sources of material. From these, the avid student of organized crime can and will explore a universe of criminality that has escaped the attention of most criminologists.

Video

- *Arts and Entertainment*
  P O Box 2284, South Burlington, Vermont (USA) 05407
  Web site: www.aetv.com 1-800-423-1212 (USA)

This home video channel has produced the most extensive video programs on organized crime, public corruption, money laundering, and drug trafficking in the world. A catalogue is available upon request.

- *David Royle Productions*
  New York, New York
  Phone 212-947-8433

Specialists in producing documentaries on organized crime.

Journals

- *Transnational Organized Crime Journal*
  C/O Frank Cass, ISBS, 5804 Northeast Hassalo Street, Portland, Oregon 97213-3644
  Phone1-800-944-6190; 503-280-8832;
  E-Mail: orders@isbs.com; Web site: Frank Cass.com.

- *Trends In Organized Crime*
  Published by Transaction Periodicals Consortium, Rutgers University, New Brunswick, New Jersey (USA) 08903; or Swets Publishing Service, Heereweg 347, 2161 CA, Lisse, The Netherlands (for Europe)

This Journal provides excerpts from international publications addressing organized crime, public corruption, drug trafficking, and criminal organizations. Proceedings conducted internationally are also addressed.

- *Journal of Contemporary Criminal Justice*
  Sage Publications, Inc., 2455 Teller Road, Thousand Oaks, California
  91320 E-mail: order@sagepub.com

Book Publishers
- *Yardbird Books*
  601 Kennedy Road, Airville, Pennsylvania 17302
  E-mail: info@yardbird.com; Web page: http:\\www.yardbird.com
Publisher specializes in books on crime and corruption in the Commonwealth of
Pennsylvania (USA). Provides a most comprehensive series on government
scandals and abuse of powers.

Personal Contacts
- *G. Robert Blakey*
  Notre Dame School of Law, South Bend, Indiana 465
  Phone 219-631-6627
A former federal prosecutor who has spent a career investigating, prosecuting,
and teaching organized crime issues. Possesses one of the most extensive
private collections of organized crime-related material in the United States.

- *Ronald Goldstock*
  New York University School of Law, 40 Washington Square S,
  New York, New York 10012. Phone 212-998-6060
A former state prosecutor who has collected a worldwide collection of
organized crime publications second only to that of Professor Blakey.

- *Frederick T. Martens*
  PO Box 1290, McAfee, New Jersey (USA) 07428
  Phone 973-209-8602
The former Executive Director of the Pennsylvania Crime Commission who has
amassed a 30 year collection of organized crime books, journals, government
publications, videos, and tapes.

- *Charles H. Rogovin*
  Temple University School of Law, 1719 N. Broad Street, Philadelphia,
  Pennsylvania 19122
  Phone 215-204-8988; Fax 215-204-1185
A former state prosecutor who has assembled a series of books and publications
that are part of his private collection.

- *Ralph Salerno*
  RD #1, Box 1055, Lake Ariel, Pennsylvania 18436
  Phone 717-689-7486;
  or 38 Grosbe Lane, Naples, Florida 33961
  Phone 813-775-2809

An authority on organized crime who maintains a private collection of material.

- *Louise Shelly*
  American University, Department of Law, Justice and Society,
  Washington, DC 20016-8022 Phone 202-885-2962;
  Fax 202-885-2907; E-mail: lshelle@americanedu.

Dr. Shelly is the foremost authority on Soviet/Russian organized crime in the former Soviet Republics.

- *Patterson Smith*
  23 Prospect Terrace, Montclair, New Jersey 07042
  Phone 973-744-3291; Fax 973-744-4501

A private collector of organized crime material who possesses books and documents seldom found in traditional libraries.

- *Adrian Woods*
  London, England
  Phone 44-1525-851-103

The world's most proficient film documentarian who possesses an outstanding array of material on organized crime.

Universities
- *Rutgers University*
  School of Criminal Justice
  15 Washington Street, 4th Floor,
  Newark, New Jersey 07102
  Phone 973-353-5522; Fax 973-353-1275

This institution houses material of an original nature on organized crime. Its librarian, Phyliss Schultze, is well-versed in obtaining documents that are unavailable in libraries.

- *Sam Houston State University*
  College of Criminal Justice
  Huntsville, Texas 77341
  Phone 409-294-1632; Fax 409-294-1653

This institution serves as secretariat of the International Association for the Study of Organized Crime (IASOC), and publishes it's newsletter, *Criminal Organizations*.

- *University of Illinois at Chicago*
  Office of International Criminal Justice,
  1033 W. Van Buren, m/c 777, Chicago, Illinois 60607
  Phone 312-996-9595; Fax 312-413-0458.

This organization was the official office of the International Association for the Study of Organized Crime from 1996-1999, and publishes *Crime and Justice International*, a monthly magazine.

- *York University*
  Osgood School of Law, Centre for the Study of Organized Crime, 4700 Keele Street, Downsview, Ontario, Canada, M3J 2R5
  Phone 416-736-5015

A Canadian think-tank dedicated to the study of organized crime on an international level.

Agencies
- *Department of Justice, State of California*
  Office of Attorney General, 4949 Broadway, Sacramento, California 95820
  Phone 916-227-4045

Publishes numerous monographs on organized crime and related issues.

- *Chicago Crime Commission*
  79 West Monroe, Suite 605, Chicago, Illinois 60603
  Phone 312-372-0104; Fax 312-372-6286

A privately funded crime commission dedicated to maintaining a spotlight on organized crime.

- *National Institute of Justice*
  810 7th Street, NW, Washington, DC 20531
  Phone 202-307-6394; Fax 202-307-6394

Provides free reports and monographs on organized crime.

- *New Jersey State Commission of Investigation*
  28 State Street, 10th Floor, Trenton, New Jersey (USA) 08625
  Phone 609-292-6767; Fax 609-633-7366.

An independent bi-partisan government commission that publishes reports on organized crime and public corruption.

- *New York State Commission of Investigation*
  270 Broadway, New York, New York 10007
  Phone 212-577-0700

A bi-partisan, government agency which publishes reports on organized crime and public corruption.

- *Centre for Business and Public Sector Ethics*
  Lilac Place, Champney's Walk, Cambridge, England CB3 9AW
  Phone 44-223-68056; Fax 44-223-32704.

- *Centre for International Financial Crime Studies*
  College of Law, University of Florida, PO Box 117625,
  Gainesville, Florida 32611-7625

- *Crime Research Bureau*
  5 Cannon Lane, London, England NW3 1EL
  Phone 44-171-435-7351; Fax 44-171-794-6575

Its director, Martin Short, is world renowned for his documentary research of criminal organizations.

- *Financial Crimes Enforcement Network (FINCEN)*
  2070 Chain Bridge Road, Suite 200, Vienna, Virginia 22182
  Phone 703-905-3591; Fax 703-905-3690;
  E-mail: morris@fincen.treas.gov

- *Institute of Advanced Legal Studies*
  University of London, Charles Clare House,
  17 Russell Square, London WC1B-5DR
  Phone 44-171-637-1731;
  Fax 44-171-580-9613

Its director, Dr. Barry Rider, is world-renowned in the study of organized crime and public corruption.

- *International Association of Law Enforcement Intelligence Analysts*
  PO Box 82-108, South Florida, 33082-1086
  or PO Box 903198, Sacramento, California 94203-1980
  Phone 609-984-1035

An organization dedicated to the advancement of organized crime intelligence analysis.

- *The Centre for International Documentation on Organized and Economic Crime*
  Rainbow Hill House, Hartford Road, Forest Row,
  East Sussex, RH18 5LU England
  Phone 44-1342-822416; Fax 44-1342-824419

- *National Strategy Information Center*
  1730 Rhode Island Avenue, NW, Suite 500,
  Washington, DC 20036-3101
  Phone 202-429-0129; Fax 202-659-5429;
  E-Mail: nsic@ix.netcom.com

This organization provides working papers on organized crime in the United States, and countries that do business with the United States.

- *Organized Crime Research*
  273 Chase Road, Southgate, London N14 6HX England,
  Attention: Randy Cozens
  Phone 44-181-882-5400

- *Research Group on International Organized Crime*
  University of Gent, Universiteitstrad 4, B-9000 Gent, Belgium

- *Research Group on Transnational Crime*
  University of Trento School of Law, via Inama 5 38100 Trento, Italy
  Phone 39-461-882304; Fax 39-461-882303;
  E-mail: savona@risc1.gelso.unitn.it

- *Trans Union National Fraud Center*
  Four Horsham Business Center, 300 Welsh Road, Suite 200, Horsham,
  Pennsylvania (USA) 19044
  Phone 215-657-0800; Fax 215-657-7071;
  E-mail: email@nationalfraud.com

A private organization that provides investigative expertise on fraud to business and government.

- *Transparency International USA*
  1615 L Street, NW, Suite 700, Washington, DC 20016
  Phone 202-682-7048; Fax 202-857-0939

A private organization which researches corruption throughout the world.

- *United Nations Crime Centre*
  PO Box 500, A-1400, Vienna Austria

Frederick T. Martens, Executive Director (Ret.), Pennsylvania Crime Commission.

Foreign Language Abstracts

1. Grensoverschrijdende misdaad: een ervaring van onduidelijkheden

Gerhard 0. W. Mueller

Het artikel beschrijft de ontwikkelingen in de definitie van grensoverschrijdende en internationale misdaad in de overleggen van de UN-instellingen. Nadat een basisdefinitie bereikt was werden de lidstaten van de UN- en de NGO-organisaties gevraagd 18 categorieen van misdaad te beschrijven die internationale kenmerken en invloeden hebben, hoewel sommige lokaal van aard lijken te zijn. De 18 categorieen worden besproken waarbij de nadruk ligt op het bereik en het patroon van elk van de categorieen, bestaande oplossingen en de benodigde maatregelen om deze misdaden te bestrijden. Besproken worden misdaden met grensoverschrijdende kenmerken als het witwassen van geld, terrorisme, intellectuele diefstal, piraterij, computer- en milieucriminaliteit enz. Deze misdaden 'lijden' onder de onduidelijkheid van de definitie van het concept grensoverschrijdende misdaad, noodzakelijk onderzoek en vereiste uitvoerbare maatregelen of criteria. De definiering van de concepten van grensoverschrijdende en internationale misdaden behoeft onderzoek en vraagt om maatregelen om ze effectief te bestriiden.

2. Rijk worden en gelijk worden: grensoverschrijdende bedreigingen in de 21e eeuw

Phil Williams

Het artikel onderzoekt de bedreiging van de nationale en internationale veiligheid door grensoverschrijdende criminele organisaties en grensoverschrijdend terrorisme. Het betoogt dat het bestaan van deze bedreigingen begrepen kan worden als het resultaat van twee processen globalisering en de crisis van de rijksoverheid - welke beide bijdragen aan het verkleinen van het bereik van het gezag van de rijksoverheid. De invloed van de verscheidene aspecten van globalisering - minderheden en etnische netwerken, de groei van de handel, de ontwikkeling van een wereldomvattend financieel systeem, de ontwikkeling van wereldomvattende informatie communicatie systemen en de opkomst van wereldsteden - worden onderzocht. Ook toekomstige ontwikkelingen in de georganiseerde misdaad en terrorisme worden nader belicht.

3. De georganiseerde misdaad in Oost Europa en de consequenties hiervan voor de veiligheid van de Westerse Wereld

Brunon Holyst

Dit artikel beschrijft de georganiseerde misdaad in Oost-Europese landen en vestigt de aandacht op de bedreigingen die hieruit voortkomen voor de Westerse Wereld. Politieke en economische veranderingen in de voorheen socialistische landen oefenen een invloed uit op de ontwikkeling van de dynamiek en structuur van de misdaad. Criminelen, steeds vaker met internationale connecties, profiteren van veranderingen die plaatsvinden op allerlei gebieden van het leven. Zwakheden in het staatsapparaat en het daaruit voortvloeiende verlies van het monopolie van rechtsbedeling, gaten in de wet, sociale onrust, een aanzienlijke verlaging van de levensstandaard, samen met een systematische corrumpering van het publieke, economische en politieke leven creeren een bijzonder netwerk van 'pathologische' institutionele verbanden. Internationale monetaire connecties, wereldomvattende financiele transacties, uitwisseling van grondstoffen alsmede de opening van grenzen zullen leiden tot een nog grotere internationalisatie en professionalisering van de activiteiten van de georganiseerde misdaad. De flexibiliteit van de georganiseerde misdaad (zij kan vele vormen aannemen) vormt de belangrijkste bedreiging doordat zij hierdoor van dezelfde vrijheden en sociale mogelijkheden kan profiteren als de conventionele, legitieme, legale, sociale en economische gemeenschap. De situatie in Oost Europa vergemakkelijkt waarschijnlijk politieke criminalisering.

4. De ontwikkeling en beheersbaarheid van de georganiseerde misdaad in Zuid-Afrika na de apartheid

Mark Shaw

De georganiseerde misdaad is dramatisch gegroeid onder het nieuwe Zuid-Afrikaanse democratische bestuur. Hoewel sommige vormen van de georganiseerde misdaad - met name de activiteiten van bendes in de Westerse Kaap - al bestonden tijdens het apartheidsregime, vormde dit geen bedreiging.
Straatbendes werden zelfs vaak gebruikt door overheidsagenten voor het ontwrichten van de antiapartheid activisten. Terwijl de publieke en politieke druk rond dit thema wordt opgevoerd, zijn de Zuid-Afrikaanse ordehandhavinginstellingen slecht op het bestrijden van grootschalige activiteiten van de georganiseerde misdaad voorbereid. Toch is het van groot belang dat interventies nu plaatsvinden: Zuid-Afrikaanse criminele organisaties, hoewel talrijk, zijn nog steeds relatief gefragmenteerd en kwetsbaar voor gerichte politionele acties. Een belangrijke zwakheid is echter het gebrek aan begrip en analyse van de omvang, vorm, structuur en groeipotentie van de Zuid-Afrikaanse georganiseerde m isdnad

5. Economische hervormingen en de 'Zwarte Genootschappen': de wederopkomst van de georganiseerde misdaad in China na Mao.

Mark S. Gaylord en Hualing Fu

Het culturele erfgoed van China omvat ook een traditie van georganiseerde misdaad van honderden jaren. Gedurende de eerste helft van de 20e eeuw onderhielden China's 'geheime genootschappen' een nauwe band met de Nationalistische regering van Chiang Kai-shek. Nadat de communisten in 1949 aan de macht kwamen begon Mao Zedong echter snel met het bestrijden van wat hij terecht zag als potentiele bron van oppositie van zijn nieuwe regering. Gedurende 30 jaar verdween de georganiseerde misdaad in China, ondergedoken samen met andere instituties uit het vorige tijdperk In het China na Mao is de georganiseerde misdaad (genaamd hei shehui of zwart genootschap) niet alleen weer op gedoken maar nu ook wijd verspreid. 'Zwarte gemeenschap' is een overkoepelende term voor kleine bendes struikrovers tot georganiseerde criminele groepen met duizenden leden. Opzettelijk wordt het uit het zicht gehouden, verborgen door geheimhouding, corrupte ambtenaren en het hopeloos vervaagde onderscheid tussen private en publieke sectoren.

6. Trends in de georganiseerde misdaad door de *Boryokudan* in Japan

Minoru Yokoyama

De *Boryokudan*, de inheemse Japanse groepen van de georganiseerde misdaad, hebben gedeeltes van de subcultuur van de bendes uit de feodale periode overgenomen. Het hart van hun ethiek wordt gevormd door *Ninkyo-do*, een soort ridderlijke geest. Na de economische groei van Japan na de tweede wereldoorlog werden, door geweld en hun immense rijkdom, verscheidene invloedrijke *Boryokudans Koiki* (breed gebied) -*Boryokudan*. Tegenwoordig opereren zij eerder als winstgeorienteerde organisaties vergelijkbaar met particuliere ondernemingen in kapitalistische landen dan als groepen met de geest van *Ninkyo-do*. De *Boryokudan* is hierarchisch gestructureerd waarbij een groot gedeelte van het geld afkomstig van lidmaatschapsgelden naar een 'godfather' stroomt. De meeste leden moeten veel illegale activiteiten uitvoeren om voldoende te verdienen voor het levensonderhoud en het lidmaatschapsgeld aan hun baas te kunnen voldoen. De belangrijkste bron van inkomsten voor de *Boryokudan* is de verkoop van stimulerende drugs. Lange tijd heeft de politie de praktijken van de *Boryokudan* oogluikend toegestaan. Geleidelijk aan heeft de politie echter zich ontdaan van de corrupte invloed van de *Boryokudan*. Tijdens de economische voorspoed van de tachtiger jaren hebben de *Koiko-Boryokudan* vele gewelddadige activiteiten begaan die meer zichtbaar en ontoelaatbaar werden voor het grote publiek. De publieke opinie keerde zich meer en meer tegen de Boryokudan. In 1991 werd de wet ter bestrijding van de *Boryokudan* ingesteld. Met behulp van deze wet controleert de politie strenger en met hulp van het volk de illegale activiteiten van de *Boryokudan*.

7. De toekomst van de Siciliaanse en Calabriaanse georganiseerde misdaad

Letizia Paoli

Om de toekomst van de Siciliaanse en Calabriaanse maffiagenootschappen te kunnen vaststellen moeten twee aspecten van hun acties worden onderscheiden en apart beschouwd worden: I) de participatie van de maffia in internationale illegale markten en 2) het locale machtssysteem van de maffia. Dit artikel betoogt dat de positie en de mate van betrokkenheid van de sterkste Italiaanse maffiaverbonden bij wereldwijde illegale wisselpraktijken voornamelijk afhangt van de bewegingen van de internationale politieke economie. Acties van ordehandhavers kunnen echter op de korte termijn een aanzienlijke invloed uitoefenen. Aan de andere kant; de invloed die maffiafamilies in de lokale gemeenschappen uitoefenen is vooral het resultaat van het samenspel van drie factoren: de maffiagroepen zelf, overheidsinstanties en de Italiaanse burgermaatschappij.

8. De toekomst van de traditionele georganiseerde misdaad in de Verenigde Staten

Howard Abadinsky

Sommige waarnemers betogen dat de Amerikaanse maffia praktisch verdwenen is, vooral door het succes van de federale ordehandhaving. Langjarige straffen met name voor criminelen van de georganiseerde misdaad heeft de omerta, de beruchte zwijgcode, doorbroken. Deze bewering is echter niet nieuw, de ondergang van de Amerikaanse maffia wordt al decennia lang voorspeld. Is uiteindelijk de tijd gekomen dat de maffia geen rol meer speelt in de Amerikaanse toekomst? Dit artikel beschouwt theorieen die zowel het ontstaan als het overleven van het fenomeen verklaren en vergelijkt de resultaten met wat bekend is van de hedendaagse Italiaans-Amerikaanse zeorzaniseerde misdaad.

9. De georganiseerde misdaad in de Verenigde Staten: enkele tegenwoor dige stromingen

Robert J Kelly

Van de Amerikaanse maffia, La Cosa Nostra, kan niet gezegd worden dat zij vernietigd is ondanks een gecombineerde aanval van de ordehandhavers. Aangezien de economische omstandigheden en sociaalpolitieke omgeving, die een voedingsbodem waren voor de maffia, veranderd zijn heeft zij zich omgevormd en zich geherdefinieerd. Andere etnische groepen, waarnaar ook wel verwezen wordt als de niet traditionele georganiseerde misdaad, komen op in etnische enclaves en getto's van nieuwe immigrantengemeenschappen. Het essay onderzoekt de processen van verval en hergroepering binnen La Cosa Nostra en schetst de structuren en dynamiek van de Chinese afpersingssyndicaten.

10. De georganiseerde misdaad in Israel

Menachem Amir

Het artikel brengt het onderzoek naar de georganiseerde misdaad in Israel in kaart zoals het weergegeven wordt in de media en academisch onderzoek. De geschiedenis van het onderzoek naar de georganiseerde misdaad in Israel wordt voortdurend gekarakteriseerd door discussies tussen politie, academici en media over de definitie, aard en reactie op de georganiseerde misdaad in Israel. De aard van de georganiseerde misdaad geeft het op een na belangrijkste kenmerk van de Israelische samenleving weer (het belangrijkste is veiligheid): dat van golven van immigranten die ook de criminele wereld, inclusief de georganiseerde misdaad, binnenkomen. De georganiseerde misdaad heeft dan ook het karakter van etnische opvolging, waarbij de laatste in de reeks de Russische immigranten zijn. Hun betrokkenheid bij criminaliteit en georganiseerde misdaad wordt nuhrc rhr-von.

11. Georganiseerde misdaad: een Oostenrijks gezichtspunt

Maximilian Edelbacher

De georganiseerde misdaad is de belangrijkste uitdaging voor de moderne wereld, vooral voor Europa. Een enorme verandering heeft plaatsgevonden in Europa sinds in 1989 het IJzeren Gordijn wegviel. Oostenrijks geografische positie in het centrum van Europa en haar nieuwe rol als lid van de Europese gemeenschap brengen nieuwe verantwoordelijkheden met zich mee om de georganiseerde misdaad te bestrijden. Oostenrijk is van belang voor zich ontwikkelende georganiseerde criminele bendes vanwege het witwassen van geld. Ook wordt Oostenrijk een basis voor operationele activiteiten van de georganiseerde misdaad. De nieuwe rol van Oostenrijk brengt de verantwoordelijkheid met zich mee de georganiseerde misdaad te bestrijden door nieuwe ideeen en counterstrategieen te ontwikkelen en met anderen te delen.

12. Afrikaans-Amerikaanse georganiseerde misdaad: raciale onderworp enheid en muiterij

Robert J. Kelly

Wanneer men veronderstelt dat La Cosa Nostra het hart vormt van de georganiseerde misdaad in de Verenigde Staten roept dit vanzelf de vraag op naar perifere vormen van het verschijnsel - namelijk georganiseerde misdaad in minderheidsgroeperingen of 'niet traditionele' georganiseerde misdaad. Dit artikel biedt enkele beschouwingen over specifieke vormen van de 'niet traditionele' georganiseerde misdaad, Afrikaans-Amerikaanse groepen en hun vooruitzichten op groei. Betoogt wordt dat beha drughandel de politieke mobiliteit binnen de minderheidsgemeenschap een voorwaarde vormt voor de groei en stabiliteit van de traditionele georganiseerde misdaad.

13. De wereldwijde handel in seks: mensen als de ultieme handelswaar

Sarah L. Shannon

Commerciele seksuele exploitatie van vrouwen en kinderen is een wereldwijd fenomeen geworden. In toenemende mate nemen grensoverschrijdende criminele organisaties deel aan deze zeer lucratieve handel. De feiten die de wereldwijde handel in seks omgeven zijn weerzinwekkend. Wanneer effectieve tegenmaatregelen genomen dienen te worden is een grondig begrip van deze feiten onontbeerlijk. Daarom worden in dit artikel enkele onderscheidende kenmerken, geografische aspecten en opkomende trends van deze vleesmarkt besproken. Een korte beschouwing van de reacties op het probleem uit de hele wereld besluit het onderzoek.

14. Diefstal van kunst en antiquiteiten

Lauren Bernick

Dit hoofdstuk onderzoekt de groeiende illegale handel in kunst, antiquiteiten en cultureel eigendom. Hoewel kunstdiefstal en het plunderen van archeologische schatten al eeuwen voorkomt, hebben een aantal veranderingen in de internationale wereld en de toenemende vraag naar kunst, bijgedragen aan de huidige snelle groei van de markt. Nieuw voor de illegale kunsthandel zijn de internationale netwerken die kunstobjecten musea en veilinghuizen van de ontwikkelde landen binnensmokkelen waarbij musea, archeologische vindplaatsen en kerken over de gehele wereld het doelwit vormen. De netwerken zijn ofwel organisaties die zich uitsluitend toeleggen op kunstdiefstal, ofwel al bestaande grensoverschrijdende criminele organisaties die het lucratieve van de kunstdiefstal ontdekt hebben. Traditionele grensoverschrijdende criminele organisaties zoals de Italiaanse maffia en de Colombiaanse drugkartels gebruiken gestolen kunst om andere illegale transacties te vergemakkelijken en verbinden daarmee kunstdiefstal met het witwassen van geld en de drughandel. De stilzwijgende medewerking van de legale kunstwereld en regeringsambtenaren vormen een extra uitdaging voor de internationale ordehandhavers om de stroom van gestolen kunst over de internationale grenzen te stoppen.

15. Het witwassen van geld

David Hess, Kenneth Myers, Mchele Gideon, Sal E. Gomez en John Daly

Het witwassen van geld wordt besproken wat betreft de doelen, methoden, instrumenten, instellingen om geld wit te wassen en verscheidene witwasmogelijkheden. Ook kwetsbare instellingen en landen komenn has.

16. De georganiseerde misdaad tegen de staat: de controle ervan, onbedoelde consequenties en suggesties voor verder onderzoek

Jeffrey Ian Ross

Dit artikel analyseert het concept van misdaden tegen de staat als een vorm van georganiseerde misdaden tegen de staat, richt zich op de controle ervan, noemt een aantal gebieden waar de controle onbedoelde consequenties kan hebben en doet suggesties hoe de agenda van de staatsmisdaad te benaderen.

17. De toekomst van het narcotica terrorisme: Colombia – een gevals analyse

Peter A. Lupsha en Sung-Kwon Cho

Narcotica terrorisme wordt gedefinieerd en beschreven waarbij de noodzakelijke 'acteurs' - in zowel de criminele als de legale gemeenschappen, waaronder de staat, worden genoemd en Colombia voor een gevalsanalyse wordt gebruikt. Voorwaarden voor het ontstaan en continuering, variatie in acties en reacties, soorten en voorspellingen over de toekomst ervan binnen de context van de georganiseerde misdaad en grensoverschrijdende misdaad komen aan bod.

18. De globalisatie van de misdaad en het strafrecht: vooruitzichten en problemen

David Nelken

Dit hoofdstuk biedt een analyse van de manieren waardop processen van globalisatie invloed kunnen uitoefenen op de ontwikkelingen van de misdaad en het strafrecht. Eerst identificeert het de angsten die voortkomen uit, aan de ene kant, de vermeende groei van de grensoverschrijdende georganiseerde misdaad en, aan de andere kant, de vermeende gevaren van de grensoverschrijdende controles. Nadat verscheidene problemen die geassocieerd worden met verschillende aspecten van globalisatie onderscheiden zijn, wordt vervolgens gewaarschuwd niet te denken dat het versterken van de grensoverschrijdende controle een noodzakelijk of voldoende antwoord is op deze problemen.

Appendix:

1. De belangrijkste onopgeloste kwestie verbonden met de hedendaagse georganiseerde misdaad

2. Bronnen wat betreft de georganiseerde misdaad

1. El Crimen Transnacional: Una Experiencia no Exacta.

Gerhard O.W Mueller

Esta hoja describe el desarrollo en las definiciones del crimen transnacional e internacional de las liberaciones de las agencias pertenecientes a las N.V . Un acuerdo basico de la definicion habia llegado, unos miembros de los estados de las N.V y organizaciones no guvernamentales, han sido preguntados para describir 18 categorias de crimenes que tienen caracteristicas e impactos internacionales sin embargo,, algunos pueden parecer locales en su naturaleza.

Las 18 categorias han sido supervisadas, introducidas en sus limites y ritmos, existiendo modos y medidas necesarias para impactar estos crimenes tratandose de estos crimenes, de caracteristicas transnacionales tales como: blanqueo de dinero, terrorismo, arte, robos intelectuales, robos computacionales, crimenes ambientales, etc.

Estos crimenes sufren de definiciones no exactas, porque estas definiciones de los conceptos de crimenes transnacionales e internacionales necesitan medidas y estudios minuciosos para definirlos.

2. Ser Rico y Ser Estable: Transnacional Chantaje en el Siglo 21.

Phil Williams

Esta hoja examina el chantaje para la seguridad nacional e internacional propuesta por organizaciones de crimenes transnacionales y grupos de terroristas. Se puede decir, que las emergencias de estos chantajes pueden relacionar como resultado de dos procesos: cubierta y crisis de estados autorizados, los dos contribuyen a la contraccion de la dominacion de las autoridades. El impacto de muchos aspectos de cubierta, moral y etica, el creciemiento comercial, el desarrollo de sistemas financieros de desarrollo de la informacion global de sistemas de comunicaciones y las emergencias de ciudades globales han examinado. La tendencia futura del crimen organizado y el terrorismo tambien estan exploradas.

3. El Crimen Organizado en Europa del Este y sus Implicaciones para la Seguridad del Mundo Oeste.

Brunon Hołyst

Este articulo define el crimen organizado situado en los paises del este de Europa y nota el chantajeo que presenta para el mundo del oeste. Las transformaciones politicas y economicas de los grupos sociales del estado intentan compactar sobre las formas dinamicas y la estructura del crimen.

Los cambios que estan tomando lugar en todos los estilos de vida estan aprovechadas por los criminales que aumentan su contacto internacional. La devilidad del aparato del estado y la consegida perdida en el monopolio para la administracion de la justicia, produce huecos en la ley, agotamiento social, la baja considerable en la forma de vida, en la conjugacion con el sistema de corrupcion en publico.

La vida politica y economica crea un complejo patologico institucional. La coneccion de la currupcion internacional, financias mundiales de transaccion, los cambios como la apertura de las fronteras esto daria como resultado una enorme internalizacion y profesionalismo en la actvidad de C.O. La buena organizacion de los chantajeadores pasa por su flexibiliadad, que permite que ellos aprovechan de la misma libertad y oportunidades sociales como los legales, la situacion en la Europa del Este parece que facilita el crimen poletico.

4. El Desarrollo y el Control del Crimen Organizado despues del Racismo en el Sur de Africa.

Mark Shaw

El crimen organizado ha crecido de forma alarmante en el sur de Africa con las nuevas normas democraticas. Mientras en algunas formas del crimen organizado, notadas la actividad de las bandas en el Cabo del Oeste existe debajo de las reglas del racismo.

Las bandas de calle se han ido utilizados para destruir las actividades de los antinacistas. Mientras la presion que hace el publico y la policia esta tomando las primeras lineas, pero la ley del sur de Africa no esta preparada para el tasco que hace la escala larga y la actividad que hace el crimen organizado.

Todavia esta criticada las intervenciones que suceden hasta hoy dia: El crimen organizado en el sur de Africa ,el gran numero, todavia esta fragmentado y perjudican la accion de la policia enfocada en esto. Una devilidad mayoritaria entonces, is la falta de intender y analizar el tamano y el crecimiento de la structure y potencia del racismo en el cremen organizado en el sur de Africa.

5. Las Reformas Economicas y la Sociedad Negra:La Re-emergencias del Crimen Organizado en Post-Mao China.

Marks S. Gaylord and Hualing Fu

La herencia de la cultura de china tambien incluye el crimen organizado tradicional desde hace muchos años. En la primera mitad del siglo 20. Los chinos " sociedad secreta" disfruta con una relacion interna con Chiang Kai-Skok's "Nacionalista". Luego los comunistas han tomado el poder en 1949, Mientras Mao Zedong ha movido rapido para conectar bien y ser visto como una potencia original y de posicion en el nuevo govierno. Desde hace 30 anos, el crimen organizado ha desaparecido, sumerjiendose con otras institiciones de la nueva epoca. In la Post-Mao China, el crimen organizado (llamado hei-shehui, o socidad negra) no solo ha vuelto a parecer sino ha llegado a formar grupos de miles de miembros.

6. Tendencia Del Crimen Organizado Por *Boryokudan* en Japan.

Minoru Yokoyama

La *Boryokudan*, un equipo indojeno Japones para el crimen organizado, que han heredado algunas de sus culturas de las Bandas de edades media en Europa. Sus etnicos estan formadas de *Ninkyo-do*, el tipo de espiritu de buen hombre. Despues de la segunda guerra mundial el desarrollo en la economia Japonesa dio una fuerza a *Boryokudan*. En muchas eras eso por su violecia e inmensa riqueza. Las organizaciones orientales estan parecidas a unas empresas privadas de paises capitalistas que en funcionales. Como un grupo disciplinado debajo de las etnicas de *Ninkyo-do*.

La *Boryokudan* es una herarquia en su estructura, en que el gran tratado de dinero pasa por su miembros activos para sus mayores. Muchos de estos miembros tienen actividades ilegales para pagar la inscripcion de miembros para sus jefes. La venta de drogas estimulantes es la gran ventana que da la potencia a estos grupos.

Por muchos tiempos la policia estaba enconveniente con la actividad de *Boryokudan*. Pero la policia poco a poco ha eliminado la influencia corruptiva de los *Boryokudan*. Durante la prosperencia economica de los años 1980, el *Koiki-Boryokudan* han cometidos muchas actividades violentas, eso les hizo muy visuales y muy intolerables en mucha populacion. La opinion publica en frente a los *Boryokudan* ha aumentado. En 1991 la ley ha tomado lugar. Debajo de esta ley la policia ha controlado muchas actividades ilegales de los *Boryokudan* con la cooperacion con la gente.

7. El Crimen Organizado en el Futuro da Sicilia y Calabria.

Letizia Paoli

Segun la figura futura de la asociacion de mafia de Sicilia y Calabria, visten   factores de accion que hay que destinguir y tomar presente: 1) grupos de mafia "su participacion en los mercados internacionales ilegales". 2) el sistema local de la fuerza de la mafia. Esta hoja trata la posicion y el grado de envuelta de la poderosa mafia italiana en el mundo, los cambios primarios van a depender de la tendencia en la politica internacional de economia. Tambien la fuerza de la ley que ejerce una influencia considerada en el poco tiempo. La fuerza ejercida por familias de mafias esta en sus comunidades locales, en los paises, de los mismos grupos de mafia, en instituciones del estado en la sociedad civil Italiana.

8. El Futuro Crimen Organizado Tradicional en los Estados Unidos.

Howard Abadinsky

Algunos observadores apoyan que la mafia americana va disminuyendo y hacia fuera, primero como el resultado de la buena ley federal. Doble digito ha utilizado para bajar las figuras de los crimenes organizados. Ese silencio, sin imbargo, no es el nuevo fin la dominacion de la mafia americana ha sido predicada para muchas decadas. Pero por ultimo ha venido el tiempo que podemos decir que la mafia americana esta fuera del futuro ?
De momento, esta hoja considera teorias que explica la creencia del fenomeno y su existencia, y analizar el resultado contra lo que sabemos sobre este, el crimen organizado Italo-Americano contemporaneo.

9. El Crimen Organizado en Estados Unidos: algunas tendencias currientes.

Robert J. Kelly

La mafia americana, la Cosa Nostra, estaba debajo de las fuerzas de ataques concentradas pero no podemos decir que esta destruida. Por los cambios que ha tenido la mafia ultimamente por las condiciones economicas y las fuerzas socio-politicas, ha sido transformada y redefinida a ella misma, otros grupos etnicos refieren a ellas como no tradicionales, el crimen organizado, estan iluminadas en la etnicos de colonias y varios de las comunidades emigrantes.

10. El Crimen Organizado en Israel

Menachem Amir

Una mapa de estudio del crimen organizado en Israel como esta reflejado en los apuntes de investigacion y los estudios academicos. La historia del estudio del crimen organizado en Israel es continua y constantemente organizada por debate entre policia, academias y la medida de la definicion y la naturaleza de reaccion del crimen oragnizado en Israel. La naturaleza del crimen organizado refleja el segundo caracteristico mas importante de la sociedad israeli (la primera era de la seguridad). Los movimientos de los emigrantes que tambien incluyen estan en el crimen organizado. El crimen organizdo en Israel tambien tiene naturaleza etnica, la ultima es la de los emigrantes Rusos. Su envoltura en el crimen y el crimen organizado es tambien posible.

11. El Crimen Organizado: La Prespectiva de Austria.

Maximilian Edelbacher

El crimen organizado es la primera meta del mundo contemporaneo, especialmente en Europa. Un enorme cambio ha tenido lugar en Europa desde 1989, cuando "Iron Curtain" ha caido. La posicion geografica de Austria en el centro de Europa y sus nuevas reglas como un pais miembro de la comunidad Europia ha empezado con mucha responsabilidad para compactar el crimen organizado. Austria tiene interes en el nuevo desarrollo C.O. grupos por su actividad de lavado de dinero que se esta haciendo basico para la activdades operacionales de C.O. Las nuevas reglas de Austria han tomado en cuenta la lucha contra C.O haciendo estratejias e ideas nuevas.

12. El Crimen Organizado Africano-Americano: Una descriminacion Racista.

Robert J.Kelly

Para pensar sobre "la Cosa Nostra" como el foco del crimen organizado en Estados Unidos hoy dia su naturaleza da la consideracion de las formas periferales de los fenomenos, no tradicional, crimen organizado. Esta hoja ofrece algunos reflejos de formas especificas del crimen organizado no tradicional, grupos Africanos-Americanos y sus perspectivas de crecimiento. Aparte del trafico de droga. Esta de acuerdo que la moblidad politica dentro de la comunidad minoritaria esta requeridas para el crecimiento y la estabildad de la actividad tradicional del crimen organizado.

13. El comercio mundial del sero. Seres humanos: lo último en mercancía de compraventa.

Sarah L.Shannon

El comercio sexual de mujeres y niños esta haciendo un fenomeno mundial. Para un incremento durado, transnacional crimen organizado engancha a un negocio de mucha ganancia, las realidades que rodean el sexo global estan repulsivas. Si las medidas efectivas estan creadas, el entendimiento detallada de estas realidades es necesaria. Algun aspecto destinguido y aspecto geografico estan discutidas en este estudio. Una consideracion previa de responsabilidades globales del problema incluyen la examinacion.

14. El Robo de Arte y Antiguedades.

Lauren Bernick

Este capitulo examina el crecimiento ilegal de comercio del mejor arte, antiguedades y la propiedades culturales .A pesar de que el robo de arte y el tesoro arquelogico ha occurido desde muchos años, los elementos dentro del cambio ambiental internacional y el incremento de demanda de arte ha contribuido en la proliferacion del mercado.Una nueva cosa del mercado ilegal de arte es internacional redes , que trafica de arte robando museos, sitios arqueologicos, iglesias de todo el mundo para venderla en los museos y casas de arte en los paises desarrollados.Estos redes internacionales pueden ser organizaciones que se dedican solamente al robo de arte o organizaciones criminales establezidas que han visto que el robo de arte es muy profetable. Las organizaciones tradicionales del crimen transnacional, como la mafia Italiana y Colombiana de drogas unidas, utiliza el arte robado para facilitar otras transeciones ilegales, solo une el crimen de arte con el lavado de dinero y el tratado de drogas. El conveniente del arte legal en el mundo y los oficiales del govierno presenta una meta para la ley internacional por frenar el flujo del arte ropada atraves de las fronteras internacionales.

15. El Lavado de Dinero.

David Hess, Kenneth Myers. Michele Gedeon. Sal E.Gomez, and John Daly

El lavado de dinero esta revisado en terminos de sus objetivos, metodos, instrumentales, instituciones de lavado de dinero y muchas operaciones y oportunidades de lavado de dinero.

16. El Crimen Organizado de Estados: su control, consequencias no entendidas y propuesta del futuro estudio.

Jeffrey Ian Ross

Este articulo analiza el concepto del crimen de estado como una forma del crimen organizado, focando en su control, pone numeros de sitios donde el control puede tener a numero de consequencias no entendidas, y luego prepusta para mejorar el control del crimen de estado.

17. El Futuro Terrorismo Narcotico: Colombia-Un Caso de Estudio

Peter A.Lupsha and Sung-kwou Cho

Utilizamos a Colombia como caso de estudio, terrorismo narcotico, esta defenido y describido notando la necidad de "actores" en cada uno de los criminales y comunidades legitimas, incluyendo los estados; condiciones de su iniciacion y continuacion, variacion en acciones y reacciones, tipos y predictos sobre sus futuros dentro del contenido del crimen organizado y transnacional crimen organizado.

18. La Globalizacion del crimen y la justicia criminal: prespectivas y problemas.

David Nelken

Este capitulo ofrece analisis de la forma en el que el proceso de globalizacion pueda afectar el desarrollo del crimen y la justicia criminal. La primera identificacion el miedo de la lucha que esta rodeando, de un lado, el desarrollo de transnacional crimen organizada y, por el otro lado, el desarrollo peligroso de la transnacional accion policial. Despues de distinguir muchos problemas asociados con los diferentes aspectos de la globilizacion esta haciendo que haya propuestas de la necesidad de cuidado en el pensar de forzar la policia transnacional esta necesario o suficiente para responder a estos problemas.

Apandece:

1. La Gran Critica del Tema no Resuelta del Crimen Organizado Contemporaneo.

2. Las Fuerzas del Crimen Organizado.

1. Crime Transnacional: Uma Experiência nas Incertezas

Gerhard O.W. Mueller

O artigo descreve os desenvolvimentos na definição de crimes transnacionais e internacionais nas deliberações das agências das Nações Unidas. Uma vez que um consenso da definição foi alcançado, foi pedido aos estado membros das Nações Unidas e à organizações não governamentais para descrever 18 categorias de crimes que tenham características e impacto internacionais, entretanto algumas podem parecer locais em sua natureza.

As dezoito   categorias são revisadas, enfatizando sua abrangência e padrões, recursos existentes e as medidas necessárias para combater esses crimes. Tratou com tais crimes, com características transnacionais, como: dinheiro lavando, terrorismo, roubo intelectual e de arte, pirataria, crimes de computador, crimes ambientais, etc.

Esses crimes 'sofrem' de incertezas, como para a definição do conceito de crime transnacional, necessitam de pesquisas e medidas viáveis ou critérios. A definição dos conceitos de crimes transnacionais e internacionais necessita de pesquisa e de medidas exigidas a fim de combatê-los efetivamente.

2

Phil Williams

Este artigo examina as ameaças para a segurança nacional e internacional, imposta pelas organizações criminais transnacionais e grupos terroristas transnacionais. Argumenta que a emergência dessas ameaças pode ser compreendida como resultado de dois processos – globalização e a crise da autoridade do estado – sendo que ambos contribuem para uma redução do domínio da autoridade do estado. O impacto dos vários aspectos da globalização – diásporas e redes étnicas, o crescimento do comércio, o desenvolvimento de um sistema financeiro global, e o desenvolvimento de um sistema global de informações e comunicações, e o surgimento de cidades globais - são examinados. Também são explorados os futuros rumos do crime organizado e do terrorismo.

3. Crime organizado no Leste Europeu a suas Implicações para a Segurança do Mundo Ocidental

Brunon Hołyst

Este artigo revisa a situação do crime organizado nos estados do Leste Europeu e assinala as ameaças que estes representam para o mundo ocidental. Transformações políticas e econômicas nos previamente estados do bloco socialista exerceram um impacto sobre a forma da dinâmica e da estrutura do crime. Mudanças ocorrendo em todas as áreas da vida são exploradas pelos criminosos que estão cada vez mais ligados internacionalmente. A fraqueza do aparato estatal e a subseqüente perda no monopólio para a administração da justiça, falhas na lei, agitação social, uma considerável queda no padrão de vida, em conjunção com uma corrupção sistêmica na vida publica, econômica e social cria uma rede particular de instituições 'patológicas'.

Conexões monetárias internacionais, transações financeiras mundiais, comodidade para trocas, assim como a abertura das fronteiras irão conduzir para uma internacionalização ainda maior e profissionalismo nas atividades do crime organizado.

A principal ameaça imposta pelo crime organizado deve-se a sua flexibilidade (assume muitas formas), o que lhe permite ganhar proveito da mesma liberdade e oportunidades que são desfrutadas pela sociedade convencional, legitima, legal, social e econômica. A situação no Leste Europeu provavelmente facilita a criminalização política.

4. Pós-Apartheid. O Desenvolvimento e Controle do Crime Organizado na África do Sul

Mark Shaw

O Crime organizado tem crescido drasticamente na nova ordem democrática da África do Sul. Enquanto algumas formas de crime organizado - particularmente as atividades de gangues no Cabo Oeste - existiam sob a vigência do Apartheid , isto não constituía uma ameaça mas, até mesmo, as gangues de ruas eram freqüentemente usados por agentes do estado para parar ativistas anti-apartheid . Enquanto a pressão publica e política está em cima deste tema, as agências que aplicam as leis na África do Sul estão mal preparadas para a tarefa de enfrentar as atividades do crime organizado em grande escala. Ainda, é fundamental que ocorram intervenções agora: as organizações criminais da África do Sul, apesar de numerosas, ainda são relativamente fragmentadas e vulneráveis para uma ação policial focalizada. A principal debilidade atual, entretanto, é a falta da compreensão e análise do tamanho, forma, estrutura e cursos potenciais de crescimento do crime organizado na África do Sul.

5. Reforma Econômica e 'Sociedade Negra' : O Ressurgimento do Crime Orrganizado na China Pós Mao.

Mark S. Gaylord and Hualing Fu

A herança cultural chinesa inclui uma tradição no crime organizado, que data de centenas de anos. Na primeira metade do século XX, 'sociedades secretas' Chinesas desfrutavam de uma íntima relação com o governo nacionalista de Chiang Kai-shek. Após a tomada do poder pelos comunistas em 1949, entretanto, Mao Zedong moveu-se rapidamente para esmagar o que ele corretamente via como uma fonte potencial de oposição para seu novo governo. Por aproximadamente 30 anos, o crime organizado na China desapareceu, submergiu junto com outras instituições da era precedente. Entretanto, na China pós Mao o crime organizado (Chamado hei shehui, ou 'sociedade negra') não somente reapareceu mas está agora disseminado. 'Sociedade negra' é um termo que abrange desde pequenos bandos de salteadores de estrada até grupos de crime organizado com milhares de membros. Por definição, são escondidos da visão, obscurecidos pelo segredo, oficiais corruptos e a distinção ofuscada e sem esperanças dos setores privados e públicos.

6. Tendências do Crime Organizado Pelo *Boryokudan* no Japão

Minoru Yokoyama

O *Boryokudan*, grupos indígenas Japoneses para crime organizado, herdou algumas culturas secundárias de gangues do período feudal. O âmago de sua ética foi composto do *Ninkyo-do*, um tipo de espírito cavalheiresco. Subsequente ao crescimento da economia Japonesa após a Segunda Guerra Mundial, vários *Boryokudans* poderosos tornaram-se *Koiki* (área ampla) – *Boryokudan*, através de violência e sua imensa prosperidade. Eles atualmente operam com uma organização orientada para o lucro, funcionando de forma mais similar a empresas privadas de países capitalistas do que como grupos disciplinados sob a ética do Ninkyo-do. Os *Boryokudan* são hierarquicamente estruturados, na qual um grande montante de dinheiro baseado em taxas de membros são levados e extraídos a um 'chefão'. A maioria dos membros tem que realizar muitas atividades ilegais a fim de ganharem seu sustento, como também para pagarem a taxa de membro, para seus chefes. A principal fonte de renda para os *Boryokudan* é a venda de drogas estimulantes.

Por muito tempo a polícia foi conivente com as atividades do *Boryokudan*. Entretanto, a polícia gradualmente foi ficando livre da influência do *Boryokudan*. Durante a prosperidade econômica dos anos 80 o *Koiki-Boryokudan* cometeram muitas atividades violentas, que tornaram-se mais visíveis e mais intoleráveis para a grande população. A Opinião pública contra o *Boryokudan* aumentou. Em 1991, a Lei para fazer frente a *Boryokudan* foi decretada. Sob esta lei, a polícia controla as atividades ilegais do *Boryokudan* mais severamente, com a cooperação do povo.

7. O Futuro do Crime Organizado Siciliano e Calabriano

Letizia Paoli

A fim de se compreender o futuro das Máfias Siciliana e Calabriana, duas facetas de suas ações devem ser distinguidas e levadas em consideração separadamente: 1) participação dos grupos mafiosos nos mercados ilegais internacionais; 2) o sistema local de poder da Máfia. Este artigo argumenta que a posição e o grau de envolvimento da mais poderosa Máfia italiana nas ligas no mundo de trocas ilegais depende principalmente das tendências da política econômica internacional, ainda que ações de cumprimento da lei possam exercer uma considerável influência a curto prazo. O poder exercido pelas famílias mafiosas em suas comunidades locais, pelo contrário, é amplamente o produto da ação recíproca de três agentes coletivos: os próprios grupos mafiosos, instituições do estado e a sociedade civil italiana.

8. O Futuro do Crime Organizado Tradicional nos Estado Unidos

Howard Abadinsky

Alguns observadores argumentam que a Máfia Americana está por baixo e quase acabada, fundamentalmente como um resultado do sucesso dos esforços federais no cumprimento da lei. Sentenças de dois dígitos, dadas, tipicamente, para figuras do crime organizado levaram ao falecimento da 'omerta', o muito vangloriado código de silêncio. Porém, esta afirmação não é nova - realmente, o falecimento da Máfia Americana tem sido predito por décadas. Mas, chegou finalmente a hora em que podemos escrever que a Máfia está fora do futuro americano? Para compreensão desse tema, este artigo considera teorias que explicam tanto a criação do fenômeno como a sua existência continuada, e analisa os resultados contra o que é sabido sobre o crime organizado italiano-americano contemporâneo .

9. Crime Organizado nos Estados Unidos: Alguma Tendência Atual

Robert J. Kelly

A Máfia Americana, La Cosa Nostra, esteve sob um severo ataque da execução da lei mas não pode ser descrita como destruída. Como as condições econômicas e os ambientes sócio-políticos que nutriram a Máfia mudaram, a Máfia transformou-se e redefiniu-se. Outros grupos étnicos, referidos como crime organizado 'não tradicional', estão crescendo nos encrave étnicos e nos guetos de novas comunidade de imigrantes. O ensaio examina os processos de declínio e re-alinhamento dentro da La Cosa Nostra e esboça as estruturas e dinâmica dos anéis de extorsão chineses.

10. Crime Organizado em Israel

Menachem Amir

O artigo mapeia o estudo do crime organizado em Israel, como é refletido nas reportagens investigatórias da mídia, e em pesquisa acadêmica. A história do estudo do crime organizado em Israel é continuamente e constantemente caracterizada por debates entre polícia, acadêmicos e mídia sobre a definição, natureza e reação ao crime organizado em Israel. A natureza do crime organizado reflete a segunda mais importante característica da sociedade Israelita (sendo segurança a primeira): - as ondas de imigrantes que também entram no cenário do crime, incluindo o crime organizado. Portanto, o crime organizado em Israel tem a natureza da sucessão étnica. Os últimos são os imigrantes Russos. Seu envolvimento no crime e no crime organizado é descrito agora.

11. Crime Organizado: Uma Perspectiva Austríaca

Maximilian Adelbacher

O crime organizado é o desafio primário para o mundo contemporâneo, especialmente na Europa. Uma grande mudança ocorreu na Europa desde 1989, quando a 'Cortina de Ferro' caiu. A posição geografia da Áustria no centro da Europa, e seu novo papel com um membro da Comunidade Européia, trazem consigo novas responsabilidade para combater o crime organizado. A Áustria é de interesse para novas gangues de crime organizado, por causa de suas atividades de ' lavagem de dinheiro', tanto quanto a Áustria está se tornando a base operacional das atividade do crime organizado. O novo papel da Áustria trás consigo a responsabilidade de combater o crime organizado através da criação e partilha de novas idéias e contra-estratégias.

12. Crime Organizado Afro-Americano : Servidão Racial e Revolta.

Robert J. Kelly

Pensar sobre La Cosa Nostra como o 'núcleo' do crime organizado nos Estados hoje, naturalmente leva para a consideração das formas periféricas do fenômeno – isto é, minoritário, ou crime organizado 'não tradicional'. Este artigo oferece algumas reflexões sobre formas específicas de crimes organizado 'não tradicional', grupos Afro-americanos, e suas perspectivas de crescimento. Além do tráfico de drogas, discute-se que a mobilidade política dentro de comunidades minoritárias é um pré-requisito para o crescimento e estabilidade das atividades do crime organizado tradicional.

13. O comércio Global do Sexo: Seres Humanos como Mercadoria Básica.

Sarah L. Shannon

A exploração comercial sexual de mulheres e crianças tornou-se um fenômeno mundial. Para uma crescente extensão, organizações criminais transnacionais se engajam neste negócio altamente lucrativo. Os fatos que cercam o comércio global de sexo são repulsivos. Se, contra-medidas efetivas estão para ser criadas, é necessário um entendimento detalhado desses fatos. Portanto, algumas das características distintivas, aspectos geográficos e as tendências emergentes desse mercado de carne são discutidas neste estudo. Uma breve consideração de respostas globais para o problema conclui a análise.

14. Roubo de Arte e Antigüidades.

Lauren Bernick

Este capítulo examina o crescente comércio ilegal das artes, antigüidades e propriedades culturais. Ainda que o roubo de arte e o saqueamento de tesouros arqueológicos tem ocorrido por vários séculos, elementos dentro do variável ambiente internacional e o crescimento na demanda de arte tem contribuído para a atual proliferação do mercado. A novidade para o mercado ilegal de arte são as redes internacionais, as quais contrabandeiam objetos de arte em museus e casas de leilões tendo como alvo museus, sítios arqueológicos e igrejas por todo o mundo. As redes são organizações dedicadas exclusivamente ao roubo de arte ou são organizações criminais transnacionais já estabelecidas que encontraram no roubo de arte uma forma rentável. Organizações criminais transnacionais tradicionais, tais como a Máfia Italiana e Os Cartéis de drogas Colombianos, usam arte roubada para facilitar outras transações ilegais, assim ligando crime de arte à lavagem de dinheiro e contrabando de drogas. A conivência do mundo da arte legal e oficiais do governo representam um desafio adicional para as agências de execução do direito internacional, além de parar o fluxo de arte roubada através das fronteiras internacionais.

15. Lavagem de Dinheiro

David Hess, Kenneth Myers, Michele Gideon, Sal E. Gomez, and John Daly

A lavagem de dinheiro é revisada em termos de seus objetivos, métodos, instrumentos, instituições de lavagem de dinheiro e suas várias oportunidades, identificando países e instituições vulneráveis.

16. Crime Organizado no Estado: Seu controle, Conseqüências não Intencionais, e Sugestões para Futura Pesquisa.

Jeffrey Ian Ross

Este artigo analisa o conceito de crime do estado como uma forma de Crime organizado do estado, focando no seu controle, colocando várias áreas aonde o controle pode ter várias conseqüências não intencionais, e então sugere como avançar na agenda de controle criminal do estado.

17. O Futuro do Narco Terrorismo: Colombia- Estudo de um Caso

Peter A. Lupsha and Sung-Kwon Cho

Usando a Colômbia como um estudo de caso, narco-terrorismo, é definido e é descrito assinalando os 'atores' necessários - em ambas as comunidades criminais e legítimas, inclusive o Estado; condições para sua iniciação e continuação, variações em ações e reações, tipos e predições sobre seu futuro dentro do contexto de crime organizado e crime organizado transnacional.

18. A Globalização do Crime e da Justiça Criminal: Perspectivas e Problemas

David Nelken

Este capítulo oferece uma análise das formas através das quais os processos da globalização podem estar afetando o crime e a justiça criminal. Primeiramente, identifica o medo da competição que gira em torno da questão, de um lado, o alegado aumento do crime transnacional e, do outro, o alegado perigo do policiamento transnacional. Após a distinção dos vários problemas associados com os diferentes aspectos da globalização, sugere a necessidade para precaução na idéia de que o fortalecimento do policiamento transnacional é uma resposta necessária ou suficiente para estes problemas.

1. O mais crítico tema não resolvido associado com o crime Organizado Internacional

2. Recursos no Crime Organizado

1. Crimine transnazionale: Una esperienza nelle incertezze.

Gerhard O. W. Mueller.

.Lo studio decrive gli sviluppi nella definizione del crimine transnazionale e internazionale nelle delibere delle agenzie ONU. Una volta raggiunta una definizione comune fondamentale, agli Stati membri delle organizzazioni UN e NGO venne chiesto di descrivere 18 categorie di crimini che hanno impatto e caratterizzazione internazionali, anche se alcuni possono sembrare locali per loro natura. Le diciotto categorie vengono riviste, enfatizzandone la portata e I modelli, le risorse esistenti e le misure necessarie per combattere tali crimini. Vengono trattati crimini con caratteristiche transnazionali quali: riciclaggio del denaro, terrorismo, furto delle opere d'arte e dell'intelletto, pirateria, crimini via computer, crimini ambientali, ecc.
Questi crimini 'soffrono' delle incertezze relative alla definizzione essenziale del concetto di crimine transnazionale, ricerca necessaria e misure e criteri adottabili.
La definizione essenziale dei concetti di crimine transnazionale e internazionale neccessita di misure e ricerche applicabili allo scopo di combatterli in modo efficace.

2. Diventare ricchi e andare pari: minacce transnazionali nel ventunesiimo secolo.

Phil Williams

Questo documento esamina le minacce alla sicureza nazionale e internazionale poste da organizzazioni criminali transnazionali e gruppi terroristici transnazionali. Afferma che l'emergenza di queste minacce puo' essere compresa come risultante di due processi - globalizzazione e crisi dell'autorita' statuale - entrambi contribuenti ad una contrazione del dominio dell'autorita' statuale. Viene esaminato l'impatto di vari aspetti della globalizzazione - diaspore e reti etniche, la crescita del commercio, lo sviluppo di un sistema finanziario globale, lo sviluppo di un sistema di comunicazione informatica globale e l'emergenza di citta' globali. Sono inoltre esplorate le tendenze future del crimine organizzato e del terrorismo.

3. Il crimine organizzato nell'Europa orientale e le sue implicazioni per la sicurezza del mondo occidentale.

Brunon Holyst.

Questo articolo esamina la situazione del crimine organizzato in Europa Orientale e registra le minacce che questo presenta per il Mondo occidentale. Le trasformazioni politiche ed economiche nel blocco degli stati ex socialisti ha esercitato un impatto sulla formazione delle dinamiche e della struttura del crimine. I cambi che si verificano in tutti gli aspetti della vita vengono utilizzati da criminali che sono sempre piu' collegati internazionalmente. La debolezza dell'apparato dello stato e la conseguente perdita del suo monopolio dell'amministrazione della giustizia, smagliature delle leggi, agitazioni sociali, un considerevole abbassamento dello standard di vita, in relazione ad una corruzione sistematica nella vita pubblica, economica e politica, creano una rete particolare di legami istituzionali 'patologici'. Legami valutari internazionali, transazioni finaziarie mondiali, scambio di beni come pure l'aprirsi di frontiere condurra' ad una sempre maggiore internazionalizzazione e professionalita' nelle attivita' del crimine organizzato. La minaccia maggiore posta dal crimine internazionale sta nella sua flessibilita', (prende molte forme) che le permette di avvantaggiarsi delle stesse opportunita' di liberta' e sociali di cui usufruiscono le attivita' legittime,legali, sociali ed economiche. La situazione nell'Est Europeo puo' facilitare la criminalita' politica.

4. Lo sviluppo e il controllo del crimine organizzato nell'Africa post-Apartheid.

Mark Shaw

Il crimine organizzato e' cresciuto in modo drammatico nel nuovo ordine democratico del Sud Africa. Anche se alcune forme di crimine organizzato - in particolare attivita' di 'gang' nel Capo Ovest - esistevano durante il periodo dell'Apartheid, cio' non costituiva una minaccia, e, anzi, gruppi criminali di strada venivano utilizzati spesso da agenti dello stato allo scopo di neutralizzare attivita' anti apartheid. Pur se la pressione pubblica e politica aumenta contro tale fenomeno, le forze di polizia sono mal preparate al fine di contrastare l'attivita' della criminalita' organizzata su larga scala. E tuttavia, e' essenziale che gli interventi si effettuino ora: le organizzazioni criminali sud africane, per quanto numerose, sono ancora relativamente frammentate e vulnerabili ad una azione mirata di polizia. Una debolezza notevole, comunque, e' rappresentata dalla mancanza di comprensione e analisi delle dimensioni, forma, struttura e vie di potenziale crescita del crimine organizzato sud africano.

5. Riforma economica e 'Societa' Nera': la rinascita del crimine organizzato nella Cina post Maoista.

Mark S. Gaylord e Hualing Fu

L'eredita' culturale cinese comprende una tradizione di crimine organizzato che risale di varie centinaia di anni. Durante la prima meta' del 20mo secolo, le 'societa' segrete' cinesi hanno goduto di uno stretto legame con il governo nazionalista di Chiang Kai-Shek. A seguito dell'ascesa al potere dei comunisti, comunque, Mao Tse Tung si mosse rapidamente per schiacciare cio' che egli correttamente presupponeva come fonte di potenziale opposizione al suo nuovo governo. Per quasi trenta anni il crimine organizzato in Cina e' scomparso, sommerso, insieme con altre istituzioni dell'era precedente. Nella Cina post maoista, invece, il crimine organizzato (chiamato 'hei shehui', o societa' nera) non solo e' ricomparso, ma si e' esteso. La 'societa' nera' e' un termine omni-comprensivo per definire tutto cio' che va da piccole bande di fuorilegge da strada fino a gruppi di criminalita' organizzata con migliaia di membri. Questa e' una realta' invisibile, oscurata dalla segretezza, da funzionari corrotti e dalla sfuocata linea di demarcazione tra I settori pubblici e privati.

6. Tendenze del crimine organizzato del *Boryokudan* in Giappone.

Minoru Yokoyama

I *Boryokudan*, gruppi originari giapponesi di criminalita' organizzata, hanno ereditato una parte di sottocultura delle bande criminali del periodo feudale. L'essenza della loro etica e' stata elaborata da *Ninkyo-do*, una specie di spirito cavalleresco. In seguito alla crescita economica dopo la seconda Guerra Mondiale, molte e potenti *Boryokudans* andarono a costituire il '*Koiki*(esteso)*-Boryokudan*' mediante la violenza e l'enorme ricchezza. Attualmente operano come organizzazioni volte al profitto alla stregua di imprese private di paesi capitalisti piu' che come gruppi disciplinati sotto l'etica di *Ninkyo-do*.
I *Boryokudan* sono strutturati come una gerarchia in cui una grande quantita' di denaro derivante dalle quote di partecipazione viene pompata dal basso verso l'alto nelle tasche di un 'padrino'. La maggior parte dei mebri deve porre in essere parecchie attivita' illegali sia per guadagnarsi da vivere sia per poter pagare la quota di partecipazione al loro capo. La fonte di reddito primaria dei *Boryokudan* e' la vendita di droghe stimolanti. Per un lungo

periodo gli agenti di polizia erano conniventi con I *Boryokudan*. Ora, pero', la polizia si e' liberata della corrotta influenza dei *Boryokudan*. Nel perdurare la prosperita' economica degli anni ottanta, il '*Koiki-Boryokudan*' ha posto in essere un gran numero di azioni violente, la qual cosa e' diventata piu' evidente e piu' intollerabile per i piu' vasti strati della popolazione. L'opinione pubblica contro i *Boryokudan* e' aumentata. Nel 1991 e' stata promulgata la 'Legge per controbattere I *Boryokudan*'. Sotto gli auspici di questa legge le polizia controlla le attivita' illegali dei *Boryokudan* piu' severamente e d'intesa con la popolazione.

7. Il futuro del crimine organizzato siciliano e calabrese.

Letizia Paoli

Per intendere il futuro delle associazioni mafiose siciliane e calabresi, occorre distinguere due aspetti della loro attivita': 1) la partecipazione dei gruppi mafiosi ai mercati illegali internazionali; 2) il sistema locale del potere di mafia. Questo documento sostiene che la posizione ed il grado di coinvolgimento delle piu' potenti coalizioni di mafia nei scambi illeciti internazionali dipende soprattutto dalle tendenze della politica economica internazionale, per quanto azioni di polizia possano esercitare una influenza considerevole nel breve termine. Il potere esercitato dalle famiglie mafiose nelle loro comunita' locali, al contrario, e' in gran parte il prodotto della interazione di tre fattori collettivi: i gruppi mafiosi stessi, le istituzioni dello Stato e la societa' italiana.

8. Il futuro del crimine organizzato tradizionale negli Stati Uniti.

Howard Abadinsky

Alcuni osservatori sostengono che la Mafia americana e' in declino e quasi sul punto di scomparire, soprattutto come risultato del successo drgli sforzi di legalizzazione federali. Condanne a periodi di detenzione a due cifre, normalmente comminate ai rappresentanti del crimine organizzato, hanno portato alla fine dell'omerta', il tanto vantato codice di silenzio. Tale affermazione, tuttavia, non e' nuova e la fine della Mafia americana e' stata preannunciata per decine di anni. Ma e' finalmente giunto il tempo per cancellare la Mafia dal futuro dell'America? Per trovare una risposta, quasto studio prende in considerazioni teorie che che spiegano sia la creazione del fenomeno sia la sua esistenza ininterrotta, analizzando inoltre i risultati alla luce di cio' che si conosce del crimine organizzato Italo-Americano.

9. Crimine organizzato negli Stati Uniti: alcune linee di tendenza attuali.

Robert J. Kelly

La Mafia americana, Cosa Nostra, e' stata oggetto di un attacco organizzato da parte delle forze dell'ordine, ma non puo' considerarsi distrutta. A mano a mano che cambiavano le condizioni e gli ambienti socio-politici che avevano costituito il terreno fertile della Mafia, essa si e' trasformata e ridefinita. Altri gruppi etnici, considerati non tradizionalmente dediti al crimine organizzato, stanno sorgendo nelle enclavi e nei ghetti delle nuove comunita' di immigranti. Il saggio esamina I processi di declino e riallineamento all'interno di Cosa Nostra e descrive le strutture e la dinamica dei circoli di estorsione cinesi.

10. Il crimine organizzato in Israele

Menachem Amir

Il documento traccia lo studio del crimine organizzato in Israele cosi' come e' descritto nei rapporti dei media e in ricerche accademiche. La storia dello studio del crimine organizzato in Israele e' continuamente e costantemente caratterizzato da dibattiti tra la polizia, accademici e media sulla sua definizione, la sua natura e la reazione ad esso in Israele. La natura del crimine organizzato e' espressione della seconda piu' importante caratteristica della societa' israeliana (dopo la sicurezza): quella delle ondate di immigranti che si affacciano anche alla scena del crimine, compreso quello organizzato. Il crimine organizzato ha pertanto la caratteristica di una successione di etnie, di cui l'ultima e' quella degli immigrati russi. Il loro coinvolgimento nel crimine e nel crimine organizzato e' ora oggetto di studio.

11. Il Crimine Organizzato: una prospettiva austriaca.

Maximilian Edelbacher

Il crimine organizzato e' la sfida principale del mondo contemporaneo, specialmente in Europa. Un enorme cambiamento si e' verificato in Europa dal 1989, quando e' caduta la cortina di ferro. La posizione dell'Austria nel centro d'Europa ed il suo nuovo ruolo di membro della Comunita' Europea comporta la responsabilita' di combattere il crimine organizzato. L'Austria interessa alle bande di nuova formazione del crimine organizzato per le loro attivita' di lavaggio del denaro nonche' per il divenire l'Austria una base per attivita' operative. Il nuovo ruolo dell'Austria porta con se la responsabilita' di combattere il crimine organizzato creando e condividendo nuove necessarie idee e controstrategie.

12. Il crimine organizzato Afro-Americano: servitu' razziale e ribellione.

Robert J. Kelly

Pensare a Cosa Nostra come al cuore del crimine organizzato in America oggi, porta naturalmente alla considerazione di forme periferiche del fenomeno, e piu' precisamente crimine organizzato delle minoranze e non tradizionale. Questo documento offre alcune riflessioni su forme specifiche di crimine organizzato non tradizionale, gruppi Afro Americani e le loro prospettive di crescita. A parte il commercio della droga, vi si sostiene che la mobilita' politica all'interno della comunita' minoritaria e' un prerequisito per la crescita e la stabilita' delle attivita' tradizionali del crimine organizzato.

13. Il commercio globale del sesso: esseri umani come mercanzia primaria.

Sarah Shannon

Lo sfruttamento a scopo di commercio sessuale di donne e bambini e' diventato un fenomeno mondiale. Sempre piu' organizzazioni criminali transnazionali si impegnano in questo affare altamente lucrativo. I fatti che circondano il commercio globale del sesso sono ripugnanti. Se occorre creare contromisure efficaci, e' richiesta una comprensione dettagliata proprio di questi fatti. Pertanto alcune caratteristiche distintive, aspetti geografici e tendenze emergenti di questo mercato della carne vengono discussi in questo studio. Una breve considerazione delle risposte globali al fenomeno conclude la tesi.

14. Furto d'arte e antiquariato.

Lauren Bernick

Questo capitolo esamina il crescente commercio illecito in arte, antichita' e proprieta' culturali. Per quanto il furto d'arte e lo scavo di tesori archeologici si sia protratto per secoli, elementi all'interno del mutante ambiente internazionale e la crescente domanda di arte hanno contribuito alla attuale crescita del mercato. Sono nuove, per il mercato illecito dell'arte, reti internazionali, che contrabbandano oggetti d'arte entro i musei e le case d'asta dei paesi sviluppati spogliando musei, siti archeologici e chiese in tutto il mondo. Tali reti sono organizzazioni dedicate unicamente al furto d'arte, ovvero si tratta di organizzazioni transnazionali gia' esistenti, che hanno trovato il furto d'arte remunerativo. Organizzazioni criminali transnazionali tradizionali, come la Mafia Italiana o i cartelli colombiani della droga usano l'arte rubata come mezzo per facilitare altre transazioni illecite, cosi' che infine si collegano il crimine artistico con il riciclaggio del denaro e il commercio della droga. La connivenza del mondo artistico lecito e di funzionari governativi presenta una sfida ulteriore alle istituzioni che devono far rispettare la legge a fermare il flusso di arte rubata attraverso frontiere internazionali.

I5. Il riciclaggio

David Hess, Kenneth Myers, Michele Gideon, Sal E. Gomez e John Daly

I riciclaggio del denaro sporco e' esaminato nell'ambito dei suoi obiettivi, metodo, strumenti, istituzioni del riciclaggio e varie opportunita' di riciclaggio, identificando istituzioni e paesi vulnerabili.

16. Il crimine organizzato di Stato: il suo controllo, conseguenze indesiderate e suggerimenti per ricerche future.

Jeffrey Ian Ross

Questo articolo analizza il concetto del crimine di stato come una forma di crimine organizzato dallo stato, focalizza sul suo controllo, identifica un numero di aree ove il controllo puo' avere certe conseguenze non volute, e quindi suggerisce come procedere.

17. Il futuro del narco terrorismo: Colombia - un caso di studio.

Peter A. Lupsha e Sung-Kwon Cho

Usando la Colombia come caso di studio, il narco terrorismo viene definito e descritto analizzando i necessari protagonisti sia nell'ambito della comunita' criminale sia nell'ambito di quella legale, ivi compreso lo stato; le condizioni per l'avvio e la continuazione, le modifiche nell'azione e nella reazione, tipi e previsioni sul suo futuro nel contesto del crimine organizzato e del crimine organizzato transnazionale.

18. La globalizzazione del crimine e giustizia criminale: prospettive e problemi.

David Nelken

Questo capitolo offre una analisi dei modi in cui processi di globalizzazione possono condizionare gli sviluppi del crimine e della giustizia criminale. Prima identifica, da un lato, le paure connesse alla presunta crescita del crimine transanazionale, e, dall'altra, i presunti pericoli di una attivita' di polizia transnazionale. Avendo distinto vari problemi connessi con diversi aspetti della globalizzazione, continua suggerendo la necessita' di prudenza nel pensare che il rafforzamento della attivita' di polizia transanazionale sia una risposta necessaria o sufficiente a questi problemi.

Appendice:

1. La questione critica piu' irrisolta associata al crimine organizzato contemporaneo.

2. Risorse per il crimine organizzato.

1. Le crime transnational : une expérience dans l'incertitude

Gerhard O. W. Mueller

Cet article décrit le développement de la définition du crime transnational et international dans les délibérations des agences des Nations Unies. Dès qu'un consensus a été obtenu sur une première définition de base, on a demandé aux états membres de l'ONU et aux NGO de décrire 18 catégories de crimes ayant des caractéristiques et un impact internationaux, bien que certaines d'entre elles puissent paraître locales de nature.
La présente étude passe en revue ces 18 catégories en insistant sur leur portée, leurs schémas de fonctionnement, les ressources existantes sur le plan international pour les combattre et les mesures de répression à mettre en oeuvre. Sont traités : les types de crimes aux caractéristiques transnationaux tels que le blanchiment d'argent, le terrorisme, le vol de propriété intellectuelle ou d'objets d'art, la piraterie, le crime informatique et les crimes contre l'environnement.
Ces types de crime souffrent d'incertitudes quant à la définition du concept de crime transnational lui-même, les recherches à mener, les critères à appliquer et les mesures à prendre.
Il est nécessaire d'approfondir davantage les définitions des concepts de crimes transnational et international, et de mieux cerner les mesures à prendre pour les combattre efficacement.

2. Richesse et revanche : les menaces transnationales du XXIe siècle.

Phil Williams

Cette étude examine les menaces pour la sécurité nationale et internationale, posées par les organisations internationales de malfaiteurs et les groupes terroristes transnationaux. L'auteur soutient que l'apparition de ces menaces peut être comprise comme étant le résultat de deux processus : la mondialisation et la crise de l'autorité de l'Etat. Ces processus contribuent tout deux à la diminution du champ d'autorité étatique. L'auteur analyse l'impact des différents aspects de la mondialisation : les diasporas et réseaux éthniques, les échanges internationaux, le développement d'un système financier mondial et d'un réseau mondial de communication, l'apparition de villes mondiales. Les tendances futures du crime organisé et du terrorisme international sont également évoquées.

3. Le crime organisé en Europe de l'Est et ses implications pour la sécurité du monde Occidental.

Brunon Holyst

L'article dresse le bilan du crime organisé dans les pays de l'Europe de l'Est et relève les menaces qu'il pose pour le monde Occidental. Les transformations politiques et économiques qui ont lieu dans les pays de l'ancien bloc socialiste ont également un impact sur la structure et la dynamique du crime organisé dans ces pays. Le milieu criminel, de plus en plus lié au niveau international, exploite les changements survenus dans tous les domaines de la vie. Les faiblesses des dispositifs judiciaires et du système régissant l'administration judiciaire, les lacunes dans la législation, les troubles sociaux, la baisse considérable du niveau de vie, associés à la corruption systèmique de la vie politique, économique et sociale, créent un réseau de liens institutionnels 'pathologiques'. L'ouverture des frontières, les transactions monétaires et le commerce international aboutiront à augmenter et à renforcer le professionalisme et les liens internationaux du crime organisé. La menace la plus grave posée par le crime organisé est due à sa souplesse : sa nature protéiforme lui permet de bénéficier de la même liberté et des mêmes occasions sur le plan social que les milieux dont l'activité économique, politique, ou sociale est légitime et conventionnelle. Vraisemblablement; la situation en Europe de l'Est facilitera la criminalisation politique.

4. Le développement et la répression du crime organisé dans l'Afrique du Sud post apartheid

Mark Shaw

L'incidence de crime organisé a augmenté de manière considérable en Afrique du Sud sous le nouveau régime démocratique. Bien que certaines formes de crime organisé aient existée sous le régime de l'apartheid, notamment en ce qui concerne les activités des gangs dans la région du Cap Occidental, elles ne menaçaient pas l'ordre. En effet, l'Etat s'était souvent servi des gangs de rue dans le but de perturber l'action du mouvement contre l'apartheid. Alors que l'opinion publique se mobilise autour du problème, les forces de l'ordre se retrouvent insuffisamment préparées à la tâche de réprimer le crime organisé à grande échelle. Il serait pourtant d'une importance capitale que l'intervention policière ait lieu dès maintenant : les organisations criminelles sud-africaines, bien que nombreuses, sont encore relativement fragmentées et seraient encore vulnérables à une action policière concertée. Une des faiblesses actuelles réside dans le manque de renseignements sur la taille, la forme, la structure et les voies de croissance potentielles du crime organisé en Afrique du Sud.

5. La réforme économique et les 'sociétés noires' : la réapparition du crime organisé dans la Chine post maoïste

Mark S. Gaylord et Hualing Fu

L'héritage culturel de la Chine comporte une tradition séculaire de crime organisé. Au cours de la première moitié du Xxe siècle, les sociétés secrètes chinoises ont joui de rapports priviligiés avec le gouvernement nationaliste de Chiang Kai Shek. Cependant, après la prise de pouvoir communiste en 1949, Mao Zedong a tôt fait de prendre les mesures nécessaires pour réprimer ce qu'il croyait à juste titre une source potentielle d'opposition au nouveau régime. Pendant près de trente ans, le crime organisé avait disparu de la Chine, noyé avec bien d'autres institutions de l'époque précédente.
Appelé *hei shehui* ou 'société noire', le crime organisé a non seulement refait surface dans la Chine post maoïste, mais il s'est très largement répandu. Le terme 'société noire' recouvre une grande diversité d'organisations, allant de la petite bande de voleurs aux associations de malfaiteurs ayant des milliers de membres. A dessein, ce sont des organisations qui fleurissent en cachette, sous le sceau du secret, protégées par des fonctionnaires corrompus comme par les limites désespérément floues des secteurs public et privé.

6. Tendances actuelles du crime organisé au Japon: les *boryokudan*

Minoru Yokoyama

Les *boryokudan* sont des associations indigènes de malfaiteurs. Ces groupes sont les héritiers de la culture des gangs de l'époque féodale. Leur éthique est fondée sur le *ninkyo-do*, sorte d'esprit chevaleresque. Suite à la croissance économique de l'après-guerre, plusieurs *boryokudan* se sont transformés en *koiki-boryokudan* (*boryokudan* de grand rayonnement) en se servant de leurs immenses richesses et de la violence. De nos jours, ces groupes ont adopté un mode de fonctionnement plus proche de celui de l'entreprise privée capitaliste que de l'esprit de *ninkyo-do*.

Les *boryokudan* sont structurés en hiérarchie. De très grosses sommes d'argent provenant des cotisations versées par les membres sont canalisées vers le parrain et la plupart des membres se voient donc contraints de participer à un nombre important d'activités criminelles afin de gagner leur vie et de payer leurs cotisations au patron. Le trafic de drogue fournit la source principale de leurs revenus.

Pendant longtemps, la police avait été de connivence avec les *boryokudan*. Cependant, petit à petit, elle a pu se libérer de leur influence corruptrice. Au cours des années 1980, période de prospérité économique, les *koiki-boryokudan* se sont engagés dans de nombreuses activités violentes, ce qui les a rendus plus visibles et moins supportables aux yeux du public. La mobilisation de l'opinion publique a entraîné le passage en 1991 d'une loi visant la répression des *boryokudan*. La loi permet à la police une meilleure maîtrise des activités illégales des *boryokudan* en collaboration avec le public.

7. L'avenir du crime organisé sicilien et calabrais

Letizia Paoli

Afin de comprendre l'avenir des mafias sicilienne et calabraise, il convient de distinguer et d'analyser deux aspects de leur action: 1) la participation des mafias au commerce international illégal et 2) le pouvoir des mafias à l'échelle locale. L'auteur soutient que la position des puissantes coalitions des mafias italiennes et le degré de leur participation aux trafics illicites mondiaux dépendent en premier lieu des tendances de l'économie politique mondiale, bien qu'à court terme l'action policière puisse influer de manière considérable. Le pouvoir exercé par les mafias à l'intérieur de leurs communautés locales résulte de l'interaction de trois facteurs: les mafias elles-mêmes, les institutions de l'état et la société italienne.

8 é traditionnel aux Etats-Unis

Howard Abadinsky

Certains observateurs soutiennent que la mafia américaine est en pleine agonie, grâce surtout au succès des efforts du système judiciaire fédéral. La loi de l'*omerta*, ce code de silence tant vanté, a perdu de son emprise sous la pression des lourdes peines de prison qui sont maintenant le sort habituel des "grands" du crime lorsqu'ils passent devant les tribunaux. Cette affirmation n'a cependant rien de nouveau. En effet, on prédit la mort de la mafia américaine depuis des décennies. L'heure est-elle enfin arrivée où nous pourrions rayer la mafia de l'avenir américain? Ce dossier étudie les théories qui cherchent à expliquer la genèse et la survie du phénomène, et analyse les résultats à la lumière des connaissances actuelles sur le crime organisé italo-américain.

9. Le crime organisé aux Etats-Unis: tendances actuelles

Robert J. Kelly

La *cosa nostra*, ou mafia américaine, a durement souffert des assauts concertés de la répression judiciaire sans que l'on puisse annoncer sa destruction pour autant. Au fur et à mesure qu'ont évolué les conditions économiques et socio-politiques qui l'avaient engendrée et nourrie, la mafia a su se transformer et se redéfinir. Mené par d'autres groupes ethniques, le crime organisé de type non traditionnel est en essor dans les ghettos et enclaves peuplés de nouveaux immigrés. La présente étude analyse les processus internes à la *cosa nostra* qui ont abouti à son déclin et à son réalignement, et décrit les structures et la dynamique du racket chinois.

10. Le crime organisé en Israël

Menahem Amir

L'article étudie le crime organisé en Israël tel que le reflètent le journalisme d'investigation et la recherche universitaire. L'historique de l'étude du crime organisé en Israël se caractérise par de longues discussions entre la police, la presse et les chercheurs portant sur la définition du crime organisé dans le pays, sa nature et les réactions qu'il suscite. La nature du crime organisé reflète le deuxième trait le plus saillant de la société israélienne (le premier étant le souci de la sécurité): la formation de la population par vagues successives d'immigrants. En s'intégrant dans la société, ces immigrants rejoignent également les milieux criminels, y compris les rangs du crime organisé. Le crime organisé en Israël reflète donc cette succession ethnique. L'étude de la dernière vague en date, celle de l'immigration russe, est actuellement en cours.

11. Le crime organisé: le point de vue autrichien

Maximilian Edelbacher

Le crime organisé constitue un défi de premier ordre pour le monde contemporain et plus particulièrement pour l'Europe, qui traverse une période de grands changements depuis 1989 et la chute du rideau de fer. La position géographique de l'Autriche en plein centre de l'Europe, ainsi que son nouveau rôle d'état-membre de la communauté européenne, lui imposent de nouvelles responsabilités en ce qui concerne la lutte contre le crime organisé. Le pays intéresse les nouveaux gangs de malfaiteurs en tant que base d'opérations et de blanchiment de fonds. L'Autriche se doit donc d'assumer ses responsabilités en matière de lutte contre le crime organisé, en créant et en partageant de nouvelles stratégies de répression.

12. Le crime organisé afro-américain: asservissement raciale et mutinerie

Robert J. Kelly

Voir en la *Cosa Nostra* le noyau dur du crime organisé aux Etats-Unis, nous mène de façon naturelle à l'analyse des formes périphériques que revêt le phénomène : c'est-à-dire, le crime organisé de type non traditionnel, tel qu'il s'est développé au sein des minorités ethniques. La présente étude propose une réflexion sur le crime organisé afro-américain et ses perspectives de croissance. Mettant à part le trafic de la drogue, l'auteur soutient que la mobilité politique à l'intérieur de la minorité est la condition préalable de la croissance et de la stabilité des activités criminelles organisées de type traditionnel.

13. Le commerce mondial du sexe: l'être humain en tant que marchandise

Sarah L. Shannon

L'exploitation sexuelle des femmes et des enfants à des fins commerciales est devenue un phénomène de portée mondiale. De plus en plus, les organisations criminelles internationales se lancent dans ce secteur hautement lucratif. Bien que les données entourant le commerce mondial du sexe soient repoussantes, il faut en avoir une connaissance approfondie si l'on veut parvenir à la mise en place de structures de lutte efficaces. Ce dossier analyse certaines des caractéristiques saillantes du commerce du sexe, de sa répartition géographique, et de ses tendances actuelles. En conlusion, l'auteur examine brièvement les réponses mondiales au problème.

14. Le vol d'objets d'art et d'antiquités

Lauren Bernick

Ce chapitre examine le commerce illicite et grandissant d'objets d'art, d'antiquités et de biens culturels volés. Bien que le vol d'objets d'art et le pillage des trésors archéologiques aient lieu depuis des siècles, la prolifération actuelle des vols est due à des facteurs internes à l'environnement internationale en mutation et à la demande croissante d'oeuvres d'art. Les réseaux internationaux de vol et de recel sont un développement récent : ils délestent les musées, les sites archéologiques et les églises partout dans le monde pour en faire passer le produit dans les musées et salles de vente du monde développé. Ces réseaux peuvent être soit des organisations criminelles transnationales consacrées exclusivement au vol et au recel d'objets d'art, soit des organisations criminelles transnationales déjà bien établies qui ont compris la rentabilité de ce type d'activité. Des organisations telles que la mafia italienne ou les cartels de drogue colombien se servent des oeuvres d'art volées pour faciliter d'autres transactions illégales, reliant ainsi le trafic des oeuvres d'art au blanchiment de fonds et au trafic de la drogue. La répression du commerce international des biens culturels volés est rendue plus problèmatique encore par la connivence des fonctionnaires et du monde de l'art.

15. Le blanchiment de fonds

David Hess, Kenneth Myers, Michele Gideon, Sal E. Gomez et John Daly

Le blanchiment de fonds est étudié ici en fonction de ses objectifs, de ses méthodes, de ses outils et instruments, des institutions qui l'effectuent ainsi que des différentes opportunités de blanchiment. L'article identifie les pays et les institutions vulnérables.

16. Le crime organisé d'état : répression, conséquences involontaires et pistes de recherche

Jeffrey Ian Ross

L'article analyse le concept du crime d'état comme étant une forme de crime organisé d'état. En se concentrant sur la répression de ce type de crime, l'auteur relève les champs où elle risque d'avoir des conséquences involontaires et ensuite propose des mesures qui feraient avancer la lutte contre le crime d'état.

17. L'avenir du narco-terrorisme: la Colombie – une étude de cas

Peter A. Lupaha et Sung-Kwon Cho

Prenant la Colombie comme étude de cas, les auteurs procèdent à la définition et à la description du narco-terrorisme, précisant les acteurs qui y jouent un rôle (l'Etat, le milieu criminel et les simples citoyens), les conditions nécessaires à son implantation et à sa continuation, les variantes qui peuvent apparaître dans son déroulement ainsi que dans les réactions qu'il suscite, sa typologie et son avenir probable dans le contexte du crime organisé général et transnational.

18. La mondialisation du crime et le système judiciaire : perspectives d'avenir et problèmes

David Nelken

Ce chapitre présente une analyse des processus de mondialisation du crime organisé et démontre comment ces processus peuvent affecter l'évolution du crime et du système judiciaire. En premier lieu il identifie les peurs en concurrence autour de la montée alléguée du crime organisé transnational, d'une part, et les dangers présumés de la lutte policière transnationale, d'autre part. Après avoir dégagé la problèmatique associée aux divers aspects de la mondialisation du crime organisé, l'auteur met en garde contre le raisonnement qui voit dans le renforcement de la répression policière à l'échelle transnationale la réponse nécessaire et suffisante au problème.

Annexes:

1. Le problème non résolu le plus critique dans le domaine du crime organisé.
2. Ressources

1. Ungewißheiten über transnationales Verbrechen

Gerhard O.W. Mueller

Der Aufsatz beschreibt die Entwicklungen in der Definition von transnationalem und internationalem Verbrechen in den Beratungen der Organe der Vereinten Nationen. Nachdem Einigkeit über eine grundsätzliche Definition erzielt worden war, wurden Mitgliedsstaaten der UN und Nichtregierungsorganisationen (NGO's) gebeten, 18 Kategorien von Verbrechen zu beschreiben, die internationale Charakteristika und Einflüsse haben, auch wenn sie von lokaler Natur erscheinen mögen. Die 18 Kategorien wurden begutachtet, und zwar unter besonderer Beachtung ihrer Reichweite, Muster, bestehender Ressourcen und der benötigten Mittel zur Bekämpfung dieser Verbrechen. Behandelt wurden Verbrechen mit transnationalem Charakter, als da sind: Geldwäsche, Terrorismus, Kunstdiebstahl und Diebstahl geistigen Eigentums, Piraterie, Computer- und Umweltverbrechen usw.. Diese Verbrechen „leiden" unter Unsicherheiten bezüglich ihrer genauen Definition eines Konzeptes von transnationalem Verbrechen, benötigter Forschung und benötigter verläßlicher Messungen und Kriterien. Eine genaue Definition der Konzepte trans- und internationaler Verbrechen braucht die hier verlangte Forschung und die Meßinstrumente, um sie effektiv bekämpfen zu können.

2. Reich und gleich werden: Länderübergreifende Bedrohungen im 21. Jahrhundert.

Phil Williams

Dieses Papier untersucht die Bedrohungen für die nationale und internationale Sicherheit, die von transnationalen kriminellen Organisationen und terroristischen Gruppen ausgeht. Es wird behauptet, daß das Entstehen dieser Bedrohungen als Resultat zweier Prozesse verstanden werden kann - Globalisierung und die Krise staatlicher Autorität - von denen beide zu einer Einschränkung im Bereich staatlicher Autorität beitragen. Der Einfluß verschiedener Aspekte der Globalisierung (Diaspora und ethnische Netzwerke, Handelswachstum, die Entwicklung eines globalen finanziellen Systems, die Entwicklung eines globalen Informations- und Kommunikationssystems und das Entstehen globaler Städte) werden untersucht. Künftige Trends bei organisiertem Verbrechen und Terrorismus werden ebenfalls erkundet.

3. Organisierte Kriminalität in Osteuropa und ihre Folgen für die Sicherheit der westlichen Welt

Brunon Holyst

Dieser Artikel betrachtet die Situation des organisierten Verbrechens in osteuropäischen Staaten und erwähnt die Bedrohungen, die dadurch für die westliche Welt entstehen. Politische und ökonomische Transformationen in den früheren sozialistischen Blockstaaten übten einen Einfluß aus auf die Ausgestaltung der Dynamik und Struktur von Verbrechen. Die Veränderungen in allen Lebensbereichen werden von Kriminellen ausgebeutet, die zunehmend international vernetzt sind. Die Schwäche des Staatsapparates und daraus folgend der Verlust des Rechtsprechungsmonopols, Gesetzeslücken, soziale Unruhen, eine beträchtliche Verringerung des Lebensstandards, in Verbindung mit systemischer Korruption im öffentlichen, ökonomischen und politischen Leben erzeugt ein besonderes Netz 'pathologischer' institutioneller Verknüpfungen. Internationale Währungsverbindungen, weltweite finanzielle Transaktionen und Warenaustausch sowie die Öffnung der Grenzen werden zu einer verstärkten Internationalisierung und Professionalisierung von Aktivitäten der organisierten Kriminalität führen. Die

Hauptbedohung durch organisierte Kriminalität erwächst aus ihrer Flexibilität (sie erscheint in verschiedenen Formen), die es ihr erlaubt, von denselben Freiheiten und sozialen Möglichkeiten zu profitieren wie jene, die sich an einer konventionellen, legitimen, legalen, sozialen und ökonomischen Gesellschaft erfreuen. Die Situation in Osteuropa erleichtert wahrscheinlich eine politische Kriminalisierung.

4. Nach der Apartheid: die Entwicklung und Kontrolle der organisierten Kriminaliät in Südafrika

Mark Shaw

Organisierte Kriminalität ist in Südafrikas neuer demokratischer Ordnung dramatisch angestiegen. Während einige Formen organisierter Kriminalität - besonders „Gang"-Aktivitäten am westliche Kap - auch schon unter der Apartheid exisitierten, bedeutete dies keine Bedrohung, und tatsächlich wurden Straßengangs von staatlichen Akteuren oftmals dazu benutzt, Anti-Apartheid-Aktivitäten zu zerschlagen. Während der öffentliche und politische Druck bezüglich dieses Themas wächst, sind die südafrikanischen Organe der Verbrechensbekämpfung schlecht auf die Aufgabe vorbereitet, großflächigen Aktivitäten organisierter Kriminalität zu begegnen. Dennoch ist es von größter Bedeutung, daß Interventionen jetzt stattfinden: südafrikanische kriminelle Organisationen sind, obwohl zahlreich, noch relativ fragmentiert und verletzbar durch konzentrierte Polizeiaktionen. Eine bedeutende gegenwärtige Schwäche liegt jedoch im mangelnden Verständnis und Analyse von Umfang, Gestalt, Struktur und potentiellem Wachstum der südafrikanischen organisierten Kriminalität.

5. Ökonomische Reform und 'schwarze Gesellschaften': Das Wiederauftauchen organisierter Kriminaliät im post-maoistischen China

Mark S. Gaylord and Hualing Fu

Chinas kulturelles Erbe schließt eine hunderte Jahre alte Tradition organisierter Kriminalität ein. Während der ersten Hälfte des 20. Jahrhunderts erfreuten sich Chinas 'Geheimgesellschaften' eines intimen Verhältnisses zu Tschiang Kai Scheks nationalistischer Regierung. Nach der kommunistischen Machtübernahme 1949 ging Mao Tse Tung jedoch schnell zur Zerstörung dessen über, was er richtig als potentielle Quelle der Opposition gegenüber seiner neuen Regierung betrachtete. Für nahezu 30 Jahre verschwand organisierte Kriminalität aus China, untergetaucht zusammen mit anderen Institutionen der früheren Ära. Im post-maoistischen China jedoch ist die organisierte Kriminalität (genannt 'hei shehui', oder 'schwarze Gesellschaft') nicht nur wieder erschienen, sondern ist heute weitverbreitet. 'Schwarze Gesellschaft' ist ein allumfassender Begriff, mit dem kleine Banden von Autobahnräubern bis zu organisierten kriminellen Gruppen mit tausenden von Mitgliedern bezeichnet werden. Von der Anlage her ist die 'schwarze Gesellschaft' unsichtbar, unklar und dunkel durch Geheimhaltung und korrumpiert Beamte und die hoffnungslos verschwommene Unterscheidung zwischen privaten und öffentlichen Bereichen.

6. Entwicklungen organisierter Kriminaliät bei den *Boryokudan* in Japan

Minoru Yokoyama

Die *Boryokudan*, einheimische japanische Gruppen organisierter Kriminalität, haben einige subkulturelle Merkmale von Banden aus der feudalen Periode geerbt. Das Zentrum ihrer

Ethik wurde aus *Ninkyo-do*, einer Art Rittergeist, gebildet. Dem japanischen ökonomischen Wachstum nach dem Zweiten Weltkrieg folgend, wurden verschiedene mächtige *Boryokudans* durch Gewalt und ihre immensen Reichtümer zum *Koiki* (großflächigen)-*Boryokudan*. Sie operieren derzeit als profitorientierte Organisationen und sind eher vergleichbar mit Privatunternehmen in einem kapitalistischen Land, denn mit Gruppen, die durch die Ethik des *Ninkyo-do* diszipliniert werden. Die *Boryokudan* sind hierarchisch strukturiert; viel auf Mitgliedsgebühren basierendes Geld wird hinein- und hinauf zu einem 'Gott-Vater' gepumpt. Die meisten Mitglieder müssen, um sowohl ihren Lebensunterhalt zu verdienen als auch die erwarteten Mitgliedsgebühren an ihren Vorgesetzten zu bezahlen, eine Vielzahl krimineller Aktivitäten ausüben. Die wichtigste Quelle ihrer Einkünfte besteht für die Boryokudan im Verkauf psychoaktiver Drogen. Lange Zeit wurden die Aktivitäten der Boryokudan von der Polizei stillschweigend geduldet. Dennoch konnte sich die Polizei allmählich vom korrumpierenden Einfluß der *Borykudan* freimachen. Während der ökonomischen Blütezeit der 80er Jahre begingen die *Koiki-Boryokudan* viele Gewaltakte, die zusehends sichtbarer und für die Allgemeinbevölkerung untolerierbarer wurden. Die öffentliche Meinung gegen die *Borykudan* wuchs. 1991 wurde das Gesetz gegen die *Borykudan* in Kraft gesetzt. Unter diesem Gesetz kontrolliert die Polizei, in Kooperation mit der Bevölkerung, die illegalen Aktiviäten der *Boryokudan* strenger.

7. Die Zukunft der sozilianischen und kalabrischen organisierten Kriminalität The Future of Sicilian and Calabrian Organized Crime

Letizia Paoli

Um die Zukunft der sizilianischen und kalabrischen mafiösen Verbindungen zu verstehen, müssen zwei Facetten ihrer Aktivität voneinander unterschieden und getrennt betrachtet werden: 1) die Beteiligung von Mafiagruppen an internationalen illegalen Märkten, und 2) die die örtlichen Systeme mafiöser Macht. Dieser Aufsatz behauptet, daß die Position und der Grad der Beteiligung von Italiens machtvollsten Mafiaverbindungen am illegalen Weltmarkt zuvörderst auf den Tendenzen der internationalen politischen Ökonomie beruht, auch wenn Strafverfolgungen kurzfristig einen beachtlichen Einfluß zeigen mögen. Die Macht der Mafiafamilien in ihren örtlichen Gemeinden ist, im Gegensatz dazu, wesentlich das Produkt der Wechselspiels von drei kollektiven Akteuren: den Mafiagruppen selbst, staatlichen Institutionen und der italienische Zivilgesellschaft.

8. Die Zukunft traditioneller organisierter Kriminaliät in den Vereinigten Staaten von Amerika

Howard Abadinsky

Einige Beobachter behaupten, die amerikanische Mafia läge in den letzten Zügen, und dies wesentlich als Ergebnis der erfolgreichen nationalen Anstrengungen bei der Strafverfolgung. Zweistellige Gefängnisstrafen, zu denen Angehörige der organisierten Kriminalität typischerweise verurteilt werden, hätten zum Ableben der Omertà, dem vielgerühmten Code des Schweigens, geführt. Diese Behauptung ist jedoch nicht neu - tatsächlich wurde das Ableben der amerikanischen Mafia seit Jahrzehnten vorhergesagt. Aber ist jetzt endlich die Zeit gekommen, in der wir die Mafia aus Amerikas Zukunft streichen können? Um einen Einblick zu gewähren, berücksicht dieses Papier Theorien, die sowohl das Entstehen des Phänomens als auch dessen fortwährende Existenz erklären, und es analysiert die Ergebnisse im Vergleich zu dem, was über die gegenwärtige italienisch-amerikanische organisierte Kriminalität bekannt ist.

9. Organisierte Kriminalität in den Vereinigten Staaten von Amerika: einige gegenwärtige Entwicklungen

Robert J. Kelly

Die amerikanische Mafia, die Cosa Nostra, stand unter konzertierten Angriffen der Verbrechensbekämpfung, aber sie kann nicht als zerstört beschrieben werden. Mit dem Wandel der ökonomischen Bedingungen und der sozio-ökonomischen Umgebungen, die die Mafia gefördert haben, hat auch sie sich verändert und neu definiert. Andere ethnische Gruppen, bezeichnet als 'nicht-traditionelle' organisierte Kriminalität, wachsen in ethnischen Enklaven und Gettos neuer Einwanderergemeinden. Dieser Aufsatz untersucht die Prozesse des Niedergangs und der Wiedergruppierung innerhalb der Cosa Nostra und skizziert die Strukturen und die Dynamik von chinesischen Erpresserbanden.

10. Organisierte Kriminalität in Israel

Menachem Amir

Der Beitrag skizziert das Studium organisierter Kriminalität in Israel, wie es in Untersuchungsberichten der Medien und der akademischen Forschung reflektiert wird. Die Geschichte des Studiums organisierter Kriminalität in Israel ist anhaltend und dauernd charakterisiert durch Debatten zwischen der Polizei, Wissenschaftlern und den Medien über die Definition und die Natur von, sowie Reaktionen gegen die organisierte Kriminalität in Israel. Die Natur organisierter Kriminalität reflektiert das zweitwichtigste Charakeristikum der israelischen Gesellschaft (das wichtigste ist Sicherheit): das von Immigrantenwellen, die auch die kriminelle Szenerie inklusive der organisierten Kriminalität betreten. Organisierte Kriminalität hat daher die Natur ethnischer Nachfolge, die letzte ist die der russischen Immigranten. Ihre Beteiligung an Kriminalität und organisierter Kriminalität wird nun beschrieben.

11. Organisierte Kriminalität: eine österreichische Perspektive

Maximilian Edelbacher

Organisierte Kriminalität (OK) ist die bedeutendste Herausforderung für die gegenwärtige Welt, besonders gilt dies für Europa. Seit 1989, als der 'Eiserne Vorhang' fiel, hat ein enormer Wandel in Europa stattgefunden. Österreichs geographische Position im Zentrum Europas und seine neue Rolle als Mitglied der europäischen Gemeinschaft bringen neue Verantwortlichkeiten in der Bekämpfung der organisierten Kriminalität mit sich. Österreich ist für neu entstandenen OK-Banden wegen ihrer Geldwäsche-Aktivitäten von Interesse, und Österreich wird zur Basis für betriebliche Aktivitäten der OK. Österreichs neue Rolle bringt die Verantwortung mit sich, OK durch die Entwicklung und das Teilen neuer Ideen und Gegenstrategien zu bekämpfen.

12. Afrikanisch-amerikanische organisierte Kriminaliät: Rassistische Sklaverei und Auflehnung

Robert J. Kelly

Über die Cosa Nostra als das 'Herz' der gegenwärtigen organisierten Kriminalität in den Vereinigten Staaten nachzudenken, führt natürlicherweise zur Betrachtung der Randformen dieses Phänomens - nämlich Minderheiten- bzw. 'nicht-traditionelle' organisierte Kriminalität. Dieser Aufsatz bietet einige Betrachtungen zu spezifischen Formen von 'nicht-traditioneller' organisierter Kriminalität von afrikanisch-amerikanischen Gruppen und deren Wachstumsaussichten. Abgesehen vom Drogenhandel wird behauptet, daß politische Mobilität innerhalb der Minderheitengemeinschaften eine unabdingbare Voraussetzung für das Wachstum und die Stabilität traditioneller organisierter Kriminalität ist.

13. Weltweiter Sexhandel: Menschen als reine Ware

Sarah L. Shannon

Kommerzielle sexuelle Ausbeutung von Frauen und Kindern ist zu einem weltweiten Phänomen geworden. In zunehmendem Ausmaß engagieren sich transnationale kriminelle Organisationen in diesem hochlukrativen Geschäft. Die Fakten über den weltweiten Sexhandel sind widerwärtig. Wenn effektive Gegenmaßnahmen geschaffen werden sollen, ist ein detailliertes Verständnis ebendieser Fakten notwendig. Deshalb werden einige der unterscheidenden Merkmale, geographische Aspekte und aufkommende Trends dieses Fleischmarktes in dieser Studie diskutiert. Eine kurze Betrachtung globaler Antworten auf dieses Problem schließt die Untersuchung ab.

14. Diebstahl von Kunst und Antiquitäten

Lauren Bernick

Dieser Abschnitt untersucht den wachsenden illegalen Handel mit Kunst, Antiquitäten und Kulturgütern. Auch wenn Kunstdiebstahl und die Plünderung archäologischer Schätze seit Jahrhunderten vorkamen, haben einige Kräfte in der sich wandelnden internationalen Umwelt und die steigende Nachfrage nach Kunstgütern zur gegenwärtigen Belieferung des Marktes beigetragen. Neu im illegalen Kunstmarkt sind internationale Netzwerke, die Kunstobjekte in die Museen und Auktionshäuser der entwickelten Welt schmuggeln, indem sie weltweit auf Museen, Ausgrabungsstätten und Kirchen zielen. Die Netzwerke sind entweder Organisationen, die sich ausschließlich dem Kunstdiebstahl verschrieben haben, oder bereits bestehende transnationale kriminelle Organisationen, die den Kunstdiebstahl als profitabel erkannt haben. Transnationale kriminelle Organisationen wie die italienische Mafia und kolumbianische Drogenkartelle nutzen gestohlenen Kunstgüter, um andere kriminelle Transaktionen zu erleichtern, und verbinden dadurch Kriminalität im Kunstbereich mit Geldwäsche und Drogenhandel. Die stillschweigende Duldung durch die legale Kunstwelt und Regierungsbeamte bildet eine weitere Herausforderung für internationale Verbrechensbekämpfungsorgane beim Stoppen des Flusses gestohlener Kunst über internationale Grenzen.

15. Geldwäsche

David Hess, Kenneth Myers, Michele Gideon, Sal E. Gomez, and John Daly

Geldwäsche wird betrachtet unter den Aspekten ihrer Zwecke, Methoden, Instrumente, Institutionen der Geldwäsche und den verschiedenen Möglichkeiten, Geld zu waschen; und es werden Institutionen und Länder identifiziert, die hierfür anfällig sind.

16. Staatliche organisierte Kriminaliät: ihre Kontrolle, unbeabsichtigte Konsequenzen und Vorschläge für künftige Forschung

Jeffrey Ian Ross

Dieser Artikel analysiert das Konzept des Staatsverbrechens als eine Form von staatlicher organisierter Kriminalität, konzentriert sich auf seine Kontrolle, postuliert eine Reihe von Bereichen, wo Kontrolle eine Anzahl unbeabsichtigter Konsequenzen haben kann, und schlägt schließlich vor, wie die Kontrolle staatlicher Verbrechen verbessert werden kann.

17. Die Zukunft des Narko-Terrorismus: eine Fallstudie über Kolumbien

Peter A. Lupsha and Sung-Kwon Cho

Indem Kolumbien als Fallstudie benutzt wird, wird Drogenterrorismus durch die Benennung der notwendigen 'Akteure' definiert und beschrieben - sowohl in den kriminellen als auch in den legitimen Gemeinschaften einschließlich des Staates; benannt werden Bedingungen für seine Einführung und Dauerhaftigkeit, Variationen in Aktionen und Reaktionen, Typen und Vorhersagen zu seiner Zukunft innerhalb des Kontextes organisierter und transnational organsisierter Kriminalität.

18. Die Globalisierung der Kiminalität und der Strafjustiz: Aussichten und Probleme

David Nelken

Dieser Abschnitt bietet eine Analyse der Art und Weise, wie Prozesse der Globalisierung die Entwicklung der Kriminalität und der Strafjustiz beeinflussen könnten. Zunächst werden die konkurrierenden Ängste identifiziert, die sich einerseits um den angeblichen Anstieg transnationaler Kriminalität und andererseits um die angeblichen Gefahren transnationaler Polizeitätigkeit ranken. Nachdem eine Reihe von Problemen unterschieden wurden, die mit verschiedenen Aspekten der Globalisierung verknüpft sind, wird damit fortgefahren, Vorsicht bei der Überlegung anzumahnen, verstärkte transnationale Polizeiarbeit sei eine notwendige oder ausreichende Antwort auf diese Probleme.

APPENDIX:

1. Das wichtigste ungelöste Problem im Zusammenhang mit organisierter Kriminalität

2. Zusammenstellung der Ressourcen zu organisierter Kriminalität

1. 跨国罪行：不确定的经验
Gerhard O.W. Mueller

本文介绍联合国组织有关跨国及国际犯罪定义的发展。当该定义初步形成后，联合国的成员国及非政府组织便定出十八种有国际特性及影响的罪行，虽然当中有些犯罪有很强的地方色彩。成员国和非政府组织对这十八种罪行进行检讨，强调其范围及模式，打击这些犯罪的现有资源及所需的措施。文中所论及有跨国性质的罪行包括：洗钱、政治恐怖活动、盗窃艺术和知识财产、侵犯版权、电脑犯罪及有关环境的罪行等。跨国犯罪这概念还没有明确的定义，因此有必要在这方面加以研究并定立有关跨国犯罪的可行标准及依据。要有效地打击这些跨国犯罪及国际犯罪，我们必需先就跨国犯罪及国际犯罪的概念进行研究并定立有关的标准及措施。

2. 国际性犯罪：二十一世纪跨国性的威胁
Phil Williams

本文研究跨国犯罪组织及跨国恐怖政治活动组织对国家及国际安全所造成的威胁。作者认为构成这些威胁的原因可归咎於两个过程：全球化现象及国家权力机关的危机。这两者导致国家权力的缩小。本文会研究全球化的多方面影响，例如：散居於世界各国的同一民族人民网络，贸易发展，全球经融体制的发展，全球资讯体制的发展及国际城市的出现。另外，作者亦会研究有组织犯罪及恐怖政治活动的未来趋势。

3. 东欧有组织罪行及其对西方社会安全的影响
Brunon Hotyst

本文评论在东欧国家内有组织犯罪的情况及其对西方国家的威胁。从前奉行社会主义的集团国的政治及经济蜕变影响了形成犯罪的动力和结构。这些广泛的转变正好被那些国际联系与日俱增的罪犯利用。国家机构的弱点及其丧失执法垄断权、法律瘫痪、社会动荡、生活质数大为下降，加上在社会上、经济上及政治上全面的贪污，构成一个病态的机构网络。国际货币联系、世界金融交易、货物交易及开放边境等引致更大规模的国际性的、专业化的有组织犯罪的出现。有组织犯罪构成最主要威胁的原因在於这些罪行有非常大的灵活性（它们可以不同形式出现）。这些灵活性使罪犯可享有与传统的、合法的法律、社会及经济组织同等的自由及机会。东欧社会的这种情况可能导致政治犯罪化的出现。

4. 有组织犯罪在南非种族隔离政策结束後的发展及抑制措施
Mark Shaw

有组织罪行在南非的新民主社会秩序下剧烈地增加。一些有组织犯罪尤其是在好望角西面的帮派活动在种族隔离政策下确实存在，但并不构成威胁。实际上国家机构亦常用街头帮派来控制反隔离政策的参与者。虽然有组织犯罪已成为南非公众及政治压力的焦点，但其执法机关仍未能对有组织犯罪进行大规模的反击。但关键的是这种干预正在开始出现：虽然南非的犯罪组织数目众多，但是很零碎并且容易被集中的警察行动击破。目前一个主要的弱点就是缺乏对南非有组织犯罪的规模、形态、结构及潜在发展途径等的了解及分析。

5.　经济改革及黑社会：有组织罪行於毛泽东时代後的重新出现

Mark S. Gaylord and 傅华伶

有组织犯罪是中国文化遗产的一个组成部分。在二十世纪初，中国的「秘密社团」与蒋介石的国民政府关系非常密切。但在一九四九年，共产党上台後，毛泽东政府迅速地粉碎了他认为对其新政府有潜在反抗力的团体。在接著的三十年中，有组织犯罪组织，同其它社会组织一起在中国消失。但是，毛泽东时代过去後，有组织罪行(即黑社会)不单再次出现，而且广泛发展。「黑社会」的含义非常广，包括由几个人组成的抢劫团伙到成百上千人组成的犯罪集团。在组织上，黑社会是隐藏的，而其中的秘密，贪官的包庇及公私之间界限的日趋模糊，使这些组织变得更加难以作模。

6.　日本有组织犯罪活动的趋势

Minoru Yokoyama

日本的黑社会组织承袭了一些封建时代帮派次文化的特徵。他们的道德观的核心是武士道精神。二次大战及日本经济增长後，许多黑社会组织，凭著暴力及其财富，演变成势力庞大的犯罪组织。这些组织现在已发展到跟资本主义社会里的私有企业类同，同样是以赚钱为目标的组织，他们不再是训练式士道精神的团体。日本的黑社会组织实行帮级制度。组织内大部分的会员会费归首领所有。大部分成员必需从事许多非法活动，以赚取足够金钱维持生活及缴交会员费。这些犯罪组织的主要收入来源是从事毒品贩卖。一直以来，警方对这些犯罪组织的活动都是采取纵容的态度。但是渐渐地，警方清除了这些组织所造成的腐败影响。八十年代，经济繁荣，大规模的黑社会犯罪组织进行了很多暴力活动。对公众而言，这些罪行越来越明显及越来越令人无法忍受。公众反对这些组织的言论亦因此而增加。有关对付这些有组织犯罪集团的法例终於在一九九一年制定。透过该条法例，警方能与市民合作，严加打击有组织的犯罪活动。

7.　西西里及加拉比有组织罪行的未来及发展

Letizia Paoli

要推测西西里及加拉比秘密犯罪组织的未来发展，我们先要将他们的活动分为两大类，然後继续研究。该两大类活动为：1)犯罪组织在国际非法市场活动中的参与；2)犯罪组织的地方势力。本文认为意大利最大势力的犯罪组织联盟在世界非法交易上的地位及参与情况，虽然可受执法活动的影响，但主要的影响却来自国际政治经济的趋势。另一方面，犯罪组织的地方势力主要取决於犯罪组织本身、国家机构及意大利市民社会三个方面的相互影响。

8.　美国传统有组织罪行的未来发展

Howard Abadinsky

有观察者认为美国犯罪组织已尽於消失的主要原因是联邦法律执行的成功。对有组织罪行篇以十年以上判刑的传统导致了美国人对该犯罪组织不再保持沉默。但其实这并非一种新的言论，有关美国犯罪组织灭亡的预测在几十年前已经出现。但我们现在是否可以说犯罪组织将会在美国消失呢?本文研究有关意裔美国人的有组织罪行的形成及其继续存在的可能和後果。

9.　美国的有组织罪行：现时的趋势

Robert J. Kelly

　　虽然美国的执法部门已对美国黑手党进行了打击，但这还不能说这些组织已被消灭。这些组织随着酿成黑手党出现的经济、政治及社会环境的转变而改变。其他的种族团体，即非传统的有组织犯罪，也正在新移民社区内出现。本文对美国黑手党的末落及重新结盟的经过及中国籍的勒索党羽的结构及动态，作出检讨。

10.　以色列的有组织罪行

Menachem Amir

　　本文列出在媒介调查报告及学术研究中所反映的有关以色列有组织罪行的情况。一直以来对以色列有组织罪行的研究都是警方、学者及媒介之间围绕着对以色列有组织罪行的定义、性质及对策进行的。有组织罪行的性质反映了以色列社会第二重要的特点（首要的特点是国家安全），即新移民参与不同形式的犯罪活动，当中包括有组织犯罪活动。所以以色列有组织犯罪活动有着民族继承的性质。而目前构成这种特性的则是来自俄罗斯的移民，及其在犯罪活动及有组织的犯罪活动中的参与。

11.　有组织罪行：奥地利的观点

Maximilian Edelbacher

　　有组织犯罪是当代世界，特别是欧洲，面临的一个重大难题。一九八九年「铁幕」瓦解后，欧洲经历了重大的转变。奥地利位於欧洲的中心。作为欧洲社会的一员，奥地利亦要分担打击有组织罪行的新责任。由於从事洗钱活动的需要，由於奥地利已成为有组织犯罪活动的基地，新兴的犯罪集团开始对奥地利感兴趣。奥地利在欧洲所扮演的新角色给她带来了跟其他欧洲国家一起研究及制定有关打击有组织罪行的策略的义务。

12.　非裔美国人有组织犯罪：种族劳役与反叛

Robert J. Kelly

　　说到黑手党是现在美国有组织犯罪的核心，自然亦会谈及围绕它所出现的现象，例如：少数民族及「非传统」的有组织犯罪。本文研究「非传统性」的有组织犯罪及非裔美国犯罪集团的特色及其发展趋势。作者认为少数民族社区的政治参与是有助传统有组织犯罪活动（但不包括私贩毒品）的发展及稳定的先决条件。

13.　全球性的色情交易活动：人类成为交易货物

Sarah L. Shannon

　　对妇女及儿童商业性的性侵犯已成为遍及全球的现象。由於从事这种非法活动的收入非常可观，所以参与的跨国犯罪组织日益增加。这些全球性的色情交易十分令人厌恶。但若要制定出有效的打击措施，我们必须对有关的事实有深入的了解。本文讨论这种人肉市场的特点、地理因素、发展趋势，及全球社会的反应。

14. 艺术品及古物的盗窃

Lauren Bernick

本章探讨日益增加的艺术品及古文物的非法买卖。虽然盗窃及掠夺艺术品及古文物在过去的几个世纪也有发生，但是国际环境因素的转变及人们对艺术品需求的增加，促使这个非法市场的增长。非法艺术品市场的新现象是国际网络的出现，使那些罪犯能从世界各地的博物馆、古代遗迹及教堂偷取艺术品及古文物，然后偷运至发达国家的博物馆及拍卖行。在这些网络中，有些是专门从事艺术品盗窃的组织。另外一些则是老牌跨国犯罪组织，他们通过染指这种非法活动以谋取暴利。传统跨国犯罪组织，例如意大利的黑手党、哥伦比亚的贩毒组织等，也利用盗窃艺术品来协助他们从事其他非法活动。因此，盗窃艺术品罪行与洗钱及贩卖毒品有密切的联系。艺术界及政府官员对这种非法活动的纵容或默许对国际执法组织对遏止被盗艺术品在国际间的流通造成了一个额外的难题。

15. 洗钱

David Hess, Kenneth Myers, Michele Gideon, Sal E. Gomez, and John Daly

本文探讨洗钱的目的、方法、工具及机构，并指出容易被用於洗钱的机会、机构和国家。

16. 有组织的国家犯罪活动：控制措施，意料之外的後果及未来研究的建议

Jeffrey Ian Ross

本文对国家犯罪，即有组织的国家犯罪，进行分析研究，其重点在於讨论对国家犯罪的控制措施。本文认为这些措施在某些方面会带来一些意料之外的後果，并提出一些控制国家犯罪的建议。

17. Narco 恐怖主义的未趋势：哥伦比亚的个案研究

Peter A. Lupsha and Sung-Kwon Cho

本文研究哥伦比亚的Narco恐怖主义，并强调合法社会，包括国家，在从中扮演的角色。文中研究该恐怖主义始创和存在的条件、其行动及应变措施、形式的改变，并预测它在有组织及跨国犯罪中的未来趋势。

18. 犯罪及刑事司法的全球化：简景及难题

David Nelken

本章分析全球化对刑事罪行及刑事司法的发展可能带来的影响。文中首先指出跨国罪行的增加及跨国警察的危险的两大忧虑。在指出有关全球化所带来的多方面影响後，作者提出对於认为加强跨国警察能解决全球化的刑事罪行的看法必须加以慎谨的处理。

附 录：

19. 当代有关有组织犯罪的最重要而未能解决的问题

20. 有关有组织犯罪的文献

1. Транснациональная преступность: опыт неопределенности

Герхард О.В. Мюллер

Резюме

Статья посвящена изменению понятий транснациональной и международной преступности в ходе дискуссий, проводившихся в организациях ООН. Когда было достигнуто соглашение по поводу базового определения, страны-члены ООН и неправительственных организаций должны были представить описание 18 категорий преступлений, имеющих международный характер и влияние, хотя и представляющихся локальными по своей природе.

В статье приводится обзор этих восемнадцати категорий преступлений, включая их масштабы и конкретную картину, имеющиеся источники и меры, необходимые для борьбы с ними. Анализируются виды преступлений, имеющих транснациональный характер: отмывание денег, терроризм, кража результатов художественного и интеллектуального творчества, пиратство, компьютерные преступления, преступления против окружающей среды и пр.

Эти преступления «страдают» от неопределенности в понятии транснациональной преступности, от отсутствия единого представления о необходимых исследованиях, а также действенных мерах или критериях.

Неопределенность в понятии транснациональной и международной преступности нуждается в проведении исследований и принятии мер, необходимых для эффективной борьбы с ней.

2. Обогащение и расплата: транснациональная угроза двадцать первого века

Фил Вильямс

Резюме

В предлагаемой статье исследуется угроза для национальной и международной безопасности, которая исходит от транснациональных криминальных организаций и транснациональных террористических групп. В статье утверждается, что появление этой угрозы следует понимать как результат двух процессов – глобализации преступности и кризиса государственной власти, каждый из которых способствует сокращению пространства государственной власти, исследуется влияние различных аспектов глобализации преступности – диаспоры и этнические связи, развитие коммерции, развитие глобальных финансовых систем и информационных и коммуникационных систем и угрожающее развитие мегалополисов, а также анализируются тенденции развития организованной преступности и терроризма.

3. Организованная преступность в Восточной Европе и ее воздействие на безопасность западного мира

Брюнон Холист

Резюме

В статье приводится обзор состояния организованной преступности в странах Восточной Европы и отмечается угроза, которую она представляет для западного мира. Политические и экономические преобразования в странах бывшего социалистического блока отрицательно влияют на динамику и структуру преступности. Изменения, происходящие во всех областях жизни, используются преступниками, международные связи которых усиливаются. Слабость государственного аппарата и последующая потеря его монополии на управление правоохранительными органами, пробелы в законодательстве, социальная незащищенность, значительное снижение уровня жизни в сочетании с тотальной коррупцией общества, экономики и политики создают особую сеть «патологических» организационных связей. Международные валютные связи, финансовые транснациональные компании, товарные биржи, равно как открытие границ приведут к еще большей интернационализации и профессионализации организованной преступности.

Главная угроза организованной преступности связана с ее гибкостью (она принимает многие формы), что позволяет ей получать выгоду от той же самой свободы и социальных возможностей, которые находятся в распоряжении общества, живущего в соответствии с экономическими, социальными и юридическими правилами. Такое положение в Восточной Европе явно способствует криминализации политики.

4. Развитие организованной преступности и контроль над ней в ЮАР после отмены режима апартеида

Марк Шоу

Резюме

Организованная преступность резко возросла при новом демократическом порядке в ЮАР. Хотя некоторые формы организованной преступности, такие, как гангстерская активность западного образца, действительно существовали при режиме апартеида, они не представляли опасности: в самом деле, уличное гангстерство часто использовалось правительственными агентами для подавления активных сторонников отмены апартеида. В то время, как общественное и политическое давление в том же направлении продолжает возрастать, следственные органы ЮАР выглядят плохо подготовленными для оказания противодействия широкомасштабной организованной преступной активности. Вмешательство государства особенно важно именно сейчас, поскольку южно-африканские криминальные организации, хотя и многочисленны, но разрозненны и чувствительны к целенаправленным действиям полиции. Одна из главных сегодняшних проблем, однако, заключается в недостаточном понимании и анализе размеров, формы, структуры и возможной динамики роста южно-африканской организованной преступности.

5. Экономическая реформа и «теневое общество»: новая опасность организованной преступности в постмаоистском Китае

Марк С. Гейлорд, Хуалинг Фу

Резюме

Китайское культурное наследие включает традиции организованной преступности, которая имеет многовековые корни. В первой половине ХХ века китайские «тайные общества» использовали тесную связь с национальным правительством Чан Кай-ши. Однако после прихода коммунистов к власти в 1949 году Мао Цзе-дун быстро подавил то, что он правильно понимал как потенциальный источник оппозиции его новому правительству. Примерно на 30 лет организованная преступность в Китае исчезла вместе с другими организациями прежних времен. Но в постмаоистском Китае организованная преступность (так называемая *хей шеху* или «теневое общество») не только восстановилась, но и широко распространилась. Термин «теневое общество» перенесен с названия небольших банд на организованные преступные группы с тысячами членов. Их отличительными признаками является то, что они скрыты от глаз, защищены секретностью, подкупают чиновников и окончательно стерли разницу между общественным и частным сектором.

6. Тенденции в области организованной преступности – *бориокудан* – в Японии

Минору Йокояма

Резюме

Бориокудан – японские организованные преступные группы, состоящие из коренных жителей страны, получили в наследство гангстерскую субкультуру феодального периода. Сердцевину их этики составляет *нинкйо-до*, разновидность рыцарской духовной культуры. Одним из последствий экономического расцвета Японии после второй мировой войны стало превращение нескольких сильных групп *бориокудан* путем насилия и использования огромных богатств в *койики бориокудан* – крупные объединения. В настоящее время они действуют скорее как коммерческие организации, подобные частным предприятиям в капиталистических странах, чем прежние группы, объединенные этикой *нинкйо-до*. *Бориокудан* – иерархическая организация, где главным источником средств являются взносы ее членов, поступающие в распоряжение крестного отца. Многие члены организации обязаны заниматься нелегальной деятельностью как для собственного жизнеобеспечения , так и для уплаты требуемых взносов боссу. Наиболее важным источником дохода является продажа стимулирующих средств.

В течение длительного времени полиция потворствовала деятельности *бориокудан*, но постепенно освободилась от их коррумпирующего влияния. В период экономического процветания 80-х годов *койики бориокудан* совершили немало актов насилия, которые стали более заметными и непереносимыми для большей части населения. Общественное осуждение *бориокудан* нарастало. В 1991 году был принят Закон о борьбе с *бориокудан*. В соответствии с ним полиция более активно контролирует незаконную деятельность *бориокудан*, опираясь на поддержку общества.

7. Будущее организованной преступности Сицилии и Калабрии

Летиция Паоли

Резюме

Для того, чтобы обрисовать будущее сицилийской и калабрийской мафии, следует рассмотреть отдельно два аспекта их активности: 1) участие мафиозных структур в международных противозаконных рынках и 2) локальные мафиозные системы.

В статье утверждается, что положение и степень вовлеченности большинства наиболее сильных объединений итальянской мафии в мировой нелегальный оборот зависит главным образом от тенденций международной политики и экономики, хотя давление закона может оказать значительное, но кратковременное влияние на этот процесс. С другой стороны, активность мафиозных семейств в местных условиях, является большей частью продуктом взаимодействия трех коллективных участников: самих мафиозных групп, государственных учреждений и итальянского общества.

8. Будущее традиционной организованной преступности в США

Ховард Абадински

Резюме

Некоторые аналитики утверждают, что американская мафия находится на спаде и почти исчезла главным образом в результате успешного применения федерального законодательства. Приговоры, предусматривавшие многолетние сроки заключения (десять лет и более), которые буквально обрушились на деятелей организованной преступности, привели к исчезновению омерты, хваленого кодекса молчания. Это заключение, однако, не ново. В самом деле, упадок американской мафии предвидели за десятилетия. Но действительно ли пришло время, когда мы можем сказать, что мафия исчезла из американского будущего? Для лучшего понимания проблемы настоящая статья обращается к теориям, которые объясняют возникновение феномена и его длительное существование и анализируют то, что известно о современной организованной преступности, созданной американцами итальянского происхождения.

9. Организованная преступность в США: некоторые современное тенденции

Роберт Д. Келли

Резюме

Американская мафия, *коза ностра*, давно находится под согласованным ударом сил закона, но нельзя сказать, что этот удар ее разрушил. По мере развития экономических и социально-политических условий мафия менялась, она трансформировалась и вновь возникала. Другие этнические группы, обозначаемые как «нетрадиционные» преступные группировки, возникают в этнических анклавах и гетто новых иммигрантских сообществ. Настоящая статья исследует процессы падения и восстановления, происходящие внутри *коза ностра*, и рисует структуру и динамику китайских групп, занимающихся рэкетом.

10. Организованная преступность в Израиле

Менахем Амир

Резюме

Статья содержит результаты исследования организованной преступности в Израиле так, как они отражены в научной периодике и в академических исследованиях. История изучения организованной преступности в Израиле непрерывно и постоянно характеризуется дебатами между полицией, учеными и средствами информации, касательно определения и природы организованной преступности в Израиле и реакции на нее. Природа организованной преступности представляет собой вторую по важности проблему израильского общества (первая – это безопасность): наличие волн иммиграции, которая выходит на криминальную сцену, включаясь и в организованную преступность. Таким образом, природу организованной преступности в Израиле можно обозначить как этнически-преемственную, что характерно для русской иммиграции. В статье описывается вовлечение последней в преступность и организованную преступность.

11. Организованная преступность: ее будущее в Австрии

Максимилиан Эдельбахер

Резюме

Организованная преступность это важный вызов современному миру, в первую очередь, Европе. Резкий сдвиг в этой ситуации произошел в Европе в 1989 году, когда пал «железный занавес». Центральное географическое положение Австрии в Европе и ее новая роль в качестве члена Европейского Сообщества возложили на нее дополнительную ответственность за борьбу с организованной преступностью. Австрия является полем интереса новообразованных банд организованной преступности вследствие их действий по отмыванию денег, а также потому, что Австрия становится базой оперативной активности организованной преступности. Эта новая роль Австрии возложила на нее ответственность за борьбу с организованной преступностью путем разработки и участия в создании новых необходимых идей и стратегии противодействия.

12. Афро-американская организованная преступность: расовое угнетение и мятеж

Роберт Д. Келли

Резюме

Представление о *коза ностра*, как о сердцевине организованной преступности в США сегодня, естественно приводит к соображению о переферийных формах явления, а именно о малой или «нетрадиционной» организованной преступности. Данная статья описывает специфические формы «нетрадиционной» организованной преступности, афро-американские группы и перспективы их роста. Утверждается, что предпосылкой роста и стабильности традиционных форм организованной преступности, кроме распространения наркотиков, является политическая мобильность внутри национальных меньшинств.

13. Международная торговля сексуальными услугами: человеческое существо как абсолютный продукт потребления

Сара И. Шеннон

Резюме

Коммерческая сексуальная эксплуатация женщин и детей уже стала широко распространенным явлением. Транснациональные преступные организации во все возрастающем объеме используют этот высокоприбыльный бизнес. Ему сопутствуют отталкивающие факты. И если эффективные контрмеры еще только предстоит разработать, то детальное понимание упомянутых фактов требуется уже сейчас. Поэтому в данной статье обсуждаются некоторые из характерных явлений, географических аспектов и опасностей этого рынка плоти, а так же дается краткое заключение о контрмерах в этой области.

14. Хищение предметов искусства и антиквариата

Лорен Берник

Резюме

В статье исследуется проблема роста объема незаконной торговли предметами искусства, антиквариата и культурных ценностей. Хотя кража археологических сокровищ существует сотни лет, факторы меняющейся международной обстановки и возросший спрос на произведения искусства приводят к расширению рынка. Новым явлением в незаконном рынке произведений искусства являются международные сети, которые занимаются контрабандой предметов искусства в музеи и на аукционы развивающихся стран из музеев, археологических раскопок и храмов всего мира. Такие сети представляют собой либо организации, специализирующиеся на краже предметов искусства, либо уже утвердившиеся транснациональные преступные организации, которые занимаются прибыльной торговлей произведениями искусства. Традиционные транснациональные криминальные организации типа итальянской мафии и колумбийских наркокартелей используют украденные ценности для того, чтобы стимулировать другие незаконные мероприятия, связывая таким образом указанные преступления с отмыванием денег и торговлей наркотиками. Содействие мира искусства и правительственных органов придает дополнительную силу международным правоохранительным органам, препятствующим перемещению украденных предметов искусства через границы.

15. Отмывание денег

Давид Гесс, Кеннет Майерс, Мишель Гидеон, Сол Е. Гомес, Джон Дэйли

Резюме

Рассматривается отмывание денег применительно к реальной ситуации, целям, методам, приемам, организациям по отмыванию денег и различным возможностям этого процесса с указанием наиболее уязвимых орагнизаций и стран.

16. Государственная организованная преступность: контроль, непредсказуемые последствия и предложения относительно будущих исследований

Джеффри Ян Росс

Резюме

В статье анализируется концепция государственной преступности как формы государственной организованной преступности. Особое внимание уделяется контролю, приводится перечень областей, где контроль может иметь ряд непредсказуемых последствий, и предлагаются способы превентивного контроля государственной преступности.

17. Будущее наркотерроризма: Колумбия как пример для изучения

Питер А. Льюпша, Санг-Квон Чо

Резюме

На примере Колумбии в определение и описание наркотерроризма включается необходимость наличия «действующих лиц» как в криминальных, так и в легитимных структурах, в том числе государственных; условия для начала и продолжения их деятельности, разнообразие действий и реакций, типов и предположений относительно их будущего существования в контексте локальной и транснациональной организованной преступности.

18. Глобализация преступности и уголовная юстиция: перспективы и проблемы

Давид Нелькен

транснационального контроля есть необходимый или достаточный ответ на эти проблемы.

Приложение:

19. Наиболее острые нерешенные проблемы, связанные с современной организованной преступностью

20. Источники организованной преступности

(١) الجريمة المتخطية للحدود الدولة: تجربة في المجهول
Gerhard O. W. Mueller

تصف هذه المقالة التطورات في تعريف الجريمة القادمة من خارج حدود الدولة والجريمة الدولية حسب ما هو متداول من قبل مؤسسات الأمم المتحدة. عندما تم الوصول إلى تعريف مقبول طلب من الدول الأعضاء في الأمم المتحدة والمؤسسات الغير حكومية أن تصف ١٨ نوعاً من الجرائم التي لها طابع وتأثير دولي بالرغم من أن بعضها من الممكن أن يكون ذا طابع محلي بطبيعته.

بمراجعة الثماني عشر نوعاً منت الجرائم مع التركيز على أغراضها وأنماطها، المصادر الموجودة والإجراءات الضرورية لمقاومة مثل هذه الجرائم. إن بعض هذه الجرائم المعالجة والتي لها صفات متشابهة بين الدول مثل: تهريب العملات، القرصنة، الإرهاب، سرقة الفنون والإبداعات العقلية، جرائم الكمبيوتر وجرائم البيئة وغيرها ..... الخ.

إن هذه الجرائم "تعاني" من الغموض خاصة تعريف مصطلح الجريمة التي تتعدى الحدود، بحاجة للدراسة وبحاجة لإجراءات وأساليب قابلة للتطبيق. إن تعريف مصطلح الجريمة المتخطية حدود الدول والجرائم الدولية بحاجة للبحث ويجب إيجاد الإجراءات المناسبة لمحاربة مثل هذه الجرائم.

(٢) الاغتناء والتعادل: المخاطر التي تتخطى الحدود في القرن العشرين
Phil Williams

تتفحص هذه الدراسة المخاطر التي تهدد الأمن الوطني والدولي نتيجة للمنظمات الإجرامية والمجموعات الإرهابية الأجنبية. وتجادل بان ظهور مثل هذه المخاطر من الممكن فهمه نتيجة عمليتين- التدويل ومأزق سلطة الدولة- تساهمان الاثنتين في تقليص سيطرة سلطة الدولة. وسيتم فحص ودراسة تأثير العنصر المختلفة للتدويل – شبكات المهاجرين والأقليات، نمو التجارة، تطور النظام المالي العالمي وتطور أنظمة المعلومات والاتصالات الدولية وظهور المد العالمية. وسيتم كذلك دراسة الأنماط المستقبلية في الجريمة المنظمة والإرهاب المنظم.

(٣) الجريمة المنظمة في دول أوروبا الشرقية
ومدى تأثيرها على الأمن في العالم الغربي
Brunon Holyst

يراجع هذا المقال وضع الجريمة المنظمة في دول أوروبا الشرقية ويعلق على ما قد تسببه في العالم الغربي. إن التغيرات السياسية والاجتماعية في الدول الاشتراكية أثرت على تشكيل ديناميكية وهيكلة الجريمة. أن

التغيرات التي تحدث على جميع مستويات الحياة تستغل من قبل المجرمين الذين تزداد اتصالاتهم الدولية. أن ضعف نظام الحكم في الدولة والخسارة الناتجة عن الاستئثار بإدارة العدالة، والفجوات في القانون وقلة الاستقرار الاجتماعي والانخفاض في مستوى المعيشة، بالإضافة إلى الفساد في النظام العام، والحياة الاقتصادية والسياسة يخلق شبكة محددة من الارتباطات المؤسساتية.

إن الارتباطات الدولية للعملة والمعاملات المالية العالمية، وتبادل البضائع الأساسية بالإضافة إلى فتح الأسواق سيؤدي إلى تدويل اكبر واحتراف اكثر في نشاطات منظمات الجريمة. أن الخطر الرئيسي الذي تشكله مؤسسات الجريمة المنظمة يعود لمرونتها (تتخذ العديد من الأشكال) التي تسمح بالربح نتيجة لنفس الحرية والفرص الاجتماعية التي تتوفر للمؤسسات الاقتصادية القانونية والشرعية في المجتمع. إن الوضع في أوروبا الشرقية يسهل عملية الإجرام السياسي.

(٤) تطور وسيطرة الجريمة المنظمة في جنوب أفريقيا ما بعد التفرقة
Mark Shaw

لقد نمت الجريمة المنظمة بشكل مأساوي في ظل النظام الديمقراطي الجديد في جنوب أفريقيا، ولكن بعض أشكال الجريمة المنظمة وخاصة نشاطات العصابات في كيب الغربية- وجدت تحت ظل نظام حكم التفرقة العنصرية ولكن ذلك لم يشكل تهديداً. وعلى مستوى عصابات الشوارع فقد استخدمت من قبل عملاء الحكومة لكي يعرقلوا نشطاء مكافحة التفرقة. ولكن ضغط الرأي العام والسياسي يتزايد بالنسبة لهذا الموضوع. ومؤسسات تطبيق القانون الجنوب افريقي غير مجهزة للوقوف ضد النشاط الاجرامي المنظم والعالي المستوى. ومع ذلك فان أي تدخل يحدث الان: بالرغم من ان منظمات الاجرام عديدة في جنوب افريقيا الا انها ما زالت ضعيفة عند مواجهة رد فعل الشرطة المركز. ومن اهم نقاط الضعف الرئيسية الحالية، هو قلة فهم وتحليل حجم وشكل وهيكلة ومقدرة نمو منظمات الاجرام المختلفة في جنوب افريقيا.

(٥) الإصلاح الاقتصادي "المجتمع الأسود": عودة ظهور الجريمة المنظمة
في الصين ما بعد ماو
Mark S. Gaylord and Hualing Fu

يضم تراث الصين تقاليد الجريمة المنظمة والتي يرجع تاريخها إلى قبل مئات السنين. خلال فترة النصف الأول من القرن العشرين، فان مجتمعات الصين السرية تمتعت بعلاقة حميمة مع حكومة تشيانج كاي-شيكس Chiang Kai-shek's الوطنية. وبعد وصول الشيوعيين إلى الحكم في العام ١٩٤٩، تحك ماوتسي تونج بسرعة لتحطيم ما رآه كمصدر معارضة لحكومته الجديدة. ولمدة ٣٠ عامُ تقريباً اختفت الجريمة المنظمة في الصين، واندمجت مع مؤسسات العهد السابق ولكن فيما بعد حكم ماو في الصين فان الجريمة المنظمة "المدعوة هاي شي شو، أو "المجتمع الأسود" ليس فقط عادت للظهور - وإنما هي الآن منتشرة بشكل واسع.

"المجتمع الأسود" له مصطلح شمولي انتقل من عصابات قطاع الطرق إلى مجموعات الجريمة المنظمة مع آلاف الأعضاء. ولكن تصميم هذه المجموعات فهو مخفي ومحاط بالسرية، الكثير من المسئولين الفاسدين وقلة وضوح الفرق بين القطاع الخاص والعام.

(٦) أنماط الجريمة المنظمة من قبل بوريوكودان Boryokudan في اليابان
Minoru Yokoyama

إن البوريوكودان هم مجموعة جريمة منظمة يابانية أهلية ورثت بعض الثقافة والتقاليد منذ فترة عصابات الإقطاعيين. إن جوهر مبادئهم تكون من Ninkyo-do نوع من روح الفروسية. نتيجة لتطور اليابان اقتصادياً بعد الحرب العالمية الثانية فان العديد من البوريوكودان القوية جداً أصبحت كونيكي (مساحة واسعة) – بويوكودان – من خلال العنف وغناهم الفاحش. ويعملون في الوقت الحاضر كمنظمات تعمل من اجل الربح بشكل يشبه الشركات الخاصة في الدول الرأسمالية، وليس كمجموعات عاملة وتخضع لنظام نينكو-دو. إن البوريوكودان هم منظمين بشكل هرمي، وبذلك فان كمية هائلة من الأموال تعتمد على رسوم العضوية التي تضخ إلى الأعلى إلى الأب الروحي. وعلى معظم الأعضاء أن يقوموا بنشاطات غير قانونية لكي يحصلوا على دخلهم، وعليهم أيضاً أن يدفعوا رسوم عضوية لرئيسهم . واهم مصادر دخل أو ربح البوريوكودان هو بيع الأدوية المنشطة. ولقد كانت الشرطة ولمدة طويلة تتستر على نشاطات البوريوكودان ولكن تخلصت الشرطة تدريجياً من تأثير البوريوكودان الفاسد. وخلال الإنعاش الاقتصادي لسنة ١٩٨٠، فان كبوكي– بوريوكودان اقترفوا العديد من النشاطات العدوانية، والتي أصبحت ظاهرة بشكل اكبر وغير محتمل من قبل جميع السكان. وازداد الرأي العام المعارض والمناهض للبوريوكودان. وقر قانون خاص بكيفية التعامل مع البوريوكودان عام ١٩٩١. وفي ظل هذا القانون فان الشرطة تسيطر على النشاطات الغير قانونية لهم بشكل اكثر شدة بالتعاون مع الناس.

(٧) مستقبل الجريمة المنظمة في المجتمع Sicilian Calabrian
Letizia Paoli

لكي نستطيع أن نستوعب مستقبل منظمات المافيا السيسيليان والكلابريان، يجب أن تفرق بين وجهين لنشاطهم والأخذ بعين الاعتبار وبشكل منفصل: ١) مجموعات المافيا التي تشترك في السوق الدولية الغير قانونية. ٢) قوة منظمات المافيا المحلية. إن هذه المقالة تجادل أن وضع ونسبة الاقتصاد السياسي العالمي، بالرغم من أن تطبيق القانون قد يؤثر تأثير قصير المدى عليها إلا أن القوة التي تمارسها عائلات المافيا في مجتمعاتهم المحلية، على العكس، هي نتيجة تداخل ثلاث عوامل: مجموعات المافيا نفسها، مؤسسات الدولة والمجتمع المدني الإيطالي.

(٨) مستقبل الجريمة المنظمة التقليدية في الولايات المتحدة
Howard Abadinsky

بعض المراقبين يجادلون أن المافيا الأمريكية هبطت أو شبه انتهت نتيجة نجاح تطبيق القانون الفيدرالي ، إعطاء أحكام مكونة من رقمين لشخصيات من أفراد الجريمة المنظمة أدى إلى توقف الظاهرة إن هذا التأكيد ، ليس بجدية بالتأكيد لأنه تم التنبؤ بإنهاء المافيا الأمريكية منذ قرون . ولكن هل أتى الوقت أخيراً أن أوكلت المافيا خرجت من مستقبل أمريكا ؟؟

أن هذه المقالة تأخذ بعين الاعتبار نظريات من الممكن أن تفسر خلق مثل هذه الظاهرة واستمرارها وتحليل النتائج مقابل ما هو معروف بالجريمة المنظمة الإيطالية الأمريكية المعاهدة .

(٩) الجريمة المنظمة في الولايات المتحدة
بعض الاتجاهات المعاصرة
Robert J. Kelly

تمر المافيا الأمريكية ، LA Cosa Nosta بهجوم نتيجة تطبيق قرار قانون ولكن لا يمكن وصفها بأنها تحطمت. لان الظروف الاقتصادية والبيئة الاجتماعية والسياسية التي تطبعت بها المافيا قد تغيرت وحولت وأعادت تعريف نفسها. وتتزايد في الآونة الأخيرة بعض المجموعات من الأقلية والتي تعرف بالجريمة المنظمة "الغير تقليدية" في المقاطعات والأحياء التي تتواجد فيها مجموعات المهاجرين الجدد. تتفحص هذه المقالة عمليات هبوط وإعادة تنظيم داخل LA Cosa Nosta ورسم الهيكلية والديناميكية لعصابات التهريب الصينية.

(١٠) الجريمة المنظمة في إسرائيل
Menachem Amir

ترسم هذه المقالة دراسة الجريمة المنظمة في إسرائيل كما تعكسها تقارير التحقيقات الصحفية والبحث الأكاديمي. يتميز تاريخ الجريمة المنظمة في إسرائيل باستمرار وبشكل دائم بمناظرات ما بين الشرطة والأكاديميين والإعلام حول تعريف الجريمة المنظمة وطبيعتها وردود الفعل عليها. إن طبيعة الجريمة المنظمة تعكس ثاني أهم ميزة للمجتمع الإسرائيلي (الأولى وهي الأمن) – وهي ظاهرة المهاجرين الجدد الذين يدخلون عالم الجريمة ، بما في ذلك الجريمة المنظمة. لذلك فان الجريمة المنظمة في إسرائيل لها طابع الاقليات، والظاهرة الأخيرة وهي المهاجرين الروس، فقد ابتدأ أكتشف تورطهم في الجريمة بشكل عام والجريمة المنظمة.

(١١) الجريمة المنظمة: وجهة نظر نمساوية
Maximilian Edelbacher

إن الجريمة المنظمة هي التحدي الأول في العالم المعاصر وخاصة في أوروبا. لقد حصل تغير ضخم في أوروبا منذ عام ١٩٨٩ عندما سقطت "الستارة الحديدية ". يجلب موقع النمسا الجغرافي في وسط أوروبا وكعضو في الاتحاد الأوروبي ، الكثير من المسئوليات لمكافحة الجريمة المنظمة المتطورة حديثاً كعمليات تهريب العملات بالإضافة إلى أهمية النمسا كقاعدة لنشاطات وعمليات الجريمة المنظمة. لذلك فان دور النمسا الجديد يجلب لها مسئولية مكافحة الجريمة المنظمة من خلال خلق والمشاركة في الأفكار الجديدة والاستراتيجيات المضادة.

(١٢) الجريمة المنظمة الأفريقية \الأمريكية: العبودية العنصرية والتمرد
Robert J. Kelly

عملية التفكير بان LA Cosa Nosta هي "مركز" الجريمة المنظمة في الولايات المتحدة اليوم، من الطبيعي أن يؤدي إلى اعتبار الأشكال السطحية لهذه الظاهرة – خاصة الاقليات، أو الجريمة المنظمة الغير تقليدية. تقدم هذه الدراسة بعض الملاحظات حول أنواع محددة من الجريمة المنظمة الغير تقليدية، المجموعات الأفريقية الأمريكية ومدى نموها. بالإضافة إلى عملية تهريب المخدرات فانه يناقش أن التحرك السياسي ضمن مجتمع الأقلية هو عنصر أساسي لهذا التطور والنمو والاستقرار بالنسبة لنشاطات الجريمة المنظمة التقليدية.

(١٣) التجارة العالمية للجنس: الإنسان كبضاعة أساسية
Sarah L. Shannon

لقد أصبحت ظاهرة التجارة بالنساء والأطفال للجنس ظاهرة عالمية. وان المنظمات الإجرامية التي تتعدى حدود الدول وبدرجة كبيرة تتعامل بهذه التجارة الربح. وان الحقائق التي تحيط بتجارة الجنس العالمية لهي مثيرة للاشمئزاز. وللوصول إلى إجراءات مضادة فعالة فانه ضروري جداً فهم تفاصيل هذه الحقائق. ستناقش في هذه الدراسة بعض الخصائص المميزة مثل العوامل الجغرافية وظهور نزعات جديدة لسوق اللحوم. وتختم هذه الدراسة بردود فعل عالمية تجاه هذه المشكلة.

(١٤) سرقة الفنون والأثريات
Lauren Bernick

يتفحص هذا الفصل النمو الواضح لتجارة الفنون والأثريـات والممتلكـات التراثيـة والحضاريـة. وبـالرغم مـن إن سرقة الفنون ونهب الكنوز الأثرية حاصل منذ قرون إلا أن عناصر تغير البيئة العالمية وازديـاد الطلـب علـى الفنـون أدى إلى التزايد في السوق الحالية. وما هو حديث على السـوق الدوليـة هو الشبكات العالمية التي تهـرب قطـع الفنون إلى المتحف وبيت المزادات في الـدول المتقدمـة عـن طريـق اسـتهداف المتحف والمواقـع الأثريـة والكنائس المنتشرة في العالم. وان هذه الشبكات من الممكن أن تكون منظمات مكرسة فقط لسرقة الفنون أو أنها مؤسسات موجودة كمنظمات إجرامية متعدية لحدود الـدول والتي وجدت بان سرقة الفنون مربحـة. أن المنظمات الإجرامية المتعدية للحـدود مثل المافيا الإيطالية أو الكولومبية يستخدمون الفنـون لتسهيل عمليـة تبادل بربط عملية سرقة الفنون لتهريب العملة والمخدرات.

(١٥) تهريب الأموال
David Hess, Kenneth Myers, Michele Gideon,
Sal E. Gomez, and John Daly

يراجع هذا البحث تهريب الأموال من خلال دراسة أهدافها وطرقها وأدواتهـا ومؤسسـاتها والتعـرف علـى فرص التهريب المختلفة واكتشاف المؤسسات والدول الضعيفة.

(١٦) الجريمة المنظمة في الولاية: سيطرتها، تأثيراتها الغير مقصودة
واقتراحات لأبحاث مستقبلية
Jeffrey Ian Ross

يحلل هذا المقال مبدأ الجريمة المنظمة في الولاية الواحدة كنـوع مـن أنـواع الجريمـة المنظمة في الولاية ويركز على سيطرتها وعداد عدد من المناطق التي يكون لسيطرتها عـدد مـن النتائج الغير مقصودة. بعد ذلك يقترح كيفية رفع السيطرة على الجريمة المنظمة.

(١٧) مستقبل إرهاب المخدرات: كولومبيا – حالة للدراسة
Peter A. Lupsha and Sung-Kwon Cho

إذا أخذنا بعين كولومبيا كحالة للدراسة فان إرهاب المخدرات يعرف ويوصف ، آخذين في الاعتبار العناصر الضرورية في كل المجتمعـات الإجراميـة والشرعية، بما في ذلك الولاية: شروط المبادرة بها واستمراريتها ،

اختلاف أفعالها وردود فعلها ، أنواعها وتنبؤات عن مستقبلها ضمن وضع الجريمة المنظمة خارج الحدود الوطنية.

(١٨) شمولية الجريمة والقانون الجنائي: آمال ومشاكل
David Nelken

يقوم هذا الفصل بتحليل للطرق التي من خلالها قد تتأثر عملية الشمولية (العالمية) على تطور الجريمة والقانون الجنائي. تتعرف هذه الدراسة في البداية على المخاوف المتنافسة والتي تدور حول الافتراض بان هناك ازدياد بالجريمة المنظمة خارج الحدود الوطنية من جهة ، ومن جهة أخرى المخاطر المفترضة لشرطة خارج الحدود. بعد التعرف على العديد من العوامل المختلفة للشمولية فإنها تقترح أن هناك حاجة للحذر والتفكير أن تقوية الشرطة خارج الحدود هل هو رد ضروري وكافي لهذه المشاكل؟

Translated by
Marina Barham, MA, BA.
Director
LOGOS SERVICES CENTER
972-(0) 52-609-569

要　　約

1．国境を越える犯罪：不確実の中での経験
（著者：Gerhard O. W. Mueller）

この論文が描くのは、国連の諸機関における討議の中で、国境を越える犯罪や国際犯罪の定義がどのように発展してきたかである。基本的に同意された定義に、ひとたび到達したとき、国連の加盟諸国やNGOの諸機関は、犯罪の18のカテゴリーを描くように求められた。その18のカテゴリーは、あるものは性質において地域的と思われるかもしれないが、いずれも国際的な特徴や影響を持つものである。18のカテゴリーは再検討され、それらの範囲やパターンが強調されている。また、これらの犯罪と闘争するための現存する資源や必要な対策が、強調されている。国境を越えるという特徴を持った犯罪で、対処すべきものは、マネー・ローンダリング、テロリズム、美術品窃盗や知的所有権窃盗、海賊行為、コンピュータ犯罪、環境犯罪などである。これらの犯罪は、国境を越える犯罪という概念の、まさにその定義について、必要とされる調査について、また、必要とされる実行可能な対策あるいは基準について、不確実性を「被っている」。国境を越える犯罪や国際犯罪という概念の、まさにその定義が、調査を必要とし、それらの犯罪と効果的に闘争するために求められている対策を、必要としている。

2．金持ちになりつつ等しくなる：21世紀の国境を越えた脅威
（著者：Phil Williams）

この論文は、国境を越えた犯罪組織と国境を越えたテロリスト集団によってもたらされた、国内的および国際的な安全への脅威を、検討する。ここで主張するのは、これらの脅威の出現が、2つの過程の結果として理解できるということである。その2つとは、グローバリゼーションと国家主権の危機ということであるが、その両方とも、国家主権の領域の収縮に寄与している。グローバリゼーションは、流民や少数民族のネットワーク、貿易の増大、グローバルな財政システムの発展、グローバルな情報伝達システムの発展、およびグローバルな都市の出現といったさまざまな様相を持つが、それらの影響が検討される。組織犯罪とテロリズムの将来の傾向も、探究される。

3．東ヨーロッパにおける組織犯罪と、西洋の世界の安全にとってのその意味
（著者：Brunon Holyst）

この論文は、東ヨーロッパ諸国における組織犯罪の状況を再検討し、これが西洋の世界に呈する脅威に言及する。前社会主義ブロックの諸国家における、政治的・経済的な変容は、犯罪のダイナミックスと構造を形成する上に、影響を及ぼしている。生活の全ての領域で生じている変化は、ますます国際的な結びつきを持つようになった犯罪者によって、食い物にされている。国家機構の弱さ、司法の執行の独占をそれが結果的に失ったこと、法におけるギャップ、社会的不穏、生活水準の相当に大きな低下は、公共的・経済的・政治的な生活における組織的な腐敗と連合して、「病理的な」制度的絆の特殊な網目を生み出している。現在の国際的な結合、世界的な財政の処理、商品交換、またフロンティアの開放は、組織犯罪の諸活動における、さらに一層大きな国際化と専門化に、導くであろう。組織犯罪によってもたらされる主な脅威は、その流動性から生じている。（多くの形態の中で認められるように）、流動性は、因習的・合法的・社会的・経済的な社会において人々が享受しているのと全く同じ、自由および社会的機会から、

利益を得るのを、組織犯罪に許している。東ヨーロッパにおける状況は、政治的な犯罪化を促進する傾向にある。

４．アパルトヘイト後の南アフリカにおける組織犯罪の発展と統制
（著者：Mark Shaw）

組織犯罪は、南アフリカの新しい民主的な秩序において、劇的に増大している。ある形態の組織犯罪は、特に、西ケープにおける悪名高いギャング活動は、アパルトヘイト統治のもとで存在していたけれども、それは、脅威とはなっていなかった。確かに、街頭レベルでのギャングは、反アパルトヘイト活動家を混乱させるために、国家機関によってしばしば使われていた。現在、公的・政治的な圧力が、組織犯罪の問題について高まっているが、南アフリカの法執行機関は、大規模な組織犯罪的な活動に対処する仕事に、良く準備されていない。しかし、今介入がなされているのは、重要である。南アフリカの犯罪組織は、数が多いとはいえ、まだ相対的に断片的であり、警察の集中する活動に対して、もろさがある。しかしながら、現在抱えている主要な弱さは、南アフリカの組織犯罪の規模、形態、構造、潜在的な成長への道筋についての理解と分析を、欠いている点にある。

５．経済的改革と「黒社会」：毛沢東後の中国における組織犯罪の再出現
（著者：Mark S. Gaylord, Hualing Fu）

中国の文化的遺産には、組織犯罪の伝統が含まれており、その伝統は、数百年前にさかのぼる。２０世紀の前半を通して、中国の「秘密社会」は、蒋介石の国民党政府と親密な関係を享受していた。しかしながら、１９４９年に共産主義者が権力を持った後、毛沢東は、その組織が彼の新しい政府に対する潜在的な敵対の源であると、正確にも認めていたので、それを壊滅するために素早く動いた。ほとんど３０年もの間、中国における組織犯罪は、消滅し、前の時期の他の諸制度とともに沈潜した。しかしながら、毛後の中国においては、（「黒社会」と呼ばれる）組織犯罪は、再現しただけでなく、今や、拡大している。「黒社会」は、追い剥ぎの小さな一団から、数千の構成員を持つ組織犯罪集団まで全てを含む、総称である。計画的に、それは、視界から隠されており、私的部門と公的部門との絶望的に不明朗な区別、腐敗した公務員、および、機密によって、不明瞭にされている。

６．日本における暴力団の組織犯罪の傾向
（著者：横山実）

日本固有の組織犯罪集団である暴力団は、封建時代のギャングから、いくつかの副次文化を受け継いできた。彼らの倫理の中核は、武士道精神の一つの型である任侠道によって、構成されてきた。第二次世界大戦後の日本の経済成長の結果、いくつかの有力な暴力団は、暴力とその巨大な富を通して、広域暴力団となった。彼らは、今では、任侠道の倫理の下で統制された集団というよりは、資本主義の国における私的な企業と類似した利益追求の組織として機能している。暴力団は、階層的に構造化されているが、そこの中では、巨額な上納金が組長へと汲み上げられている。大部分の組員は、自分の生活費を稼ぐために、また、期待されている上納金をボスに支払うために、多くの違法的な活動を遂行しなければならない。暴力団にとっての最も重要な収入源は、覚醒剤の販売である。長い間、警察は、暴力団の諸活動を、見て見ぬ振りをしてきた。しかしながら、警察は、次第に暴力団の腐敗的な影響下から脱してきている。１９８０年代の経済的繁栄の間、広

域暴力団は、多くの暴力的な活動を行い、それらは、一般の人々にとって一層可視的になり、また、一層耐え難いものとなった。暴力団を指弾する世論が、増大した。１９９１年には、暴力団対策法が、制定された。この法の下で、警察は、人々と共同で、一層厳しく、暴力団の違法な諸活動を統制している。

７．シチリアとカラブリアの組織犯罪の将来
（著者：Letizia Paoli）

シチリアとカラブリアのマフィア結社の将来を予測するために、彼らの活動の二つの側面が、識別され、別々に考慮されなければならない。その二つの側面とは、第１に、マフィア集団が違法な国際市場に参画すること、第２には、マフィアの力の地方的システムということである。イタリアの最も有力なマフィアの連合体は、違法な世界的交換にかかわっているが、そのかかわりの地位および程度が、主として政治的な国際経済の傾向に依存していることを、この論文は主張する。けれども、法執行の活動は、短期的にのみ、相当大きな影響を及ぼすかもしれない。他方、マフィア家族がその地方的コミュニティで行使する力は、大部分、３つの集合的行動主体、つまり、マフィア集団それ自体、国の諸制度およびイアリアの市民社会という３つの相互作用の産物である。

８．アメリカ合衆国の伝統的な組織犯罪の将来
（著者：Howard Abadinsky）

ある観察者達が主張するところによると、アメリカのマフィアは、主として連邦レベルの法執行の努力が成功した結果、衰退し、まさに消滅しようとしている。組織犯罪の大物に下された二桁に及ぶ典型的な判決は、大いに誇示されてきた沈黙の掟の消滅、つまりオメルタの消滅に、導いた。しかしながら、この主張は、新しくはない。確かに、アメリカのマフィアの消滅は、何十年もの間、予言されてきた。しかし、私たちがアメリカの将来の視点からマフィアを書こうとするとき、その消滅の時がついにやってきた、いえるのであろうか。洞察するために、この論文は、いくつかの理論を考察するが、それらの理論は、現象の創造とその継続的存在の両方を説明し、現代のイタリア系アメリカ人の組織犯罪について知られていることに反する諸結果を、分析するものである。

９．アメリカ合衆国における組織犯罪：いくつかの現在の傾向
（著者：Robert J. Kelly）

ラ・コーザ・ノストラと呼ばれるアメリカのマフィアは、法執行の集中的な攻撃の下におかれてきた。しかし、それが破壊されたと描くことは出来ない。マフィアを育ててきた経済的条件や社会・政治的環境は、変化してきたので、それは変形し、それ自体を再定義している。「非伝統的」組織犯罪として言及される、他の少数民族の集団は、少数民族の居住地や新しい移民コミュニティのゲットーの中で勃興している。この論文では、ラ・コーザ・ノストラの衰退と再編成の過程を検討し、中国人の強奪徒党の構造とダイナミックスの概略を記述する。

１０．イスラエルにおける組織犯罪
（著者：Menachem Amir）

この論文では、イスラエルにおける組織犯罪の研究を概観するが、メディア独自の調査よる報告と学術的な調査とが、考察される。イスラエルにおける組織犯罪の研究の歴史を、常に絶えず特徴づけているのは、警察、研究者、メディアの間

での討論であるが、それは、イスラエルにおける組織犯罪の定義と性質、組織犯罪への反作用についてのものである。組織犯罪の性質は、イスラエル社会の第2の最も重要な特徴（第1は、安全というものある）を、反映している。その特徴とは、移民の波である。彼らもまた、組織犯罪を含む犯罪の現場に登場してくる。それ故に、イスラエルにおける組織犯罪は、少数民族の連続的受け入れという性質を持っており、その最後が、ロシア移民の受け入れである。犯罪や組織犯罪への彼らのかかわりが、今、記述されている。

11．組織犯罪：オーストリアの視点
（著者：Maximilian Edelbacher）
組織犯罪は、現代の世界に対する主要な挑戦であるが、特にヨーロッパにおいて、そうである。「鉄のカーテン」が崩れた1989年以降、巨大な変化が、ヨーロッパに起こった。オーストリアは、ヨーロッパの中心という地理的な位置と、ヨーロッパ共同体の構成員としてのその新しい役割のために、組織犯罪への闘争という新しい責任を担っている。新たに発展してきた組織犯罪ギャングにとって、「マネー・ローンダリング」の活動をするために、また、組織犯罪の作戦活動の基地とするために、オーストリアが重要になっている。オーストリアの新しい役割は、新たに必要とされる理念や対抗戦略を創造し、それらを分かちあうことで、組織犯罪と闘争するための責任を担う。

12．アフリカ系アメリカ人の組織犯罪：人種的隷属と反抗
（著者：Robert J. Kelly）
今日アメリカ合衆国の組織犯罪の「中核」として、ラ・コーザ・ノストラを考えることは、当然、少数民族の組織犯罪あるいは「非伝統的」組織犯罪といった、現象の周辺的な諸形態への考慮に導く。この論文は、「非伝統的」組織犯罪の特殊な形態、つまり、アフリカ系アメリカ人の集団と、その成長の見通しについて、若干の考察を行う。薬物取引は別にして、少数民族のコミュニティの中での政治的な移動性が、伝統的な組織犯罪活動の成長と安定の必要条件であると、主張する。

13．グローバルな性の貿易：究極的な商品としての人間
（著者：Sarah L. Shannon）
女性と子どもの性を商業的に搾取することは、世界的な規模の現象となってきた。ますます大きな範囲で、国境を越える犯罪組織が、この非常に儲かる事業にかかわっている。グローバルな性の貿易をめぐる事実は、ぞっとするようなものである。もし有効な対抗策を創造しようとするならば、まさにこれらの事実を詳しく理解することが、要求される。それ故に、この人肉の市場の顕著な特徴、地理的様相、および、出現しつつある傾向のいくつかが、この研究で論じられる。その問題に対するグローバルな応答についての短い考察で、検討を終える。

14．美術品および骨董品の窃盗
（著者：Lauren Bernick）
この章では、美術品、骨董品および文化財の増大している違法な貿易を、検討する。美術品窃盗と、考古学的宝物の略奪は、数世紀の間、起こってきたけれども、変化している国際環境の中での諸要素と、美術への増加している要求が、市場の現在の増殖に寄与している。違法な美術市場に、新たに、国際的なネットワーク

が出来ている。そのネットワークは、世界的な規模で、博物館、考古学的遺跡および教会を標的にして、発展した国々の博物館や競売会社に、美術品を密輸している。そのネットワークを構成しているのは、もっぱら美術品窃盗に打ち込んでいる組織か、あるいは、美術窃盗が儲かると知って参入した、国境を越える既存の犯罪組織のいずれかである。イタリアのマフィアやコロンビアの薬物カルテルといった、国境を越える伝統的な犯罪組織は、盗まれた美術品を他の違法な売買を促進するために使う。たとえば、美術品の犯罪を、マネー・ローンダリングや薬物取引に結びつける。美術の不法な世界と政府の役人とのもたれ合いは、盗まれた美術品の国境を越える流出を阻止しようとする、国際的法執行機関に対して、もう一つの挑戦となっている。

１５．マネー・ローンダリング
（著者：David Hess, Kenneth Myers, Michele Gideon, Sal E. Gomez , John Daly)

ここでマネー・ローンダリングが再検討されるのは、その目的物、方法、手段、マネー・ローンダリングの制度、および、マネー・ローンダリングのいろいろな機会の見地からである。それは、マネー・ローンダリングにもろい制度や国を確認するためである。

１６．国家組織犯罪：その統制、意図しない結果、および、将来の調査への示唆
（著者：Jeffrey Ian Ross)

この論文は、国家組織犯罪の一つの形態としての国家犯罪の概念を分析し、その統制に焦点を当てる。また、統制が多数の意図しない結果を持ちうる、多くの領域を、仮定してみる。それから、国家犯罪統制のための行動綱領を、いかに進めるかについて、示唆する。

１７．麻薬テロリズムの将来：コロンビアの事例の研究
（著者：Peter A. Lupsha, Sung-Kwon Cho)

事例研究としてコロンビアを使って、麻薬テロリズムが、定義される。また、国家を含む、合法的なコミュニティと、犯罪的なそれとの両方の、必要な「行動主体」に注目して、麻薬テロリズムを描くことにする。そこでは、組織犯罪と国境を越える組織犯罪の脈絡の中で、その将来についての予知と型、活動と反作用の変動、その加入と存続のための条件が、描かれる。

１８．犯罪と刑事司法のグローバリゼーション：展望と問題点
（著者：David Nelken)

この章では、グローバリゼーションの過程が、犯罪と刑事司法の発展に影響を与えるかもしれないやり方について、分析を提供する。それは、まず、競合する恐怖を確認する。それらの恐怖は、一方では、国境を越える組織犯罪の申し立てられている増加、他方では、国境を越える警察活動の申し立てられている危険性をめぐって、起こっている。グローバリゼーションの異なる様相と結びついたいろいろな問題を識別した後、さらに、「国境を越える警察活動の強化が、これらの問題に対する必要な、あるいは、十分な応答である」と考えることに、注意が必要であることを、示唆する。

Index